# Microsoft® 365 Office®

## ALL-IN-ONE

3rd Edition

**by Paul McFedries**

for dummies®
A Wiley Brand

**Microsoft® 365 Office® All-in-One For Dummies®, 3rd Edition**

Published by: **John Wiley & Sons, Inc.,** 111 River Street, Hoboken, NJ 07030-5774, www.wiley.com



For general information on our other products and services, please contact our Customer Care Department within the U.S. at 877-762-2974, outside the U.S. at 317-572-3993, or fax 317-572-4002. For technical support, please visit https://hub.wiley.com/community/support/dummies.

Wiley publishes in a variety of print and electronic formats and by print-on-demand. Some material included with standard print versions of this book may not be included in e-books or in print-on-demand. If this book refers to media such as a CD or DVD that is not included in the version you purchased, you may download this material at http://booksupport.wiley.com. For more information about Wiley products, visit www.wiley.com.

Library of Congress Control Number: 2025930414

ISBN 978-1-394-29505-0 (pbk); ISBN 978-1-394-29506-7 (ebk); ISBN 978-1-394-29507-4 (epdf)

SKY10097191_012825

# Contents at a Glance

# Table of Contents

# Introduction

You've heard of Microsoft Office, but what's all this about Office "365." Is that how many days it's going to take you to learn how to use this thing? Is that how many headaches you're going to have to suffer through before you know what you're doing? Is that how many tissues you'll need to wipe away the tears caused by your struggles to tame this beast of a suite? Is that how many questions I'm going to ask before I get to my point?

To be honest, I have no idea what the "365" of Office 365 is supposed to mean. What I *can* tell you is that, although from the outside Office 365 appears hideously complex and impossible to master, once you get inside it's nowhere near as bad as it seems.

Or, I should say, Office 365 isn't as complicated as it looks *if* you have a guide who knows the easiest and simplest ways to navigate the Office landscape. Office 365 is a powerful set of tools *if* you have a teacher who can reduce convoluted Office tasks to simple steps that get the job done. Office 365 makes sense *if* you have an interpreter who can translate esoteric Office lingo into plain English.

Where are you supposed to find a guide, a teacher, and an interpreter for Office 365? Reader, you're looking right at it!

## About This Book

Welcome to *Microsoft 365 Office All-in-One For Dummies,* 3rd Edition! The "All-in-One" part of the title means, first, that you don't need to buy a bunch of books to learn Office 365; all you need is this one. Sweet! But that "All-in-One" in the title also means that this book is your guide, teacher, and interpreter for Office 365. Bliss!

What the "All-in-One" part of the title does *not* mean is that this book tells you everything there is to know about Office 365. First, such a book would be ten times the size and, second, such a book would be *incredibly boring!* Knowing Office 365's abstruse technical minutiae and arcane for-geeks-only settings won't help you get your work (or play) done, so you won't find any of that nonsense in this book. Instead, I introduce every Office 365 feature with just enough background to give you some context, then I get right down to the business of showing you how to use that feature to do your thing, whatever that might be.

Does this mean you have to start on Page 1 and read right through to the end? Well, you certainly *could* do that if you wanted to; there's no law against it (at least, none that I know of). But, happily, you don't have to read the entire book from start to finish. *Office 365 All-in-One For Dummies*, 3rd Edition, is a reference book, so you can dip in and out of the book as needed to get just the info you need to accomplish a task. To help you with that, I've tried to organize everything in a sensible way, with lots of useful headings to help you get your bearings quickly. The book also offers a detailed table of contents and an index created by a professional indexer so, despite the book's formidable size, you can find anything you need quickly and easily.

# Foolish Assumptions

This book isn't a primer on using a computer or working with your device's operating system. This is a book on Office 365, pure and simple. This means I assume the following:

- You have an Office 365 subscription and you have installed it on your computer.
- You know how to wield a mouse (or a trackpad) and know your way around a keyboard.
- You use the Windows 10 or 11 operating system. Office 365 works on machines that run Windows 10 or higher, not machines that run Windows 8.1, Windows 8, or Windows 7.
- You know how to perform basic Windows tasks, such as starting and closing apps, switching between running apps, and navigating the file system.
- You brush and floss your teeth regularly.

# Conventions Used in This Book

I want you to understand all the instructions in this book, and in that spirit, I've adopted a few conventions.

Where you see boldface letters or numbers in this book, it means to type the letters or numbers. For example, "Type **25** in the Percentage text box" means to do exactly that: Type the number 25.

Besides using the menu and toolbar, you can run many Office 365 commands using shortcut keys, which are typically some combinations of keys. For example, the shortcut Ctrl+S runs the vital Save command to save the document you're currently working on. What "Ctrl+S" means is that you hold down the Ctrl key, tap the S key, and then release Ctrl.

On a computer with a touchscreen or trackpad, instead of clicking a mouse you can tap your finger on the screen or the trackpad to initiate tasks. In this book, the word *click* does double duty. *Click* means either to click a mouse button or to tap your finger on a touchscreen or trackpad. To keep from littering the pages of the book with instructions to "click the mouse or tap a touchscreen or trackpad," I just use the word *click*. You're welcome!

# Icons Used in This Book

To help you get the most out of this book, I've sprinkled a few icons here and there. Here's what the icons mean:

REMEMBER

This icon points out juicy tidbits that are likely to be useful to you — so please don't forget them.

TIP

Think of these icons as the fodder of advice columns. They offer (I hope) wise advice or a bit more information about a topic under discussion.

WARNING

Look out! In this book, you see this icon when I'm trying to help you avoid mistakes that can cost you time, money, or embarrassment.

TECHNICAL STUFF

When you see this icon, you've come across material that isn't critical to understand but will satisfy the curious. Think "inquiring minds want to know" when you see this icon.

# Beyond the Book

In addition to the information you find in the book, this book includes these online bonuses:

- **Cheat Sheet:** Go to `www.dummies.com` and search *Office 365 All-in-One For Dummies* to find the Cheat Sheet for this book. Here you'll find some extra goodies to make your time with Office 365 a little more productive.
- **Updates:** Occasionally, there are updates to technology books. If this book does have technical updates, they will be posted at `www.dummies.com` (search this book's title to get to the right page).

# 1

# Common Office Tasks

# Contents at a Glance

IN THIS CHAPTER

- » Getting comfy with Office 365
- » Introducing the Office 365 applications
- » Exploring the Office 365 terrain
- » Opening, saving, and closing Office 365 files

# Chapter 1

# Getting Your Bearings

When I arrive in a new town — especially one that's distant enough that jet lag could be an issue — I like to drop off my bags at the hotel and then spend a few hours walking around the neighborhood. This not only keeps me awake so that tomorrow's jet lag will be less of an issue, but it also gives me the lay of the land so it's easier for me to find my way around my temporary home.

If you think of Office 365 as a kind of digital city, then the same idea applies. No, you're unlikely to experience jet lag when you start using Office 365, but the place will be unfamiliar, so a quick tour is in order so that you know where the more important landmarks can be found and what you need them for.

Let this chapter serve as your initial ramble around the Office 365 neighborhood. I introduce you to Office 365 and its applications; give you a tour of the interface; and show you the basics of saving, opening, and closing files. There's nothing complicated here, but everything you learn will provide you with a good foundation for the rest of the book.

# Saying "Hello" to Office 365

Office 365 is a subscription service from Microsoft that enables you to install a suite of applications. Wait, what? A *suite*? Yep. My dictionary defines a *suite* as "a connected series of rooms to be used together." While you may be thinking of a hotel suite, you're not too far off. Office 365 is a kind of software suite. You can, in fact, define Office 365 as "a connected series of Microsoft apps to be used together." Now don't get me wrong. The Office 365 apps are all awesome when used by themselves, but when they're connected, they make your work life easier, more efficient, and more productive.

## Meeting the Office 365 applications

Okay, so what are these apps that I've been going on and on about? Table 1-1 provides a list of the major apps, with pointers to where you can find more info about them later in this book.

WARNING

You need to be running Windows 10 or later on your computer to run Office 365 applications. The applications don't run on computers running earlier versions of Windows. What if you have a Mac? Yep, sure, you can run Office 365, but you won't have access to certain applications, such as Access. The Mac versions of the Office 365 apps are a little different than their Windows counterparts, so I don't cover the Mac apps in this book.

REMEMBER

If you're new to Office 365, don't be daunted by the prospect of having to learn so many different applications. The Office 365 programs have a ton of common elements, including many of the same toolbar elements and shortcut keys. These common features mean that once you learn them in one Office 365 program, you don't have to re-learn them in the next app you tackle.

### "OFFICE 365" OR "MICROSOFT 365"?

March 2020 will go down in infamy as the month the Great Pandemic began in earnest and most of the world shut down to ride out the storm at home. That same month, Microsoft made the bizarre decision to "rebrand" their insanely popular and widely known suite of applications from the familiar "Office 365" to the head-scratching "Microsoft 365." Maybe it's because the pandemic had everyone otherwise preoccupied, or maybe it's because the name "Microsoft 365" is inherently meaningless, but you'd be hard-pressed to find anyone outside of Microsoft who refers to the suite with that new moniker. That's why I use good, old *Office 365* throughout this book. However, just remember that if you hear anyone speaking of "Microsoft 365," they're just using a new name for Office 365.

**TABLE 1-1** The Main Office 365 Applications

| App | What You Can Do with It | Where to Find More Info |
|---|---|---|
| Word 365 | Create, edit, and collaborate on word-processing documents. You can change the layout, add bulleted and numbered lists, work with headers and footers, format text, paragraphs, and pages, and more. | Book 2 |
| Excel 365 | Create, edit, and collaborate on spreadsheets. You can build formulas, sort and filter data, analyze data, and more. | Book 3 |
| PowerPoint 365 | Create, edit, and collaborate on presentations. You can change the theme, show your presentation, create slides that include text, images, shapes, and more. | Book 4 |
| Outlook 365 | Send and receive email messages. You can also share files as attachments, organize messages, control email conversations, and more. Outlook also lets you maintain a calendar of appointments and an address book of contacts. | Book 5 |
| Access 365 | Create, maintain, and organize databases of information. | Book 6 |
| Microsoft Teams | Set up and join online meetings. You can invite people to a meeting, share resources, record and live stream a meeting, and more. | Book 7 |

## Getting to know the Office 365 cloud services

Besides the applications listed in Table 1-1, an Office 365 subscription entitles you to these goodies from the cloud:

- **Storing and sharing files online with OneDrive.** Besides storing your Office 365 files on your computer, you can also save them to OneDrive, Microsoft's online file storage service. Why would you do such a thing? Having your Office 365 files online means that you can access them using any device that has internet access, so your documents are available no matter where your travels take you. Most Office 365 subscriptions offer a generous 1TB (that's one terabyte, or a thousand gigabytes) of storage space on OneDrive. You can also invite others to work on files you store on OneDrive. (Book 8 explains how to store and share files with OneDrive.)
- **The opportunity to use the web (online) versions of Word, Excel, Outlook, and PowerPoint.** What if you're away from your computer and the device you're using doesn't have Office 365 installed? Think nothing of it! Your Office 365 subscription entitles you to use the web versions of Word, Excel, Outlook, and PowerPoint. These web versions are nearly identical to their desktop cousins, but they live online so you access them using your favorite web browser. Yep, you're right: That *is* cool.

TECHNICAL STUFF

## WHAT'S ALL THIS ABOUT A CLOUD?

I mentioned the term *cloud* a couple of times now, so let me take a few minutes of your precious time to explain what I'm talking about. In many network diagrams (schematics that show the overall layout of a network's infrastructure), the designer is most interested in the devices that connect to the network, not in the network itself. After all, the details of what happens inside the network to shunt signals from source to destination are often extremely complex and convoluted, so all that minutiae would serve only to detract from the network diagram's larger message of showing which devices can connect to the network, how they connect, and their network entry and exit points.

When the designers of a network diagram want to show the network but not any of its details, they almost always abstract the network by displaying it as a cloud symbol. (It is, if you will, the yadda-yadda-yadda of network diagrams.) At first, the cloud symbol represented the workings of a single network, but in recent years it has come to represent the internet (the network of networks).

So far, so good. Earlier in this millennium, some folks had the bright idea that, rather than store files on local computers, you could store them on a server connected to the internet, which meant that anyone with the proper credentials could access the files from anywhere in the world. Eventually, folks started storing programs on internet servers, too, and started telling anyone who'd listen that these files and applications resided "in the cloud" (meaning on a server — or, more typically, a large collection of servers that reside in a special building called a *data center* — accessible via the internet).

All the online Office 365 components (the web versions of Word, Excel, Outlook, and so on) are examples of such apps — in the rarefied world of cloud computing geeks, these apps are described as *software as a service*, or *SaaS* — and they all reside inside Microsoft's cloud service called, almost poetically, Microsoft Azure. These apps, as well as any data you store in OneDrive, live "in the cloud." That's also why you need an internet connection to use the Office 365 cloud services: They require that connection to access all that cloud stuff.

## Finding out what software and Office 365 version you have

Follow these steps to find out which version of Office 365 you have and which Office 365 applications are installed on your computer:

1. **Open any Office 365 application.**
2. **Click the File tab.**

   This tab appears in the upper-left corner of the screen. The backstage view opens after you click the File tab (refer to "Heading backstage via the File tab," later in this chapter for more info).
3. **On the left side of the backstage view, click the Account category.**

   As shown in Figure 1-1, the Account window opens. Under "This Product Contains" is an icon for each Office 365 application that's installed on your computer.

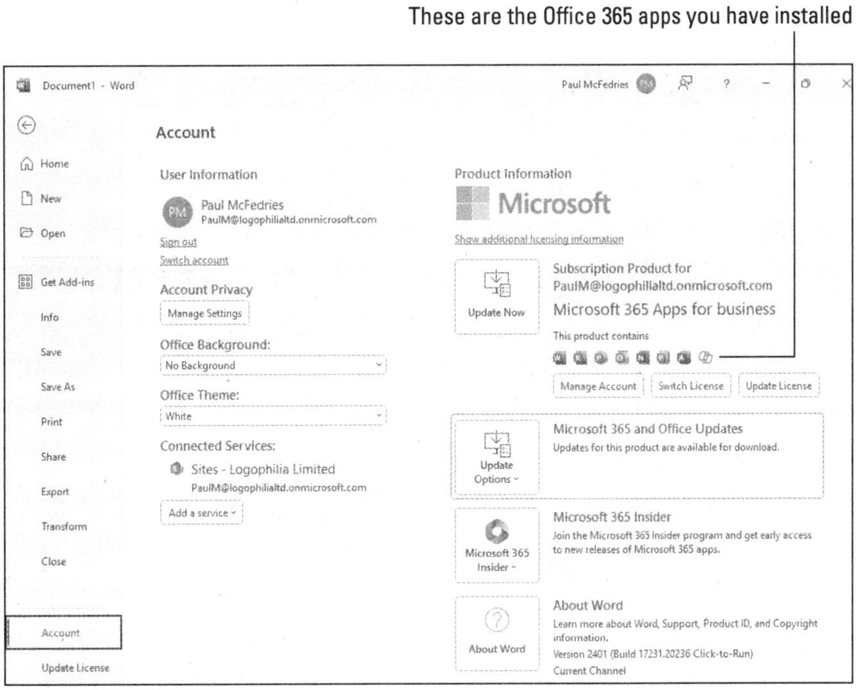


**FIGURE 1-1:** The Account window tells you which Office 365 applications are installed.

TIP

Here's an alternative way to open the Account window: Click your name in the upper-right corner of any Office 365 application window and choose the Office User Info link on the drop-down menu.

4. **Return to the Office 365 application and click the Back button (shown in the margin) in the Account window.**

   The backstage view closes.

## UPDATING OFFICE 365

From time to time, Microsoft updates Office 365 software. The updates are performed automatically. Follow these steps to find out when your version of Office 365 was last updated and update your software, if necessary:

1. **In any Office 365 application, click the File tab.**
2. **In the backstage view, click Account to open the Account window (refer to Figure 1-1).**
3. **Click the Update Options button and choose one of the following options on the drop-down menu.**

- **Update Now:** Checks whether an update is needed and updates the software, if need be
- **View Updates:** Opens a web page that displays when the software was last updated

# Managing your Microsoft account

All subscribers to Office 365 must have a Microsoft account. To find out whether your account is paid up, change the password to your account, pay your subscription fee, or do anything pertaining to your account, follow these steps:

1. **Open any Office 365 application.**
2. **In the upper-right corner of the screen, click your name.**

   A drop-down menu appears.

   If your name doesn't appear in the upper-right corner of the screen, you aren't signed in to your Microsoft account. Click the Sign In button and enter your sign-in credentials.
3. **Select the View Account link on the drop-down menu.**

   If you're using an Office 365 personal account, the link will be named My Microsoft Account, instead. Nothing wrong with an Office 365 personal account, of course, but note that this book assumes you have a business account. Just sayin'.

   Your web browser drops you off at a `Microsoft.com` page where you can investigate everything you need to know about your account.

# Navigating the Office 365 Apps

The major Office 365 apps offer a similar look and a similar collection of basic tools. As proof, Figure 1-2 shows the top part of three app windows — Word (top), Excel (middle), and PowerPoint (bottom) — and points out the main features, which I discuss throughout the next few sections.

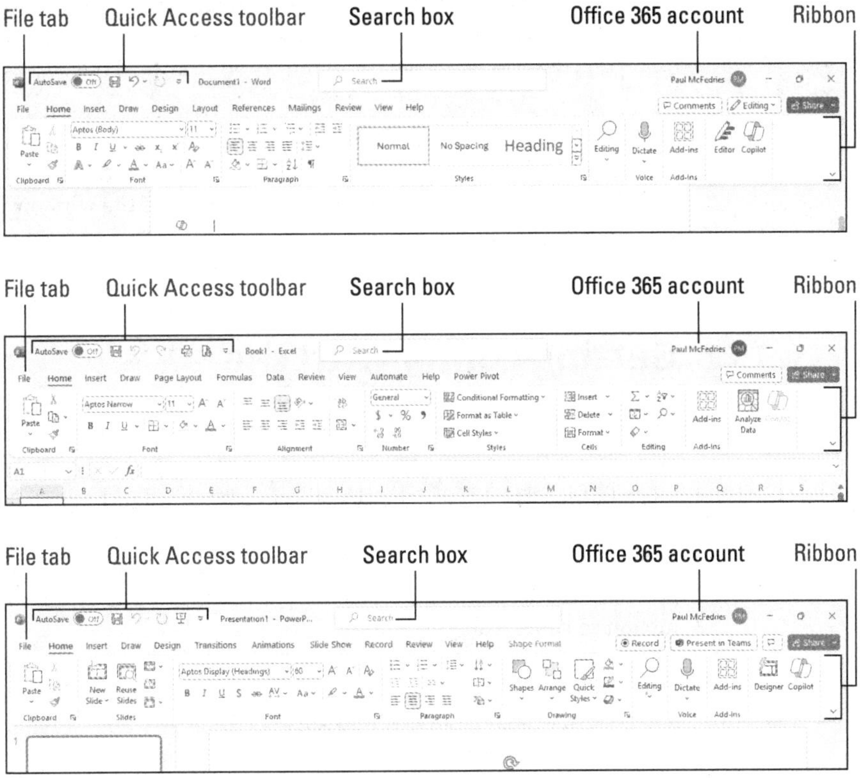


**FIGURE 1-2:** Word (top), Excel (middle), and PowerPoint (bottom) offer similar features.

## Heading backstage via the File tab

Taking a look at Figure 1-2, near the upper-left corner of each Office 365 app window is the File tab. When you click the File tab, the app opens a window similar to the one you saw earlier in Figure 1-1. Microsoft calls this the *backstage* view, presumably because it offers "behind-the-scenes" features related to the currently open document and to the app itself.

The backstage view is split vertically into two areas:

- **Navigation pane:** This is the strip that runs down the left side of the backstage view and includes commands such as Home, New, Info, Save, Account, and Options. You learn about each of these navigation commands as you go through this book.
- **Current window:** The rest of the backstage view displays the content and features that are related to whatever command is currently selected in the Navigation pane. For example, clicking Account in the backstage Navigation pane displays Office 365 account-related stuff, as shown earlier in Figure 1-1.

To leave backstage view and return to the application window, click the Back button (shown in the margin) at the top of the Navigation pane. (You might be sorely tempted to click the X in the upper-right corner of the window to get out of backstage view, but don't do it! That's the Close button and it will close your current document, which is probably not what you want.)

## Getting comfy with the all-important Ribbon

As I point out earlier in Figure 1-2, the Ribbon is the strip that runs across every app window. I'm not exaggerating even a little when I tell you that the royal road to being a productive Office 365 user is to get comfortable with the Ribbon. Why? Because with very few exceptions (such as the backstage view I introduce in the previous section) almost everything you do in every Office 365 app will involve the Ribbon in some way.

The Ribbon is all-important because it's home to almost all the knickknacks and doodads that enable you to make each Office 365 app do your bidding. Want to format some text? Use the Ribbon. Want to insert a photo or drawing? Use the Ribbon. Want to change the view? You got it — use the Ribbon.

The top part of the Ribbon is home to a collection of commands called *tabs*. The File tab that I mention in the previous section ("Heading backstage via the File tab") is a bit of an odd duck because clicking it displays the backstage view. When you click the rest of the tabs — Home, Insert, Draw, and so on — the Ribbon changes to display the commands and controls associated with that tab.

For example, clicking the Home tab displays commands mostly related to formatting and working with text, as shown on the top in Figure 1-3. Clicking the Insert tab, as shown on the bottom of Figure 1-3, displays a new collection of Ribbon commands and features related to inserting stuff, such as table, images, and links.

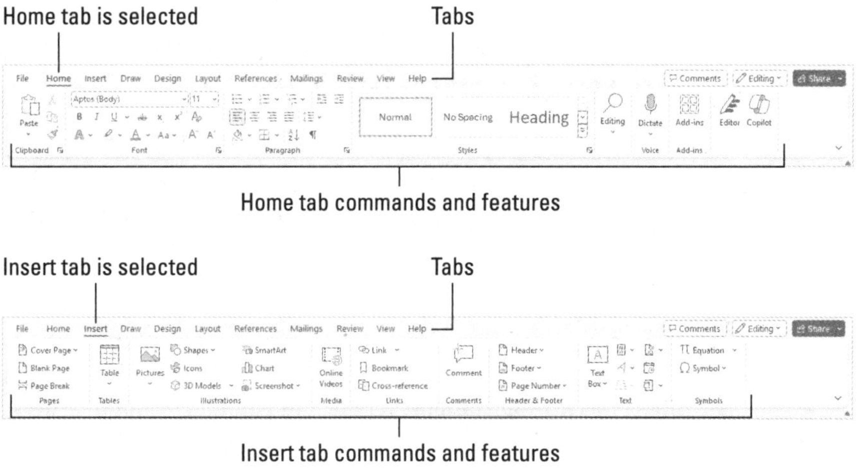


**FIGURE 1-3:** In Word's Ribbon, the Home tab (top) displays one set of commands, while the Insert tab (bottom) displays another.

**REMEMBER**

You can tell at a glance which tab is currently selected by looking for the underline under the tab name.

Surprisingly, the Ribbon is customizable. To learn how to remake the Ribbon in your own specifications, refer to Book 1, Chapter 4.

## COLLAPSING AND SHOWING THE RIBBON

To get more room to view items onscreen, consider collapsing the Ribbon. When the Ribbon is collapsed, only tab names on the Ribbon appear; the buttons and galleries are hidden from view.

Use these techniques to collapse the Ribbon:

- Press Ctrl+F1.
- Right-click any part of the Ribbon and then click Collapse the Ribbon on the shortcut menu.

- Click the Ribbon Display Options button (shown in the margin) in the bottom-right corner of the Ribbon and click Show Tabs Only.

Use these techniques to show the Ribbon when it's collapsed:

- Press Ctrl+F1.
- Right-click a tab and then click to deselect Collapse the Ribbon.

- Click a tab to display the Ribbon, click the Ribbon Display Options button (shown in the margin), and then click Always Show Ribbon.

## Commands only when you need 'em: context-sensitive tabs

One of the more confusing aspects of the Ribbon is that while some tabs — such as Home, Insert, and View — stay onscreen full-time, other tabs appear to come and go willy-nilly. Fortunately, this behavior is neither willy nor nilly. What's happening is that some tabs show up only when certain types of document content are selected.

For example, Figure 1-4 shows a photo inserted into a Word document. When I click the photo to select it, a new tab named Picture Format materializes on the Ribbon. This tab contains a bunch of commands and features related to working with images. When I click outside the photo to deselect it, the Picture Format tab also goes away because it's no longer needed. Because tabs such as Picture Format only appear when the appropriate content is selected, such tabs are described as, in exquisite geek-speak, *context-sensitive.*

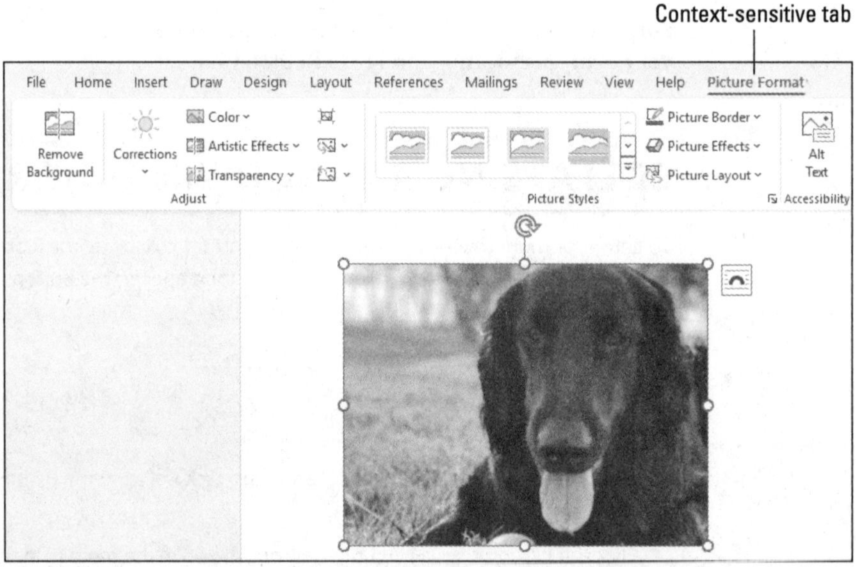


**FIGURE 1-4:** When I select the photo, the Picture Format context-sensitive tab shows up on the Ribbon.

## Taking a closer look at Ribbon tabs

As you use Office 365, you'll be spending a ton of time working inside one tab or another in every app you use. So, it pays to take a bit of extra time now to examine these tab things to understand how they work.

## Running commands with buttons and drop-down lists

The most obvious thing to notice about any tab is that it's festooned with little doohickeys: most. Most are cute, little pictures, but some are controls you normally associate with dialog boxes, such as check boxes and drop-down lists.

Each of the little icons — which are known generally as *controls* — is almost always one of the following:

- **Button:** Runs a command, which performs some sort of task. For example, every Home tab has a Bold button (refer to Figure 1-5) that, when clicked, applies bold formatting to the selected text.
- **Drop-down list:** Displays a drop-down menu with a set of commands from which you can choose the one you want to run. All tab drop-down list icons have a teensy downward pointing arrow, as pointed out in Figure 1-5. Note, too, that some drop-down lists don't use an icon, such as the Font and Font Size lists pointed out in Figure 1-5.
- **Button and drop-down list:** Does double-duty by offering both a drop-down list and a button that, if clicked, applies the default (or sometimes the most recently chosen) option from the drop-down list. For example, the Paste control, pointed out in Figure 1-5, has a button on top and a drop-down list below.

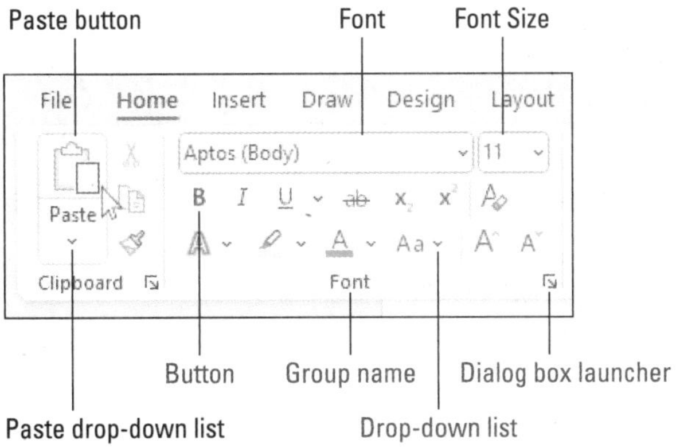


**FIGURE 1-5:** The tab controls offer buttons and drop-down lists galore.

Depending on the width of the app window, buttons and drop-down lists might be shown as just an icon or, with a wider window, might also be labeled with a word or phrase.

TIP

If a tab control is just an icon, you can learn the name of the control and find out what it does by hovering the mouse pointer over the control to display a pop-up description.

## Gawking at galleries

Built into some tabs are galleries. A *gallery* presents you with visual options for modifying the selected text or object. For example, Figure 1-6 shows Word's Styles gallery, which offers a collection of styles you can apply to your text (refer to Book 2, Chapter 3).

**FIGURE 1-6:** Word's Styles gallery.

The number of gallery items that appear depends on the window width, with wider windows showing more items. (In the version of Word's Styles gallery shown in Figure 1-6, three items are shown: Normal, No Spacing, and Heading.) However, you can use the following three controls on the right side to control the gallery display:

- **Scroll up:** Scrolls the displayed gallery items up one row
- **Scroll down:** Scrolls the displayed gallery items down one row
- **Open:** Displays all (or most) of the gallery in a separate pop-up window

When you move the pointer over a gallery choice, the item on your page or slide — the table, chart, or diagram, for example — changes appearance. In galleries, you can preview different choices before you click to select the choice you want.

## Getting to grips with groups

Take a close look at any tab in any Office 365 app and you'll notice a curious thing: At seemingly random intervals, vertical lines appear that don't do anything when you click them. Ah, there's nothing random about these lines. Their purpose is to organize the controls on each tab into groups, where a *group* is a collection of related buttons, drop-down lists, galleries, or whatever. The name of each group appears below the controls. For example, the Home tab in Word includes several groups, including the Font group, which offers quite a few buttons and drop-down lists related to formatting text (check out Book 1, Chapter 2).

REMEMBER

If your app window isn't wide enough to display all the controls in a tab, the app will collapse one or more groups, where each of those groups is displayed as a single icon labeled with the name of the group and a drop-down arrow. Click a collapsed group to display its controls.

Many groups have a *dialog box launcher* (shown in the margin) in the lower-right corner. This is a button that, not surprisingly, launches a dialog box that contains even more options related to the group.

## Accessing stuff quickly I: The Quick Access toolbar

The Ribbon is a convenient way to run commands in the Office 365 apps, but sometimes it's not the fastest way. Depending on which tab is displayed, whether any tab groups are collapsed, and other factors, it can take four or five clicks to finally run a single command.

To save wear and tear on everyone's clicking finger, the Office 365 apps all offer a handy feature called the Quick Access toolbar, which appears near the upper-left corner of the app window (refer to Figure 1-2). The "quick access" part of the name means that the toolbar offers one-click access to several useful commands, such as Undo and Save. Nice!

You can also click the Customize Quick Access Toolbar button (shown in the margin) on the right side of the Quick Access toolbar to get two-click access to even more commands and to customize the toolbar. Want the particulars on how to customize the Quick Access toolbar? Pop over to Book 1, Chapter 4.

## Accessing stuff quickly II: Mini-toolbars and shortcut menus

The Office 365 apps are loaded with features. That largesse means the apps can do almost anything you need them to do, but at the cost of often being unable to locate the command that does what you want. (Cue the frustration, the gnashing of teeth, the pulling of hair.)

Fortunately, the Office 365 apps offer a few features that make it easier to access the program's commands. For example, context-sensitive tabs show up when you select certain types of content (as I describe earlier in the "Commands only when you need 'em: context-sensitive tabs" section).

That idea of making commands available when you need them is behind the *mini-toolbar* feature, which is a toolbar that shows up onscreen to help you perform a task. For example, when you select text with the mouse in Word, a mini-toolbar materializes as shown in Figure 1-7. In this case, the mini-toolbar offers commands related to working with the selected text, so you don't need to hunt around the Ribbon for the same commands.

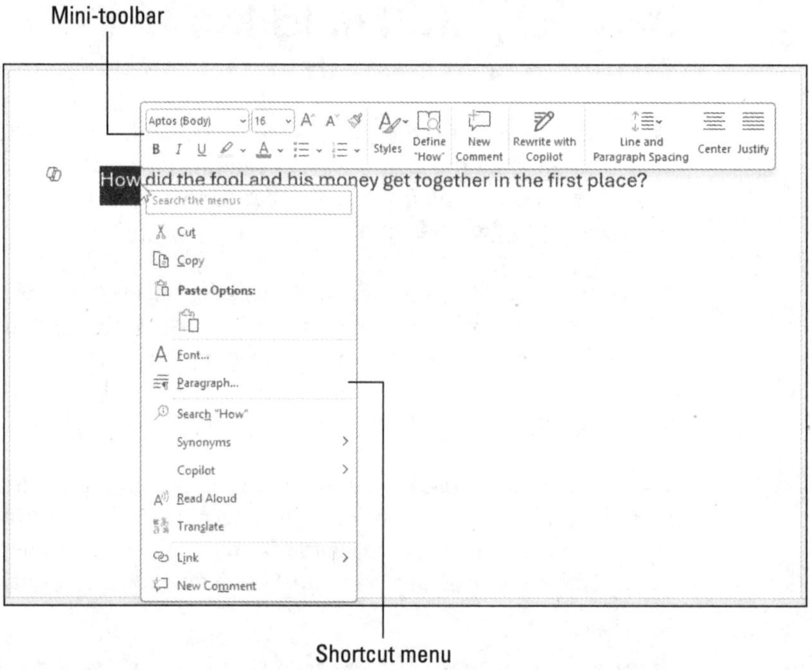


**FIGURE 1-7:** A mini-toolbar (top) and shortcut menu (bottom).

Similar to mini-toolbars are the shortcut menus you get when you right-click something, as shown in Figure 1-7. Right-click just about anything and you get a shortcut menu of some kind. Again, the shortcut menu that shows up contains commands that are related to whatever you right-clicked.

REMEMBER

In Word, Excel, and PowerPoint, a mini-toolbar *and* a shortcut menu appear when you right-click text.

# Accessing stuff quickly III: Keyboard shortcuts

The Ribbon and features such as mini-toolbars and shortcut menus are mouse-friendly, but that doesn't mean that the Office 365 apps are mouse-only programs. All the apps offer keyboard techniques for running commands, which can be handy when you're typing something because it means you can keep your hands on the keyboard to, say, apply some formatting, rather than switching over to the mouse to click the equivalent Ribbon button.

First, all the Office 365 apps offer many keyboard shortcuts. For example, you can toggle the Ribbon between collapsed and full by pressing Ctrl+F1. (refer to the "Collapsing and showing the Ribbon" sidebar). This means you hold down Ctrl, press F1, then release Ctrl. As you go through this book, I tell you a feature's keyboard shortcut, if one is available.

Second, Office 365 offers Alt+key shortcuts that enable you to run a command by pressing a series of keys. Here's the procedure to follow:

1. **Press the Alt key.**

   Letters — they're called *KeyTips* — appear on the Ribbons' tab names.

2. **Press a tab's KeyTip to open that tab.**

   For example, pressing **h** opens the Home tab.

   In the opened tab, KeyTips now appear for each button, drop-down list, and gallery.

3. **Press the letter or letters associated with the command you want to run.**

   If a given control has a two-letter KeyTip, press the first letter, then press the second letter.

   The Office 365 app runs the command.

   If the command displays a drop-down list or a gallery, more KeyTips appear in the displayed list or gallery.

4. **Repeat Step 3 as needed until you're done.**

## SEARCHING FOR HELP

In all Office 365 applications, the Search box (pointed out earlier in Figure 1-2) appears at the top of the window. Follow these steps the next time you can't locate a command in an Office 365 application:

1. Click the magnifying glass or the word *Search* (or press Alt+Q). Your Office 365 application presents a list of tasks in a drop-down menu. On the list, tasks you attempted recently appear under the heading "Recently Used Actions," and tasks Office 365 thinks you'd like to try appear under the heading "Suggested Actions."
2. If the task you want to complete is on the list, click it. Otherwise, type a word or two to describe the task that needs to be completed. A new task list appears.
3. Click your task on the list, enter a different term to describe the task, or choose a Help topic on the list.

# Saving Your Files

Soon after you create a new file, be sure to save it. And save your file from time to time while you work on it as well. Until you save your work, it resides in the computer's electronic memory, a precarious location. If a power outage occurs or your computer crashes, you lose all the work you did since the last time you saved your file. (And if you haven't yet saved a new file, you lose all your work, period.) Make it a habit to save files every few minutes or so or when you complete an important task.

REMEMBER

The above applies only if you save your work locally on your PC. An alternative is to save your documents on OneDrive, as I mention earlier. A big advantage to using OneDrive is that Office 365 saves your document changes automatically, so you never have to worry about losing important work. Book 8, Chapter 2, is the place to be to learn all about OneDrive.

## Saving a file

To save a file, use any of the following three techniques:

- Click the Quick Access toolbar's Save button (shown in the margin).
- Press Ctrl+S.
- Click the File tab and then click Save.

## Saving a new file for the first time

Follow these steps to save a file for the first time (or save a file under a different name or in a different location):

1. **Click the File tab and then click Save As.**

   The Save As window opens (refer to Figure 1-8).

   If the Save This File dialog box appears, instead, you can type a name, choose a storage location, and click Save; or you can click More Options to open the Save As window. Note that you can head directly to the Save As dialog box by pressing F12.

2. **Type a descriptive name for the file.**
3. **If the current location (pointed out in Figure 1-8) isn't where you want to store the file, select This PC to rummage through folders on your computer.**

   You can also list network and OneDrive locations in the Open and Save As windows. (Refer to Book 8, Chapter 2 to learn more about OneDrive.)

4. **Select the folder where you expect to find or want to save the file.**

   The window provides a few techniques for finding that folder:

   - **Recent Folders:** Click the name of a folder you opened recently.
   - **New Folder:** Click to open the Create New Folder dialog box, type the name of the folder, then click OK. The app creates a new subfolder in the current location.
   - **More Options:** Click the More Options button, then use the Save As dialog box to locate and select a folder.

5. **Click Save.**

   The app saves the file.

## Saving AutoRecovery information

To ensure against data loss owing to computer and power failures, Office 365 saves files on its own every ten minutes. (Unless, as I mention earlier, your document is stored on OneDrive, in which case Office 365 saves the document as soon as you make any change.) These files are saved in an AutoRecovery file. After your computer fails, you can try to recover some of the work you lost by getting it from the AutoRecovery file, which appears automatically the next time you start the Office 365 app.

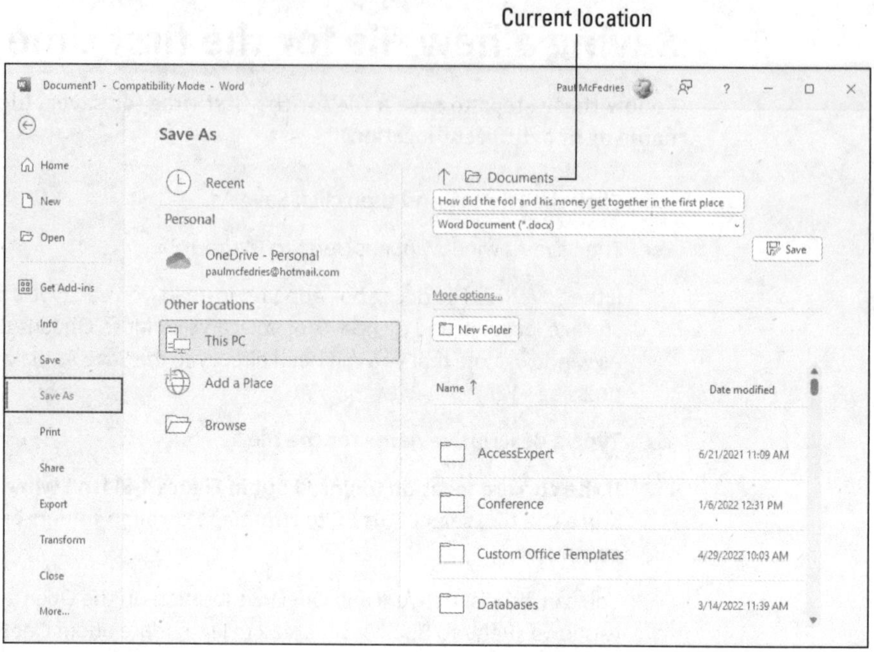


**FIGURE 1-8:** Use the Save As window to save a new file for the first time.

Office 365 saves AutoRecovery files every ten minutes, but if you want the program to save the files more or less frequently, you can change the AutoRecovery setting by following these steps:

1. **On the File tab, click Options.**

   The Options dialog box appears.

2. **Select the Save category.**
3. **Enter a Minutes setting in the Save AutoRecover Information Every box.**
4. **Click OK.**

# Opening and Closing Files

To get to work on a file, you have to open it first. And, of course, you close a file when you're finished working on it and want to stop and smell the roses.

## Opening a file

Follow these steps to open a file:

1. **On the File tab, click Open (or press Ctrl+O).**

   The Open window appears. It lists files you recently opened.

2. **If the name of the file you want to open is on the Recent list, click the name to open the file.**

   If the name isn't on the list, go to Step 3.

3. **Click the location — This PC, OneDrive, a network folder — where the file is located.**

   Click This PC if the file is located on your computer.

4. **Select the folder and file you want to open.**

   There are a couple of ways you can select the folder and file:

   - If the folder appears in the backstage view's Open window, click the folder, then click the file.
   - If the folder isn't listed in the Open window, click the Browse button to display the Open dialog box, navigate to the folder, click the file, and then click Open.

   Your file opens.

TIP

Another way to open a file is to locate it in File Explorer, then double-click it.

## Closing a file

To close a file, save your file and use one of these techniques:

- On the File tab, click Close.
- Click Close (shown in the margin) in the upper-right corner of the window.
- Press Alt+F4.

IN THIS CHAPTER

» Dealing with capitalization

» Adding symbols and links

» Speaking words of wisdom

» Selecting, moving, copying, and deleting text

» Playing around with the font, size, and color of text

# Chapter 2

# Populating Documents with Text

I'm going to go out on the world's sturdiest limb here and say that it's an extremely rare Office 365 user who doesn't work with text in some way. Even the rightmost of right-brain artists still need to caption or describe their creations; even the leftmost of left-brain types still need to label or annotate their worksheets. So, whether you spend time in Word, Excel, Outlook, or PowerPoint, you spend time wrestling with words.

In this book's Introduction, one of the "foolish assumptions" I made about you is that you know your way around a keyboard, by which I mean you know how to type. Sure, "typing" for you might mean hunting-and-pecking with two forefingers but, even so, you know how to make your keyboard make words.

So, while this chapter has a bit to say about getting text into a document, it's not a primer about typing text, per se. Instead, you explore a few interesting tidbits about entering text, such as changing case, inserting symbols, forging hyperlinks, and speaking text. The bulk of the chapter deals with the text-related tasks that are common to all the Office 365 apps, including selecting text; moving, copying, and deleting text; and formatting text.

# Messing with Capitalization

Early typesetters stored their letters in a giant case that had two compartments: the lower compartment held the regular letters, while the upper compartment held the capitals. That's why, today, we speak of regular letters being *lowercase*, while capital letters are *uppercase*. More generally, we use the word *case* to refer to how letters are capitalized in words and sentences. Table 2-1 explains the different cases as they're used in Office 365.

**TABLE 2-1** Cases for Headings and Titles

| Case | Description | Example |
|---|---|---|
| Sentence Case | The first letter in the first word is capitalized; all other words are lowercase. | The rain in spain |
| Lowercase | All letters are lowercase even if they are proper names. | the rain in spain |
| Uppercase | All letters are uppercase no matter what. | THE RAIN IN SPAIN |
| Capitalize Each Word | The first letter in each word is capitalized. | The Rain In Spain |

Notice that Office 365's different capitalization methods aren't all that smart. That is, a case such as lowercase changes *everything* to lowercase letters, even when the text includes a proper name (such as *Spain*) that should have a capital first letter.

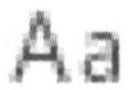


To change case in Word and PowerPoint, select the text you want to alter, go to the Home tab, click the Font group's Change Case button (shown in the margin), and then click one of the following options on the drop-down list:

- **Sentence case:** Renders the letters in sentence case
- **lowercase:** Makes all the letters lowercase
- **UPPERCASE:** Converts all the letters to capitals
- **Capitalize Each Word:** Capitalizes the first letter in each word (even, unfortunately, not-normally-capitalized words such as *the*, *a*, and *an*)
- **tOGGLE cASE:** Reverses the case of each letter (that is, changes uppercase to lowercase and lowercase to uppercase). Choose this option if you accidentally enter letters with the Caps Lock key pressed.

TIP

You can also change case by pressing Shift+F3. Each time you press this key combination, Word and PowerPoint cycle the selected text through uppercase, lowercase, and sentence case.

# Entering Symbols, Foreign Letters, and Other Oddball Characters



What's on your keyboard doesn't represent every possible character you can add to a document — far from it. There are dozens, nay hundreds, okay *thousands* of other symbols and foreign characters available to you. Are you writing an article about the euro currency, but don't know how to enter the € symbol? Are you writing a history of United Nations Secretaries-General, but can't find the letter ö so you can write Dag Hammarksjöld?

Have no fear. You can enter any symbol and foreign character by following these steps:

1. **On the Insert tab, in the Symbols group, click the Symbol button.**

   Excel and PowerPoint take you directly to the Symbol dialog box (refer to Figure 2-1).

   Word, Outlook, and Publisher display a menu of recently used symbols. If the symbol you seek appears, go right ahead and click it and then skip the rest of these steps with a glad heart. Otherwise, click More Symbols to open the Symbol dialog box.

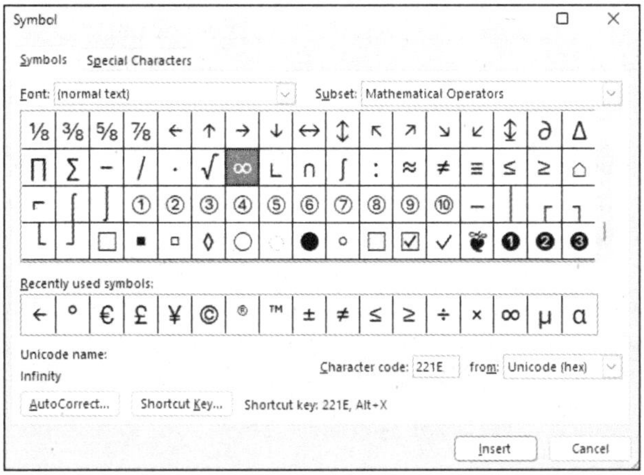


**FIGURE 2-1:** To enter a symbol or foreign character, select it and click the Insert button.

2. **If you're looking to insert a symbol, not a foreign character, choose Webdings or Wingdings 1, 2, or 3 in the Font drop-down list.**

   Webdings and the Wingdings fonts offer all kinds of weird and wacky symbols.

3. **Click the symbol or foreign character you want to insert.**

   You may have to scroll to find the one you want. You can also use the Subset list to choose a particular set of characters, such as Arrows or Currency Symbols.

4. **Click the Insert button to enter the symbol.**
5. **Repeat Steps 2 through 4 to insert any other symbols you require.**
6. **Click Close to shut down the dialog box.**

TIP

Word's Symbol dialog box offers a Shortcut Key for most symbols. In some cases, the shortcut key combo is straightforward, such as Alt+Ctrl+C for the copyright symbol and Alt+0165 (that is, hold down Alt and press the numbers 0165 on the numeric keypad) for the Yen currency symbol. Some shortcuts are a bit strange, though. For example, Word's Symbol dialog box says the shortcut for the infinity symbol is 221E, Alt+X (refer to Figure 2-1). Huh? What this means is that you type **221E**, then press Alt+X. Word then changes the 221E text into the infinity sign.

# Forging Hyperlinks

A *hyperlink* is an electronic shortcut from one place to another. If you've spent any time on the internet, you know what a hyperlink is. Clicking hyperlinks on the internet takes you to different web pages or different places on the same web page. In the Office applications, you can use hyperlinks to connect readers to your favorite web pages or to a different page, slide, or file. You can fashion a link out of a word or phrase as well as any object — a graphic image, text box, shape, or picture.

The next few sections explain how to insert a hyperlink to another place in your file as well as create links to web pages. You also discover how to enter an email hyperlink that makes it easy for others to email you.

REMEMBER

The Office applications create a hyperlink for you automatically when you type a word that begins with *www.* and ends with *.com* or *.net*. The programs create an automatic email hyperlink when you enter letters that include the at symbol (@) and end in *.com* or *.net*.

## Linking a hyperlink to a web page

It could well be that a web page on the internet has all the information your readers need. In that case, you can link to the web page so that viewers can visit it in the course of viewing your file. When a viewer clicks the link, a web browser opens and the web page appears.

Follow these steps to hyperlink your file to a web page on the internet:

1. **Select the text or object that will form the hyperlink.**

   For example, select a line of text or phrase if you want viewers to be able to click it to go to a web page.

2. **On the Insert tab, in the Links group, click the Link button (or press Ctrl+K).**

   The Insert Hyperlink dialog box drops by, as shown in Figure 2-2. You can also open the dialog box by right-clicking an object or text and choosing Link on the shortcut menu.

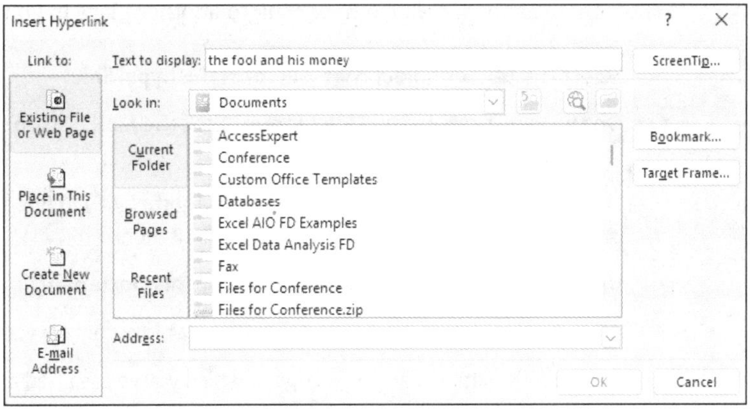


**FIGURE 2-2:** Enter the web page target in the Address text box to create a hyperlink to a web page.

3. **Under Link To on the left, select Existing File or Web Page.**

4. **In the Address text box, enter the address of the web page to which you want to link.**

   From easiest to hardest, here are techniques for entering web page addresses:

   - **Copy and paste the address:** If you have the web page open in a browser, use the browser to copy the address, then paste it into the Address text box.

   - **Browse for the address:** Click the Browse the Web button to open your web browser, navigate to the web page, copy the page's address in your web browser, and paste the address in the Address text box.

- **Choose a recent page:** Click Browsed Pages to open a dialog box that lists web pages you recently visited after you click this button. Click a web page.
- **Type the web page address:** If you happen to know the address, you can type it directly into the Address text box.

5. **Click the ScreenTip button, enter a ScreenTip in the Set Hyperlink ScreenTip dialog box, and click OK.**

   Viewers can read the ScreenTip you enter when they move their pointers over the hyperlink.

6. **Click OK to convert the selected text or object into a hyperlink.**

   I would test the hyperlink if I were you to make sure that it takes viewers to the right web page. To test a hyperlink, Ctrl+click it or right-click it and choose Open Hyperlink on the shortcut menu.

## Creating a hyperlink to another place in your file

Follow these steps to create a hyperlink to another place in your file:

1. **Select the text or object that will form the hyperlink.**
2. **On the Insert tab, in the Links group, click the Link button (or press Ctrl+K).**

   The Insert Hyperlink dialog box shows up. Another way to open this dialog box is to right-click and choose Link in the shortcut menu.

3. **Under Link To on the left, select Place in This Document.**

   What appears in the dialog box depends on which program you're working in:

   - Word: Bookmarks and headings to which you've assigned a heading style
   - Excel: Boxes for entering cell references and defined cell names
   - PowerPoint: A list of slides in your presentation, as well as links to the first, last, next, and previous slide, as shown in Figure 2-3

4. **In the Select a Place in This Document list, click the target of the hyperlink.**
5. **Click the ScreenTip button, type a ScreenTip, and click OK.**

   When viewers move their pointers over the link, the words you type appear in a tooltip. Type a description of the hyperlink's destination.

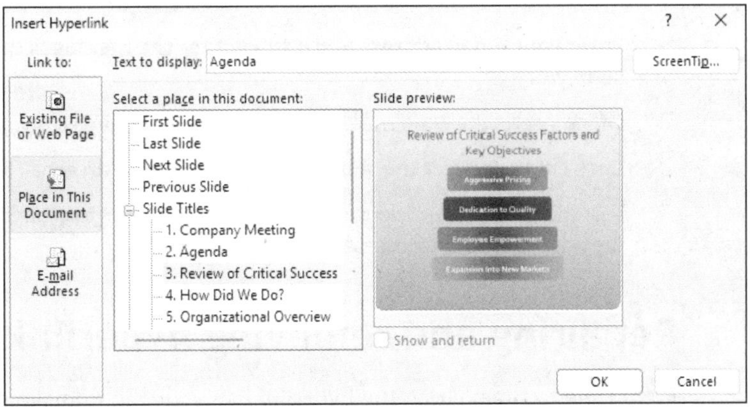


**FIGURE 2-3:** You can create a hyperlink to a different place in a file, such as to another slide.



6. **Click OK to convert the selected text or object to a hyperlink.**

   To test your hyperlink, move the pointer over it. The ScreenTip description you wrote should appear. Ctrl+click the link to check that it takes you to the right place.

## Creating an email hyperlink

An *email hyperlink* is one that opens an email program. These links are sometimes found on web pages so that anyone visiting a web page can conveniently send an email message to the person who manages the web page. When you click an email hyperlink, your default email program opens. And if the person who set up the link was thorough about it, the email message is already addressed and given a subject line.

TIP

Include an email hyperlink in a file if you're distributing the file to others and would like them to be able to comment on your work and send the comments to you.

Follow these steps to put an email hyperlink in a file:

1. **Select the words or object that will constitute the link.**
2. **On the Insert tab, in the Links group, click the Link button (or press Ctrl+K).**

   The Insert Hyperlink dialog box appears.
3. **Under Link To on the left, click Email Address.**

   Text boxes appear for entering an email address and a subject message.

4. **Enter your email address and a subject for the messages that others will send you.**

   Office inserts the word mailto: before your email address as you enter it.

5. **Click OK to convert the selected text or object to an email hyperlink.**

   Test the link by Ctrl+clicking it. Your default email program opens. The email message is already addressed and given a subject.

## Repairing and removing hyperlinks

From time to time, check the hyperlinks in your file to make sure that they still work. Clicking a hyperlink and having nothing happen is disappointing. Hyperlinks get broken when web pages and parts of files are deleted.

To repair or remove a hyperlink, right-click the link and choose Edit Link on the shortcut menu (or click in the link and then click the Link button on the Insert tab). The Edit Hyperlink dialog box appears. This dialog box looks and works just like the Insert Hyperlink dialog box. Sometimes you can repair a link simply by editing it in this dialog box.

- **Repairing a link:** Select a target in your file or a web page and click OK.
- **Removing a link:** Click the Remove Link button. You can also remove a hyperlink by right-clicking the link and choosing Remove Link on the shortcut menu.

# Dictating the Words

Where Word, PowerPoint, and Outlook are concerned, you can be a dictator. You can dictate words rather than type them. As long as you speak slowly, and as long as the microphone on your computer works, Office can understand the words (most of them, anyway) and enter them for you.

Start by making sure that Office knows which language you want to speak. On the Home tab, click the down arrow on the Dictate button and select a language or regional language from the drop-down list.

Place the cursor where you want the words to appear and follow these steps to dictate to Word, PowerPoint, or Outlook:



1. **On the Home tab, in the Voice group (or on the Message tab in Outlook), click the Dictate button (shown in the margin).**

   A dialog box for recording your voice appears onscreen, as shown in Figure 2-4.

FIGURE 2-4: Dictating to Microsoft Word.

2. **The app should activate the Microphone button automatically. If not, click the Microphone button (shown in the margin).**

   The app activates dictation mode.

3. **Start talking slowly and clearly.**

   To enter a punctuation mark, say its name. For example, to enter a period, say "period."

   To start a new paragraph, say "new paragraph."

   REMEMBER

   Don't use your keyboard while dictating. Using your keyboard tells Office that you want to type the words, not speak them.

4. **Click the Microphone button again to stop dictating.**



# Manipulating Text Like a Pro

Whether you type, paste, or dictate text, or get Copilot to create text for you, it's unlikely you'll want to let the text just sit there in its original condition. Fortunately, all the Office 365 programs offer a wide range of features and techniques for manipulating text, whatever its origin.

The next few sections describe the many techniques that are available for selecting, deleting, copying, and moving text. You find an inordinate number of tips on these pages because so many shortcuts for manipulating text are available. Master the many shortcuts and you cut down considerably on the time you spend editing text. You're welcome.

## Selecting text

Before you can do anything to text — move it, boldface it, delete it, translate it — you have to select it. Here are speed techniques for selecting text:

| To Select | Do This |
|---|---|
| A word | Double-click the word. |
| A few words | Drag over the words. From the keyboard, position the cursor at the start of the first word, hold down Ctrl and Shift, then press the right arrow key until all the words you want are selected. |

| To Select | Do This |
|---|---|
| A paragraph | Triple-click inside the paragraph (in Word, PowerPoint, and Outlook messages). |
| A block of text | Click the start of the text, hold down the Shift key, and click the end of the text. In Word you can also click the start of the text, press F8, and click at the end of the text. |
| All text | Press Ctrl+A. |

TIP

Word offers a special command for selecting text with similar formats throughout a document. You can use this command to make wholesale changes to text. Select an example of the text that needs changing, and on the Home tab, in the Editing group, click the Select button and then click Select All Text with Similar Formatting. Then choose formatting commands to change all instances of the text that you selected.

## Moving or copying text

Office 365 offers a couple of ways to move or copy text from place to place. Select the text you want to work with and then use one of these techniques to move or copy it:

- **Dragging and dropping:** Position the mouse over the text and then drag the text to move it to the new location. If you want to copy the text, instead, hold down the Ctrl key while you drag.

- **Using the Clipboard:** Move the text by clicking the Cut button (shown in the margin) in the Home tab's Clipboard group, pressing Ctrl+X, or right-clicking the text and clicking Cut on the shortcut menu. The text is moved to an electronic holding tank called the Clipboard. Position the cursor where you want the text moved, and then paste the text by clicking the Paste button in the Home tab's Clipboard group, pressing Ctrl+V, or right-clicking and choosing Paste.

  Copy the text by clicking the Copy button (shown in the margin) in the Home tab's Clipboard group, pressing Ctrl+C, or right-clicking the text and clicking Copy on the shortcut menu. Position the cursor where you want the copy to appear, then paste the text by clicking the Paste button, pressing Ctrl+V, or right-clicking and choosing Paste.

## A LOOK AT THE PASTE OPTIONS

Text adopts the formatting of neighboring text when you move or copy it to a new location. Using the Paste options, however, you can decide for yourself what happens to text formatting when you move or copy text from one place to another. To avail yourself of the Paste options:

- On the Home tab, in the Clipboard group, open the drop-down list on the Paste button to display the Paste Options submenu.
- Right-click to display the Paste options on the shortcut menu.

- Click the Paste Options button (shown in the margin) to open the Paste Options submenu. This button appears after you paste text by clicking the Paste button or pressing Ctrl+V.

Choose a Paste option to determine what happens to text formatting when you move or copy text to a new location:

- **Keep Source Formatting:** The text keeps its original formatting. Choose this option to move or copy text formatting along with text to a different location.
- **Merge Formatting (Word only):** The text adopts the formatting of the text where it is moved or copied.
- **Keep Text Only:** The text is stripped of all formatting.

In Word, you can decide for yourself what the default activity is when you paste within a document, between documents, and between programs. Go to the File tab and choose Options. In the Options dialog box, go to the Advanced category, and under Cut, Copy, and Paste, choose default options.



## Taking advantage of the Clipboard task pane

The Office Clipboard is a piece of work. After you copy or cut text with the Cut or Copy command, the text is placed on the Clipboard. The Clipboard holds the last 24 items that you cut or copied. You can open the Clipboard task pane and view the last 24 items you cut or copied to the Clipboard and cut or copy them anew, as shown in Figure 2-5.

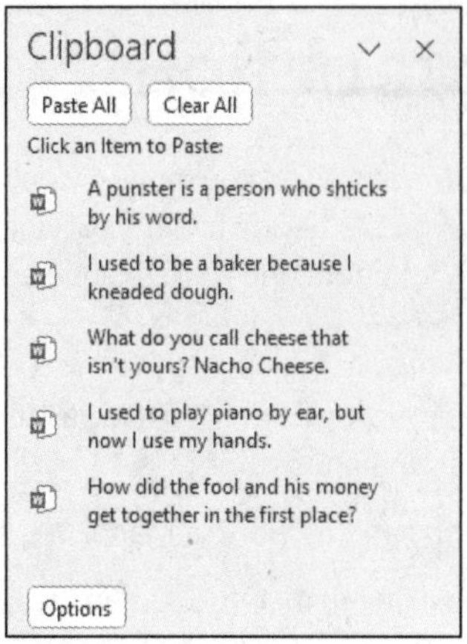


**FIGURE 2-5:** The Clipboard task pane in action.

To open the Clipboard task pane, go to the Home tab and click the Clipboard group's dialog box launcher (shown in the margin). Icons next to the items tell you where they came from. To copy an item, click it or open its drop-down list and choose Paste. The Clipboard, which is available to all Office applications, is especially useful for copying text and graphics from one Office application to another.

## Deleting text

To delete text, select it and press the Delete key. To replace existing text with new text, first select the existing text, then start typing the new text. The letters you type immediately take the place of and delete the text you selected.

REMEMBER

You can always click the Undo button (shown in the margin; or press Ctrl+Z) if you regret deleting text. The Undo button is located on the Quick Access toolbar.

And if you regret your regret and decide that you didn't want to undo your most recent edit after all, you can click the Redo button (shown in the margin; or press Ctrl+Y). The Redo button is right next to Undo on the Quick Access toolbar.

# Formatting Text for Fun and Profit

When you write just for yourself, it really doesn't matter what the text looks like. However, the words you type in your PowerPoint presentations, Outlook email messages, and even some of your Word documents and Excel workbooks will be read by other folks. And just like you wouldn't go to a party without giving at least some thought to what you wear, nor should your words go out in public unadorned. Adding a judicious amount of formatting to your text can make it clearer, more forceful, and easier to read overall.

When I talk about formatting text, what I mean is the text's font, the size of the letters, the color of the letters, and whether text effects or font styles such as italic or boldface are applied to the text.

A *font* is a collection of letters, numbers, and symbols in a particular *typeface*, which is a distinctive look that has been applied to each character. Some fonts give your text a classy, formal look, while others present your words with a more modern, clean feel.



*Font styles* include boldface, italic, and underline. By convention, headings are boldface. Italic is used for emphasis and to mark foreign words in text. Office 365 also provides a number of *text effects*, also known as *text attributes*, which include strikethrough (~~like this~~), superscripts (for example, $e = mc^2$), and subscripts (for example, $H_2O$).

WARNING

The Office 365 apps all come with an impressive collection of fonts and quite a few styles and effects. The temptation might be to throw a ton of formatting at your text, thinking that it makes it interesting or fun. Sorry, but all you'll really be doing is making your text annoying and unreadable. Please use fonts and text effects responsibly.

The following sections look at the different ways to change the font, font size, and color of text, as well as how to assign font styles and text effects to text.

## THE FORMAT PAINTER: A FAST WAY TO CHANGE THE LOOK OF TEXT

When you're in a hurry to change the look of text and reformat paragraphs, consider using the Format Painter. This nifty tool works something like a paintbrush. You drag it over text to apply — or, in a sense, *paint* — existing formatting onto the text. Follow these instructions to use the Format Painter:

1. Click within or select the text that has the formatting you want to apply elsewhere.
2. On the Home tab, in the Clipboard group (or the Format Text tab in an Outlook message), click the Format Painter button (shown in the margin), or press Ctrl+Shift+C.

*(continued)*

*(continued)*

If you want to apply the formatting to two or more places, double-click the button, instead of just clicking it.

The mouse pointer changes to a paintbrush.

3. Drag the pointer across text to which you want to copy the formats.

   Format Painter applies the formatting from the original text to the new text. If you clicked the Format Painter button once, the Office 365 app automatically turns off Format Painter, so you can skip the rest of the steps.

4. If you double-clicked the Format Painter button, repeat Step 3 for each of the other places to which you want to copy the formatting.

5. Click the Format Painter button or press Esc when you finish using the Format Painter.

At the opposite end of the spectrum from the Format Painter button is the Clear All Formatting button (shown in the margin) on the Home tab in the Font group. You can select text and click this button to strip the selected text of all its formats, whatever they may be.

## Formatting text: let me count the ways

You'll spend quite a bit of your precious time formatting text, so those formatting tasks will go easier if you know all the ways that the Office 365 apps offer to format the selected text or any new text you type after selecting the formatting:

- **Home tab Font group:** Use the controls in this group to select a font, apply a font size, and apply any of the font styles and effects.
- **Mini-toolbar:** Use the controls in this toolbar — which appears immediately after you select the text with the mouse — to apply a subset of the text formatting commands.

- **Font dialog box:** On the Home tab, click the Font group dialog box launcher (shown in the margin), or press Ctrl+D. In the Font dialog box that shows up, select a font, font size, text styles or effects, then click OK.
- **Shortcut menu:** Right-click the selected text, click Font to open the Font dialog box, choose your formatting, then click OK.

## Upgrading text with a new font

The default fonts used by each Office 365 app are fine, but are you sure you want to settle for just fine? I thought not. So, why not upgrade your documents with a nicer font? It might take a bit of experimenting to find a font that works for you, but those experiments are made easier by the previews that the Office 365 apps display when you use the Font list from the Home tab or the mini-toolbar. Pull down the Font drop-down list, hover the mouse pointer over a font, and the selected text displays a preview of the font, as shown in Figure 2-6. If that's the font you want to apply, click it to make it so.

**FIGURE 2-6:** Hover the mouse pointer over a font in the Home tab's Font drop-down list to display a preview of the font for the selected text.

**WARNING**

Avoid using too many different fonts because a file with too many fonts looks like alphabet soup. The object is to choose a font that helps set the tone. An aggressive sales pitch calls for a strong, bold font; a technical presentation calls for a font that is clean and unobtrusive. Make sure that the fonts you select help communicate your message.

## Making text larger or smaller

Font size enables you to create a kind of hierarchy for your text, with more important text, such as titles and headings, formatted with a larger size, and less important text, such as footnotes, formatted with a smaller size. Just so you know, font size is measured in *points*, where in most apps the default size is 16 points. (It probably doesn't help you to know that there are 72 points to an inch, especially if you're not even sure what an "inch" is. My advice? Don't worry about it even a little bit.)

Select your text and use one of these techniques to change the font size of the characters:

- **Font Size drop-down list:** On the Home tab, in the mini-toolbar, or in the Font dialog box, open the Font Size drop-down list and choose a font size.
- **Increase Font Size button:** Click this button (shown in the margin) or press Ctrl+] to increase the point size to the next value on the Font Size drop-down list. You can find the Increase Font Size button on the Home tab in the Font group and on the mini-toolbar.
- **Decrease Font Size button:** Click this button (shown in the margin) or press Ctrl+[ to decrease the point size to the previous value on the Font Size drop-down list. You can find the Decrease Font Size button on the Home tab in the Font group and on the mini-toolbar.

TIP

If the font size you want isn't on the Font Size drop-down list, enter the size. For example, to change the font size to 13.5 points, type **13.5** in the Font Size box and press Enter.

## Applying styles to text

There are four — count 'em, four — font styles that you can apply to the selected text:

- **Regular:** This style is just Office's way of denoting an absence of any applied font style. In the Font dialog box, select Regular in the Font Style list, then click OK.
- **Bold:** Bold text, like the word at the start of this bullet, calls attention to itself. Either click Bold (shown in the margin) on the Home tab's Font group or in the mini-toolbar, or, in the Font dialog box, select Bold in the Font Style list, then click OK.

- **Italic:** Italic is used for emphasis, when introducing a new term, and to mark foreign words such as *violà*, *gung hay fat choy*, and *Qué magnifico!* You can also italicize titles to make them a little more elegant. Either click Italic (shown in the margin) on the Home tab's Font group or in the mini-toolbar, or, in the Font dialog box, select Italic in the Font Style list, then click OK.
- **Underline:** Underlined text also calls attention to itself, but use underlining sparingly. Either click Underline (shown in the margin) on the Home tab's Font group or in the mini-toolbar, or, in the Font dialog box, select an item in the Underline Style list, then click OK.

To remove a font style from the selected text, click the Bold, Italic, or Underline button a second time. You can also select text and then click the Clear Formatting button on the Home tab (in Word, PowerPoint, and Publisher).



## Fancifying text with effects

Text effects have various uses, some utilitarian and some strictly for yucks. Be careful with text effects. Use them sparingly and to good purpose. To apply a text effect, either use the Home tab's Font group (or the Format Text tab in Outlook messages) or the Font dialog box.

Here's a rundown of the different text effects (not all these effects are available in PowerPoint, Excel, Publisher, and Outlook):

- **Strikethrough and double strikethrough:** By convention, `strikethrough` is used to show where passages are struck from a contract or other important document. `Double strikethrough`, for all I know, is used to show where passages are struck out forcefully. Use these text effects to demonstrate ideas that you reject. Strikethrough is available on the Home tab (shown in the margin). Both Strikethrough and Double Strikethrough are available as check boxes in the Font dialog box.
- **Subscript:** A *subscript* is a character that is lowered in the text, like so: $C_{12}H_{22}O_{11}$. Subscript is available on the Home tab (shown in the margin) and as a check box in the Font dialog box. For kicks, you can also press Ctrl+=.
- **Superscript:** A *superscript* is a character that is raised in the text, as in this example: $a^2 + b^2 = c^2$. Superscript is available on the Home tab (shown in the margin) and as a check box in the Font dialog box. You can also press Ctrl+Shift+plus sign.

- **Small Caps:** A small cap is a small version of a capital letter. You can find many creative uses for small caps. An all-small-cap title looks elegant. Be sure to type lowercase letters in order to create small caps. Type an uppercase letter, and Office refuses to turn it into a small cap. Not all fonts can produce small capital letters. Small Caps is available as a check box in the Font dialog box.
- **All Caps:** The All Caps text effect merely capitalizes all letters. Use it in styles to make sure that you enter text in all capital letters. All Caps is available as a check box in the Font dialog box.
- **Equalize Character Height (PowerPoint only):** This effect makes all characters the same height and stretches the characters in text. You can use it to produce interesting effects in text box announcements. Equalize Character Height is available as a check box in the Font dialog box.

## Coloring text

You can add a bit of visual interest, perhaps even a dash of pizzazz, by changing the color of a word or phrase. For example, you might want to make all your headings dark blue, your document subtitle a light gray, a warning label red, and so on. As with all other things related to text formatting, the key here is moderation: A few colors here and there can enhance your document; a few dozen colors all over the place will make your document the laughingstock of your next Teams meeting.

WARNING

Before you change the color of text, examine the current background color of the document. It's vital that you choose a text color with sufficient contrast that the text will be readable against the background color.

Select the text that needs touching up and then use one of these techniques to change its color:

- On the Home tab's Font group or on the mini-toolbar, click the Font Color button (shown in the margin) to display the drop-down list shown in Figure 2-7, then click a color.
- In the Font dialog box, open the Font Color drop-down list, choose a color, and then click OK.

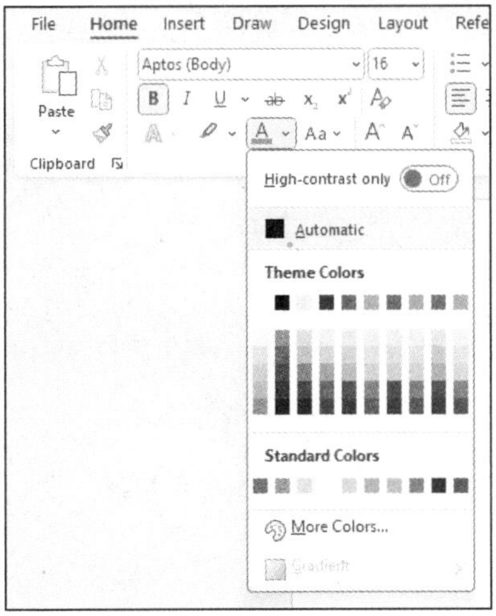


**FIGURE 2-7:** Choosing a font color on the mini-toolbar.

TIP

The Font Color drop-down list offers theme colors and standard colors. You are well advised to choose a theme color. These colors are deemed *theme colors* because they jibe with the theme you chose for your file. For info on Word's themes, check out Book 2, Chapter 6; to learn about PowerPoint themes, head over to Book 4, Chapter 2.

IN THIS CHAPTER

» Undoing mistakes and repeating actions

» Zooming to get a better view of your work

» Getting multiple views of a single file

» Entering laborious-to-type text with the AutoCorrect command

# Chapter 3
# Becoming Enviously Efficient

Unless you're either a workaholic or an artist (not that the two are mutually exclusive, mind you), chances are you want to get your Office 365 work done as quickly as possible so that you can move on to other activities that are more interesting or more fun. Getting things done usually means a nose-to-the-proverbial-grindstone mindset where you just focus on your work and promise yourself that the YouTube cat videos can wait until you get home.

However, there's another way to speed up your work: become a ridiculously efficient Office 365 user. In one sense, that's one of the goals of this book because throughout I show you the fastest way to complete most tasks, tell you about any shortcut keys that you can use, tell you (and show you) exactly where a command is located on the Ribbon, and more.

Then there's this brief chapter, which takes you on a whirlwind tour of shortcut techniques that can save you time and effort no matter which Office 365 application you're working in. With these speed-enhancing tools in your back pocket, you'll be able to get your Office 365 chores done quickly and then get away from your computer. You're welcome!

# Undoing and Repeating Commands

If I were to choose two commands for the Hall of Fame, they would be the Undo command and the Repeat command. One allows you to reverse actions you regret doing, and the other repeats a previous action without your having to choose the same commands all over again. Undo and Repeat are explained forthwith.

## Undoing a mistake

Fortunately for you, all is not lost if you make a big blunder because Office has a marvelous little tool called the Undo command. This command "remembers" your previous editorial and formatting changes. As long as you catch your error in time, you can undo your mistake.

Click the Undo button (shown in the margin) on the Quick Access toolbar, or press Ctrl+Z, to undo your most recent change. If you made your error and went on to do something else before you caught it, open the drop-down list on the Undo button. It lists your most recent actions, as shown in Figure 3-1. Find the action you want to undo, then click it.

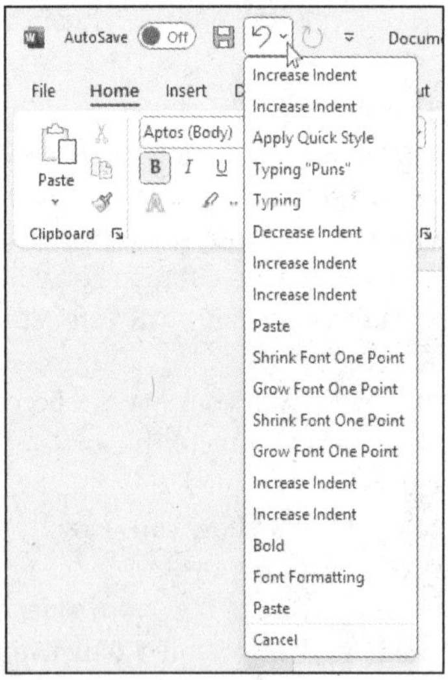


**FIGURE 3-1:** You can reverse multiple actions using the Undo drop-down list.

WARNING

It's vital to remember that clicking an action far down the Undo list doesn't just reverse that action; it also reverses *all* the actions above it on the list! For example, if you undo the 19th action on the list, you also undo the 18 more recent actions above it.

## Repeating an action — and quicker this time

The Quick Access toolbar offers a button called Repeat that you can click to repeat your last action. This button can be a mighty, mighty timesaver. For example, if you just changed fonts in one heading and you want to change another heading in the same way, select the heading you want to change and click the Repeat button (shown in the margin) or press either F4 or Ctrl+Y. Move the pointer over the Repeat button to display, in a pop-up box, what clicking Repeat will do.

After you click the Undo button, the Repeat button changes names and becomes the Redo button. Click the Redo button to "redo" the command you just "undid." In other words, if you regret clicking the Undo button, you can turn back the clock by immediately clicking Redo.

# Zooming In, Zooming Out

Your eyes don't come equipped with built-in magnifying glasses, which makes the Zoom controls all the more valuable. You can find these controls on the View tab and in the lower-right corner of the window, as shown in Figure 3-2. Use them freely and often to enlarge (or shrink) what's on the screen so that your eyes don't have to work so hard.



Meet the Zoom controls:

- **Zoom button:** On the View tab, in the Zoom group, click the Zoom button to display the Zoom dialog box, shown in Figure 3-2. (You can also get the Zoom dialog box onscreen by clicking the Zoom level percentage value shown to the right of the Zoom slider.) From there, you can select an option button or enter a percent measurement.
- **Zoom slider:** Drag this slider left to reduce the Zoom level or right to increase the Zoom level.
- **Zoom In:** Click this button on the right side of the Zoom slider to zoom in using 10-percent increments (or to the next highest 10-percent increment).
- **Zoom Out:** Click this button on the left side of the Zoom slider to zoom out using 10-percent increments (or to the next lowest 10-percent increment).
- **Mouse wheel:** If your mouse has a wheel, you can hold down the Ctrl key and rotate the wheel forward to zoom in or backward to zoom out.

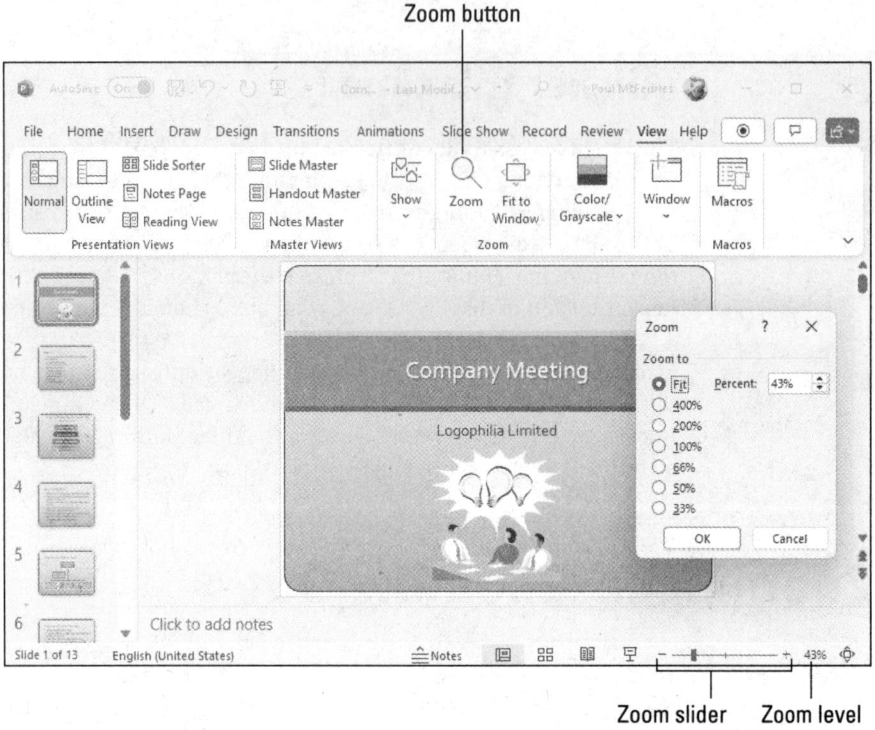


**FIGURE 3-2:** The Zoom controls.

TIP

Each Office program offers its own special Zoom commands in the Zoom group on the View tab. In Word, for example, you can display one page or two pages; in Excel, you can click the Zoom to Selection button to enlarge a handful of cells. Make friends with the Zoom commands. They never let you down.

# Viewing a File Through More Than One Window

By way of the commands in the Window group in the View tab, you can be in two places simultaneously, at least where Office is concerned. You can work on two files at one time. You can place files side by side on the screen and do a number of other things to make your work a little easier.

On the View tab, Word, Excel, and PowerPoint offer these buttons in the Window group:

» **New Window:** Opens another window on your file so that you can be two places simultaneously in the same file. To go back and forth between windows, click a taskbar button or click the Switch Windows button and choose a window name on the drop-down list. Click a window's Close button when you finish looking at it.

- **Arrange All:** Arranges open windows onscreen so that all are visible. Similar to Arrange All, the Cascade command in PowerPoint displays open windows so that they overlap.
- **Split:** Divides the document window horizontally and enables you to navigate the upper and lower sections separately, which makes it easy to view two different parts of the document at the same time.
- **Switch Windows:** Opens a drop-down list with open windows so that you can travel between windows.

You can also take advantage of these Window buttons in Word and Excel to compare files:

- **View Side by Side:** Displays files side by side so that you can compare and contrast them.
- **Synchronous Scrolling:** Permits you to scroll two files at the same rate so that you can proofread one against the other. To use this command, start by clicking the View Side by Side button. After you click the Synchronous Scrolling button, click the Reset Window Position button so that both files are displayed at the same size onscreen.
- **Reset Window Position:** Makes files being shown side by side the same size onscreen to make them easier to compare.



# Correcting Typos on the Fly

The unseen hand of Office 365 corrects some typos and misspellings automatically. For example, try typing "accomodate" with one *m* — Office corrects the misspelling and inserts the second *m* for you. Try typing "perminent" with an *i* instead of an *a* — the invisible hand of Office corrects the misspelling, and you get *permanent.* While you're at it, type a colon and a close parenthesis :) — you get a smiley face.

As good as the AutoCorrect feature is, you can make it even better. You can also add the typos and misspellings you often make to the list of words that are corrected automatically.

Office corrects common spelling errors and turns punctuation mark combinations into symbols as part of its AutoCorrect feature. No doubt, you make your own typing errors and spelling errors time and time again. If these errors aren't part of the default AutoCorrect database, you can tell Office to correct them for you automatically. You do that by entering the misspelling and its corrected spelling in the AutoCorrect dialog box by following these steps:

1. **On the File tab, choose Options.**

   The Options dialog box appears.

2. **Click the Proofing category on the left.**
3. **Click the AutoCorrect Options button.**

   The AutoCorrect dialog box opens and displays the AutoCorrect tab.

   As shown in Figure 3-3, the AutoCorrect tab lists words that are corrected automatically. Scroll down the Replace list and have a look around. Go ahead. Make yourself at home.

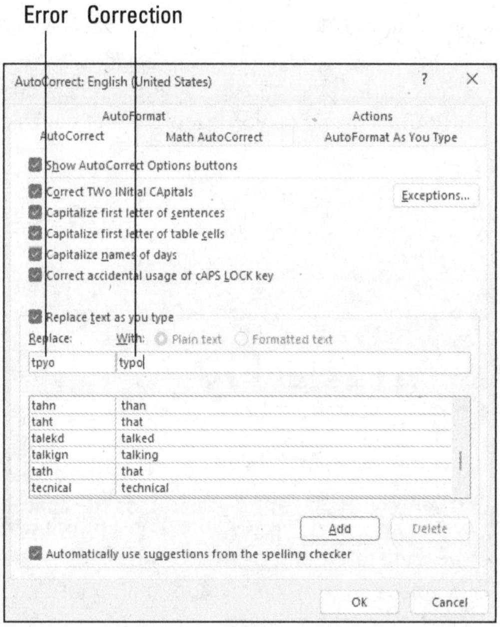


**FIGURE 3-3:** As you type, words in the Replace column are replaced automatically with words in the With column.

TIP

You can remove misspellings and typos from the list of words that are corrected automatically. To remove a word from the list of corrected words, select it in the AutoCorrect dialog box and click the Delete button.

4. **Use the Replace text box to type the error you want to correct.**
5. **Use the With text box to type the correction.**
6. **Click Add.**

   AutoCorrect adds the error and your correction.
7. **Repeat Steps 4 through 6 to specify any other corrections you need to add.**
8. **Click OK to close the AutoCorrect dialog box.**
9. **Click OK to close the Options dialog box.**

## Entering Text Quickly with the AutoCorrect Command

TIP

As the "Correct" part of its name implies, the AutoCorrect command I discuss in the previous section is a whiz at fixing misspellings on-the-fly as you type. The "secret" — if that's not too grandiose a term here — of AutoCorrect is that it maintains a list of errors and, when it comes across one of those errors as you're typing, it automatically fixes the error with zero fuss.

However, if you look carefully at AutoCorrect's list of "errors," you'll find plenty that aren't mistakes at all. For example, AutoCorrect will replace "(c)" with the copyright symbol "©." Hmm. Doesn't that mean that instead of typing a long or complex word or phrase, you can instead load a shorter code into AutoCorrect and it will enter the longer text for you automatically whenever you type the code? Why, yes, it does, and it's a fantastic timesaver.

For example, if your line of work means that you have to regularly type the word "antidisestablishmentarianism," you can enter, say, "antid" as the error in AutoCorrect, and "antidisestablishmentarianism" as the replacement, as shown in Figure 3-4. Then when you type "antid" and press the spacebar in a document, AutoCorrect fills out the entire word for you.

You can use this technique for any laborious-to-type text that you use regularly: scientific terms, boilerplate phrases, long-winded jargon, you name it. Follow the steps in the previous section to enter each "correction" into the AutoCorrect tab.

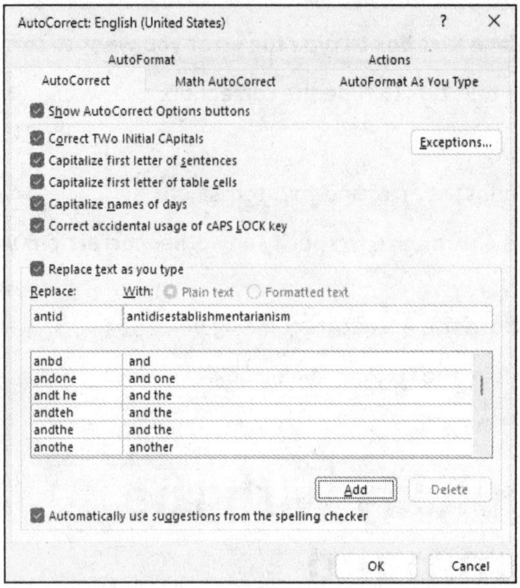


**FIGURE 3-4:** With a little cunning, you can use AutoCorrect to enter hard-to-type text.

WARNING

When coming up with a shorter code to enter into the Replace text box, don't use a word or any sequence of characters that refers to something else that you might need to type as-is someday. If you do, the AutoCorrect mechanism might kick in when you least expect it. Enter three to five characters that never appear together.

IN THIS CHAPTER

» Renovating the Ribbon

» Revamping the Quick Access toolbar

» Rearranging the status bar

» Redoing the screen background and Office theme

» Reconfiguring Word's keyboard shortcuts

Chapter 4

# Making Office 365 Your Own

When you install Office 365 on your computer, Microsoft sets up each app with a default configuration for common tools such as the Ribbon, the Quick Access toolbar, and the status bar. How did they arrive at that configuration? They tested many, many variations of those tools on hundreds — perhaps it was even thousands — of users to find an arrangement that seemed to work best for most folks. In other words, the default Office 365 configuration is one that works fine for the average user most of the time.

If that sounds, well, rather *bland*, that's because it is. Microsoft doesn't know you, so all it can do is configure its software to be reasonably functional for the average user. I don't know you, either, but I bet you don't think of yourself as an "average user." At least, I'd *hope* you don't, because the way you'll use Office 365 is unique to you. That uniqueness means that the "average" defaults set up by Microsoft almost certainly aren't going to work ideally for you.

The great news is that Microsoft also offers some powerful tools for customizing Office 365 to suit your style and the way you work and play. Sure, customizing Office 365 might sound ambitious, but it will make you more efficient and productive and, if it doesn't, you can always put things back to their default configuration without much bother. This chapter tells you everything you need to know to remake Office 365 to suit your own inimitable style.

## Giving the Ribbon a Facelift

The Ribbon is your main way of accessing the commands, features, and tools in all the Office 365 apps. But the Ribbon isn't perfect in its out-of-the-box configuration. For example, I'm sure the Ribbon contains lots of commands you'll never use. Similarly, the Ribbon might be missing a command or two that you use often. And, finally, the Ribbon's default configuration might require too many clicks for you to access some commands that you use frequently.

If you find yourself irritated by the Ribbon for any or even all of these annoyances, take heart: The Ribbon offers a power set of customization tools that enable you to reconfigure the Ribbon to suit the way you work.

To wreak havoc on, er, I mean, to reconfigure the Ribbon, begin by using one of these techniques in the Office 365 app you want to customize:

- » Choose File ➪ Options, then click the Customize Ribbon category in the Options dialog box.
- » Right-click any part of the Ribbon, then click Customize the Ribbon.

The app displays the Customize Ribbon tab of the Options dialog box, which contains controls for customizing the Ribbon, as shown in Figure 4-1. The right side of the dialog box ("Customize the Ribbon") lists the names of tabs, groups within tabs, and commands within groups that are currently on the Ribbon. One way to customize the Ribbon is to arrange the right side of the dialog box to your liking.

The left side of the dialog box ("Choose Commands From") presents every tab, group, and command in your Office 365 program. Another way to customize the Ribbon is select an item on the left side of the dialog box and add it to the Ribbon, either to an existing tab or to a new tab.

Keep reading to find out how to display tabs, groups, and commands in the Options dialog box and how to do all else that pertains to customizing the Ribbon. In case you make a hash of the Ribbon, you also find instructions for restoring the Ribbon to its original state.

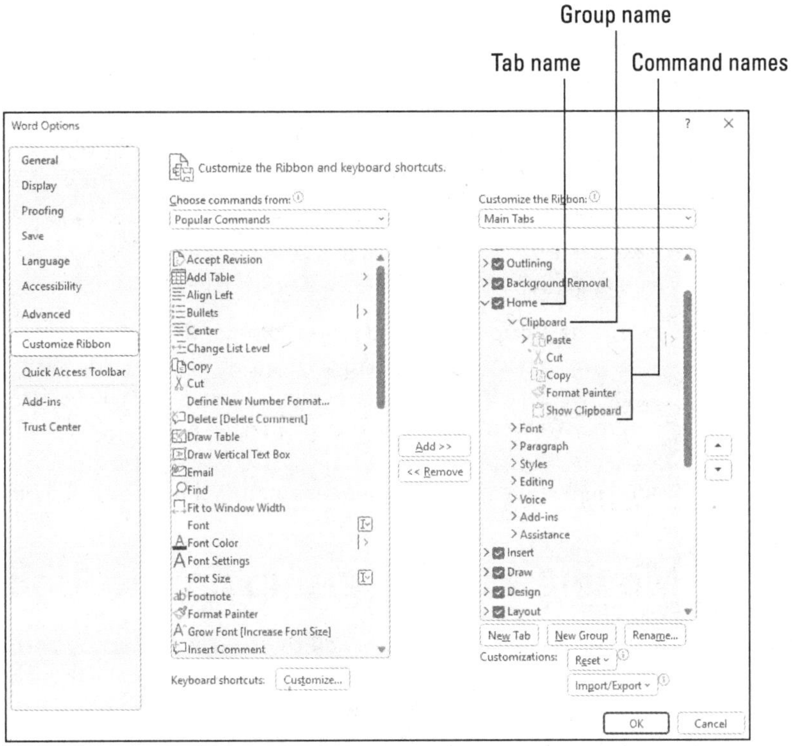


**FIGURE 4-1:** Not surprisingly, the Customize Ribbon category of the Options dialog box lets you customize the Ribbon.

## Displaying and selecting tab, group, and command names

To customize the Ribbon, you need to display and select tab names, group names, and command names in the Options dialog box (refer to Figure 4-1). Start by opening the drop-down lists and choosing a display option:

- **Choose Commands From (left side of dialog box):** Choose an option to locate the tab, group, or command you want to add to the Ribbon. For example, choose All Commands to display an alphabetical list of all the commands in the Office program you're working in; choose Main Tabs to display a list of tabs.
- **Customize the Ribbon (right side of dialog box):** Choose an option to display the names of all tabs, main tabs, or tool tabs. Tool tabs are the context-sensitive tabs that appear after you insert or click something. For example, the Table Tools tabs appear when you construct tables in Word.

After you choose display options on the drop-down lists, you can display the names of groups and commands (refer to Figure 4-1):

- **Displaying group names:** Click the right-pointing arrow (shown in the margin) next to a tab name to display the names of the tab's groups.
- **Displaying command names in groups**: Click the right-pointing arrow (shown in the margin) next to a group name to display the names of the group's commands.
- **Hiding group names and group commands:** Click the downward-pointing arrow (shown in the margin) next to a tab name to hide the tab's group names. Click the downward-pointing arrow (shown in the margin) next to a group name to hide the group's command names.

After you display the tab, group, or command name, click to select it.

## Moving a tab or group on the Ribbon

To change the position of a tab on the Ribbon or a group within a tab, select the name of the tab or group on the right side of the Customize Ribbon section of the Options dialog box. Then use either of the following techniques to change the location of the selected tab or group:

- **Move the tab or group up:** Drag the name of the tab or group up or click the Move Up button (shown in the margin) until the tab or group is in the position you prefer. Note that moving an item up in the list is equivalent to moving it to the left on the Ribbon.
- **Move the tab or group down:** Drag the name of the tab or group down or click the Move Down button (shown in the margin) until the tab or group is in the position you prefer. Note that moving an item down in the list is equivalent to moving it to the right on the Ribbon.

WARNING

Be careful when moving groups. Move a group too far and you run the risk of moving it to a different tab on the Ribbon.

## Creating new tabs and groups

Create new tabs and groups on the Ribbon for commands that are especially useful to you. Follow these steps on the Customize Ribbon category of the Options dialog box to create a new tab or group:

1. **On the right side of the dialog box, display and select the name of a tab or group.**

   - **Tab:** If you're creating a tab, select a tab name. The tab you create will appear after the tab you select.
   - **Group:** If you're creating a group, select a group name. The group you create will appear after the group you select.

2. **Click the New Tab or New Group button.**

   Your Office program creates a new tab or group called "New Tab (Custom)" or "New Group (Custom)." If you created a tab, Office also creates a new group inside your new tab.

3. **Click the Rename button to give the tab, group, or both a name.**

   In the Rename dialog box, enter a descriptive name and click OK. If you're naming a group, the Rename dialog box gives you the opportunity to select an icon to help identify the group.

4. **Add groups, commands, or both to your newly made tab or group.**

   For instructions, refer to "Adding an item to the Ribbon," next.

## Adding an item to the Ribbon

Follow these steps to add a tab, group, or command to the Ribbon:

1. **On the left side of the Customize Ribbon category of the Options dialog box, select the tab, group, or command you want to add.**

   For example, to add the Tables group to the Home tab, select the Tables group.

   WARNING

   Commands can be added only to custom groups. To add a command to the Ribbon, create a new group for the command (check out "Creating new tabs and groups," earlier in this chapter).

2. **On the right side of the dialog box, select the tab or custom group where you want to place the item.**

   If you're adding a tab to the Ribbon, select a tab. The tab you add will go after the tab you select.

3. **Click the Add button.**

   The app adds the item to the tab or group.

## Removing an item from the Ribbon

Follow these steps to remove a tab, group, or command from the Ribbon:

1. **On the right side of the Customize Ribbon category of the Options dialog box, select the tab, group, or command you want to remove.**
2. **Click the Remove button.**

   The app removes the item from the tab or group.

WARNING

Except for tabs you create yourself, you can't remove tabs from the Ribbon. And you can't remove a command unless you remove it from a group you created yourself.

## Renaming tabs and groups

Sorry, you can't rename a command. Follow these steps to rename a tab or group:

1. **On the right side of the Customize Ribbon category of the Options dialog box, select the tab or group you want to rename.**
2. **Click the Rename button.**

   The Rename dialog box appears.
3. **Enter a new name and click OK.**

   When renaming a group that you created yourself, you can also choose a symbol for the group in the Rename dialog box, as shown in Figure 4-2.

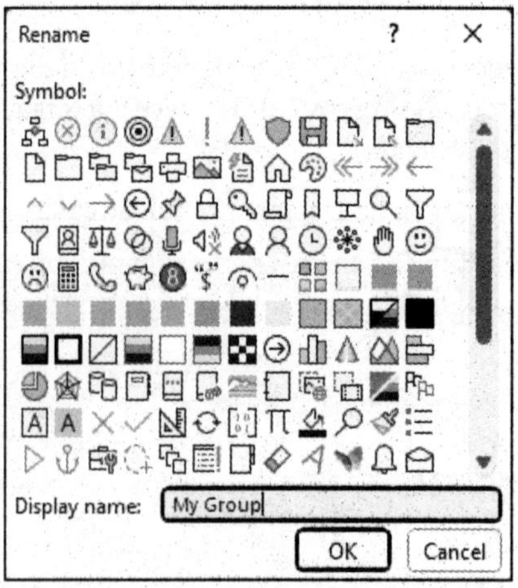


**FIGURE 4-2:** When renaming a group, you can also select a symbol for the group.

## Resetting your Ribbon customizations

If you make a hash of the Ribbon, all is not lost because you can restore the original settings. In the Options dialog box, click the Reset button and choose one of these commands on the drop-down list:

- **Reset Only Selected Ribbon Tab:** Select a tab name on the right side of the Options dialog box and choose this command to restore a tab to its original state.
- **Reset All Customizations:** Choose this command to restore the Ribbon in its entirety. All changes you made are reversed.

You can also remove tabs and groups you created if you discover you don't need them. Refer to "Removing an item from the Ribbon," earlier in this chapter.

# Refurbishing the Quick Access Toolbar

No matter where you go in Office, the Quick Access toolbar lurks in the upper-left corner of the screen. This toolbar offers the AutoSave, Save, Undo, and Redo buttons. However, which buttons appear on the Quick Access toolbar is entirely up to you. You can put your favorite buttons on the toolbar to keep them within reach. And if the Quick Access toolbar gets too crowded, you can move it below the Ribbon to give it some room to grow.

## Adding a button to the Quick Access toolbar

Use one of these techniques to add a button to the Quick Access toolbar:

- On the Ribbon, right-click a button you want to add to the toolbar and then click Add to Quick Access Toolbar on the shortcut menu. You can add a Ribbon group to the Quick Access toolbar by right-clicking the group name and clicking Add to Quick Access Toolbar.

- Click the Customize Quick Access Toolbar button (shown in the margin) and click to activate (that is, place a check mark beside) a button that appears in the drop-down list.
- Choose File ➪ Options, then click the Quick Access Toolbar category in the Options dialog box (or right-click any button or tab and choose Customize Quick Access toolbar on the shortcut menu). You come face to face with the

Quick Access Toolbar category of the Options dialog box, as shown in Figure 4-3. In the Choose Commands From list, select the name of the button you want to add to the Quick Access toolbar, then click the Add button.

TIP

To restore the Quick Access toolbar to its original buttons, click the Reset button in the Options dialog box and click Reset Only Quick Access Toolbar on the drop-down list.

## Changing the position of a button on the Quick Access toolbar

Follow these steps to change the position of a button on the Quick Access toolbar:

1. **Click the Customize Quick Access toolbar button and choose More Commands on the drop-down list.**

   The Quick Access toolbar category of the Options dialog box appears (refer to Figure 4-3). You can also open this dialog box by right-clicking any button or tab and choosing Customize Quick Access toolbar.

2. **Select the name of a button on the right side of the dialog box and click one of the following:**

   - **Move Up:** Moves the button up, which is equivalent to moving the button to the left on the Quick Access toolbar.
   - **Move Down:** Moves the button down, which is equivalent to moving the button to the right on the Quick Access toolbar.

   Repeat as needed until the button is in the position you prefer.

3. **Click OK.**

## Removing a button from the Quick Access toolbar

Use one of these techniques to remove a button from the Quick Access toolbar:

- » Right-click the button and choose Remove from Quick Access toolbar on the shortcut menu.
- » Right-click any button or tab and choose Customize Quick Access toolbar. The Quick Access toolbar category of the Options dialog box appears. On the right side of the dialog box, select the button you want to remove, then click the Remove button.

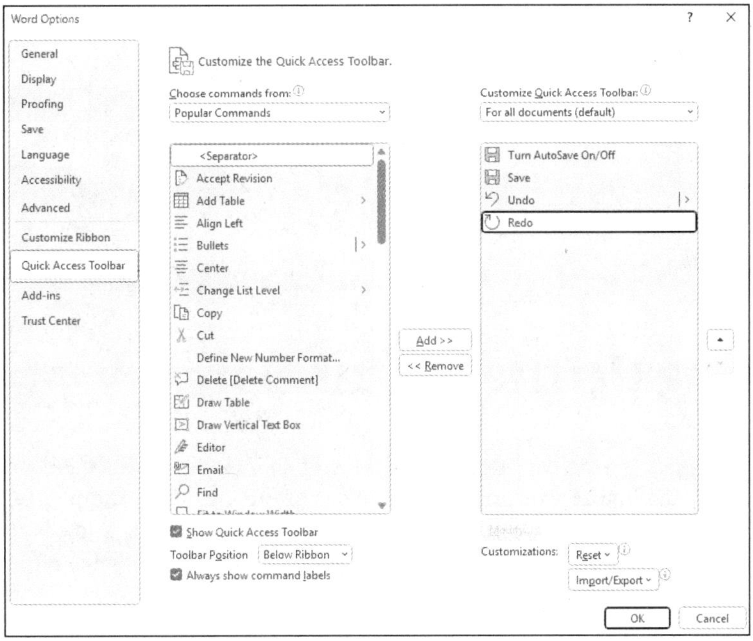


**FIGURE 4-3:** Add, remove, and reorder Quick Access toolbar buttons in the Options dialog box.

REMEMBER

You can click the Reset button in the Options dialog box and then click Reset Only Quick Access Toolbar to remove all the buttons you added to the Quick Access toolbar.

## Placing the Quick Access toolbar above or below the Ribbon

If your Quick Access toolbar contains many buttons, consider placing it below the Ribbon, not above it (refer to Figure 4-4). Follow these instructions to place the Quick Access toolbar above or below the Ribbon:

- **Quick Access toolbar below the Ribbon:** Right-click the toolbar, and on the shortcut menu, click Show Quick Access toolbar Below the Ribbon.
- **Quick Access toolbar above the Ribbon:** Right-click the toolbar, and on the shortcut menu, click Show Quick Access toolbar Above the Ribbon.

TIP

You can hide the Quick Access toolbar altogether. To do so, right-click a button on the toolbar and click Hide Quick Access Toolbar. To display the toolbar again, right-click anywhere on the Ribbon and click Show Quick Access toolbar.

FIGURE 4-4: You can move the Quick Access toolbar to below the Ribbon.

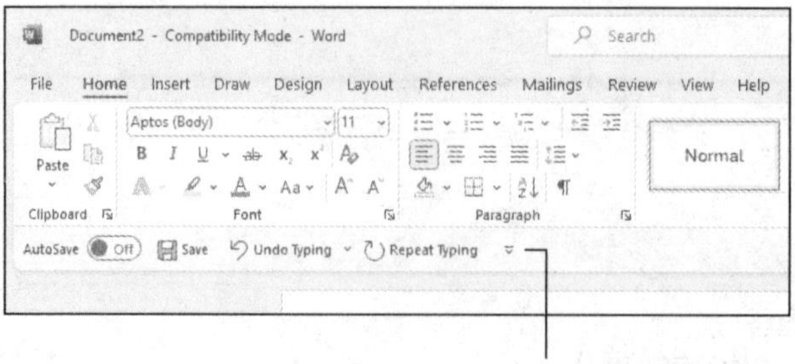


Quick Access toolbar below the Ribbon

# Sprucing Up the Status Bar

The status bar along the bottom of the window gives you information about the file you're working on. The Word status bar, for example, tells you which page you're on, how many pages are in your document, and several other things. In PowerPoint, the status bar tells you which slide is selected. It also presents the view buttons and zoom controls.

To choose what appears on the status bar, right-click the status bar. A drop-down list similar to the one in Figure 4-5 shows up. By selecting and deselecting items in this list, you can decide what appears on the status bar.

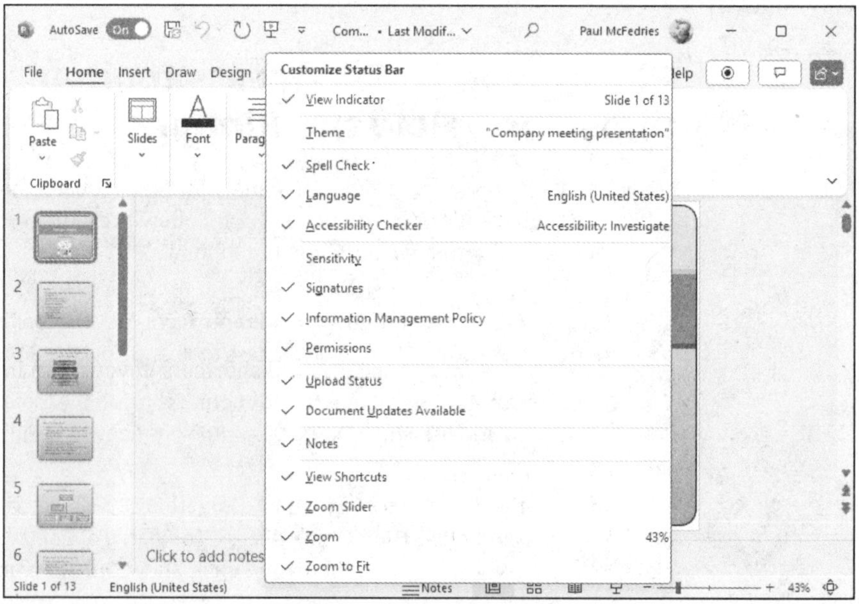


FIGURE 4-5: Right-click the status bar to customize it.

# Changing the Screen Background and Office Theme

You can change the screen background and Office theme. The *screen background* is the fluff that appears along the top of Office application windows. The *Office theme* is the color (or lack thereof) that appears around the perimeter of Office application windows. You are encouraged to experiment with screen backgrounds and Office themes until you find a combination that works for you.

Follow these steps to choose a screen background and Office theme:

1. **Choose File ⇨ Account.**

   The Account screen appears.

2. **Open the Office Background drop-down list and choose an option.**
3. **Open the Office Theme drop-down menu and choose an option.**

   Choosing the Black theme changes Office screens to so-called *dark mode.* Some people believe dark mode prevents eyestrain. In dark mode, text is white; it appears against a black background.

REMEMBER

A screen background and Office theme you apply in one Office program applies to all the other programs as well.

# Customizing Keyboard Shortcuts in Word

In Microsoft Word, you can change the keyboard shortcuts. If you don't like a keyboard shortcut in Word, you can change it and invent a keyboard shortcut of your own. You can also assign keyboard shortcuts to symbols, macros, fonts, building blocks, and styles.

Follow these steps to choose keyboard shortcuts of your own in Microsoft Word:

1. **Choose File ⇨ Options.**

   The Word Options dialog box shows up.

2. **Click the Customize Ribbon category.**

3. **Click the Customize button (you can find it at the bottom of the dialog box next to the words "Keyboard Shortcuts").**

   The Customize Keyboard dialog box makes an appearance, as shown in Figure 4-6.

4. **In the Categories list, choose the category with the command to which you want to assign the keyboard shortcut.**

   At the bottom of the list are the Macros, Fonts, Building Blocks, Styles, and Common Symbols categories.

5. **Choose the command name, macro, font, building block, style, or symbol name in the Commands list.**

6. **In the Press New Shortcut Key box, type the keyboard shortcut.**

   Press the actual keys. For example, if the shortcut is Ctrl+8, press the Ctrl key and the 8 key — don't type C-t-r-l-+8.

   If you try to assign a shortcut that has already been assigned, the words "Currently assigned to" and a command name appear below the Current Keys box. You can override the preassigned keyboard assignment by entering a keyboard assignment of your own.

   To delete a keyboard shortcut, display it in the Current Keys box, select it, and click the Remove button.

7. **If you want the keyboard shortcut changes you make to apply to the document you're working on, not to all documents created with the template you're working with, open the Save Changes In drop-down list and choose your document's name.**

8. **Click the Assign button.**

9. **When you finish assigning keyboard shortcuts, click Close to close the Customize Keyboard dialog box.**

REMEMBER

You can always get the old keyboard shortcuts back by clicking the Reset All button in the Customize Keyboard dialog box.

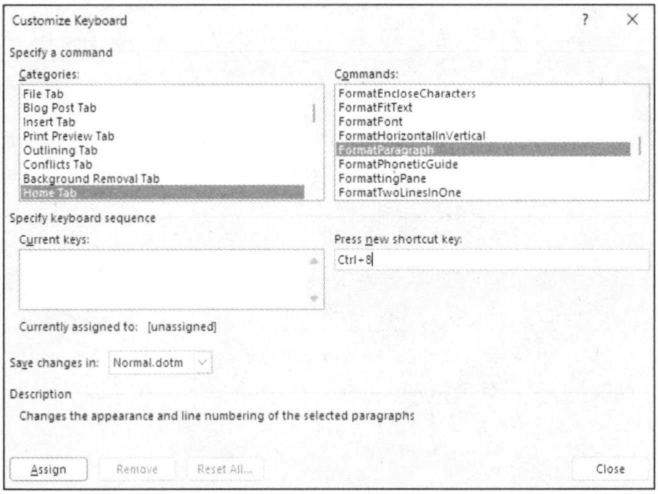


**FIGURE 4-6:** Assigning keyboard shortcuts to Word commands.

IN THIS CHAPTER

» Adding visual flair to your documents

» Sprucing up your work with shapes, images, and other graphics

» Learning the best ways to select, move, resize, and format graphics

» Applying eye-catching effects such as shadows, 3D, color gradients, and textures

# Chapter 5
# Handling Graphics and Photos

When most people think about using the Office programs, they generally think about text, whether it's writing sentences and paragraphs in Word, adding formulas and labels in Excel, creating slide titles and bullets in PowerPoint, and so on. It's certainly true that most of the work people do in Office — from papers to purchase orders to presentations — is, and should remain, text-based.

However, if you *only* think text when you think of Office, you're missing out on a whole other dimension. The main Office 365 programs — Word, Excel, PowerPoint, and Outlook — have extensive graphics tools that you can take advantage of to improve the clarity of your work or just to add a bit of pizzazz to liven up an otherwise drab document.

Even better, these graphics tools work the same across apps, so once you learn how to use them, you can apply your knowledge to any Office app. This chapter shows you how to create, edit, and enhance graphics in the Office programs.

# Plopping a Shape into a Document

A shape is an object, such as a line or rectangle, that you draw within your document. You can use shapes to point out key features in a document, enclose text, create flowcharts, and enhance the look of a document. In Office 365, you can use nine shape types:

- **Lines:** Straight lines, squiggles, freeform polygons, arrows, connectors, and curves
- **Rectangles:** Four-sided figures of various kinds, including rounded and snipped corners
- **Basic Shapes:** Triangles, circles, boxes, cylinders, hearts, and many more
- **Block Arrows:** Two-dimensional arrows of various configurations
- **Equation Shapes:** Two-dimensional images for the basic arithmetic symbols, such as plus (+) and equals (=)
- **Flowchart:** The standard shapes used for creating flowcharts
- **Stars and Banners:** Stars, starbursts, scrolls, and more
- **Callouts:** Boxes and lines for creating callouts to document features
- **Action Buttons (PowerPoint only):** Buttons such as forward and backward that represent standard slide show actions

In Word, Excel, PowerPoint, and Outlook, you access these graphic objects via the new ribbon interface. Follow these steps:

1. **Click the Insert tab.**
2. **In the Illustrations group, cull down the Shapes menu to display the list of shapes, as shown in Figure 5-1.**

Note, too, that after you select at least one shape, the top of the Shapes list sprouts a section titled Recently Used Shapes that displays the shapes you've used most recently.

## Inserting a line

You can use lines to point out important document information, create a freeform drawing, or as part of a more complex graphic, such as a company logo. Follow these steps to create a line:

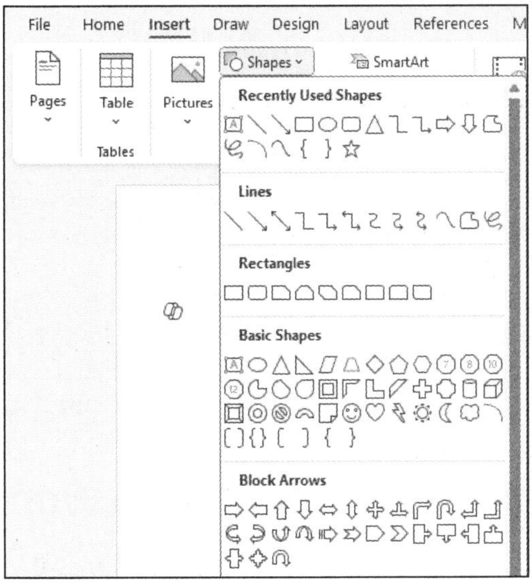


**FIGURE 5-1:** In Office 365, the shapes reside in the Shapes menu on the Insert tab.

1. **On the Insert tab, in the Illustrations group, click Shapes, and then click the shape you want in the Lines section.**
2. **Position the crosshair where you want to begin the line.**
3. **Press and hold down the left mouse button.**
4. **Drag the mouse pointer to where you want the line to end.**

   If you're drawing a squiggle, drag the mouse pointer in the shape of the line you want.

   TIP

   To restrict straight lines and arrows to horizontal, vertical, and angles in 45-degree increments, hold down the Shift key while you drag the mouse.
5. **Release the mouse button. Selection handles appear on each end of the line and the Shape Format contextual tab appears.**
6. **If you're drawing a freeform polygon, repeat Steps 2 through 5, and then double-click when you're done.**

## Inserting any other shape

You can use the other shapes either on their own — for example, to point out features with callouts or block arrows or to enhance text with stars or banners — or as part of a more complex graphic. Follow these steps to insert a non-line shape:

1. **On the Insert tab, in the Illustrations group, click Shapes, and then click the shape you want to insert.**

2. **Position the crosshair where you want to begin the shape.**
3. **Press and hold down the left mouse button.**
4. **Drag the mouse pointer until the shape has the size and form you want.**

   TIP

   To make your rectangles square, your ellipses circular, and your angled lines at 45 degrees, hold down the Shift key while dragging the mouse.
5. **Release the mouse button.**

   Selection handles appear around the shape and the Shape Format contextual tab appears. You find out more about the Shape Format tab later in this chapter (refer to the "Messing Around with Graphic Objects" section).

## Creating a drawing canvas in Word

When you work with shapes in a Word document, you may find yourself combining two or more shapes to create a more complex drawing. Although an effective technique, it can also be a hassle because you often need to perform some action on all the shapes in the drawing at the same time (such as moving them to a different location in the document). This requires selecting each element of the drawing, which can take time.

A solution to this problem is to first create a drawing canvas in your Word document. When you then draw your shapes inside this canvas, Word treats them like a single object. Here are the steps to follow to create a drawing canvas for your shapes:

1. **Select the position within the document where you want the canvas to appear.**
2. **Click the Insert tab.**
3. **In the Illustrations group, pull down the Shapes menu and then click New Drawing.**

   Word adds the drawing canvas to the document.

# Livening Up a Document with a Picture

Although the drawing tools that come with Office are handy for creating simple graphics effects, a more ambitious image requires a dedicated graphics program. With these programs, you can create professional-quality graphics and then import them into your Office document. You can even set up a link between the inserted picture and the original file, so that any changes you make to the original are automatically reflected in the document copy.

To insert an existing graphics file in your document, follow these steps:

1. **In your document, position the cursor where you want the picture to appear.**
2. **Click the Insert tab.**
3. **In the Illustrations group, click Pictures and then click This Device.**

   The Insert Picture dialog box rolls in.
4. **Click the graphics file you want to insert.**
5. **Pull down the Insert list and click one of the following commands:**
   - *Insert:* Click this command to insert a copy of the picture into the document. Use this command when it doesn't matter if changes are made to the original file.
   - *Link to File:* To save space, click this command to insert the picture as a link to the original file. Use this command when you want edits to the original file to be updated in your document, but you don't want a copy of the picture in the document.
   - *Insert and Link:* Click this command to insert a copy of the picture into the document and to maintain a link to the original file. Use this command when you want edits to the original file to be updated in your document, but you also want a copy within the document just in case the original is deleted.

REMEMBER

If you're using Office on a notebook computer and the picture you're inserting comes from a network folder, use the Insert and Link command. This way, even when you disconnect your computer from the network when you travel outside the office, you'll still see the picture in your document.

The program inserts the picture into the document and displays the Picture Format contextual tab.

# Sprucing Up Your Work with a Stock Image

If you don't have the time or the skill to create your own images, consider using stock images. Stock images are ready-to-insert photos, icons, illustrations, and other professional-quality artwork that can often add just the right touch to a newsletter, brochure, or presentation. Office 365 gives you access to hundreds of stock images in dozens of different categories, from Science and Scenery to Animals and Art.

Here are the steps to follow to insert a stock image:

1. **In your document, position the cursor where you want the image to appear.**
2. **Click the Insert tab.**
3. **In the Illustrations group, click Pictures and then click Stock Images.**

   The Stock Images dialog box appears, as shown in Figure 5-2.

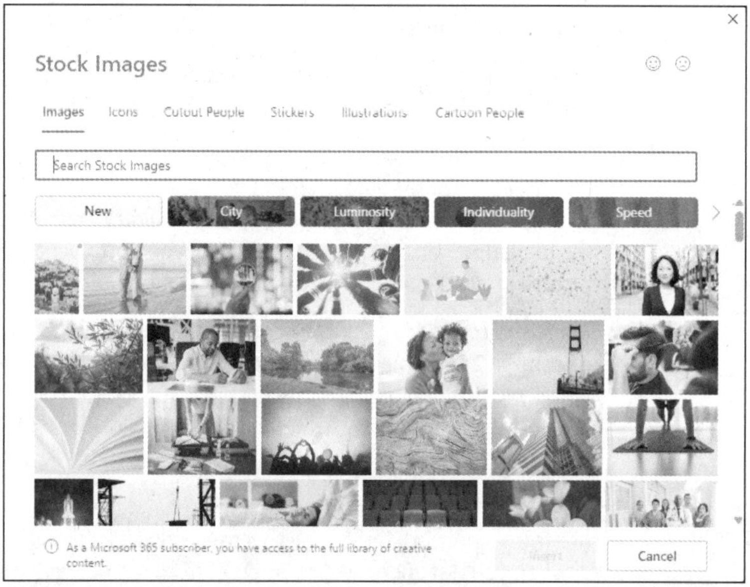


**FIGURE 5-2:** The Stock Images dialog box is home to hundreds of ready-to-use images.

4. **Click the type of stock image you want: Images, Icons, Cutout People, and so on.**
5. **Either click a category button or use the Search text box to type a word or phrase that describes the type of image you want.**

   The stock images that match the category or your search text appear.
6. **Click the stock image you want to use.**

   Technically, you're free to click as many images as you want. Each time you click an image, it gets added to the selection.

7. **Click Insert.**

   The program inserts the stock image into the document and displays the Picture Format contextual tab.

# Cobbling Together a SmartArt Graphic

A SmartArt graphic combines text, predefined shapes — and in some cases arrows and images — into a diagram that you use to convey some concept graphically. You use SmartArt to illustrate concepts in text categories:

- **List:** These are concepts that are sequential or that form a progression or a group. Most of these SmartArt graphics consist of shapes arranged in vertical or horizontal lists.
- **Process:** These are concepts that progress from one stage to another, where the overall progress has a beginning and an end. In most of these SmartArt graphics, each stage is represented by a shape and accompanying text, and one-way arrows lead you from one shape to the next.
- **Cycle:** These are concepts that progress from one stage to another in a repeating pattern. In most of these diagrams, each stage is represented by a shape and accompanying text, and one-way arrows lead you from one shape to the next. The most common structure is a circle, with the last stage leading back to the first stage.
- **Hierarchy:** These are concepts that either show the relative importance of one thing over another or show how one thing is contained within another. These SmartArt graphics look like organization charts.
- **Relationship:** These are concepts that show how two or more items are connected to each other. In most of these diagrams, each item is represented by a shape and accompanying text, and all the shapes either reside within a larger structure, such as a pyramid, or are positioned relative to one another, such as in a Venn diagram.
- **Matrix:** These are concepts that show the relationship between the entirety of something and its components, organized as quadrants. These SmartArt graphics have one shape that represents the whole and four shapes that represent the component quadrants.
- **Pyramid:** These are concepts with components that are proportional to each other or interconnected in some way. In most of these SmartArt graphics, the component shapes are arranged in a triangle pattern.

» **Picture:** These are concepts where one or more images are used to convey information, whether it's a central image or multiple satellite images.

» **`Office.com`:** This category is a miscellany of SmartArt designs from `office.com`.

Here are the steps required to insert a SmartArt diagram:

1. **In your document, position the cursor where you want the SmartArt to appear.**
2. **Click the Insert tab.**
3. **In the Illustrations group, click SmartArt.**

   The Choose a SmartArt Graphic dialog box pops up.
4. **On the left side of the dialog box, click the type of SmartArt you want.**

   **Figure 5-3 shows the dialog box with the Cycle category selected.**

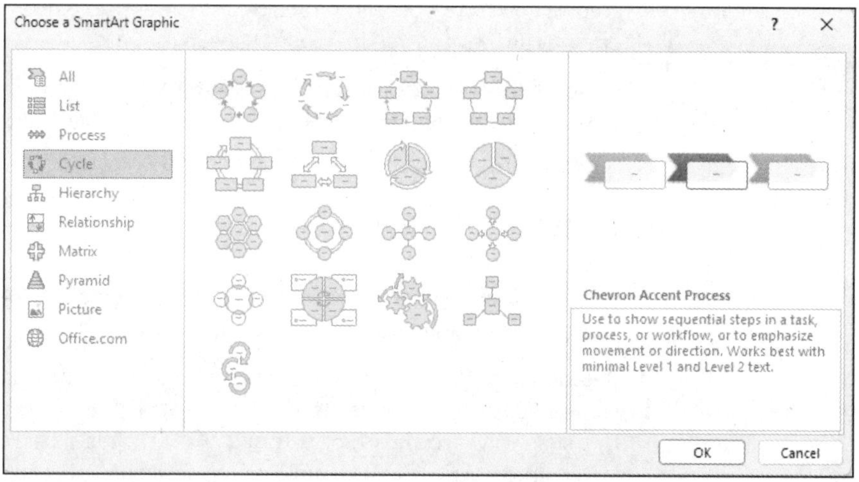


**FIGURE 5-3.** Click a SmartArt category to get started.

5. **In the middle section of the dialog box, click the SmartArt graphic you want.**

   When you click a SmartArt type, the right side of the dialog box shows a description as well as a larger, in-color version of the SmartArt diagram.
6. **Click OK.**

   The program inserts a skeleton of the SmartArt graphic into the document and displays the SmartArt Design and Format contextual tabs.

7. **Use the Type Your Text Here box to type the text for each shape in the SmartArt.**

   You can also click the [Text] placeholder inside each shape to add the text directly.

# Tossing In a Text Box

The graphics you add to your documents will usually consist of images, but sometimes you'll need to augment those images with some text. For example, you might want to add a title and subtitle or insert a label. To add text to an existing image, you draw a text box and then type your text within that box. Here are the steps to follow:

1. **Click the Insert tab.**
2. **In the Text group, click Text Box.**
3. **If you're using Word, click Draw Text Box.**
4. **Position the crosshair where you want to begin the text box.**
5. **Press and hold down the left mouse button.**
6. **Drag the mouse pointer until the text box has the size and form you want.**

   TIP

   To make your text box square, hold down the Shift key while dragging the mouse.
7. **Release the mouse button.**

   Selection handles appear around the shape and the Shape Format contextual tab appears.
8. **Type your text in the box.**

# Turning Text into a Work of Art with WordArt

WordArt takes a word or phrase and converts it into a graphic object that applies artistic styles, colors, and shapes to the text. WordArt is therefore useful for newsletter titles, logos, and any time you want text to really stand out from its surroundings.

Here are the steps to follow to insert WordArt into a document:

1. **Either select the text that you want to convert to WordArt or select the position within the document where you want a new WordArt object to appear.**
2. **Click the Insert tab.**
3. **In the Text group, click WordArt.**

   A gallery of WordArt styles appears. Note that the WordArt styles you see depend on the application. For example, Excel and PowerPoint display a different set of styles than Word and Publisher.
4. **Click the WordArt style you want to use.**

   The program inserts the WordArt object and displays the Shape Format contextual tab.
5. **If you're inserting a new WordArt object, type the text.**

# Creating a Drop Cap in Word

A *drop cap* is the first letter in a paragraph that has been formatted with a much larger size and placed in a separate frame so that it appears "beside" the first few lines of the paragraph or in the margin. You usually only use a drop cap in the first paragraph of a document or in the first paragraph of each important section of a document. Here are the steps to follow to create a drop cap in Word:

1. **Place the insertion point cursor inside the paragraph you want to work with.**
2. **On the Insert tab, in the Text group, click Drop Cap.**

   Word displays a gallery of drop cap styles.
3. **Click the drop cap style you want to use: Dropped or In Margin.**

   You can also click Drop Cap Options to display the Drop Cap dialog box, which enables you to set the drop cap font, the number of lines to drop (essentially, the size of the frame), and the distance from the text. Click OK when you're done.

   Word creates a frame around the first letter of the paragraph, positions the frame according to the drop cap style you chose, and formats the font size of the letter.

# Messing Around with Graphic Objects

Inserting a line, shape, picture, or other graphic object is usually only half the battle. To complete your work with the graphic, you usually need to spend a bit of time formatting and editing the object to get it just right. This may include some or all of the following: sizing the graphic; rotating it; moving it; grouping or aligning it with other objects; and formatting the object's fill, lines, and shadow effects. The rest of this chapter provides you with the details of these and other techniques for working with graphic objects.

## Selecting graphic objects

Every graphic object has an invisible rectangular frame. For a line or rectangle, the frame is the same as the object itself. For all other objects, the frame is a rectangle that completely encloses the shape or image. Before you can format or edit a graphic object, you must select it, which displays selection handles around the frame.

If you just want to work with a single object, you can select it by clicking it with your mouse. If you need to work with multiple objects, Office 365 gives you several methods, and the one you choose depends on the number of objects and their layout within the document.

The simplest scenario is when you've just a few objects to select. In this case, hold down the Shift key and click each object. If you click on an object by accident, keep the Shift key held down and click the object again to deselect it.

The next easiest method is when the objects you want to select are all in roughly the same part of the document. In this case, you use the Select tool to click and drag a box around the objects you want to select. Here are the steps to follow:

1. **Click the Home tab.**
2. **The next step depends on the program:**
   - In Word, PowerPoint, and Outlook, in the Editing group, click Select and then click Select Objects.
   - In Excel, in the Editing group, click Find & Select and then click Select Objects.
3. **Position the mouse pointer at the top-left corner of the area you want to select.**

4. **Drag the pointer to the bottom-right corner of the area you want to select.**

5. **When the selection area completely encloses each object you want to select, release the mouse button.**

   The app selects each object in the selection area.

6. **To end the selection, press the Esc key.**

Finally, you can also instruct the program to select all the objects in a document. Here are the techniques you use in various programs:

» In Word and PowerPoint, on the Home tab in the Editing group, click Select and then click Select All.

» In Excel, on the Home tab in the Editing group, click Find & Select and then click Go To Special to open the Go To Special dialog box. Select Objects and then click OK.

After you've selected multiple objects, you can perform actions on all the objects at once, including sizing, moving, deleting, and rotating. You can also format all the selected objects, but your formatting of the objects may be limited if you've selected objects that use different formatting tools.

## Sizing a graphic object

If a graphic is too large or too small for your needs, or if the object's shape isn't what you want, you can resize the image to change its dimensions or its shape. The following procedure outlines the steps to work through:

1. **Select the object you want to size.**

   The program displays selection handles around the object's frame.

2. **Position the mouse pointer over the handle you want to move (the pointer changes to a two-headed arrow):**

   - To change the size horizontally or vertically, use the appropriate handle on the middle of a side.
   - To change the size in both directions at once, use the appropriate corner handle.

3. **Drag the handle to the position you want (the pointer changes to a crosshair).**

   TIP

   To keep the same proportions when sizing an object, hold down the Shift key and drag a corner handle.

4. **Release the mouse button.**

   The program redraws the object and adjusts the frame size.

## Reshaping a graphic object

One of the most obscure aspects of Office graphics editing is the reshaping handle, which you can use to reshape some aspect of a graphic object. Why is it so obscure? Probably for two reasons:

- It only appears with certain types of graphic objects, including certain shapes, text boxes, and WordArt.
- What it "reshapes" varies widely from one type of image to the next. For example, it reshapes the borders around a text box, the smile in a smiley face shape, and the relative sizes of the shaft and head of an arrow.

The reshaping handle is quite useful, so it's time to bring it out of obscurity.

To see the reshaping handle, click the graphic object you want to work with. If you see one or more yellow handles, then the object supports reshaping. Here is how it works:

1. **Click the graphic object you want to reshape.**
2. **Move the mouse pointer over the yellow reshaping handle.**

   The mouse pointer changes to a wedge shape.

3. **Drag the reshaping handle until the aspect of the graphic object affected by the handle is the shape you want.**

## Rotating a graphic object

Most graphic objects get inserted into a document without any rotation: Horizontal borders appear horizontal, and vertical borders appear vertical. (The exception here is WordArt objects in Word, which often appear initially at an angle.) A non-rotated image is probably what you'll want most of the time, but for some occasions an image tilted at a jaunty angle is just the right touch for a document. Many objects come with a rotation handle that you can use to rotate the object clockwise or counterclockwise, as described in the following steps:

1. **Click the graphic object you want to reshape.**
2. **Move the mouse pointer over the rotation handle, which is the circular arrow.**

   As shown in Figure 5-4, the mouse pointer changes to a circular arrow.
3. **Drag the rotation handle until the graphic object is at the angle you want:**
   - Drag the handle clockwise to rotate the object clockwise.
   - Drag the handle counterclockwise to rotate the object counterclockwise.

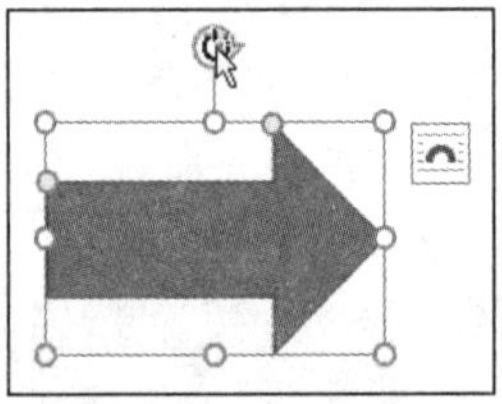

**FIGURE 5-4:** Drag the rotation handle to rotate the graphic object.

## Moving a graphic object

If a graphic isn't in the position you want within the document, you can move the object to a different part of the document by following these steps:

1. **Select the object you want to move.**

   The program displays selection handles around the object's frame.
2. **Position the mouse pointer on any edge of the object, but not over any selection handle.**

   A four-headed arrow appears along with the normal mouse pointer.
3. **Drag the object to the position you want.**

   As you drag the object, you see either an outline or a faded version of the object that shows you the new position.

   TIP

   To move an object only horizontally or vertically, hold down the Shift key while dragging.
4. **Release the mouse button.**

   The program redraws the object in the new position.

## Aligning graphic objects

If your document includes multiple graphic objects, you may want to enhance the appearance of the document by aligning some or all the objects with each other. For example, if you have a series of images down the left side of the document, the series will probably look best if the left edges of the objects all line up.

This sounds like a time-consuming chore, but the Office apps have alignment tools that can perform such tasks automatically. Here are the steps you need to follow:

1. **Select the graphic objects you want to align.**
2. **Click the contextual tab that appears (such as the Shape Format tab, if you selected shapes).**

3. **In the Arrange group, click Align (shown in the margin).**
4. **Click one of the alignment commands:**
   - *Align Left:* Aligns the objects on the left edges of their frames.
   - *Align Center:* Aligns the objects on the horizontal center of their frames.
   - *Align Right:* Aligns the objects on the right edges of their frames.
   - *Align Top:* Aligns the objects on the top edges of their frames.
   - *Align Middle:* Aligns the objects on the vertical middle of their frames.
   - *Align Bottom:* Aligns the objects on the bottom edges of their frames.
   - *Distribute Horizontally:* Aligns the objects so that they are evenly spaced horizontally.
   - *Distribute Vertically:* Aligns the objects so that they are evenly spaced vertically.

## Copying graphic objects

If you want multiple copies of the same object, you don't have to draw each one. Instead, follow the steps outlined next to make as many copies of the object as you need:

1. **Click the object you want to copy.**

   The app displays selection handles around the object's frame.

2. **Hold down the Ctrl key and position the mouse pointer inside the object.**

   For some objects, you may need to point at the object frame, instead. The pointer changes to an arrow with a plus sign.

3. **Drag the object to the position where you want the copy to appear.**

   As you drag the mouse, a copy of the object comes along for the ride.

4. **Release the mouse button.**

   A copy of the object now resides where you released the mouse.

## Deleting a graphic object

To delete a graphic object, click it and then press Delete. The app deletes the object. If you delete a graphic object accidentally, immediately click Undo (shown in the margin) or press Ctrl+Z to reverse the deletion.

## Grouping graphic objects

I mention earlier that combining two or more shapes, text boxes, or other graphic objects to create a more complex image is common. Needing to work with all those objects at once is also common. For example, you might want to change the colors of all the objects or resize or rotate them together.

You can work with all the objects together by selecting them, but this method can become laborious if you must do it frequently. A better way is to create a *group* consisting of all the objects. A group is a collection of objects that the app treats as a single object. That is, you can format, resize, and rotate the group the same way that you perform these actions on a single object. Also, to select an entire group of objects, you can select just one object from the group.

To group two or more objects, follow these steps:

1. **Select the objects you want to include in the group.**
2. **Click the contextual tab that appears (such as the Shape Format tab, if the selected objects are shapes).**

3. **In the Arrange group, click Group Objects (shown in the margin), and then click Group.**

   Alternatively, you can right-click any selected object, click Group in the context menu that appears, and then click Group.

   The program creates an invisible, rectangular frame around the objects.

To ungroup objects, follow these steps:

1. **Select the group.**
2. **Click the contextual tab that appears (such as the Shape Format tab, if the grouped objects are shapes).**
3. **In the Arrange group, click Group Objects (shown in the margin), and then click Ungroup.**

   Alternatively, you can right-click the group, click Group in the context menu that appears, and then click Ungroup.

   The program removes the group but leaves the individual objects selected.

# Stacking overlapped graphic objects

When you have two graphic objects that overlap, the most recently created object covers part of the earlier object. The newer object is stacked "in front" of the older one. You can change the stacking order either by sending an object toward the back of the stack or by bringing an object toward the front of the stack.

Follow these steps to send an object back in the stack:

1. **Click the object you want to work with.**
2. **Click the contextual tab that appears (such as the Picture Format tab, if the selected object is a picture).**
3. **In the Arrange group, do one of the following:**
   - *To send the object back one level in the stack:* Click the Send Backward button.
   - *To send the object all the way to the back of the stack:* Pull down the Send Backward list and then click Send to Back.

Follow these steps to bring an object toward the front of the stack:

1. **Click the object you want to work with.**
2. **Click the contextual tab that appears (such as the Shape Format tab, if the selected object is a shape).**
3. **In the Arrange group, do one of the following:**
   - *To bring the object forward one level in the stack:* Click the Bring Forward button.
   - *To bring the object all the way to the front of the stack:* Pull down the Bring Forward list and then click Bring to Front.

TIP

You can also change an object's stacking order by right-clicking the object and then using the Send to Back button or list or the Bring to Front button or list.

## Stacking graphic objects and text in Word

Word views the document text as a kind of layer in the overall document stack. This means, for example, that you can send one or more graphic objects behind the text to create a sort of watermark effect. However, the document text layer is separate from the graphic objects. In essence, Word maintains three layers:

- The document text.
- The stack of graphic objects that are behind the document text. In this case, you can use the techniques from the previous section to change the stacking order for those objects behind the text.
- The stack of graphic objects that are in front of the document text. In this case, you can use the techniques from the previous section to change the stacking order for those objects in front of the text.

Here are the steps to follow to send a graphic object behind the document text:

1. **Click the object you want to work with.**
2. **Click the contextual tab that appears (such as the Shape Format tab, if the selected object is a shape).**
3. **In the Arrange group, pull down the Send Backward menu and then click Send Behind Text.**

   Alternatively, right-click the object, click the Sent to Back list, and then click Send Behind Text.

Here are the steps to follow to bring a graphic object in front of the document text:

1. **Click the object you want to work with.**
2. **Click the contextual tab that appears (such as the Shape Format tab, if the selected object is a shape).**
3. **In the Arrange group, pull down the Bring Forward menu and then click Bring in Front of Text.**

   Alternatively, right-click the object, click the Bring to Front list, and then click Bring in Front of Text.

## Wrapping text around a graphic object in Word

When you add a graphic object to a Word document, most of the time that image must coexist with the document text. It's unlikely that you want the object to cover the text, so you need to decide how the text will "react" to the image. Will it stop above the image and then restart below the image? Will it wrap around the image frame? Will it wrap around the image itself? These questions represent just a few of the possibilities that Word offers you for combining text and graphics in a document.

TIP

When you insert a graphic object, Word applies the In Line with Text wrapping (described in the steps that follow) by default. To set a different default, choose File ➪ Options to launch the Word Options dialog box, click Advanced, and then use the Insert/Paste Pictures As list to click the wrapping you prefer (again, I run through the wrapping possibilities in the steps that begin any second now).

Follow these steps to set the text wrapping option for a graphic object in a Word document:

1. **Click the graphic object you want to work with.**
2. **Click the contextual tab that appears (such as the Picture Format tab, if the selected object is a picture).**
3. **To set the position of the image within the page, in the Arrange group, click Position and then click one of the preset position options, shown in Figure 5-5.**

   Notice that the position in the In Line With Text section automatically applies top and bottom text wrapping (refer to Step 5 for the details) and the nine positions in the With Text Wrapping section automatically apply tight text wrapping (again, refer to Step 5).
4. **To set the text wrapping, click Wrap Text and then click one of the following options from the list shown in Figure 5-6:**
   - *In Line With Text:* Moves the graphic object along with the text as you insert and delete text before the object.
   - *Square:* Wraps the text around the graphic object's frame.
   - *Tight:* Wraps the text along the edges of the image itself.

     TECHNICAL STUFF

     In a tight text wrapping, the text may wrap in a strange way if the image is an unusual shape. To fix this problem, click Edit Wrap Points in the Wrap Text list to display a series of edit handles around the image. Drag the edit handles to define the edges around which Word places the surrounding text in a tight text wrap.

**FIGURE 5-5.** Use the Position gallery to set both the position and the text wrapping for the image.

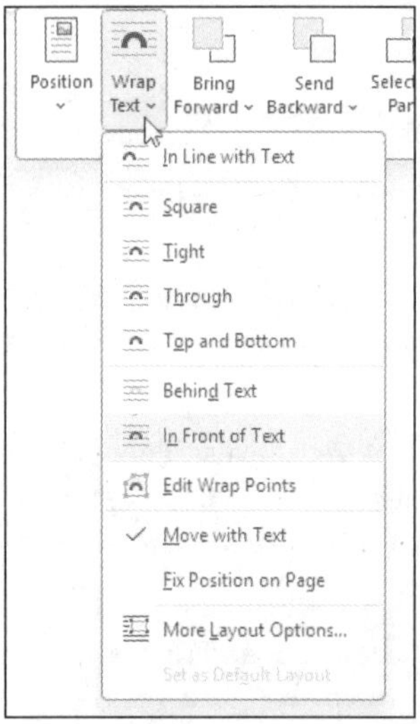


**FIGURE 5-6.** Use the Text Wrap gallery to set the text wrapping for the image.

- *Through:* This is the same as the tight text wrapping, except Word also wraps the text into any open space within the image.
- *Top and Bottom:* Stops the text above the graphic object and resumes the text on a new line below the object.
- *Behind Text:* Moves the graphic object behind the text layer, as described in the previous section.
- *In Front of Text:* Moves the graphic object in front of the text layer, as described in the previous section.

- *More Layout Options:* Displays the Layout dialog box with the Text Wrapping tab displayed, which enables you to set precise values for position and wrapping.

## Formatting the fill

In a graphic object, the *fill* is the area inside the edges of the image. The fill is usually white, but Office enables you to format the fill with a solid color, a color gradient, a picture, or a texture. This feature is useful for adding a bit of pizzazz to a plain shape, or to match an image's interior with the document's background or color scheme. You can format the fill for shapes, text boxes, and WordArt graphics.

Here are the steps to follow to format a graphic object's fill:

1. **Click the graphic object you want to work with.**
2. **Click the contextual tab that appears (such as the Shape Format tab, if the selected object is a shape).**

3. **In the Shape Styles group, click the Shape Fill button (shown in the margin) to apply the current fill color (which is indicated by the horizontal strip that appears under the paint bucket).**

   To apply some other fill, pull down the Shape Fill list and click one of the following:

   - *Theme Colors:* Formats the fill with a solid color from the current theme. In the color palette, click the color swatch you want to use for the fill.
   - *Standard Colors:* Formats the fill with a solid color from the standard Office colors. In the color palette, click the color swatch you want to use for the fill.
   - *No Fill:* Removes any fill you've added to the image.
   - *More Fill Colors:* Displays the Colors dialog box, which gives you a fistful of ways to define a custom color.
   - *Picture:* Formats the fill with a picture. Click this button to display the Insert Pictures dialog box. From here, you can insert a local file, or insert a stock image, online picture, or icon.
   - *Gradient:* Formats the fill with a color gradient where one color blends into a second color. Click this button to display the Gradient gallery, and then click the predefined gradient you want to use for the fill. To define your own gradient, click More Gradients.

- *Texture:* Formats the fill with a texture. Click this button to display the Texture gallery, then click a texture that appeals. You can also click More Textures to display the Format Shape task pane with the Fill options displayed, as shown in Figure 5-7. (To get here, you can also right-click the object and then click Format Shape.)

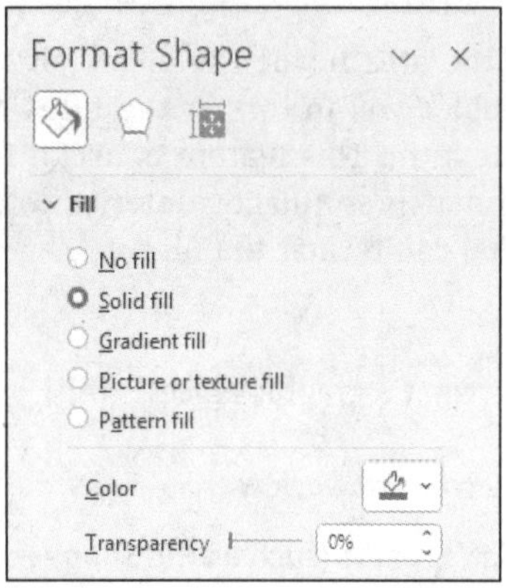


**FIGURE 5-7:** The Format Shape task pane's Fill options.

## Formatting lines

By default, Office usually creates the outline of a shape, text box, or similar image using thin, solid, black lines, but you can format all three aspects of an object's outline. That is, you can change the thickness, style (such as dotted or dashed), and color. You can also add or remove arrows if the image is a line shape. You can format the outline for shapes, text boxes, and WordArt graphics, and you can apply similar formatting for the borders around pictures and SmartArt items.

Here are the steps to follow to format a graphic object's outline:

1. **Click the graphic object you want to work with.**
2. **Click the contextual tab that appears (such as the Shape Format tab, if the selected object is a shape).**
3.  **In the Shape Styles group, click the Shape Outline button (shown in the margin) to apply the current outline color (which is indicated by the horizontal strip that appears at the bottom of the icon).**

   To format the object's outline in some other way, pull down the Shape Outline menu and use the following:

   - *Theme Colors:* Formats the outline with a solid color from the current theme. In the color palette, click the color swatch you want to use for the outline.

- *Standard Colors:* Formats the outline with a solid color from the standard Office colors. In the color palette, click the color swatch you want to use for the outline.
- *No Outline:* Click this command to remove the outline from the image.
- *More Outline Colors:* Displays the Colors dialog box, which gives you oh-so-many ways to define a custom color.
- *Weight:* Formats the thickness of the outline. Click this button to display the Weight gallery and then click the weight you want to use for the outline.
- *Sketched:* Formats the outline to look like it was drawn by hand. Click this button to display the Sketched gallery and then click the format you want.
- *Dashes:* Formats the outline style, such as dashed or dotted. Click this button to display the Dashes gallery, and then click the style you want to use for the outline.
- *Arrows:* Adds an arrowhead to a line shape. Click this button to display the Arrows gallery, and then click the arrowhead you want to use.
- *More Lines:* Displays the Format Shape task pane with the Line options displayed, as shown in Figure 5-8. The More Lines command is available at the bottom of the Weight, Sketched, Dashes, and Arrows galleries.

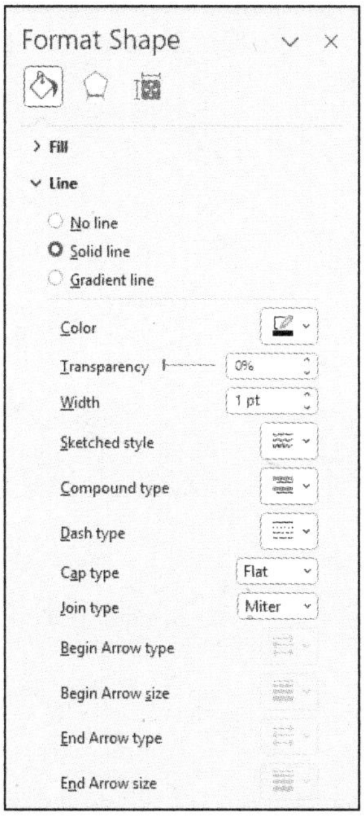


**FIGURE 5-8:** The Format Shape task pane's Line options.

## Applying a shadow effect

You can make an image stand out from the document by applying a shadow effect. For example, the classic drop shadow effect makes an image look as though it's floating over the page. You can also add perspective shadows that give the illusion of depth. You can apply shadow effects to shapes, text boxes, WordArt graphics, pictures, and SmartArt items.

Here are the steps to follow to apply a shadow effect to a graphic object:

1. **Click the graphic object you want to work with.**
2. **Click the contextual tab that appears (such as the Picture Format tab, if the selected object is a picture).**
3.  **In the Shape Styles group, click Shape Effects (shown in the margin).**
4. **Click Shadow.**

   The Shadow gallery appears.

5. **Click the style you want to use for the shadow.**

   Alternatively, you can click Shadow Options to open the Format Shape task pane with the Shadow options displayed, as shown in Figure 5-9. With these options you can choose a preset shadow, change the color, and tweak the shadow transparency, size, blur, and more.

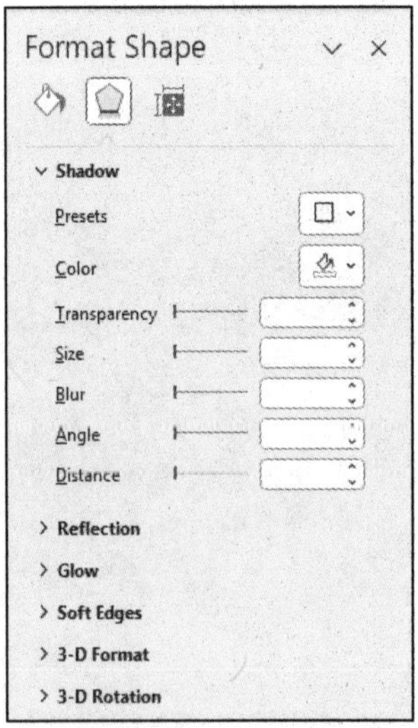


**FIGURE 5-9:** The Format Shape task pane's Shadow options.

## Applying other effects

To make an image stand out from the herd, the Office 365 apps offer several special effects that you can apply. I talk about the shadow special effect in the previous section, but there are several other effects that you can throw at an image to liven it up. You can apply special effects to shapes, text boxes, WordArt graphics, pictures, and SmartArt items.

Here are the steps to follow to apply special effects to a graphic object:

1. **Click the graphic object you want to work with.**
2. **Click the Format tab.**
3. **Click the contextual tab that appears (such as the Shape Format tab, if the selected object is a shape).**

4. **In the Shape Styles group, click Shape Effects (shown in the margin).**
5. **In the list that appears, you can apply the following effects:**
   - *Preset:* Offers ready-to-apply effects that are combinations of the Shadow, Reflection, Glow, Soft Edges, Bevel, and 3-D Rotation effects.
   - *Reflection:* Adds a transparent mirror image of the graphic. You can choose how close the reflection is to the original picture and how large the reflection is.
   - *Glow:* Adds a fuzzy border around the image. You can choose the color and size of the border.
   - *Soft Edges:* Feathers the edges of the image so that the edges gradually become transparent, and the image seems to fade into the document.
   - *Bevel:* Gives the image a three-dimensional look by making the edges appear to be beveled. You can choose from several bevel styles.
   - *3-D Rotation:* Rotates the picture so that the picture appears to be three-dimensional. You can choose the rotation angle.

REMEMBER

The special effects are also available via the Format Shape task pane, as shown earlier in Figure 5-9. In each special effect gallery, click the *Effect* Options command that appears at the bottom of the gallery (where *Effect* is the name of the gallery, such as Reflection Options in the Reflection gallery).

## Formatting and editing shapes

Besides the general formatting tools that I talk about in the past few sections, Office also offers sets of tools that are specific to particular image types. In this section you learn about the tools available for shapes, and the next section shows you the tools for pictures.

To see the formatting and editing options available for a shape, follow these steps:

1. **Click the shape you want to work with.**
2. **Click the Shape Format contextual tab.**

Figure 5-10 shows the ribbon layout that appears.

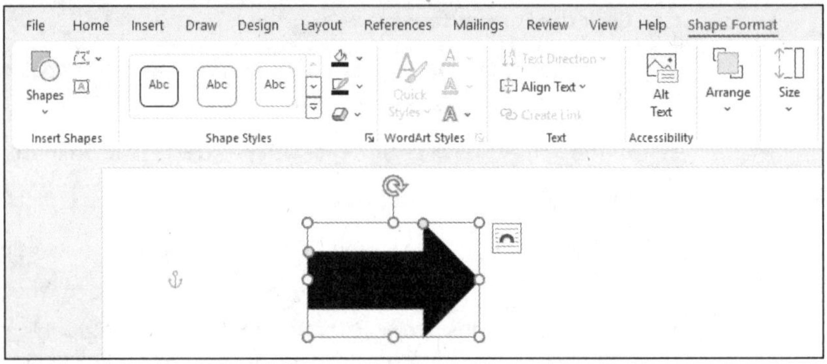


**FIGURE 5-10:** The Shape Format contextual tab shows up when you click a shape object.

In the Insert Shapes group, you can click Edit Shape (shown in the margin) and then click one of the following:

- **Change Shape:** Displays the Shapes gallery so that you can change the image to a different shape.
- **Edit Points:** Enables you to modify a shape by moving its vertices. Clicking this command displays edit handles at each vertex of the shape. Drag the edit handles to move the vertices.

The Shape Styles group offers several drawing styles with preformatted fills, shadow effects, and 3D effects. You can click a style directly in the Shape Styles list, or you can pull down the list to view the Shape Styles gallery.

Use the Arrange group to format the shape's position, text wrapping, and alignment, as described earlier in this chapter.

Use the Size group to change the dimensions of the selected shape by changing the values displayed in the Height and Width spin boxes.

# Formatting and editing pictures

Office 365 offers several tools for formatting and editing pictures, including tools that enable you to perform relatively sophisticated tasks such as recoloring the image and changing its brightness and contrast. Office also offers useful effects beyond the shadow and 3D effects I introduced earlier in this chapter.

To see the formatting and editing options available for a picture, follow these steps:

1. **Click the picture you want to work with.**
2. **Click the Picture Format contextual tab.**

Figure 5-11 shows the ribbon layout that appears.

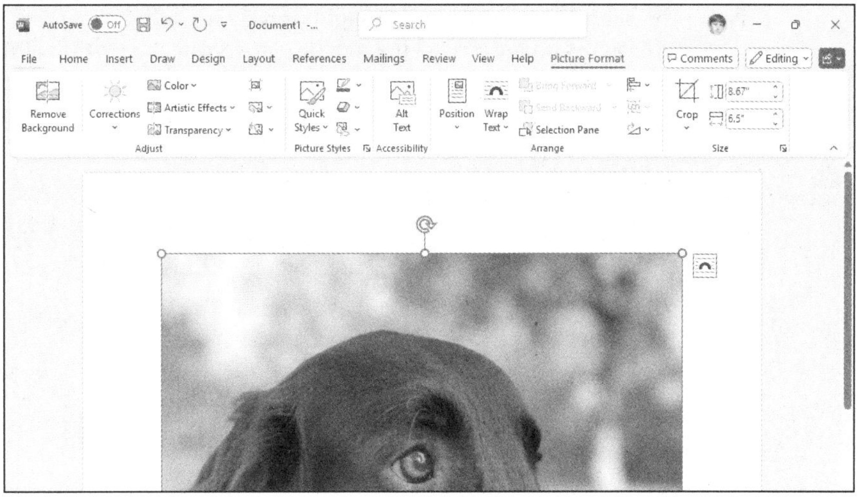


**FIGURE 5-11:** The Picture Format contextual tab shows up when you click a picture object.

The Adjust group gives you six choices:

- **Corrections:** Enables you to sharpen or soften the picture, adjust the brightness of the picture, and change the picture contrast.
- **Color:** Applies a coloring effect to the picture, such as sepia, washout, or a color accent.
- **Artistic Effects:** Applies an effect that makes the picture appear to have been made using a specific artistic medium or technique.
- **Transparency:** Sets the transparency of the picture.

- **Compress Pictures**. Applies compression to all the pictures in the document to reduce the size of the document.
- **Change Picture**. Enables you to change the current picture to a different picture.
- **Reset Picture:** Click this button to undo any editing and formatting that you've applied to the picture. If you also want to undo any sizing you've applied, drop down the Reset Picture list and then click Reset Picture & Size.

The Picture Styles group offers a gallery of styles with preformatted shapes, outlines, and 3D effects.

Use the Arrange group to format the picture's position, text wrapping, and alignment, as described earlier in this chapter.

Use the Size group to change the dimensions of the selected picture by changing the values displayed in the Height and Width spin boxes. You can also click Crop to crop the image by clicking and dragging over the portion of the picture that you want to keep.

# 2 Word 365

# Contents at a Glance

IN THIS CHAPTER

» Forging a new Word document

» Playing around with the view

» Exploring speedy selection, editing, and formatting techniques

» Navigating a Word document

# Chapter 1

# Getting Up to Speed with Word

All the Office 365 programs require at least some written input. From email messages in Outlook to bullet points in PowerPoint to memo fields in Access, you always end up working with text in one form or another when you work with Office 365.

However, when you have some *real* writing to do, the Office 365 tool of choice is, of course, Word and its word-processing pedigree. Whether you're firing off a 3-page memo to the troops or putting together a 300-page book, Word can handle any text task you throw at it.

Unfortunately, most Word training doesn't involve much more than typing in a bit of text and formatting it with boldface type or italics. It's like having a Formula 1 racing car in the driveway and using it only to pop out to the corner store for a quart of milk.

Word is loaded with useful and powerful features that can help you to not only create beautiful documents but also create those documents in record time. The chapters here in Book 2 are designed to introduce you to these features and other techniques for getting the most out of Word. This chapter gets you off to a good start by examining a number of handy and powerful techniques for viewing, selecting, and navigating text in Word.

# Cranking Out a Shiny, New Word Document

Everything you create in Word — whether it's a newsletter, a report, a memo, or a proclamation — is called a *document*. Underneath (so to speak) every document is a special kind of file called a *template*, which provides the initial formatting — the fonts, styles, margin specifications, layouts, and other stuff — that give the document its appearance.

Blank Word documents are based on the Normal template, which contains Word's default formatting. However, when you create a document, you get a chance to choose some other template to establish your document's initial appearance. If your aim is to create an academic report, flyer, newsletter, calendar, résumé, or other sophisticated document, you might be able to spare yourself some formatting work by choosing the appropriate template when you create your document. (Book 2, Chapter 3 explains templates in detail and how to create your own templates.)

Follow these basic steps to create a document:

1. **Choose File ⇨ New.**

   The New window, shown in Figure 1-1, appears.

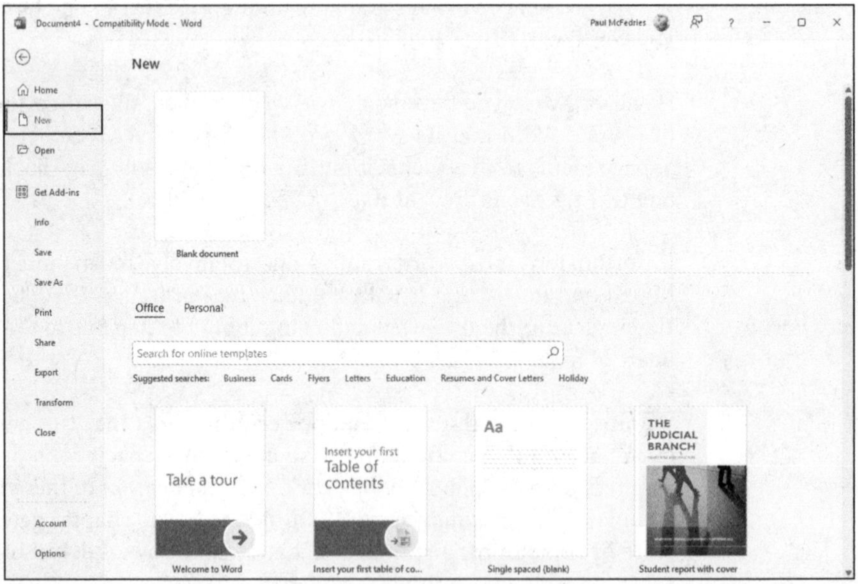


**FIGURE 1-1:** To create a document, choose a template in the New window.

2. **Click the template you want to use as the basis for your new document.**

   A preview window appears with a description of the template you chose, as shown later in Figure 1-2.

3. **Click the Create button in the preview window.**

   Your new Word document opens.

Use these techniques in the New window to choose a template and create a document:

- **Create a document based on the Normal template:** Click Blank Document to create a bare-bones document with few styles. Blank Document is the default template for creating documents. (By pressing Ctrl+N, you can create a new document without opening the New window.)
- **Create a document from a displayed template:** Click a template to examine it in a preview window similar to the one shown in Figure 1-2. Click the Create button in the preview window to create a document from the template.



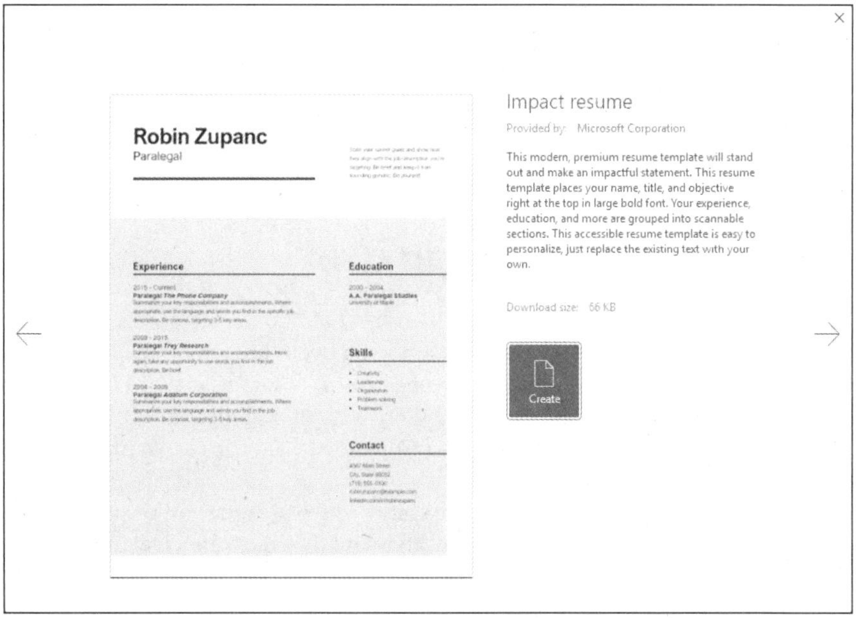


**FIGURE 1-2:** When you click a template in the New window, Word displays a preview.

- **Create a document from an online template:** Type a search term in the Search For Online Templates text box and then press Enter. (Alternatively, you can click one of the suggested search terms that appear just below the text box). Templates that match your search term appear in the New window. You can click a template to examine it closely in a preview window (refer to Figure 1-2). Click the Create button to create a document from the template.

- **Create a document from a personal template:** On the Personal tab, click to select a template and create a document. A personal template is one that you created or copied to your computer or network. Book 2, Chapter 3 explains how to create templates. The Personal tab appears in the New window only if you've created templates or copied them to your computer.

TIP

To find out which template was used to create a document, choose File ⇨ Info to open the Info window, click the Show All Properties link (it's located in the lower-right corner of the window). The Properties list appears. Among other things, it tells you the template with which the document was created.

# Fussing with the View

You might think that there's only one way to view a document. That is, you create a new document or open an existing one, and there it is on your screen, end of story. Not so fast. Word actually gives you quite a few ways to view your document from different angles, so to speak. Why on earth would you ever want to do such a thing? Believe it or not, a different view can make it easier or more efficient to work with a document. The next couple of sections explain how merely changing the view can make your Word life easier.

## Views you can use

Page layout, which is the subject of Book 2, Chapter 2, is all about working with the "big picture," but it's a not-so-well-known — or perhaps it's more accurate to say it's a not-so-well-*understood* — fact that Word has various "big pictures" to choose from. These are Word's *views* and instead of always using the default view, you should be changing from one to another as your page layout needs change.

Figure 1-3 shows these views. The pages that follow explain how to change views, the six different views, and why to select one view over another. (Be sure to visit Book 1, Chapter 3 as well; it describes how to view a document through more than one window and how to open a second window in a document.)

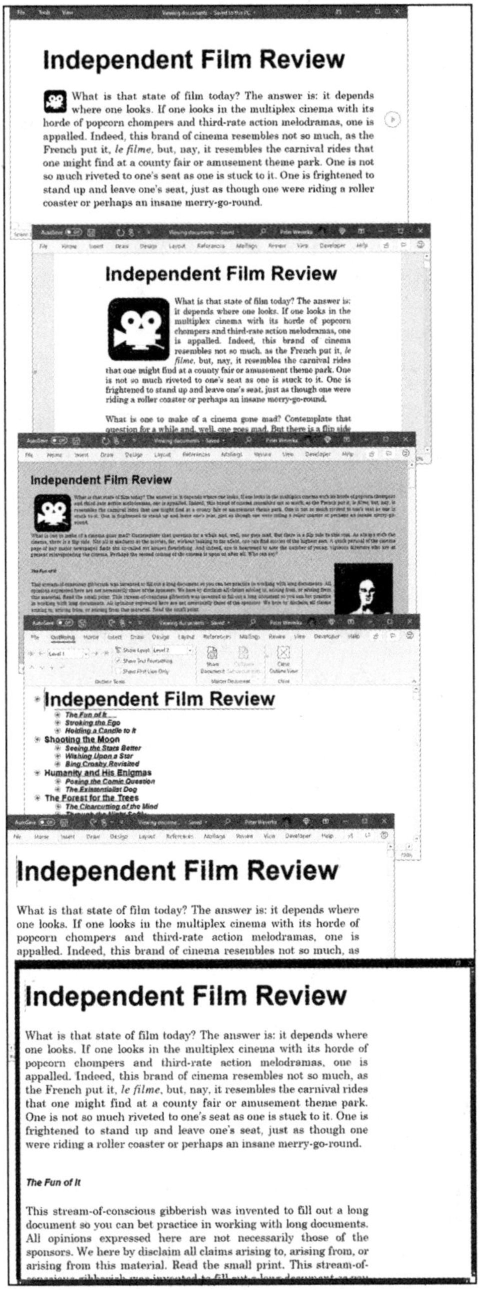


**FIGURE 1-3:** The different document views (top to bottom): Read Mode, Print Layout, Web Layout, Outline, Draft, and Focus Mode.

## Changing the view

Use these techniques to change views:

- Click one of the four View buttons on the right side of the status bar, pointed out in Figure 1-4.
- On the View tab, click one of the five buttons in the Views group or the Focus button in the Immersive group (again, check out Figure 1-4).

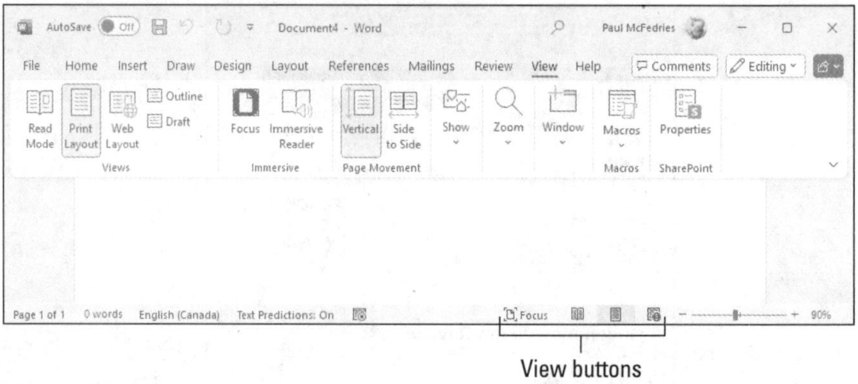


**FIGURE 1-4:** You can change the view using either the status bar or the View tab.

## Read mode

Read mode (the status bar button is shown in the margin) enables you to focus on the text itself and proofread your documents. You can't enter or edit text in Read mode and most everything else — including the Ribbon, the Quick Access toolbar, and the search box — is stripped away. All you get are the text and artwork in your documents. Read mode is designed for reading documents on tablet computers. (To leave Read mode, choose View ➪ Edit Document.)

## Print Layout view

Print Layout view (the status bar button is shown in the margin) shows how your document will appear when you print it. Graphics, headers, footers, and even page borders appear in Print Layout view. This view also clearly shows where page breaks occur (where one page ends and the next begins). In Print Layout view, you can click the One Page, Multiple Pages, or Page Width button on the View tab's Zoom group to display more or fewer pages on your screen.

## Web Layout view

Web Layout view (the status bar button is shown in the margin) shows how your document would appear as a web page. Background colors appear (if you chose a theme or background color for your document). Text is wrapped to the window rather than around the artwork in the document.

## Outline view

Outline view shows how your work is organized by displaying only the headings in your document. You can get a sense of how your document unfolds and easily move sections of text backward and forward in a document. In other words, you can reorganize a document in Outline view. Book 2, Chapter 8 explains outlines in torturous detail.

## Draft view

Draft view enables you to focus on the words in your document. Pictures, shapes, and other distractions don't appear in this view, nor do page breaks (although Draft view does show section breaks). As the name implies, Draft view is best for writing first drafts.

## Focus Mode view

Focus Mode view makes reading a document easier because it's designed to prevent eyestrain. You can enter text in Focus Mode view, but that's about it. All editing commands are stripped from the screen. Press the Esc key to leave Focus Mode view.

TIP

Word provides a special screen called the Immersive Reader for people who have poor eyesight and need help reading. The screen offers tools for focusing on lines of text, breaking words into syllables, changing the background color of the page, and hearing the words read aloud. Choose View ➪ Immersive Reader to open the Immersive Reader screen.

## READ MODE ZOOMING

While you're in Read mode, you can double-click a table, image, or chart to enlarge it onscreen for easier viewing. After the item gets enlarged, you can click the Zoom button (shown in the margin) to enlarge it several times more.

To shrink an item back to size, press Esc or click onscreen (don't click the item itself).

## Splitting the screen

Besides opening a second window on a document (a subject of Book 1, Chapter 3), you can be two places at one time in a Word document by splitting the screen. One reason you might do this: You're writing a long report and want the introduction to support the conclusion, plus you want the conclusion to fulfill all promises made by the introduction. Achieving both goals can be difficult to do sometimes, but you can make it easier by splitting the screen so that you can be two places at one time as you write your introduction and conclusion.

*Splitting* a window means to divide it into north and south halves. In a split screen, two sets of scroll bars appear so that you can travel in one half of the screen without disturbing the other half. Follow these steps to split the screen:

1. **Choose View ⇨ Split (in the Window group).**

   You can also split the screen by pressing Ctrl+Alt+S.

   A gray line appears onscreen, as shown in Figure 1-5.

2. **Drag the gray line until the line is where you want the split to be.**

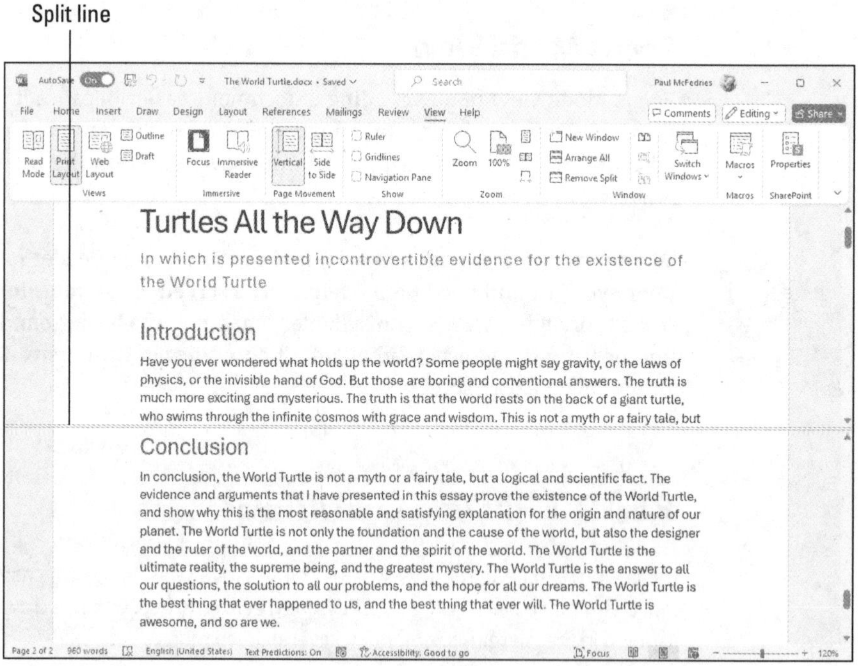


**FIGURE 1-5:** A split screen, with one view of a document on top and another view on the bottom, separated by a split line.

When you tire of this split-screen arrangement, choose View ➪ Remove Split (in the Window group), drag the line to the top or bottom of the screen, or press Ctrl+Alt+S again. You can also double-click the line that splits the screen in two.

TIP

In a split screen, you can choose a different view for the different halves. For example, click in the top half of the screen and choose Outline view to display your document in outline form, then click in the bottom half and choose Draft view to display the other half in Draft view. This particular combo is useful when you're writing the document introduction because it enables you to view the document's headings.



# Snappier Ways to Edit and Format Text

If, as writing coaches the world over have reminded us again and again, the essence of writing is rewriting, then the essence of Word must be its text-editing features and techniques. At first blush, there doesn't seem to be too much to this topic. After all, what's involved in text editing other than knowing how to use the Backspace and Delete keys? You'd be surprised. There are actually a few useful editing techniques you ought to know to make revising your prose faster and more efficient, as the next few sections show.

## Selecting text lickety-split

Book 1, Chapter 2 explains how to enter text and change its appearance and size. After you enter text, you inevitably have to copy, move, or delete it, but you can't do those tasks until you select it first. Table 1-1 describes shortcuts for selecting text.

REMEMBER

If a bunch of highlighted text is onscreen and you want it to go away but it won't (because you pressed F8), press the Esc key.

TIP

After you press F8, all the keyboard shortcuts for moving the cursor also work for selecting text. For example, press F8 and then press Ctrl+Home to select everything from the cursor to the top of the document. Later in this chapter, the "Keys for getting around quickly" section describes keyboard shortcuts for getting from place to place.

**TABLE 1-1** Shortcuts for Selecting Text

| To Select This | Do This |
|---|---|
| A word | Double-click the word. |
| A line | Click in the left margin next to the line. |
| Some lines | Drag the mouse pointer over the lines or drag it down the left margin. |
| A sentence | Ctrl+click the sentence. |
| A paragraph | Double-click in the left margin next to the paragraph; or triple-click inside the paragraph. |
| A mess of text | Click at the start of the text, hold down the Shift key, and click at the end of the text. |
| A gob of text | Put the cursor where you want to start selecting, press F8, and press an arrow key, drag the mouse, or click at the end of the selection. |
| Text with the same formats | On the Home tab, in the Editing group, click Select and then click Select Text with Similar Formatting. |
| A document | Hold down the Ctrl key and click in the left margin; triple-click in the left margin; press Ctrl+A; or choose Home ➪ Select ➪ Select All. |

## Editing text from the keyboard

When you are busy typing, having to reach for the mouse to perform a quick edit is often a hassle. However, in many situations you can bypass the mouse and keep your fingers over the keyboard. Table 1-2 presents my favorite keyboard-based techniques for editing text.

**TABLE 1-2** The Most Useful Word Keyboard Editing Shortcuts

| Press | To |
|---|---|
| Ctrl+Backspace | Delete from the current cursor position to the beginning of the word. |
| Ctrl+Delete | Delete from the current cursor position to the end of the word. |
| Shift+Home, Delete | Delete from the current cursor position to the beginning of the line. |
| Shift+End, Delete | Delete from the current cursor position to the end of the line. |
| Ctrl+Shift+Down arrow, Delete | Delete from the current cursor position to the end of the paragraph. |
| Ctrl+Shift+Up arrow, Delete | Delete from the current cursor position to the beginning of the paragraph. |
| Shift+F3 | Cycle the case of the current word or selection through UPPERCASE, lowercase, and Title Case. |
| Alt+Shift+Down arrow | Move the current paragraph down by one paragraph. |
| Alt+Shift+Up arrow | Move the current paragraph up by one paragraph. |

## Formatting from the keyboard

When you have a ton of typing to get through, the last thing you want to do is switch over to the mouse to get your formatting chores accomplished. Fortunately, you may not have to bother much with the mouse because Word offers a huge number of formatting shortcuts via the keyboard. Table 1-3 offers the complete list.

**TABLE 1-3** Word's Formatting Keyboard Shortcuts

| Press | To Apply the Following Format |
|---|---|
| Ctrl+B | Bold |
| Ctrl+I | Italics |
| Ctrl+U | Underline |
| Ctrl+Shift+D | Double underline |
| Ctrl+Shift+W | Underline each word in the selection |
| Ctrl+Shift+A | Uppercase |
| Shift+F3 | Cycle case |
| Ctrl+Shift+K | Small caps |
| Ctrl+= | Subscript |
| Ctrl++ | Superscript |
| Ctrl+Shift+Q | Symbol font |
| Ctrl+> | Grow font |
| Ctrl+] | Grow font size by one point |
| Ctrl+< | Shrink font |
| Ctrl+[ | Shrink font size by one point |
| Ctrl+D or Ctrl+Shift+F | Display the Font dialog box with Font selected |
| Ctrl+Shift+P | Display the Font dialog box with Size selected |
| Ctrl+Shift+N | Normal style |
| Alt+Ctrl+1 | Heading 1 style |
| Alt+Ctrl+2 | Heading 2 style |
| Alt+Ctrl+3 | Heading 3 style |

*(continued)*

**TABLE 1-3** ***(continued)***

| Press | To Apply the Following Format |
|---|---|
| Ctrl+Shift+S | Display the Apply Styles pane |
| Ctrl+L | Align left |
| Ctrl+E | Center |
| Ctrl+R | Align right |
| Ctrl+J | Justify |
| Ctrl+T | Increase hanging indent |
| Ctrl+Shift+T | Decrease hanging indent |
| Ctrl+M | Increase indent |
| Ctrl+Shift+M | Decrease indent |
| Ctrl+Shift+L | Bullet |
| Ctrl+1 | Set paragraph line spacing to 1 |
| Ctrl+5 | Set paragraph line spacing to 1.5 |
| Ctrl+2 | Set paragraph line spacing to 2 |
| Ctrl+* | Show/Hide ¶ (formatting symbols) |
| Ctrl+Shift+C | Copy formatting from selection |
| Ctrl+Shift+V | Paste formatting to selection |
| Ctrl+Space or Ctrl+Shift+Z | Clear character formatting |
| Ctrl+Q | Clear paragraph formatting |

You can also use the keyboard to create a quick border between two paragraphs. The official way to do this is to display the Home tab, drop down the Borders tool (shown in the margin) in the Paragraph group, and then click either Top Border (if the cursor is in the second of the two paragraphs) or Bottom Border (if the cursor is in the first paragraph).

From the keyboard, you create a border by typing one of six characters — hyphen (-), underscore (_), equal sign (=), pound sign (#), tilde (~), or asterisk (*) — three times and then pressing Enter. Table 1-4 summarizes these key combinations and the border types they forge.

**TABLE 1-4** Keyboard Shortcuts to Create Borders

| Press | To Create the Following Border |
|---|---|
| ---+Enter | Thin |
| ___+Enter | Thick |
| ===+Enter | Double |
| ###+Enter | Triple (two thin, one thick) |
| ~~~+Enter | Wavy |
| ***+Enter | Dotted |

TIP

These automatic borders are one of Word's AutoFormat features. If you prefer not to use them, create a border, click the AutoCorrect Options button (shown in the margin) that appears beside the border, then click Stop Automatically Creating Border Lines.

## VIEWING THE HIDDEN FORMATTING SYMBOLS

¶

Word has a set of hidden formatting symbols that mark document features such as line breaks, tabs, paragraph breaks, and spaces. It's often useful to display these symbols when you're editing and laying out a document. For example, if you notice some unwanted vertical space between a table and the following text, displaying the hidden formatting symbols might show you that the space is caused by an extra paragraph break. To display the hidden formatting symbols, go to the Home tab and, in the Paragraph group, click the Show/Hide ¶ button (displayed in the margin) or press Ctrl+Shift+8. Click the button again (or press Ctrl+Shift+8 again) to hide the symbols.

Here's how the hidden symbols appear onscreen and how to enter them from the keyboard.

| Symbol | How to Enter |
|---|---|
| Line break (↲) | Press Shift+Enter |
| Optional hyphen (-) | Press Ctrl+hyphen |
| Paragraph (¶) | Press Enter |
| Space (·) | Press the spacebar |
| Tab (→) | Press Tab |

# Navigating Like a Pro

Getting around in a two- or three-page document is no big deal, but once your Word creations get longer than that, you'll need some techniques to make navigation easier. Sure, using the scroll bar will take you to and fro, but Word offers quite a few other navigation aids that'll help you get from here to there easier and more efficiently.

## Keys for getting around quickly

One of the fastest ways to go from place to place (especially if you already have your hands on the keyboard) is to press the keys and key combinations listed in Table 1-5.

**TABLE 1-5** Keys for Moving Around Documents

| Press | To Move |
|---|---|
| PgUp | Up the length of one screen |
| PgDn | Down the length of one screen |
| Home | To the start of the line |
| End | To the end of the line |
| Ctrl+PgUp | To the previous page in the document |
| Ctrl+PgDn | To the next page in the document |
| Ctrl+Home | To the top of the document |
| Ctrl+End | To the bottom of the document |

TIP

Another useful navigation shortcut is to press Shift+F5, which moves the cursor to the location of your most recent edit. Press Shift+F5 again to move the edit before that. Keep pressing Shift+F5 to keep moving back through your edits. Pressing Shift+F5 is useful when you want to return to the place where you made an edit but can't quite remember where that place is.

## Navigating by heading or by page

In really long documents, often the quickest way to navigate is to make use of the aptly named Navigation pane, which enables you to go anywhere in any size document with just a click or two.

To display the Navigation pane, go to the View tab and, in the Show group, select the Navigation Pane check box. You then use the following techniques:

- **Navigating to a heading:** In the Navigation pane, click the Headings tab, which displays all the headings in your document, as shown in Figure 1-6. (To learn how to apply heading styles, check out Book 2, Chapter 3). Click a heading in the Navigation pane and Word jumps immediately to that heading in your document. Here are a couple of useful techniques for managing the Navigation pane display:

  - *Controlling the displayed heading levels:* Right-click any heading in the Navigation pane, click Show Heading Levels, and then click the level you want to display. To display a heading's hidden subheadings, click the expansion triangle (shown in the margin) that appears to the left of the heading.

  - *Expanding or collapsing all headings:* Right-click any heading in the Navigation pane and then click either Expand All to display every heading, or Collapse All to display only the top-level headings. To collapse a single heading, click the collapse triangle (shown in the margin) that appears to the right of the heading.



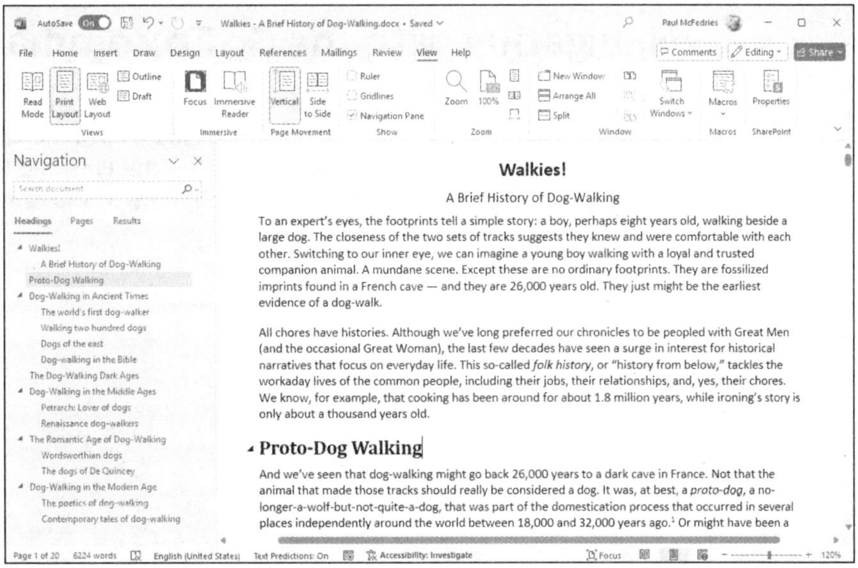


**FIGURE 1-6:** In the Navigation pane's Headings tab, click a heading to navigate directly to that heading in the document.

» **Navigating to a page:** In the Navigation pane, click the Pages tab, which displays a thumbnail image of each page in the document, as shown in Figure 1-7. Click a page thumbnail in the Navigation pane to leap directly to that page in the document. To control the width of the Navigation pane (for example, a wider pane shows more page thumbnails), drag the right border of the Navigation pane.

**FIGURE 1-7:** In the Navigation pane's Pages tab, click a page thumbnail to jump to that page in the document.

## Navigating with the Go To command

Another fast way to go from place to place in a long document is to use the Go To command. On the Home tab, in the Editing group, open the Find button's drop-down list and then click Go To. Word launches the Find and Replace dialog box with the Go To tab displayed, as shown in Figure 1-8. You can also crank up this dialog box by pressing Ctrl+G or F5.

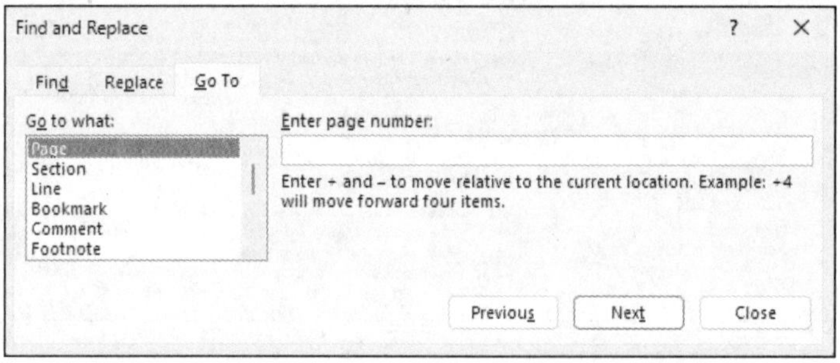


**FIGURE 1-8:** Navigating with the Go To command.

The Go to What list in this dialog box contains a collection of document features, including Page, Section, Bookmark (refer to the next section), Footnote, and Heading. Select the feature type you want to use to navigate, then use either of the following techniques to navigate:

- **Enter a specific feature number or name:** Depending on the type of feature you choose in the Go to What list, the Enter control on the right will be either a text box into which you type a number (for example, the number of the page to which you want to jump) or a list from which you select an item (such as the bookmark to which you want to leap). Click Go To to make it so.
- **Traverse the feature one item at a time:** Click the Next button to navigate to the next instance of whatever feature you selected in the Go to What list; click the Previous button to go to the previous instance.



## Bookmarks for hopping around

In some long documents, you may have a location or three that you visit frequently. It might be a table of contents (refer to Book 2, Chapter 8), an index (Book 2, Chapter 8, as well), or some place that's important to you in some way. In the same way that a physical bookmark makes it easy to find a particular location in a printed book, a Word bookmark makes it easy to navigate to any location in a Word document.

Follow these instructions to work with bookmarks in your Word documents:

- **Inserting a bookmark:** Click the location or object in your Word document where you want the bookmark to go, visit the Insert tab, and then, in the Links group, click the Bookmark button. (You can also run the Bookmark command by pressing Ctrl+Shift+F5.) In the Bookmark dialog box that shows up, type a descriptive name in the Bookmark Name text box. Note that bookmark names can't start with numbers or include blank spaces. When you're done, click Add.
- **Navigating to a bookmark:** On the Insert tab, in the Links group, click the Bookmark button (or press Ctrl+Shift+F5) to open the Bookmark dialog box, double-click the bookmark (or click the bookmark and then click Go To), and then click Close.
- **Deleting a bookmark:** On the Insert tab, in the Links group, click the Bookmark button (or press Ctrl+Shift+F5) to open the Bookmark dialog box, click the bookmark you want to nuke, click Delete, and then click Close.

IN THIS CHAPTER

- » Starting new lines, sections, and pages
- » Modifying margins and indents
- » Augmenting pages with headers and footers
- » Cobbling together bulleted and numbered lists
- » Dealing with tabs and hyphenation

# Chapter 2
# Laying Out Pages Just So

One of the consequences of Office 365's monopolization of the productivity suite market (and, most particularly, Word 365 in the word-processing market) is that people — particularly businesspeople — now have high expectations. That is, because so many users have access to powerful formatting techniques, people have come to expect that the documents they read will have a relatively high level of visual appeal. Send someone a plain, unformatted memo and, although they may not delete it without a glance, they're likely to shake their heads at such a ragtag specimen. So, although you need to always ensure your content is up to snuff (accurate, grammatically correct, and so on), you also need to spend some time making sure that the content is visually appealing.

To that worthy end, in this chapter you can explore Word's extensive collection of page layout tools, where *layout* refers to the arrangement of the elements on the page. That might seem trivial to you now, but you discover in this chapter that designing (or laying out) your document pages with care can make a big difference to the clarity and readability of your documents and how well you get your message across.

# Them's the Breaks

In a Word document, a *break* is a transition between two consecutive parts of the same type. For example, when you press Enter to start a new paragraph, you create a *paragraph break* between the two paragraphs.

You can also populate your documents with breaks at the line, page, and section levels.

## Take a line break

When you type, your text naturally breaks onto a new line once your typing hits the right margin. However, what if you want to start a new line *before* your typing reaches the right margin and you don't want to start a new paragraph?

In that case, my friend, what you need is a *line break.* When the cursor is positioned where you want the break to occur, press Shift+Enter (known as a *soft return* in word-processing lingo). Word starts a new line, just like that.

¶ To display your line breaks, open the Home tab and, in the Paragraph group, click the Show/Hide ¶ button (shown in the margin). Line breaks are marked with the ↲ symbol. To remove a line break, position the cursor just to the left of the ↲ symbol, then press Delete.

## Give me a page break

As you *populate* or add content to a document, the text and other objects naturally flow from one page to the next. The transition from one page to the next is called a *soft page break* because the document content flows back and forth over the break as you add and delete stuff.

However, sometimes it's important for a particular heading, table, or other object to always appear at the top of its own page. You can ensure that by inserting a *hard page break,* which means that Word creates a new page and positions whatever content that immediately follows the page break at the top of the new page. No matter how much content you add or delete before the hard page break, that content remains anchored at the top of its page.

To insert a hard page break, position the cursor immediately before the content that you want to appear at the top of the new page, then click one of the following buttons on the Insert tab, in the Pages group:

- **Page Break:** Word inserts a hard page break and starts a new page at the cursor position. (You can also press Ctrl+Enter or go to the Layout tab's Page Setup group, click the Breaks button, and click Page on the drop-down list.)
- **Blank Page:** Word inserts two hard page breaks at the cursor position. That is, you end up with a blank page, followed by another new page that has at the top the content that followed the cursor.

REMEMBER

Figure 2-1 shows, in Draft view, the difference between a soft page break and a hard page break. In Draft view, soft page breaks are marked with a dotted line; hard page breaks are marked with the words `Page Break` and a dotted line. You can tell where hard page breaks are in Print Layout and Draft view by clicking the Home tab's Show/Hide ¶ button (shown in the margin).

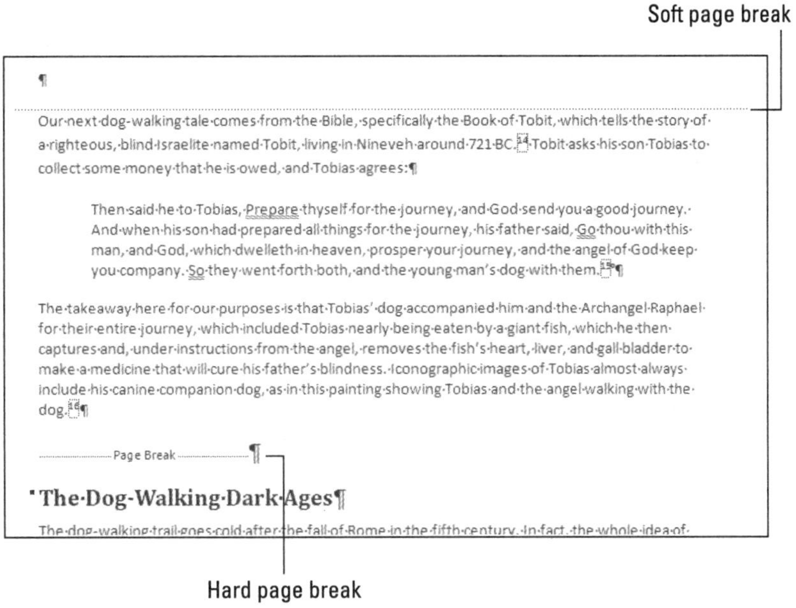


**FIGURE 2-1:** In Draft view, a soft page break (top) and hard page break (bottom).

To delete a hard page break, switch to Draft view (or activate the Show/Hide ¶ button), double-click the words `Page Break`, and press the Delete key.

# Catch a section break

In Word-related training sessions and question-and-answer periods, some of the most common complaints and queries center around using multiple page layouts in a single document:

- How can I have different headers (or footers) for different parts of a document?
- I have a long table on one page. For that one page, how can I change the text direction and set it up with landscape orientation?
- Can I switch from a two-column layout to a three-column layout for part of a document?

Most people end up splitting a single document into multiple documents to accomplish these and similar tasks. However, you don't have to break up your document just because you want to break up the page layout. The secret to doing this is the *section*, a document part that stores page layout options such as the following:

- Margins
- Page size and page orientation
- Headers and footers
- Columns
- Line numbering
- Text direction
- Footnotes and endnotes

When you create a document, Word gives it a single section that comprises the entire document. However, you're free to create multiple sections within a single document, and you can then apply separate page layout formatting to each section. The transition from one section to another is called a *section break.*

Follow these steps to create a new section:

1. **Click where you want to insert a section break.**
2. **On the Layout tab, in the Page Setup group, click the Breaks button.**

   Word displays a list of break types.
3. **Under Section Breaks on the drop-down list, select a section break:**

   - **Next Page:** Inserts a page break as well as a section break so that the new section can start at the top of a new page (the next one). Select this option to start a new chapter, for example.

- **Continuous:** Inserts a section break in the middle of a page. Select this option if, for example, you want to introduce newspaper-style columns in the middle of a page.
- **Even Page:** Starts the new section on the next even page. This option is good for two-sided documents in which the headers on the left- and right-side pages are different.
- **Odd Page:** Starts the new section on the next odd page. You might choose this option if you have a book in which chapters start on odd pages. (By convention, that's where they start.)

REMEMBER

To delete a section break, make sure that you're in Draft view so that the section breaks appear, click the dotted line, and press the Delete key.

WARNING

In the same way that paragraph marks store formats for a paragraph, section breaks store formats for an entire section. When you delete a section break, you apply new formats, because the section is folded into the section that formerly followed it and the section you deleted adopts that next section's formats. Because it's easy to accidentally delete a section break and create havoc, I recommend working in Draft view when your document has many section breaks. In Draft view, you can tell where a section ends because `Section Break` and a double dotted line appear onscreen. The only way to tell where a section ends in Print Layout view is to click the Show/Hide ¶ button on the Home tab. (You can make section information appear on the status bar. Right-click the status bar and choose Section on the pop-up menu.)



# Managing Margins

One of the most common page layout changes is to adjust the *margins,* the blank space to the left and right, as well as above and below the document text (including the header and footer). The standard margins are one inch on all sides. Decreasing the margins fits more text on each page (which is useful when printing a long document), but it can also make the printout appear cluttered and uninviting. If you increase the margins, you get less text on each page, but the added white space can make the document more appealing.

Follow these steps to change the margins:

1. **Position the cursor according to the following guidelines:**
   - If your document has only one section and you want to change the margins for the entire document, position the cursor anywhere within the document.

- If your document has multiple sections and you want to change the margins for a single section, position the cursor anywhere within that section.
- If your document has multiple sections and you want to change the margins for the entire document, select the entire document.

2. **On the Layout tab, in the Page Setup group, click Margins.**

   Word displays a menu of margin settings.

3. **Click the margin option you want.**

   Word applies the margins.

Word's Page Setup dialog box has a Margins tab that enables you to set up more advanced margin settings:

» You can set specific margin sizes for the Top, Bottom, Left, and Right margins.

» You can set the size and position of the *gutter,* extra white space added (usually) to the inside margin to handle document binding.

» You can specify where you want Word to apply the new margins: the current section, the whole document, or from the insertion point forward.

To work with these margin options, choose Page Layout ➪ Margins ➪ Custom Margins to display the Margins tab, shown in Figure 2-2.

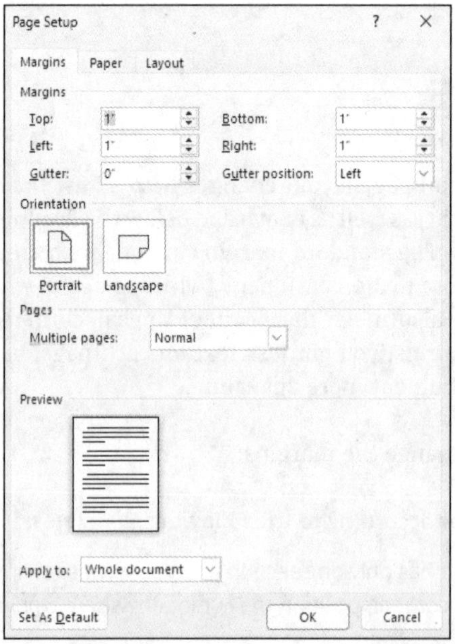


**FIGURE 2-2:** In the Page Setup dialog box, use the Margins tab to specify your margin settings.

# Shifting Text Sideways with Indents

An *indent* is the space between some text and its nearest vertical margin. For example, a *left indent* is the space between the left edge of some text and the point where the left margin begins (that is, the rightmost edge of that margin). Similarly, a *right indent* is the space between the right edge of some text and the point where the right margin begins.

You can use indents to control the horizontal positioning of text in a document. Indents are margins that affect individual lines or entire paragraphs. You might use an indent to distinguish a particular paragraph on a page — for example, a long quote or block quote.

You can indent entire paragraphs in your document from the left and right margins. You also can indent only the first line of a paragraph or all lines *except* the first line of the paragraph. You can set indents using buttons on the Ribbon, the ruler, and the Paragraph dialog box.

## Indenting via the Ribbon



To set indents from the Ribbon, first position the cursor inside the paragraph you want to shift. If you want to indent multiple paragraphs, select them. Display the Home tab then, in the Paragraph group, click the following buttons:

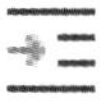

- **Increase Indent:** Shifts the paragraph (or selected paragraphs) a half-inch to the left (that is, a half-inch farther away from the left margin). If you created tab stops, Word indents the text to the next tab stop. (Refer to "Getting Things to Line Up Nice and Neat with Tabs," later in this chapter.) You can also run the Increase Indent command by pressing Ctrl+M.

- **Decrease Indent:** Shifts the paragraph (or selected paragraphs) a half-inch to the right (that is, a half-inch closer to the left margin). If you created tab stops, Word indents the text to the previous tab stop. You can also run the Decrease Indent command by pressing Ctrl+Shift+M.

This is the fastest way to indent text, although you can't indent first lines or indent from the right margin this way.

Another, more precise, way to indent text via the Ribbon is to open the Layout tab then, in the Paragraph group, under the Indent heading, use the following controls to set the indents on the current or selected paragraphs:

- **Left:** Sets how far the text is indented from the left margin. In the text box, type an indent value, or use the arrows to increase or decrease the indent value.
- **Right:** Sets how far the text is indented from the right margin. In the text box, type an indent value, or use the arrows to increase or decrease the indent value.

## "Eyeballing" it with the ruler

You can also change indentations by using the ruler to "eyeball" it. This technique requires some dexterity with the mouse or your finger, but it offers some precision about where paragraphs and the first lines of paragraphs are indented. If necessary, display the ruler by going to the View tab and, in the Show group, selecting the Ruler check box. Then click in or select the paragraph or paragraphs that need indenting and use these techniques to re-indent them:

- **Indenting an entire paragraph from the left margin:** Drag the *left-indent marker* on the ruler to the right. Figure 2-3 shows where this marker is located. Dragging the left-indent marker moves the first-line indent marker as well.

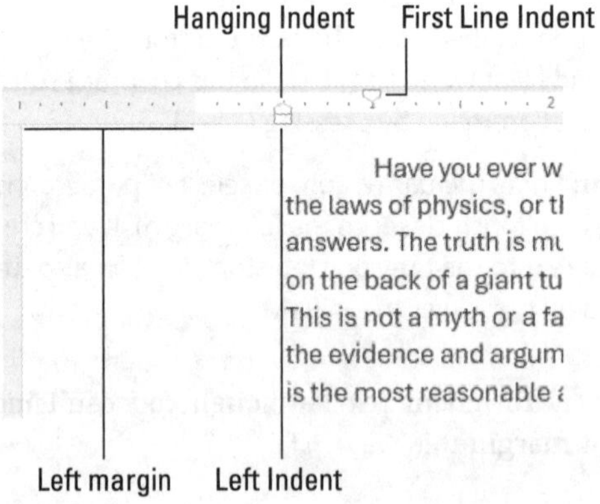


**FIGURE 2-3:** Indenting from the left margin with the ruler.

- **Indenting the first line of a paragraph:** Drag the *first-line indent marker* to the right (refer to Figure 2-3). This marker determines how far the first line of the paragraph is indented.

- **Making a hanging indent:** Drag the *hanging indent marker* to the right of the first-line indent marker (refer to Figure 2-3). A *hanging indent* is one in which the first line of a paragraph appears to "hang" into the left margin because the second and subsequent lines are indented to the right of the start of the first line. Bulleted and numbered lists employ hanging indents.
- **Indenting an entire paragraph from the right margin:** Drag the *right-indent marker* to the left (refer to Figure 2-4).

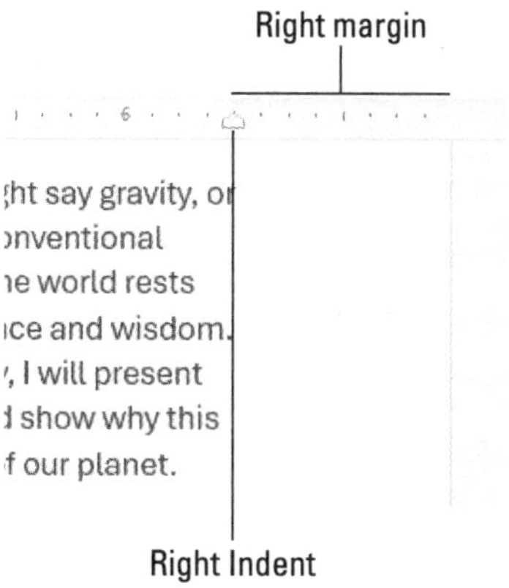


**FIGURE 2-4:** Indenting from the right margin with the ruler.



Notice the shaded areas on the left (pointed out in Figure 2-3) and right (pointed out in Figure 2-4) side of the ruler. These areas represent the page's side margins.

## Indenting via the Paragraph dialog box

Yet another way to indent a paragraph or first line is to visit the Paragraph dialog box. Click in or select the paragraph or paragraphs in question, go to the Home or Layout tab then, in the Paragraph group, click the Paragraph dialog box launcher (shown in the margin). Word coughs up the Paragraph dialog box and displays the Indents and Spacing tab, shown in Figure 2-5. Use the Left and Right spin boxes to change the indentation settings. If you want to indent the first line or create a hanging indent, use the Special drop-down list to choose First Line or Hanging and enter a measurement in the By box.

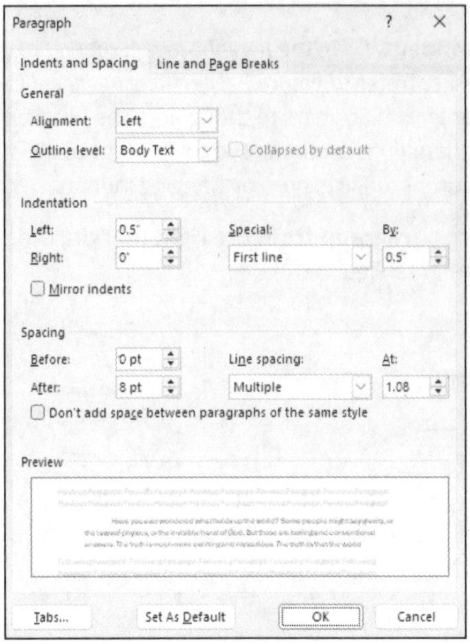


**FIGURE 2-5:** Indenting via the Paragraph dialog box.

# Making Heads and Tails of Headers and Footers

A *header* is a section that appears near the top of each page between the top margin and the first line of text. Any text, graphics, or properties you insert in a header appears at the top of every page in the document. Typical header contents include the document author, the document title, and the date the document was created or modified.

A *footer* is a section that appears near the bottom of each page between the bottom margin and the last line of text. Anything you insert in a footer appears at the bottom of every page in the document. Typical footer contents include the page number and document filename.

## Adding a prefab header or footer

All Word documents have a header and footer, but most of the time they're "invisible" because they don't contain any content. You can change that by adding text, images, document properties, or fields to the header or footer.

Word comes with several predefined headers and footers, which makes adding these elements to your document very easy:

- **To insert a predefined header:** On the Insert tab, in the Header & Footer group, click Header to display a gallery of header styles, then click the style you prefer.
- **To insert a predefined footer:** On the Insert tab, in the Header & Footer group, click Footer to display the footer gallery, then click the style you prefer.

## Editing a header and footer

If you want to get the most control over your headers and footers, then you need to go beyond Word's predefined styles and work with a document's headers and footers directly. You can either modify an existing design or create a header and footer from scratch:

- **To edit a header:** On the Insert tab, in the Header & Footer group, click Header and then click Edit Header.
- **To edit a footer:** On the Insert tab, in the Header & Footer group, click Footer and then click Edit Footer.



TIP

If you want to modify an existing header or footer, you can open it for editing by double-clicking the header or footer.

As shown in Figure 2-6, Word separates the regular text and the header or footer with a dashed line labeled either Header or Footer, and it also displays the Header & Footer contextual tab. You use the box above (for a header) or below (for a footer) the dashed line to define and format the header or footer, either by manually inserting text and applying formatting, or by using the controls in the Header & Footer tab. When you've finished working with the header or footer, close it either by choosing Header & Footer ➪ Close Header and Footer or by double-clicking the document.

## Populating a header or footer

You define a header or footer by adding some kind of content to it. Before you get to that stage, you should know that headers and footers often have two preset tab tops: a center tab in the middle of the box and a right tab on the right edge of the box. This enables you to place content on the left side of the header/footer, in the middle, and on the right.

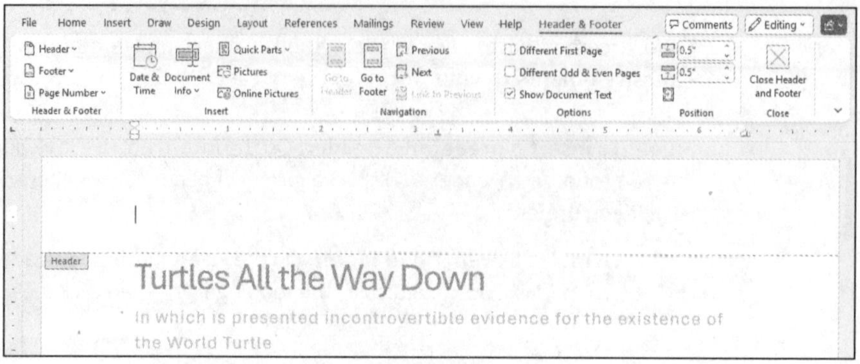


**FIGURE 2-6:** When you open a header or footer for editing, Word displays a box for the header or footer as well as the Header & Footer contextual tab.

Here are your choices for adding content to a header/footer:

- **Text:** Type any text, such as a brief document description, a note to the reader, or your company name.
- **Page numbers:** Choose Header & Footer ➪ Page Number, click where you want the page numbers to appear (such as Top of Page) to display a gallery of page number styles, then click the style you want to use. You can also choose Header & Footer ➪ Page Number ➪ Format Page Numbers to change various page number options.

TIP

If you want the page numbers to start over at a certain point in your document, create a new section at that point. Edit the header or footer for the new section, select the page number field, and choose Header & Footer ➪ Page Number ➪ Format Page Numbers. Select the Start At option and then use the spin box to specify the starting page number for the section.

- **The current date and/or time:** Choose Header & Footer ➪ Date & Time to display the Date and Time dialog box, and then click the format you want to use. If you want Word to update the displayed date and time automatically each time you open the document, select the Update Automatically check box. Click OK to insert the date and/or time.
- **A document property:** Choose Header & Footer ➪ Document Info to display a list of properties, including Author, File Name, and Document Title. You can click Document Property to display even more properties. Click the property you want to insert.
- **A field:** Choose Header & Footer ➪ Quick Parts ➪ Field and then use the Field dialog box to insert the field code.
- **Picture:** Choose Header & Footer ➪ Pictures or Header & Footer ➪ Online Pictures. (Refer to Book 1, Chapter 5 for the details on using these graphics commands.)

## Creating a unique first-page header or footer

By default, once you define the content for one header, Word displays the same content in every header in the document. The same is true for footers, where Word displays the same content in every footer.

However, you'll often stumble upon situations where this default behavior isn't what you want. One common requirement is to use a different header/footer on the first page of a document. For example, many texts use *no* header or footer on the first page. Another example is when you want to insert document instructions or notes in the first header or footer, but you don't want that text repeated on every page.

For these kinds of situations, you can tell Word that you want the first page's header and footer to be different than the headers and footers in the rest of the document. You set this up by displaying the Header & Footer tab and then selecting the Different First Page check box. Word changes the labels of the first page header and footer to First Page Header and First Page Footer.

## Creating unique odd and even page headers or footers

Many documents require different layouts for the header or footer on odd and even pages. A good example is the book you're reading. Notice that the even page footer has the page number on the left, followed by the mini-book number and title, while the odd page footer has the page number on the right, preceded by the chapter number and title.

To handle this type of situation, you can configure your document with different odd and even page headers and footers by displaying the Header & Footer tab, then selecting the Different Odd & Even Pages check box. Word changes the labels of the page headers to Even Page Header and Odd Page Header and of the footer to Even Page Footer and Odd Page Footer.

## Navigating headers and footers

If your document uses just a single header and not footer throughout, then "navigating" the headers is trivial because you can make changes by editing the header on any page in the document. This is also true if your document uses a single footer throughout and no header.

If your document uses a single header *and* a single footer, life is a bit more complicated, but not by much:

- When you're working in the header, you can immediately jump to the footer by choosing Header & Footer ⇨ Go to Footer.
- When you're working in the footer, you can immediately leap up to the header by choosing Header & Footer ⇨ Go to Header.

Header/footer navigation requires a bit more care after you've set up different first page or odd and even page headers and footers:

- **To move "forward" through the headers or footers:** Choose Header & Footer ⇨ Next. For example, if you're currently in the First Page Header, this command takes you first to the Even Page Header and then to the Odd Page Header.
- **To move "backward" through the headers or footers:** Choose Header & Footer ⇨ Previous. For example, if you're currently in the Odd Page Footer, this command takes you first to the Even Page Footer and then to the First Page Footer.

## Creating unique section headers and footers

If your document has multiple sections (refer to "Catch a section break," earlier in this chapter), by default Word doesn't treat the headers and footers differently for each section: The header is the same throughout the document, as is the footer. One exception to this rule is that you can have a unique first page header in each section of the document. To set up this feature, move the insertion point into the header of the section you want to work with, then, on the Header & Footer tab, select Different First Page.

However, what if your document requires a different header and footer for each section? You can do this, but first you have to understand why Word treats all the headers and footers the same in a document with multiple sections. The secret is that when you create a new section, Word sets up the section's header with a link to the previous section's header (the footer also gets a link to the previous section's footer). This link configures the two headers to always use the same content. If you change the text or formatting in one header, the linked header changes as well. This link is noted by the phrase *Same as Previous* that appears on the right side of the header or footer box, as shown in Figure 2-7.

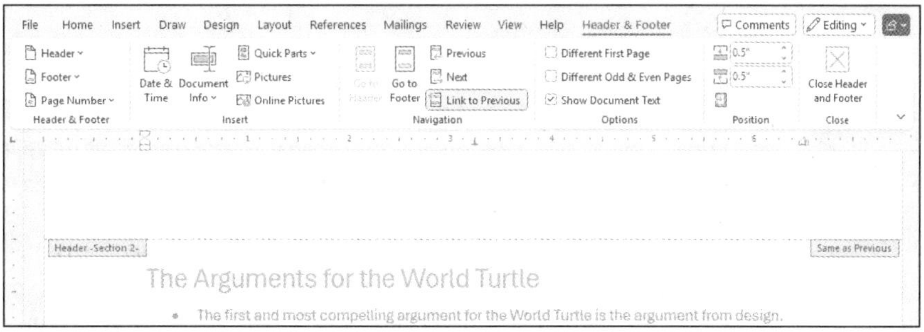


**FIGURE 2-7:** The Same as Previous label tells you this section's header is linked to the previous section's header.

Therefore, the secret to creating a unique header or footer for a section is to break the link with the previous section's header or footer. You do that by clicking to deactivate the Header & Footer tab's Link to Previous button (it's in the Navigation group).

# Breathing Room: Setting the Spacing

One of the most potent ways to make people *not* want to read your writing is to try and cram as much text on each page as possible. The more cramped the page, the less inviting it is to read. Assuming, you know, you actually *want* folks to read your prose, then you can make your pages much more reader-friendly by opening things up with generous amounts of space.



One way to open up a page is to give it generous margins, as I describe earlier in the "Managing Margins" section. However, Word also offers two other methods for injecting some welcome space into a document: setting the spacing that appears between each line and adjusting the spacing between each paragraph.

## Adjusting the space between lines

Within a multi-line paragraph, notice that there's a bit of nothingness between the bottom of one line and the top of the line below it. That nothingness is called the *line spacing*, and it plays a big role in how readable your paragraphs are:

- If the line spacing is set too small, then the lines crash into each other, making them difficult or even impossible to read.
- If the line spacing is set too large, then the lines seem to float away from each other, making it hard to scan from the end of one line to the beginning of the next.

By default, Word assigns a line-spacing value of 1.08 for all new documents. What this value means is that the actual line spacing that Word sets is equal to 1.08 multiplied by the font size of the text. So, text that uses a 20-point font will have a line spacing of 21.6 points. If you set that text's line spacing to, say, 1.4 (a common value for readable text), then the actual line spacing becomes 28 points.

To set the line spacing, either select the lines you want to change, or put the cursor anywhere within a paragraph if you're changing the line spacing for the entire paragraph. Then, on the Home tab in the Paragraph group, click the Line and Paragraph Spacing button (shown in the margin) and choose a line-spacing value on the drop-down list.

To take advantage of more line-spacing options, open the Paragraph dialog box, shown earlier in Figure 2-5. Use either of these techniques to open the Paragraph dialog box:

- On to the Home tab or Layout tab, click the Paragraph dialog box launcher (shown in the margin).
- On the Home tab in the Paragraph group, click the Line and Paragraph Spacing button (shown in the margin) and click Line Spacing Options on the drop-down list.

In the Spacing section, the Line Spacing drop-down list offers the following options:

- **Single:** Sets the line spacing to 1.0.
- **1.5 lines:** Sets the line spacing to 1.5.
- **Double:** Sets the line spacing to 2.0.
- **At Least:** Sets the line spacing to the number of points you enter in the At box. However, this value is a minimum. If a line has one or more characters set at a larger font size, Word will increase the line spacing as needed.
- **Exactly:** Sets the line spacing to the number of points you enter in the At box. Note that this is a fixed value that Word applies no matter the font size.
- **Multiple:** Sets the line spacing to the number you type in the At box multiplied by the default line-spacing value. Entering **1** is the same as choosing the Single option; entering **2** is the same as choosing the Double option. However, you usually use Multiple to get non-standard line-spacing values, such as 1.4-spacing (type **1.4** in the At box) or triple-spacing (type **3** in the At box).

TIP

To quickly single-space text, click the text or select it if you want to change more than one paragraph, and press Ctrl+1. To quickly double-space text, select the text and press Ctrl+2. Press Ctrl+5 to put one and a half lines between lines of text.

The Design tab offers a command called Paragraph Spacing for changing the overall appearance of paragraphs. Click the Paragraph Spacing button and choose an option on the drop-down list to make paragraphs and lines of text more compact, tight, open, or relaxed.

## Adjusting the space between paragraphs

Rather than press Enter to put a blank line between paragraphs, you can open the Paragraph dialog box and enter a point-size measurement in the Before or After text box (refer to Figure 2-5). The Before and After measurements place a specific amount of space before and after paragraphs.

Go to the Home tab and, in the Paragraph group, use one of these techniques to adjust the amount of space between paragraphs:

- Click the Line and Paragraph Spacing button (shown in the margin) and choose Add Space Before Paragraph or Add Space After Paragraph on the drop-down list. These commands add 10 points of blank space before or after the paragraph that the cursor is in.
- Click the Paragraph dialog box launcher (shown in the margin) to open the Paragraph dialog box (refer back to Figure 2-5), and enter point-size measurements in the Before and After boxes (or choose Auto in these boxes to enter one blank line between paragraphs in whatever your line-spacing choice is). Selecting the Don't Add Space between Paragraphs of the Same Style check box tells Word to ignore Before and After measurements if the previous or next paragraph is assigned the same style as the paragraph that the cursor is in.



# Making Lists, Optionally Checking Them Twice

Lists are one of the most common document structures. Whether it's a to-do list, a list of action items, a grocery list, or a list of steps to follow, breaking items out so that they appear individually instead of running them all together in a paragraph can make those items easier to read.

If you do want to include a list in your document, what's the best way to go about it? You can use separate paragraphs or headings and number them yourself or add, say, asterisks (*) at the beginning of each. I suppose that would work, but hold your list horses — there's a better way. Word has a couple of commands designed to give you much more control over your list-building chores.

## Putting your affairs in order with numbered lists

To include a numbered list of items —a top-ten list, bowling league standings, or any kind of ranking — don't bother adding the numbers yourself. Instead, you can use the Numbering command in Word to generate the numbers for you.

Before I get to the specifics, you should know that Word is happy to create multi-level numbered lists, where each level has its own numbering format. Here's the default numbering format:

- The top level of the list uses regular numbers followed by periods (1., 2., 3., and so on).
- The second level of the list uses lowercase letters followed by periods (a., b., c., and so on).
- The third level of the list uses lowercase Roman numerals followed by periods (i., ii., iii., and so on).

To forge a numbered list of your own, follow these steps:

1. **If you have some existing text that you want to convert to a numbered list, select that text.**

   Make sure that each item in your existing text is in its own paragraph.

2. **On the Home tab, in the Paragraph group, click Numbering (shown in the margin).**

   Word displays a menu of numbered-list formats.

3. **Select the numbering scheme you want to use.**

   If you selected some text in advance, Word converts the text to a numbered list. To add an item to that list, place the cursor at the end of the last item and then press Enter or Return.

4. **For a second-level item, press Tab; for a third-level item, press Tab again.**

5. **Enter your item text and then press Enter or Return to create a new item in the list.**

6. **Repeat Steps 4 and 5 until your list is complete.**

7. **To tell Word you've finished entering list items, press Enter or Return a second time.**

## Scoring points with bulleted lists

The numbered lists that I discuss in the preceding section aren't suitable for every type of list. If you just want to enumerate a few points, a bulleted list might be more your style. They're called *bulleted* lists because Word displays a cute little dot, called a *bullet*, to the left of each item.

Most bulleted lists are one level, but Word doesn't mind creating lists that have two or even three levels. Here's the default bullet format:

- The top level of the list uses filled-in discs.
- The second level of the list uses circles (discs that aren't filled in).
- The third level of the list uses filled-in squares.



To throw together a bulleted list, follow these steps:

1. **If you have existing text that you want to convert to a bulleted list, select that text.**

   For best results, each item in the text should be in its own paragraph.

2. **On the Home tab, in the Paragraph group, click Bullets (shown in the margin).**

   Word offers you a menu of bulleted list formats.

3. **Choose the bullet scheme you want to use.**

   If you selected text in advance, Word converts the text to a bulleted list. To add an item to the list, place the cursor at the end of the last item and then press Enter or Return.

4. **For a second-level item, press Tab; for a third-level item, press Tab again.**

5. **Enter your item text and then press Enter or Return to create a new item in the list.**

6. **Repeat Steps 4 and 5 until your list is complete.**

7. **To tell Word you've finished entering list items, press Enter or Return a second time.**

## AUTOMATIC LISTS: LOVE 'EM OR HATE 'EM

Word creates automatic lists for you whether you like it or not. To try it out, type the number 1, type a period, and press the spacebar. Word immediately creates a numbered list. In the same manner, Word creates a bulleted list when you type an asterisk (*) and press the spacebar.

Some people find this kind of behind-the-scenes skullduggery annoying. If you are one such person, do one of the following to keep Word from making lists automatically:

- Immediately after Word creates the list, click the AutoCorrect Options button (shown in the margin) and then click either (depending on the type of list) Stop Automatically Creating Numbered Lists or Stop Automatically Creating Bulleted Lists.
- Choose File ➪ Options to open the Word Options dialog box, click the Proofing category, and click the AutoCorrect Options button. In the AutoCorrect dialog box, on the AutoFormat As You Type tab, deselect the Automatic Numbered Lists and Automatic Bulleted Lists check boxes. Click OK, then click OK in the Word Options dialog box.

# Managing a multilevel list

A *multilevel list* is a list with entries at different levels, where the initial entries are on the first level, subordinate entries are on the second level, entries that are subordinate to the second level are on the third level, and so on. Confusingly, the higher the level number, the lower the item is in the list hierarchy. That is, first-level items are at the top, second-level items are below the first, then come third-level items, and so on.

To create a multilevel list, you declare what kind of list you want, and then, as you enter items for the list, you indent the items that you want to be subordinate. Follow these steps to create a multilevel list:

1. **If you have existing text that you want to convert to a multilevel list, select that text.**

   For best results, each item in the text should be in its own paragraph.

2. **On the Home tab, in the Paragraph group, click Multilevel List (shown in the margin).**

   Word offers you a menu of multilevel list formats.

3. **Choose the multilevel scheme you want to use.**

   If you selected text in advance, Word converts the text to a multilevel list.

4. **To add an item to the list, place the cursor at the end of the last item and then press Enter or Return. Repeat until your list is complete.**

5. **Designate the levels for each subordinate item. For each item that you want to be a subordinate, select the item and then do one of the following:**

   - To drop the item to a lower level (that is, a higher level number), click Increase Indent (shown in the margin) or press Tab or Ctrl+M. Repeat until the item is at the level you want.
   - To raise the item to a higher level (that is, a lower level number), click Decrease Indent (shown in the margin) or press Shift+Tab or Ctrl+Shift+M. Repeat until the item is at the level you want.

# Getting Things to Line Up Nice and Neat with Tabs



Documents read much better if they're properly indented and if their various parts line up nicely. The best way to do this is to use tabs instead of spaces whenever you need to create some room in a line. Why? Well, a single space can take up different amounts of room, depending on the font and size of the characters you're using. So, your document can end up with a ragged appearance if you try to use spaces to indent your text. Tabs, on the other hand, are fastidiously precise: Whenever you press the Tab key, the insertion point moves ahead exactly a half an inch — no more, no less.

You can make things even more precise by defining your own *tab stops*, which are points on the ruler that Word uses to align text. Word lets you set five kinds of tab stops (the symbols in the margin are the icons that Word uses on the ruler to identify each tab stop type):

- **Left:** Text lines up with the tab on the left. This tab type is represented by a right-facing triangle on the ruler at the top of your document.
- **Right:** Text lines up with the tab on the right. The ruler shows this tab type as a left-facing triangle.

» **Center:** Text is centered on the tab. This tab type is represented by a diamond shape on the ruler.

» **Decimal:** Numbers are aligned on their decimal points.

» **Bar:** Within each line of the paragraph where the tab is set, Word adds a vertical bar that aligns with the tab.

Display the ruler (on the View tab, in the Show group, select the Ruler check box) and follow these steps to change tabs or change where tabs appear on the ruler:

1. **Click inside the paragraph you want to tab-ify, or select the paragraphs you want to work with.**
2. **Position the mouse pointer on the bottom edge of the ruler at the spot where you want the tab to appear, then double-click the ruler.**

   The Tabs dialog box reports for duty.
3. **In the Tab Stop Position list box, click the tab you just created.**
4. **In the Alignment section, select the radio button for the type of tab stop you want to set.**
5. **If you want to include a tab leader (a series of punctuation marks — usually periods — that connect the end of the previous text to the tab stop), select a radio button in the Leader section.**
6. **Click OK to set the tab.**

TIP

After you select your paragraphs, a quicker method for setting multiple tabs is to click the Tab box that appears on the far left side of the ruler as many times as necessary to choose the kind of tab you want. Symbols on the tab box indicate which type of tab you're choosing. Then click the ruler where you want the tab to go. You can click as many times as you want and enter more than one kind of tab.

To move a tab stop, drag it to a new location on the ruler. Text that is aligned with the tab stop moves as well. To remove a tab stop, drag it off the ruler. When you remove a tab stop, text to which it was aligned is aligned to the next remaining tab stop on the ruler, or to the next default tab stop if you didn't create any tab stops of your own.

Sometimes it's hard to tell where tabs were put in the text. To find out, click the Home tab's Show/Hide ¶ button (shown in the margin) to display the formatting characters, including the arrows that show where the Tab key was pressed.

# Hyphenating Text

A raging debate among desktop publishers — that is, folks who use an app such as Word to design publications — is going on even as you read this: Should you justify text — that is, align the text on both the left and right margins — or should you justify only the left margin and leave the right margin ragged? The answer is, "It depends." Many people perceive justified text as a formal look and, therefore, more desirable for formal documents. Others insist that the drawbacks of right justification outweigh the perhaps more casual approach of a ragged right margin.

When you *justify* text, Word forces extra spaces between words to make the right margin even — or *flush* — with the right side of the page. These extra spaces can cause "rivers" of unwanted white space to run through your text. When you justify text in columns, Word has fewer words to work with and might insert whole blocks of spaces to even out the margin. Readers find these blocks extremely distracting.

On the other hand, ragged right margins don't force extra spaces into text and therefore don't cause white space rivers and blank areas. Extra white space at the right margin also helps open up your text, but sometimes your right edges can end up *too* ragged, particularly if you use many long words.

You can solve both problems using Word's hyphenation feature, which hyphenates longer words rather than wrapping them onto the next line:

- In justified text, this means you get more text on each line, so you're less likely to have rivers of white space, and blank areas are filled in with partial words.
- In right-ragged text, Word fills in the right edge of each line with either entire words, if they fit, or with partial words as part of the hyphenation process, so the raggedness of the right margin is greatly reduced.

Unfortunately, if you hyphenate to reduce raggedness, you run the risk of having hyphens ending too many lines, which is another visual distraction for the reader. Fortunately, you can control this, too, by setting the maximum number of consecutive hyphenated lines that Word will allow in your document.

TIP

If you have a paragraph that you don't want hyphenated, you can tell Word to skip it. Position the cursor inside the paragraph, display either the Home tab or the Layout tab, then click the Paragraph group's dialog box launcher icon (shown in the margin). In the Line and Page Breaks tab, select the Don't Hyphenate check box, then click OK.

Use either of the following methods in the Layout tab's Page Setup group to hyphenate your document:

- Click Hyphenation and then click Automatic to have Word hyphenate the document using the default settings.
- Click Hyphenation and then click Manual to apply the hyphenation yourself. For each potential hyphenation, Word displays the Manual Hyphenation dialog box, shown in Figure 2-8. Use the arrow keys to select the hyphen position you want Word to use, and then click Yes (or click No to avoid hyphenating this word).

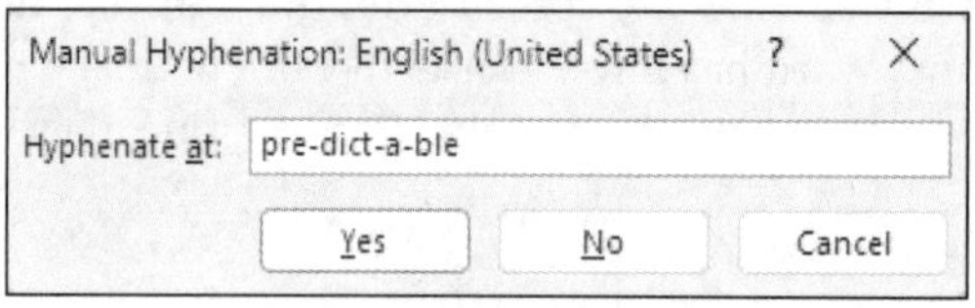


**FIGURE 2-8:** With a manual hyphenation, you control where Word places each hyphen.

To control the number of consecutive hyphens that Word can use, choose Layout ⇨ Hyphenation ⇨ Hyphenation Options to display the Hyphenation dialog box, use the Limit Consecutive Hyphens To spin box to set the limit you prefer, then click OK.

TIP

If you have words that always use hyphens — for example, Wi-Fi and Band-Aid — you probably don't want lines to break at such hyphens. In that case, replace the regular hyphen with a nonbreaking hyphen by pressing Ctrl+Shift+-.

IN THIS CHAPTER

» Understanding why styles are indistinguishable from magic

» Applying styles

» Creating your own styles

» Altering a style

» Creating a new template

# Chapter 3

# Making Looking Good Look Easy: Styles

Formatting is essential if you want to produce good-looking documents that get noticed. The problem is that formatting always seems to take up *so much* time.

Suppose that you want to add a title to a document. Titles usually appear in a larger, sans serif font, so you type the text, select it, and then use the Font and Font Size commands to set up the appropriate formatting. For good measure, you also center the title. It looks not bad, but you decide that the text needs to be bold. So, you select the text again and apply the bolding. Things are looking good, but then you decide to apply a larger type size. Once again, you select the text and make the size adjustment. After fiddling with a few more options (maybe underlining or dark blue text would look good), you finally get the title exactly right. You've just wasted ten minutes of your busy day, but, hey, that's the reality of working with Word, right?

Wrong. You don't have to stand for this! By learning how to use styles, you can accomplish the same chore in five seconds instead of five minutes! That might sound like a bold claim, but it's a true and I'll prove it to you in this chapter, which is entirely devoted to working with styles in Word 365.

# Getting Acquainted with Styles

A *style* is nothing more than a predefined collection of formatting and layout settings. Word comes with a few built-in styles, including a style named Title. This means that rather than fuss around with formatting options, you can just select the text you want to use as the title and then apply the Title style, which takes just two or three clicks. Word immediately applies all the Title style's predefined formatting options — which might consist of a larger font size, bold text, increased line spacing, and centered between the margins — just like that. Total time? Yep: about five seconds.

What if you don't like the default formatting of the Title style? That's not a problem because it's also easy to define your own version of each built-in style. For example, you can format some text with an 18-point, bold, dark blue, Verdana font that's centered between the left and right margins and then tell Word to use that formatting instead of its default formatting for the Title style. You'd then enter the document title, select it, and apply the Title style. In the blink of an eye, Word formats the text as 18-point, bold, dark blue Verdana, centered between the left and right margins. That's right: With a single command, Word can throw any number of character, line, or paragraph formatting options at the selected text.

## Learning how styles make your life better

Here's a short list of just some of the benefits you gain when you use styles:

- The most obvious, of course, is the time you save. After you've invested the initial few minutes to define your version of a style, applying any style takes only a few mouse clicks.
- You eliminate the trial-and-error that goes into many formatting chores. After you've decided on a look that you like, you can capture it in a style for all time.
- If you change your mind, however, a style can be quickly edited. Does this mean that you have to go back and reapply the style throughout the document? No way. Any text that's formatted with that style is automatically updated with the revised style. This feature alone is worth the price of admission.
- Styles make it easy to create documents that have a consistent look and feel because you can access your styles from any document.
- Styles reduce the number of keystrokes and mouse clicks you need to get the job done. In this age where repetitive strain injuries such as carpal tunnel syndrome are reaching almost epidemic proportions, anything that reduces the wear-and-tear on our sensitive anatomy is a welcome relief.

If it all sounds too good to be true, well, there's a downside: Styles can save you so much time that you may run out of things to do during the day. (Pause while the laughter dies down.)

## Understanding the connection between styles and templates

One common styles question is, where do they come from? Well, you can make up your own styles, as you learn a bit later in the "Concocting a New Style" section. However, when you're just getting started in the style game, you can use the styles that are available in every Word document.

Okay, but where do *those* styles come from? So many questions! Okay, every Word document is based on a *template* and every Word template comes with, among other things, its own predefined set of styles.

For example, suppose you create a simple document with the Blank Document template (by choosing File ⇨ New and clicking Blank Document, or by pressing Ctrl+N). That template has 16 predefined styles for formatting titles, subtitles, headings, quotations, and more.

Figure 3-1 illustrates how choosing styles from a template changes text formatting. On the left is a document with no styles applied, just plain, unadorned (read: dull) text. In the middle is the Styles pane (which I show you how to display in just a sec in the "Applying a style" section), which lists the 16 styles in the Blank Document template — from Normal, No Spacing, and Heading 1 at the top, down to Book Title and List Paragraph at the bottom. On the right is the same text with some styles applied: Title, Subtitle, Heading 1, and Heading 2. With just these few styles, the document on the right becomes much easier to read and much more inviting. That's the power and the magic of styles!



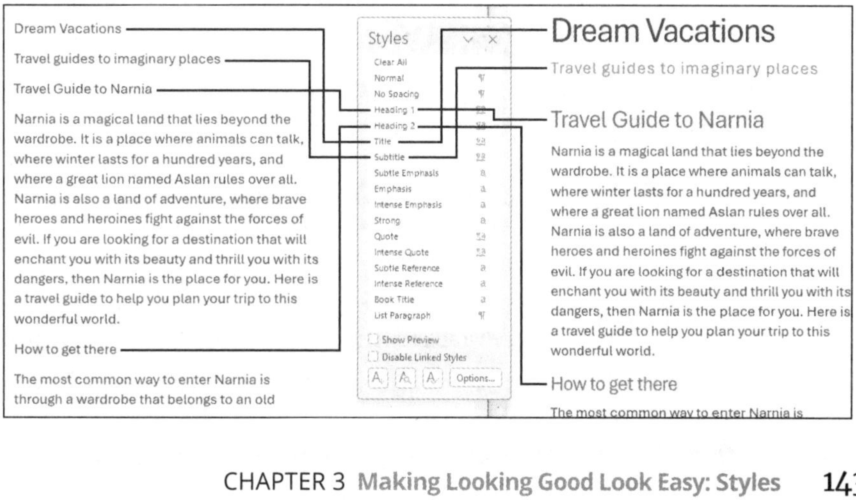


**FIGURE 3-1:** A document without styles (left) and the same text with style (right).

## Checking out the style types

In the Styles pane (refer to Figure 3-1), notice that each style is displayed with its name on the left and a cryptic symbol in the right. The symbol associated with each style name tells you what type of style you're dealing with. Word offers three style types:

- **Paragraph style:** Applies the style's formatting to entire paragraphs. A paragraph style can include these settings: font, paragraph, tab, border, language, bullets, numbering, and text effects. Paragraph styles are marked with the paragraph symbol (¶).
- **Character style:** Applies the style's formatting to the individual characters in the selected text (or the subsequent text, if you apply the style at the cursor). A character style can include these settings: font, border, language, and text effects. When you apply a character style to text, the character-style settings override the paragraph-style settings. For example, if the paragraph style calls for 14-point Arial font but the character style calls for 12-point Times Roman font, the character style wins. Character styles are marked with the letter *a.*
- **Linked (paragraph and character) style:** Applies both the style's paragraph formatting and the style's character formatting throughout a paragraph. These styles are marked with the paragraph symbol (¶) as well as the letter *a.*

# Making Your Documents Stylish

Word offers several ways to apply a style, and you're invited to choose the one that works best for you. To help you make that decision, the next few sections explain the different methods for applying a style.

## Applying a style

REMEMBER

Before fancifying your document with a style, you first need to select the part of your document to which you want the style applied:

- **A single paragraph:** Click anywhere in the paragraph to which you want to apply a paragraph style. This works because paragraph styles apply to all the text in a paragraph.
- **Two or more paragraphs:** Select all or part of each paragraph to which you want to apply a paragraph style. (Book 2, Chapter 1 explains how to select text in Word.)
- **Text:** Select the characters to which you want to apply a character style.

Next, apply the style with one of these techniques:

- **Styles gallery:** On the Home tab, in the Styles group, choose a style in the Styles gallery. Figure 3-2 shows where the Styles gallery is located. The formatted letters above each style name in the gallery give you a preview of what your style choice will do to paragraphs or text. You can also "live-preview" styles on the Styles gallery by moving the pointer over style names.

- **Styles pane:** On the Home tab, click the Styles dialog box launcher (shown in the margin) button to open the Styles pane, as shown in Figure 3-2, and then click a style. Select the Show Preview check box at the bottom of the Styles pane to display formatted style names in the pane and get an idea of what the different styles are. You can drag the Styles pane to different locations on your screen. It remains onscreen after you leave the Home tab.

- **Apply Styles task pane:** Choose a style on the Apply Styles task pane, as shown in Figure 3-2. To display this task pane, go to the Home tab, click the Styles gallery's Open button (shown in the margin), and click Apply Styles. You can drag the Apply Styles task pane to a corner of the screen. The Apply Styles task pane remains onscreen after you leave the Home tab.

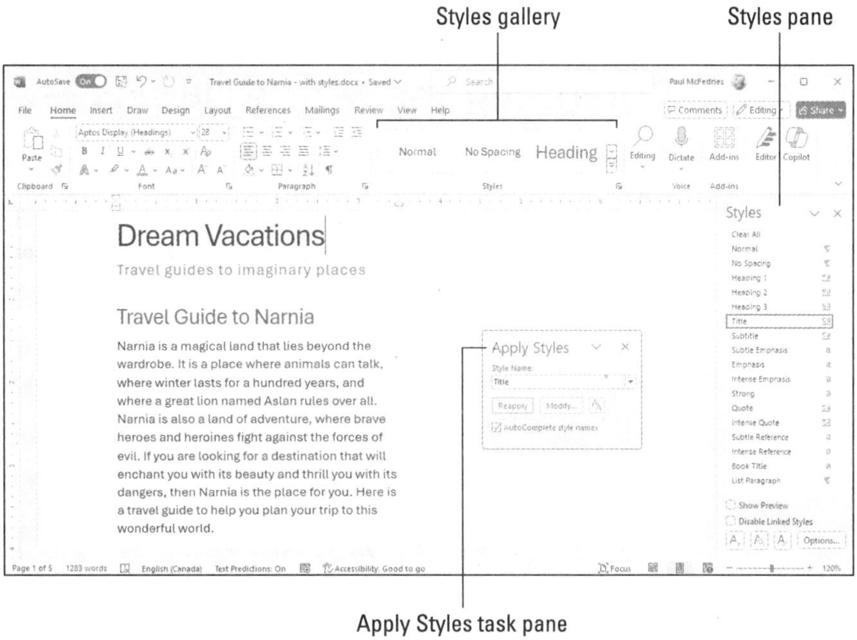


**FIGURE 3-2:** The three ways to apply a style.

## KEYBOARD SHORTCUTS FOR APPLYING STYLES

A handful of keyboard shortcuts can be very handy when applying paragraph styles:

- Normal: Ctrl+Shift+N
- Heading 1: Ctrl+Alt+1
- Heading 2: Ctrl+Alt+2
- Heading 3: Ctrl+Alt+3
- Next higher heading: Alt+Shift+←
- Next lower heading: Alt+Shift+→

You can assign keyboard shortcuts to styles. Book 1, Chapter 4 explains how.

REMEMBER

To strip a paragraph or text of its style and give it the generic Normal style, select the paragraph or text and then click either Clear Formatting in the Styles gallery or Clear All at the top of the Styles pane.

# Experimenting with style sets

A *style set* is a slight variation on the styles in the template that you chose when you created your document. Style sets include Classic, Elegant, Fancy, and Modern. Choosing a style set imposes a slightly different look on your document — you can make it classier, more elegant, fancier, or more modern. All templates, even those you create yourself, offer style sets. Style sets are a convenient way to experiment with the overall appearance of a document.

To experiment with style sets, go to the Design tab and choose an option in the Style Set gallery, shown in Figure 3-3.

To return to the original styles in a template, open the Style Set gallery and choose Reset to the Default Style Set.

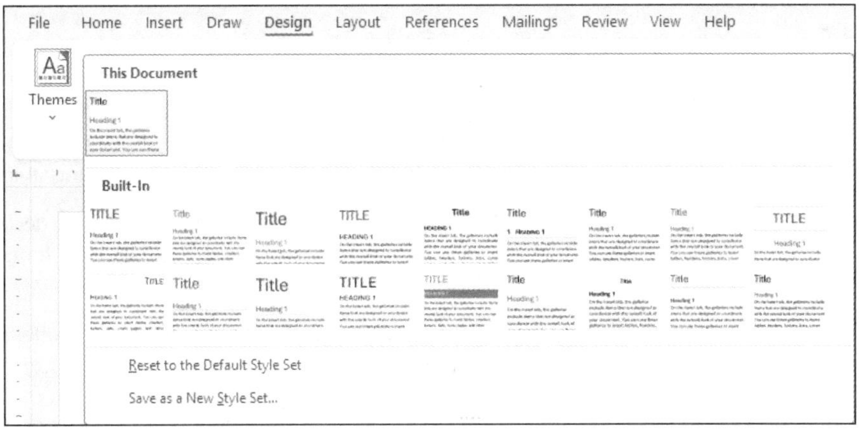


**FIGURE 3-3:** The Style Set gallery.

## Choosing which style names appear on the Style menus

One of the challenges of applying styles is finding the right style to apply in the Styles gallery, Styles pane, or Apply Styles task pane (refer to Figure 3-2). All three can become crowded with style names. To make finding and choosing styles names easier, you can decide for yourself which names appear on the three style menus.

### Styles gallery

In the Styles gallery, remove a style name by right-clicking it and choosing Remove from Style gallery.

### Styles pane and Apply Styles task pane

To decide for yourself which style names appear in the Styles pane and Apply Styles task pane, display the Styles pane (by clicking the Styles dialog box launcher button on the Home tab) and click the Options button (found near the bottom of the pane). The Style Pane Options dialog box appears, shown in Figure 3-4. Use the following options to tell Word which style names appear in the Styles pane and Apply Styles task pane:

- **Select Styles to Show:** Choose All Styles to show all style names. The other options place a subset of names in the window and task pane. Recommended style names are those that Microsoft thinks you need most often.

» **Select How List Is Sorted:** Choose an option to describe how to list styles. Except for Based On, these options are, I think, self-explanatory. The Based On option lists styles in alphabetical order according to which style each style is based on (later in this chapter, "Creating a style from the ground up" explains how the Based On setting is used in constructing styles).

» **Select Formatting to Show as Styles:** Choose options to declare which styles to list — those that pertain to paragraph level formatting, fonts, and bulleted and numbered lists.

» **Select How Built-In Style Names Are Shown:** Choose options to tell how to handle built-in styles, the obscure styles that Word applies on its own when you create tables of contents and other self-generating lists.

» **Apply to this document or to the template as well:** Click the Only in This Document option button to apply your choices only to the document you're working on; click the New Documents Based on This Template option button to apply your choices to your document and to all future documents that you create with the template you're using.

## DETERMINING WHICH STYLE IS IN USE

How can you tell which style has been applied to a paragraph or text? Sometimes you need to know which style is in play before you decide whether applying a different style is necessary.

Click the paragraph or text and use these techniques to find out which style was applied to it:

- **Refer to the Styles gallery and Styles pane to find out which style is selected.** The selected style is the one that was applied to your paragraph or text.

- **Click the Style Inspector button (shown in the margin).** The Style Inspector pane opens and lists the current style.
- **Press Shift+F1.** The Reveal Formatting task pane opens. It displays the style that's applied to the paragraph or text.

If you're especially keen to know about styles in your document, you can make style names appear to the left of the text in Outline and Draft view. Choose File ⇨ Options. In the Word Options dialog box, go to the Advanced tab, scroll down to the Display section, and enter .5 or another measurement in the Style Area Pane Width in Draft and Outline Views box. You can drag the border of the Style Area pane to enlarge or shrink it.

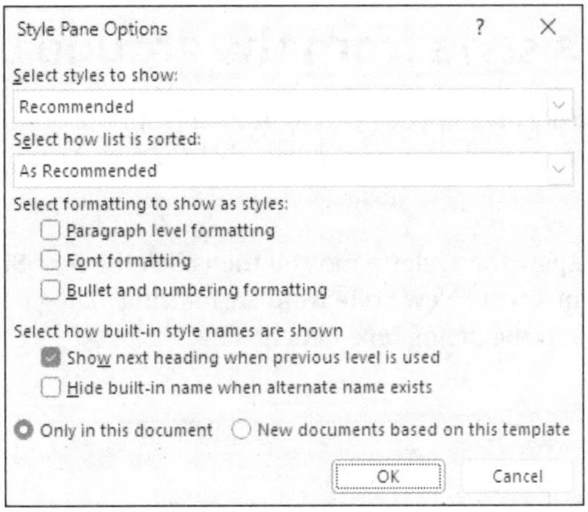


**FIGURE 3-4:** Deciding which names to put in the Styles pane and Apply Styles task pane.

# Concocting a New Style

You can create a new style by creating it from a paragraph or building it from the ground up. To do a thorough job, build it from the ground up because styles you create this way can be made part of the template that underlies the document you're currently working in and can be copied to other templates. (Later in this chapter, "Creating and Managing Templates" explains templates.)

## Creating a style from a paragraph

If your document includes a paragraph that has all the formatting you want to shoehorn into a style, you can convince Word to create a new style based on the paragraph by following these steps:

1. **Click anywhere in the paragraph that has the formatting you want to turn into a style.**
2. **On the Home tab, open the Styles gallery and click Create a Style.**

   The Create New Style from Formatting dialog box drops by.
3. **Type a name for your new style.**
4. **Click OK.**

   REMEMBER

   A style you create this way becomes a part of the document you're working on; it isn't made part of the template from which you created your document.

## Creating a style from the ground up

To make a style truly useful, you need to build it from the ground up and add it to a template so that the style becomes available in future documents based on that template.

To get started, display the Styles pane and then click the New Style button (shown in the margin). The Create New Style from Formatting dialog box opens, as shown in Figure 3-5. Fill in the dialog box and click OK.

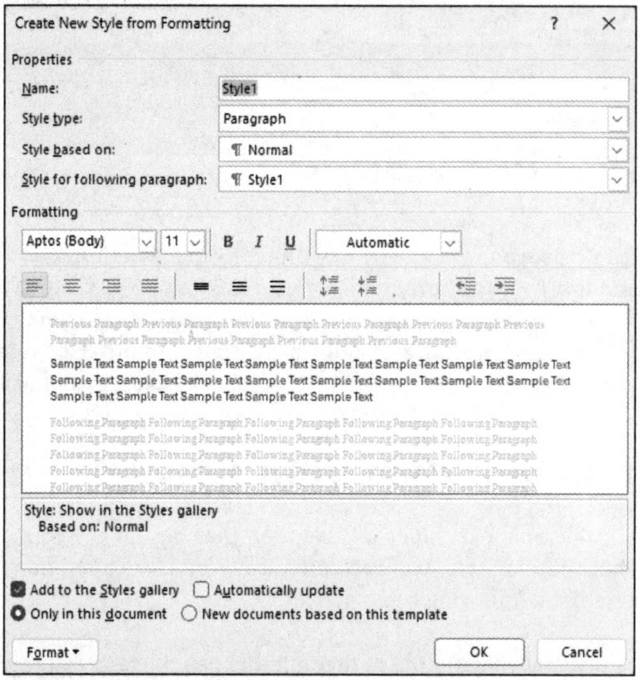


**FIGURE 3-5:** Creating a brand-spanking-new style.

Here's a rundown of the options in the Create New Style from Formatting dialog box:

- **Name:** Type a descriptive name for the style.
- **Style Type:** On the drop-down list, choose a style type ("Checking out the style types," earlier in this chapter, describes the style types).
- **Style Based On:** If your new style is similar to a style that is already part of the template with which you created your document, choose the style to get a head start on creating the new one. Be warned, however, that if you or someone else changes the Based On style, your new style will inherit those changes and be altered as well.

WARNING

- **Style for Following Paragraph:** Choose a style from the drop-down list if the style you're creating is always followed by an existing style. For example, a new style called Chapter Title might always be followed by a style called Chapter Intro Paragraph. For convenience, someone who applies the style you're creating and presses Enter automatically applies the style you choose here on the next line of the document. Applying a style automatically to the following paragraph saves you the trouble of having to apply the style yourself.
- **Formatting:** Choose options from the menus or click buttons to fashion or refine your style. Alternatively, you can click the Format button, as I describe in the last item in this list.
- **Add to Styles Gallery:** Select this check box to make the style's name appear in the Styles gallery, Styles pane, and Apply Styles task pane.
- **Automatically Update:** Normally, when you make a formatting change to a paragraph, the style assigned to the paragraph does not change at all, but the style does change if you select this box. Selecting this box tells Word to alter the style itself each time you alter a paragraph to which you've assigned the style. With this box selected, all paragraphs in the document that were assigned the style are altered each time you change a single paragraph that was assigned the style.
- **Only in This Document/New Documents Based on This Template:** To make your style a part of the template from which you created your document as well as the document itself, click the New Documents Based on This Template option button. This way, new documents you create that are based on the template you are using can also make use of the new style.
- **Format:** Click this button, click a formatting category (such as Font or Paragraph) in the list that appears, then use the dialog box that shows up to set the formatting you want for your bouncing baby style.

# Tweaking a Style



What if you decide at the end of an 80-page document that you're not happy with the formatting of the 35 introductory paragraphs to which you assigned the Intro Para style? Do you need to modify the formatting of all 35 paragraphs by hand? Don't be silly!

If (as I describe in the previous section) you selected the Automatically Update check box in the Create New Style from Formatting dialog box when you created the style, all you have to do is alter the formatting of any paragraph to which you assigned the Intro Para style. Just like that, Word propagates that formatting change to all the other introductory paragraphs. Sweet!

However, if you decided against updating styles automatically, you can still change the introductory paragraphs throughout your document. Here are the steps to follow to modify a style that isn't updated automatically:

1. **Click in any paragraph, table, or list to which you've assigned the style; if you want to modify a character style, select one or more characters to which you've assigned the style.**
2. **In the Styles pane or Apply Styles task pane, make sure that the name of the style that you want to modify is selected.**

   If the right name isn't selected, select it now in the Styles pane or Apply Styles task pane.
3. **In the Styles pane, move the mouse pointer over the style name to display the style's drop-down arrow, open the style's drop-down list, and then click Modify, as shown in Figure 3-6; in the Apply Styles task pane, click the Modify button.**

   The Modify Style dialog box pops by. Does the dialog box seem familiar? Yep: It's identical to the Create New Style from Formatting dialog box that you used to create the style in the first place (refer to Figure 3-5).
4. **Change the settings in the Modify Styles dialog box and click OK.**

   The previous section in this chapter explains the settings.

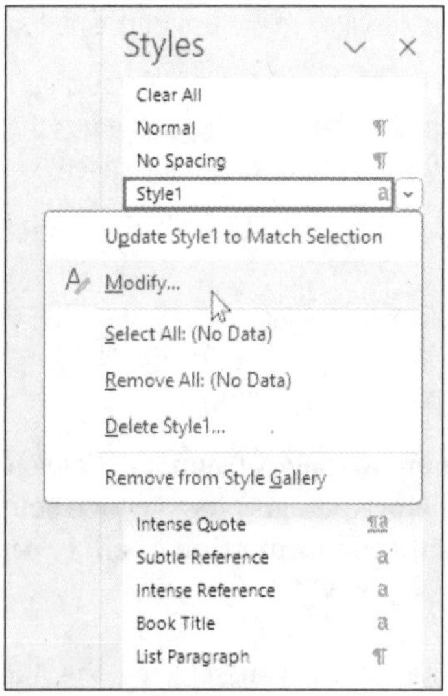


**FIGURE 3-6:** Tweaking a style.

After you modify a style, all paragraphs or text to which the style was assigned are instantly changed. You don't have to go back and reformat text and paragraphs throughout your document.

# Creating and Managing Templates

As I explain at the start of this chapter, every document you create is fashioned from a *template*. The purpose of a template is to store items that you want to reuse in new documents so that you don't have to reinvent the wheel each time. Templates store prefab text, objects, and formatting, but for the purposes of this chapter, it's important to remember that templates also store styles.

For example, when you select Blank Template in the New window or press Ctrl+N, you create a document with the Normal template, a relatively simple template with few styles. When you create a document with a template from `Office.com` or a template from the New window, more styles are usually available to you because these templates are usually more sophisticated.

To save time formatting your documents, you're invited to create templates with styles that you know you'll need to use again and again. You can create a new template on your own or create a template by assembling styles from other templates and documents. Styles in templates can, like styles in documents, be modified, deleted, and renamed.

REMEMBER

To create a document from a template you created yourself, open the New window (on the File tab, choose New), click the Personal tab, and select your template (refer to Book 2, Chapter 1 for details).

TIP

To find out which template was used to create a document, go to the File tab and choose Info. Then click the Show All Properties link in the Info window. A list of document properties appears, including the name of the template used to create the document.

## Creating a new template

How do you want to create a new template? You can do it on your own or assemble styles from other templates. Read on.

## Creating a template on your own

One way to create a template is to start by opening a document with many or all the styles you use regularly. When you save this document as a template, you pass along the styles in the document to the template, and you save yourself the trouble of creating styles for the template after you create it.

Follow these steps to create a template on your own:

1. **Create a new document or open a document with styles that you can recycle.**
2. **On the File tab, choose Save As.**

   The Save As window opens.
3. **Click This PC.**
4. **Click the Browse button.**

   The Save As dialog box appears.
5. **Open the Save As Type menu and choose Word Template (*.dotx).**

   The Save As dialog box opens to the folder where templates are stored on your computer.
6. **Enter a name for your template.**
7. **Click the Save button.**

Create, modify, and delete styles as necessary (check out "Concocting a New Style" and "Tweaking a Style," earlier in this chapter).

## Assembling styles from different documents and templates

Suppose that you like a style in one document and you want to copy it to another so that you can use it there. Or you want to copy it to a template to make it available to documents created with the template. Read on to find out how to copy styles between documents and between templates.

### COPYING A STYLE FROM ONE DOCUMENT TO ANOTHER

Copy a style from one document to another when you need the style on a one-time basis. Follow these steps:

1. **Select a paragraph that was assigned the style you want to copy.**

   Be sure to select the entire paragraph. If you want to copy a character style, select the text to which you have assigned the character style.

2. **Press Ctrl+C or right-click and choose Copy to copy the paragraph to the Clipboard.**

3. **Switch to the document you want to copy the style to and press Ctrl+V or click the Paste button on the Home tab.**

4. **Delete the text you just copied to your document.**

   The style remains in the Styles pane and Styles gallery even though the text is deleted. You can call upon the style whenever you need it.

## COPYING STYLES TO A TEMPLATE

Use the Organizer to copy styles from a document to a template or from one template to another. After making a style a part of a template, you can call upon the style in other documents. You can call upon it in each document you create or created with the template. Follow these steps to copy a style into a template:

1. **Open the document or template with the styles you want to copy.**

   Later in this chapter, "Opening a template so that you can modify it" explains how to open a template.

2. **In the Styles pane, click the Manage Styles button (shown in the margin).**

   The Manage Styles dialog box appears.

3. **Click the Import/Export button.**

   The Organizer dialog box appears, shown in Figure 3-7. Styles in the document or template that you opened in Step 1 appear in the In list box on the left side.

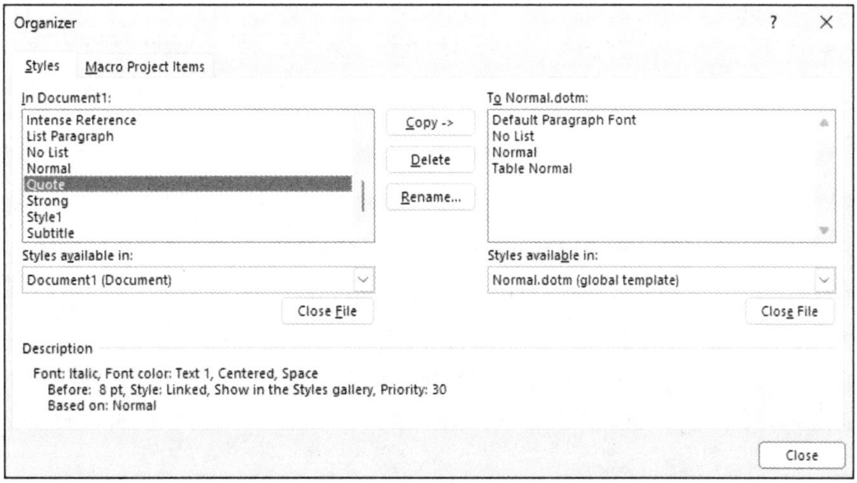


**FIGURE 3-7:** Copying styles to a template.

4. **Click the Close File button on the right side of the dialog box.**

   The button changes names and becomes the Open File button.

5. **Click the Open File button and, in the Open dialog box, find and select the template to which you want to copy styles; then, click the Open button.**

   The names of styles in the template you chose appear on the right side of the Organizer dialog box.

6. **In the Organizer dialog box, Ctrl+click to select the names of styles on the left side of the dialog box that you want to copy to the template listed on the right side of the dialog box.**

   As you click the names, they become highlighted.

7. **Click the Copy button.**

   The names of styles that you copied appear on the right side of the Organizer dialog box.

8. **Click the Close button and click Save when Word asks whether you want to save the new styles in the template.**

## ATTACHING A DIFFERENT TEMPLATE TO A DOCUMENT

It happens in the best of families. You create or are given a document, only to discover that the wrong template is attached to it. For times like those, Word gives you the opportunity to switch templates. Follow these steps:

1. **On the Developer tab, click the Document Template button.**

   The Templates and Add-Ins dialog box appears. If the Developer tab isn't displayed on your screen, choose File ➪ Options, visit the Customize Ribbon category in the Word Options dialog box, select the Developer check box, and click OK.

2. **Click the Attach button to open the Attach Template dialog box.**
3. **Find and select the template you want and click the Open button.**

   You return to the Templates and Add-ins dialog box, where the name of the template you chose appears in the Document Template box.

4. **Select the Automatically Update Document Styles check box.**

   Doing so tells Word to apply the styles from the new template to your document.

5. **Click OK.**

## Opening a template so that you can modify it

Follow these steps to open a template in Word so that you can mess around with the template:

1. **On the File tab, choose Open.**

   The Open window shows up.

2. **Click This PC.**
3. **Click the Browse button.**
4. **In the Open dialog box, go to the Templates folder where you store templates.**
5. **Select the template.**
6. **Click the Open button.**

The template opens in the Word window. Style modifications that you make in the template become available to all documents that were fashioned from the template.

## Modifying, deleting, and renaming styles in templates

Modify, delete, and rename styles in a template the same way you do those tasks to styles in a document (refer to "Tweaking a Style," earlier in this chapter). However, in the Modify Style dialog box, select the New Documents Based on This Template option button before clicking OK.

Your style modifications will apply to all documents you create in the future with your template. For the style modifications to take effect in documents you already created with your template, tell Word to automatically update document styles in those documents. Follow these steps:

1. **Save and close your template if it is still open.**

   If any documents you fashioned from the template are open, close them as well.

2. **Open a document that you want to update with the style modifications you made to the template.**

3. **Go to the Developer tab.**

   To display this tab, if necessary, choose File ➪ Options, go to the Customize Ribbon category in the Word Options dialog box, select the Developer check box, and click OK.

4. **Click the Document Template button.**

   The Templates and Add-ins dialog box opens. It should list the path to the Templates folder and the template you modified. If the wrong template is listed, click the Attach button and select the correct template in the Attach Template dialog box.

5. **Select the Automatically Update Document Styles check box.**
6. **Click OK.**

IN THIS CHAPTER

- » Creating and formatting tables
- » Decorating a table with styles, colors, and borders
- » Doing math calculations in a Word table
- » Discovering an assortment of table tricks

# Chapter 4
# Building a Table with Your Bare Hands

Text in Word generally flows along from one line to another, one paragraph to another, one page to another, and so on. However, flowing text isn't always the best choice for displaying certain kinds of information. In Book 2, Chapter 2, for example, I introduce bulleted and numbered lists, which are perfect ways to present lists of things.

In this chapter, you pick up a bit of computer carpentry when I show you how to build and work with tables, which offer yet another alternative way to display information in Word. Don't worry, though, if you can't tell a hammer from a hacksaw: The kinds of tables you deal with are purely digital because, in Word, a table is a rectangular grid of rows and columns in a document. You can enter all kinds of info into a table, including text, numbers, and graphics.

This chapter delves into tables in Word. You learn how to build tables, how to populate them with data, how to format them, and even how to add Excel-like formulas. You also get the hang of a few useful table tricks that can impress people at your next cocktail party.

# What Is a Table?

Most Word documents consist of text in the form of sentences and paragraphs. However, including lists of items within a document is common, particularly where each item in the list includes two or more details. For a short list with just a few details, the quickest way to add the list to a document is to type each item on its own line and press Tab between each detail. You could then add tab stops (refer to Book 2, Chapter 2) to the ruler to line up the items into proper columns.

However, a tab-separated list quickly becomes unwieldy as the number of items and details grows. For these more complex lists, you should build a *table*, a rectangular structure with the following characteristics:

- Each item in the list gets its own horizontal rectangle called a *row.*
- Each set of details in the list gets its own vertical rectangle called a *column.*
- The rectangle formed by the intersection of a row and a column is called a *cell* and you use the table cells to hold the data.

In other words, a Word table is very similar to an Excel worksheet and an Access datasheet. Figure 4-1 shows a sample table.

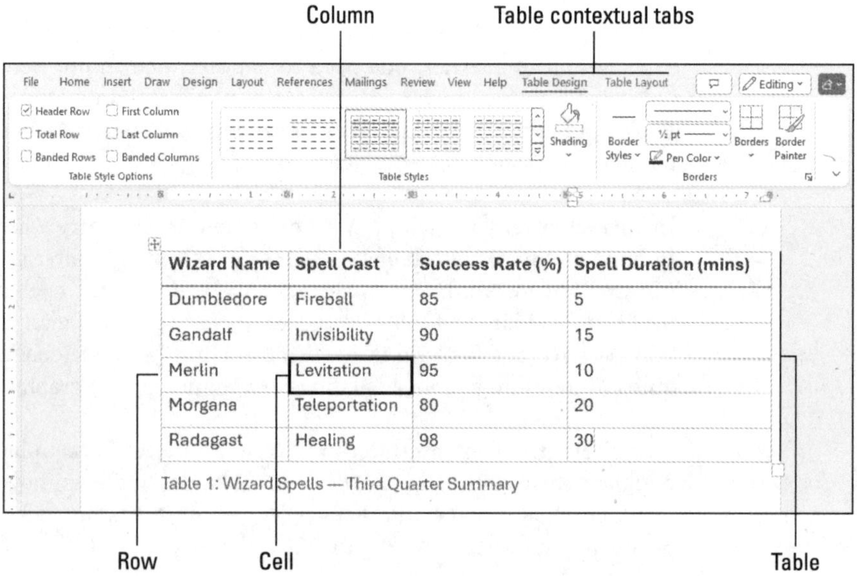


**FIGURE 4-1:** A table hanging out in a Word document.

# Constructing a Table

The Word programmers seem to be more than a little obsessed with tables because they built into the program no less than six methods for constructing them, which is excessive even by Word's standards. However, one of those methods actually inserts an Excel spreadsheet (which is useful if you need to make complex calculations; if your needs are simpler, then you don't need a full-blown Excel object in your document), and two others are either too complex or require too many clicks. That leaves you with just three very simple methods for creating a table, and the next three sections take you through the details of each method.

## Converting text to a table

If you already have a list where each column is separated by a tab, comma, or some other consistent character, you can convert that list to a table. Here are the steps to follow:

1. **Select the list.**
2. **Choose Insert ➪ Table ➪ Convert Text to Table.**

   Word displays the Convert Text to Table dialog box, shown in Figure 4-2.

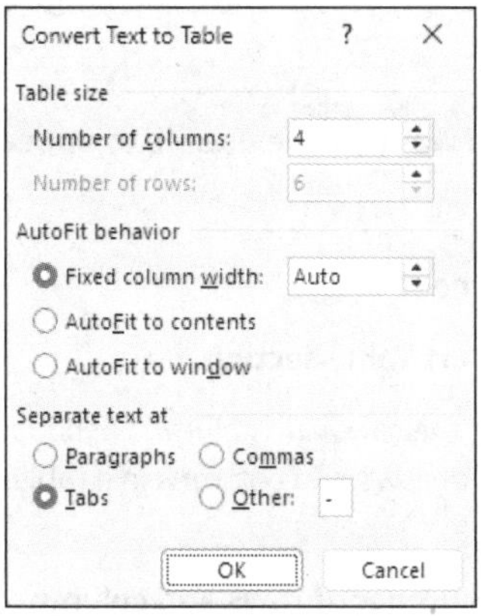


**FIGURE 4-2:** You can semi-magically convert plain text into an honest-to-goodness table.

3. **Adjust the Number of Columns value, if necessary.**

   ¶

   If the value shown in the Number of Columns spin box is wrong, and the correct separation character is selected (refer to Step 4), it usually means that you have one or more incorrect separation characters in your text, such as a space instead of a tab. To check, click Cancel to return to your document, click the Home tab's Show/Hide ¶ button (shown in the margin), and then examine your text's separation characters.

4. **In the AutoFit Behavior section, select an option to set how wide you want your table columns:**

   - *Fixed Column Width:* Gives each column the same width. Either use Auto to let Word figure out the width automatically or use the spin box to set the width you prefer.
   - *AutoFit to Contents:* Makes each column just wide enough to fit its widest item.
   - *AutoFit to Window:* Makes the table as wide as the document (excluding the left and right margins) and distributes the columns across that width.

5. **In the Separate Text At section, select the radio button that corresponds to the character you used to separate each column in your text.**

   If you separated your columns with a character other than a paragraph mark, tab, or comma, select Other and then type the character in the text box provided.

6. **Click OK.**

   Word goes right ahead and converts the list to a table.

## Creating a blank table from scratch

If you just need a simple, blank table with no more than eight rows and ten columns, follow these steps:

1. **Position the cursor where you want the new table to appear.**
2. **Choose Insert ⇨ Table.**

   Word displays a menu of table choices.

3. **Move your mouse into the Insert Table section.**

   As you move the pointer among the rows and columns of squares, Word displays the equivalent number of rows and columns in a table, as shown in Figure 4-3.

4. **When the pointer is over the number of rows and columns you need, click the mouse.**

   With nary a complaint, Word constructs a table with the specified number of rows and columns.

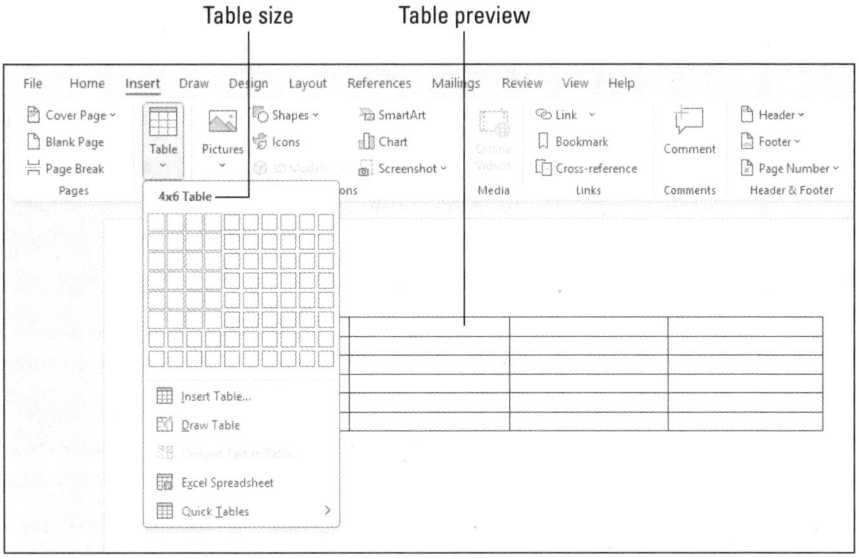


**FIGURE 4-3:** Move your mouse pointer over the number of rows and columns you want in your simple table.

## Creating a table from a template

If you don't want to spend much time formatting your table after you create it, you can build it from one of Word's table templates, which come conveniently preformatted. Here are the steps to follow:

1. **Position the insertion point where you want the new table to appear.**
2. **Choose Insert ➪ Table ➪ Quick Tables.**

   Word displays a gallery of table templates.
3. **Click the template you want to use.**

   Word inserts the table with dummy text.

# Selecting Table Bits and Pieces

Before you can populate a table with data or change the layout or formatting of a table, you need to select the part of the table you want to work with. Here are the techniques to use:

- **Select a cell:** Move the mouse over the left edge of the cell (the pointer changes to an upward-right pointing arrow) and click.

- **Select two or more nonadjacent cells:** Select the first cell, hold down Ctrl, and then select the other cells.
- **Select two or more adjacent cells:** Drag the mouse over the cells.
- **Select a row.** Move the mouse pointer to the left of the row and click. You can also click inside the row and then choose Table Layout ➪ Select ➪ Select Row.
- **Select two or more nonadjacent rows.** Select the first row, hold down Ctrl, and then select the other rows.
- **Select two or more adjacent rows.** Move the mouse pointer to the left of the first row and then drag the mouse down to select the next rows.
- **Select a column.** Move the mouse pointer above the column (the mouse pointer changes to a downward-pointing arrow) and click. You can also click inside the column and then choose Table Layout ➪ Select ➪ Select Column.
- **Select two or more nonadjacent columns.** Select the first column, hold down Ctrl, and then select the other columns.
- **Select two or more adjacent columns.** Move the mouse pointer above the first column and then drag the mouse to the right to select the next columns.

- **Select the entire table.** Move the mouse pointer over the table handle (shown in the margin) that appears above and to the left of the table (the pointer changes to a four-headed arrow) and click. You can also choose Table Layout ➪ Select ➪ Select Table.

# Populating the Table

After you've created the table, you can start entering text and numbers. All you have to do is place the cursor in the cell you want to fill and start typing.

Here are some shortcuts for moving the cursor in a table:

| Press | Moves the Cursor to the |
|---|---|
| Tab | Next column in the current row or, if the cursor is in the last column, the first column in the next row |
| Shift+Tab | Previous column in the current row or, if the cursor is in the first column, the last column in the previous row |
| ↓ | Row below |
| ↑ | Row above |
| Alt+Home | Start of the current row |

| Press | Moves the Cursor to the |
|---|---|
| Alt+End | End of the current row |
| Alt+Page Up | Top of the current column |
| Alt+Page Down | Bottom of the current column |

# Messing with the Table Layout

After you create your table, you may need to adjust the layout by resizing rows and columns, inserting or deleting rows and columns, and so on. You can do these things and much more using the Table Layout contextual tab that appears after you create a new table or click an existing table.

## Resizing a column width or row height

You may find that a particular column is either not wide enough to hold your data or is too wide for the existing data. Word gives you the following methods for changing the column width:

- Move the mouse pointer to the left edge of any cell in the column. The pointer changes to a vertical bar with left- and right-pointing arrows. Drag the left edge of the cell to get the width you want.

- Select any cell in the column and then in the Table Layout tab's Cell Size group, use the Table Column Width spin box (the icon for which is shown in the margin) to set the new width.
- To adjust the width of a column to fit its widest data item, move the mouse pointer to the left edge of any cell in the column and then double-click.
- To adjust the width of all columns to fit their widest data items, choose Table Layout ➪ AutoFit ➪ AutoFit Contents.

- To give each column the same width, choose Table Layout ➪ Distribute Columns (shown in the margin).

Similarly, you may want a taller row height so you can get more data into a row. Word gives you the following methods for changing the row height:

- Move the mouse pointer to the bottom edge of any cell in the row. The pointer changes to a horizontal bar with up- and down-pointing arrows. Click and drag the edge of the cell to get the height you want.

- Select any cell in the row and then in the Table Layout tab's Cell Size group, use the Table Row Height spin box (the icon for which is shown in the margin) to set the new height.
- To adjust the height of a row to fit its tallest data item, move the mouse pointer to the bottom edge of any cell in the row and then double-click.

- To give each row the same height, choose Table Layout ➪ Distribute Rows (shown in the margin).

## Resizing the entire table

To change the width or height (or both) of a table, select the table and use one of these techniques to change its size:

- **Dragging:** Drag the top, bottom, or side of the table. You can also drag the lower-right corner to change the size vertically and horizontally.
  - **Table Properties dialog box:** On the Table Layout contextual tab, in the Table group, click Properties to display the Table tab of the Table Properties dialog box. Select the Preferred Width check box, enter a measurement in the text box, and then click OK.

## Shoehorning columns and rows into a table

If you have to add more data to your table, Word gives you several tools that enable you to expand the table as needed. If you're adding new items to the table, then you need to add more rows; if you are adding more details to each item, then you need to add more columns.

When you need to add another row, you can add the row either at the end of the table or within the table, as follows:

- **Adding a new row at the end of the table:** Click inside the bottom-right cell (that is, the last column of the last row) and press Tab.
- **Adding a new row above an existing row:** Click inside the existing row and then choose Table Layout ➪ Insert Above. You can also right-click the existing row and then choose Insert ➪ Insert Rows Above.
- **Adding a new row below an existing row:** Click inside the existing row and then choose Table Layout ➪ Insert Below. You can also right-click the existing row and then choose Insert ➪ Insert Rows Below.

Adding a new column is similar, except no simple method exists for inserting a column at the end:

- **Adding a new column to the left of an existing column:** Click inside the existing column and then choose Table Layout ➪ Insert Left. You can also right-click the existing column and then choose Insert ➪ Insert Columns to the Left.
- **Adding a new column to the right of an existing column:** Click inside the existing column and then choose Table Layout ➪ Insert Right. You can also right-click the existing column and then choose Insert ➪ Insert Columns to the Right.

TIP

If you want to insert multiple rows or columns, you can insert them all in one fell swoop by first selecting the same number of existing rows or columns. For example, if you select two rows and then choose Table Layout ➪ Insert Below, Word inserts two rows below the selected rows.

Another way to insert one row or one column is to take advantage of Word's so-called One-Click button (shown in the margin):

- **Insert a row:** Position the mouse pointer on the left edge of the table, between the two rows where you want the new row to show up. When the One-Click button appears, click it to insert one row.
- **Insert a column:** Position the mouse pointer on the top edge of the table, between the columns where you want to insert the new column. When the One-Click button appears, click it to insert one column.

## Deleting table elements

Got a table element — that is, a cell, column, row, or even the entire table — that has worn out its welcome? Go ahead and delete that element by selecting it, choosing Table Layout ➪ Delete, and then clicking one of the following commands:

- **Delete Cells:** Deletes the selected cell or cells. Word displays the Delete Cells dialog box to ask whether you want to shift the remaining cells to the left or up, or if you'd rather delete the entire row or column.
- **Delete Columns:** Deletes the selected column or columns.
- **Delete Rows:** Deletes the selected row or rows.
- **Delete Table:** Deletes the entire table.

## Moving a column or row

If your table's columns or rows aren't in the order you prefer, that's no problem because you can move a column or row without much trouble. Here are the steps to follow:

1. **Select the column or row you want to move.**

   If you want to move multiple columns or rows, select them.

2. **Position the mouse pointer anywhere inside the selected column or row.**
3. **Drag the selected element as follows:**
   - *Column:* Drag the column left or right until the cursor appears in the column to the left of which you want to move the column you're dragging, then drop the column there.
   - *Row:* Drag the row up or down until the cursor appears in the row above which you want to move the row you're dragging, then drop the row there.

## SORTING, OR REORDERING A TABLE

*Sorting* means to rearrange all the rows in a table on the basis of data in one or more columns. For example, a table that shows candidates and the number of votes they received could be sorted in alphabetical order by the candidates' names or in numerical order by the number of votes each candidate received. Both tables present the same information, but the information is sorted in different ways.

The difference between ascending and descending sorts is as follows:

- Ascending arranges text from A to Z, numbers from smallest to largest, and dates from earliest to latest.
- Descending arranges text from Z to A, numbers from largest to smallest, and dates from latest to earliest.

When you rearrange a table by sorting it, Word rearranges the formatting as well as the data. Therefore, if possible, it's best to do your sorting before you format the table.

Follow these steps to sort a table:

1. **On the Table Layout contextual tab, in the Data group, click the Sort button.**

   The Sort dialog box shows up.

2. **In the first Sort By drop-down list, choose the column you want to sort with.**

   When you sort a table, Word ignores the *header row* — the first row in the table — and doesn't move it. However, if you want to include the header row in the sort, select the No Header Row option button in the Sort dialog box.

3. **If necessary, open the first Type drop-down list and choose Text, Number, or Date to specify the type of data you're sorting.**

4. **Select the Ascending or Descending option button to declare whether you want an ascending or descending sort.**

5. **If necessary, on the first Then By drop-down list, choose the tiebreaker column.**

   If two items in the Sort By columns are alike, Word looks to your Then By column choice to break the tie and place one row before another in the table.

6. **Click OK.**

# Refinishing Your Table

After you enter text in the table, lay out the columns and rows, and make them the right size, the fun begins. Now you can dress up your table and make it snazzy. You can choose colors for columns and rows. You can play with the borders that divide the columns and rows and shade columns, rows, and cells by filling them with gray shades or a black background. Read on to find out how to do these tricks.

## Designing a table with a table style

TIP

The fastest way to get a good-looking table is to select a table style in the Table Styles gallery, as shown in Figure 4-4. A *table style* is a ready-made assortment of colors and border choices. You can save yourself a lot of formatting trouble by selecting a table style. After you select a table style, you can modify it by selecting or deselecting check boxes in the Table Style Options group on the Table Design tab.

Click anywhere in your table and follow these steps to apply a table style:

1. **Click the Table Design tab.**

2. **Click the Table Styles gallery's Open button (shown in the margin).**

   Word opens the Table Styles gallery.

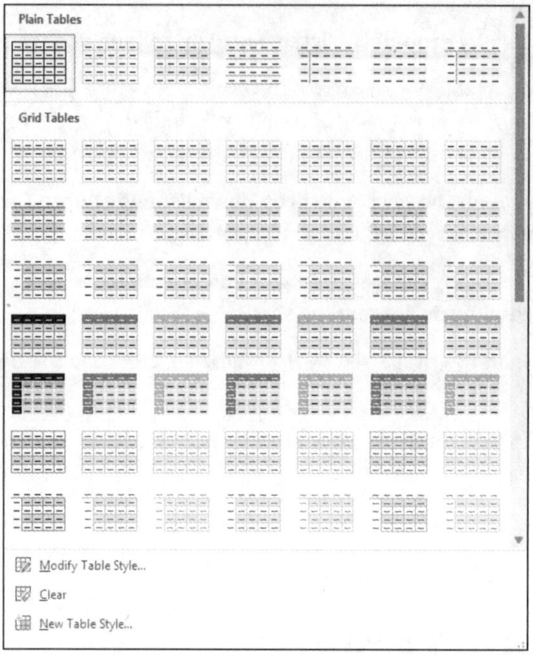


**FIGURE 4-4:** The Table Styles gallery.

3. **Move the pointer over table style choices to live-preview the formatting on your table.**
4. **Click the table style that catches your eye.**

   Word applies the style's formatting to your table.

To remove a style from a table, click inside the table, open the Table Styles gallery, and click Clear.

TIP

For consistency's sake, choose a similar table style — or better yet, the same table style — for all the tables in your document. This way, your work doesn't become a showcase for table styles.

## Calling attention to different rows and columns

On the Table Design tab, in the Table Style Options group, Word offers check boxes for calling attention to different rows or columns. For example, you can make the first row in the table, called the header row, stand out by selecting the Header Row check box. If your table presents numerical data with total figures in the last row, you can call attention to the last row by selecting the Total Row check box. Select or deselect these check boxes on the Table Design tab to make your table easier to read and understand:

- **Header Row and Total Row:** These check boxes make the first row and last row in a table stand out. Typically, the header row is a different color or contains boldface text because it is the row that identifies the data in the table. Click the Header Row check box to make the first row stand out; if you also want the last row to stand out, click the Total Row check box.
- **Banded Columns and Banded Rows:** *Banded* means "striped" in Office lingo. For striped columns or striped rows — columns or rows that alternate in color — select the Banded Columns or Banded Rows check box.
- **First Column and Last Column:** Often the first column stands out in a table because it identifies what type of data is in each row. Select the First Column check box to make it a different color or boldface its text. Check the Last Column check box if you want the rightmost column to stand out.

## Decorating your table with borders and colors

Besides relying on a table style, you can play interior decorator on your own. You can slap color on the columns and rows of your table, draw borders around columns and rows, and choose a look for borders. The Table Design tab offers many commands that pertain to table decoration. Use these commands to shade table columns and rows and draw table borders.

### Designing borders for your table

Follow these steps to fashion a border for your table or a part of your table:

1. **Click inside your table and then click the Table Design tab.**
2. **Select the part of your table that needs a new border.**

   To select the entire table, go to the Table Layout contextual tab, click the Select button, and click Select Table.
3. **Create a look for the table borders you will apply or draw.**

   Use all or some of these techniques to devise a border:

   - **Border style:** Open the drop-down list on the Border Styles button and choose the border style that most resembles the one you want.

- **Line style:** Open the Line Style drop-down list and choose a style.
- **Line weight:** Open the Line Weight drop-down list and choose a line thickness.

TIP

If a table on the current page already has the border you like, you can "sample" the border. Open the drop-down list on the Border Styles button and click Border Sampler. The pointer changes to an eyedropper. Click the border you want to select its style, weight, and color settings.

4. **Open the drop-down list on the Borders button and choose where to place borders on the part of the table you selected in Step 2.**

You can also change borders by clicking the Borders group button and making selections in the Borders and Shading dialog box, as shown in Figure 4-5.

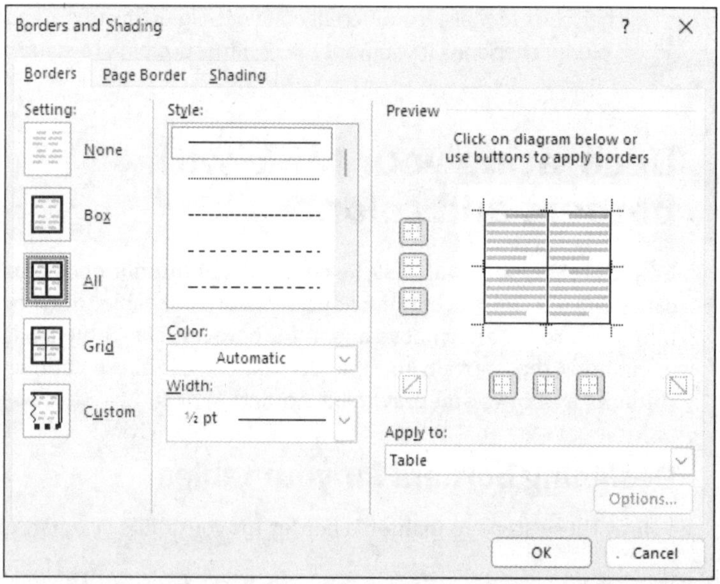


**FIGURE 4-5:** You can draw borders with the Borders and Shading dialog box.

## Selecting colors for columns, rows, or your table

Follow these steps to paint columns, rows, or your table a new color:

1. **Select the part of the table that needs a paint job.**
2. **In the Table Design tab, open the drop-down list on the Shading button and choose a color.**

# Getting Your Geek on with Table Formulas

Word tables are useful for organizing text into rows and columns and for providing an attractive layout option for lists and other data. But tables get especially powerful and dynamic when you apply formulas to the numeric data contained within a table's rows or columns. For example, if you have a table of sales for various departments, you could display the total sales in a cell at the bottom of the table. Similarly, if your table lists the gross margins from all company divisions, you could display the average gross margin in a cell.

## Understanding formula fields

To add calculations to a table, you must insert a field that uses a formula. Here are the general steps to follow to insert a field manually into a table cell:

1. **Click the cell into which you want to insert the field.**
2. **Press Ctrl+F9.**

   Word inserts a blank field that includes only the braces: { and }.
3. **Type your field code between the braces.**
4. **Press F9 to see the field result.**

All formula fields have the same general structure: an equal sign (=), followed by one or more operands — which can be a literal value, the result of another field, the contents of a bookmark, a table reference, or a function result — separated by one or more operators — the symbols that combine the operands in some way, such as the plus sign (+) and the greater-than sign (>). These field formulas come in two varieties: arithmetic and comparison.

*Arithmetic formulas* are by far the most common type of formula. They combine operands with mathematical operators to perform calculations. I've summarized the mathematical operators used in arithmetic formulas in Table 4-1.

For example, suppose you want to know the average number of words per page in your document. That is, you need to divide the total number of words (as given by the NumWords field) by the total number of pages (as given by the NumPages field). Here's a formula field that does this:

```
{= { NumWords } / { NumPages } }
```

**TABLE 4-1** **Word's Formula Field Arithmetic Operators**

| Operator | Name | Example | Result |
|---|---|---|---|
| + | Addition | {=10+5} | 15 |
| – | Subtraction | {=10–5} | 5 |
| * | Multiplication | {=10*5} | 50 |
| / | Division | {=10/5} | 2 |
| % | Percentage | {=10%} | 0.1 |
| ^ | Exponentiation | {=10^5} | 100000 |

A *comparison formula* is an expression that compares two or more numeric operands. If the expression is true, the result of the formula is 1. If the statement is false, the formula returns 0. Table 4-2 summarizes the operators you can use in comparison formulas.

**TABLE 4-2** **Word's Formula Field Comparison Operators**

| Operator | Name | Example | Result |
|---|---|---|---|
| = | Equal to | {=10=5} | 0 |
| > | Greater than | {=10>5} | 1 |
| < | Less than | {=10<5} | 0 |
| >= | Greater than or equal to | {=10>=5} | 1 |
| <= | Less than or equal to | {=10<=5} | 0 |
| <> | Not equal to | {=10<>5} | 1 |

For example, suppose you want to know whether a document's current size on disk (as given by the FileSize field) is greater than 50,000 bytes. Here's a comparison formula field that checks this:

```
{= { FileSize } > 50000}
```

Finally, Word also offers a number of functions that you can plug into your formula fields. Table 4-3 lists the available functions.

**TABLE 4-3** Word's Formula Field Functions

| Function | Returns |
|---|---|
| ABS(x) | The absolute value of x |
| AND(x,y) | 1 if both x and y are true; 0 otherwise. |
| AVERAGE(x,y,z,. . .) | The average of the list of values given by x,y,z,. . . ., . . . |
| COUNT(x,y,z,. . .) | The number of items in the list of values given by x,y,z,. . . ., . . . |
| DEFINED(x) | 1 if the expression x can be calculated; 0 otherwise. |
| FALSE | 0 |
| INT(x) | The integer portion of x |
| MIN(x,y,z,. . .) | The smallest value in the list of values given by x,y,z,. . . ., . . . |
| MAX(x,y,z,. . .) | The largest value in the list of values given by x,y,z,. . . ., . . . |
| MOD(x,y) | The remainder after dividing x by y |
| NOT(x) | 1 if x is false; 0 if x is true. |
| OR(x,y) | 1 if either or both x and y are true; 0 if both x and y are false. |
| PRODUCT(x,y,z,. . .) | The result of multiplying together the items in the list of values given by x,y,z,. . . ., . . . |
| ROUND(x,y) | The value of x rounded to the number of decimal places specified by y |
| SIGN(x) | 1 if x is positive; –1 if x is negative. |
| SUM(x,y,z,. . .) | The sum of the items in the list of values given by x,y,z,. . . ., . . . |
| TRUE | 1 |

## Referencing table cells

The trick to using formulas within tables is to reference the table cells correctly. The easiest way to do this is to use the relative referencing that's built into Word tables, as outlined in Table 4-4.

**TABLE 4-4** Word's Relative Referencing for Table Calculations

| Relative Reference | Refers To |
|---|---|
| ABOVE | All the cells above the formula cell in the same column |
| BELOW | All the cells below the formula cell in the same column |
| LEFT | All the cells to the left of the formula cell in the same row |
| RIGHT | All the cells to the right of the formula cell in the same row |

For example, the following formula field sums all the numeric values in the cells above the formula cell in the same column:

```
{ =SUM(ABOVE) }
```

If you need to refer to specific cells in your formula, use absolute referencing, which is very similar to the cell referencing used by Excel. That is, the table columns are assigned the letters A (for the first column), B (second column), and so on; the table rows are assigned the numbers 1 (for the first row), 2 (second row), and so on. Table 4-5 provides you with some examples.

**TABLE 4-5** **Examples of Absolute Table Cell References**

| Absolute Reference | Refers To |
|---|---|
| A1 | The cell in the first row and first column |
| D5 | The cell in the fifth row and fourth column |
| A1,D5 | The cells A1 and D5 |
| A1:D5 | The rectangular range of cells created by A1 in the top-left corner and D5 in the bottom-right corner |
| B:B | All the cells in the second column |
| 3:3 | All the cells in the third row |

For example, if you have an invoice with a subtotal in cell F10 and you want to calculate 5% tax on that subtotal, the following formula will do the trick:

```
{ =F10 * 0.05 }
```

# Picking Up a Few Table Tricks

The rest of this chapter details a handful of neat table tricks to make your tables stand out in a crowd. Why should all tables appear alike? Read on to discover how to align table text, merge and split cells, repeat header rows for multipage tables, and wrap text around a table.

## Aligning text in columns and rows

Aligning text in columns and rows is a matter of choosing how you want the text to line up vertically and how you want it to line up horizontally. Follow these steps to align text in a table:

1. **Select the cells, columns, or rows, with text that you want to align (or select your entire table).**
2. **Click the Table Layout contextual tab.**
3. **In the Alignment group, click an Align button.**

Figure 4-6 shows where the Align buttons are on the Table Layout contextual tab and how these options align text in a table.

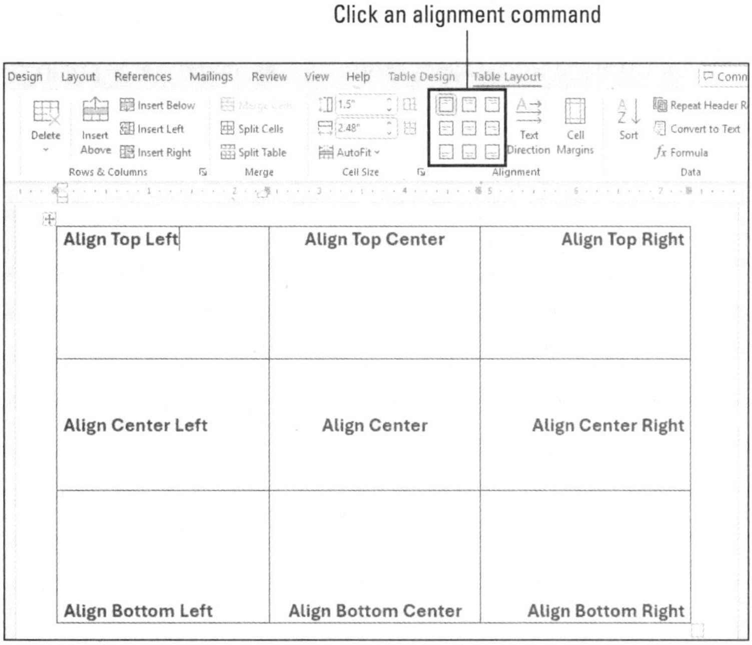


**FIGURE 4-6:** Word offers nine ways to align text.

## Merging and splitting cells

Although most people use tables to store lists of data, using a table to lay out a page in a particular way is also common. For example, if you're building a Word document that looks like an existing paper form or invoice, you'll almost certainly need to use a table to do it. However, on most forms, not all the fields — which will be the cells in the table you create — are the same width: You might have a small field for a person's age, a much wider field for an address, and so on. Changing the row width doesn't work because you need to change the sizes of individual cells.

The best way to do this is to build your table normally and then merge two or more cells together. For example, if you merge two cells that are side-by-side in the same row, you end up with a single cell that's twice the width of the other cells.

Here are the steps to follow to merge two or more cells:

1. **Select the cells you want to merge.**

   You can select cells in a single row, a single column, or in multiple rows and columns. However, the selection must be a rectangle of adjacent cells.

2. **On the Table Layout contextual tab, in the Merge group, click Merge Cells.**

   Word combines all the selected cells into a single cell.

The opposite problem occurs when you're building a page layout that requires a smaller field than the standard column width. In this case, you can get a smaller table cell by splitting an existing cell in half. This feature is also useful if you have merged two or more cells and would like to return those cells to their original configuration.

Here are the steps to follow to split a cell into two or more cells:

1. **Select the cell you want to split.**
2. **On the Table Layout contextual tab, in the Merge group, click Split Cells.**

   Word displays the Split Cells dialog box.

3. **Specify the Number of Columns into which you want to split the cell.**
4. **Specify the Number of Rows into which you want to split the cell.**
5. **Click OK.**

   Word splits the cell.

## Repeating headers for multipage tables

If your table spans two or more pages, you can make the table more readable by cajoling Word into repeating the table's header row at the top of every subsequent page on which the table appears.

Here's how it's done:

1. **Place the cursor in the header row or select the header rows if your table includes more than one header row.**
2. **On the Table Layout contextual tab, in the Data group, click to activate the Repeat Header Rows button.**

   Header rows appear only in Print Layout view, so don't worry if they don't appear in Draft view.

## Wrapping text around a table

If a table isn't very wide, it can leave an unsightly gap in your document. To prevent this, you can ask Word to wrap the surrounding text around the table, as shown in Figure 4-7.

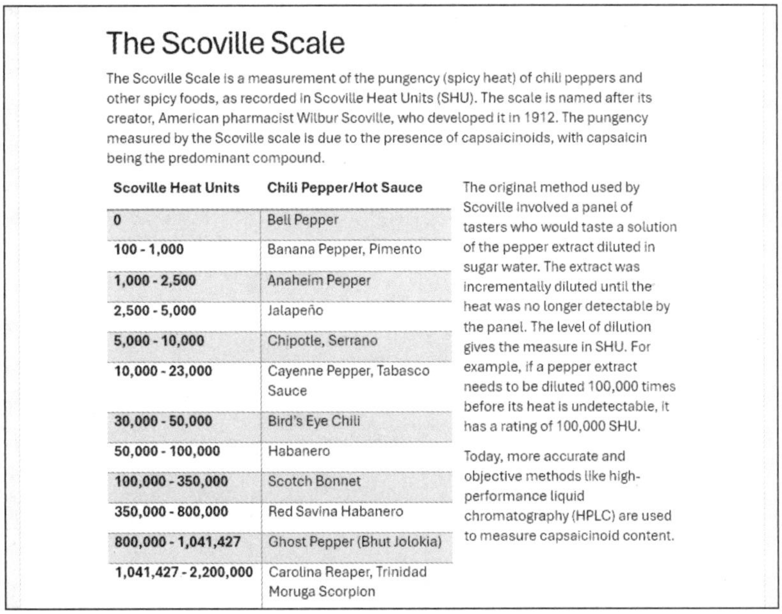

The Scoville Scale

The Scoville Scale is a measurement of the pungency (spicy heat) of chili peppers and other spicy foods, as recorded in Scoville Heat Units (SHU). The scale is named after its creator, American pharmacist Wilbur Scoville, who developed it in 1912. The pungency measured by the Scoville scale is due to the presence of capsaicinoids, with capsaicin being the predominant compound.

| Scoville Heat Units | Chili Pepper/Hot Sauce |
|---|---|
| 0 | Bell Pepper |
| 100 - 1,000 | Banana Pepper, Pimento |
| 1,000 - 2,500 | Anaheim Pepper |
| 2,500 - 5,000 | Jalapeño |
| 5,000 - 10,000 | Chipotle, Serrano |
| 10,000 - 23,000 | Cayenne Pepper, Tabasco Sauce |
| 30,000 - 50,000 | Bird's Eye Chili |
| 50,000 - 100,000 | Habanero |
| 100,000 - 350,000 | Scotch Bonnet |
| 350,000 - 800,000 | Red Savina Habanero |
| 800,000 - 1,041,427 | Ghost Pepper (Bhut Jolokia) |
| 1,041,427 - 2,200,000 | Carolina Reaper, Trinidad Moruga Scorpion |

The original method used by Scoville involved a panel of tasters who would taste a solution of the pepper extract diluted in sugar water. The extract was incrementally diluted until the heat was no longer detectable by the panel. The level of dilution gives the measure in SHU. For example, if a pepper extract needs to be diluted 100,000 times before its heat is undetectable, it has a rating of 100,000 SHU.

Today, more accurate and objective methods like high-performance liquid chromatography (HPLC) are used to measure capsaicinoid content.

**FIGURE 4-7:** Wrap text to prevent unsightly gaps in your documents.

Follow these steps to wrap your table:

1. **Click inside your table.**
2. **On the Table Layout contextual tab, in the Table group, click Properties.**

   The Table Properties dialog box opens and displays the Table tab.
3. **Under Text Wrapping, select the Around option.**
4. **Click OK.**

   Word wraps the surrounding text around the table.

IN THIS CHAPTER

» Repairing spelling and grammatical errors

» Getting the Editor to look over your work

» Digging up that just-so word in the thesaurus

» Finding text — and (optionally) replacing it

# Chapter 5
# Polishing Your Prose

Words. Whether you're a logophile (a lover of words) or a logophobe (one who has an aversion to words), you can't leave home without 'em. Whether you suffer from logomania (the excessive use of words) or logographia (the inability to express ideas in writing), you can't escape 'em. So far in Book 2, you've seen ways to edit words, ways to organize them, and ways to get them all dressed up for the prom, but when it comes down to using them, well, you've been on your own.

Now that changes, because in this chapter you explore a few powerful tools that'll help you buff your words until they shine. I speak, of course, of Word's many proofing tools — including the spell checker, the grammar checker, the Editor, and the thesaurus — and a few other prose-polishing features such as Find & Replace and Translator. Judicious use of these tools will at the very least help you become a better wordsmith. Who knows? With these tools in hand, you may become a full-fledged logolept (a word maniac).

# Correcting Spelling Slip-Ups

One of the easiest ways to lose face in the working world or marks in the academic world is to hand in a piece of writing that contains spelling mistakes. No matter how professionally organized and formatted your document appears, a simple spelling error will stick out and take your reader's mind off your message. However, mistakes do happen, especially if your document is a large one. To help you catch these errors, Word offers a spell-checking utility, which is part of Word's Editor feature.

REMEMBER

A version of the spell-checking feature is also available with Excel, PowerPoint, Access, the Outlook editor, and most other Office 365 programs. Most of the features and techniques you learn about in this section also apply to those programs.

## Working with on-the-fly spell checking

As you type in Word, the spell checker operates in the background and examines your text for errors. When you type a white space character (that is, you press the spacebar, Tab, or Enter), the spell checker compares the previous word with its internal dictionary; if it can't find the word in the dictionary, it signals a spelling error by placing a wavy red line under the word.

To deal with the error, right-click the underlined term. Word displays a shortcut menu with the Spelling submenu displayed. That submenu offers the following:

- **Suggested corrections:** The spell checker usually offers one or more suggested corrections for the misspelled word. You have two ways to proceed here:
  - Click one of those suggestions to correct the word.
  - Click the right-pointing arrow to the right of a suggestion. In the menu that appears, click Read Aloud to hear the suggestion; click Change All to replace every instance of the error with the suggestion; click Add to AutoCorrect so that, when you misspell the word in the future, Word will automatically correct it; or click AutoCorrect Options to open the AutoCorrect dialog box and set up an AutoCorrect entry manually.
- **Add to Dictionary:** If the word is spelled correctly and you don't want Word to flag it again, click Add to Dictionary to insert the term into your custom dictionary. (You find out more about your custom dictionary later in this chapter in the "Managing your custom dictionary" section.)
- **Ignore All:** If you know the word is spelled correctly throughout the document, click Ignore All to remove the red underlines from all instances of the word in the current document and any other document you use in the current Word session. If you restart Word, it will again flag this word as an error.

» **See More:** Click this command to open the Editor pane, which I discuss a bit later in the "Getting the Editor on the Job" section.

TIP

If you don't want Word to check your spelling on-the-fly, choose File ⇨ Options to display the Word Options dialog box. Click Proofing, deselect the Check Spelling as You Type check box, and then click OK to put the new setting into effect.

## Checking spelling directly

You can also invoke the spell checker directly, which is useful if you've turned off Word's on-the-fly spell checking. To get started, use either of the following methods:

» In the Review tab's Proofing group, click the Spelling & Grammar drop-down arrow, and then click Spelling.

» Press F7.

Word opens the Editor pane, which displays the first error in the document, as shown in Figure 5-1. (If you just see the Editor score at the top of the pane, congratulations: your document is free of spelling errors!)

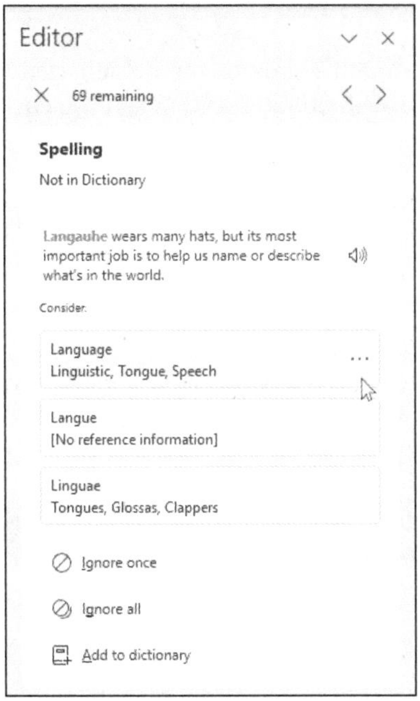


**FIGURE 5-1:** A direct spell-check displays errors in the Editor pane.

As with the Spelling menu I discuss in the previous section, for each error the Editor displays one or more suggested corrections. For each error, click a suggestion or click one of the following:

- **Ignore Once:** Skip this instance of the word.
- **Ignore All:** Skip all instances of the word in the current Word session.
- **Add to Dictionary:** Add the unknown word to your custom dictionary.

For even more options, hover the mouse pointer over a suggestion, click the See More button that materializes (shown in the margin), and then click a command: Change All, Add to AutoCorrect, Read Aloud, or Spell Out.

## Managing your custom dictionary

The dictionary that Word uses to check spelling is extensive and includes Fortune 1000 company names, ethnic names, many recently coined words (such as FOMO — fear of missing out), computer lingo, and the names of countries and large U.S. towns.

That still leaves out a large chunk of the English language, however. To account for this lack, you can use custom dictionaries to hold words you use frequently that the spell checker doesn't recognize.

You saw earlier that you can add words to the default custom dictionary. The default custom dictionary is called CUSTOM.DIC. When you click Add to Dictionary either in the context menu or in the Editor pane box, the spell checker inserts the unknown word into this dictionary.

What if you add a word accidentally and want to remove it? What if you have a list of words you want to add to CUSTOM.DIC? To accomplish these tasks, follow these steps:

1. **Choose File ⇨ Options to open the Word Options dialog box, then click Proofing.**
2. **Click Custom Dictionaries.**

   Word displays a list of your custom dictionaries. (In the next section, you learn how to create new dictionaries.)
3. **Click CUSTOM.DIC.**
4. **Click Edit Word List.**

   Word displays the CUSTOM.DIC dialog box.

5. **You have three choices:**
   - *To add a word to the dictionary:* Type the word in the Word(s) text box and click Add.
   - *To delete a word from the dictionary:* Click the word in the Dictionary list and then click Delete.
   - *To delete all words from the dictionary:* Click Delete All. When Word asks you to confirm, click OK.
6. **Click OK to return to the Custom Dictionaries dialog box.**
7. **Click OK to return to the Word Options dialog box.**
8. **Click OK.**



## Creating a new custom dictionary

Rather than adding words to CUSTOM.DIC one at a time, you can let the spell checker know about a large number of words by creating a custom dictionary that contains all the words. You can create as many different dictionaries as you need. For example, you could have a dictionary for technical terms used in your industry, another for employee or customer names, and another for common abbreviations.

If you only have a few words to add to the custom dictionary, use the following steps to create it:

1. **Choose File ⇨ Options to open the Word Options dialog box, then click Proofing.**
2. **Click Custom Dictionaries.**
3. **Click New.**

   The Create Custom Dictionary dialog box slides in.
4. **In the File Name text box, type a name for the file, then click Save.**

   Word creates the new dictionary.

   WARNING

   Be sure to save your new custom dictionary in the default UProof folder for easy access later.
5. **Click the new custom dictionary in the Dictionary List. (Make sure the dictionary's check box is selected.)**
6. **Click Edit Word List and follow the steps from the previous section to add your words to the dictionary.**
7. **Click OK to return to the Word Options dialog box.**
8. **Click OK.**

If you have a fistful of words you want to put in a custom dictionary, adding them one by one is too time-consuming. A better method is to add the words to a text file and then import the text file as a dictionary. Here are the steps to follow:

1. **Open Notepad or some other text editor.**
2. **Type your words into the text file, pressing Enter after each one.**
3. **Save the text file:**
   - Give the filename the .dic extension.
   - Save the file in the UProof folder (usually C:\Documents and Settings*User*\Application Data\Microsoft\UProof, where *User* is your Windows username).
4. **Choose File ⇨ Options to open the Word Options dialog box, then click Proofing.**
5. **Click Custom Dictionaries.**
6. **Click Add to display the Add Custom Dictionary dialog box.**
7. **Click the text file you created and then click Open.**
8. **Click OK to return to the Word Options dialog box.**
9. **Click OK.**

TIP

You can designate your custom dictionary as the spell checker's default dictionary, which means that each time you run the Add to Dictionary command, the unknown word is added to your custom dictionary instead of CUSTOM.DIC. In the Custom Dictionaries dialog box, click your dictionary and then click Change Default.

## Customizing the spell checker

The spell checker comes with several options that enable you to customize the way the feature operates. To work with these options, choose File ⇨ Options and then click Proofing. Here are the options you're most likely to use:

- **Ignore words in UPPERCASE:** When selected, the spell checker ignores all words typed entirely in uppercase letters.
- **Ignore words that contain numbers:** When selected, the spell checker ignores all words that contain numeric values.

- **Ignore internet and file addresses:** When selected, the spell checker ignores all words that contain internet addresses (such as `https://paulmcfedries.com/`) or file paths (such as \\Server\user\).
- **Flag repeated word:** When selected, the spell checker treats a repeated word as an error.
- **Enforce accented uppercase in French:** When selected, the spell checker treats unaccented uppercase French characters as an error.
- **Suggest from main dictionary only:** When selected, the spell checker only suggests replacement words from the main spell checker dictionary; in other words, it doesn't suggest replacements from CUSTOM.DIC or any of your custom dictionaries.



# Fixing Grammar Gaffes

A misspelled word is not the only blunder that can mar an otherwise well-constructed document. A lapse in grammar can also jolt the reader and cause them to wonder about the intelligence (or, at least, the proofreading diligence) of the writer. To avoid this scenario, be sure to check your document for grammatical correctness. Word's Editor feature has a grammar component that can help you locate and fix many grammar woes.

I should mention here that the grammar checker is not as proficient at finding errors as the spell checker. Grammar rules are a tricky business, and catching grammatical errors is difficult even for expert editors (the professional editors reading these words nod knowingly). Word's grammar checker often misses completely obvious grammar problems and flags perfectly correct sentences as errors. Therefore, I suggest that you take the grammar checker's suggestions with the proverbial grain of salt.

## Working with on-the-fly grammar checking

Like the spell checker, the grammar checker also operates in the background and scours your text for errors. When you start a new sentence, the grammar checker examines the previous sentence for problems and, if it finds any, it signals a grammatical spelling error by placing a double blue underline beneath the offending word or phrase.

To handle the error, right-click the underlined text. Word displays a shortcut menu with the Grammar submenu displayed. That submenu offers the following:

- **Suggested corrections:** The grammar checker usually offers one or more suggested corrections for the error. You have two ways to proceed:
  - Click one of those suggestions to correct the text.
  - Click the right-pointing arrow to the right of a suggestion. In the menu that appears, click Read Aloud to hear the suggestion.
- **Ignore Once:** If you know the text is correct, click this command to skip this instance of the error in the current document.
- **Don't check for this issue:** Click this command to tell the grammar checker to no longer flag the rule underlying this error.
- **Options for Grammar:** Displays the Grammar Settings dialog box, which enables you to choose which grammar rules get checked.
- **See More:** Click this command to open the Editor pane, which I discuss a bit later in the "Getting the Editor on the Job" section.

TIP

If you don't want Word to check your grammar on-the-fly, choose File ⇨ Options to display the Word Options dialog box. Click Proofing, deselect the Mark Grammar Errors as You Type check box, and then click OK.

## Checking grammar directly

You can also invoke the grammar checker directly, which is useful if you've turned off Word's on-the-fly grammar checking. To invoke the grammar checker, use either of the following methods:

- In the Review tab's Proofing group, click Spelling & Grammar.
- Press F7.

Word opens the Editor pane, which displays the first error in the document. If this is a spelling error, click Back (X), then click Grammar to see the first grammar error.

As with the Grammar menu I discuss in the previous section, for each error the Editor displays one or more suggested corrections. For each error, click a suggestion or click one of the following:

- **Ignore Once:** Skip this instance of the error.
- **Stop checking for this:** Skip all instances of the error in the current Word session.

For even more options, hover the mouse pointer over a suggestion, click the See More button that materializes (shown in the margin), and then click a command: Read Aloud or Spell Out.

# Getting the Editor on the Job



The spell checker and grammar checker are part of Word's Editor feature which, like the flesh-and-blood editors who make writers look good, word-wise, can help you polish your prose to a high shine. The Editor improves your writing not only by offering corrections for any spelling and grammatical glitches in your document, but also by suggesting alternate word choices that can improve your document along several different refinement axes, including clarity, conciseness, and formality.

The Editor pane leads off with a value called the Editor Score, which is a percentage between 0 and 100 that gives you an overall sense of what kind of shape your document is in. The more spelling and grammar transgressions are in the document, and then more refinements the Editor has suggested, the lower the Editor score.

Happily, a low Editor Score doesn't mean you need to scrap your document entirely. Mend the document's spelling slips, patch up its grammar problems, and implement a few of the editor's suggested refinements, and watch the Editor Score rise accordingly. You can shoot for 100% if you have the time and patience but know that a score over 90% is fine for most documents.

To display the Editor pane, Word offers the following choices:

- On the Home tab, in the Editor group, click Editor.
- On the Review tab, in the Proofing group, click Editor.
- Press F7.

The Editor pane slides onto the screen and you see your document's Editor Score at the top, as shown in Figure 5-2.

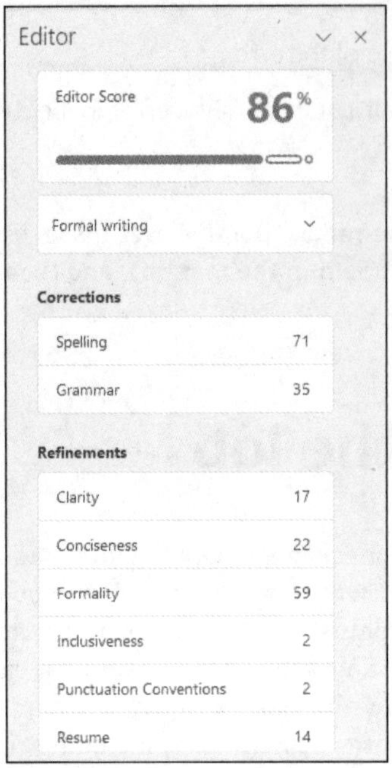


**FIGURE 5-2:** You can use the Editor to improve your writing.

Below the Editor Score, the pane is divided into the following elements and sections:

- **How formal will this document be?:** This is the list that appears just below the Editor Score. Before you do anything else with the Editor, you should use this list to select the formality level of your document: Formal, Professional, or Casual. This selection will change how the Editor analyzes your document and will likely affect your Editor Score and the number and type of the suggested refinements.
- **Corrections:** This section shows you how many spelling and grammar errors the Editor found in your document. You can click Spelling to address the spelling mishaps, or you can click Grammar to correct the grammar miscues.
- **Refinements:** This section shows you how many issues the Editor found in your document related to word-choice categories such as Clarity and Conciseness. Click a refinement category and then, for each issue, you can do one of the following:
  - **Apply a suggested fix:** If the Editor offers one or more suggested ways to address the issue, you can click one of the suggestions to make it so.
  - **Correct the issue manually:** If the Editor doesn't have a suggested fix, you can edit the text manually to address the problem.

- **Ignore Once:** Skip this instance of the issue.
- **Stop checking for this:** Skip all instances of the issue in the current Word session.

» **Similarity:** Click this box to have the Editor check whether any of your text is similar to online sources.

» **Insights:** Click this box to display The Readability Statistic dialog box, which shows various document stats, such as word count, average sentences per paragraph, average words per sentence.



# Using the Splendiferous Thesaurus

Did you know that the English language boasts about 600,000 words (plus another 400,000-or-so technical terms and another 2,250,000 Gen Z slang terms)? So why use a boring word like *boring* when gems such as *prosaic* and *insipid* are available? What's that? Vocabulary was never your best subject? No problem-o. Word's built-in Thesaurus can supply you with enough synonyms (words with a similar meaning) and even antonyms (words with the opposite meaning) to keep even the biggest word hound happy.

WARNING

That said, even though Word is happy to provide you with a list of synonyms for a word, it doesn't mean that every one of those synonyms is appropriate. The key point to remember with the Thesaurus is that the words it provides are only *similar* in meaning to the original word. If you want to give an unfamiliar synonym a whirl, be sure to check out its definition first, just to make sure it's carrying the lexical weight you want it to carry.

The quickest way to get a list of synonyms for a word is to right-click the word and then click Synonyms in the shortcut menu. As shown in Figure 5-3, Word displays a list of synonyms (for, in this case, the word *cheeky*). If you see a word that tickles your inner editor, click it to replace the original with the synonym.

To get a longer list of synonyms or to search for the perfect synonym, click the word in question and open the Thesaurus task pane with one of these techniques:

» Press Shift+F7.

» Right-click the word and choose Synonyms ➪ Thesaurus.

» On the Review tab, in the Proofing group, click Thesaurus.

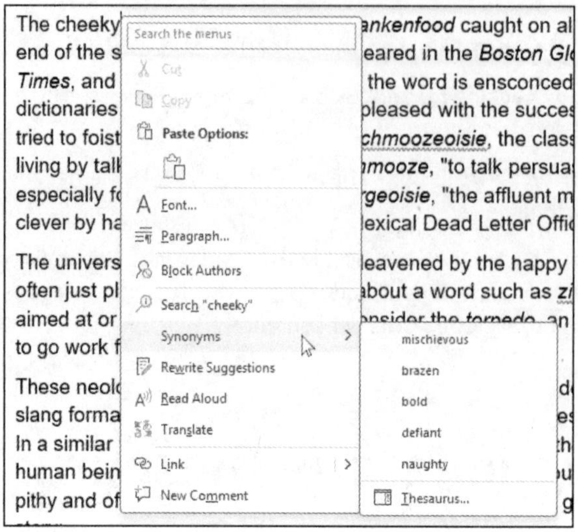


**FIGURE 5-3:** You can right-click a word to display a few synonyms.

The Thesaurus task pane opens, as shown in Figure 5-4. It offers a list of synonyms and sometimes includes an antonym (labeled as "(Antonym)" in the list). Now you're getting somewhere:

- **Choosing a synonym:** Move the pointer over the synonym you want, open its drop-down list, and choose Insert.
- **Finding a synonym for a synonym:** If a synonym intrigues you, click it. The task pane displays a new list of synonyms.
- **Searching for synonyms:** If you can't find a synonym that works, try using the search box near the top of the Thesaurus pane to search for a similar word.

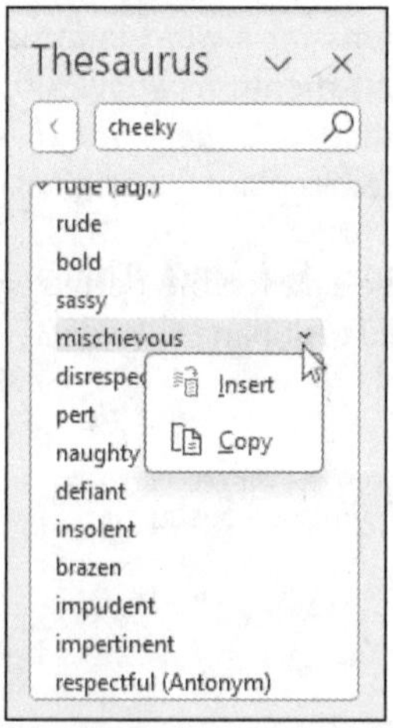


**FIGURE 5-4:** The Thesaurus task pane offers a longer list of synonyms.

# Finding and Replacing Text

If you've ever found yourself lamenting a long-lost word adrift in some humongous mega-document, the Word folks can sympathize (because it has probably happened to them a time or two). In fact, they were even kind enough to build a special Find feature into Word to help you locate missing text. And that's not all: You can use this feature also to seek out and replace every instance of one word or phrase with another. Sound like fun? Well, okay, maybe not, but it *is* handy, so you might want to read this section anyway.



## The basics: Finding stray words and phrases

If you need to find a certain word or phrase in a short document, it's usually easiest just to scroll through the text. But if you're dealing with more than a couple of pages, don't waste your time rummaging through the whole file. Bring the Find feature onboard and let it do the searching for you:

1. **Press Ctrl+F or go to the Home tab and click the Find button.**

   The Navigation pane appears so that you can enter search criteria.

2. **Type the word or phrase in the search text box.**

   After you type the word or phrase, the Navigation pane's Results tab lists each instance of the term you're hunting for and Word highlights each instance of the term in your document.

3. **Click an instance of the search term in the Results tab to scroll to that location in your document.**

   To go from search term to search term, you can also scroll in the Results tab, click the Previous button (up arrow) or Next button (down arrow), or press Ctrl+Page Up or Ctrl+Page Down.

## Narrowing your search

To narrow your search, click the Search for More Things button (shown in the margin) on the far right of the Navigation pane's search bod, as shown in Figure 5-5. Then choose an option on the drop-down list:

- **Options:** Opens the Find Options dialog box so that you can select options to narrow your search (refer to Figure 5-5). Table 5-1 explains these options.
- **Advanced Find:** Opens the Find tab of the Find and Replace dialog box so that you can select options to narrow the search (check out Figure 5-5).

Table 5-1 explains these options. (You can also open this dialog box on the Home tab, in the Editing group, by opening the drop-down menu on the Find button and choosing Advanced Find.) Choose Advanced Find if you want to search using font, paragraph, and other formats as well as advanced search criteria. By clicking the Format button and Special button, you can search for text that was formatted a certain way, as well as for special characters such as paragraph marks and page breaks.

- **Find (Graphics, Tables, Equations, Footnotes/Endnotes, Comments):** Search for a particular object type. For example, choose Tables to search for tables.

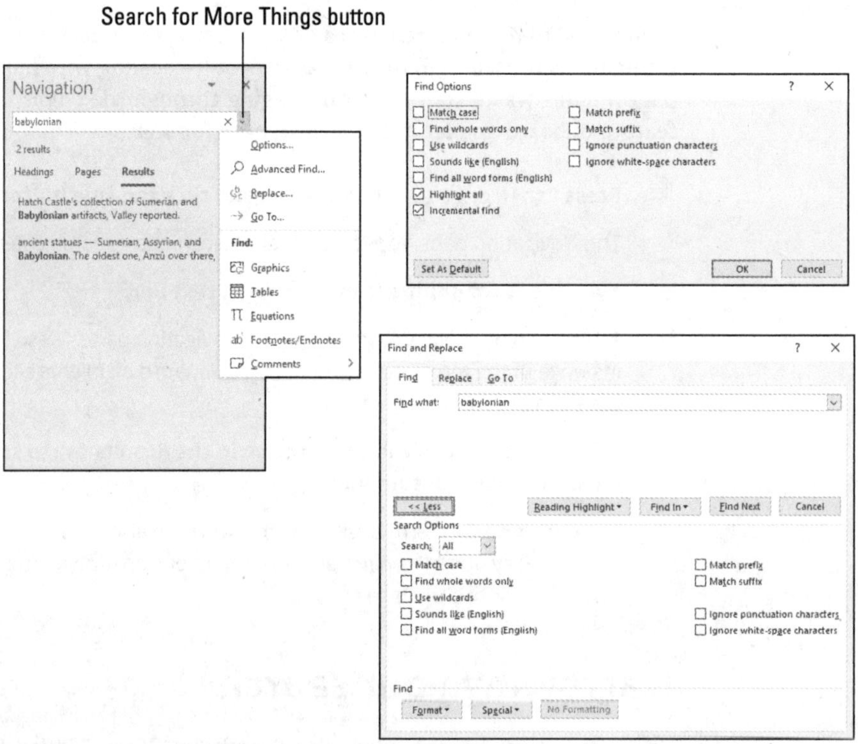


**FIGURE 5-5:** Conducting a narrow search.

REMEMBER

Click the More button in the Find and Replace dialog box to see all the search options.

WARNING

After you finish conducting a search for formatted text, don't forget to click the No Formatting button in the Find and Replace dialog box. (You can't conduct a normal search again unless you turn format searching off.)

**TABLE 5-1** **Search Options in the Find Options and Find and Replace Dialog Box**

| Option | Description |
|---|---|
| Match Case | Searches for words with upper- and lowercase letters that exactly match those in the search text box. When the Match Case option is selected, a search for *bow* finds *bow,* but not *Bow* or *BOW.* |
| Find Whole Words Only | Normally, a search for *bow* yields *elbow, bowler, bow-wow,* and all other words with the letters *b-o-w* (in that order). Choose this option and you get only *bow.* |
| Use Wildcards | Choose this option to use wildcards in searches. (See "Using wildcard operators to refine searches," later in this chapter.) |
| Sounds Like | Search for words that sound like the one in the Search text box. A search for *bow* with this option selected finds *beau,* for example. However, it doesn't find *bough.* This command isn't very reliable. |
| Find All Word Forms | Takes into account verb conjugations and plurals in searches. With this option, you get *bows, bowing,* and *bowed* as well as *bow.* |
| Highlight All[1] | Highlights search results on the page. (Click the Reading Highlight button in the Find and Replace dialog box and then click Highlight All.) |
| Match Prefix | A *prefix* is a syllable appearing before the root or stem of a word to alter its meaning. For example, *co-, mid-, non-,* and *un-* are prefixes in the words *coauthor, midtown, nonviolent,* and *unselfish.* Choose this option and enter a prefix (without a hyphen) in the Find What text box to locate words that begin with the prefix you enter. |
| Match Suffix | A *suffix* is a syllable or two appearing at the end of a word that alters its meaning. For example, *-age, -ish,* and *-ness* are suffixes in the words *spillage, smallish,* and *darkness.* Choose this option and enter a suffix (without a hyphen) in the Find What text box to find words that end with the same suffix. |
| Ignore Punctuation Characters | Search in text for word phrases without regard for commas, periods, and other punctuation marks. For example, a search for *Yuma Arizona* finds *Yuma, Arizona* (with a comma) in the text. |
| Ignore White Space Characters | Search in text for word phrases without regard for white space caused by multiple blank spaces or tab entries. |
| Format (button)[2] | Search for text formatted a certain way. For example, search for boldface text. After you click the Format button in the Find and Replace dialog box, you can choose a format type on the drop-down list — Font, Paragraph, Tabs, Language, Frame, Style, or Highlight. A Find dialog box opens so that you can describe the format you're looking for. Select options in the dialog box to describe the format and click OK. |
| Special (button)[2] | Search for special characters such as paragraph marks and em dashes. (See "Searching for special characters," later in this chapter.) |

*a[1] Find Options dialog box only*

*b[2] Find and Replace dialog box only*

## Using wildcard operators to refine searches

Word permits you to use wildcard operators in searches. A *wildcard operator* is a character that represents characters in a search expression. Wildcards aren't for everybody. Using them requires a certain amount of expertise, but after you know how to use them, wildcards can be invaluable in searches and macros. Table 5-2 explains the wildcard operators that you can use in searches. Click the Use Wildcards check box if you want to search using wildcards.

**TABLE 5-2** Wildcards for Searches

| Operator | What It Finds | Example |
|---|---|---|
| ? | Any single character | **b?t** finds *bat, bet, bit,* and *but.* |
| * | Zero or more characters | **t*o** finds *to, two,* and *tattoo.* |
| [*xyz*] | A specific character, *x, y,* or *z* | **t[aeiou]pper** finds *tapper, tipper,* and *topper.* |
| [*x-z*] | A range of characters, *x* through *z* | **[1-4]000** finds *1,000, 2,000, 3,000,* and *4,000,* but not *5,000.* |
| [!*xy*] | Not the specific character or characters, *xy* | **p[!io]t** finds *pat* and *pet,* but not *pit* or *pot.* |
| < | Characters at the beginning of words | **<info** finds *information, infomaniac,* and *infomercial.* |
| > | Characters at the end of words | **ese>** finds *these, journalese,* and *legalese.* |
| @@ | One or more instances of the previous character | **sho@@t** finds *shot* and *shoot.* |
| {*n*} | Exactly *n* instances of the previous character | **sho{2}t** finds *shoot* but not *shot.* |
| {*n*,} | At least *n* instances of the previous character | **^p{3,}** finds three or more paragraph breaks in a row, but not a single paragraph break or two paragraph breaks in a row. |
| {*n*,*m*} | From *n* to *m* instances of the previous character | **10{2,4}** finds *100, 1000,* and *10000,* but not *10* or *100000.* |

WARNING

You can't conduct a whole-word-only search with a wildcard. For example, a search for **f*s** not only finds *fads* and *fits* but also all text strings that begin with *f* and end with *s,* such as *for the birds.* Wildcard searches can yield many, many results and are sometimes useless.

TIP

To search for an asterisk (*), question mark (?), or other character that serves as a wildcard search operator, place a backslash (\) before it in the text box.

## Searching for special characters

Table 5-3 describes the *special characters* you can look for in Word documents. To look for the special characters listed in the table, enter the character directly in the text box or click the Special button in the Find and Replace dialog box, and then choose a special character from the pop-up list. Be sure to enter lowercase letters. For example, you must enter **^n**, not **^N**, to look for a column break. *Note:* A caret (^) precedes special characters.

**TABLE 5-3**

### Special Characters for Searches

| To Find/Replace | Enter |
|---|---|
| Column break | ^n |
| Field[1] | ^d |
| Manual line break (↵) | ^l |
| Manual page break | ^m |
| No-width non break | ^z |
| No-width optional break | ^x |
| Paragraph break (¶) | ^p |
| Section break[1] | ^b |
| Section character | ^% |
| Tab space (→) | ^t |
| **Punctuation Marks** | |
| 1/4 em space | ^q |
| Caret (^) | ^^ |
| Ellipsis | ^i |
| Em dash (—) | ^+ |
| En dash (–) | ^= |
| Full-width ellipses | ^j |
| Nonbreaking hyphen | ^~ |
| Optional hyphen | ^- |
| White space (one or more blank spaces)[1] | ^w |

*(continued)*

**TABLE 4-3** *(continued)*

| To Find/Replace | Enter |
|---|---|
| **Characters and Symbols** | |
| Foreign character | You can type foreign characters in the Find What and Replace With text boxes |
| ANSI and ASCII characters and symbols | ^*nnnn*, where *nnnn* is the four-digit code |
| Any character[1] | ^? |
| Any digit[1] | ^# |
| Any letter[1] | ^$ |
| Clipboard contents[2] | ^c |
| Contents of the Find What box[2] | ^& |
| **Elements of Reports and Scholarly Papers** | |
| Endnote mark[1] | ^e |
| Footnote mark[1] | ^f |
| Graphic[1] | ^g |

*a[1] For use in Find operations only*

*b[2] For use in Replace operations only*

TIP

Before searching for special characters, go to the Home tab and, in the Paragraph group, click the Show/Hide ¶ button (shown in the margin). That way, you see special characters — also known as *hidden format symbols* — onscreen when Word finds them.

TIP

Creative people find many uses for special characters in searches. The easiest way to find section breaks, column breaks, and manual line breaks in a document is to enter **^b**, **^n**, or **^l**, respectively, and start searching. By combining special characters with text, you can make find-and-replace operations more productive. For example, to replace all double hyphens (--) in a document with em dashes (—), enter -- in the Find What text box and **^m** in the Replace With text box. This kind of find-and-replace operation is especially useful for cleaning documents that were created in another application and then imported into Word.

## Conducting a find-and-replace operation

If you do a lot of writing, one of the features you'll come to rely on the most is *find-and-replace*, where Word seeks out a particular bit of text and replaces it with something else. This may not seem like a big deal for a word or two, but if you need to change a couple of dozen instances of *irregardless* to *regardless*, it can be a real time-saver.

Searching and replacing is, as you might imagine, not all that different from plain old searching. Here's how it works:

1. **Press Ctrl+H or go to the Home tab and, in the Editing group, click the Replace button.**

   The Find and Replace dialog box appears.

2. **In the Find What text box, type the text that needs to be replaced.**

   Earlier in this chapter, "The basics: Finding stray words and phrases" explains how to construct a search. Try to narrow your search so you find only the text you're looking for.

3. **In the Replace With text box, type the replacement text.**

   You can select replacement text from the drop-down list.

4. **Click the Find Next button.**

   Word highlights the next instance of your search term.

   If Word displays the "No results found" dialog box, your document doesn't contain the search term, so you might need to refine your Find What text.

5. **Tell Word what you want to happen next by clicking one of these buttons:**

   - *Next:* Bypass this instance of the search term and move on to the next one.
   - *Replace:* Change this instance of the search term to the Replace With text and move on to the next instance.
   - *Replace All:* Change every instance of the search term to the Replace With text.
   - *Cancel:* Bail out of the operation altogether and move on with your life.

WARNING

Clicking Replace All sure seems like the easy way to get this chore finished faster, but some caution is required. Double-check (and maybe even triple-check) your Find What and Replace With text and try to think of any ways a Replace All operation can go wrong. For example, you might want to replace the word *egret* with the word *heron*. That's your business, but know that if you run Replace All willy-nilly, you might also change *regret* to *rheron* and *allegretto* to *allheronto*.

Be sure to examine your document after you conduct a find-and-replace operation. You never know what the powerful Replace command will do. If the command makes a hash of your document, click the Undo button.

IN THIS CHAPTER

» Embellishing documents with themes

» Decorating documents with borders, backgrounds, and watermarks

» Arranging document text in newspaper-style columns or linked text boxes

» Customizing documents with page setup options

# Chapter 6

# Designing Fancy-Schmancy Documents

When your to-do list is longer than your arm and the next item on that list involves creating a Word document, it can be tempting to just pound out the text, apply some token formatting, run a quick spell check, and move on to the next item. Hey, no judgement. We're all busy. And that slapdash approach is totally fine if you're the only one who'll read the document.

But, these days, it's far more likely that others will read any document you create. It could be the others on your team, colleagues in your department, or folks elsewhere in your organization. When a document's life cycle goes from your-eyes-only to their-eyes-too, then you really should take a bit more care with how the document looks overall and how you present the information.

If you just groaned at the thought of putting all that effort into a Word document, I hear you. But here's the good news: Word offers quite a few tools for fancifying a humdrum document, none of those tools has a steep learning curve (or any learning curve at all), and most can be applied with just a few mouse clicks. In other words, as you learn in this chapter, making your Word documents both fancy and schmancy doesn't have to take a lot of time or a lot of effort.

# Giving a Document a Makeover with a Theme

By far the easiest and fastest way to apply high-quality design and formatting to a document is to use a theme. A *theme* is a predefined collection of formatting options that control the colors, fonts, and background used with each page in the document. Word built-in themes are nice on their own, but you can also customize any aspect of the theme to tweak the design to suit your personal style or match your organization's style guidelines.

## Applying a prefab theme

Applying one of Word's predefined themes takes just a few mouse clicks, as the following steps show:

1. **Click the Design tab.**
2. **In the Document Formatting group, click Themes.**

   Word unveils the Themes gallery, as shown in Figure 6-1.

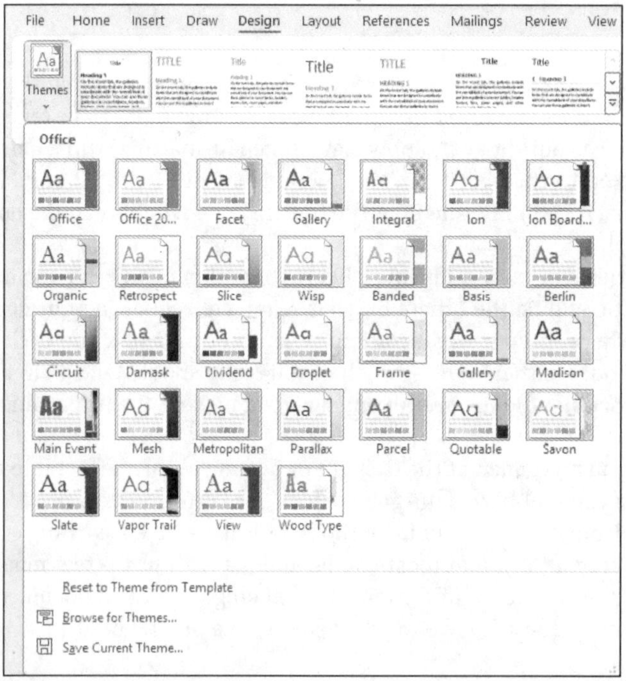


**FIGURE 6-1:** Use Word's Themes gallery to apply a prefab theme to your document.

TIP

Before committing to a theme, remember that if you hover the mouse pointer over a swatch in the Themes gallery, Word temporarily applies the theme to the displayed page so you can preview the theme design.

3. **Click a theme that appeals to you.**

   Word applies the theme to all the pages in the document.

## Trying different theme colors

If the colors that come with a predefined theme aren't sparking your joy, you can change them individually. However, if you want to avoid the drudgery of getting your text, line, background, and fill colors to match, Word comes with more than 20 built-in color schemes that do the hard work for you. Follow these steps to apply a color scheme:

1. **Click the Design tab.**
2. **In the Document Formatting group, click Colors.**

   Word unfurls the Theme Colors gallery of color schemes, as shown in Figure 6-2. Each color scheme has eight color swatches: The first is the background color, the second is the text color, and the rest are "accent" colors that Word uses with content such as charts and SmartArt diagrams.

3. **Click a color scheme that looks good.**

   Word applies the color scheme to the document.



## Creating your very own custom color scheme

If a built-in color scheme isn't quite right for your needs or you want to create a color scheme to match your company's brand colors, you need to create a custom scheme. Follow these steps:

1. **If you want to use an existing color scheme as your starting point, open the Design tab, click Colors, and then click the color scheme you want to use as your base.**
2. **In the Design tab, click Colors, and then click Customize Colors.**

   Word displays the Create New Theme Colors dialog box, shown in Figure 6-3.

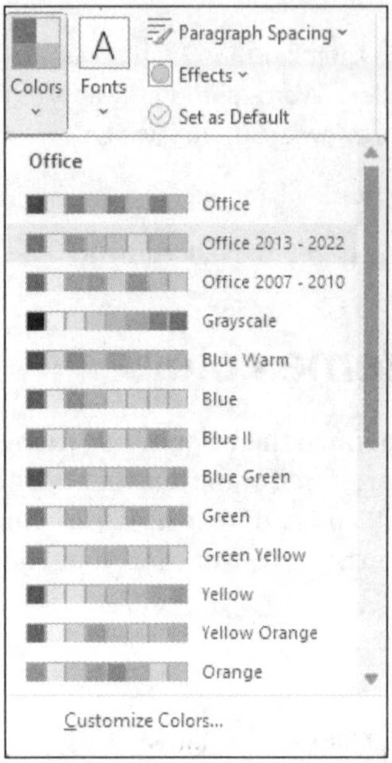


**FIGURE 6-2:** Use Word's Theme Colors gallery to choose a color scheme for your document.

3. **Use the following drop-down lists to select the text and background colors:**
   - *Text/Background - Dark 1:* The dark text color that Word applies when you choose a light background color.
   - *Text/Background - Light 1:* The light text color that Word applies when you choose a dark background color.
   - *Text/Background - Dark 2:* The dark background color that Word applies when you choose a light text color.
   - *Text/Background - Light 2:* The light background color that Word applies when you choose a dark text color.
4. **Use the Accent drop-down lists (Accent 1 through Accent 6) to choose the accent colors.**
5. **Use the following drop-down lists to choose link colors:**
   - *Hyperlink:* The color of the link text before the link is clicked.
   - *Followed Hyperlink:* The color of the link text after the link is clicked.
6. **In the Name text box, type a name for the new color scheme.**
7. **Click Save.**

   Word saves your custom color scheme and adds it to the Theme Colors gallery in a new section at the top of the gallery named Custom.

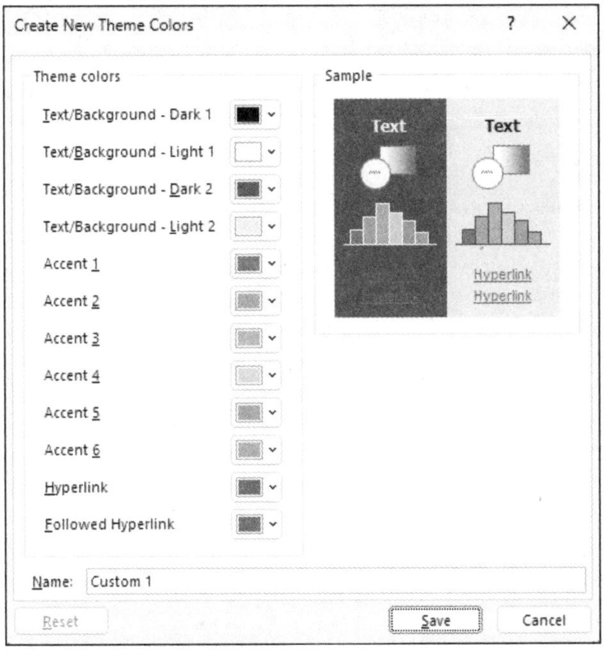


**FIGURE 6-3:** Use the Create New Theme Colors dialog box to create a custom color scheme.



## Giving different theme fonts a whirl

Each theme defines two fonts: a larger font for title text and a smaller font for body text. The typeface is usually the same for both types of text, but some themes use two different typefaces, such as Aptos Display for titles and Aptos for body text. You can change the fonts used in the current theme by following these steps:

1. **Click the Design tab.**
2. **In the Document Formatting group, click Fonts.**

   Word reveals the Theme Fonts gallery, as shown in Figure 6-4.
3. **Click the fonts you want to use.**

   Word applies the font scheme to the document.

## Fabricating a custom theme font combo

If none of Word's theme font pairs are exactly what you want to use in your document, you can create your own custom combination. Follow these steps:

1. **If you want to use an existing font pair as your starting point, open the Design tab, click Fonts, and then click the theme font combination you want to use as your base.**

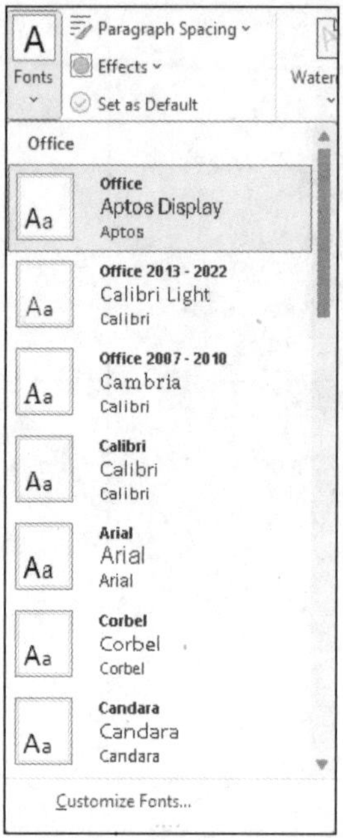


**FIGURE 6-4:** Use Word's Theme Fonts gallery to choose fonts for your document.

2. **In the Design tab, click Fonts, and then click Customize Fonts.**

   Word displays the Create New Theme Fonts dialog box, shown in Figure 6-5.

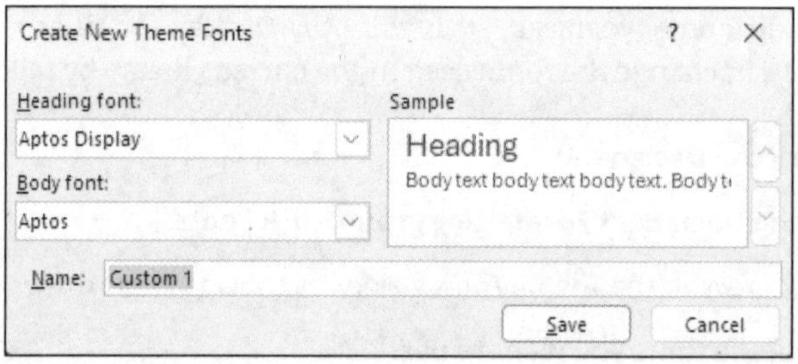


**FIGURE 6-5:** Use the Create New Theme Fonts dialog box to create your custom font combination.

3. **Use the Heading font list to click the typeface you want to use for titles.**
4. **Use the Body font list to click the typeface you want to use for the body text.**
5. **In the Name text box, type a name for the new theme fonts.**
6. **Click Save.**

   Word saves your custom theme font combination and adds it to the Theme Fonts gallery in a new section at the top of the gallery named Custom.

## Applying theme effects

Word defines a number of effects that govern the look of objects such as shapes, SmartArt diagrams, and chart markers. Here are the steps to follow to apply these theme effects:

1. **Click the Design tab.**
2. **In the Document Formatting group, click Effects.**

   Words calls up the Theme Effects gallery.
3. **Click the effect you want to use.**

   Word applies the selected effect to the document.

## Creating a custom theme

If you go to the trouble of choosing a theme and then customizing that scheme with effects and with either predefined or custom colors and fonts, you probably don't want to go through the entire process the next time you want the same theme for a document. Fortunately, you don't have to because Word enables you to save all of your theme details as a custom theme. Here are the steps to follow:

1. **Use the techniques from the past few sections to customize a theme and its colors, fonts, and effects.**
2. **Click the Design tab.**
3. **In the Document Formatting group, click Themes.**

   Word unveils the Themes gallery.
4. **Click Save Current Theme.**

   Word displays the Save Current Theme dialog box.
5. **In the File Name text box, type a name for the custom theme.**
6. **Click Save.**

   Word saves the theme as an Office Theme file and adds it to the Theme gallery in a new section at the top of the gallery named Custom.

TIP

If you want to use your custom theme as the default theme for all new documents, make sure the theme is applied, open the Design tab, and then in the Document Formatting group, click Set as Default.

# Adding Some Finishing Touches

Some page design embellishments are in the service of making a document easier to read, but then there are those adornments that are only about making a document easier on the eyes. In the sections that follow, you learn about two ways to increase a document's curb appeal.

## Setting page borders

An attractive border around a page can add a nice touch to a document printout. (Word also shows page borders when you work with a document in Page Layout view.) Word enables you to add a border to a single page, each page in a section, or every page in a document. The border can be a solid or dotted line, a drop shadow, 3D, or even artwork (such as balloons for use around a birthday party invitation).

Follow these steps to add a page border to your document:

1. **If your document has multiple sections and you want to add borders for the page in a particular section, position the cursor anywhere within that section.**
2. **On the Design tab, in the Page Background group, click Page Borders.**

   Word displays the Borders and Shading dialog box with the Page Border tab selected.
3. **In the Setting section, click the basic border type you want.**
4. **Click the border Style, Color, and Width you want.**
5. **If you want to use artwork instead of a line, use the Art list to click the image you want.**
6. **Click the buttons in the Preview section to toggle the border on and off for the indicated sides.**
7. **In the Apply to list, click one of the following options:**
   - *Whole Document:* Applies the border to every page in the document.
   - *This Section:* Applies the border to every page in the current section.
   - *This Section - First Page Only:* Applies the border to the first page in the current section.
   - *This Section - All Except First Page:* Applies the border to every page in the current section except the first page.
8. **Click OK.**

   Word applies the page border as instructed.

# Setting the page background

In almost all cases, documents look their best and are easiest to read when you use dark-colored text on a light-colored background, with black on white being the ideal. However, special situations may arise where you prefer to shake things up and use, say, white text in a dark blue background, or some other effect. You can also add a *watermark*, semitransparent text or a washed-out picture that appears behind the document text. The next two sections show you how to create these custom page backgrounds.

## Adding a custom fill effect

If you just want to format the page background with a solid color, open the Design tab, in the Page Background group click Page Color, and then click the color you want in the palette that appears.

If a more elaborate fill effect is what you're looking for, follow these steps:

1. **On the Design tab, in the Page Background group, click Page Color and then click Fill Effects.**

   Word coughs up the Fill Effects dialog box.

2. **Click one of the following tabs and use its controls to set up the effect you want.**

   - *Gradient:* Create a gradient fill effect in which one color fades either into different shades of the same color (click One color) or into a different color (click Two colors and then click the colors).
   - *Texture:* Click a texture to use as the background.
   - *Pattern:* Cover the page background with a pattern that has a foreground and background color.
   - *Picture:* Cover the page background with a picture.

3. **Click OK.**

   Word applies the fill effect.

## Adding a custom watermark

Word comes with several predefined watermarks for the following text: CONFIDENTIAL, DO NOT COPY, DRAFT, SAMPLE, ASAP, and URGENT. To apply one of these watermarks to your document, open the Design tab, in the Page Background group click Watermark, and then click the watermark text and style you want.

You can also create a custom watermark that uses your own text as well as the font, size, and color you prefer. You can also choose a picture to use as a watermark, which Word displays with a washed-out effect.

Follow these steps to apply a custom watermark to your document:

1. **On the Design tab, in the Page Background group, click Watermark and then click Custom Watermark.**

   Word calmly displays the Printed Watermark dialog box.

2. **You have two watermark options:**

   - *Picture watermark:* Select this option to use an image as your watermark. Click Select Picture to choose the image, and then use the Scale list to choose how Word scales the image on the page.
   - *Text watermark:* Select this option to create a watermark using text. Use the Text combo box to either select a predefined message or to type your own. Use the Font, Size, Color, and Layout options to format the watermark.

3. **Click OK.**

   Word applies the custom watermark to your document.

# Corralling Text into Columns

If you're putting together a brochure, a newsletter, or any document where you want to mimic the layout of a newspaper or magazine, you probably want your text to appear in two or more columns. When you use columns, as the text in the first column reaches the bottom of the page, it continues at the top of the next column. It's only when the text reaches the bottom of the last column that it continues on the next page. Figure 6-6 shows a document laid out in two columns.

Follow these steps to lay out text in columns:

1. **Position the cursor according to the following guidelines:**

   - If your document has only one section and you want to use columns for the entire document, position the insertion point anywhere within the document.
   - If your document has multiple sections and you want to use columns for a single section, position the insertion point anywhere within that section.
   - If your document has multiple sections and you want to use columns for the entire document, select the entire document.

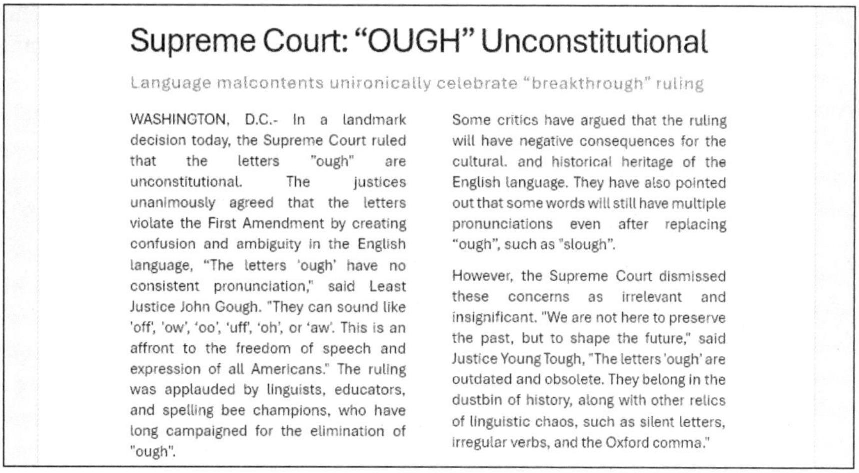

## Supreme Court: "OUGH" Unconstitutional

Language malcontents unironically celebrate "breakthrough" ruling

WASHINGTON, D.C.- In a landmark decision today, the Supreme Court ruled that the letters "ough" are unconstitutional. The justices unanimously agreed that the letters violate the First Amendment by creating confusion and ambiguity in the English language. "The letters 'ough' have no consistent pronunciation," said Least Justice John Gough. "They can sound like 'off', 'ow', 'oo', 'uff', 'oh', or 'aw'. This is an affront to the freedom of speech and expression of all Americans." The ruling was applauded by linguists, educators, and spelling bee champions, who have long campaigned for the elimination of "ough".

Some critics have argued that the ruling will have negative consequences for the cultural. and historical heritage of the English language. They have also pointed out that some words will still have multiple pronunciations even after replacing "ough", such as "slough".

However, the Supreme Court dismissed these concerns as irrelevant and insignificant. "We are not here to preserve the past, but to shape the future," said Justice Young Tough, "The letters 'ough' are outdated and obsolete. They belong in the dustbin of history, along with other relics of linguistic chaos, such as silent letters, irregular verbs, and the Oxford comma."

**FIGURE 6-6:** A document using a two-column layout.

2. **On the Layout tab, in the Page Setup group, click Columns.**

   Word displays a menu of column options.

3. **Click the column option you want to apply:**

   - *One:* Arranges the text in a single column (use this option to revert your text from columned to un-columned).
   - *Two:* Arranges the text into two columns.
   - *Three:* Arranges the text into three columns.
   - *Left:* Arranges the text into two columns, with a narrow left column and a wide right column.
   - *Right:* Arranges the text into two columns, with a narrow right column and a wide left column.

Word's Columns dialog box enables you to set up more advanced column settings:

- More than three columns (the max depends on the column widths, spacing, and the page orientation).
- Whether you want a vertical line separating each column.
- A width for each column.
- The amount of space between each column.
- Where you want Word to apply the columns. If you selected text in advance, then your choices are the selected text, the selected sections, or the whole document; if you positioned the cursor, then your choices are the current section, this point forward, or the whole document.

To work with these column options, choose Layout ➪ Columns ➪ More Columns to display the Columns dialog box, shown in Figure 6-7.

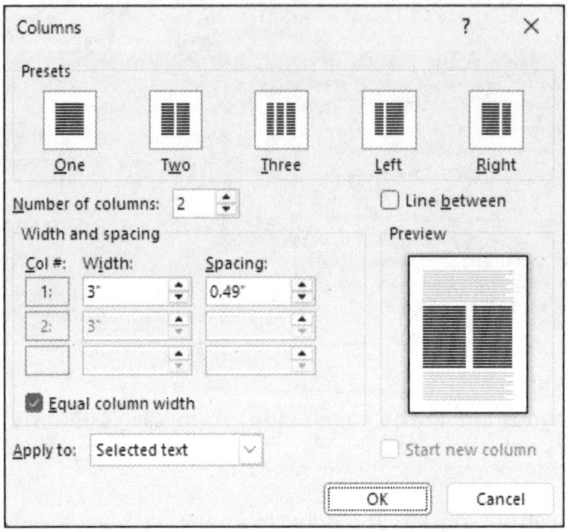


**FIGURE 6-7:** The Columns dialog box offers settings for more sophisticated columns.

# Laying Out Text in Linked Text Boxes

When you use columns (as I describe in the previous section, "Corralling Text into Columns"), the text flows from one column to the next, and from the last column on one page to the first column on the next. That's usually the narrative flow you want, but there might be times when you need the text to "jump" from one part of the document to another. For example, you might have several articles in a single document, and you want to show just the beginning of each article on the first page. To make life easier for your reader, including some kind of "jump text" along with each front-page article, such as "To continue reading, see page 5" is a good idea.

One way to do this would be to cut the first paragraph or two from each article and paste this text on your first page. That would probably work if you're no longer modifying the document, but what if you're still making changes to the text? What you need is some way for text to flow from the front-page portion of the article to the continuation later in the document.

You can't do this with columns, but you can do it with *linked text boxes*, which are two or more text box objects that you set up to allow text to flow from one text box to the next (thus creating what Word calls a *story*). Because the text boxes are separate objects (to learn how to work with them individually, refer to Book 1, Chapter 5), you can put them anywhere in your document (for example, one on the front page and one on page 5), and you can set up a link to the next text box in the chain. The next few sections provide you with the details.

## Linking two text boxes

Here are the steps to follow to create a link between two text boxes:

1. **On the Insert tab, in the Text group, click Text Box, and then click Draw Text Box.**
2. **Drag in your document to create the text box the size and shape you want.**
3. **Repeat steps 1 and 2 to create a second text box.**
4. **Click inside the first text box, right-click the border of the text box, and then click Create Text Box Link.**

   The mouse pointer changes to a pitcher.
5. **Click inside the second text box.**

   Word sets up the link between the two text boxes.

With the link in place, go ahead and start typing your text into the first text box. When the text reaches the bottom of the first text box, it flows into the top of the second text box.

REMEMBER

You're not stuck with using just two text boxes. Word lets you link up to 32 text , although in practice you'll rarely use more than a few. The best way to link three or more text boxes is to first create all your text boxes, and then create all the links. For the latter, link the first to the second, then link the second to the third, and so on. Once all that's done, then add your text using the first text box.

## Navigating linked text boxes

If you have a chain of text boxes throughout a document, navigating from one to another can be time-consuming. If you're near the bottom of one text box, you can hold down the right arrow key and Word automatically moves the insertion point into the next text box. Similarly, you can hold down the left arrow key near the top of a text box to move the cursor into the previous text box.

Fortunately, Word provides two much easier methods:

- **To move forward:** Right-click the border of any text box in the chain except the last one, and then click Next Text Box.
- **To move backward:** Right-click the border of any text box in the chain except the first one, and then click Previous Text Box.

## Creating a navigation link to the second text box

If the next text box in a story occurs later in the document, you don't want your readers to scroll through the document to continue reading. Instead, you should create a hyperlink at the end of the first text box that the reader can Ctrl+click to jump to the rest of the story.

WARNING

Only create the navigation link after you've finished inserting and editing all the text in the story. Otherwise, if you add more text before the hyperlink, the link text might flow into the next text box.

The first thing you need to do is set up a bookmark for the text box you want to jump to. Here are the steps to follow:

1. **Select the text box you want to hyperlink to.**
2. **On the Insert tab, in the Links group, click Bookmark.**

   Word offers up the Bookmark dialog box.
3. **Type a Bookmark name.**

   REMEMBER

   For bookmark names, the first character must be a letter and each subsequent characters can be a letter, a number, or an underscore (_). Spaces and other special characters aren't allowed in bookmark names.
4. **Click Add.**

   Word creates the bookmark.

Now you're ready to set up the hyperlink by following these steps:

1. **Position the cursor at the bottom of the first text box.**
2. **On the Insert tab, in the Links group, click the top half of the Link button.**

   Word introduces you to the Insert Hyperlink dialog box.

3. **In the Text to Display box, type the text you want the reader to click.**

4. **Click Place in This Document, click the bookmark for the second text box, and then click OK.**

   Word inserts the link to the bookmark.

# Trying Out More of Word's Page Setup Options

Word's options and features for setting up pages are legion, but few of us use them with any regularity. That's a shame because Word's page setup tools are often useful and quite easy to implement, once you get to know them. The next few sections take you through a few of Word's page setup features.

## Changing the page orientation

By default, page text runs across the short side of the page, and down the long side. This is called *portrait* orientation. Alternatively, you can configure the text to run across the long side of the page and down the short side, which is called *landscape* orientation.

You'd use the landscape orientation mostly when you have text or an image that's too wide to fit across the page in portrait orientation. If you're using letter-size paper and your margins are set to 0.75 inches, then you have only seven inches of usable space across the page. A wide image, a table with many columns, or a long line of programming code are just a few of the situations where this width might not be enough. If you switch to landscape, however, then the usable space grows to 9.5 inches, a substantial increase.

Follow these steps to change the page orientation:

1. **Position the insertion point according to the following guidelines:**
   - If your document has only one section and you want to change the page orientation for the entire document, position the insertion point anywhere within the document.
   - If your document has multiple sections and you want to change the page orientation for a single section, position the insertion point anywhere within that section.

- If your document has multiple sections and you want to change the page orientation for the entire document, select the entire document.

2. **On the Layout tab, in the Page Setup group, click Orientation.**
3. **Click either Portrait or Landscape.**

   Word changes the page orientation.

## Changing the paper size

Word assumes that you'll be printing your documents on standard letter-size paper, which is 8.5 inches by 11 inches. If you plan on using a different paper size, then you need to let Word know what you'll be using so that it can print the document correctly. This is also a section-by-section option, so you can set up different sections of your document to use different size paper.

However, getting the proper printout isn't the only reason for configuring Word to use a different page size. An old trick is to tell Word you're using a larger paper size than you actually are. Word will then print the page as if you're using the larger size, which with some experimentation means you can get Word to print right to (or pretty close to) the edge of a regular sheet of paper or an envelope.

Follow these steps to change the paper size:

1. **Position the insertion point according to the following guidelines:**
   - If your document has only one section and you want to change the paper size for the entire document, position the insertion point anywhere within the document.
   - If your document has multiple sections and you want to change the paper size for a single section, position the insertion point anywhere within that section.
   - If your document has multiple sections and you want to change the paper size for the entire document, select the entire document.
2. **On the Layout tab, in the Page Setup group, click Size.**

   Word displays a menu of paper sizes.
3. **Click the paper size you want.**

   Word changes the paper size.

If you want to specify a custom size, choose Layout ⇨ Size ⇨ More Paper Sizes to open the Page Setup dialog box with the Paper tab displayed (refer to Figure 6-8), and then use the Width and Height spin boxes to set the size you want.

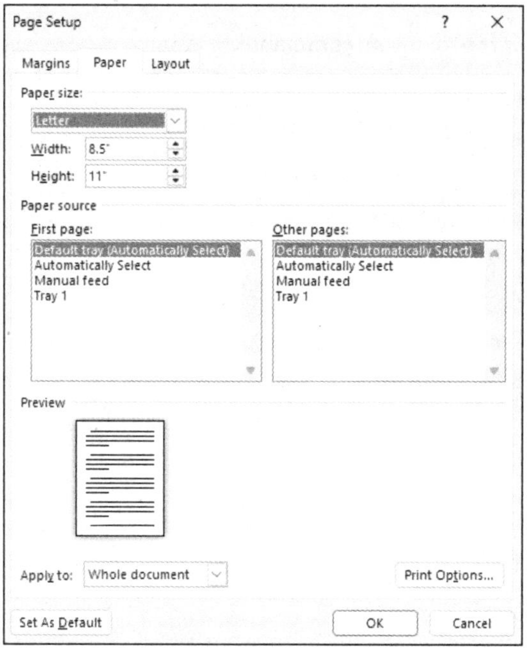


**FIGURE 6-8:** Use the Paper tab in the Page Setup dialog box to specify a custom paper size.



## Adding line numbers

Some documents require the lines to be numbered so that the reader (or writer) can more easily reference a particular line. Legal documents most often require line numbers, but they are also useful for programming code and literary analysis. You can also apply line numbers by section, so you can add them to some or all of a document.

Follow these steps to add line numbers:

1. **Position the insertion point according to the following guidelines:**
   - If your document has only one section and you want to turn on line numbers for the entire document, position the insertion point anywhere within the document.
   - If your document has multiple sections and you want to turn on line numbers for a single section, position the insertion point anywhere within that section.
   - If your document has multiple sections and you want to turn on line numbers for the entire document, select the entire document.
2. **On the Layout tab, in the Page Setup group, click Line Numbers.**

   Word displays a menu of line numbering commands.

3. **Click one of the following commands:**

- *None:* Turns off line numbers.
- *Continuous:* Turns on line numbers for the section or document and the line numbers don't restart with each new section or page.
- *Restart Each Page:* Turns on line numbers and resets the numbering to 1 at the beginning of each page.
- *Restart Each Section:* Turns on line numbers and resets the numbering to 1 at the beginning of each section.
- *Suppress for Current Section:* Hides line numbers for the current section. Line numbers in subsequent sections don't change.
- *Line Numbering Options:* Displays the Layout tab of the Page Setup dialog box. Click Line Numbers to display the Line Numbers dialog box, which enables you to select a starting line number, the value by which to increase each number, and other advanced options.

IN THIS CHAPTER

» Printing envelopes

» Printing labels

» Mail merging for form letters and bulk mailing

# Chapter 7

# Printing Envelopes and Labels

We live in an email and text world nowadays, meaning that most of our written communication is delivered electronically. However, that's not to say that hard copy messages are obsolete— — far from it. Many people still rely on the post office for the delivery of bills, bill payments, account statements, résumés, letters, and many other forms of correspondence.

If you still send things via the "snail mail" method, then you probably take care to ensure that what goes inside the envelope is accurate and easy to understand. That's good, but you should also apply the same level of meticulousness to what goes *outside* the envelope. Simply scrawling a name and address on the front might be quick, but it's not a good idea for two reasons. First, the post office or the recipient might misread the address and deliver the envelope to the wrong person or location. Second, if you're trying to impress the recipient (if you're sending a résumé and cover letter, for example), then a handwritten address isn't a good start because it looks unprofessional.

You can avoid both problems by creating envelopes and labels in Word. This ensures a neat, accurate address on the front of the envelope, and adding features such as your return address is easy. In this chapter you explore not only printing envelopes and labels but also bulk mailings with Word's mail merge feature.

# Addressing an Envelope

Printing a nice, neat delivery address on an envelope isn't the easiest Word task, but I guarantee that it won't tax your brain all that much. (Later in this chapter, "Churning Out Letters, Envelopes, and Labels for Mass Mailings" explains how to print more than one envelope at a time). To prove it, here are the steps to print a delivery address (and, optionally, a return address) on an envelope:

1. **On the Mailings tab, in the Create group, click the Envelopes button.**

   The Envelopes tab of the Envelopes and Labels dialog box appears, as shown in Figure 7-1.

**FIGURE 7-1:** Printing on an envelope.

2. **If Word didn't pick up the delivery address automatically from the document, specify the delivery address using one of the following methods:**
   - If you copied the address from another program, click inside the Delivery address box and press Ctrl+V.

   - If the recipient is an Outlook contact, click the Insert Address button (shown in the margin) above the Delivery address box, click the contact, and then click OK.
   - Type the address in the Delivery address box.

3. **(Optional) Specify a return address using one of the following methods:**

   - If you have an Outlook contact for yourself, click the Insert Address button above the Return address box, click your contact, and then click OK.
   - Type the address in the Return address box.

   If Word entered a return address automatically, but you don't want to include a return address on this envelope, select the Omit check box.

4. **Click the Options button, and in the Envelope Options dialog box, tell Word what size your envelopes are and how your printer handles envelopes.**

   Tell Word about your envelopes on the Envelope Options and Printing Options tabs, and click OK:

   - **Envelope Options tab:** Choose an envelope size, a font for printing the delivery and return address, and a position for the addresses. The sample envelope in the Preview shows you what your position settings do when the envelope is printed.
   - **Printing Options tab:** Choose a technique for feeding envelopes to your printer. Consult the manual that came with your printer, select one of the Feed Method boxes, click the Face Up or Face Down option button, and open the Feed From drop-down list to tell Word which printer tray the envelope is in or how you intend to stick the envelope in your printer.

5. **Print the envelope using one of the following techniques:**

   - *Print the envelope now:* First make sure your printer is up and running with the appropriate envelope loaded. When it's ready, click the Print button.
   - *Print the envelope along with the document later:* Insert the envelope into the document by clicking the Add to Document button. Word adds a new page to the top of the document (by inserting a hard page break) and displays the return and mailing addresses. Later, when you're ready to print, you can choose File ➪ Print to send both the envelope and the document to the printer.

   If you specified a return address in Step 4 and this was the first time you've done that, Word displays a dialog box asking whether you want to save the address as the default return address.

6. **Click Yes, if you do. Otherwise, click No.**

# Addressing a Label (or a Page of Labels)

Instead of printing an address directly on an envelope, you can instead place the address on a label and then stick the label on the envelope. This is handy if you're using envelopes that are too big to fit in your printer or if you're using padded envelopes that could cause a printer to jam. Of course, labels have many other uses: name tags, file folders, and so on. And if you need multiple copies of the same label (such as your return address), you can print an entire sheet of labels. (Later in this chapter, "Churning Out Letters, Envelopes, and Labels for Mass Mailings" explains how to print multiple labels as part of a mass mailing.)

Before you start printing, however, take note of the label's brand name and product number because Word will ask you for this info during the label-printing process.

Follow these steps to print a single label or a sheet full of identical labels:

1. **On the Mailings tab, in the Create group, click the Labels button.**

   The Envelopes and Labels dialog box appears and displays the Labels tab, as shown in Figure 7-2.

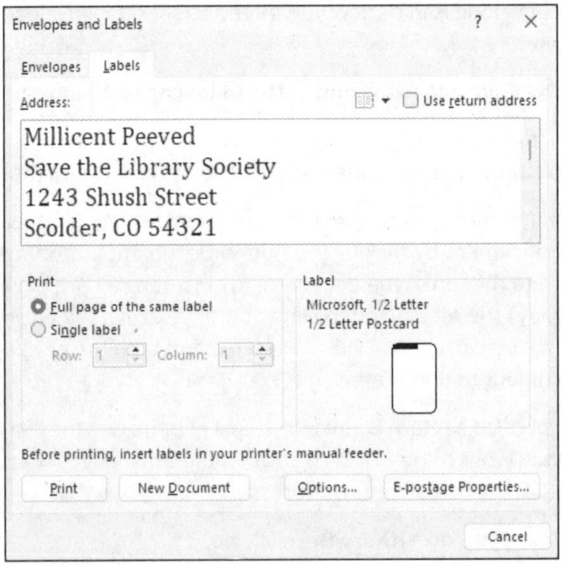


**FIGURE 7-2:** Printing labels.

2. **If Word didn't pick up the delivery address automatically from the document, specify the delivery address using one of the following methods:**

   - If you copied the address from another program, click inside the Address box and press Ctrl+V.

   - If the recipient is an Outlook contact, click the Insert Address button (shown in the margin) above the Address box, click the contact, and then click OK.
   - Type the address in the Address box.
   - If you want to create labels for your own address, select the Use Return Address check box and Word should enter your address in the Address box. If not, you'll need to enter the address manually.

3. **The Print group gives you the following options:**

   - *Full Page of the Same Label:* Select this option to have Word fill the page with multiple copies of a single label.
   - *Single label:* Select this option to print only one label. Use the Row and Column spin boxes to specify where you want the label printed.

4. **The Label group shows the currently selected label. To change the label, click Options and then use the Label Options dialog box to click the label you're using. Note that you can also use this dialog box to select the printer type and label tray. Click OK when you're done.**

   If none of the listed labels match your label's dimensions, you can customize an existing label type to the size you need:

   **a.** In the Product number list, click a label that has dimensions that are similar to the label size you need.

   **b.** Click New Label to open the Label Details dialog box.

   **c.** In the Label name text box, type a name for your new label.

   **d.** Use the spin boxes to set the margins and dimensions of the label, as well as the number of labels across and down.

   **e.** Click OK to return to the Label Options dialog box.

   **f.** Make sure your custom label is selected in the Product number list and then click OK to return to the Labels tab.

5. **Print or create the labels:**

   - *Print the label or labels now:* Make sure your printer is running and the labels are inserted, then click Print.

- *Print the label or labels along with the document later:* Insert the labels into the document by clicking New Document. Word creates a new document for the labels. Later, when you're ready to print, you can choose File ➪ Print to send both the labels and the document to the printer.

# Churning Out Letters, Envelopes, and Labels for Mass Mailings

If you have form letters, envelopes, or letters that you need to send out to a bunch of people, don't bother personalizing each item by hand. Instead, get Word to do all the hard work by combining the form letter, envelope, or label document with information from a data source. The *data source* is the item that contains the names and addresses of the mailing recipients. A Word table, an Excel worksheet, a Microsoft Access database table or query, or an Outlook contacts list can serve as the data source.

Word calls this process *merging.* During the merge, names and addresses from the data source are plugged into the appropriate places in the form letter, envelope, or label document. When the merge is complete, you can either save the form letters, envelopes, or labels in a new file or start printing right away.

The following pages explain how to prepare the data source and merge addresses from the data source with a document to create the mailing. Then you discover how to print the form letters, labels, or envelopes after you've generated them.

TIP

Word offers a mail-merge wizard (*wizard* is Microsoft's name for a step-by-step procedure you can follow to accomplish a task). If you want to try your hand at using the wizard to complete a mail merge, go to the Mailings tab, click the Start Mail Merge button, and choose Step by Step Mail Merge Wizard on the drop-down list. Good luck to you!

## Preparing the data source

If you intend to get addresses for your form letters, labels, or envelopes from an Outlook contact list on your computer, you're ready to go. However, if you haven't entered the addresses yet or you are keeping them in a Word table, Excel worksheet, Access database table, or Access query, make sure that the data is in good working order:

» **Word table:** Save the table in its own file and enter a descriptive heading at the top of each column. In the merge, when you tell Word where to plug in address and other data, you'll do so by choosing a heading name from the top of a column. In Figure 7-3, for example, the column headings are Contact Name, Company Name, Address, and so on. (Book 2, Chapter 4 explains how to construct a Word table.)

| Contact Name | Company Name | Address | City | Region | Country | Postal Code |
|---|---|---|---|---|---|---|
| **Alejandra Camino** | Romero y tomillo | Gran Vía, 1 | Madrid | | Spain | 28001 |
| **Alexander Feuer** | Morgenstern Gesundkost | Heerstr. 22 | Leipzig | | Germany | 04179 |
| **Ana Trujillo** | Ana Trujillo Emparedados y helados | Avda. de la Constitución 2222 | México D.F. | | Mexico | 05021 |
| **Anabela Domingues** | Tradição Hipermercados | Av. Inês de Castro, 414 | São Paulo | SP | Brazil | 05634-030 |
| **André Fonseca** | Gourmet Lanchonetes | Av. Brasil, 442 | Campinas | SP | Brazil | 04876-786 |
| **Ann Devon** | Eastern Connection | 35 King George | London | | UK | WX3 6FW |
| **Annette Roulet** | La maison d'Asie | 1 rue Alsace-Lorraine | Toulouse | | France | 31000 |
| **Antonio Moreno** | Antonio Moreno Taquería | Mataderos 2312 | México D.F. | | Mexico | 05023 |
| **Aria Cruz** | Familia Arquibaldo | Rua Orós, 92 | São Paulo | SP | Brazil | 05442-030 |
| **Art Braunschweiger** | Split Rail Beer & Ale | P.O. Box 555 | Lander | WY | USA | 82520 |
| **Bernardo Batista** | Que Delícia | Rua da Panificadora, 12 | Rio de Janeiro | RJ | Brazil | 02389-673 |

**FIGURE 7-3:** You can use a Word table as a data source for a mail merge.

» **Excel worksheet:** Arrange the worksheet in table format with a descriptive heading atop each column and no blank cells in any columns. Word will plug in addresses and other data by choosing heading names.

» **Access database table or query:** Make sure that you know the field names in the database table or query where you keep the addresses. During the merge, you will be asked for field names. By the way, if you're comfortable in Access, query a database table (as I explain in Book 6, Chapter 3) for the records you will need. As you find out shortly, Word offers a technique for choosing only the records you want for your form letters, labels, or envelopes. However, by querying first in Access, you can start off with the records you need and spare yourself from having to choose records in Word.

A Word table, Excel worksheet, or Access table or query can include more than address information. Don't worry about deleting information that isn't required for your form letters, labels, and envelopes. As you find out soon, you get to decide which information to take from the Word table, Excel worksheet, or Access table or query.

## Merging the document with the data source

After you prepare the data source, the next step in generating form letters, labels, or envelopes for a mass mailing is to merge the document with the data source. Follow these general steps to do so:

1. **Create or open a document.**
   - **Form letters:** Either create a new document and write your form letter, being careful to leave out the parts of the letter that differ from recipient to recipient, or open a letter you have already written and delete the addressee's name, the address, and other parts of the letter that are particular to each recipient.
   - **Envelopes or labels:** Create a new document.
2. **On the Mailings tab, in the Start Mail Merge group, click the Start Mail Merge button.**
3. **On the drop-down list, click the type of mailing: Letters, Envelopes, or Labels.**
4. **Prepare the groundwork for creating form letters, envelopes, or labels for a mass mailing.**

   What you do next depends on what kind of mass mailing you want to attempt:

   - **Form letters:** You're ready to go. The text of your form letter already appears onscreen if you followed the directions for creating and writing it in Step 1.
   - **Envelopes:** The Envelope Options dialog box shows up, where, on the Envelope Options and Printing Options tabs, you tell Word what size envelope you will print on. Check out "Addressing an Envelope," earlier in this chapter, for instructions about filling out these tabs (refer to Step 4). A sample envelope appears onscreen.
   - **Labels:** The Label Options dialog box jogs onto the screen, where you tell Word what size labels to print on. Refer to "Addressing a Label (or a Page of Labels)," earlier in this chapter, if you need advice for filling out this dialog box (refer to Steps 4 and 5).
5. **On the Mailings tab, in the Start Mail Merge group, click the Select Recipients button and choose an option on the drop-down list to direct Word to your data source.**

   Earlier in this chapter, "Preparing the data source" explains what a data source is. Your options are as follows:

   - **Addresses from a Word table, Excel worksheet, Access database table, or Access query:** Click Use an Existing List. The Select Data Source dialog box materializes. Locate the Word file, the Excel worksheet, or the Access database, select it, and click Open.

If you select an Excel worksheet or Access database, the Select Table dialog box shows up for work. Select the worksheet, table, or query you want and click the OK button.

- **Addresses from Microsoft Outlook:** Click the Choose from Outlook Contacts option (Outlook must be your default email program to get addresses from Outlook). Then, in the Select Contacts dialog box, choose Contacts and click OK. The Mail Merge Recipients dialog box appears (skip to Step 7).

6. **Click the Edit Recipient List button.**

The Mail Merge Recipients dialog box appears, as shown in Figure 7-4.

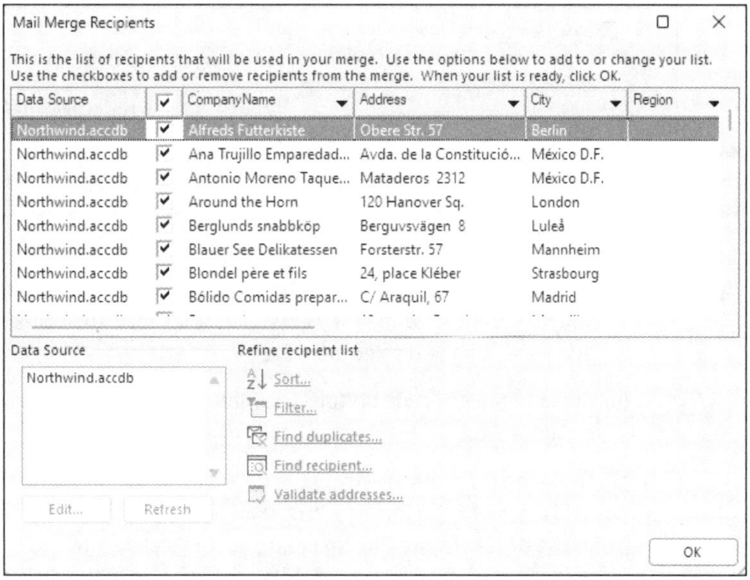


**FIGURE 7-4:** Choosing who gets mail.

7. **In the Mail Merge Recipients dialog box, select the names of people to whom you will send mail; then click OK.**

To select recipients' names, select or deselect the boxes to the right of the Data Source column.

8. **Enter the address block on your form letters, envelopes, or labels.**

The *address block* is the address, including the recipient's name, company, title, street address, city, and ZIP code. If you're creating form letters, click in the sample letter where the address block will go. If you're printing on envelopes, click in the middle of the envelope where the delivery address will go. Then follow these steps to enter the address block:

**(a)** On the Mailings tab, in the Write & Insert Fields group, click the Address Block button. The Insert Address Block dialog box appears, as shown in Figure 7-5.

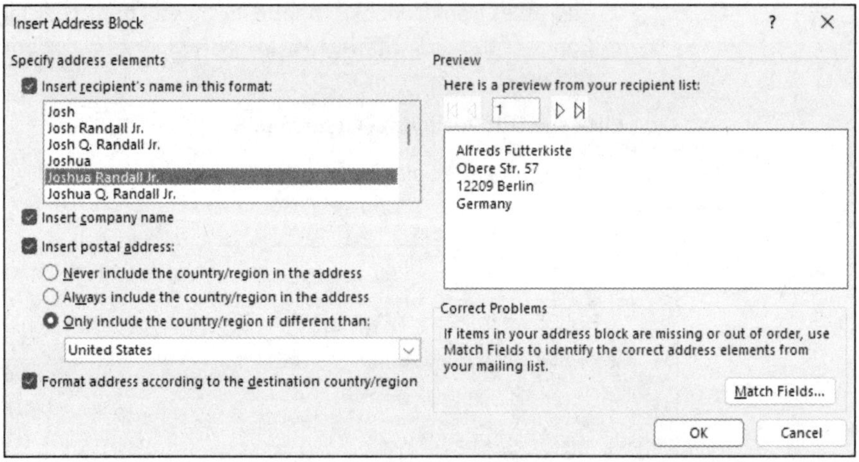


**FIGURE 7-5:** Creating the address block.

**(b)** Choose a format for entering the recipient's name in the address block. As you do so, examine the Preview window; it shows the actual names and addresses that you selected in Step 7.

**(c)** Click the Match Fields button. The Match Fields dialog box slides in, shown in Figure 7-6.

**(d)** Using the drop-down lists on the right side of the dialog box, match the fields in your data source with the address block fields on the left side of the dialog box. In Figure 7-6, for example, the CompanyName field is the equivalent of the Company field on the left side of the dialog box, so CompanyName is chosen from the drop-down list to match Company.

**(e)** Click OK in the Match Fields dialog box and the Insert Address Block dialog box. The <<AddressBlock>> field appears in the document where the address will go. Later, when you merge your document with the data source, real data will appear where the field is now. Think of a field as a kind of placeholder for data.

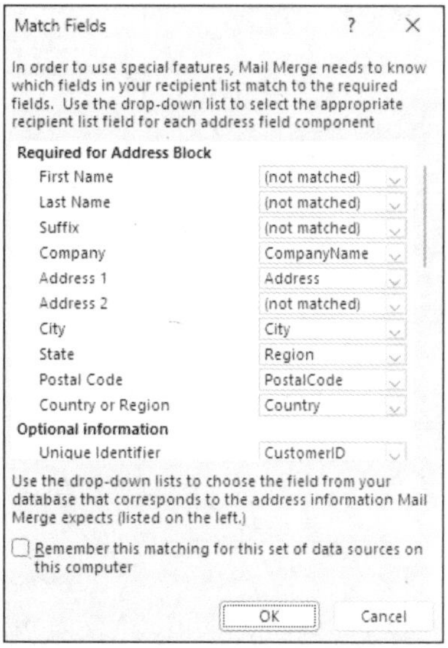


**FIGURE 7-6:** Linking the address block with address fields.

9. **On the Mailings tab, in the Preview Results group, click the Preview Results button to display real data rather than fields.**

   Now you can determine whether you entered the address block correctly. If you didn't enter it correctly, click the Match Fields button (it's in the Write & Insert Fields group) to open the Match Fields dialog box and make new choices.

10. **Put the finishing touches on your form letters, labels, or envelopes:**

    - **Form letters:** Click where the salutation ("Dear John") will go and then, on the Mailings tab, in the Write & Insert Fields group, click the Greeting Line button. The Insert Greeting Line dialog box pops up, shown in Figure 7-7. Make choices in this dialog box to determine how the letters' salutations will read.

      The body of your form letter may well include other variable information such as names and birthdays. To enter that stuff, click in your letter where variable information goes then, on the Mailings tab, in the Write & Insert Fields group, click the Insert Merge Field button. The Insert Merge Field dialog box appears and lists fields from the data source. Select a field, click the Insert button, and click the Close button. (You can also open the drop-down list on the Insert Merge Field button and choose a field from the data source.)

      If you're editing your form letter and you want to know precisely where the variable information you entered is located, click the Highlight Merge Fields button. The variable information is highlighted in your document.

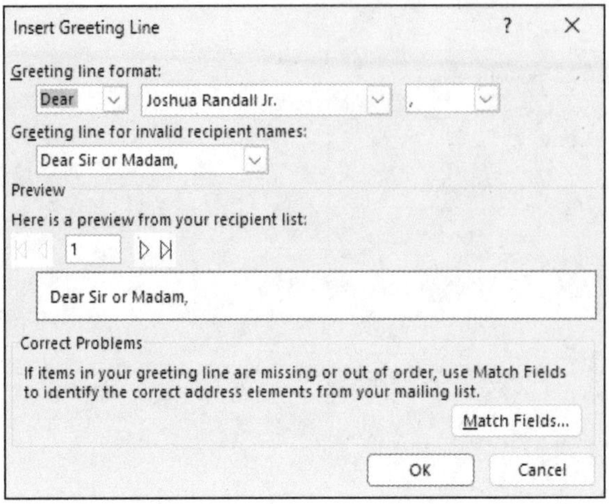


**FIGURE 7-7:** Entering the greeting.

- **Envelopes:** To position the address block correctly, you may have to press the Enter key and tab keys to move it to the center of envelope. If you don't like the fonts or font sizes on the envelope, select an address, go to the Home tab, and change fonts and font sizes there.

  To enter a return address, click in the upper-left corner of the envelope and enter it there.

- **Labels:** Click the Update Labels button to enter all recipients' labels in the sample document.

11. **Make sure the Preview Results button is selected and then, on the Mailings tab, in the Preview Results group, use the following buttons to navigate the recipients to check whether you've entered information correctly:**

- *First Record:* Navigates to the first recipient.
- *Previous Record:* Navigates to the previous recipient.
- *Next Record:* Navigates to the next recipient.
- *Last Record:* Navigates to the final recipient.

You can also type a record number in the text box and press Enter.

The items that appear onscreen are the same form letters, envelopes, or labels you'll get when you've finished printing.

If an item is incorrect, open the data source and correct it there. When you save the data source, the correction is made in the sample document.

At last — you're ready to print the form letters, envelopes, or labels. Take a deep breath and keep reading.

## Printing form letters, envelopes, and labels

After you have gone to the trouble to prepare the data file and merge it with the document, you're ready to print your form letters, envelopes, or labels. Start by loading paper, envelopes, or sheets of labels in your printer:

- **Form letters:** Form letters are easiest to print. Just put the paper in the printer.
- **Envelopes:** Not all printers are capable of printing envelopes one after the other. Sorry, but you probably have to consult the dreary manual that came with your printer to find out the correct way to load envelopes.
- **Labels:** Load the label sheets in your printer. Again, you might want to consult the printer manual to ensure you have the labels facing the right way.

Now, to print the form letters, envelopes, or labels, save the material in a new document or send it straight to the printer:

- **Saving in a new document:** On the Mailings tab, in the Finish group, click the Finish & Merge button and then click Edit Individual Documents (or press Alt+Shift+N). The Merge to New Document dialog box makes an appearance. Click OK. After Word creates the document, save it and print it. You can go into the document and make changes here and there before printing. In form letters, for example, you can write a sentence or two in different letters to personalize them.
- **Printing right away:** On the Mailings tab, in the Finish group, click the Finish & Merge button and then click Print Documents (or press Alt+Shift+M) to print the form letters, envelopes, or labels without saving them in a document. Click OK in the Merge to Printer dialog box and then negotiate the Print dialog box.

TIP

Save the form letters, labels, or envelopes in a new document if you intend to print them at a future date or ink is running low on your printer and you may have to print in two or more batches. Saving in a new document permits you to generate the mass mailing without having to start all over again with the merge process and all its tedium.

IN THIS CHAPTER

» Organizing your document with Outline view

» Going pro with everything from footnotes and captions to citations and bibliographies

» Making navigation a snap with a table of contents, a table of figures, and an index

Chapter 8

# Advanced (But Useful) Document Design

If you want to take your documents to a higher level, Word certainly has powerful tools that can help you get there. However, as any carpenter or cook will tell you, powerful tools alone are not enough to ensure a good result. You have to know how to wield those tools, of course, but you also need to know *why* you want to use those tools. In other words, when you use a tool, you should have some sort of objective in mind.

One very useful objective is to ensure your document presents its information in a manner that's both logical and consistent. Another laudable goal is to create a document that has high-quality, trustworthy information. A third goal is a document that provides features that make it easy for the reader to determine what's in the document and to find that specific information.

The Word features you read about in this chapter can help you realize all of these goals (and many others). An outline helps you build a document with a logical, consistent structure. The judicious use of footnotes, endnotes, and citations, and the addition of a comprehensive bibliography ensure others treat your information as trustworthy. And inserting a table of contents, table of figures, and a high-quality index can help readers know what's in your document and find the information they need.

# Keeping a Document Organized with an Outline

Most documents have titles, headings, and subheadings that determine the underlying organizational structure of the document. An outline is a summary of this structure that shows how the document is organized. If certain parts of the document look out of place or in the wrong order, you can use the outline structure to quickly reorganize the document.

Note that in Word you don't "create" an outline. Instead, the outline builds itself naturally out of the document's Heading styles — Heading 1 through Heading 9. If you don't use these styles, you can still work with an outline by defining the appropriate outline levels for your own styles.

## Switching to Outline view

To display and work with your document's outline, on the View tab, in the Views group, click Outline. Word changes the document view as follows:

- Word hides graphics, headers, footers, page breaks, page borders, and page backgrounds.

- For each paragraph formatted with a Heading style (as well as the Title and Subtitle styles), Word displays the Expand/Collapse icon (shown in the margin) to the left of the paragraph.
- Title and Heading 1 paragraphs are displayed flush with the left margin, and lower-level headings are displayed indented from the left margin (with Heading 3 indented further than Heading 2, Heading 4 indented further than Heading 3, and so on).
- Each heading is assigned a level number in the outline, and the level number corresponds to the Heading style number: Heading 1 is Level 1, Heading 2 is Level 2, and so on. (For the record, Title is also Level 1 and Subtitle is also Level 2.)
- Non-heading paragraphs — which Word labels as Body Text — are displayed with a bullet to the left of the paragraph.

Figure 8-1 shows a document in Print Layout view, and Figure 8-2 shows the same document in Outline view. Note that, in Outline view, Word also displays the style area pane to the left of the document, which tells you the style applied to each paragraph.

**TIP**

You can control the width of the style area pane by choosing File ➪ Options, clicking Advanced, then, in the Display group, typing a width in the Style Area Pane Width in Draft and Outline Views text box. Click OK to make it so.

Word also adds the Outlining tab to the Ribbon, as shown in Figure 8-2. You use the controls on this tab to work with your outline, as I discuss in the next few sections.

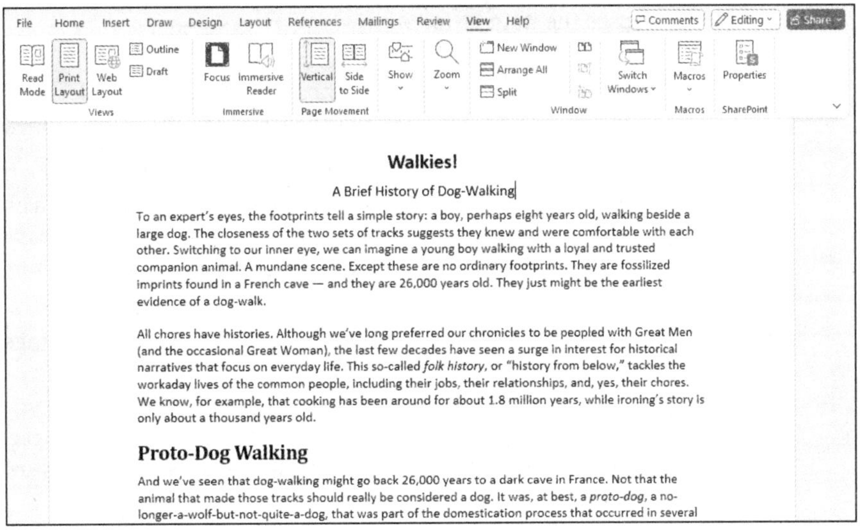


**FIGURE 8-1:** A document in Print Layout view.

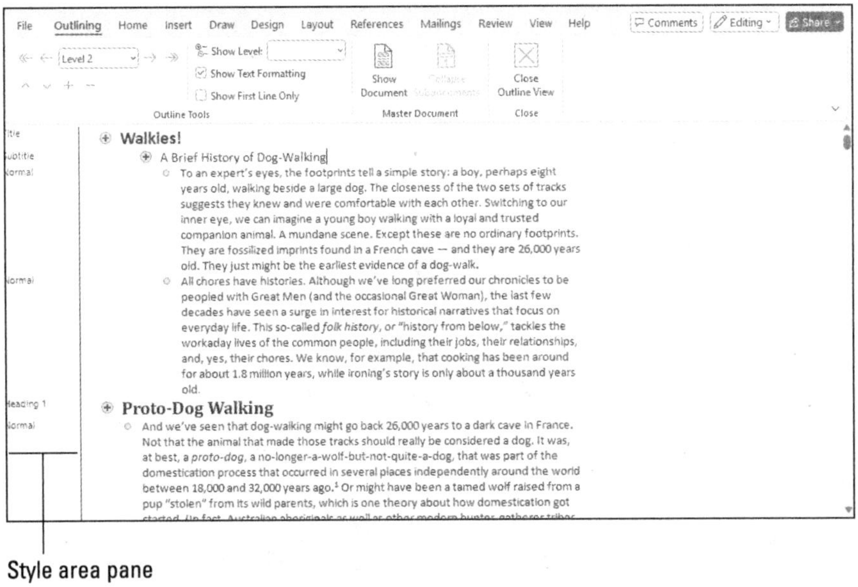


**FIGURE 8-2:** The same document in Outline view.

## Collapsing and expanding outline levels

You'll most often use an outline to get an overall view of your document structure. The initial outline view that shows all the headings and body text isn't much good for that, so you need to *collapse* some or all of the outline items to hide the body text and some or all of their subheadings.

To collapse an outline level, position the cursor inside the level and then choose Outlining ⇨ Collapse (shown in the margin), or press Alt+_ (underscore). Word collapses the item as follows:

- The first time you run the Collapse command Word hides all the body text within the level, including the body text of all the item's subheadings.
- Each subsequent time you run the Collapse command, Word hides the lowest level within the item. For example, if a Heading 1 item contains Heading 2 and Heading 3 subheadings, the second Collapse command hides the Heading 3 items, and the third Collapse command hides the Heading 2 items.

TIP

If you want to hide all of an item's body text and subheadings, double-click the item's Expand/Collapse (+/-) icon.

Figure 8-3 shows an outline with all the body text collapsed. Viewing only a document's headings is a great way to get a feel for the overall structure of the document.

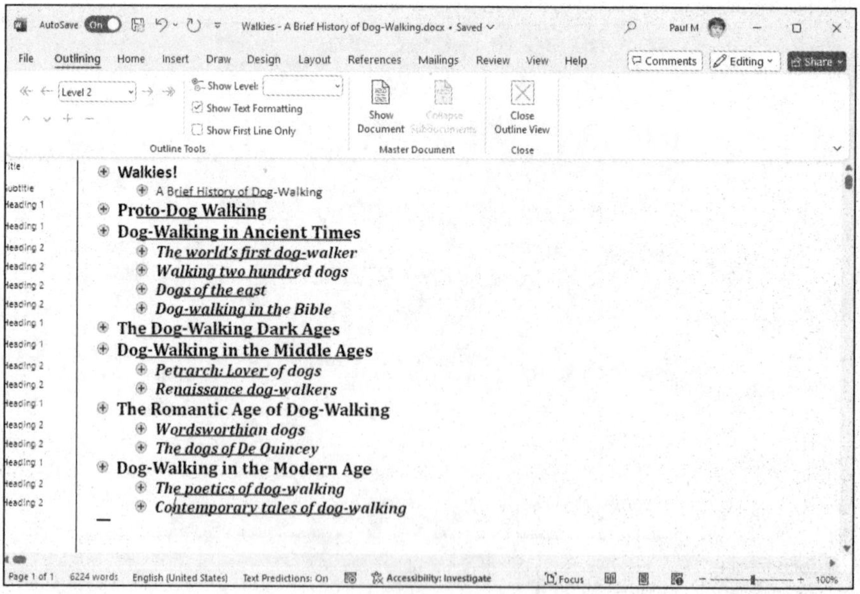


**FIGURE 8-3:** An outline collapsed to show just the document's headings.

To expand an outline level, position the cursor inside the level and then choose Outlining ⇨ Expand (shown in the margin), or press Alt++ (plus). Word expands the item's subheadings and body text in the opposite order that it collapses them.

## Changing the number of levels displayed

If you're working with a large document that has many levels of subheadings, viewing or working with the lowest levels may not be practical. For example, when examining the soundness of a document's structure, you really only have to display the first two or three levels and you can ignore anything lower.

One way to hide the lowest levels in a document's outline is to position the cursor in the highest-level item and then collapse the item until the levels you don't need are hidden.

However, this method isn't practical if you have a number of items at the highest level. A much faster solution in this case is to use the Outlining tab's Show Level list to click the highest level you want to display in the outline. For example, if you click Level 3, Word automatically collapses the outline to show just the Heading 1, Heading 2, and Heading 3 items.

## Promoting and demoting outline items

Probably the most common problem associated with document structure is a paragraph with the wrong heading style. For example, if a paragraph is supposed to be a subheading of a Heading 2 item, then the paragraph should be styled as Heading 3. Anything else — such as Heading 2 or Heading 4 — is incorrect and results in an improper document structure.

Unless you use wildly different formatting for each heading style, this kind of problem is very hard to notice when you're working in any of Word's regular views. However, it's just the kind of thing that Outline view specializes in, because an item with the wrong heading style will stick out (in some cases literally) from the surrounding headings.

Not only that, but Outline view also makes fixing the problem very easy by enabling you to quickly *promote* or *demote* items. Promoting an item means moving it to a higher outline level (for example, Level 4 to Level 3); demoting an item means moving it to a lower outline level (for example, Level 2 to Level 3). Note that in both cases Word also changes the paragraph's heading style (for example, a paragraph promoted or demoted to Level 3 will now use the Heading 3 style).

Use the Outlining tab tools summarized in Table 8-1 to promote and demote outline items.

**TABLE 8-1 Word's Outline Promoting and Demoting Tools**

| Click | To |
|---|---|
|  | Promote the current item to Heading 1 |
|  | Promote the current item one level (you can also press Alt+Shift+left arrow) |
| Level 1 | Assign a specific outline level to the current item |
|  | Demote the current item one level (you can also press Alt+Shift+right arrow) |
|  | Demote the current item to Body Text |

## Rearranging outline items

After incorrect heading styles, probably the next most common problem with document structure is a heading that appears in the wrong place. Almost all documents have a proper flow where the information is presented to the reader in a logical sequence. For example, information presented early in the document shouldn't rely on information presented later in the document. Similarly, readers often have an easier time understanding a document when it goes from the general to the specific, where broader concepts appear at the beginning and subsequent text expands on each concept with more detailed information.

Again, the flow of a document's information is often hard to decipher in the regular views, but the Outline view makes it easy to grasp the flow of concepts — expressed as the document's headings — and to determine whether each one follows logically from what has come before. As a bonus the Outlining tab has two tools that enable you to move items up or down in the document:

» Choose Outlining ⇨ Move Up (shown in the margin) or press Alt+Shift+up arrow to move the current item up one item in the outline.

» Choose Outlining ⇨ Move Down (shown in the margin) or press Alt+Shift+down arrow to move the current item down one item in the outline.

WARNING

A collapsed outline item "contains" all of its body text and subheadings, so if you delete the outline item, you also delete everything contained in the item. For this reason, deleting document text while using Outline view is generally not a good idea.

## Defining outline levels for custom styles

Besides the Title and Subtitle styles, Word's default outlines are based on the Heading 1 through Heading 9 styles, which correspond to outline levels 1 through 9. However, what if your documents don't use the Heading styles? For example, you may have to follow corporate style guidelines and templates that dictate other styles for titles, subtitles, headings, and subheadings.

In this case, you can still use the Outline view, but first you must modify your custom heading styles to assign each one the corresponding outline level. Here are the steps to follow:

1. **In Word's Home tab, click the Styles group's dialog box launcher (shown in the margin).**

   Word displays the Styles pane.

2. **Right-click the style you want to work with and then click Modify.**

   The Modify Style dialog box shows up.

3. **Click Format and then click Paragraph.**

   The Paragraph dialog box drops in.

4. **Use the Outline Level list to click the outline level you want to associate with the style.**
5. **Click OK to return to the Modify Style dialog box.**
6. **Click OK.**
7. **Repeat steps 2 through 6 for each of the other heading styles you want to assign an outline level.**

# The Bird's-Eye View: Creating a Table of Contents

As a book reader, you need no introduction to the idea of a table of contents (TOC). In fact, if you're like most savvy computer book buyers, you probably take a good long look at a book's TOC before deciding whether to purchase it.

However, you may not be as familiar with TOCs as they apply to Word documents. That's not surprising if you normally deal only with documents that are just a few pages long. However, when a document gets to be 10 or 20 pages long with multiple headings and subheadings, putting a TOC at or near the beginning of the document is a good idea for the following reasons:

- The TOC gives the reader a good sense of the overall structure of the document.
- You can include page numbers in the TOC, which enables the reader of a document printout to easily find a particular section.
- You can set up the TOC entries as hyperlinks to the corresponding sections within the document, so your readers are always just a Ctrl+click away from any section.

Like the items that appear in Outline view, Word also generates the entries that comprise a TOC from a document's Heading styles. (Although, as I show a bit later in the "Defining TOC levels for custom styles" section, you can also create a TOC from any other set of styles.) This concept makes sense because a TOC is, by definition, a listing of the main headings in a document, as they appear within that document.

The next few sections show you how to create and work with TOCs in Word.

## Creating a predefined TOC

The easiest way to generate a TOC is to use one of Word's predefined TOC styles. Here are the steps to follow:

1. **Position the cursor according to the following guidelines:**
   - If you want the TOC to be the first page of the document, move the cursor to the beginning of the document.
   - If you want the TOC on a separate page within the document, create a blank page (choose Insert ➪ Blank Page) where you want the TOC to appear and move the cursor to the top of that blank page.
   - If you want the TOC within the existing document text, move the cursor to the place where you want the TOC to appear.
2. **Choose References ➪ Table of Contents.**

   Word displays a gallery of its predefined TOCs. There's not much of a selection here, admittedly. Both the Automatic Table 1 and Automatic Table 2 templates generate TOCs from the first three heading levels; the only difference is that the former uses the title "Contents" while the latter uses the title "Table of Contents".

**3. Click the TOC template you prefer.**

Word inserts the predefined TOC. Figure 8-4 shows an example.

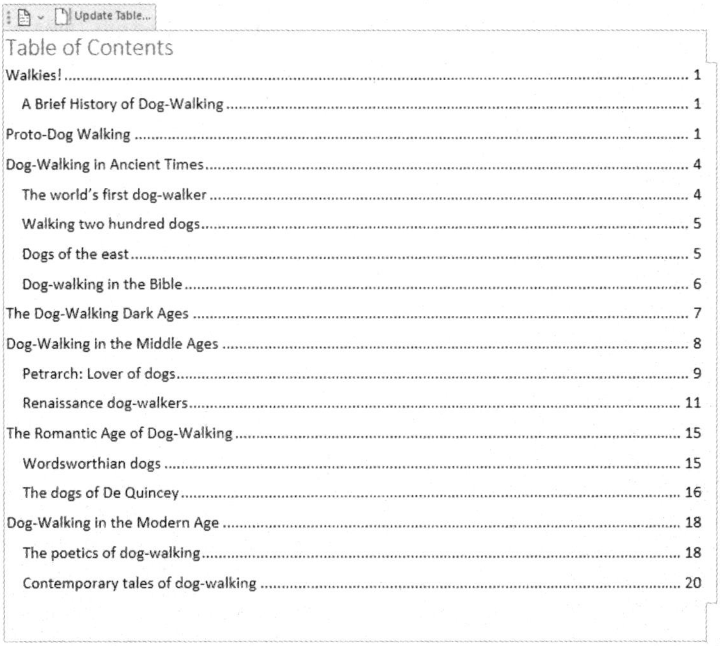
Update Table...

Table of Contents

Walkies! ........ 1

A Brief History of Dog-Walking ........ 1

Proto-Dog Walking ........ 1

Dog-Walking in Ancient Times ........ 4

The world's first dog-walker ........ 4

Walking two hundred dogs ........ 5

Dogs of the east ........ 5

Dog-walking in the Bible ........ 6

The Dog-Walking Dark Ages ........ 7

Dog-Walking in the Middle Ages ........ 8

Petrarch: Lover of dogs ........ 9

Renaissance dog-walkers ........ 11

The Romantic Age of Dog-Walking ........ 15

Wordsworthian dogs ........ 15

The dogs of De Quincey ........ 16

Dog-Walking in the Modern Age ........ 18

The poetics of dog-walking ........ 18

Contemporary tales of dog-walking ........ 20

**FIGURE 8-4:** One of Word's predefined TOC styles.

## Creating a custom TOC

The predefined TOCs all have the following characteristics:

- Right-aligned page numbers.
- Headings and page numbers separated by dot leaders.
- Entries formatted as hyperlinks (Ctrl+click any entry to jump to that section within the document).
- A maximum of three heading levels. That is, the TOC includes Heading 1, Heading 2, and Heading 3 items, but not Heading 4 and below.

There's a good chance that you may not want one or more of these characteristics in your TOC. For example, you probably don't want page numbers if you're using the TOC as a simple record of the document's headings. As another example, if you have a complex document that uses five or six heading levels, then you may want a detailed TOC that includes every heading.

To create a custom TOC, you need to use the Table of Contents dialog box to configure the TOC from scratch. Here are the steps to follow:

1. **Position the cursor where you want the TOC to appear.**
2. **Choose References ⇨ Table of Contents ⇨ Custom Table of Contents.**

   Word coaxes the Table of Contents dialog box onto the screen, as shown in Figure 8-5.

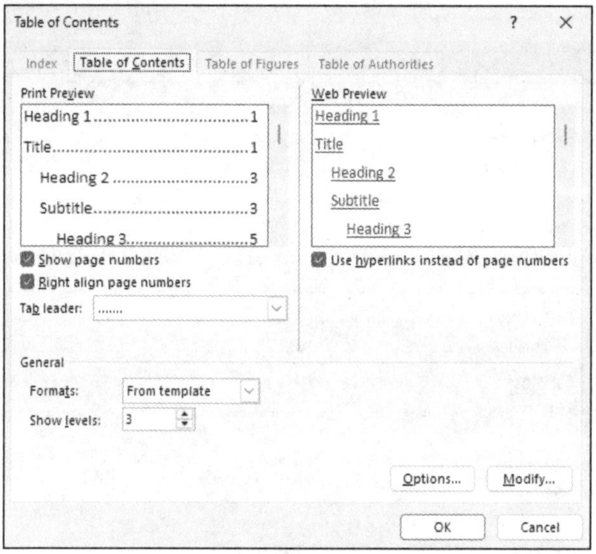


**FIGURE 8-5:** Use the Table of Contents dialog box to define a custom TOC.

3. **If you want to base your custom TOC on a template, use the Formats list to choose the template you want to start off with.**
4. **(Optional) If you don't want page numbers in the TOC, deselect the Show Page Numbers check box.**
5. **(Optional) If you left the Show Page Numbers check box selected, deselect the Right Align Page Numbers check box to have the page numbers appear immediately after the headings in the TOC.**
6. **(Optional) If you have both the Show Page Numbers and Right Align Page Numbers check boxes selected, use the Tab Leader list to choose the leader you want to appear between the headings and the page numbers.**
7. **(Optional) If you want page numbers in the Web Layout view, deselect the Use Hyperlinks Instead of Page Numbers check box.**

REMEMBER

The Use Hyperlinks Instead of Page Numbers check box is misnamed. When this check box is selected, Word still uses page numbers in Page Layout, Outline, and Draft views, but it doesn't display page numbers in the Web Layout and Full Screen Reading views. In all views, the headings are formatted as hyperlinks.

8. **Use the Show Levels spin box to choose the number of levels you want in the TOC.**

9. **Click OK.**

   Word inserts the custom TOC.

TIP

If you think you'll be reusing your custom TOC for other documents, you can avoid having to recreate the TOC from scratch each time by saving it as a building block that appears in the Table of Contents gallery. Here are the steps to follow:

1. **Select your custom TOC.**

2. **Choose References ⇨ Table of Contents ⇨ Save Selection to Table of Contents Gallery.**

   Word displays the Create New Building Block dialog box, shown in Figure 8-6.

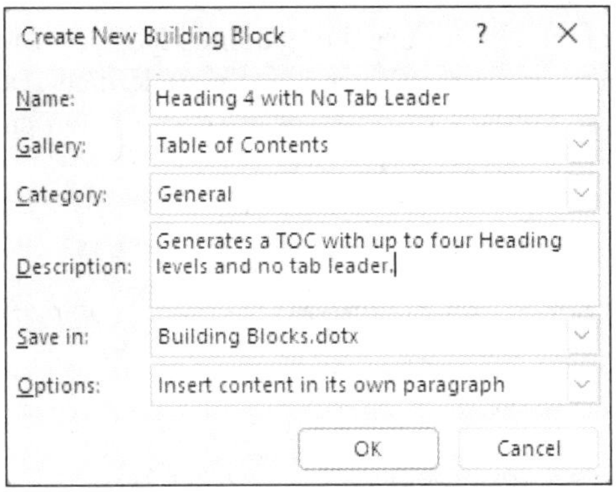


**FIGURE 8-6:** Use the Create New Building Block dialog box to save your custom TOC for later use.

3. **Type a Name and Description for the custom TOC.**

4. **Click OK.**

   Word saves your custom TOC as a building block.

To reuse your custom TOC, choose References ⇨ Table of Contents and then click the building block name you provided in step 3.

## Updating a TOC

If you add or delete headings, change heading text, or insert body text so that your page numbers change, your TOC will not reflect the current document structure. To fix this, you must update the TOC by following these steps:

1. **Choose References ➪ Update Table.**

   Alternatively, right-click the TOC and then click Update Field button at the top of the TOC. Word displays the Update Table of Contents dialog box.

2. **Select one of the following options:**

   - *Update page numbers only:* Click this option if your document headings have not changed.
   - *Update entire table:* Click this option to update the page numbers and headings.

3. **Click OK.**

   Word updates the table of contents.

## Defining TOC levels for custom styles

If you have documents that don't use the Heading styles for titles, subtitles, headings, and subheadings, you can still use Word's predefined TOC styles or create a custom TOC. However, you must first associate each of your custom styles with a TOC level. Here are the steps required:

1. **Position the cursor where you want the TOC to appear.**
2. **Choose References ➪ Table of Contents ➪ Custom Table of Contents Field.**

   Word displays the Table of Contents dialog box.

3. **Click Options.**

   Word convinces the Table of Contents Options dialog box to show up.

4. **In the Available Styles list, find a style you want to use for the TOC and type a number in the corresponding TOC Level text box.**

   For the highest-level style, type 1, for the next highest type 2, and so on.

5. **Repeat step 4 to define the TOC levels for all the styles you want in your TOC.**
6. **Click OK to return to the Table of Contents dialog box.**
7. **Configure the other TOC options and then click OK to insert the TOC.**

TIP

You might have a non-heading — such as a figure or table caption — that you want to include in your TOC. In this case, select the text and then choose References ➪ Add Text. In the menu that appears, click the TOC level you want to assign to the text: Level 1, Level 2, Level 3, or Level 4.

# Organizing Images with Captions and Tables of Figures

A *table of figures* (TOF) is most commonly a listing of the figures or illustrations in a document, and it usually appears just after the TOC. (Less commonly, a TOF can also be a listing of a document's tables or equations.) Like a TOC, the TOF can also include page numbers and you can set up each TOF entry as a hyperlink. You can also create separate TOFs for a document's tables and its equations.

## Inserting a caption

What figures, tables, and equations all have in common is that you can insert a caption above or below each of these items. The caption serves to identify the item by providing it with a unique number (such as Figure 1 or Table A) and often a brief description. Word builds a TOF by gathering the captions and using each caption text as an entry in the TOF. Again, you create separate TOFs using the captions for figures, tables, and equations (which makes the term "table of figures" regrettably misleading because a TOF can also be a "table of tables" or a "table of equations").

So, before you can build a TOF, you must add captions to the figures, tables, and equations in your document. Here are the steps to follow:

1. **Select the picture, table, or equation you want to caption.**

2. **On the References tab, in the Captions group, click Insert Caption (shown in the margin).**

   Alternatively, right-click the object, and then click Insert Caption.

   Word displays the Caption dialog box, shown in Figure 8-7.

3. **In the Label list, choose the type of object you're captioning: Equation, Figure, or Table.**
4. **Type your caption in the Caption text box.**
5. **Use the Position list to click the caption position you prefer: Above Selected Item or Below Selected Item.**

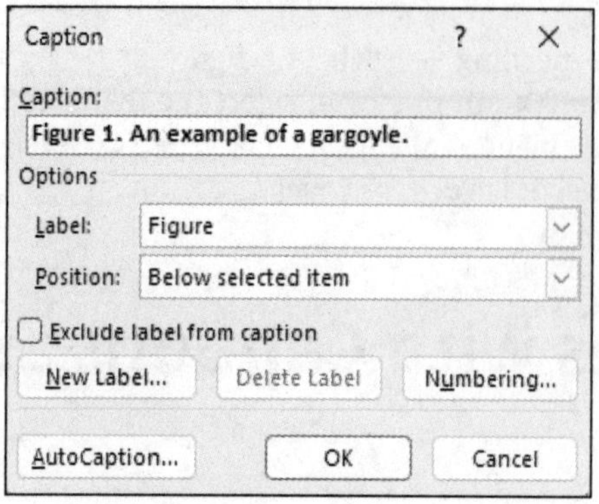


**FIGURE 8-7:** Use the Caption dialog box to type your caption and select caption options.

6. **If you don't want the label ("Equation," "Figure," or "Table") in the caption, select the Exclude Label from Caption check box.**
7. **To customize the caption numbering, follow these sub-steps:**
   **a)** Click Numbering to open the Caption Numbering dialog box.
   **b)** Use the Format list to choose a number format (such as letters or Roman numerals).
   **c)** If you want to include the chapter number in the caption, select the Include Chapter Number check box and then choose when each chapter starts (the default is each time you use the Heading 1 style) and the separator you prefer.
   **d)** Click OK.
8. **Click OK.**

   Word inserts the caption. Figure 8-8 shows an example.

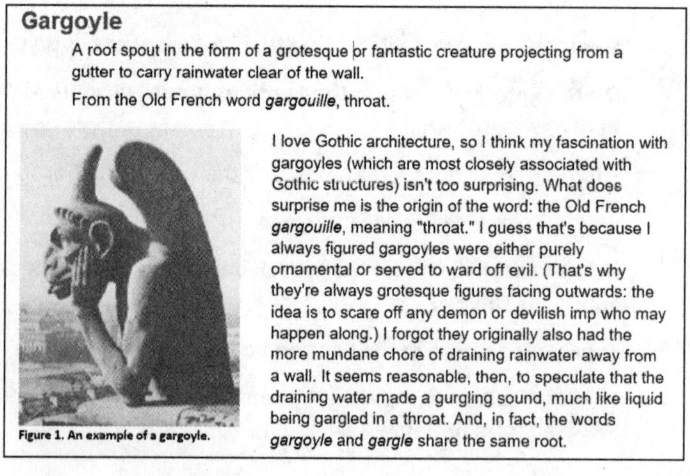
Gargoyle
A roof spout in the form of a grotesque or fantastic creature projecting from a gutter to carry rainwater clear of the wall.
From the Old French word gargouille, throat.
I love Gothic architecture, so I think my fascination with gargoyles (which are most closely associated with Gothic structures) isn't too surprising. What does surprise me is the origin of the word: the Old French gargouille, meaning "throat." I guess that's because I always figured gargoyles were either purely ornamental or served to ward off evil. (That's why they're always grotesque figures facing outwards: the idea is to scare off any demon or devilish imp who may happen along.) I forgot they originally also had the more mundane chore of draining rainwater away from a wall. It seems reasonable, then, to speculate that the draining water made a gurgling sound, much like liquid being gargled in a throat. And, in fact, the words gargoyle and gargle share the same root.
Figure 1. An example of a gargoyle.

**FIGURE 8-8:** An example caption added to a figure.

# Creating a TOF

Word doesn't come with predefined TOFs, so you need to create one from scratch. Here are the steps to follow:

1. **Use your best overhand throwing technique to toss the cursor to the spot you want the TOF to show up.**

2. **On the References tab, in the Captions group, click Table of Figures Dialog (shown in the margin).**

   Word displays the Table of Figures dialog box, shown in Figure 8-9.

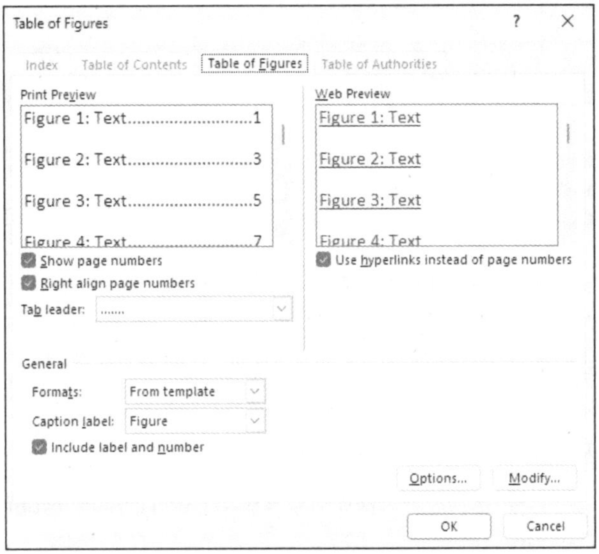


**FIGURE 8-9:** Use the Table of Figures dialog box to define a custom TOF.

3. **If you want to base your custom TOF on a template, use the Formats list to choose the template you want to start off with.**
4. **(Optional) If you don't want page numbers in the TOF, deselect the Show Page Numbers check box.**
5. **(Optional) If you left the Show Page Numbers check box selected, deselect the Right Align Page Numbers check box to have the page numbers appear immediately after the figure references in the TOF.**
6. **(Optional) If you have both the Show Page Numbers and Right Align Page Numbers check boxes selected, use the Tab Leader list to choose the leader you want to appear between the figure references and the page numbers.**

7. **(Optional) If you want page numbers in the Web Layout view, deselect the Use Hyperlinks Instead of Page Numbers check box.**

REMEMBER

The Use Hyperlinks Instead of Page Numbers check box is misnamed. When this check box is selected, Word still uses page numbers in Page Layout, Outline, and Draft views, but it doesn't display page numbers in the Web Layout and Full Screen Reading views. In all views, the figure references are formatted as hyperlinks.

8. **Use the Caption Label list to choose the caption label: Equation, Figure, Table, or (none).**
9. **Click OK.**

   Word inserts the custom TOF.

## Updating a TOF

If you add or delete figures, tables, or equations, change caption text, or insert body text so that your page numbers change, your TOF won't reflect the current document structure. To fix this, you must update the TOF by following these steps:

1. **On the References tab, in the Captions group, click Update Table of Figures (shown in the margin).**

   Alternatively, right-click the TOF and then click Update Field.

   Word displays the Update Table of Figures dialog box.

2. **Select one of the following options:**
   - *Update Page Numbers Only:* Select this option if your document headings have not changed.
   - *Update Entire Table:* Select this option to update the page numbers and headings.
3. **Click OK.**

   Word updates the table of figures.

## Creating a custom TOF label

By default, Word gives you three choices for caption labels: Equation, Figure, and Table. However, you can also create a custom label and then use that label to create a new TOF out of captions that use your custom label. For example, you might have a document that includes many charts. By creating a custom "Chart" label, you could then add captions to each chart ("Chart 1," "Chart 2," and so on) and then create a TOF just for the charts.

First create the custom label by following these steps:

1. **Select the object you want to caption.**
2. **On the References tab, in the Captions group, click Insert Caption (shown in the margin).**

   Alternatively, right-click the object, and then click Insert Caption.

   Word promotes the Caption dialog box.
3. **Click New Label.**

   Word offers up the New Label dialog box.
4. **Type your custom label in the Label text box and then click OK.**
5. **Choose the other caption options you want to use and then click OK.**

The next time you choose References ➪ Insert Caption, the Caption dialog box displays your custom label in the Label list. (If not, click the custom label in the list.)

REMEMBER

If you create a custom label by accident or you no longer need a custom label, choose References ➪ Insert Caption, click the custom label in the Label list, and then click Delete Label.

Once you add all your captions using the custom label, follow these steps to create a TOF using those captions:

1. **Position the cursor where you want the TOF to appear.**
2. **Choose References ➪ Table of Figures Dialog.**

   Word displays the Table of Figures dialog box.
3. **Use the Caption label list to click your custom caption label.**
4. **Choose the other TOF options you want to use and then click OK.**

# Supplementing Your Text with Footnotes and Endnotes

A *footnote* is a (usually) short note at the bottom of a page that provides extra info about something mentioned in the regular text on that page. Word indicates a footnote with a *reference mark*, which is a number or other symbol (such as * or †) that appears as a superscript in both the regular text and in a special footnote box at the bottom of the page. You can also place all your footnotes at the end of a section or at the end of the document, in which case they're called — no surprises, here — *endnotes.*

You might think that working with footnotes and endnotes is painfully complicated and fussy. Yep, sure, it would be if you tried to do everything manually, but there's no need for that. Word not only makes footnotes and endnotes straightforward to insert, but Word also keeps track of the reference marks and updates the numbers or symbols automatically no matter where you insert new notes in the document. Word also ensures that a footnote and the text to which it refers always appear on the same page, which is no mean feat. Finally, Word also gives you many useful options for creating custom footnotes and endnotes. The next few sections tell you all you need to know.

## Adding a default footnote

A default Word footnote appears at the bottom of the current page and uses Arabic numerals (1, 2, 3, and so on) as the reference marks. Here are the steps to follow to insert a default footnote:

1. **Plop the cursor where you want the footnote reference mark to appear.**
2. **On the References tab, in the Footnotes section, click Insert Footnote (shown in the margin), or press Ctrl+Alt+F.**

   Word inserts the reference mark in the text and in the footnote area.
3. **In the footnote area, type your footnote text to the right of the reference mark.**

Figure 8-10 shows an example footnote.

REMEMBER

If the footnote reference mark appears near the top of the page, you may need to scroll down to display the footnote text. You can avoid this scrolling by placing the mouse pointer over the reference mark. Word then displays the footnote text in a banner.

## Adding a default endnote

A default Word endnote appears at the end of the current document and uses lowercase Roman numerals (i, ii, iii, and so on) as the reference marks. Here are the steps to follow to insert a default endnote:

1. **Position the cursor where you want the endnote reference mark to appear.**

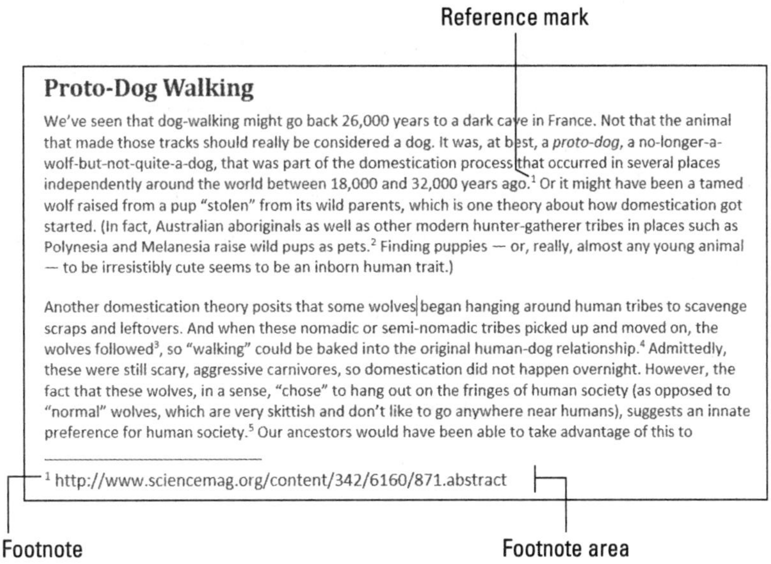


**Proto-Dog Walking**

We've seen that dog-walking might go back 26,000 years to a dark cave in France. Not that the animal that made those tracks should really be considered a dog. It was, at best, a *proto-dog*, a no-longer-a-wolf-but-not-quite-a-dog, that was part of the domestication process that occurred in several places independently around the world between 18,000 and 32,000 years ago.[1] Or it might have been a tamed wolf raised from a pup "stolen" from its wild parents, which is one theory about how domestication got started. (In fact, Australian aboriginals as well as other modern hunter-gatherer tribes in places such as Polynesia and Melanesia raise wild pups as pets.[2] Finding puppies — or, really, almost any young animal — to be irresistibly cute seems to be an inborn human trait.)

Another domestication theory posits that some wolves began hanging around human tribes to scavenge scraps and leftovers. And when these nomadic or semi-nomadic tribes picked up and moved on, the wolves followed[3], so "walking" could be baked into the original human-dog relationship.[4] Admittedly, these were still scary, aggressive carnivores, so domestication did not happen overnight. However, the fact that these wolves, in a sense, "chose" to hang out on the fringes of human society (as opposed to "normal" wolves, which are very skittish and don't like to go anywhere near humans), suggests an innate preference for human society.[5] Our ancestors would have been able to take advantage of this to

[1] http://www.sciencemag.org/content/342/6160/871.abstract

**FIGURE 8-10:** When you add a default footnote, Word inserts the note number as a reference mark in the text and in the footnote section.

2. **On the References tab, in the Footnotes section, click Insert Endnote (shown in the margin) or press Ctrl+Alt+D.**

   Word inserts the reference mark in the text and in the endnote area.

3. **In the endnote area, type your endnote text to the right of the reference mark.**

TIP

After you've added several footnotes to a document, you may decide that you prefer to use endnotes, instead. Fortunately, you don't have to recreate all the notes from scratch. Instead, on the References tab, click the dialog box launcher (shown in the margin) in the lower-right corner of the Footnotes group. In the Footnote and Endnote dialog box that puts in an appearance, click Convert, select Convert All Footnotes to Endnotes, and then click OK.

# Creating custom footnotes and endnotes

If Word's default footnotes and endnotes don't do it for you, there are plenty of customization options you can apply to get the notes you want. Here are just some of the customization possibilities:

- You can position the footnote area below the last line of the page instead of at the bottom of the page.
- You can gather your endnotes at the end of sections in which they appear instead of at the end of the document.

» For the reference marks, you can use Arabic numerals, uppercase or lowercase letters, uppercase or lowercase Roman numerals, or symbols such as the following: *, †, ‡, §. In fact, you can use any symbol available in the Symbol dialog box.

» You can start the reference marks at a specific number, letter, or symbol.

» You can have the reference marks restart with each page or each section.

To create a custom footnote or endnote that uses some or all of these options, follow these steps:

1. **Stick the cursor where you want the reference mark to appear.**

2. **On the References tab, click the dialog box launcher (shown in the margin) in the lower-right corner of the Footnotes tab.**

   Word displays the Footnote and Endnote dialog box, shown in Figure 8-11.

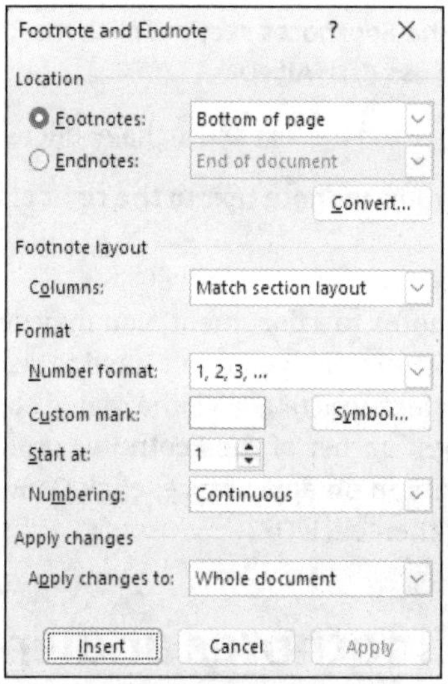


**FIGURE 8-11:** Use the Footnote and Endnote dialog box to set up a custom footnote or endnote.

3. **Click the location you want:**
   - **Footnotes.** Select this option to create a footnote, and then use the list to choose either Bottom of Page (the default) or Below Text.
   - **Endnotes.** Select this option to create an endnote, and then use the list to choose either End of Document (the default) or End of Section.

4. **Select the reference marks you want to use. You have two choices:**
   - In the Number Format list, choose a predefined reference mark style.

- For custom reference marks, click Symbol to display the Symbol dialog box, click the symbol you want, and then click OK. Repeat to add other symbols to the Custom mark text box.

5. **If you chose a predefined number format, use the Start At spin box to click the starting number, letter, or symbol you want to use.**
6. **In the Numbering list, click Continuous (the default), Restart Each Section, or Restart Each Page.**
7. **Click Insert.**

   Word inserts the reference mark in the text and in the footnote or endnote area.

8. **Type your footnote or endnote text.**

# Navigating footnotes and endnotes

Once you add a few footnotes or endnotes to a document, you may need to navigate them to view or edit the text or to add formatting. Scrolling through the document is one way to do this, but this method is way too slow if you're working with a long document. Fortunately, Word offers several faster ways to navigate notes:

- Choose References ➪ Next Footnote (shown in the margin) to jump to the next footnote in the document.
- Choose References ➪ Next Footnote ➪ Previous Footnote to jump to the previous footnote in the document. (Note that in this case you pull down the Next Footnote menu instead of just clicking the button.)
- Choose References ➪ Next Footnote ➪ Next Endnote to jump to the next endnote in the document.
- Choose References ➪ Next Footnote ➪ Previous Endnote to jump to the previous endnote in the document.

- Choose References ➪ Show Notes to jump to the footnote or endnote area for the current page.
- Double-click a reference mark in the text to jump from that reference mark to its associated footnote or endnote.
- Double-click a reference mark in the footnote or endnote area to jump from that footnote or endnote to the associated reference mark in the text.

TIP

If a footnote or endnote reference mark is in the wrong position, you can move it to another location. Even if you move the mark to another page, Word moves the note along with it. Select the reference mark, press Ctrl+X, move the cursor to the new position, and then press Ctrl+V.

# Naming Names: Inserting Citations and Bibliographies

In a scholarly document, if you reference someone else's results, ideas, or work, you must provide a citation for that reference so that other people can check out the original work for themselves. The documentation style of the citation depends on the citation guidelines that your company, publisher, or teacher uses. The most popular documentation styles come from the Modern Language Association (MLA), *The Chicago Manual of Style* (Chicago), and the American Psychological Association (APA).

Word offers comprehensive tools for inserting citations, working with citation styles, creating and managing sources, and inserting bibliographies based on your document's sources. The next few sections take you through the details.

## Inserting a citation

If you have just a few references that require citations in your document, or if you want to insert citations as you go (that is, each time you reference another person's work), Word's Insert Citation command enables you to create and insert sources one at a time. On the other hand, if you cite many sources in your document, you might prefer to add all those sources at the same time and then insert the citations from this list. You learn how to do so later in this chapter (refer to the later section "Managing your sources").

Here are the steps to follow to create a source and insert it as a citation:

1. **Wrestle the cursor into the position where you want the citation to appear.**
2. **On the References tab, in the Citations & Bibliography group, use the Style list to choose the documentation style you prefer.**
3. **On the References tab, in the Citations & Bibliography group, click Insert Citation and then click Add New Source.**

   After thinking it over briefly, Word displays the Create Source dialog box.
4. **In the Type of Source list, choose the type of source material you used.**
5. **Type the bibliographic data in the text boxes provided, which vary depending on the type of source you chose.**

   For example, Figure 8-12 shows the basic bibliographic fields for a journal article.

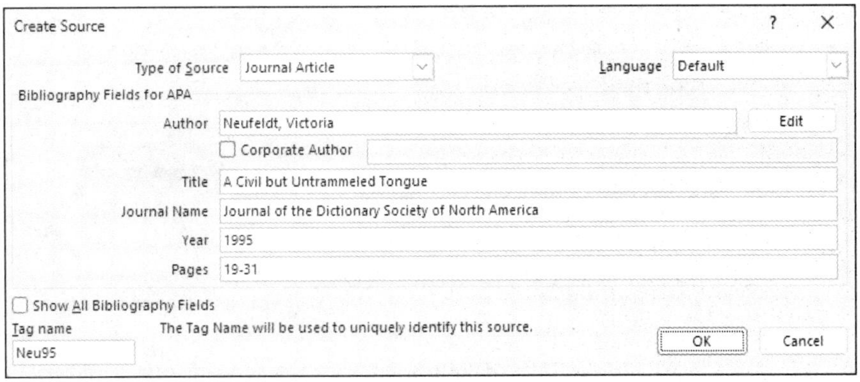


**FIGURE 8-12:** The bibliographic fields that appear in the Create Source dialog box depend on the type of source.

6. **Click OK.**

   Word inserts the citation (check out Figure 8-13, in the next section).

TIP

If a field you require is not shown in the Create Source dialog box, select Show All Bibliography Fields. Word adds text boxes for every bibliographic field associated with the current source type.

For each source you create, Word adds the entry to the document's list of sources. When you choose References ➪ Insert Citation, Word displays this source list, so you can reuse a source by clicking it in the list.

TECHNICAL STUFF

Note, too, that Word also maintains a master list of sources. This is an XML file named BookData.xml and you can find yours in the following subfolder of your Windows user folder:

```
Application Data\Microsoft\Bibliography
```

## Editing a citation's source

If you want to make changes to a citation's source, you can do it by following these steps:

1. **Click the citation you want to work with.**

   Word displays a Citation Options field menu around the citation.

2. **Click the menu, as shown in Figure 8-13, and then choose Edit Source.**

   Word displays the Edit Source dialog box.

TIP

You can also display the Edit Source dialog box by right-clicking the citation and then clicking Edit Source.

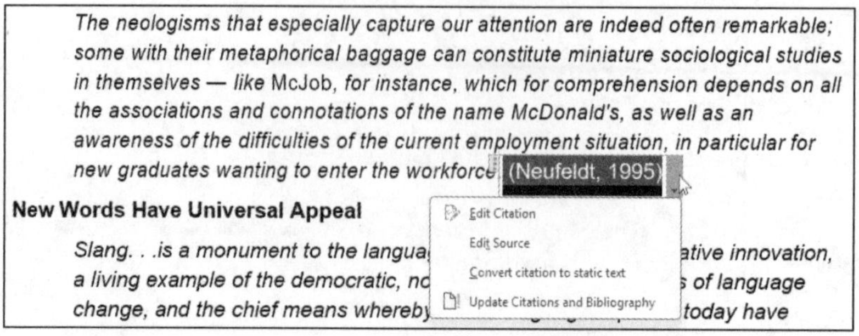

The neologisms that especially capture our attention are indeed often remarkable; some with their metaphorical baggage can constitute miniature sociological studies in themselves — like McJob, for instance, which for comprehension depends on all the associations and connotations of the name McDonald's, as well as an awareness of the difficulties of the current employment situation, in particular for new graduates wanting to enter the workforce
(Neufeldt, 1995)
New Words Have Universal Appeal
Edit Citation
Edit Source
Convert citation to static text
Update Citations and Bibliography
Slang. . .is a monument to the langua
ative innovation,
a living example of the democratic, nc
of language
change, and the chief means whereby
today have


**FIGURE 8-13:** Click the citation and then click the Citation menu to display a list of options.

3. **In the Type of Source list, click the type of source material you used.**
4. **Type the bibliographic data in the text boxes provided, which vary depending on the type of source you chose.**
5. **Click OK.**

   Word updates the citation.

## Suppressing a citation's fields

Depending on the documentation style you're using, you may want to remove some or all of the following source fields from the citation: Author, Date, or Title. Here's how you do so:

1. **Click the citation you want to work with.**

   Word displays the Citation Options field menu around the citation.
2. **Click the menu and then choose Edit Citation.**

   The Edit Citation dialog box appears.
3. **Select any of the following check boxes to suppress the corresponding field: Author, Date, and/or Title.**
4. **If you want to add the page numbers where the reference occurs, type a page number or page range in the Pages text box.**
5. **Click OK.**

   Word updates the citation.

## Managing your sources

Word maintains a list of sources in the current document as well as a master list of sources that you've added in all documents. If you have a ton of sources to add, Word offers a handy Source Manager feature you can use to quickly add all the sources you need. You can also use this dialog box to copy sources from the master list to the current document, which makes it easy to reuse sources in different documents. Manage Sources also enables you to edit and delete sources and perform searches for the source you need.

To work with Source Manager, on the References tab, in the Citations & Bibliography group, click Manage Sources (shown in the margin) to open the dialog box shown in Figure 8-14.

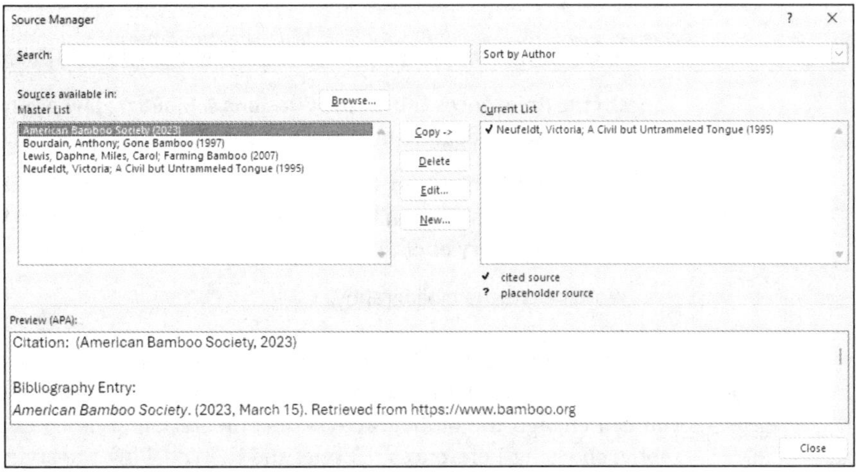


**FIGURE 8-14:** Use the Source Manager to add, edit, delete, and copy bibliographic sources.

The list on the left is the master list of sources, while the list on the right is the list of sources added to the current document. Sources with check marks beside them have been used in citations.

Source Manager enables you to work with sources by using the following buttons:

- **Copy:** Copies the selected source from the master list to the current document.
- **Delete:** Removes the selected source from the current document or the master list.
- **Edit:** Displays the Edit Source dialog box, which enables you to make changes to the selected source.
- **New:** Displays the Create Source dialog box, which enables you to create a new source.
- **Sorting:** Sorts the sources by the specified field.

- **Search:** Filters the source lists to show just those that contain in any field the word or phrase you type into the text box.
- **Close:** Shuts down Source Manager.

## Inserting a bibliography

After you add all of your document's sources, you can assemble those sources into a bibliography. Here are the steps to follow:

1. **Place the cursor where you want the bibliography to appear.**
2. **On the References tab, in the Citations & Bibliography group, click Style and then click the documentation style you want to use for the bibliography.**
3. **On the References tab, in the Citations & Bibliography group, click Bibliography (shown in the margin) and then either click a bibliography from the gallery or click Insert Bibliography.**

   Word inserts the bibliography.

TIP

If you add, edit, or delete sources in your document, be sure to update your bibliography. Right-click the bibliography and then click Update Field. Note, too, that you can change the bibliography's documentation style by clicking the bibliography, choosing References ⇨ Style, and then clicking the style you want to use.

# Making an Index, Checking It Twice

I think it's safe to say that one of the first things a savvy computer book buyer (someone such as yourself) does before making a decision on a book is to give the book's TOC a good going-over. In many cases, the second thing is giving the book's index a good look, too. Even if you don't check out the index *before* buying a book, there's a good chance you make regular use of the index *after* buying it. In almost all nonfiction books, a good index is an essential feature.

Is it essential in your Word documents? That depends on several factors:

- **Length:** The longer the document, the more likely an index is necessary or expected.

- **Complexity:** The more complex a document's subject matter, the more likely an index helps cut through that complexity and enables your readers to find what they want.
- **Audience:** Some people simply *expect* an index and are inordinately upset if a document does not include one.

If you have a document that has some or all of these factors, then you ought to consider adding an index. However, I should mention early on that creating an index is tedious, time-consuming, finicky work. Although some techniques are available that you can use to lighten the load, you should not make the decision to include an index lightly.

If you really need an index, but don't have the time to build one yourself, you have two alternatives: hire a professional indexer or purchase indexing software. Both routes are expensive (at least hundreds of dollars), but the resulting index will almost certainly be of much higher quality than one you build yourself.

On the other hand, although building a quality index for a large document such as a book requires special training, Word's indexing tools are all you really need for more modest projects. The next two sections take you through Word's methods for marking index entries, and then you'll learn how to build the index from those entries.

## Marking index entries directly in the document

The most straightforward — but also the most time-consuming — method for marking entries is to go through your document and mark the entries directly. Here's the basic method:

1. **Select the text you want to use as an index entry.**

2. **On the References tab, in the Index group, click Mark Entry (shown in the margin).**

   Alternatively, press Alt+Shift+X.

   Word displays the Mark Index Entry dialog box.

3. **In the Main Entry text box, type the text that you want Word to use as the index entry (the default is the text you selected).**

4. **Click Mark or, if the selected text appears in multiple places in the document, click Mark All.**

   Word leaves the dialog box open for more entries.

5. **Repeat steps 1, 3, and 4 to mark other entries in the document.**

TIP

After you mark your first index entry, Word turns on its formatting marks to display the otherwise hidden index fields. To hide these marks, choose Home ➪ Show/Hide ¶ (or press Ctrl+*).

The Mark Index Entry dialog box contains three sections with controls that you can use to fine-tune the index marking:

- **Index:** The text you select appears in the Main Entry text box. If you want this text to be a subentry, instead, cut the text, paste it in the Subentry text box, and then type the Main Entry text. Figure 8-15 shows an example.

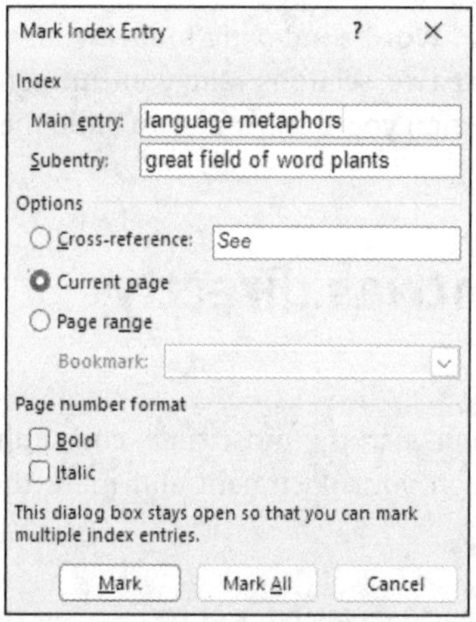


**FIGURE 8-15:** An example of a main entry and a subentry.

- **Options:** The Current Page option is the default, and this creates an index entry that points to the page or pages in which the entry appears in the document. If you want to refer the reader to a different index entry, select Cross-Reference and then type the entry name. If you want the entry to refer to a range of pages, first create a bookmark for the page range, then select Page Range and choose the bookmark name in the list.
- **Page number format:** Select Bold and/or Italic if the index entry is important in some way. For example, these formats are often used to highlight entries that define the concept or that discuss the concept in a major way.

# Marking index entries with a concordance file

The process of selecting each entry in the document can really slow you down. If you have a good idea of the words and phrases you want to include in your index, you can set up a separate *concordance file,* a Word document that includes these words and phrases, either as main entries or as subentries. You can then use Word's AutoMark feature to mark all the concordance items as index entries.

The concordance file is a regular Word document, which you create by following these steps:

1. **Insert a two-column table.**
2. **In the left column, type the word or phrase that you want Word to look for in the document you are indexing.**
3. **In the right column, type the word or phrase that you want Word to use as the index entry. If you want to create both a main entry and a subentry, separate them with a colon.**
4. **Repeat steps 1 through 3 for the other words and phrases you want to mark.**

With the concordance file completed and saved, you now follow these steps to mark the entries:

1. **Switch to the document you want to index.**
2.  **On the References tab, in the Index group, click Insert Index (shown in the margin).**

   Word displays the Index dialog box.
3. **Click AutoMark.**

   Word displays the Open Index AutoMark File dialog box.
4. **Click the concordance file and then click Open.**

   Word marks all the concordance items as index entries.

TIP

If you make an error when marking an index entry or mark text that you don't want in the index, be sure to delete the index field to avoid having an inaccurate or cluttered index. Double-click one of the braces around the field and then press Delete.

## Creating the index

Once you have your entries marked, you can go ahead and create the index. Here are the steps to follow:

1. **Finagle the cursor to where you want the index to reside.**

2. **On the References tab, in the Index group, click Insert Index (shown in the margin).**

   Word displays the Index dialog box.

3. **If you want to base your custom index on a template, use the Formats list to click the template you want to start off with.**
4. **(Optional) Select the Right Align Page Numbers check box to have the page numbers aligned with the right margin.**
5. **(Optional) If you have the Right Align Page Numbers check box selected, use the Tab Leader list to choose the leader you want to appear between the index entries and the page numbers.**
6. **Select Indented to show the subentries on separate lines; otherwise, select Run-In to show each group of the subentries in a single paragraph.**

   Note that selecting Run-In disables the Right Align Page Numbers check box.

7. **Click OK.**

   Word inserts the custom index.

## Updating an index

If you add or delete index entries or insert body text so that your page numbers change, your index will not reflect the current document structure. To fix this, you must update the index by using either of the following techniques:

- On the References tab, in the Index group, click Update Index (shown in the margin).
- Right-click the index and then click Update Field.

IN THIS CHAPTER

» Getting acquainted with Copilot and AI

» Prompting Copilot to write new content, rewrite existing text, or improve a document

» Summoning the help of your new Copilot overlord

# Chapter 9

# Writing and Editing with Copilot at Your Side

Some people are "natural" writers in the sense that writing just flows without much in the way of fuss. These lucky few are never at a loss for written words. The blank screen of a new Word document is an invitation. A quick crack of the knuckles and away they go.

For everyone else — and that would be pretty much everyone — writing is decidedly a chore. Whether it's a memo, a report, an essay, an article, or a blog post, the thought of pounding out all those words is painful and procrastination-inducing. The blank screen of a new Word document with its blinking cursor produces the same level of anxiety as watching a ticking time bomb.

If you identify with the second group, I'm here to tell you that it doesn't have to be that way. Nowadays you can take advantage of the text-creating powers of modern artificial intelligence (AI) to generate writing ideas or even entire first drafts. Even better, if your Office 365 account includes a subscription to Microsoft's Copilot service, you have direct access to a powerful AI model in any Word document. In Word, you can use AI to write new text from a request, refine existing text, summarize a too-long-to-read document, and much more.

In this chapter, you get to know Microsoft Copilot and then delve into everything it can do to help you make all your writing less of a chore and more of a creative adventure. The knuckle-cracking is optional.

## Getting to Know Copilot

On a commercial airliner, the cockpit portion of the crew usually consists of a captain and a copilot. The captain is in charge of the flight and the copilot often takes on more mundane tasks such as making sure the aircraft is ready for flight and working the radio and navigation. However, in practice the captain and the copilot share most duties, and the copilot will often take over the plane when the captain needs a break. The captain is the commanding officer and could get the plane from here to there on their own, but that task is made much easier by having a copilot to share the burden.

In the same way, up till now you've been the commanding officer of your job and have been able to do that job on your own, but wouldn't that task be much easier if you had a copilot to share the burden?

In the past, having a "copilot" would mean having some sort of assistant at your beck and call, which these days is a pipe dream for all but those in the C-suite. Amazingly, now just about anyone can have their own assistant in the form of artificial intelligence. Specifically, folks can now enlist the assistance of *generative AI,* which is AI that can generate content (writing and, depending on the context, sometimes also things like images and charts) based on a simple request — or *prompt,* in AI-speak.

That might sound like magic but, as the British sci-fi writer Arthur C. Clarke once wrote: "Any sufficiently advanced technology is indistinguishable from magic." Today's generative AI models have been trained on immense amounts of data — which is why they're known as *large language models*, or *LLMs* for short — and that vast training set, combined with some of the most painfully complicated math ever created, means that these models can perform eyebrow-raising, impressive feats of text creation.

WARNING

Yep, today's generative AI models are mind-bendingly good at pulling sophisticated text snippets seemingly out of thin air, but they have a dark side. Specifically, generative AI models tend to make things up out of whole cloth, a trait known somewhat euphemistically as *hallucinating.* That dark side doesn't matter so much for creative endeavors such as short stories and poems, but it can be a huge problem for more factual documents. If an AI produces "facts" in a response, it's your responsibility to check that they're actual facts, not hallucinations.

## Meeting your new assistant

You might have heard of (or even used) ChatGPT, which is the most famous example of generative AI (with the "Chat" part referring to the ChatGPT interface, which is much like what you see in a typical chat app). ChatGPT is great, but you don't need to bother with it because there's a good chance you have generative AI built right into your Office 365 account. Microsoft is a partner of OpenAI, the company that makes ChatGPT, which means that Microsoft has access to the latest version of GPT (which as I write these words is GPT-4), the LLM that powers ChatGPT. Microsoft has taken that access and used it as the basis of their own generative AI: Microsoft Copilot.



With the powerful combination of Word and Copilot, you can use relatively simple text prompts to do any of the following:

- Generate a first draft of all the text for a new document
- Add new text based on the existing content of a document
- Rewrite a document's existing text
- Ask questions
- Do research
- Brainstorm writing ideas

Copilot is really a personal assistant that can help you with just about any writing task.

WARNING

In the first bullet, above, note my use of the phrase "first draft." Believe me, you'll be sorely tempted to take Copilot's generated text as is and sign your name under it. The busier you are, the greater that temptation will be. I get it: You just want to get your work done. But at the very least you should carefully read what Copilot produces and feel free to edit the heck out of it not only to fix the inevitable errors and inconsistencies, but also to put the text into your own voice. And, these days, there's a good chance you work for a company that has strict guidelines on the use of AI-generated text, so how you use Copilot to generate text should fall within those guidelines. Either way, you'll sleep better at night.

## Checking for Copilot access

How do you know whether you have access to Copilot? The easiest way to check is to open any existing Word document or create a new Word document, then look for the following:

- The Copilot icon (shown on the left) in the document margin to the left of whatever line currently holds the cursor.
- In a freshly made document, the message Select the icon or press Alt+i to draft with Copilot.
- The Copilot command on the Home tab, usually on the far right of the tab, beside the Editor icon.

Figure 9-1 shows all three Copilot indicators.

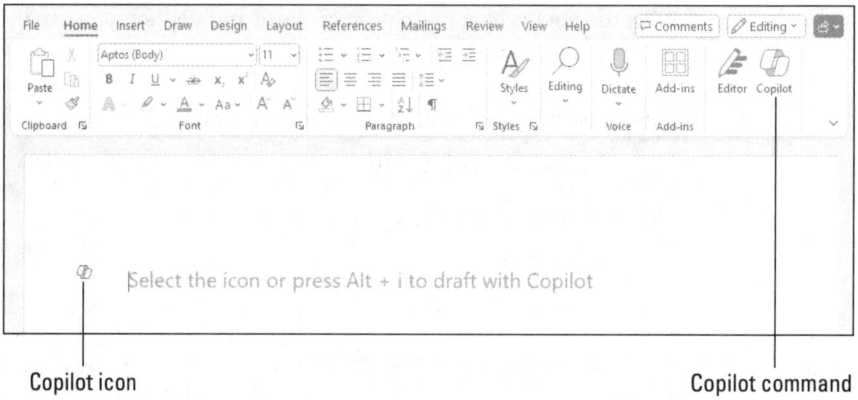


**FIGURE 9-1:** Your Office 365 account includes Copilot if you see the Copilot icon and the Copilot command.

REMEMBER

In case you're wondering, the answer to the question, "Can I turn off Copilot?" is "Nope, sorry." Word (or any Office 365 app that uses Copilot) doesn't have an option for disabling Copilot. If, for some reason, you really don't want anything to do with Copilot, begging and pleading with your Office 365 administrator to disable the service is your only recourse here. Good luck!

# Drafting New Text

*Writer's block* is an all-too-common affliction in which an author finds it impossible to start or continue a piece of writing. Many a writer has owned up to a crippling *blank page fear*, where the white expanse of the not-yet-typed-on page is seen as a cold and forbidding place that evokes terror instead of creativity.

These and similar authorial maladies will soon become things of the past at least for anyone whose version of Word is tricked out with Microsoft Copilot! A simple text prompt can produce everything from essays to emails, brochures to blog posts.

The key to using Copilot is the *prompt*, which is a sentence or two that describes the writing you want Copilot to generate. Most prompts are short, to-the-point descriptions of what you're looking for. However, to help ensure that you get text you can work with, it helps to craft your prompts with the following points in mind:



- **What you want to write:** A letter, a social media post, a memo, an ad, an email, or perhaps just a document title or image caption. If you want the output to include specific elements, be sure to specify them in your prompt.
- **Who you're writing to:** A customer, a recruiter, a friend, your team, your company, and so on.
- **Why you're writing this text:** To persuade, to thank, to motivate, and so on.
- **How you want it written:** Formal, funny, enthusiastic, heartfelt, and so on.

You don't need to include all four points in every prompt, but most prompts will include at least three of the four. Here are some examples:

Social media post announcing our new line of bell-bottom shorts

Ad copy to persuade consumers that bell-bottom shorts are a thing

Testy cease-and-desist letter to an overly persistent job recruiter

Motivational speech to the team, especially to those who insist on taking weekends off

Word has three methods for displaying a box to prompt AI:

- **Copilot icon:** If your document already has some writing, position the cursor where you want the generated text to appear. The Copilot icon (shown in the margin) appears to the left of the line that contains the cursor. Click that icon.
- **Keyboard:** Press Alt+i.
- **Context menu:** If your document already has some writing, right-click the document where you want the generated text to appear. In the context menu that appears, click Draft with Copilot.

Whichever method you choose, above the document Word displays a few suggested prompts as well as the Draft with Copilot dialog box that you use to enter your own prompt as shown in Figure 9-2.

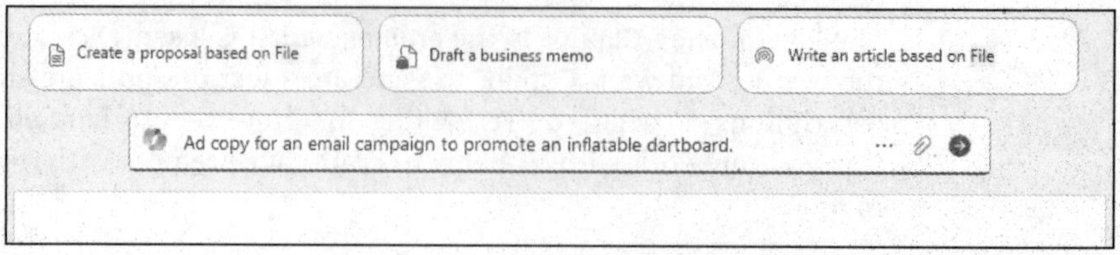


**FIGURE 9-2:** In the Draft with Copilot dialog box, type the prompt that tells the AI what you want.

REMEMBER

Your prompts can be as long as 2,000 characters, so feel free to be as specific as you need. The numbers in the lower-left corner of the text box tell you how many characters you've typed out of your 2,000-character allotment.

When your prompt is ready, click Generate (shown in the margin) and the AI goes to work converting your prompt to the requested text. Figure 9-3 shows an example result.

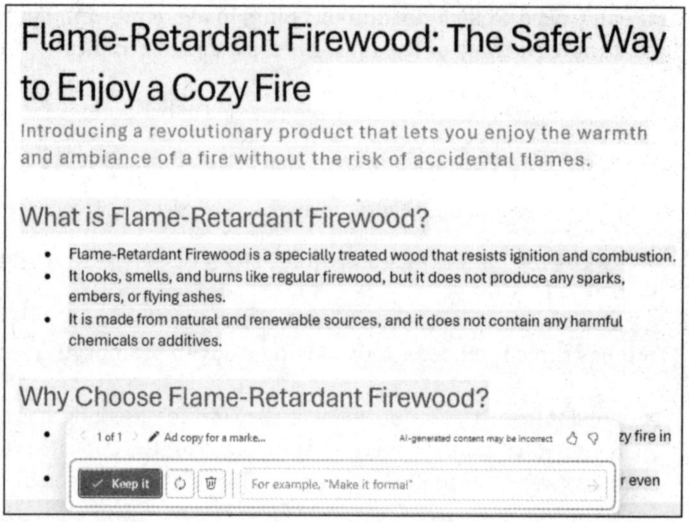


**FIGURE 9-3:** Some Copilot-generated text based on the prompt shown in Figure 9-2.

You have five possible paths from here:

- **Give the draft the thumbs up:** If you're happy with the draft, click Keep It to leave the text in your document.

- **Try again:** If you think Copilot can do better, click Regenerate (shown in the margin) to have Copilot create an entirely new draft for you.
- **Modify the prompt:** If you want to adjust the prompt and then regenerate the text, click Edit Prompt (shown in the margin) to redisplay the Draft with Copilot dialog box with your prompt ready for editing, make your changes, and then click Generate. Note that if you're not getting the results you want, try editing your prompt to make it much more specific about what you need from Copilot.
- **Reject it:** If the draft is a write-off and you'd prefer to start over, click Discard It (shown in the margin).
- **Refine it:** Use the text box to specify how you want Copilot to modify the draft, then click Generate (shown in the margin). Here are some example refinements:
  - *Make it funnier.*
  - *Make it more formal.*
  - *Make it more casual.*
  - *Lengthen it by adding more details.*
  - *Shorten it by removing details.*

Again, remember that this is a draft that Copilot has generated for you, so at this point you should give the generated text both a once-over and a twice-over to look for errors and to put the text into your own voice.



# Adding Text to an Existing Document

If you have a document that's partially complete and you're stuck for what to write next, Copilot can help you get unstuck. The AI offers an Inspire Me feature that examines what's in the document and then suggests what could come next. Here's how this works:

1. **Start a new line at the bottom of the document.**
2. **Click the Copilot icon (shown in the margin) or press Alt+i.**

   The version of the Draft with Copilot dialog box shown in Figure 9-4 appears.
3. **Click Inspire Me.**

   Copilot generates some new text based on your document's existing text.

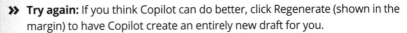

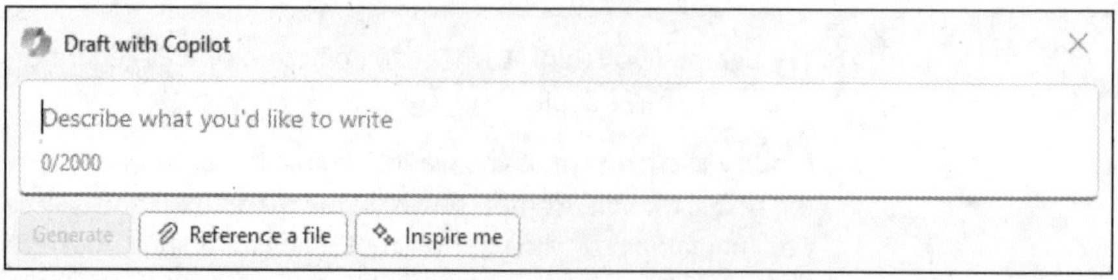


**FIGURE 9-4:** The Draft with Copilot dialog box that appears when your document has existing text.

4. **Choose how you want to handle the generated text:**
   - **Keep It:** Leaves the text in your document.
   - **Regenerate:** Creates a new draft.
   - **Edit Prompt:** Redisplays the Draft with Copilot dialog box with your prompt ready for editing. Make your edits and then click Generate.
   - **Discard It:** Ends the operation without inserting the generated text.
   - **Refine text box:** Modifies the generated text. Type a prompt that specifies how you want Copilot to refine the draft, then click Generate (shown in the margin).

# Transforming Existing Text

Copilot isn't just a whiz at crafting new text: You can also ask it to rewrite existing text for you, and it even lets you select the overall tone of the revised text (professional, casual, and so on).

Follow these steps to get Copilot to rewrite some existing text:

1. **Select the text you want Copilot to revise.**
2. **Ask Copilot to rewrite the selected text for you:**
   - Click the Copilot icon to the left of the selected text, then click Auto Rewrite in the menu that appears.
   - Click Auto Rewrite in the mini-toolbar.
   - Right-click the selected text and then use the context menu to choose Copilot ➪ Auto Rewrite.

   Copilot takes a few seconds to conjure up a few rewrites, then the Rewrite with Copilot dialog box appears, as shown in the Figure 9-5.

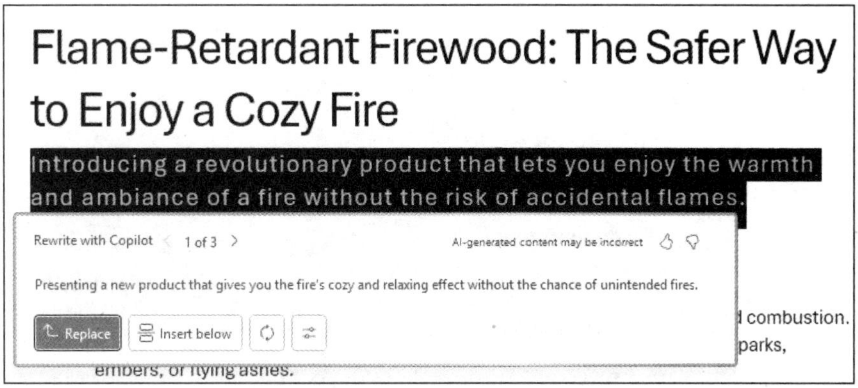
Flame-Retardant Firewood: The Safer Way to Enjoy a Cozy Fire
Introducing a revolutionary product that lets you enjoy the warmth and ambiance of a fire without the risk of accidental flames.
Rewrite with Copilot
1 of 3
AI-generated content may be incorrect
Presenting a new product that gives you the fire's cozy and relaxing effect without the chance of unintended fires.
Replace
Insert below
combustion.
parks,
embers, or flying ashes.

**FIGURE 9-5:** The Rewrite with Copilot dialog box shows Copilot's revised versions of the selected text.

3. **Click Next (shown in the margin) to run through Copilot's rewrites of the text.**

4. **(Optional) If you think Copilot was phoning it in, click Regenerate (shown in the margin) to create a new set of rewrites.**

5. **(Optional) To select a different tone for the rewrite, click Adjust Tone (shown in the margin), click a tone in the list that appears — Neutral, Professional, Casual, Imaginative, or Concise — and then click Regenerate.**
6. **When you find a rewrite you like, click one of the following buttons to add the rewrite to your document:**
   - *Replace:* Replaces the selected text with the rewrite. Click this button if you're sure the rewrite is superior to the original.
   - *Insert Below:* Inserts the rewrite into the document, just below the selected text. Click this button if you're not sure about the rewrite and you want to compare it with the original.

REMEMBER

If you don't like any of Copilot's rewrites, you can abandon the entire procedure by pressing Esc or clicking anywhere in the document outside of the Rewrite with Copilot dialog box.

# Referencing a File

I talk earlier (refer to "Adding Text to an Existing Document") about how Copilot's Inspire Me feature can generate a draft of some new text based on a document's existing text. That's cool and all, but what if the existing text resides in another document? That's not even close to a problem because as long as the file is on your OneDrive, you can include a reference to that file in your Copilot prompt. Copilot will analyze that file and generate some fresh text based on your prompt and the file's contents.

Here's how it works:

1. **Start a new document or start a new line at the bottom of an existing document.**
2. **Click the Copilot icon (shown in the margin) or press Alt+i.**

   The Draft with Copilot dialog box shows up.
3. **Type your prompt up to the point where you want to reference the file.**

   For example, you might type something along the lines of "Write something similar to the content of. . . "
4. **Click Reference a File or press slash (/).**

   Copilot displays a list of files you've worked on recently, as shown in Figure 9-6.

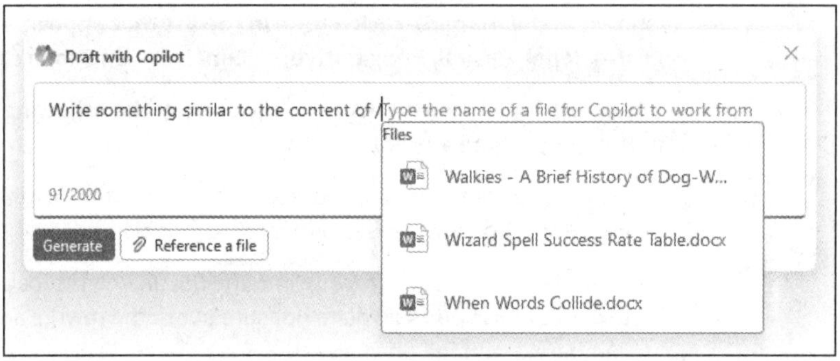


**FIGURE 9-6:** Type a slash (/) or click Reference a File to add a file to your prompt.

5. **To reference another file, start typing the file name until the file appears in the list.**
6. **Click the file you want to include in your prompt.**
7. **Complete the prompt, if needed, and then click Generate.**
8. **Choose how you want to handle the generated text:**
   - **Keep It:** Keeps the text in your document.
   - **Regenerate:** Asks Copilot to give it another shot.
   - **Edit Prompt:** Opens the Draft with Copilot dialog box with your prompt displayed. Edit the prompt as you see fit, then click Generate.

- **Discard It:** Tells Copilot to forge the whole thing.

- **Refine text box:** Asks Copilot to modify the generated text based on the prompt you type. Click Generate (shown in the margin) to make the modification happen.

# Getting Copilot's Help with a Document



In Word, Copilot's main job is to generate text drafts based on whatever guidance you provide in your prompt. But Copilot has many other talents, and you can take advantage of those talents for tons of useful tasks. In particular, Copilot can examine whatever document you have open and help you with that document, such as summarizing it or improving it.

You access Copilot's extra features via the Copilot task pane, which you display by heading over to the Home tab and clicking the Copilot button (it's usually on the far right of the tab, next to the Editor button). Figure 9-7 shows the Copilot pane.

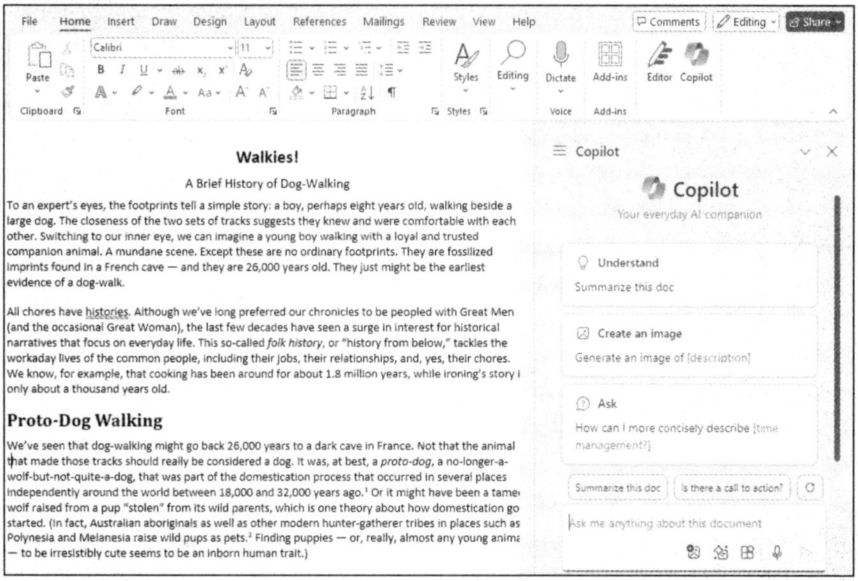


**FIGURE 9-7:** On the Home tab, click the Copilot button to open the Copilot pane.

The focal point of the Copilot pane is the large text box near the bottom, which is where you type your prompt. The text box is also home to four icons:

- **View Prompts:** Displays a menu of possible prompts to help you get started.
- **Manage Search and Plug-ins:** Opens the Search and Plug-ins dialog box, which you can use to configure where Copilot can search for answers and controls which plug-ins you want it to use (a *plug-in* enables Copilot to access a particular app).
- **Microphone:** Enables you to use a connected microphone to dictate your prompts rather than typing them.
- **Send:** Delivers your prompt to Copilot for processing. (You can also press Enter to submit a prompt.)

Not sure what to type in the prompt box? Perhaps a few examples might help.

## Understanding a document

If you're given a long or complex document, reading and rereading it until you understand what's it's trying to say can take up a big chunk of your day. Forget that. Instead, put Copilot to work to help you understand the document.

Here are some Copilot prompts you can use to help you understand the contents of whatever document is displayed next to the Copilot pane:

- *Explain this document in* X *sentences.* (Replace *X* with a number, such as *three* or *five*.)
- *Summarize this document.*
- *Summarize this document in* X *key points.* (Replace *X* with a number, such as *four* or *six*.)
- *What does the document say about* Y*?* (Replace *Y* with a concept or topic covered in the document.)
- *What arguments does this document make?*
- *What are the main benefits of* Y*?* (Replace *Y* with a concept or topic covered in the document.)
- *What are the pros and cons of* Y*?* (Replace *Y* with a concept or topic covered in the document.)

## Improving a document

If you want to improve a document that you've written or that you're editing, Copilot is happy to help. Here are a few Copilot prompts you can use to ask Copilot for advice on how to improve whatever document is displayed next to the Copilot pane:

- *What's a more concise way to describe* Y? (Replace *Y* with a concept or topic covered in the document.)
- *What would be a good font combination for the heading and body text of this document?*
- *What are some strong titles for this document?*
- *Can you make some suggestions for a subtitle for this document?*
- *What are some ways I can make this document read better?*
- *What are some ways I can make this document funnier?*
- *Give me some background info on* Y. (Replace *Y* with a concept or topic you want to cover in the document.)
- *How do I* Z? (Replace *Z* with a Word task you want to perform on the document, such as *insert an image* or *add a table of contents*.)

REMEMBER

The Copilot pane isn't just for tasks related to the open document. Using the Copilot pane's text box, you're free to prompt the AI about pretty much anything. You can ask questions, research topics, brainstorm ideas, even have a chat session.

# 3 Excel 365

# Contents at a Glance

IN THIS CHAPTER

» Getting to know Excel's Start screen and program window

» Working through worksheets and creating workbooks

» Populating a worksheet with data

» Using AutoFill and Flash Fill to enter lists and serial data

# Chapter 1

# Excel: The 50-Cent Tour

If you're new to Excel, launching the program for the first time can be headache-inducing. So many icons! So many lines! So little guidance! The problem is that you've been catapulted into what appears to be a strange and exotic landscape without a map, a guidebook, or even a "You are here" sign. You wouldn't travel to Upper Volta or lower Manhattan without these tools in your travel kit, so why are you visiting Excel that way?

Ah, but your purchase of this book shows that you are, indeed, a savvy and sophisticated traveler. Now you've got the guidebook you need to learn the language, customs, and tourist hotspots of Excel. And the map? That's what this chapter is all about. Here you take a guided tour that points out the main features of the Excel landscape; shows you the best ways to navigate from the spreadsheet equivalent of Point A to Point B; and tells you how to call for help should the need arise.

Oh, and by the way: You are *here*. Let's go!

## Getting Comfy with the Excel Window

When you first open a new, blank workbook by clicking the Blank Workbook thumbnail in the Home screen, Excel opens a single worksheet (with the generic name, Sheet1) in a new workbook file (with the generic filename, Book1) inside a program window such as the one shown in Figure 1-1.

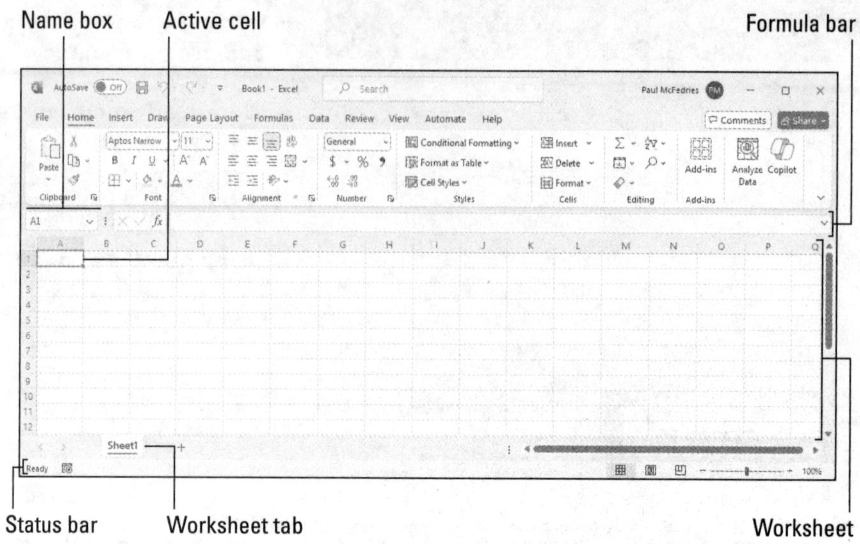


**FIGURE 1-1:** The Excel program window as it appears after first opening a blank workbook.

The Excel program window is made up of the standard Office 365 elements such as the File menu button, the Quick Access toolbar, and the Ribbon, as well as the following unique features (pointed out in Figure 1-1):

- **Worksheet:** This is your Excel work area, which consists of a series of columns (identified by the letters along the top: A, B, C, and so on) and a series of rows (identified by the numbers running down the left: 1, 2, 3, and so on). The intersection of each column and row is called a *cell* and you enter your Excel data and formulas into these cells. You use a horizontal scroll bar on the bottom to move left and right through the sheet and a vertical scroll bar on the right edge to move up and down through the sheet.
- **Worksheet tab:** Displays the name of each worksheet (although the default new workbook comes with just one worksheet).
- **Active cell:** The currently highlighted cell in the worksheet.
- **Formula bar:** Displays the contents (if any) of the active cell. You can also use it to enter and edit cell data and formulas.
- **Name box:** Displays the address of the active cell.
- **Status bar:** This bar keeps you informed of the program's current mode and any special keys you engage, and it enables you to select a new worksheet view and to zoom in and out on the worksheet.

## ASSIGNING 26 LETTERS TO 16,384 COLUMNS

When it comes to labeling the 16,384 columns of an Excel worksheet, our alphabet with its measly 26 letters is simply not up to the task. To make up the difference, Excel first doubles the letters in the cell's column reference so that Column AA follows Column Z (after which you find Column AB, AC, and so on) and then triples them so that Column AAA follows Column ZZ (after which you get Column AAB, AAC, and the like). At the end of this letter tripling, the 16,384th and last column of the worksheet ends up being XFD, so that the last cell in the 1,048,576th row has the cell address XFD1048576.

## Fooling around with the Formula bar

The Formula bar displays the cell address and the current contents of the active cell and enables you to add and edit the contents of the active cell. The address of a cell is determined by its column letter(s) followed immediately by its row number. For example, the top-left cell of each worksheet is at the intersection of Column A and Row 1, so it's address is A1.



The Formula bar is divided into three sections:

- **Name box:** The leftmost section displays the address of the active cell or the cell's defined range name, if it has one (see Book 3, Chapter 5 to learn more about defining range names).
- **Formula bar buttons:** The second, middle section usually has only the Insert Function button (labeled *fx*) enabled. When you start making or editing a cell entry, the Cancel (an *X*) and Enter (a check mark) buttons are also enabled.



- **Cell contents:** The third white area to the immediate right of the Insert Function button takes up the rest of the bar and expands as necessary to display long cell entries that won't fit in the normal area. This area contains a Formula Bar button (shown in the margin) on the far right that enables you to expand the Formula bar display to show really long formulas that span more than a single row; click the button again to contract the cell contents area back to its normal single row.

The cell contents section of the Formula bar is important because it *always* shows you the contents of the cell even when the worksheet does not. (When you're dealing with a formula, Excel displays only the formula result in the cell and not the formula itself.) You can edit the contents of the cell in this area at any time. By the same token, when the cell contents area is blank, you know that the cell is empty as well.

## Touring the worksheet area

The worksheet area is where most of the Excel spreadsheet action takes place because it contains the cells where you enter and edit your labels, values, and formulas.

Keep in mind that to enter or edit data in a cell, that cell must be the active cell. Excel indicates the active cell in four ways:

- The cell pointer — the dark green border surrounding the cell's perimeter — appears in the cell.
- The address of the cell appears in the Name box of the Formula bar.
- The cell's column letter(s) and row number are shaded (in a green color on most monitors) in the column headings and row headings that appear at the top and left of the worksheet area, respectively.
- The background color of the cell's column heading and row heading changes from light gray to dark gray.

### Moving around the worksheet

Excel offers a fistful of methods for moving the cell pointer around the worksheet to the cell where you want to enter new data or edit existing data:

- Click the desired cell — assuming that the cell is displayed within the section of the sheet currently visible in the worksheet area.
- Click the Name box, type the address of the desired cell directly into this box, and then press Enter.
- Press F5 or Ctrl+G to open the Go To dialog box, type the address of the desired cell into its Reference text box, and then click OK.
- Use the cursor keys listed in Table 1-1 to move the cell pointer to the desired cell.
- Use the horizontal and vertical scroll bars at the bottom and right edges of the worksheet area to move the part of the worksheet that contains the desired cell. Then click the cell to put the cell pointer in it.

**TABLE 1-1** **Keystrokes for Moving the Cell Pointer**

| Keystroke | Where the Cell Pointer Moves |
|---|---|
| → or Tab | Cell to the immediate right |
| ← or Shift+Tab | Cell to the immediate left |
| ↑ | Cell up one row |
| ↓ | Cell down one row |
| Home | Cell in Column A of the current row |
| Ctrl+Home | First cell (A1) of the worksheet |
| Ctrl+End or End, Home | Cell in the worksheet at the intersection of the last column that has any data in it and the last row that has any data in it. (That is, the last cell of the so-called active area of the worksheet.) |
| PgUp | Cell one screenful up in the same column |
| PgDn | Cell one screenful down in the same column |
| Ctrl+→ or End, → | First occupied cell to the right in the same row that is either preceded or followed by a blank cell. If no cell is occupied, the pointer goes to the cell at the very end of the row. |
| Ctrl+← or End, ← | First occupied cell to the left in the same row that is either preceded or followed by a blank cell. If no cell is occupied, the pointer goes to the cell at the very beginning of the row. |
| Ctrl+↑ or End, ↑ | First occupied cell above in the same column that is either preceded or followed by a blank cell. If no cell is occupied, the pointer goes to the cell at the very top of the column. |
| Ctrl+↓ or End, ↓ | First occupied cell below in the same column that is either preceded or followed by a blank cell. If no cell is occupied, the pointer goes to the cell at the very bottom of the column. |
| Ctrl+Page Down | Last occupied cell in the next worksheet of that workbook. |
| Ctrl+Page Up | Last occupied cell in the previous worksheet of that workbook. |

**Note:** *In the case of those keystrokes that use arrow keys, you must either use the arrows on the cursor keypad or have the Num Lock key disengaged on the numeric keypad of your keyboard.*



## Surfing the sheets in a workbook

Each new workbook you open in Excel contains a single blank worksheet, aptly named Sheet1, with 16,384 columns and 1,048,576 rows (giving you a truly staggering total of 17,179,869,184 blank cells!). Should you still need more worksheets in your workbook, you can add them by clicking the New Sheet button (shown in the margin) that appears to the immediate right of Sheet1 tab.

## ONE GOOD REASON FOR ADDING EXTRA SHEETS TO A WORKBOOK

You may wonder why on earth anyone would ever need more than one worksheet, given just how many cells each sheet contains. The simple truth is that it's all about how you choose to structure a particular workbook rather than running out of places to put the data. For example, say you need to create a workbook that contains budgets for all the various departments in your corporation; you may decide to devote an individual worksheet to each department (with the actual budget worksheet tables laid out in the same manner on each sheet) rather than placing all the tables in different sections of the same sheet. Using this kind of one-sheet-per-budget layout makes it much easier for you to find each budget, print each one as a separate page of a report, and, if ever necessary, consolidate their data in a separate summary worksheet.

On the left side of the bottom of the worksheet area, the sheet tab scroll buttons appear, followed by the actual tabs for the worksheets in your workbook and the New Sheet button. To activate a worksheet for editing, you select it by clicking its sheet tab. Excel lets you know what sheet is active by displaying the sheet name on its tab in green, boldface type as well as underlining the tab and making the tab appear to be connected to the worksheet area above.

REMEMBER

You can use the Ctrl+Page Down and Ctrl+Page Up shortcut keys to select the next and previous sheets, respectively, in your workbook. When the tab bar is full, you can also click the following buttons:

- **Next Sheet:** The ellipsis (. . .) button on the right side of the sheet tabs immediately left of the New Sheet button. Clicking this button selects the first non-visible tab to the right.
- **Previous Sheet:** The ellipsis (. . .) button on the left side of the sheet tabs to the immediate left of the first visible sheet tab. Clicking this button selects the first non-visible tab to the left.

If your workbook contains too many sheets for all their tabs to be displayed at the bottom of the worksheet area, use the sheet tab scroll buttons to bring new tabs into view (so that you can then click the tab you want to activate):

- **Next:** Click this button (shown in the margin) to scroll the next hidden sheet tab into view on the right. Ctrl+click the Next button to scroll the last sheet into view.

» **Previous:** Click this button (shown in the margin) to scroll the next hidden sheet into view on the left. Ctrl+click the Previous button to scroll the first sheet into view.

TIP

Right-click either sheet tab scroll button to display the Activate dialog box listing the names of all the worksheets in the workbook in order from first to last. To activate a worksheet, either double-click its name or click the name and then click OK.

## Taking a closer look at the status bar

The status bar is the last component at the very bottom of the Excel program window. (See Figure 1-2.)

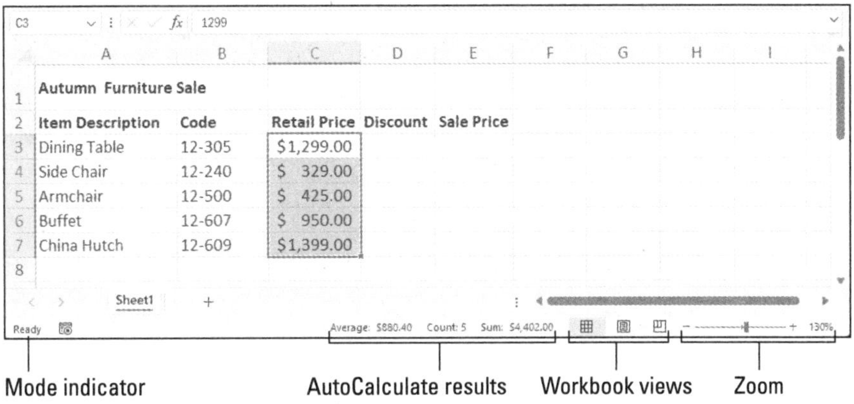


**FIGURE 1-2:** The Excel status bar.

The status bar contains the following items:

» **Mode indicator:** Indicates the current state of the Excel program (READY, ENTER, EDIT, and so on).

» **AutoCalculate results:** Displays the AVERAGE, COUNT, and SUM of all the numerical entries in the active cell selection.

» **Workbook views:** Enables you to select between three views for the worksheet area: Normal, the default view that shows only the worksheet cells with the column and row headings; Page Layout view, which adds rulers and page margins and shows page breaks for the worksheet; and Page Break Preview, which enables you to adjust the paging of a report.

» **Zoom:** Enables you to zoom in and out on the cells in the worksheet area by dragging the slider to the right or left, respectively.

You can customize the status bar by right-clicking it and then activating or deactivating the commands in the shortcut menu that appears.

# Creating Fresh Workbooks

When you launch Excel (without also opening an existing workbook file, such as by double-clicking an Excel file in File Manager), the Start screen presents you with two choices for creating a new workbook:

- Open a new workbook based on the design in one of the other templates displayed in the Start screen or available in the New screen (click the More Templates link in the Home screen or click the New button in the Navigation pane).
- Open a new workbook (with the generic filename, Book1), consisting of a single, totally blank worksheet (with the generic worksheet name, Sheet1) by clicking the Blank Workbook template.

The sections that follow expand on these choices, starting with creating a workbook from a template.

## Taking it from a template

Spreadsheet templates are the way to go if you can find one that uses the design of the worksheet that you want to build (or is close to it, anyway). There are many templates to choose from when you initially launch Excel and then click the New option in the Navigation pane. (Refer to Figure 1-3.) The templates displayed on the New screen run the gamut from budgets and schedules to profit and loss statements, invoices, sales reports, and calendars.

If none of the templates displayed on the New screen fit the bill, you can search for templates. This screen contains suggested links to common searches: Business, Personal, Planners and Trackers, Lists, Budgets, Charts, and Calendar. When you click one of these links, the New screen displays your choices in that particular category.

TIP

If the type of template you're looking for doesn't fit any of the categories listed in the Suggested Searches, you can run your own template search. Click the Search for Online Templates text box, type one or more keywords describing the type of template (such as **finance**), and then press Enter or click the Start Searching button (the magnifying glass icon). Excel displays the search results, as shown in Figure 1-4, which displays the templates that Excel uncovers based on a search for **finance**.

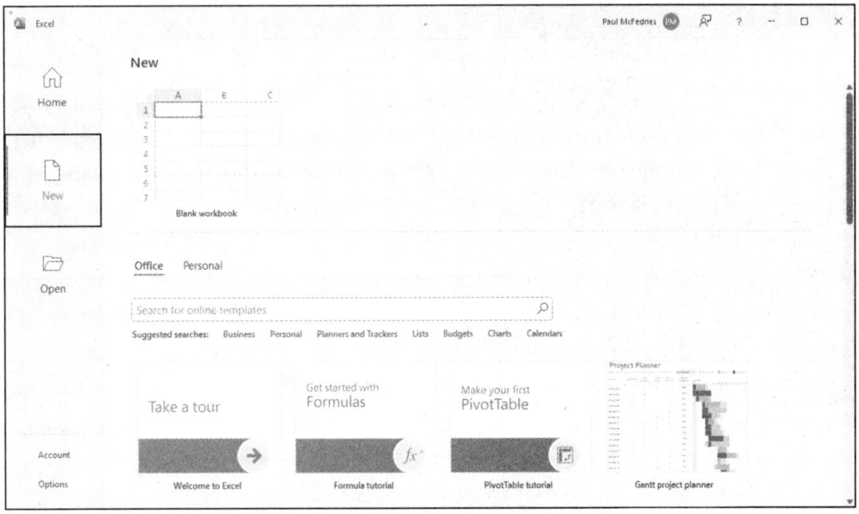


**FIGURE 1-3:** The New screen is home to a fistful of templates you can use to get a head start on building a new workbook.

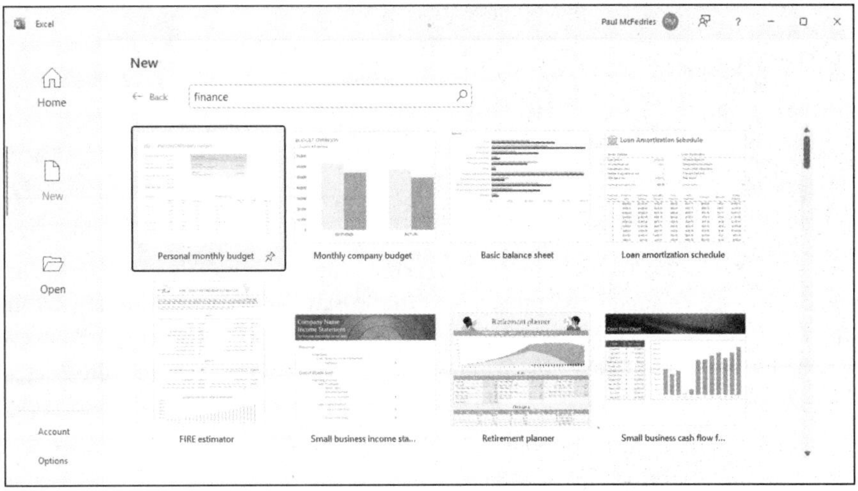


**FIGURE 1-4:** Searching for finance-related templates.

**REMEMBER**

Instead of using ready-made templates, you can create your own templates from your favorite Excel workbooks. After you save a copy of a workbook as a template file, Excel automatically generates a copy of the workbook whenever you open the template file. This way, you can safely customize the contents of the new workbook without any danger of inadvertently modifying the original template.

## Downloading the template to use

When you locate a template with a design that you can adapt to your worksheet needs, you can download the template. Click the template's thumbnail on the

New screen. Excel then opens a dialog box similar to the one shown in Figure 1-5, containing a more extensive description of the template and its download file size. To download the template and create a new Excel workbook from it, click the Create button. Excel creates the new workbook and gives it the same name as the template, but with a "1" tacked on to the end (for example, Monthly Company Budget1).

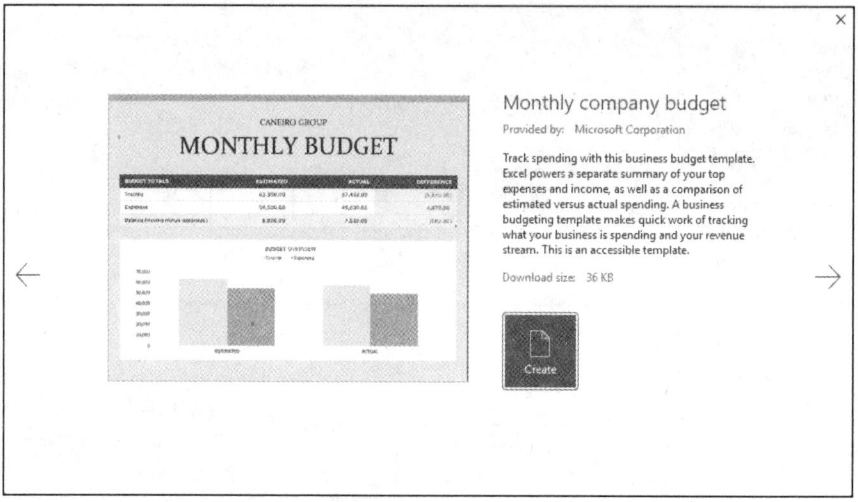


**FIGURE 1-5:** When you click a template thumbnail, Excel displays more details about the template.

If you return to the New screen (by choosing File ⇨ New), the template you downloaded now appears next to the Blank Workbook template, as shown in Figure 1-6. You can click the downloaded template to create another new workbook based on that file (which will have a "2" tacked on to the filename).

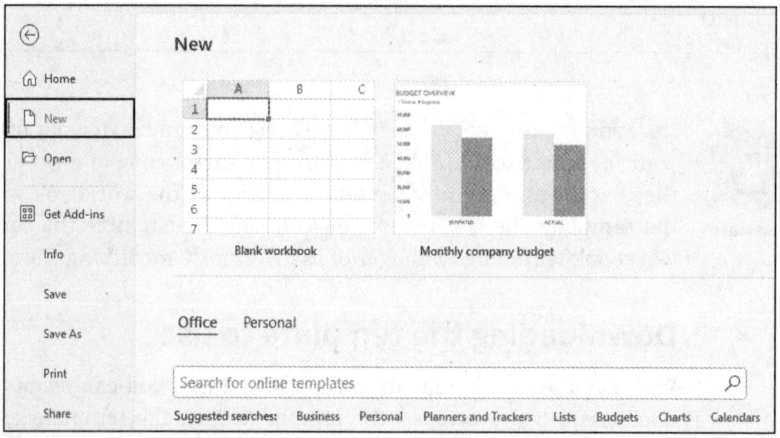


**FIGURE 1-6:** The downloaded template now appears in the New screen.

To customize a worksheet generated from one of the installed templates, you replace the placeholder entries in the new worksheet with your own data. Note that when filling in or replacing the data in a worksheet generated from one of these ready-made templates, you have access to all the cells in the worksheet: those that contain standard headings as well as those that require personalized data entry.

After you finish filling in the personalized data, save the workbook just as you would a workbook that you had created from scratch.

## Saving changes to your customized templates

You can save the customization you do to the templates you download to make the workbooks you create from them easier to use and quicker to fill out. To save your changes as a new template file, follow these steps:

1. **Choose File ⇨ Save As.**

   The Save As screen opens where you select the location where the customized template file is to be saved.

2. **Select This PC.**

   Excel selects the Documents folder, which is the place you want to be.

   If you really want to store your personal templates elsewhere (say, on your OneDrive), you're free to do so. Just note that you'll have to jump through a few extra hoops to tell Excel where you store your custom templates. I show you how to navigate those hoops right after these steps. For now, just remember the location you select because you'll need it later.

3. **Use the Enter File Name Here text box to type filename you want to use.**

4. **In the Save as Type list (which appears just below the Enter File Name Here text box), select Excel Template (*.xltx).**

   If you need your new template file to be compatible with earlier versions of Excel (versions 97 through 2003), click Excel 97–2003 Template (*.xlt) rather than Excel Template (*.xltx). When you do this, Excel saves the new template file in the older binary file format (rather than the newer XML file format) with the old `.xlt` filename extension instead of the newer `.xltx` filename extension. If your template contains macros that you want the user to be able to run when creating the worksheet, click Excel Macro-Enabled Template (*.xltm).

   If you're using the default Documents folder as the save location, Excel changes the selected folder to a subfolder of Documents named Custom Office Templates as soon as you change the file type from Excel Workbook to Excel Template.

5. **Click Save.**

   Excel saves your custom template in the location you selected.

   After the Save As dialog box closes, you still need to close the customized workbook file in the Excel work area.

6. **Choose File ⇨ Close or press Ctrl+W to close the customized workbook file.**

If you saved your customized template file in any folder other than the one currently listed as the Default Personal Template Location in the Excel Options dialog box, you need to tell Excel about this folder and where it is by following these steps:

1. **Choose File ⇨ Options ⇨ Save.**

   Excel opens the Excel Options dialog box and selects the Save tab.

2. **Click the Default Personal Templates Location text box and enter the complete filename path for the folder where you saved your initial personal template file.**

   For example, if you created a Templates subfolder within the Documents folder on my personal OneDrive to store all my personal Excel template files, you would enter the following pathname in the Default Personal Templates Location text box:

   ```
   C:\Users\Paul\OneDrive\Documents\Templates
   ```

3. **Click OK to put the new setting into effect.**

After designating the location of your personal templates folder as described in the preceding steps, the next time you open the New screen (choose File ⇨ New), you see two new headings below the Blank Workbook template (and above the Search box):

- **Office:** Click this heading to view and search for Office Excel templates.
- **Personal:** Click this heading to view your custom templates.

To generate a new workbook from one of your custom templates, click the Personal heading to display thumbnails for all the templates you've saved in the designated personal templates folder. To open a new Excel workbook from one of your custom templates, click the template's thumbnail.

## Creating your own workbook templates

You certainly don't have to rely on workbook templates created by other people. Indeed, often you can't do this because, even though other people may generate the type of template that you need, their design doesn't incorporate and represent the data in the manner that you prefer or that your company or clients require.

When you can't find a ready-made template that fits the bill or that you can easily customize to suit your needs, create your own templates from workbooks that you've created or that your company has on hand. The easiest way to create your own template is to first create an actual workbook prototype, complete with all the worksheets, text, data, formulas, graphics, and macros that it requires to function.

When readying the prototype workbook, make sure that you remove all headings, miscellaneous text, and numbers that are specific to the prototype and not generic enough to appear in the new template. You may also want to protect all generic data, including the formulas that calculate the values that you or your users input into the worksheets generated from the template and headings that never require editing. (See Book 8, Chapter 4 for information on how to protect certain parts of a worksheet from changes.)

After making sure that both the layout and content of the boilerplate data are hunky-dory, use the Save As command to save the workbook in the Excel Template (.xltx) file format in your personal templates folder so that you can then generate new workbooks from it. (For details on how to save a workbook as a template, refer to the steps in the previous section, "Saving changes to your customized templates.")



As you may have noticed when looking through the sample templates included in Excel (refer to Figure 1-4, for example) or browsing through the templates that you can download from the Microsoft `Office.com` website found at `http://office.microsoft.com`, many worksheet templates hide the familiar worksheet grid of cells, preferring a look very close to that of a paper form instead. When converting a sample workbook into a template, you can also hide the grid, use cell borders to underscore or outline key groups of cells, and color different cell groups to make them stand out. (For information on how to do this kind of stuff, refer to Book 3, Chapter 2.)

REMEMBER

You can add inline notes to parts of the template that instruct coworkers on how to properly fill in and save the data. These notes are helpful if your coworkers are unfamiliar with the template and may be less skilled in using Excel. (See Book 8, Chapter 4 for details about adding notes to worksheets.)

## Opening a new blank workbook

Although you can open a new workbook when you first start Excel, you'll often need to open a blank workbook after you've started working with Excel. The easiest way to open a blank workbook is to press Ctrl+N. Excel responds by opening a new workbook, which is given a generic Book name with the next unused number (Book2, if you opened Excel with a blank Book1). You can also do the same thing in backstage view by choosing File ➪ New and then selecting the Blank Workbook thumbnail.

As soon as you open a blank workbook, Excel makes its document window active. To then return to another workbook that you have open (which you would do if you wanted to copy and paste some of its data into one of the blank worksheets), move the mouse pointer over the Excel button on the Windows taskbar and then click the workbook thumbnail or press Alt+Tab until its file icon is selected in the dialog box that appears in the middle of the screen.

# Data Entry 101

I want to pass on a few basic rules of data entry:

- You must first select the cell where you want to make the data entry.
- Any entry that you make in a cell that already contains data replaces the existing entry.
- Every data entry that you make in a cell must be completed with some sort of action, such as clicking the Enter button on the Formula bar (shown in the margin; note that this button is only enabled when you're entering data), which is shown in Figure 1-7; pressing the Enter key, the Tab key, or one of the arrow keys; or clicking a different cell.

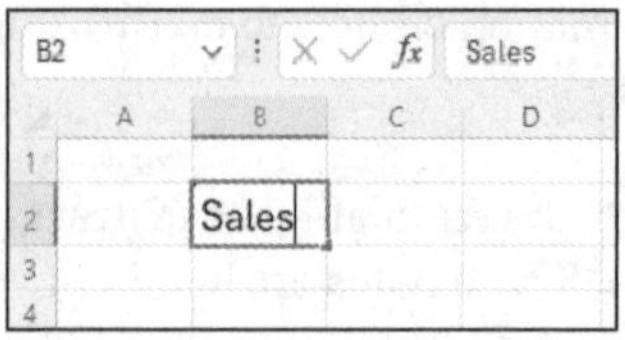


**FIGURE 1-7:** One way to complete a cell entry is to click the Enter button in the Formula bar.

The first rule sounds so obvious that it should go without saying, but you'd be surprised how many times you look at the cell where you intend to add new data and then just start entering that data without realizing that you haven't yet moved the active cell to that cell. As a result, the data entry that you're making is not destined to go into the cell that you intended. In fact, you're in the process of making the entry in whatever cell currently contains the active cell — if that cell already contains data, you're in the process of replacing its entry with the one you meant to go somewhere else!

REMEMBER

This is why the third rule is so important: Even if you're in the process of messing up your worksheet by entering data in the wrong cell (and, if that cell has data, by also destroying a perfectly good entry), you haven't messed anything up until you complete the entry (by, for example, pressing Enter). That reprieve means you can avoid the data entry error by clicking the Cancel button on the Formula bar (shown in the margin) or by pressing Escape. The erroneous data entry then disappears from the Formula bar (and the original data entry — if it exists — remains intact), and you're then free to move the active cell to the desired cell and redo the entry there.

## Data entry keyboard style

The only trick to entering data from the keyboard is to figure out the most efficient way to complete the entry in the active cell (and Excel gives you many choices in this regard).

One possibility is to complete any data entry by pressing the Enter key. Pressing Enter not only completes the entry in the cell, but also moves the active cell down to the cell in the next row. Pressing the Enter key is the efficient choice when you're entering data in a single column because it means that Excel automatically selects the cell in the next row for you. Sweet!

Another way to move the active cell down is to complete the cell entry by pressing the ↓ key. Note, however, that this only works for new entries, not when you're editing an existing entry.

A third possibility is to press the → key. Pressing → both completes the entry and moves the active cell to the next cell to the right. (Again, this only works for new entries.) Pressing → is the efficient option when you want to enter the data in a single row because it means that Excel automatically selects the cell in the next column for you. Thanks! (To be nerdily complete here, note that you can achieve the same effect by pressing the Tab key.)

Table 1-2 offers a list of the keys that you commonly use to complete data entries. Keep in mind, however, that any key combination that moves the active cell (refer to Table 1-1 for a list of these keystrokes) also completes the data entry that you're making, as does clicking another cell in the worksheet.

**TABLE 1-2** Keys Used in Completing Data Entry

| Press | To Have the Cell Pointer Move |
|---|---|
| Enter | Down one row |
| ↓ | Down one row |
| → | Right one column |
| Tab | Right one column |
| Shift+Tab | Left one column |
| ← | Left one column |
| Shift+Enter | Up one row |
| ↑ | Up one row |

TIP

What if you want to complete the data entry and stay in the same cell? Alas, you can't do that from the keyboard. Instead, you need to click the Enter button on the Formula bar (presumably this is what Microsoft intended; otherwise, why have the button?). Clicking Enter leaves the active cell on the cell in which you entered the data. Clicking Enter is the efficient move when you want to keep working on the same cell, say, by applying some text or numeric formatting. However, clicking Enter is not at all efficient when the mouse pointer isn't close to it or when you prefer to move the active cell to a different cell for your next entry.

TIP

If you have more than one cell selected (see Book 3, Chapter 2 for more on this) and then press Ctrl+Enter to complete the data entry that you're making in the active cell of this selected range, Excel simultaneously enters that data entry into all the cells in the selection. You can use this technique to enter a single label, value, or formula in many places in a worksheet at one time.

## Entering text labels

Sometimes a text entry is too long to fit in a cell. How Excel accommodates text entries that are too wide depends on whether data is in the cell to the right of the one you entered the text in:

- If the cell to the right is empty, Excel lets the text spill into the next cell.
- If the cell to the right contains data, the entry gets cut off. Nevertheless, the text you entered is in the cell. Nothing gets lost when it can't be displayed onscreen. You just can't see the text or numbers except by glancing at the Formula bar, where the contents of the active cell can be seen in their entirety.

## Entering numeric values

REMEMBER

When a number is too large to fit in a cell, Excel displays pounds signs (###) instead of a number or displays the number in scientific notation (8.78979E+15). You can always glance at the Formula bar, however, to find out the number in the active cell. As well, you can always widen the column to display the entire number (as explained in Book 3, Chapter 2).

To enter a fraction in a cell, enter a 0 or a whole number, a blank space, and the fraction. For example, to enter 3/8, type a **0**, press the spacebar, and type **3/8**. To enter 5 3/8, type **5**, press the spacebar, and type **3/8**. For its purposes, Excel converts fractions to decimal numbers, as you can see by looking in the Formula bar after you enter a fraction. For example, 5 3/8 displays as 5.375 in the Formula bar.

## Entering date and time values

Dates and times can be used in calculations, but entering a date or time value in a cell can be problematic because these values must be entered in such a way that Excel can recognize them as dates or times, not text.

### Entering date values

You can enter a date value in a cell in just about any format you choose, and Excel understands that you're entering a date. For example, enter a date in any of the following formats and you'll be all right:

| | |
|---|---|
| m/d/yy | 7/31/25 |
| m-d-yyyy | 7-31-2025 |
| d-mmm-yy | 31-Jul-25 |

Here are some basic things to remember about entering dates:

- **Date formats:** You can quickly apply a format to dates by selecting cells and using one of these techniques:
  - On the Home tab, open the Number Format drop-down list and choose Short Date (*m/d/yyyy;* 7/31/2025) or Long Date (*day of the week, month, day, year;* Wednesday, July 31, 2025).
  - On the Home tab, click the Number group button to open the Number tab of the Format Cells dialog box. Choose the Date category and then choose a date format.

- **Current date:** Press Ctrl+; (semicolon) to enter the current date.
- **Current year's date:** If you don't enter the year as part of the date, Excel assumes that the date you entered is in the current year. For example, if you enter a date in the *m/d* (7/31) format during the year 2025, Excel enters the date as 7/31/25. As long as the date you want to enter is the current year, you can save a little time when entering dates by not entering the year because Excel enters it for you.
- **Dates on the Formula bar:** No matter which format you use for dates, dates are displayed in the Formula bar in the format that Excel prefers for dates: *m/d/yyyy* (7/31/2025). How dates are displayed in the worksheet is up to you.

REMEMBER

- **20th and 21st century two-digit years:** When it comes to entering two-digit years in dates, the digits 30 through 99 belong to the 20th century (1930–1999), but the digits 00 through 29 belong to the 21st century (2000–2029). For example, 7/31/25 refers to July 31, 2025, not July 31, 1925. To enter a date in 1929 or earlier, enter four digits instead of two to describe the year: **7-31-1929**. To enter a date in 2030 or later, enter four digits instead of two: **7-31-2030**.

## Entering time values

Excel recognizes time values that you enter in the following ways:

| | |
|---|---|
| *h:mm* AM/PM | 3:31 AM |
| *h:mm:ss* AM/PM | 3:31:45 PM |

Here are some things to remember when entering time values:

- **Use colons:** Separate hours, minutes, and seconds with a colon (:).
- **Time formats:** To change to the *h:mm:ss* AM/PM time format, select the cells, go to the Home tab, open the Number Format drop-down list, and choose Time. You can also change time formats by clicking the Number group button on the Home tab and selecting a time format on the Number tab of the Format Cells dialog box.
- **AM or PM time designations:** Unless you enter AM or PM with the time, Excel assumes that you're operating on military time. For example, 3:30 is considered 3:30 a.m.; 15:30 is 3:30 p.m. Don't enter periods after the letters *am* or *pm* (don't enter a.m. or p.m.).
- **Current time:** Press Ctrl+Shift+; (semicolon) to enter the current time.

- **Times on the Formula bar:** On the Formula bar, times are displayed in this format: *hours:minutes:seconds,* followed by the letters AM or PM. However, the time format used in cells is up to you.

## Combining date and time values

You can combine dates and time values by entering the date, a blank space, and the time:

- 7/31/21 3:31 am
- 7-31-21 3:31:45 pm

# You AutoFill me

Few Excel features are more helpful than the AutoFill feature, which enables you to fill in a series of entries in a row or column — all by entering only the first item (or, in some cases, the first two or three items) in the series. You can sometimes use the AutoFill feature to quickly input row and column headings for a new data table or to number the records in a table. For example, when you need a row of column headings that list the 12 months for a sales table, you can enter *January* or *Jan.* in the first column and then have AutoFill input the other 11 months for you in the cells in columns to the right. Likewise, when you need to create a column of row headings at the start of a table with successive part numbers that start at L505-120 and proceed to L505-128, you enter L505-120 in the first row and then use AutoFill to copy the part numbers down to L505-128 in the cells below.

The key to using AutoFill is the Fill handle, which is the small black square that appears in the lower-right corner of the active cell. When you position the mouse on the Fill handle, it changes from the normal thick, white-cross pointer to a thin, black-cross pointer. This change in shape is your signal that when you drag the Fill handle in a single direction, either down or to the right, Excel either copies the active cell entry to all the cells that you select or uses it as the first entry in a consecutive series, whose successive entries are then automatically entered in the selected cells.

Note that you can immediately tell whether Excel will copy the cell entry or use it as the first in a series to fill in by the ScreenTips that appear to the right of the mouse pointer. As you drag through subsequent cells, the ScreenTip indicates which entry will be made if you release the mouse button at that point. If the ScreenTip shows the same entry as you drag, you know Excel didn't recognize the entry as part of a consecutive series and is copying the entry verbatim. If, instead, the ScreenTips continue to change as you drag through cells showing you successive entries for the series, you know that Excel has recognized the original entry as part of a consecutive series.

Figures 1-8 and 1-9 illustrate how AutoFill works. In Figure 1-8, I entered January as the first column heading in Cell B2 (using the Enter button on the Formula bar to keep the active cell in B2, ready for AutoFill). Next, I positioned the mouse pointer on the AutoFill handle in the lower-right corner of B2, then I dragged the Fill handle to the right until I reached Cell M2 (and the ScreenTip stated December).

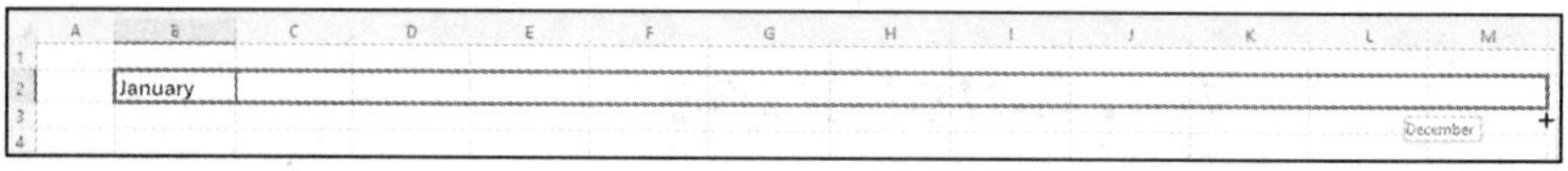


**FIGURE 1-8:** Dragging the Fill handle to fill in a series with the 12 months of the year.

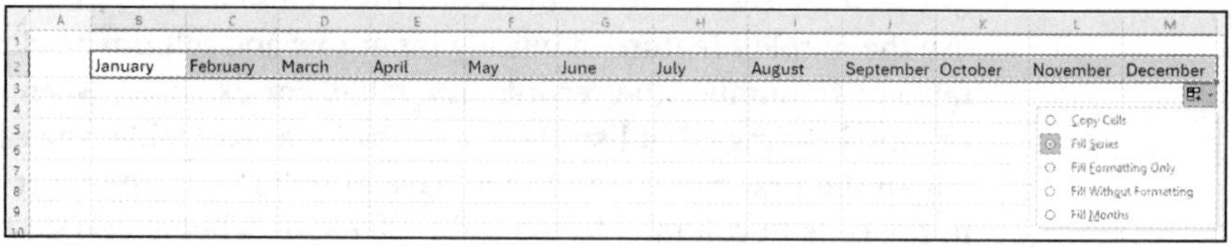


**FIGURE 1-9:** The series of monthly column headings with the AutoFill Options drop-down menu.

Figure 1-9 shows the series that was entered in the cell range B2:M2 when I released the mouse button with Cell M2 selected. For this figure, I also clicked the drop-down button attached to the AutoFill Options button (shown in the margin) that automatically appears whenever you use the Fill handle to copy entries or fill in a series to show you the items on this drop-down menu. This menu contains a Copy Cells option button that enables you to override Excel's decision to fill in the series and have it copy the original entry (January, in this case) to all the selected cells.

Note that you can also override Excel's natural decision to fill in a series or copy an entry before you drag the Fill handle. To do so, hold down the Ctrl key (which adds a tiny plus sign to the upper-right corner of the Fill handle). Continue to hold down the Ctrl key as you drag the Fill handle and notice that the ScreenTip now shows that Excel is no longer filling in the series, but copying the entry as expected.

## AutoFill via the Fill button on the Ribbon

Instead of using the Fill handle, you can also fill in a series using the Fill button on the Excel Ribbon. To use the Fill button on the Home tab of the Ribbon to accomplish your AutoFill operations, follow these steps:

1. **Enter the first entry (or entries) upon which the series is to be based in the first cell(s) to hold the new data series in your worksheet.**
2. **Select the cell range where the series is to be created, across a row or down a column, being sure to include the cell with the initial entry or entries in this range.**
3. **On the Home tab, in the Editing group, click the Fill button (shown in the margin) and then tap Series on its drop-down menu.**

   Excel opens the Series dialog box.
4. **In the Type group, select the AutoFill option button.**
5. **Click OK.**

   Excel enters a series of data based on the initial value(s) in your selected cell range just as though you'd selected the range with the fill handle.



Note that the Series dialog box contains a bunch of options that you can use to further refine and control the data series that Excel creates. In a linear data series, if you want the series to increment more than one step value at a time, you can increase it in the Step Value text box. Likewise, if you want your linear or AutoFill series to stop when it reaches a particular value, you enter that into the Stop Value text box.

REMEMBER

When you're entering a series of dates with AutoFill that increment on anything other than the day, remember the Date Unit options in the Series dialog box enable you to specify other parts of the initial date to increment in the series. Your choices include Weekday, Month, or Year.

## AutoFill series with custom increments

Normally, when you drag the Fill handle to fill in a series of data entries, Excel increases or decreases each entry in the series by a single unit (a day, month, hour, or whatever). You can, however, get AutoFill to fill in a series of data entries that uses a custom increment, such as every two days, every third month, or every hour-and-a-half.

Figure 1-10 illustrates several series all created with AutoFill that use custom increments:

- The first example in Row 2 shows a series of times with 45-minute increments, starting with 8:00 a.m. in Cell A2 and extending to 2:00 p.m. in Cell I2.
- The second example in Row 4 contains a series of weekdays with two-day increments, starting on Monday in Cell A4 and extending to Saturday in Cell G4.
- The third example in Row 6 shows a series of numbers created with a custom increment of 15, starting with 35 in Cell A6 and increasing to 155 in Cell I6.
- The fourth example in Row 8 shows a series of months created with a custom increment of 2, starting with Jan in Cell A8 and ending with Nov in Cell F8.
- The final example in Row 10 shows a series of numbers created with a custom increment of -25 (so, really, a *decrement*), starting with 100 in Cell A10 and decreasing to -100 in Cell I10.

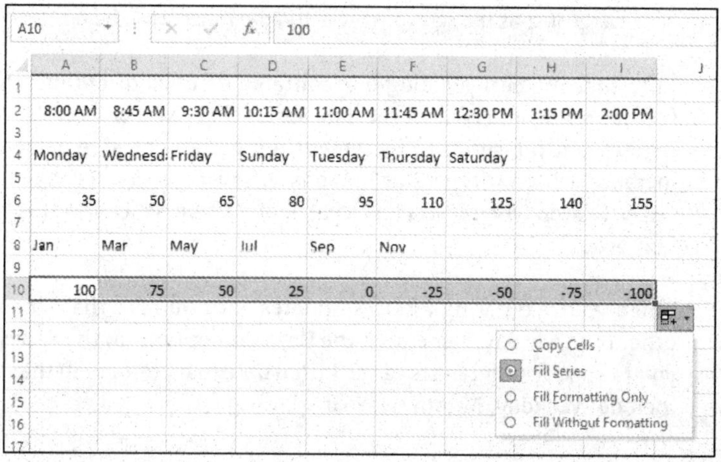


**FIGURE 1-10:** Some series created with AutoFill by using custom increments.

To create a series that uses a custom increment, follow these four general steps:

1. **Enter the first two entries in the series in consecutive cells above one another in a column or side by side in a row.**

   Enter the entries one above the other when you intend to drag the Fill handle down the column to extend the series. Enter them side by side when you intend to drag the Fill handle to the right across the row.

2. **Position the cell pointer in the cell with the first entry in the series and drag through the second entry.**

   Both entries must be selected (indicated by being enclosed within the expanded active cell) before you use the Fill handle to extend the series. Excel analyzes the difference between the two entries and uses this difference as its increment in filling in the data series.

3. **Drag the Fill handle down the column or across the row to extend the series.**

   In this case, Excel fills the series by using the increment value. Check the ScreenTips to make sure that Excel is using the correct increment in filling out your data series.

4. **Release the mouse button when you reach the desired end of the series (indicated by the entry shown in the ScreenTip appearing next to the black-cross mouse pointer).**

## Creating custom AutoFill lists

Just as you can use AutoFill to create a series with a custom increment, you can also cajole AutoFill into creating a custom list using items that you specify. For example, suppose that you often enter a standard series of city locations as the column or row headings in new worksheets. Instead of copying the list of cities from one workbook to another, you can create a custom list containing all the cities in the order in which they normally appear in your worksheets. After you create a custom list in Excel, you can then enter the first item in a cell and use the Fill handle to extend the series either down a column or across a row.

To create a custom series, you can either enter the list of entries in the custom series in successive cells of a worksheet before you open the Custom Lists dialog box, or you can type the sequence of entries for the custom series in the List Entries list box located on the right side of the Custom Lists tab in this dialog box, as shown in Figure 1-11.

If you already have the data series for your custom list entered in a range of cells somewhere in a worksheet, follow these steps to create the custom list:

1. **Click the cell with the first entry in the custom series and then drag the mouse or Touch pointer through the range until all the cells with entries are selected.**

   The expanded active cell should now include all the cells with entries for the custom list.

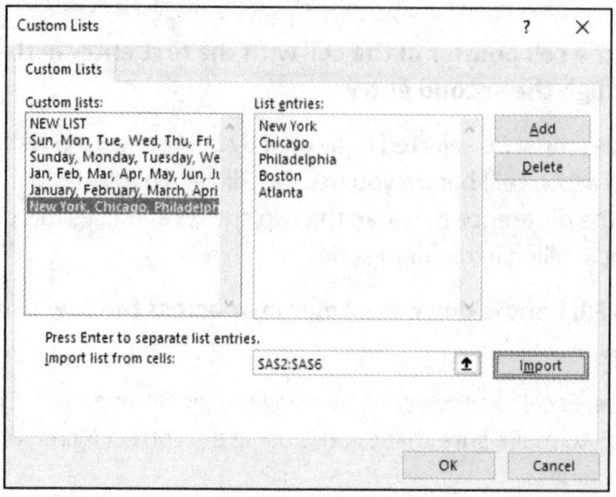


**FIGURE 1-11:** Creating a custom list of cities for AutoFill.

2. **Choose File ⇨ Options ⇨ Advanced and then scroll down and click the Edit Custom Lists button located in the General section.**

   The Custom Lists dialog box opens with its Custom Lists tab, where you now should check the accuracy of the cell range listed in the Import List from Cells text box. (The range in this box lists the first cell and last cell in the current selected range separated by a colon — you can ignore the dollar signs following each part of the cell address.)

3. **Click the Import button to add the entries in the selected cell range to the List Entries box on the right and to the Custom Lists box on the left side of the Custom Lists tab.**

   Excel adds the data entries in the selected cell range to both the List Entries and the Custom Lists boxes.

4. **Click OK to close the Custom Lists dialog box, and then click OK to close the Excel Options dialog box.**

If you don't have the entries for your custom list entered anywhere in the worksheet, you must follow the second and third steps listed previously and then take these three additional steps instead:

1. **Click the List Entries box and then type each of the entries for the custom list in the order in which they are to be entered in successive cells of a worksheet.**

   Press the Enter key after typing each entry for the custom list so that each entry appears on its own line in the List Entries box or separate each entry with a comma.

2. **Click the Add button to add the entries that you've typed to the Custom Lists box.**

   Note that when Excel adds the custom list that you just typed to the Custom Lists box, it automatically adds commas between each entry in the list — even if you pressed the Enter key after making each entry. It also automatically separates each entry on a separate line in the List Entries box — even if you separated them with commas instead of carriage returns.

3. **Click OK to close the Custom Lists dialog box, and then click OK to close the Excel Options dialog box.**

After you've created a custom list by using one of these two methods, you can fill in the entire data series by entering the first entry of the list in a cell and then dragging the Fill handle to fill in the rest of the entries. If you ever decide that you no longer need a custom list that you've created, you can delete it by clicking the list in the Custom Lists box in the Custom Lists dialog box and then clicking the Delete button. Excel then displays an alert box indicating that the list will be permanently deleted when you click OK. Note that you can't delete any of the built-in lists that appear in this list box when you first open the Custom Lists dialog box.

REMEMBER

You can also fill in any part of the series by entering any one of the entries in the custom list and then dragging the Fill handle in the appropriate direction (down and to the right to enter succeeding entries in the list or up and to the left to enter preceding entries).



## Flash Fill to the rescue

Excel's handy Flash Fill feature gives you the ability to take a part of the data entered into one column of a worksheet table and enter just that data in a new table column using only a few keystrokes. The series of entries appear in the new column the moment Excel detects a pattern in your initial data entry that enables it to figure out the data you want to copy. The beauty is that all this happens without the need for you to construct or copy any kind of formula.

The best way to understand Flash Fill is to see it in action. Figure 1-12 contains a new data table consisting of four columns. The first column already contains the full names of clients (first, middle, and last). The second, third, and fourth columns need to have just the first, middle, and surnames, respectively, entered (so that particular parts of the clients' names can be used in the greetings of form emails and letters as in, "Hello Keith," or "Dear Mr. Harper,").

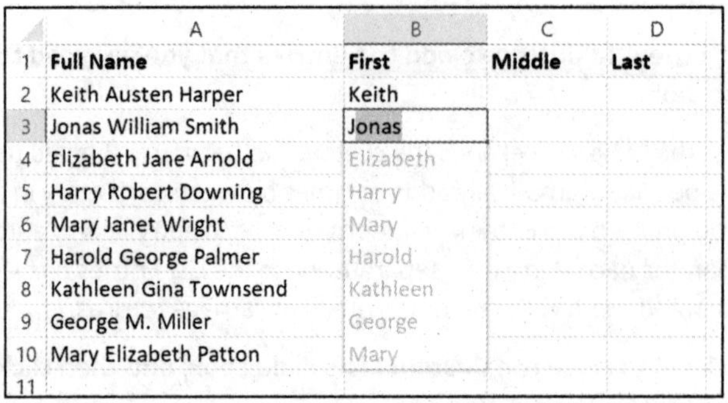
A
B
C
D
1 Full Name
First
Middle
Last
2 Keith Austen Harper
Keith
3 Jonas William Smith
Jonas
4 Elizabeth Jane Arnold
Elizabeth
5 Harry Robert Downing
Harry
6 Mary Janet Wright
Mary
7 Harold George Palmer
Harold
8 Kathleen Gina Townsend
Kathleen
9 George M. Miller
George
10 Mary Elizabeth Patton
Mary
11

**FIGURE 1-12:** New data table containing full names that need to be split up in separate columns with Flash Fill.

Rather than manually entering the first, middle, or last names in the respective columns (or attempting to copy the entire client name from Column A and then editing the parts not needed in the First Name, Middle Name, and Last Name columns), you can use Flash Fill to quickly and effectively do the job. And here's how you do it:

1. **Type** Keith **in Cell B2 and complete the entry with the ↓ or Enter key.**

   When you complete this entry with the ↓ key or Enter key on your keyboard, Excel moves the cell pointer to Cell B3, where you have to type only the first letter of the next name for Flash Fill to get the picture.

2. **In Cell B3, type only** J, **the first letter of Jonas, the second client's first name.**

   Flash Fill immediately does an AutoFill type maneuver by suggesting the rest of the second client's first name, Jonas, as the text to enter in this cell. At the same time, Flash FIll suggests entering all the remaining first names from the full names in Column A in Column B.

3. **Complete the entry of Jonas in Cell B3 by clicking the Enter button or pressing an arrow key.**

   The moment you complete the data entry in Cell B3, the First Name column is done: Excel enters all the other first names in Column B at the same time!

To complete this example name table by entering the middle and last names in Columns C and D, respectively, you repeat these steps in those columns. You enter the first middle name, **Austen**, from Cell A2 in Cell C2 and then type **W** in Cell C3. Complete the entry in Cell C3 and the middle name entries in that column are done. Likewise, you enter the first last name, **Harper**, from Cell A2 in Cell D2 and then type **S** in Cell D3. Complete the entry in Cell D3, and the last name entries for Column D are done, finishing the entire data table.

REMEMBER

Flash Fill works perfectly at extracting parts of longer data entries in a column provided that all the entries follow the same pattern and use same type of separators (spaces, commas, dashes, and the like). For example, in Figure 1-12, there's an anomaly in the full name entries in Cell A9 where only the middle initial with a period is entered instead of the full middle. In this case, Flash Fill enters M in Cell C9, and you have to manually edit its entry to add the necessary period. Also, remember that Flash Fill's usefulness isn't restricted to all-text entries as in my example Client Name table. It can also extract parts of entries that mix text and numbers, such as ID numbers (AJ-1234, RW-8007, and so forth).

IN THIS CHAPTER

» Selecting cells

» Adjusting column widths and row heights

» Getting cells and data into the right format

» Using the Format Painter to quickly copy formatting

# Chapter 2

# Sprucing Up a Worksheet

When it comes to populating a worksheet with data, Excel doesn't put a lot of hurdles in your path. Most of the time, you click the cell you want to use, type your label, data, or formula, press Enter, and — voilà! — you've got yourself a cell entry. Repeat as needed and soon enough your worksheet is done.

Or is it? The problem with Excel's data entry process is that it tends to produce worksheets that are, well, unattractive: All the text is the same size and the same color; some longer cell entries appear truncated; columns of data and labels are misaligned. It's a mess! So, sure, Excel makes it easy to add data, but to make that data look presentable requires more work.

Why should you care about how your worksheets look? After all, most of the time you're the only person who'll seem them, right? Perhaps. But even if your eyeballs are the only ones that will grace your worksheets, there are lots of advantages to taking a bit of extra time to make things look nice. *Formatting* a worksheet — the process of adding fonts and colors, adjusting column widths and row heights, aligning data, adding borders, and much more — makes the worksheet easier to read, helps you find errors, and gives you a hand spotting trends and performing other types of data analysis. And all those advantages are doubled if you plan to share your workbooks with colleagues and coworkers.

In this chapter, you explore Excel's extensive worksheet formatting options. After a brief foray into selecting cells, you dive into the deep end of formatting cells, ranges, rows, and columns. Your worksheets are going to look *so* good by the time you're done with this chapter.

# Selecting Cells and Ranges

Before you can modify the appearance of anything in a worksheet, you must first select the cells you want to mess with.

In Excel, you can select a single cell, a block of cells (known as a *cell range,* or, usually, just a *range*), or a collection of discontinuous cell ranges (also known as a *nonadjacent range*).

REMEMBER

The address of a range is always noted in a formula by the upper-left and lower-right cells that you select, separated by a colon (:). For example, if you select Cell A1 as the first cell and Cell H10 as the last cell, the range address would be A1:H10.

In the sections that follow, I walk you through the techniques you can use to select cells using either the mouse or the keyboard.

## Selecting cells with the mouse

Excel offers several methods for selecting cells with the mouse. With each method, you start by selecting one of the cells that occupies the corner of the range that you want to select. The first corner cell that you click becomes the *active cell* (indicated by its cell reference in the Formula bar's Name box), and the range that you then select becomes anchored on this cell.

After you select the active cell in the range, drag the pointer to extend the selection until you've highlighted all the cells that you want to include.

Here are some tips:

- To extend a range in a block that spans several columns, drag right or left from the active cell.
- To extend a range in a block that spans several rows, drag down or up from the active cell.

» To extend a range in a block that spans several columns and rows, drag diagonally from the active cell in the most logical directions (up and to the right, down and to the right, up and to the left, or down and to the left).

If you ever extend the range too far in one direction, you can always reduce it by dragging in the other direction. If you've already released the mouse button and you find that the range is incorrect, click the active cell again. (Clicking any cell in the worksheet deselects a selected range and activates the cell that you click.) Then select the range of cells again.

TIP

You can always tell the active cell that forms the anchor point of a range because it's the only cell within the range that you've selected that isn't highlighted and is the only cell reference listed in the Formula bar's Name box. As you extend the range by dragging the thick white-cross mouse pointer, Excel indicates the current size of the range in columns and rows in the Name box (as in 4R x 3C when you've highlighted a range that's four rows long and three columns wide), as shown in Figure 2-1. However, as soon as you release the mouse button, Excel replaces this row and column notation with the address of the active cell.

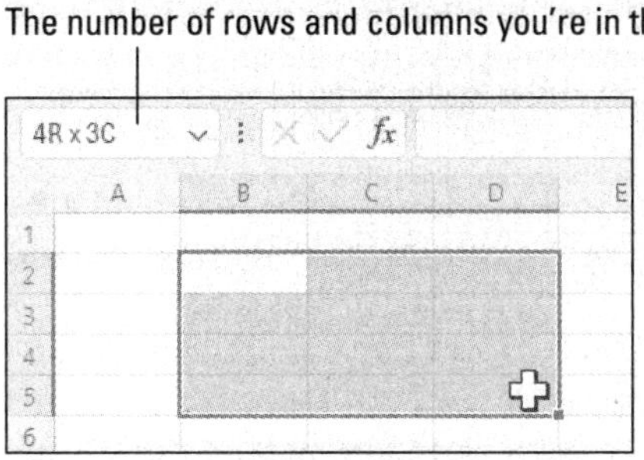


**FIGURE 2-1:** As you drag the mouse, the Name box tells you how many rows and columns you've selected.

You can also use the following shortcuts when selecting cells with the mouse:

» To select a single-cell range, click the cell.

» To select all cells in an entire column, position the mouse pointer in the column header (the pointer changes to a downward-pointing arrow) and then click. To select several adjacent columns, drag through their column headers.

» To select all cells in an entire row, position the mouse pointer in the row header (the pointer changes to a right-pointing arrow) and then click. To select several adjacent rows, drag through the row headers.

» To select all the cells in the worksheet, click the box in the upper-left corner of the worksheet at the intersection of the row and column headers (shown in the margin). You can also select every cell from the keyboard by pressing Ctrl+A.

» To select a range without dragging, click the first cell in the range, hold down the Shift key, click the last cell in the range, and then release the Shift key. Excel selects all the cells in between the first and last cells that you click.

» To select a nonadjacent selection consisting of several discontinuous ranges, drag through the first cell range and then hold down the Ctrl key as you drag through the other ranges. After you've marked all the cell ranges to be included in the nonadjacent selection, you can release the Ctrl key.

## Selecting cells with the keyboard

Excel also makes it easy for you to select cell ranges with a keyboard by using a technique known as *extending a selection.* To use this technique, you move the cell cursor to the first cell you want to include in the range; then press F8 to turn on Extend Selection mode (indicated by Extend Selection on the status bar) and use the direction keys to move the pointer to the last cell in the range. Excel selects all the cells that the cell cursor moves through until you turn off Extend Selection mode (by pressing F8 again).

You can use the mouse as well as the keyboard to extend a selection when Excel is in Extend Selection mode: Click the active cell, press F8, and then click the last cell to mark the range.

You can also select a cell range with the keyboard without turning on Extend Selection mode. Here, you use a variation of the Shift+click method by moving the cell pointer to the first cell of the range, holding down the Shift key, and then using the direction keys to extend the range. After you've highlighted all the cells that you want to include, release the Shift key.

To mark a nonadjacent selection of cells with the keyboard, you need to combine the use of Extend Selection mode with that of Add to Selection mode. To turn on Add to Selection mode (indicated by Add to Selection on the status bar), you press Shift+F8. To mark a nonadjacent selection by using Extend Selection and Add to Selection modes, follow these steps:

1. **Move the cell cursor to the first cell of the first range you want to select.**
2. **Press F8 to turn on Extend Selection mode.**
3. **Use the arrow keys to extend the cell range until you've highlighted all its cells.**

4. **Press Shift+F8 to turn off Extend Selection mode and turn on Add to Selection mode instead.**
5. **Move the cell cursor to the first cell of the next cell range you want to add to the selection.**
6. **Press F8 to turn off Add to Selection mode and turn Extend Selection mode back on.**
7. **Use the arrow keys to extend the range until all cells are highlighted.**
8. **Repeat Steps 4 through 7 until you've selected all the ranges that you want included in the nonadjacent selection.**
9. **Press F8 to turn off Extend Selection mode.**

# Adjusting Columns and Rows

Along with knowing how to select cells for formatting, you really also have to know how to adjust the width of your columns and the heights of your rows. Why? Because often in the course of assigning different formatting to certain cell ranges (such as new font and font size in boldface type), you may find that data entries that previously fit within the original widths of their column no longer do and that the rows that they occupy seem to have changed height all on their own.

Most of the time, you don't need to be concerned with the heights of the rows in your worksheet because Excel automatically adjusts them up or down to accommodate the largest font size used in a cell in the row and the number of text lines (in some cells, you may wrap their text on several lines, as I describe in the "Formatting Cells from the Ribbon" section). Instead, you'll spend a lot more time adjusting the column widths to suit the entries for the formatting that you assign to them.



## Fitting the column to its contents automatically

The easiest way to adjust the width of a column to suit its longest entry is to use the AutoFit feature. AutoFit examines the content in the selected column or columns and then adjusts the width of each column so that it's just a bit wider than the column's widest entry.

» **To use AutoFit on a single column:** Position the mouse pointer on the right edge of that column in the column header. You'll know you've got it right when the pointer changes to a double-headed arrow. Double-click the mouse and Excel adjusts the column width just like that.

- **To use AutoFit on multiple columns at one time:** Select the columns by dragging through them in the column header or by Ctrl+clicking the column letters and then double-clicking the right edge of one of the selected columns when the pointer changes to a double-headed arrow.

These AutoFit techniques work well for adjusting all columns except for those that contain really long headings (such as the worksheet title that often spills over several blank columns in Row 1), in which case AutoFit makes the columns far too wide for the bulk of the cell entries.

For those situations, use the AutoFit Column Width command, which adjusts the column width to suit only the entries in the cells of the column that you have selected. This way, you can select all the cells except for any really long ones in the column that purposely spill over to empty cells on the right, and then have Excel adjust the width to suit. Select the cells in the column that you want the new width to fit, click the Home tab, click the Format button in the Cells group, and then click AutoFit Column Width.

## Adjusting columns the old-fashioned way

AutoFit is nothing if not quick and easy. If you need more precision in adjusting your column widths, you have to do this manually either by dragging its border with the mouse or by entering new values in the Column Width dialog box.

- **To manually adjust a column width with the mouse:** Position the mouse pointer on the right edge of that column in the column header (look for the pointer changing to a double-headed arrow), then drag to the left (to narrow) or to the right (to widen) as required. As you drag the column border, a ScreenTip appears above the mouse pointer indicating the current width in both characters and pixels. When you have the column adjusted to the desired width, release the mouse button to set it.
- **To adjust a column width in the Column Width dialog box:** Position the cell pointer in any one of the cells in the column that you want to adjust, click the Home tab, click the Format button in the Cells group, and then click Column Width to open the Column Width dialog box. Type the new width (as the number of characters; use a value between 0 and 255) in the Column Width text box and then click OK.

TIP

You can apply a new column width that you set in the Column Width dialog box to more than a single column by selecting the columns (either by dragging through their letters on the Column header or holding down Ctrl as you click them) before you open the Column Width dialog box.

## Hiding a column or two

You can use the Hide command to temporarily remove columns of data from the worksheet display. When you hide a column, you're essentially setting the column width to 0. Hiding columns enables you to remove the display of sensitive or supporting data that needs to be in the worksheet but may not be appropriate when you share your screen with others.

To hide a column, put the cell pointer in a cell in that column; to hide more than one column at a time, select the columns either by dragging through their letters on the Column header or by holding down Ctrl as you click them. Click the Home tab, click the Format button in the Cells group, and then click Hide & Unhide ⇨ Hide Columns.

Excel lets you know that certain columns are missing from the worksheet by removing their column letters from the Column header so that if, for example, you hide Columns D and E in the worksheet, Column C is followed by Column F on the Column header.

To restore hidden columns to view, select the visible columns on either side of the hidden one(s) — indicated by the missing letter(s) on the column headings — and then click the Home tab, click the Format button in the Cells group, and then click Hide & Unhide ⇨ Unhide Columns.

Because Excel also automatically selects all the redisplayed columns, you need to deselect these columns before you do any formatting or editing that will affect all their cells. To deselect the columns, click a single cell anywhere in the worksheet or select whatever cell range that you want to work with.



## Fiddling with rows

The controls for adjusting the height of the rows in your worksheet parallel those that you use to adjust column widths. The big difference is that Excel always applies AutoFit to the height of each row so that even though you find an AutoFit Row Height option under Cell size on the Format button's drop-down menu, you won't find much use for it.

Instead, you'll probably end up manually adjusting the heights of rows with the mouse or by entering new height values and occasionally hiding rows with sensitive or potentially confusing data. Follow these instructions for each type of action:

- **To adjust the height of a row with the mouse:** Position the mouse on the lower edge of the row's border in the Row header and then drag up or down when the mouse pointer changes to a double-headed, vertical arrow. As you drag, a ScreenTip appears to the side of the pointer, keeping you informed of the height in characters and also in pixels.
- **To change the height of a row in the Row Height dialog box:** Click the Home tab, click the Format button in the Cells group, and then click Row Height. Enter the value for the new row height in the Row Height text box and then click OK.
- **To hide a row:** Position the cell cursor in any one of the cells in that row and then click the Home tab, click the Format button in the Cells group, and then click Hide & Unhide ➪ Hide Rows from the drop-down menu. To then restore the rows that you currently have hidden in the worksheet, select the rows above and below the hidden rows, click the Home tab, click the Format button, and then click Hide & Unhide ➪ Unhide Rows.

REMEMBER

As with adjusting columns, you can change the height of more than one row and hide multiple rows at the same time by selecting the rows before you drag one of their lower borders, open the Row Height dialog box, or click Format ➪ Hide & Unhide ➪ Hide Rows on the Home tab.

# Formatting Cells from the Ribbon

In the Ribbon's Home tab, the formatting buttons that appear in the Font, Alignment, and Number groups enable you to apply all kinds of cell formatting. Table 2-1 offers a complete rundown on the use of each of these formatting buttons.

REMEMBER

Don't forget the shortcut keys: Ctrl+B for toggling bold in the cell selection, Ctrl+I for toggling italics, and Ctrl+U for toggling underlining.

**TABLE 2-1** **The Formatting Command Buttons in the Home Tab's Font, Alignment, and Number Groups**

| Group | Button Name | Function |
|---|---|---|
| Font | | |
| | Font | Displays a Font drop-down menu from which you can assign a new font for the entries in your cell selection |
| | Font Size | Displays a Font Size drop-down menu from which you can assign a new font size to the entries in your cell selection. Click the Font Size text box and enter the desired point size if it doesn't appear on the drop-down menu. |
| | Increase Font Size | Increases the font size of the entries in your cell selection |
| | Decrease Font Size | Decreases the font size of the entries in your cell selection |
| | Bold | Applies and removes boldface in the entries in your cell selection |
| | Italic | Applies and removes italics in the entries in your cell selection |
| | Underline | Applies and removes underlining in the entries in your cell selection |
| | Borders | Opens a Borders drop-down menu from which you can assign a new border style to or remove an existing border style from your cell selection |
| | Fill Color | Opens a drop-down Color palette from which you can assign a new background color for your cell selection |
| | Font Color | Opens a drop-down Color palette from which you can assign a new font color for the entries in your cell selection |
| Alignment | | |
| | Top Align | Aligns the entries in your cell selection with the top border of their cells |
| | Middle Align | Vertically centers the entries in your cell selection between the top and bottom borders of their cells |
| | Bottom Align | Aligns the entries in your cell selection with the bottom border of their cells |
| | Orientation | Opens a drop-down menu with options for changing the angle and direction of the entries in your cell selection |
| | Wrap Text | Wraps all entries in your cell selection that spill over their right borders onto multiple lines within the current column width |
| | Align Left | Aligns all the entries in your cell selection with the left edge of their cells |
| | Center | Centers all the entries in your cell selection within their cells |
| | Align Right | Aligns all the entries in your cell selection with the right edge of their cells |

*(continued)*

**TABLE 2-1** *(continued)*

| Group | Button Name | Function |
|---|---|---|
| | Decrease Indent | Decreases the margin between entries in your cell selection and their left cell borders by one character |
| | Increase Indent | Increases the margin between the entries in your cell selection and their left cell borders by one character |
| | Merge & Center | Merges your cell selection into a single cell and then centers the combined entry in the first cell between its new left and right borders. Click the Merge and Center drop-down button to display a menu of options that enable you to merge the cell selection into a single cell without centering the entries, as well as to split up a merged cell back into its original individual cells. |
| Number | | |
| | Number Format | Displays the number format applied to the active cell in your cell selection. Click its drop-down button to open a drop-down menu where you can assign one of Excel's major Number formats to the cell selection. |
| | Accounting Number Format | Opens a drop-down menu from which you can select the currency symbol to be used in the Accounting number format. When you select the $ English (United States) option, this format adds a dollar sign, uses commas to separate thousands, displays two decimal places, and encloses negative values in a closed pair of parentheses. Click More Accounting Formats to open the Number tab of the Format Cells dialog box where you can customize the number of decimal places and/or currency symbol used. |
| | Percent Style | Formats your cell selection using the Percent Style number format, which multiplies the values by 100 (for display purposes only) and adds a percent sign with no decimal places |
| | Comma Style | Formats your cell selection with the Comma Style Number format, which uses commas to separate thousands, displays two decimal places, and encloses negative values in a pair of parentheses |
| | Increase Decimal | Adds a decimal place to the values in your cell selection |
| | Decrease Decimal | Removes a decimal place from the values in your cell selection |

# Formatting Numbers, Dates, and Time Values

When you enter a number that Excel recognizes as belonging to one of its formats, Excel assigns the number format automatically. Enter **45%**, for example, and Excel assigns the Percentage number format. Enter **$4.25**, and Excel assigns the Currency number format. Besides assigning formats by hand, however, you can assign them to cells from the get-go and spare yourself the trouble of entering dollar signs, commas, percent signs, and other extraneous punctuation. All you have to do is enter the raw numbers. Excel does the window dressing for you.

Excel offers five number-formatting buttons on the Home tab in the Number group. Select cells with numbers in them and click one of these buttons to change how numbers are formatted:

- **Accounting Number Format:** Places a dollar sign (or any currency sign you choose after opening the drop-down list on this button) before the number and gives it two decimal places
- **Percent Style:** Places a percent sign after the number and converts the number to a percentage
- **Comma Style:** Places commas in the number
- **Increase Decimal:** Increases the number of decimal places by one
- **Decrease Decimal:** Decreases the number of decimal places by one

To choose among many formats and to format dates and time values as well as numbers, select the cells, go to the Home tab, and use one of these techniques:

- Open the Number Format drop-down list and select an option.
- Click the Number group's dialog box launcher (shown in the margin) and make selections on the Number tab of the Format Cells dialog box. Choose a category and select options to describe how you want numbers or text to appear. You can also open the Format Cells dialog box by right-clicking and choosing Format Cells on the shortcut menu.

To strip formats from the data in cells, select the cells, go to the Home tab, in the Editing group, click the Clear button, and then choose Clear Formats.



# Hiring Out the Format Painter

The Home tab's Clipboard group includes the Format Painter button, which copies formatting from the current cell and applies it to cells that you "paint" by dragging its special thick-white cross-plus-paintbrush mouse pointer through them. Format Painter provides a quick-and-easy way to take a bunch of different formats (such as a particular font, border, and alignment) that you applied individually to a cell in the worksheet and then apply them in one fell swoop to a new range of cells.

To use the Format Painter, follow these steps:

1. **Position the cell cursor in a cell that contains the formatting that you want copied to another range of cells in the worksheet.**

   The selected cell becomes the sample cell whose formatting is taken up by Format Painter and copied in the cells that you "paint" with its special mouse pointer.

2. **In the Home tab's Clipboard group, click the Format Painter button (shown in the margin).**

   Excel adds a paintbrush icon to the standard thick white-cross mouse pointer, indicating that the Format Painter is ready to copy the formatting from the sample cell.

3. **Click the cell or click and drag the mouse pointer through the range of cells that you want formatted identically to the sample cell.**

   When you release the mouse button, the cells in the range that you just selected with the Format Painter become formatted the same way as the sample cell. Excel deactivates the Format Painter button automatically.

TIP

If you want to keep the Format Painter activated so that you can use it to format more than one range of cells in the worksheet, you need to double-click the Format Painter button in Step 2, above. The Format Painter button remains selected (indicated by the shading) until you click its command button again. During this time, you can "paint" as many different cells or ranges in the worksheet as you desire.

IN THIS CHAPTER

» Learning basic cell editing techniques

» Zooming in and out on the worksheet

» Freezing columns and rows on the screen

» Copying and moving worksheet data

Chapter 3

# Fiddling with Your Worksheets

Are you the kind of person who meticulously plans every element of a worksheet before you even think about entering your labels, data, and formulas? Of course you aren't! Nobody is! Why not? Because we all have *way* too much on our plates to spend precious time merely planning the layout of a worksheet. Can you imagine?

When all you need is a quick-and-dirty worksheet model to perform some analysis or run a few calculations, you don't need any preliminaries. Just get in there and start banging away. Nothing wrong with working that way, but just remember the "dirty" side of the "quick-and-dirty" approach. When you leap before you look to build a worksheet, the result is almost always not a pretty sight.

Again, nothing wrong with an unsightly worksheet as long as it gets the job done, right? But a "dirty" worksheet might not just be tough to look at. It might also be tough to understand or even be downright wrong because of errors in your data or your formulas. And if you hope to share that worksheet with colleagues or clients, then you'll need to make things more comprehensible, for sure.

Fortunately, Excel offers an extensive set of editing tools that can help you whip a worksheet into shape. In this chapter, you find out how to make basic editing changes in a worksheet by modifying the contents of a cell as well as how to do more complex editing in your worksheets. These techniques include how to use the Undo and Redo features, zoom in and out on data, move and copy data, and delete data entries and insert new ones.

# Editing a Cell

The biggest thing to remember about basic cell editing is that you have to put the cell pointer (also known as the cell cursor) on the cell you want to modify. When modifying a cell's contents, you can replace the entry entirely, delete characters from the entry, and/or insert new characters into the entry:

- **Replacing a cell's contents:** Select the cell, type your new entry, and then press Enter (or use whatever completion technique you prefer). Excel replaces the existing data entry with your typing. While you're typing the new entry, you can cancel the replacement and restore the original cell entry by clicking the Formula bar's Cancel button or by pressing Escape.
- **Deleting characters in a cell entry:** Open the cell for editing by selecting the cell and pressing F2 or by double-clicking the cell. Either technique puts Excel into Edit mode (indicated by Edit on the status bar). Alternatively, select the cell and click inside the Formula bar. You now have an insertion point cursor either inside the cell or in the Formula bar. Use the Home, End, or ← and → keys to move the insertion point to the right of the first character you want to delete and press Backspace until you've removed all the unnecessary or incorrect characters. (Alternatively, move the insertion point to the left of the first character you want to delete, and then press Delete until you've removed all the characters you no longer need.)
- **Inserting new characters in a cell entry:** Open the cell for editing by selecting the cell and pressing F2 or by double-clicking the cell. Either technique puts Excel into Edit mode (indicated by Edit on the status bar). Alternatively, select the cell and click inside the Formula bar. You now have an insertion point cursor either inside the cell or in the Formula bar. Use the Home, End, or ← and → keys to move the insertion point to the location in the entry where you want to insert the new characters and then start typing.

## Changing your mind with Undo and Redo

Excel supports multiple levels of undo that you can use to recover from potentially costly editing mistakes that would require data re-entry or extensive repair operations. The most important thing to remember about the Undo command is that it is cumulative, meaning that you may have to select it multiple times to reverse several actions that you've taken before you get to the one that sets your worksheet right again.

You can select the Undo command either by clicking the Undo button on the Quick Access toolbar (shown in the margin) or by pressing Alt+Backspace or Ctrl+Z. Excel then reverses the last edit you made in the worksheet.

On the Quick Access toolbar, you can click the drop-down button attached to the Undo command button (or press Alt+3) to display a menu of the actions that you've recently taken in the worksheet. Instead of undoing one action at a time, you undo multiple actions by clicking the last of the actions you want to undo in the drop-down menu. Excel then restores the worksheet to the state that it was in before you took all the actions that you chose from this drop-down menu.

After you use the Undo feature to reverse an editing change, the Redo button (shown in the margin) on the Quick Access toolbar becomes active. The Redo command item on the Redo button's drop-down menu has the name of the latest type of editing that you just reversed with the Undo button, such as Redo Clear when the last action you took was to restore a cell entry that you just deleted.

You use the Redo command to restore the worksheet to the condition that it was in before you last clicked the Undo command. As with using the Undo button on the Quick Access toolbar, when you click the drop-down button attached to the Redo button, you can repeat multiple actions by clicking the last of the actions you want repeated (assuming that you used the Undo command multiple times). You can also restore edits that you've undone one at a time by pressing Ctrl+Y.

TIP

## EDITING IN THE CELL VERSUS ON THE FORMULA BAR

When doing simple editing to a cell's contents, you might wonder whether it's better to edit the contents in the cell directly or edit the contents in the Formula bar. When editing short entries that fit entirely within the current column width, it really is a matter of personal choice. Some people prefer editing on the Formula bar because it's out of the way of other cells in the same region of the worksheet. Other people prefer editing on the Formula bar because they find it easier to click the insertion point with the I-beam mouse pointer at precisely the place in the entry that needs editing. (When you press F2 to edit in the cell, Excel always positions the insertion point at the very end of the entry,

*(continued)*

(continued)

and when you double-click in the cell, you really can't tell exactly where you're putting the insertion point until you finish double-clicking, at which time the flashing insertion point appears.)

When it comes to editing longer cell entries (that is, text entries that spill over into empty neighboring cells, and numbers that, if their digits weren't truncated by the number format assigned, wouldn't fit within the current cell width), you probably will want to edit their contents on the Formula bar. You can click the Formula Bar button (the carat symbol turned downward) to display the entire contents of the cell without obscuring any of the cells of the worksheet.

## Clearing cells

Sometimes you need to delete an entry that you made in a cell of the worksheet without replacing it with any other contents. Excel refers to this kind of deletion as *clearing* the cell. This is actually more correct than referring to it as "emptying" the cell because although the cell may appear empty when you delete its contents, it may still retain the formatting assigned to it, and therefore it isn't truly empty.

For this reason, on the Home tab, in the Editing group, clicking the Clear button (shown in the margin) opens a drop-down menu with these options:

- **Clear All:** Gets rid of both the contents and the formatting assigned to the current cell selection.
- **Clear Formats:** Removes only the formatting assigned to the current cell selection without getting rid of the contents.
- **Clear Contents:** Gets rid of only the contents in the current cell selection without getting rid of the formatting assigned to it. (This is the equivalent of pressing the Delete key.)
- **Clear Comments and Notes:** Removes only the comments and notes assigned to the cells in the selection without touching either the contents or the formatting.
- **Clear Hyperlinks:** Displays the Clear Hyperlinks button below and to the right of the selection. Click that button and then click either Clear Hyperlinks Only (which removes the hyperlinks without also removing the hyperlink formatting) or Clear Hyperlinks and Formats (which removes both the hyperlinks and the hyperlink formatting).
- **Remove Hyperlinks**: Removes the hyperlink and its formatting.

## Deleting cells

The Clear All option I mention in the previous section is great when you need to truly empty a cell of all formatting and contents while at the same time retaining that empty cell in the worksheet. However, what about when you need to get rid of the cell as well as all its contents?

In this case, you want to both clear the duplicate entry and remove the newly emptied cell while at the same time pulling up the cells with the rest of the numbers in the list below along with the cell at the end that contains the formula that sums the values together. Excel offers just such a command on the Home tab, in the Cells group, in the form of the Delete button and its drop-down menu.

When you select the cell (or cells) you want to expunge and then click the Delete button, Excel dutifully removes the selected cell(s) from the worksheet and then does one of the following:

- **Shifts cells up:** Excel always does this if there is at least one non-empty cell below the deleted cell in the same column. If there is no non-empty column below the deleted cell, then Excel does the following, instead.
- **Shifts cells to the left:** Excel does this if there is at least one non-empty cell to the right of the deleted cell in the same row.

REMEMBER

When you use the Delete command, Excel zaps everything, including the contents, formatting, and any and all attached comments. Don't forget about the Undo button on the Quick Access toolbar or Ctrl+Z in case you ever zap something you shouldn't have!

That's a tad confusing, I know, and Excel's default shifting of nearby cells might not be what you want. To gain more control over the deletion process, click the Delete button's drop-down menu and then click Delete Cells. The Delete dialog box appears, similar to the one shown in Figure 3-1. This dialog box lets you choose how you want the remaining cells to be shifted when the selected cell (or cells) is removed from the worksheet.

Figures 3-1 and 3-2 illustrate how Delete Cells works in the example where a duplicate entry has been mistakenly entered in a column of numbers that is totaled by a summing formula. In Figure 3-1, I selected Cells A5:B5, which contain duplicate entries, before clicking the Delete button's drop-down button and then clicking Delete Cells from its drop-down menu to display the Delete dialog box.

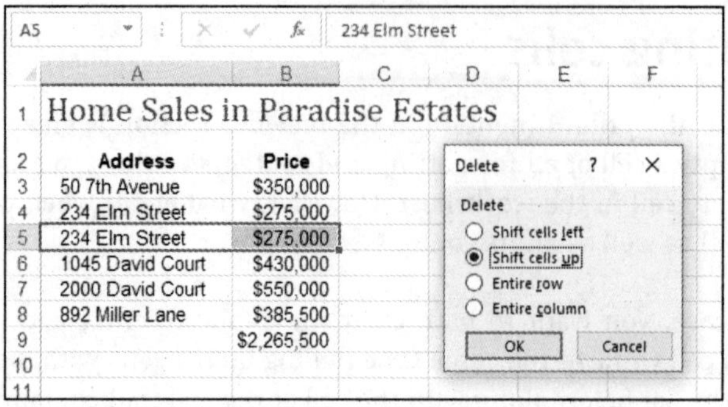


**FIGURE 3-1:** When you select Delete Cells, Excel asks how you want the remaining cells to be shifted.

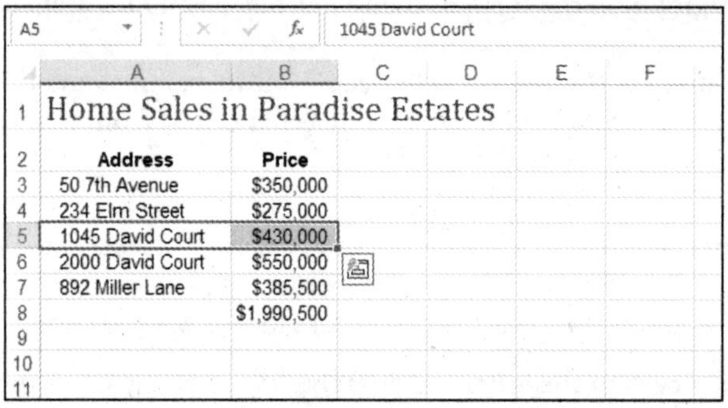


**FIGURE 3-2:** Worksheet after deleting the cell with the duplicate entry.

When the Delete dialog box opens, the Shift Cells Left option is automatically selected. That's not what I want here. Instead, I want Excel to shift the remaining cells up to fill in the blank cells, so that's why I've selected the Shift Cells Up option in Figure 3-1. Figure 3-2 shows the same worksheet after clicking OK in the Delete dialog box. Notice how Excel pulled up the entries in the cells below when it deleted the duplicate in Cell B5, while at the same time automatically recalculating the summing formula to reflect the total of the remaining entries.

## Inserting cells

On the Home tab, in the Cells group, the Insert command is the opposite of the Delete button immediately below it. That is, rather than removing cells for your worksheet, you use Insert to create new cells in your worksheet.

For example, suppose that you discover that you've left out three numbers from a column of summed numbers and that these values should have appeared in the middle of the column. You could shift the bottom half of the column down three cells to create some room, but that can be a pain if you're dealing with a long column of values. Instead, you can use the Insert command to get Excel to do the work for you.

To make this edit, select the first data row that needs to be shifted down to make room for the missing entries. If you were just inserting a single entry, you can leave it at that. However, to let Excel know how many rows you want to insert, you drag the selection down until you've selected the number of rows you want inserted. For example, you'd select three rows if you wanted to insert three entries.

Figures 3-3 and 3-4 (sample workbook: Home Sales.xlsx for both) illustrate this situation. In Figure 3-3, I selected the cell range A5:B7, where cells for the three missing entries are to be inserted. I then clicked the drop-down button on the Insert button followed by Insert Cells on its drop-down menu. The Insert dialog box opens with the Shift Cells Right option button selected. Because I needed to have the cells in the selected range moved down to make room for the missing entries, I then selected the Shift Cells Down option.

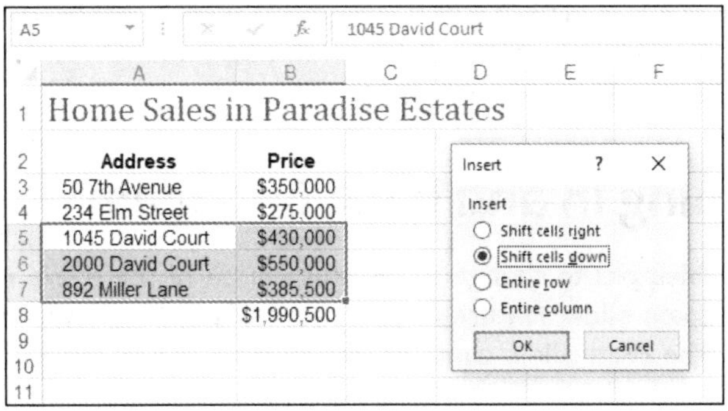


**FIGURE 3-3:** Inserting three blank cells for missing entries in two columns of a table while shifting the existing entries down. (Sample workbook: Home Sales.xlsx)

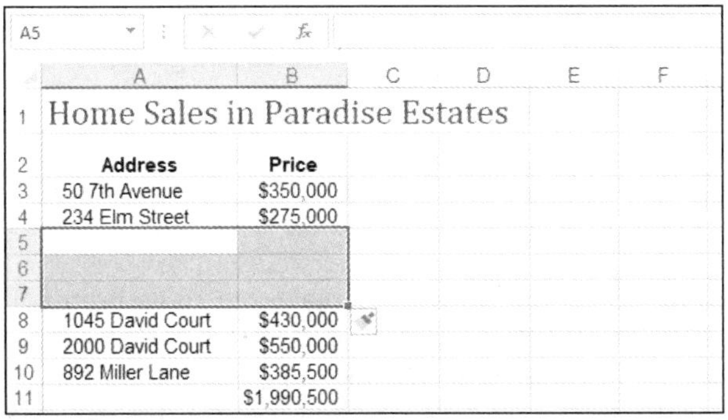


**FIGURE 3-4:** The worksheet table after entering the missing entries in the newly inserted blank cells. (Sample workbook: Home Sales.xlsx)

After clicking OK in the Insert dialog box, Excel moves down the existing entries as shown in Figure 3-4. This leaves the previously occupied range A5:B7 with three blank data rows, where I can input my missing entries.

TIP

If you know that you want to move existing cells down with the Shift Cells Down option when inserting new cells in the current cell selection, you don't have to bother with opening the Insert dialog box at all: Click the Insert button (rather than its drop-down button), and Excel instantly inserts new cells while moving the existing ones down.

# A Worksheet with a View

Excel provides a number of features that can help you find your way and keep your place in a worksheet that needs editing. Among these are its Zoom feature, which enables you to increase or decrease the magnification of the worksheet window, thus making it possible to switch from a really up-close view to a really far-away view in seconds, and its Freeze Panes feature, which enables you to keep pertinent information, such as column and row headings, on the worksheet window as you scroll other columns and rows of data into view.

## Zooming in and back out again

Excel enables you to change the magnification of the active worksheet window with its Zoom slider feature on the status bar in the lower-right corner of the window. The Zoom slider contains two buttons, one on either end:

- **Zoom Out (-):** Reduces the worksheet area's magnification percentage by 10 percent each time you click the button.
- **Zoom In (+):** Increases the worksheet area's magnification percentage by 10 percent each time you click the button.

You can also quickly change the worksheet area's magnification percentage by dragging the slider's button to the left (to zoom out) or to the right (to zoom in).

REMEMBER

When you first open the worksheet, the Zoom slider button is always located in the very center of the Zoom slider, putting the worksheet area magnification at 100%. As you click the Zoom Out or Zoom In button or drag the slider button, Excel keeps you informed of the current magnification percentage by displaying it to the immediate right of the Zoom In button on the status bar. Note too, that 10% is the lowest percentage you can select by dragging the button all the way to the left on the slider, and 400% is the highest percentage you can select by dragging the button all the way to the right.

Although the Zoom slider is always available on the status bar in any worksheet you have open, you can also change the worksheet area's magnification percentage via the Ribbon: On the View tab, in the Zoom group, click the Zoom button. Excel opens the Zoom dialog box, where you have three ways to change the Zoom level:

- Select one of the preset magnification percentages: 200%, 100%, 75%, 50%, or 25%.
- Select the Custom option and then use the Custom text box to enter any magnification percentage between a minimum of 10% and a maximum of 400%.
- Select the Fit Selection option to have Excel change the magnification so that the selected cell range takes up the entire height or width of the worksheet area. Alternatively, select your cell range, and then click the View tab's Zoom to Selection button.

Figures 3-5 and 3-6 illustrate how you can use the Zoom feature to first zoom out to locate a region in a large worksheet that needs editing and then zoom in on the region to do the editing. In Figure 3-5, I zoomed out on the Income Analysis to display all its data by selecting a 50% magnification setting. At the 50% setting, I could just barely make out the headings and read the numbers in the cells. I then located the cells that needed editing and selected their cell range (J20:L25) in the worksheet.

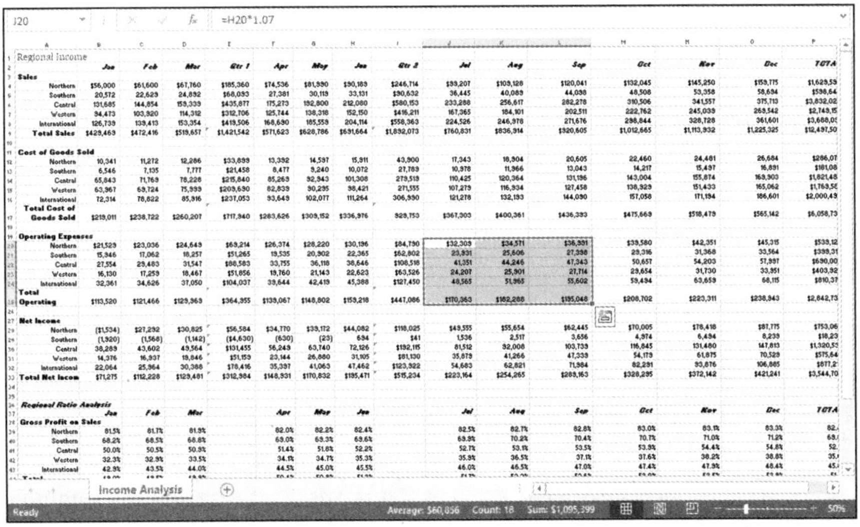


**FIGURE 3-5:** The Income Analysis worksheet after zooming out to a 50% magnification setting. (Sample workbook: Income Analysis.xlsx)

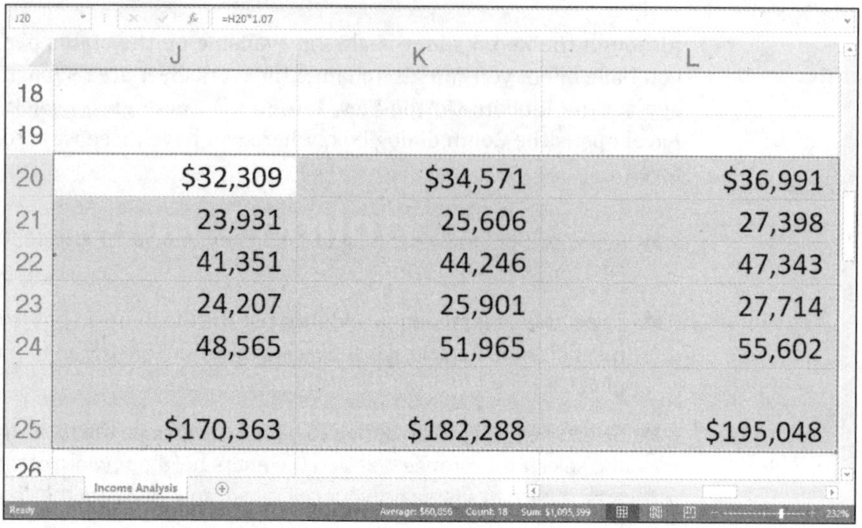


**FIGURE 3-6:** Worksheet at 232% magnification after zooming in on the cell range J20:L25. (Sample workbook: Income Analysis.xlsx)

I then clicked the Zoom to Selection command button on the View tab, and Figure 3-6 shows the result. As shown on the status bar, Excel boosted the magnification from 50% up to 232% to get the range to fit (in this case) the width of the worksheet area.

TIP

Because Excel immediately puts the slider button at whatever point you click, you can instantly return the magnification percentage to the normal 100% after selecting any other magnification. Click the vertical line at the midpoint in the Zoom slider on the status bar. Alternatively, in the View tab's Zoom group, click the 100% button.

## Freezing window panes

Excel's Freeze Panes feature enables you to specify one or more rows and/or columns that stay put while you scroll the worksheet. For example, if you freeze row 1 (the top row) of the worksheet, the data in that row remains visible no matter how far down you scroll in the worksheet. Similarly, if you freeze column A (the leftmost column) of the worksheet, the data in that column remains visible no matter how far right you scroll in the worksheet.

How is this useful? Well, Figure 3-6 could be the poster child for why you need the Freeze Panes feature. Although zooming in on the range of cells that needs editing makes their data entries more readable, it also removes all the column and row labels that enable you to figure out what data you're examining. If I had used the

Freeze Panes command to freeze Column A with the row labels and Row 2 with the column labels, they would remain displayed on the screen — regardless of the magnification settings that I select or how I scroll through the cells.

To use the Freeze Panes feature in this manner, you first position the cell pointer in the cell that's located to the immediate right of the column or columns that you want to freeze and immediately beneath the row or rows that you want to freeze. Now, in the View tab's Window group, click Freeze Panes to drop down the menu, and then select the Freeze Panes command.

TIP

To freeze the top row of the worksheet (assuming that it contains column headings) from anywhere in the worksheet (it doesn't matter where the cell cursor is), display the View tab and choose Freeze Panes ➪ Freeze Top Row. If you want to freeze the first column (assuming that it contains row headings) from anywhere in the worksheet, display the View tab and select Freeze Panes ➪ Freeze First Column.

Figures 3-7 and 3-8 illustrate how this works. Figure 3-7 shows the Income Analysis worksheet after freezing Column A and Rows 1 and 2. To do this, I positioned the cell cursor in Cell B3 before choosing Freeze Panes from the Freeze Panes button's drop-down menu. Notice the thin black line that runs down Column A and across Row 2, marking which column and rows of the worksheet are frozen on the display and that now remain in view — regardless of how far you scroll to the right to new columns or scroll down to new rows.

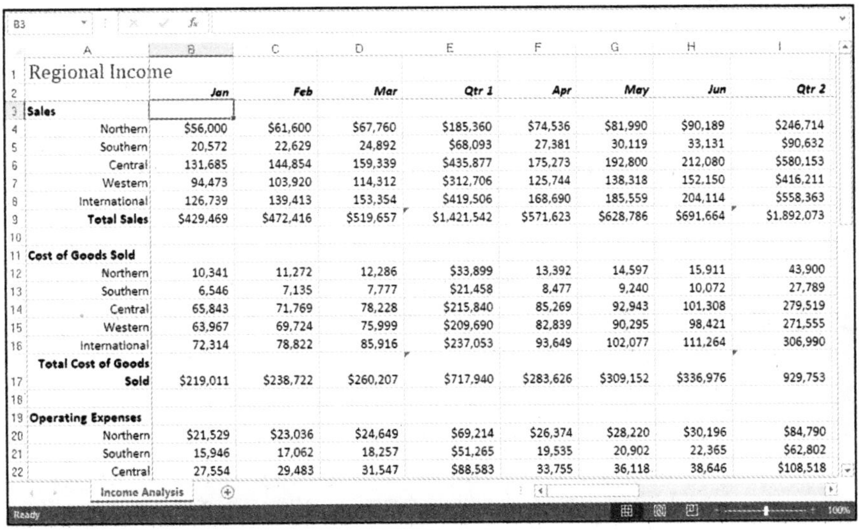

| | A | B | C | D | E | F | G | H | I |
|---|---|---|---|---|---|---|---|---|---|
| 1 | Regional Income | | | | | | | | |
| 2 | | Jan | Feb | Mar | Qtr 1 | Apr | May | Jun | Qtr 2 |
| 3 | Sales | | | | | | | | |
| 4 | Northern | $56,000 | $61,600 | $67,760 | $185,360 | $74,536 | $81,990 | $90,189 | $246,714 |
| 5 | Southern | 20,572 | 22,629 | 24,892 | $68,093 | 27,381 | 30,119 | 33,131 | $90,632 |
| 6 | Central | 131,685 | 144,854 | 159,339 | $435,877 | 175,273 | 192,800 | 212,080 | $580,153 |
| 7 | Western | 94,473 | 103,920 | 114,312 | $312,706 | 125,744 | 138,318 | 152,150 | $416,211 |
| 8 | International | 126,739 | 139,413 | 153,354 | $419,506 | 168,690 | 185,559 | 204,114 | $558,363 |
| 9 | Total Sales | $429,469 | $472,416 | $519,657 | $1,421,542 | $571,623 | $628,786 | $691,664 | $1,892,073 |
| 10 | | | | | | | | | |
| 11 | Cost of Goods Sold | | | | | | | | |
| 12 | Northern | 10,341 | 11,272 | 12,286 | $33,899 | 13,392 | 14,597 | 15,911 | 43,900 |
| 13 | Southern | 6,546 | 7,135 | 7,777 | $21,458 | 8,477 | 9,240 | 10,072 | 27,789 |
| 14 | Central | 65,843 | 71,769 | 78,228 | $215,840 | 85,269 | 92,943 | 101,308 | 279,519 |
| 15 | Western | 63,967 | 69,724 | 75,999 | $209,690 | 82,839 | 90,295 | 98,421 | 271,555 |
| 16 | International | 72,314 | 78,822 | 85,916 | $237,053 | 93,649 | 102,077 | 111,264 | 306,990 |
| 17 | Total Cost of Goods Sold | $219,011 | $238,722 | $260,207 | $717,940 | $283,626 | $309,152 | $336,976 | 929,753 |
| 18 | | | | | | | | | |
| 19 | Operating Expenses | | | | | | | | |
| 20 | Northern | $21,529 | $23,036 | $24,649 | $69,214 | $26,374 | $28,220 | $30,196 | $84,790 |
| 21 | Southern | 15,946 | 17,062 | 18,257 | $51,265 | 19,535 | 20,902 | 22,365 | $62,802 |
| 22 | Central | 27,554 | 29,483 | 31,547 | $88,583 | 33,755 | 36,118 | 38,646 | $108,518 |



**FIGURE 3-7:** The income worksheet after freezing Column A and Rows 1:2 in the worksheet display.

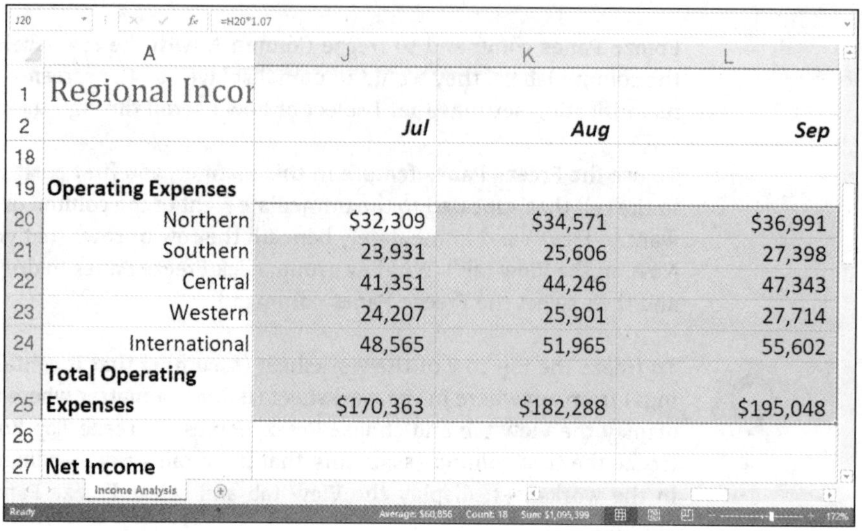


**FIGURE 3-8:** The income worksheet after zooming in on the cell range J20:L25 after freezing panes.

As Figure 3-8 shows, frozen panes stay on the screen even when you zoom in and out on the worksheet. For Figure 3-8, I repeated the steps I took in changing the magnification for Figures 3-5 and 3-6 (only this time with the frozen panes in place). First, I zoomed out on the Income Analysis worksheet by dialing the 50% magnification setting on the Zoom slider; second, I selected the range J20:L25 and then clicked the Zoom to Selection button on the View tab.

Figure 3-8 shows the result. Note that with the frozen panes in place, this time Excel only selected a 172% magnification setting instead of the original 232% setting. This lower magnification setting is worth it because all the important information has been added to the cell range.

To unfreeze the panes after you've finished editing, click the Unfreeze Panes option on the Freeze Panes button's drop-down menu. (This option replaces Freeze Panes at the top of the menu.)

# Copying and Moving Stuff Around

Moving and copying worksheet data are among the most common tasks that you perform when editing a typical worksheet. Excel offers two basic methods for moving and copying a cell selection in a worksheet: First, you can use drag-and-drop to place the cells in a new location; second, you can cut or copy the contents to the Clipboard and then paste them into the desired area. Moving and copying data to new areas in a worksheet are basically very straightforward procedures.

You need to keep a few things in mind, however, when rearranging cell entries in a worksheet:

- When you move or copy a cell, Excel moves everything in the cell, including the contents, formatting, and any note assigned to the cell. (See Book 8, Chapter 4, for information on adding notes to cells.)
- If you move or copy a cell so that it overlays an existing entry, Excel replaces the existing entry with the contents and formatting of the cell that you're moving or copying. This means that you can replace existing data in a range without having to clear the range before moving or copying the replacement entries. It also means that you must be careful not to overlay any part of an existing range that you don't want replaced with the relocated or copied cell entries.
- When you move cells referred to in formulas in a worksheet, Excel automatically adjusts the cell references in the formulas to reflect their new locations in the worksheet.
- When you copy formulas that contain cell references, Excel automatically adjusts the cell references in the copies relative to the change in their position in the worksheet. (See Book 3, Chapter 5 for details on copying formulas in a worksheet.)

REMEMBER

For situations in which you need to copy only a single data entry to cells in a single row or to cells in a single column of the worksheet, you can use AutoFill to extend the selection left or right or up or down by dragging the fill handle. (See Book 3, Chapter 1 for information about using AutoFill to extend and copy a cell entry.)

# Copying and moving with drag-and-drop

Drag-and-drop provides the most direct way to move or copy a range of cells in a single worksheet. To move a range, select the cells, position the pointer on any one of the edges of the range (the pointer's cursor changes to a white arrowhead pointing to the center of a black cross with four black arrowheads), drag the range to its new position in the worksheet, and then release the mouse button.

## Moving cells with drag-and-drop

As you drag a cell range using drag-and-drop, Excel displays only the outline of the range with a ScreenTip that keeps you informed of its new cell or range address. After you've positioned the outline of the selected range so that the outline surrounds the appropriate cells in a new area of the worksheet, release the mouse button or your finger or stylus from the touchscreen. Excel moves the selected cells (including the entries, formatting, and comments) to this area.

If the outline of the cell selection that you're dropping encloses any cells with existing data entries, Excel displays an Alert dialog box asking whether you want to replace the contents of the destination cells. If you click OK in this dialog box, the overlaid data entries are completely zapped when they're replaced by the incoming entries. If you inadvertently overwrite useful data, not to worry: Immediately press Ctrl+Z (or click the Quick Access toolbar's Undo command) to reverse the move and restore the zapped cells.

### Copying cells with drag-and-drop

You can use drag-and-drop to copy cell ranges as well as to move them. To modify drag-and-drop so that the feature copies the selected cells rather than relocating them, hold down the Ctrl key when you position the mouse pointer on one of the edges of the selected range. Excel indicates that drag-and-drop is ready to copy rather than move the cell selection by changing the mouse pointer to an outline pointer with a small plus sign in the upper-right. When the pointer assumes this shape, drag the outline of the selected cell range to the desired position and release both the Ctrl key and mouse button.

## Copying and moving with copy, cut, and paste

Despite the convenience of using drag-and-drop, you may still prefer to use the more traditional method of copying or cutting and then pasting selections when moving or copying cells in a worksheet. Cut, Copy, and Paste uses the Clipboard (a special area of memory shared by all Windows programs), which provides a temporary storage area for the data in your cell selection until you paste the selection into its new position in the worksheet. Here are the basic techniques:

- **Moving a cell selection:** On the Home tab, in the Clipboard group, click the Cut command (shown in the margin), or press Ctrl+X or Shift+Delete.

- **Copying a cell selection:** On the Home tab, in the Clipboard group, click the Copy command (shown in the margin), or press Ctrl+C or Ctrl+Insert.

When you cut or copy a selection to the Clipboard, Excel displays a marquee around the cell selection (sometimes called *marching ants*), and the following message appears on the status bar:

```
Select destination and press ENTER or choose Paste
```

To complete the move or copy operation, select the first cell in the range where you want the relocated or copied selection to appear and then press the Enter key, click the Home tab's Paste button (shown in the margin), or press Ctrl+V or Shift+Insert. Excel then completes the move or copy operation, pasting the range as required, starting with the active cell. When selecting the first cell of a paste range, be sure that you have sufficient blank cells below and to the right of the active cell so that the range you're pasting doesn't overwrite any existing data that you don't want Excel to replace.

WARNING

Unlike when moving and copying a cell selection with drag-and-drop, the cut-and-paste method doesn't warn you when it's about to replace existing cell entries in cells that are overlaid by the incoming cell range — it just goes ahead and replaces them with nary a beep or an alert! If you find that you moved the selection to the wrong area or replaced cells in error, immediately click the Undo button on the Quick Access toolbar or press Ctrl+Z to restore the range to its previous position in the worksheet.

## "Paste it again, Sam"

When you complete a copy operation with cut-and-paste by clicking the Paste button in the Clipboard group at the beginning of the Ribbon's Home tab instead of pressing the Enter key, Excel copies the selected cell range to the paste area in the worksheet without removing the marquee from the original range. You can continue to paste the selection to other areas in the worksheet without having to recopy the cell range to the Clipboard. If you don't need to paste the cell range in any other place in the worksheet, you can press Enter to complete the copy operation. If you don't need to make further copies after using the Paste command, you can remove the marquee from the original selection by pressing the Escape key.

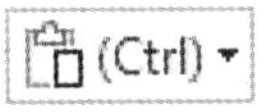

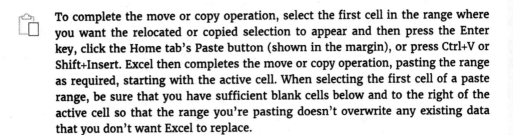

Also, when you paste a cell selection that you've copied to the Clipboard (this doesn't apply when pasting cells that you've cut to the Clipboard), Excel displays the Paste Options button (shown in the margin) in the lower-right corner of the cell selection (marked with the word Ctrl). When you position the mouse pointer over this Paste Options button (or press the Ctrl key), a palette of buttons divided into three sections (Paste, Paste Values, and Other Paste Options) appears as shown in Figure 3-9.

The buttons in these three sections of the Paste Options palette offer you the following choices for refining your paste operation. The eight buttons that appear in the Paste section are

- **Paste (P):** Excel pastes everything in the cell selection (text, values, formulas, and cell formatting).
- **Formulas (F):** Excel pastes all the text, numbers, and formulas in the current cell selection without their formatting.

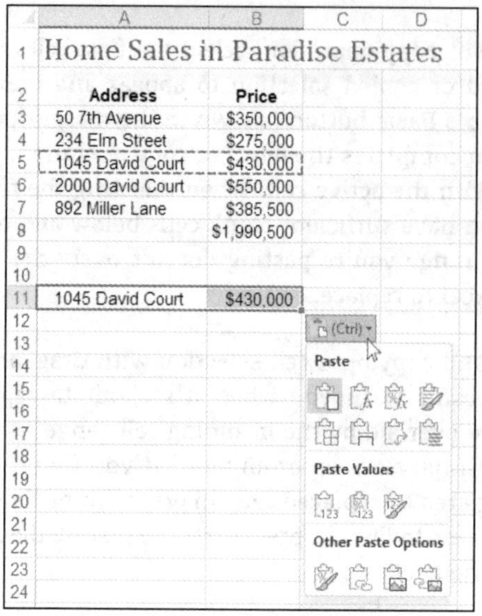


**FIGURE 3-9:** The Paste Option button's palette with the option buttons that commonly appear after pasting a cell selection that's been copied to the Clipboard.

- **Formulas & Number Formatting (O):** Excel pastes the number formats assigned to the copied values along with their formulas.
- **Keep Source Formatting (K):** Excel copies the formatting from the original cells and pastes this into the destination cells (along with the copied entries).
- **No Borders (B):** Excel pastes everything in the cell selection without copying any borders applied to its cell range.
- **Keep Source Column Widths (W):** Excel makes the width of the columns in the destination range the same as those in the source range when it copies their cell entries.
- **Transpose (T):** Excel changes the orientation of the pasted entries. For example, if the original cell entries run down the rows of a single column of the worksheet, the transposed pasted entries run across the columns of a single row.
- **Merge Conditional Formatting (G):** Excel combines the Conditional Formatting rules of the source and destination ranges. This button doesn't appear if neither range has any Conditional Formatting rules applied.

The three buttons that appear in the Paste Values section of the Paste Options palette are

- **Values (V):** Excel pastes only the calculated results of any formulas in the source cell range.

- **Values & Number Formatting (A):** Excel pastes the calculated results of any formulas along with all the formatting assigned to the values in the source cell range into the destination range.
- **Values & Source Formatting (E):** Excel pastes the calculated results of all formulas along with all formatting assigned to source cell range.

The four buttons that appear in the Other Paste Options section of the Paste Options palette are

- **Formatting (R):** Excel pastes only the formatting (and not the entries) copied from the source cell range to the destination range.
- **Paste Link (N):** Excel creates linking formulas in the destination range so that any changes that you make to the entries in cells in the source range are also reflected in the corresponding cells of the destination range.
- **Picture (U):** Excel pastes only the pictures in the copied cell selection.
- **Linked Picture (I):** Excel pastes a link to the pictures in the copied cell selection.

## Taking it out of the Clipboard task pane

When the Office Clipboard is open, Excel puts the contents of all cell selections that you copy and paste (using the Copy and Paste command buttons or their keyboard equivalents) into the Office Clipboard. In fact, the Office Clipboard stores the contents of up to the last 24 copied-and-pasted cell selections (before replacing them with new copied-and-pasted selections) not only from Excel, but from every Office program. Up to that point, you can examine the contents of the Office Clipboard and even paste your cell selections in other places in your worksheet or in documents open in other programs that you're running.

To open the Clipboard task pane on the left side of the Excel program window, click the dialog box launcher (shown in the margin) in the lower-right corner of the Home tab's Clipboard group.

When the Clipboard task pane is displayed, it shows all the individual cut or copied items that have been placed there (up to a maximum of 24). While this pane is open, Excel also places there all selections that you cut or copy in the worksheet, even those that you paste by pressing the Enter key as well as those you don't paste elsewhere.

REMEMBER

If you want Excel to place all selections that you cut and copy in the worksheet into the Office Clipboard even when the Clipboard task pane is not open, click Options at the bottom of the Clipboard pane and then click to activate the Collect Without Showing Office Clipboard option.

To paste an item on the Clipboard into a cell of one of your worksheets, click the cell and then click the item in the Clipboard task pane.

TIP

If you're using the Clipboard a lot with Cut, Copy, and Paste in a worksheet, you can have Excel automatically display the Clipboard task pane as you do the editing. Open the Clipboard task pane, click the Options button at the very bottom, and then click to activate the Show Office Clipboard Automatically option. When this setting is selected, Excel automatically opens the Clipboard task pane if you put more than two items in the Clipboard during your work session. To have Excel display the Clipboard task pane when you press Ctrl+C twice in a row (Ctrl+CC), click to activate the Show Clipboard When Ctrl+C Pressed Twice option from the Options menu.

## Inserting rather than replacing copied cells

When you use combinations of Cut, Copy, and Paste to move or copy a cell selection, you can have Excel paste the data into the worksheet without replacing existing entries in overlaid cells. In the Home tab's Cells group, click Insert and then click either Insert Cut Cells or Insert Copied Cells (depending on whether you cut or copied the cells to the Clipboard) instead of clicking the normal Paste command. Excel displays the Insert dialog box, where you can choose between the following options:

- **Shift Cells Right:** Excel moves the existing cells to the right to make room for the moved or copied cells.
- **Shift Cells Down:** Excel moves the existing cells down to make room for the moved or copied cells.

TIP

If you want to shift existing cells down to make room for the ones you've cut or copied to the Clipboard, you can click the Home tab's Insert button rather than dropping down its menu.

IN THIS CHAPTER

- » Inserting and deleting columns and rows in a worksheet
- » Splitting the worksheet into separate panes
- » Outlining data in a worksheet
- » Inserting, deleting, and reordering worksheets in a workbook

Chapter 4

# Taming Your Worksheets

Although many of Excel's advanced features are designed with specific groups of users in mind (scientists, engineers, and so on), others are intended to make everyone's life easier. These tools reward a bit of effort in the short term with improved productivity in the long term. Such is the case with the worksheet-related features that are the subject of this chapter. All these features have two things in common: They can make your day-to-day work more efficient, and they can help you get more out of your Excel investment.

In this chapter, you start by exploring ways to reorganize information in a single worksheet. These ways include inserting and deleting columns and rows and splitting the worksheet into panes. You also learn how to apply outlining to worksheet data that enables you to expand and collapse data details by showing and hiding columns and rows. You also discover methods that enable you to reorganize and manipulate the worksheets in a workbook, including renaming worksheets, adding and deleting worksheets, hiding worksheets, and more.

## Revamping a Worksheet

Most worksheets start off simply enough, but as you add data, labels, and formulas, that simplicity soon gives way to, at best, a more sophisticated data model or, at worst (and, alas, more likely), a confusingly chaotic and sprawling data mess.

Once your worksheet grows to the point where you find it hard to locate the data you want or to even make sense of what the worksheet is trying to do, it's time to take matters in hand and rearrange the data. Many times, this involves deleting unnecessary columns and rows to bring the data ranges and tables closer to each other. At other times, you may need to insert new columns and rows in the worksheet to create some breathing room between the groups of data.

Within the sprawl of a large worksheet, your main challenge is often keeping tabs on all the information spread out throughout the sheet. At times, you may find that you need to split the worksheet window into panes so that you can view two disparate regions of the worksheet together in the same window and compare their data. For large ranges and tables, you may want to outline the worksheet data so that you can immediately collapse the information down to the summary or essential data and then just as quickly expand the information to show some or all the supporting data.

## Being cautious when deleting and inserting columns and rows

WARNING

The first thing to keep in mind when inserting or deleting columns and rows in a worksheet is to be sure that you're not about to adversely affect data in unseen rows and columns of the sheet. You might think such adverse effects only apply to deleting rows and columns, but inserting columns or rows can be almost as detrimental if, by inserting them, you split apart existing data tables or ranges whose data should always remain together.

One way to guard against inadvertently deleting existing data or splitting apart a single range is to use the Zoom slider on the status bar to zoom out on the sheet and then check visually for intersecting groups of data in the hinterlands of the worksheet. You can do this quickly by dragging the Zoom slider button to the left to the 25% setting. Of course, even at the smallest zoom setting of 10%, neither all the columns nor all the rows in the worksheet appear, and because everything's so tiny at that setting, you can't always tell whether the column or row you intend to fiddle with intersects those data ranges that you can identify.

Another way to check is to press End+→ or End+↓ to move the cell pointer from range to range across the column or row affected by your column or row deletion. Remember that pressing End plus an arrow key when the cell pointer is in a blank cell jumps the cell pointer to the next occupied cell in its row or column. That means if you press End+→ when the cell pointer is in, say, cell A52 (that is, Column A, Row 52) and the pointer jumps to cell XFD52 (that is, Column XFD,

Row 52, which is the end of the worksheet in that row), you know that there isn't any data in that row that would be eliminated by your deleting that row or shifted up or down by your inserting a new row. So too, if you press End+↓ when the cell pointer is in column D and the cell pointer jumps down to cell D1048576, you're assured that no data is about to be purged or shifted left or right by that column's deletion or a new column's insertion at that point.

When you're sure that you aren't about to make any problems for yourself in other, unseen parts of the worksheet by deleting or inserting columns, you're ready to make these structural changes to the worksheet.



# Deleting columns or rows

Assuming you've checked that deleting entire columns or rows won't mess up any surrounding data, the next two sections tell you how to get rid of any worksheet columns or rows you no longer need.

## Deleting one or more columns

When you delete a column, all the data entries within the cells of that column are immediately zapped. At the same time, all remaining data entries in succeeding columns to the right move left to fill the blank left by the now-missing column.

Excel offers three methods for removing one or more columns from a worksheet:

- Select the column or columns (refer to Book 3, Chapter 2) then, on the Home tab in the Cells group, click Delete.
- Select the column or columns, right-click any selected column header, and then click Delete.
- Select a cell in each column then, on the Home tab in the Cells group, drop down the Delete menu and click Delete Sheet Columns.

REMEMBER

Pressing the Delete key is *not* the same as clicking the Delete button on the Home tab of the Ribbon. When you press the Delete key after selecting columns or rows in the worksheet, Excel clears the data entries in their cells without adjusting any of the existing data entries in neighboring columns and rows. Click the Delete command button on the Home tab when your purpose is *both* to delete the data in the selected columns or rows *and* to fill in the gap by adjusting the position of entries to the right and below the ones you eliminate.

### Deleting one or more rows

When you delete a row, all the data entries within the cells of that row are immediately eliminated, and the remaining data entries in rows below move up to fill in the gap left by the missing row.

Excel offers three methods for taking out one or more rows from a worksheet:

- Select the row or rows (refer to Book 3, Chapter 2) then, on the Home tab in the Cells group, click Delete.
- Select the row or rows, right-click any selected row header, and then click Delete.
- Select a cell in each row then, on the Home tab in the Cells group, drop down the Delete menu and click Delete Sheet Rows.

WARNING

Should your row or column deletions remove data entries referenced in formulas, the #REF! error value replaces the calculated values in the cells of the formulas affected by the elimination of the original cell references. You must then either restore the deleted rows or columns or re-create the original formula and then recopy it to get rid of these nasty formula errors.

## Inserting new columns or rows

Assuming you're sure that inserting entire columns or rows won't damage any surrounding data on your worksheet, the next two sections tell you how to shoehorn new columns or rows into your worksheet.

REMEMBER

Whenever your column or row insertions reposition data entries that are referenced in other formulas in the worksheet, Excel automatically adjusts the cell references in the formulas affected to reflect the movement of their columns left or right or rows up or down.

### Inserting one or more columns

When you insert a blank column, Excel moves the existing data in the selected column to the right, while simultaneously moving any other columns of data on the right over one.

Excel offers three methods for inserting one or more columns into a worksheet:

- Select the column or columns (refer to Book 3, Chapter 2) to the left of which you want the new columns to appear then, on the Home tab in the Cells group, click Insert.

- Select the column or columns to the left of which you want the new columns to appear, right-click any selected row header, and then click Insert.
- Select a cell in each column to the left of which you want the new columns to appear then, on the Home tab in the Cells group, drop down the Insert menu and click Insert Sheet Columns.

### Inserting one or more rows

When you insert a blank row, Excel moves the existing data in the selected row down, while simultaneously adjusting any other rows of existing data that fall below it down by one.

Excel offers three methods for inserting one or more rows into a worksheet:

- Select the row or rows (refer to Book 3, Chapter 2) above which you want the new rows to appear then, on the Home tab in the Cells group, click Insert.
- Select the row or rows above which you want the new rows to appear, right-click any selected row header, and then click Insert.
- Select a cell in each row above which you want the new rows to appear then, on the Home tab in the Cells group, drop down the Insert menu and click Insert Sheet Rows.

## Splitting the worksheet into panes

Excel enables you to split the active worksheet window into two or four panes. After splitting up the window into panes, you can use the Excel workbook's horizontal and vertical scroll bars to bring different parts of the same worksheet into view. This is great for comparing the data in different sections of a table that would otherwise not be legible if you zoomed out far enough to have both sections displayed in the worksheet window.

You can split a worksheet window in three ways:

- **Two horizontal panes:** Position the cell pointer in Column A of the worksheet in the cell where you want the horizontal division to take place. Every row above that cell appears in the top pane, while the cell's row and every row below it appears in the bottom pane.
- **Two vertical panes:** Position the cell pointer in the first row of the column where the split is to occur. Every column to the right of that cell appears in the

right pane, while the cell's column and every column to its left appears in the left pane.

- **Four panes:** Position the cell pointer in the cell in the column to the right of where you want the vertical dividing line and in the row below where you want the horizontal dividing line. After you create the split, the cell pointer is in the upper-left corner of the lower-right pane.

To perform the split, in the View tab's Window group, click the Split button (shown in the margin).

Excel carves the worksheet into the number of panes you asked for and separates the panes with a vertical and/or a horizontal split bar. To modify the size of a pane, position the mouse pointer on the appropriate split bar. When the pointer changes to either a double-headed arrow (if you're adjusting two panes) or a four-headed arrow (if you're adjusting four panes), drag the bar until the pane is your preferred size and then release the mouse button.

When you split a window into panes, Excel automatically synchronizes the scrolling, depending on how you split the worksheet. When you split a window into two horizontal panes, as shown in Figure 4-1, the worksheet window contains a single horizontal scroll bar and two separate vertical scroll bars. This means that all horizontal scrolling of the two panes is synchronized, while the vertical scrolling of each pane remains independent.

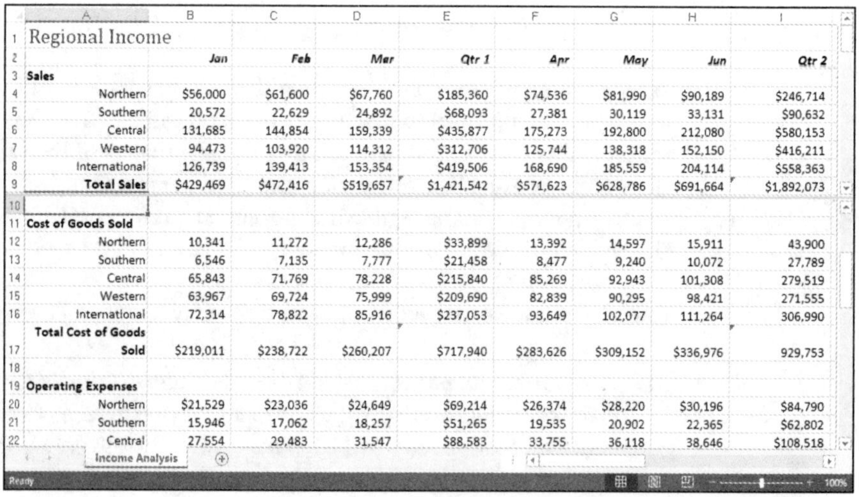

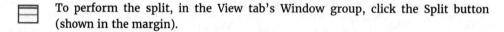

| | A | B | C | D | E | F | G | H | I |
|---|---|---|---|---|---|---|---|---|---|
| 1 | Regional Income | | | | | | | | |
| 2 | | Jan | Feb | Mar | Qtr 1 | Apr | May | Jun | Qtr 2 |
| 3 | **Sales** | | | | | | | | |
| 4 | Northern | $56,000 | $61,600 | $67,760 | $185,360 | $74,536 | $81,990 | $90,189 | $246,714 |
| 5 | Southern | 20,572 | 22,629 | 24,892 | $68,093 | 27,381 | 30,119 | 33,131 | $90,632 |
| 6 | Central | 131,685 | 144,854 | 159,339 | $435,877 | 175,273 | 192,800 | 212,080 | $580,153 |
| 7 | Western | 94,473 | 103,920 | 114,312 | $312,706 | 125,744 | 138,318 | 152,150 | $416,211 |
| 8 | International | 126,739 | 139,413 | 153,354 | $419,506 | 168,690 | 185,559 | 204,114 | $558,363 |
| 9 | **Total Sales** | $429,469 | $472,416 | $519,657 | $1,421,542 | $571,623 | $628,786 | $691,664 | $1,892,073 |
| 10 | | | | | | | | | |
| 11 | **Cost of Goods Sold** | | | | | | | | |
| 12 | Northern | 10,341 | 11,272 | 12,286 | $33,899 | 13,392 | 14,597 | 15,911 | 43,900 |
| 13 | Southern | 6,546 | 7,135 | 7,777 | $21,458 | 8,477 | 9,240 | 10,072 | 27,789 |
| 14 | Central | 65,843 | 71,769 | 78,228 | $215,840 | 85,269 | 92,943 | 101,308 | 279,519 |
| 15 | Western | 63,967 | 69,724 | 75,999 | $209,690 | 82,839 | 90,295 | 98,421 | 271,555 |
| 16 | International | 72,314 | 78,822 | 85,916 | $237,053 | 93,649 | 102,077 | 111,264 | 306,990 |
| 17 | **Total Cost of Goods Sold** | $219,011 | $238,722 | $260,207 | $717,940 | $283,626 | $309,152 | $336,976 | 929,753 |
| 18 | | | | | | | | | |
| 19 | **Operating Expenses** | | | | | | | | |
| 20 | Northern | $21,529 | $23,036 | $24,649 | $69,214 | $26,374 | $28,220 | $30,196 | $84,790 |
| 21 | Southern | 15,946 | 17,062 | 18,257 | $51,265 | 19,535 | 20,902 | 22,365 | $62,802 |
| 22 | Central | 27,554 | 29,483 | 31,547 | $88,583 | 33,755 | 36,118 | 38,646 | $108,518 |



**FIGURE 4-1:** The Regional Income worksheet with the window divided into two horizontal panes at Row 10.

When you split a window into two vertical panes, as shown in Figure 4-2, the situation is reversed. The worksheet window contains a single vertical scroll bar and two separate horizontal scroll bars. This means that all vertical scrolling of the two panes is synchronized, while horizontal scrolling of each pane remains independent.

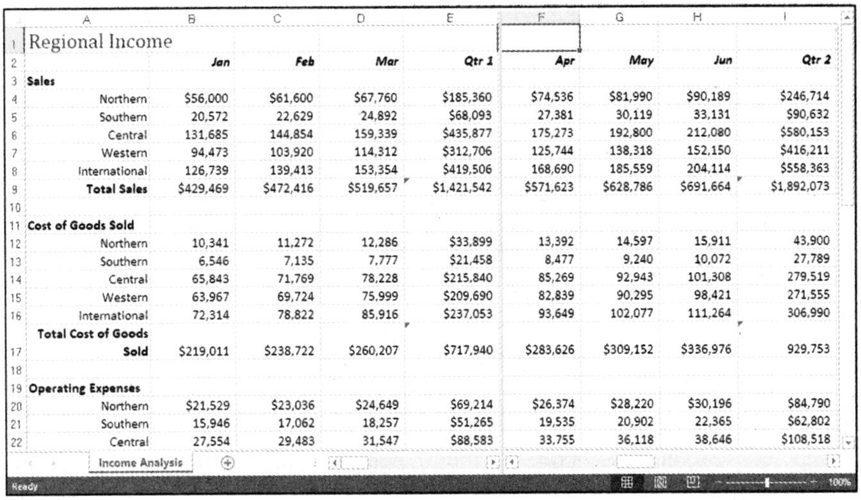


**FIGURE 4-2:** The Regional Income worksheet with the window divided into two vertical panes at Column F.

When you split a window into two horizontal and two vertical panes, as shown in Figure 4-3, the worksheet window contains two horizontal scroll bars and two separate vertical scroll bars. This means that vertical scrolling is synchronized in the top two window panes when you use the top vertical scroll bar and synchronized for the bottom two window panes when you use the bottom vertical scroll bar. Likewise, horizontal scrolling is synchronized for the left two window panes when you use the horizontal scroll bar on the left, and it's synchronized for the right two window panes when you use the horizontal scroll bar on the right.

To remove all panes from a window when you no longer need them, either click the View tab's Split button or drag the split bar (with the black double-headed split arrow cursor) either for the horizontal or vertical pane until you reach one of the edges of the worksheet window. You can also remove a pane by positioning the mouse pointer on a pane-dividing bar and then, when it changes to a double-headed or four-headed split arrow, double-clicking it.

REMEMBER

You can freeze panes in the window so that information in the upper pane and/or in the leftmost pane remains in the worksheet window at all times, no matter what other columns and rows you scroll to or how much you zoom in and out on the data. (See Book 3, Chapter 3 for more on freezing panes.)

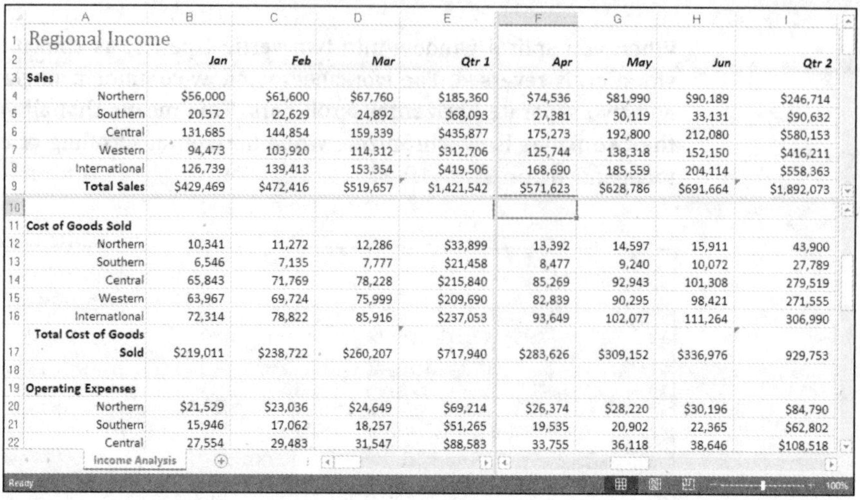

| | A | B | C | D | E | F | G | H | I |
|---|---|---|---|---|---|---|---|---|---|
| 1 | Regional Income | | | | | | | | |
| 2 | | Jan | Feb | Mar | Qtr 1 | Apr | May | Jun | Qtr 2 |
| 3 | Sales | | | | | | | | |
| 4 | Northern | $56,000 | $61,600 | $67,760 | $185,360 | $74,536 | $81,990 | $90,189 | $246,714 |
| 5 | Southern | 20,572 | 22,629 | 24,892 | $68,093 | 27,381 | 30,119 | 33,131 | $90,632 |
| 6 | Central | 131,685 | 144,854 | 159,339 | $435,877 | 175,273 | 192,800 | 212,080 | $580,153 |
| 7 | Western | 94,473 | 103,920 | 114,312 | $312,706 | 125,744 | 138,318 | 152,150 | $416,211 |
| 8 | International | 126,739 | 139,413 | 153,354 | $419,506 | 168,690 | 185,559 | 204,114 | $558,363 |
| 9 | Total Sales | $429,469 | $472,416 | $519,657 | $1,421,542 | $571,623 | $628,786 | $691,664 | $1,892,073 |
| 10 | | | | | | | | | |
| 11 | Cost of Goods Sold | | | | | | | | |
| 12 | Northern | 10,341 | 11,272 | 12,286 | $33,899 | 13,392 | 14,597 | 15,911 | 43,900 |
| 13 | Southern | 6,546 | 7,135 | 7,777 | $21,458 | 8,477 | 9,240 | 10,072 | 27,789 |
| 14 | Central | 65,843 | 71,769 | 78,228 | $215,840 | 85,269 | 92,943 | 101,308 | 279,519 |
| 15 | Western | 63,967 | 69,724 | 75,999 | $209,690 | 82,839 | 90,295 | 98,421 | 271,555 |
| 16 | International | 72,314 | 78,822 | 85,916 | $237,053 | 93,649 | 102,077 | 111,264 | 306,990 |
| 17 | Total Cost of Goods Sold | $219,011 | $238,722 | $260,207 | $717,940 | $283,626 | $309,152 | $336,976 | 929,753 |
| 18 | | | | | | | | | |
| 19 | Operating Expenses | | | | | | | | |
| 20 | Northern | $21,529 | $23,036 | $24,649 | $69,214 | $26,374 | $28,220 | $30,196 | $84,790 |
| 21 | Southern | 15,946 | 17,062 | 18,257 | $51,265 | 19,535 | 20,902 | 22,365 | $62,802 |
| 22 | Central | 27,554 | 29,483 | 31,547 | $88,583 | 33,755 | 36,118 | 38,646 | $108,518 |



**FIGURE 4-3:** Splitting the worksheet window into four panes: two horizontal and two vertical at Cell F10.

# Outlining a worksheet

The Outline feature enables you to control the level of detail displayed in a worksheet range or table. To outline a range or table, the data must use a uniform layout with a row of column headings identifying each column of data and summary rows that subtotal and total the data in rows above (like the CG Music Sales data shown in Figure 4-4).

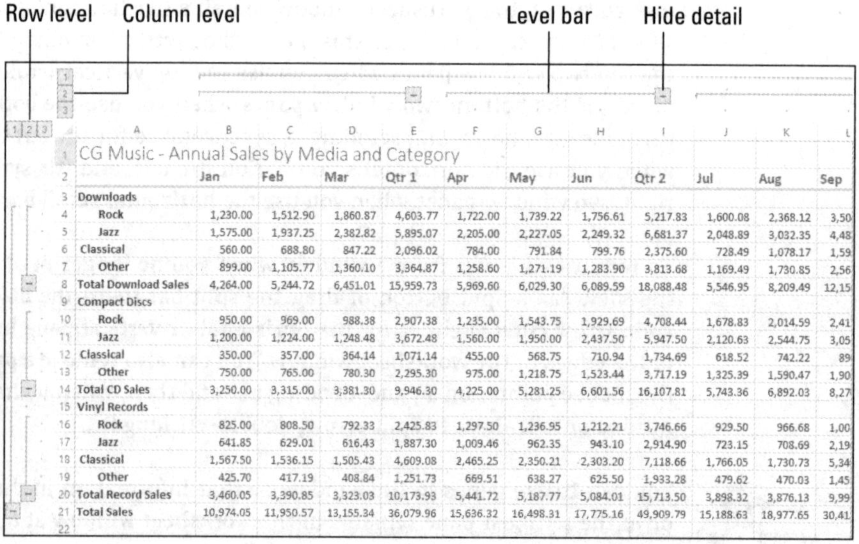


| | A | B | C | D | E | F | G | H | I | J | K | L |
|---|---|---|---|---|---|---|---|---|---|---|---|---|
| 1 | CG Music - Annual Sales by Media and Category | | | | | | | | | | | |
| 2 | | Jan | Feb | Mar | Qtr 1 | Apr | May | Jun | Qtr 2 | Jul | Aug | Sep |
| 3 | Downloads | | | | | | | | | | | |
| 4 | Rock | 1,230.00 | 1,512.90 | 1,860.87 | 4,603.77 | 1,722.00 | 1,739.22 | 1,756.61 | 5,217.83 | 1,600.08 | 2,368.12 | 3,50 |
| 5 | Jazz | 1,575.00 | 1,937.25 | 2,382.82 | 5,895.07 | 2,205.00 | 2,227.05 | 2,249.32 | 6,681.37 | 2,048.89 | 3,032.35 | 4,48 |
| 6 | Classical | 560.00 | 688.80 | 847.22 | 2,096.02 | 784.00 | 791.84 | 799.76 | 2,375.60 | 728.49 | 1,078.17 | 1,59 |
| 7 | Other | 899.00 | 1,105.77 | 1,360.10 | 3,364.87 | 1,258.60 | 1,271.19 | 1,283.90 | 3,813.68 | 1,169.49 | 1,730.85 | 2,56 |
| 8 | Total Download Sales | 4,264.00 | 5,244.72 | 6,451.01 | 15,959.73 | 5,969.60 | 6,029.30 | 6,089.59 | 18,088.48 | 5,546.95 | 8,209.49 | 12,15 |
| 9 | Compact Discs | | | | | | | | | | | |
| 10 | Rock | 950.00 | 969.00 | 988.38 | 2,907.38 | 1,235.00 | 1,543.75 | 1,929.69 | 4,708.44 | 1,678.83 | 2,014.59 | 2,41 |
| 11 | Jazz | 1,200.00 | 1,224.00 | 1,248.48 | 3,672.48 | 1,560.00 | 1,950.00 | 2,437.50 | 5,947.50 | 2,120.63 | 2,544.75 | 3,05 |
| 12 | Classical | 350.00 | 357.00 | 364.14 | 1,071.14 | 455.00 | 568.75 | 710.94 | 1,734.69 | 618.52 | 742.22 | 89 |
| 13 | Other | 750.00 | 765.00 | 780.30 | 2,295.30 | 975.00 | 1,218.75 | 1,523.44 | 3,717.19 | 1,325.39 | 1,590.47 | 1,90 |
| 14 | Total CD Sales | 3,250.00 | 3,315.00 | 3,381.30 | 9,946.30 | 4,225.00 | 5,281.25 | 6,601.56 | 16,107.81 | 5,743.36 | 6,892.03 | 8,27 |
| 15 | Vinyl Records | | | | | | | | | | | |
| 16 | Rock | 825.00 | 808.50 | 792.33 | 2,425.83 | 1,297.50 | 1,236.95 | 1,212.21 | 3,746.66 | 929.50 | 966.68 | 1,00 |
| 17 | Jazz | 641.85 | 629.01 | 616.43 | 1,887.30 | 1,009.46 | 962.35 | 943.10 | 2,914.90 | 723.15 | 708.69 | 2,19 |
| 18 | Classical | 1,567.50 | 1,536.15 | 1,505.43 | 4,609.08 | 2,465.25 | 2,350.21 | 2,303.20 | 7,118.66 | 1,766.05 | 1,730.73 | 5,34 |
| 19 | Other | 425.70 | 417.19 | 408.84 | 1,251.73 | 669.51 | 638.27 | 625.50 | 1,933.28 | 479.62 | 470.03 | 1,45 |
| 20 | Total Record Sales | 3,460.05 | 3,390.85 | 3,323.03 | 10,173.93 | 5,441.72 | 5,187.77 | 5,084.01 | 15,713.50 | 3,898.32 | 3,876.13 | 9,99 |
| 21 | Total Sales | 10,974.05 | 11,950.57 | 13,155.34 | 36,079.96 | 15,636.32 | 16,498.31 | 17,775.16 | 49,909.79 | 15,188.63 | 18,977.65 | 30,41 |
| 22 | | | | | | | | | | | | |

**FIGURE 4-4:** Automatic outline applied to the CG Music sales data with three levels of detail displayed.

After outlining a range, you can condense the range's display when you want to work with only particular levels of summary information, and you can just as easily expand the outlined range to display levels of detail data as needed. Being able to control which outline level is displayed in the worksheet makes it easy to print summary reports with levels of data as well as to chart just the summary data.

Worksheet outlines are a little different from the outlines you created in high school and college. In those outlines, you placed the headings at the highest level (I.) at the top of the outline with the intermediate headings indented below. Most worksheet outlines, however, seem backward in the sense that the highest-level summary row and column are located at the bottom and far right of the table or list of data, with the columns and rows of intermediate supporting data located above and to the left of the summary row and column.



The reason that worksheet outlines often seem "backward" when compared to word-processing outlines is that, most often, to calculate your summary totals in the worksheet, you naturally place the detail levels of data above the summary rows and to the left of the summary columns that total them. When creating a word-processing outline, however, you place the major headings above subordinate headings, while at the same time indenting each subordinate level, reflecting the way we read words from left to right and down the page.

## Creating the outline

To create an outline, position the cell pointer in the range or table containing the data to be outlined. In the Data tab's Outline group, click Group and then click Auto Outline.

By default, Excel assumes that summary rows in the selected data table are below their detail data, and summary columns are to the right of their detail data, which is normally the case. If, however, the summary rows are above the detail data, and summary columns are to the left of the detail data, Excel can still build the outline, but you need to adjust some settings.

In the Data tab's Outline group, start by clicking the dialog box launcher (shown in the margin) in the lower-right corner of the group. In the Settings dialog box that appears, deselect the Summary Rows below Detail and/or Summary Columns to Right of Detail check boxes. Also, you can have Excel automatically apply styles to different levels of the outline by selecting the Automatic Styles check box. (For more information on these styles, refer to the "Applying outline styles" section, later in this chapter.) To have Excel create the outline, click Create; if you click OK, instead, Excel closes the dialog box without outlining the selected worksheet data.

Figure 4-4 shows the first part of the outline created by Excel for the CG Music Sales worksheet. Note the outline symbols that Excel added to the worksheet when it created the outline. Figure 4-4 identifies most of these outline symbols (the Show Detail button with the plus sign is not displayed in this figure; check out Figure 4-6), and Table 4-1 explains their functions.

**TABLE 4-1** **Outline Buttons**

| Button | Name | Function |
|---|---|---|
| 1 2 3 | Row Level (1-8) and Column Level (1-8) | Displays a desired level of detail throughout the outline (1, 2, 3, and so on up to 8). When you click an outline's level bar rather than a numbered Row Level or Column Level button, Excel hides only that level in the worksheet display, the same as clicking the Hide Detail button (explained below). |
| + | Show Detail | Expands the display to show the detail rows or columns that have been collapsed |
| – | Hide Detail | Condenses the display to hide the detail rows or columns that are included in its row or column level bar |

TIP

If none of the outline doodads identified in Figure 4-4 and Table 4-1 appear, it means that Excel is configured not to show them. Choose File ⇨ Options to open the Excel Options dialog box and display the Advanced tab. In the Display Options for This Worksheet section, select the Show Outline Symbols If an Outline Is Applied check box, and then click OK. Alternatively, you can press Ctrl+8 to toggle the display of the outline symbols.

## Applying outline styles

You can apply predefined row and column outline styles to your data.

To apply these styles when creating the outline, don't use the Auto Outline method. Instead, in the Data tab's Outline group, click the dialog box launcher (shown in the margin) in the lower-right corner to open the Settings dialog box, select the Automatic Styles check box, and then click Create.

If your outline is already displayed, you can still apply the outline styles. First, select all the cells in the outlined range. In the Data tab's Outline group, click the dialog box launcher in the lower-right corner to open the Settings dialog box, select the Automatic Styles check box, and then click Apply Styles.

Figure 4-5 shows you the sample CG Music Sales table after I applied the automatic row and column styles to the outlined table data. In this example, Excel applied two row styles (RowLevel_1 and RowLevel_2) and two column styles (ColLevel_1 and ColLevel_2) to the worksheet table.

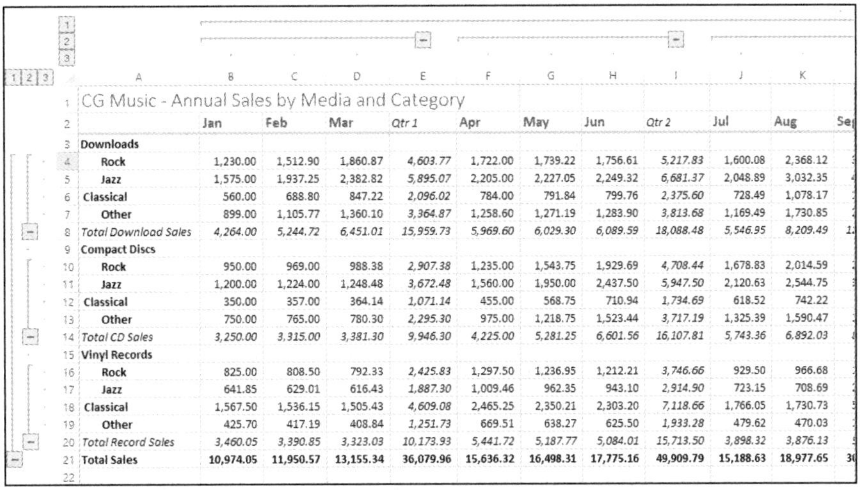

| | A | B | C | D | E | F | G | H | I | J | K |
|---|---|---|---|---|---|---|---|---|---|---|---|
| 1 | CG Music - Annual Sales by Media and Category | | | | | | | | | | |
| 2 | | Jan | Feb | Mar | *Qtr 1* | Apr | May | Jun | *Qtr 2* | Jul | Aug |
| 3 | **Downloads** | | | | | | | | | | |
| 4 | **Rock** | 1,230.00 | 1,512.90 | 1,860.87 | *4,603.77* | 1,722.00 | 1,739.22 | 1,756.61 | *5,217.83* | 1,600.08 | 2,368.12 |
| 5 | **Jazz** | 1,575.00 | 1,937.25 | 2,382.82 | *5,895.07* | 2,205.00 | 2,227.05 | 2,249.32 | *6,681.37* | 2,048.89 | 3,032.35 |
| 6 | **Classical** | 560.00 | 688.80 | 847.22 | *2,096.02* | 784.00 | 791.84 | 799.76 | *2,375.60* | 728.49 | 1,078.17 |
| 7 | **Other** | 899.00 | 1,105.77 | 1,360.10 | *3,364.87* | 1,258.60 | 1,271.19 | 1,283.90 | *3,813.68* | 1,169.49 | 1,730.85 |
| 8 | *Total Download Sales* | *4,264.00* | *5,244.72* | *6,451.01* | *15,959.73* | *5,969.60* | *6,029.30* | *6,089.59* | *18,088.48* | *5,546.95* | *8,209.49* |
| 9 | **Compact Discs** | | | | | | | | | | |
| 10 | **Rock** | 950.00 | 969.00 | 988.38 | *2,907.38* | 1,235.00 | 1,543.75 | 1,929.69 | *4,708.44* | 1,678.83 | 2,014.59 |
| 11 | **Jazz** | 1,200.00 | 1,224.00 | 1,248.48 | *3,672.48* | 1,560.00 | 1,950.00 | 2,437.50 | *5,947.50* | 2,120.63 | 2,544.75 |
| 12 | **Classical** | 350.00 | 357.00 | 364.14 | *1,071.14* | 455.00 | 568.75 | 710.94 | *1,734.69* | 618.52 | 742.22 |
| 13 | **Other** | 750.00 | 765.00 | 780.30 | *2,295.30* | 975.00 | 1,218.75 | 1,523.44 | *3,717.19* | 1,325.39 | 1,590.47 |
| 14 | *Total CD Sales* | *3,250.00* | *3,315.00* | *3,381.30* | *9,946.30* | *4,225.00* | *5,281.25* | *6,601.56* | *16,107.81* | *5,743.36* | *6,892.03* |
| 15 | **Vinyl Records** | | | | | | | | | | |
| 16 | **Rock** | 825.00 | 808.50 | 792.33 | *2,425.83* | 1,297.50 | 1,236.95 | 1,212.21 | *3,746.66* | 929.50 | 966.68 |
| 17 | **Jazz** | 641.85 | 629.01 | 616.43 | *1,887.30* | 1,009.46 | 962.35 | 943.10 | *2,914.90* | 723.15 | 708.69 |
| 18 | **Classical** | 1,567.50 | 1,536.15 | 1,505.43 | *4,609.08* | 2,465.25 | 2,350.21 | 2,303.20 | *7,118.66* | 1,766.05 | 1,730.73 |
| 19 | **Other** | 425.70 | 417.19 | 408.84 | *1,251.73* | 669.51 | 638.27 | 625.50 | *1,933.28* | 479.62 | 470.03 |
| 20 | *Total Record Sales* | *3,460.05* | *3,390.85* | *3,323.03* | *10,173.93* | *5,441.72* | *5,187.77* | *5,084.01* | *15,713.50* | *3,898.32* | *3,876.13* |
| 21 | **Total Sales** | **10,974.05** | **11,950.57** | **13,155.34** | **36,079.96** | **15,636.32** | **16,498.31** | **17,775.16** | **49,909.79** | **15,188.63** | **18,977.65** |
| 22 | | | | | | | | | | | |

**FIGURE 4-5:** The outline after applying automatic styles with the Settings dialog box.

The RowLevel_1 style is applied to the entries in the first-level summary row (Row 21) and makes the font appear in bold. The ColLevel_1 style is applied to the data in the first-level summary column (Column R, which isn't shown in the figure), and it, too, makes the font bold. The RowLevel_2 style is applied to the data in the second-level rows (Rows 8, 14, and 20), and this style adds italics to the font. The ColLevel_2 style is applied to all second-level summary columns (Columns E, I, M, and Q), and it also italicizes the font. (Note that Columns M and Q are also not visible in Figure 4-5.)

**TIP**

Sometimes Excel can get a little finicky about applying styles to an existing outline. If, in the Settings dialog box, you click the Automatic Styles check box, click the Apply Styles button, and nothing happens to your outline, re-create the outline by selecting the Data tab's Group ➪ Auto Outline command in the Outline group. Excel displays an alert dialog box asking you to confirm that you want to modify the existing outline. When you click OK, Excel redisplays your outline, this time with the automatic styles applied.

## Displaying and hiding different outline levels

The real effectiveness of outlining worksheet data becomes apparent when you start using the outline symbols to change the way the data are displayed in the worksheet. By clicking the appropriate row or column level symbol, you can immediately hide detail rows and columns to display just the summary information in the table. For example, Figure 4-6 shows you the CG Music Sales table after clicking the number 2 Row Level button and number 2 Column Level button. Here, only the first- and second-level summary information appears; that is, the totals for the quarterly and annual totals for the three types of music sales.

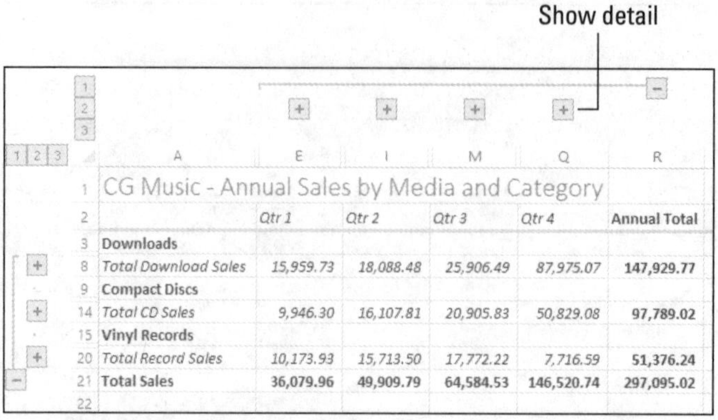


**FIGURE 4-6:** Collapsed worksheet outline showing first- and secondary-level summary information.

TIP

You can also hide and display levels of the outlined data via the Ribbon. First, position the cell cursor in the column or row. Then, in the Data tab's Outline group, click either Hide Detail or Show Detail. The great thing about using these buttons or their hot key equivalents is that they work even when the outline symbols are not displayed in the worksheet.

Figure 4-7 shows you the same table, this time after clicking the number 1 Row Level button and number 1 Column Level button. Here, only the first-level summary for the column and the row appears, that is, the grand total of the annual CG Music sales. To expand this view horizontally to display the total sales for each quarter, you would click the number 2 Column Level button. To expand this view even further horizontally to display each monthly total in the worksheet, you would click the number 3 Column Level button. So too, to expand the outline vertically to display totals for each type of media, you would click the number 2 Row Level button. To expand the outline one more level vertically to display the sales for each type of music as well as each type of media, you would click the number 3 Row Level button.

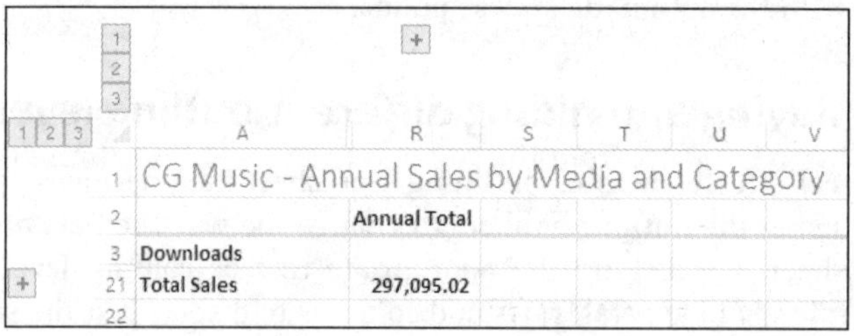

CG Music - Annual Sales by Media and Category
Annual Total
Downloads
Total Sales 297,095.02


**FIGURE 4-7:** Totally collapsed worksheet outline showing only the first-level summary information.

When displaying different levels of detail in a worksheet outline, you can use the Hide Detail and Show Detail buttons along with the Row Level and Column Level buttons. For example, Figure 4-8 shows you another view of the CG Music outlined sales table. Here, in the horizontal dimension, all three column levels have been expanded, including the monthly detail columns for each quarter. In the vertical dimension, however, only the detail rows for the Download sales have been expanded. The detail rows for the CD and Vinyl Record sales are still collapsed.

| | A | E | I | M | Q | R |
|---|---|---|---|---|---|---|
| 1 | CG Music - Annual Sales by Media and Category | | | | | |
| 2 | | *Qtr 1* | *Qtr 2* | *Qtr 3* | *Qtr 4* | **Annual Total** |
| 3 | **Downloads** | | | | | |
| 4 | **Rock** | *4,603.77* | *5,217.83* | *7,473.02* | *25,377.42* | **42,672.05** |
| 5 | **Jazz** | *5,895.07* | *6,681.37* | *9,569.12* | *32,495.48* | **54,641.04** |
| 6 | **Classical** | *2,096.02* | *2,375.60* | *3,402.35* | *11,553.95* | **19,427.92** |
| 7 | **Other** | *3,364.87* | *3,813.68* | *5,461.99* | *18,548.21* | **31,188.76** |
| 8 | *Total Download Sales* | *15,959.73* | *18,088.48* | *25,906.49* | *87,975.07* | **147,929.77** |
| 9 | **Compact Discs** | | | | | |
| 14 | *Total CD Sales* | *9,946.30* | *16,107.81* | *20,905.83* | *50,829.08* | **97,789.02** |
| 15 | **Vinyl Records** | | | | | |
| 20 | *Total Record Sales* | *10,173.93* | *15,713.50* | *17,772.22* | *7,716.59* | **51,376.24** |
| 21 | **Total Sales** | **36,079.96** | **49,909.79** | **64,584.53** | **146,520.74** | **297,095.02** |
| 22 | | | | | | |

**FIGURE 4-8:** Worksheet outline expanded to show only details for Download sales for all four quarters.



To create this view of the outline, you click the number 2 Column Level and Row Level buttons, and then click only the Show Detail (+) button located to the left of the Total Download Sales row heading. When you want to view only the summary-level rows for each media type, you can click the Hide Detail (–) button to the left of the Total Download Sales heading, or you can click its level bar (drawn from the collapse symbol up to the first music type to indicate all the detail rows included in that level).

REMEMBER

Excel adjusts the outline levels displayed on the screen by hiding and redisplaying entire columns and rows in the worksheet. Therefore, changes that you make that reduce the number of levels displayed in the outlined table also hide the display of all data outside of the outlined table that are in the affected rows and columns.

TIP

After selecting the rows and columns you want to display, you can then remove the outline symbols from the worksheet display to maximize the amount of data displayed onscreen. To do this, press Ctrl+8.

## Removing an outline

To delete an outline from your worksheet, display the Data tab, and then in the Outline group, click the drop-down button attached to the Ungroup button and then click Clear Outline. Note that removing the outline doesn't affect the data in any way — Excel merely removes the outline structure. Also note that it doesn't matter what state the outline is in at the time you select this command. If the outline is partially or totally collapsed, deleting the outline automatically displays all the hidden rows and columns in the data table or list.

# Overhauling a Workbook

Any new workbook that you open comes with a single blank worksheet. Although most of the workbooks you create and work with may never expand beyond this one sheet, it helps to know how to deal with multi-sheet workbooks for those situations when scattering all your information all over a single sprawling worksheet isn't practical.

## Renaming a worksheet

When you add new worksheets to a new workbook, Excel gives each one a default sheet name along the lines of Sheet2, Sheet3, and so on. Boring! And not helpful because these default names don't describe the content of the worksheet. To make it easier to navigate and work with multi-sheet workbooks, you should give all your worksheets descriptive names.

To rename a worksheet, you take these steps:

1. **Bring the worksheet tab into view, if it's not already.**
2. **Double-click the worksheet tab.**

   Alternatively, on the Home tab, in the Cells group, click Format and then click Rename Sheet. You can also right-click the sheet tab and then click Rename.

   Excel opens the tab name text for editing and positions the insertion point at the end of the name.
3. **Replace or edit the name on the sheet tab and then press Enter.**

   Note that the name must be unique in the workbook, no longer than 31 characters, and can include any character except the following: \ / ? * [ ] and :.

REMEMBER

When you rename a worksheet, keep in mind that Excel then uses that sheet name in any formulas that refer to cells in that worksheet. So, for instance, if you rename Sheet2 to Sales and then create a formula in Cell A10 of Sheet1 that adds its Cell B10 to Cell C34 in Sheet2, the formula in Cell A10 becomes

```
=B10+Sales!C34
```

This is in place of the more obscure =B10+Sheet2!C34. For this reason, keep your sheet names short and to the point so that you can easily and quickly identify the sheet and its data without creating excessively long formula references.

## Outfitting a workbook with designer sheets

Excel makes it easy to color-code the worksheets in your workbook. This makes it possible to create a color scheme that helps either identify or prioritize the sheets and the information they contain.



REMEMBER

When you color a sheet tab, note that the tab appears in that color only when it's not the active sheet. The moment you select a color-coded sheet tab, it becomes white with just a gradient of the assigned color appearing under the sheet name. Note, too, that when you assign darker colors to a sheet tab, Excel automatically reverses out the sheet name text to white when the worksheet is not active.

### Color-coding sheet tabs

To assign a new color to a sheet tab, follow these three steps:

1. **Click the tab you want to color.**

   Don't forget that you have to select and activate the sheet whose tab you want to color, or you end up coloring the tab of whatever sheet happens to be current at the time you perform the next step.

2. **On the Home tab, in the Cells group, click the Format button and then click Tab Color.**

   Excel displays a color palette.

   An alternative way to display the color palette is to right-click the tab and then click Tab Color on the shortcut menu that appears.

3. **Click the color you want to assign to the current sheet tab.**

REMEMBER

To remove color-coding from a sheet tab, repeat Steps 1 and 2, and then click the No Color command near the bottom of the color palette.

### Assigning a graphic image as the sheet background

If coloring the sheet tabs isn't enough for you, you can also assign a graphic image to be used as the background for all the cells in the entire worksheet. Just be aware that the background image must either be very light in color or use a greatly reduced opacity so that your intended audience can read your worksheet data over the image. This probably makes most graphics that you have readily available unusable as worksheet background images. It can, however, be quite effective if you have a special corporate watermark graphic (such as the company's logo at extremely low opacity) that adds just a hint of a background without obscuring the data being presented in its cells.

To add a local graphic file as the background for a worksheet, take these steps:

1. **Click the sheet tab.**

   Don't forget that you have to select and activate the sheet for which the graphic file will act as the background, or you end up applying the background to whatever sheet happens to be current at the time you perform the following steps.

2. **In the Page Layout tab's Page Setup group, click the Background command.**

   Excel opens the Insert Pictures dialog box.

3. **Click the Browse button to the right of the From a File link.**

   Excel opens the Sheet Background dialog box.

4. **Open the folder that contains the image you want to use, click the image file, and then click Insert.**

   Excel applies the image as the background for all cells in the current worksheet. (Usually, the program does this by stretching the graphic so that it takes up all the cells that are visible in the workbook window. In the case of some smaller images, the program does this by tiling the image so that it's duplicated across and down the viewing area.)

REMEMBER

A graphic image that you assign as the worksheet background doesn't appear in the printout, unlike the pattern and background colors that you assign to ranges of cells in the sheet.

To remove a background image, click the Page Layout tab's Delete Background command (which replaces the Background button when you assign a background image to a worksheet).

TIP

You can also turn online graphics into worksheet backgrounds. Select the Page Layout tab's Background command and use the Bing Image Search text box to search for the image you want to use. When you find an online image that suits your style, and the image isn't protected by copyright (most are, so be careful), double-click its thumbnail (or click the thumbnail and then click Insert) to download the image and insert it into the current worksheet as the sheet's background.

## Adding worksheets

You can add as many worksheets as you need to build out your workbook model. To add a new worksheet, click the New Sheet button (shown in the margin), which always appears immediately to the right of the last sheet tab in the workbook.

Excel inserts a new worksheet after whatever sheet was active when you clicked New Sheet and the program assigns it the next available sheet number (Sheet2, Sheet3, Sheet4, and so on).

REMEMBER

You can also insert a new sheet (and not necessarily a blank worksheet) into the workbook by right-clicking a sheet tab and then clicking Insert at the top of the tab's shortcut menu. Excel opens the Insert dialog box containing different file icons that you can select — Worksheet, Chart, MS Excel 4.0 Macro, and MS Excel 5.0 Dialog, along with a variety of different worksheet templates. Click Worksheet to insert a blank worksheet; click Chart to insert a specialized chart sheet (refer to Book 3, Chapter 7); click MS Excel 4.0 Macro to insert a macro sheet (this is obsolete); click MS Excel 5.0 to insert a sheet for a custom dialog box (also obsolete); or click a template to insert a worksheet that follows a template design. Note that when you insert a new sheet using the Insert dialog box, Excel inserts the new sheet to the left of the worksheet that's active (in contrast to clicking the New Sheet button, which inserts the new sheet to the right of the active worksheet).

TIP

If you find that a single worksheet just never seems sufficient for the kind of workbooks you normally create, you can change the default number of sheets that are automatically available in all new workbook files that you open. To do this, open the Excel Options dialog box (File ⇨ Options). In the General tab, use the Include This Many Sheets spin box to specify the default number of worksheets you want to appear in each new workbook you create (up to a maximum of 255).

## Deleting worksheets

To remove a worksheet, follow these steps:

1. **Click the tab you want to remove.**
2. **On the Home tab, in the Cells group, click the Delete button.**
3. **Click Delete Sheet.**

   Alternatively, right-click the worksheet's tab and then click Delete from its shortcut menu.

   If Excel detects that the worksheet contains some data, the program then displays an alert dialog box cautioning you that the worksheet you're about to zap will be permanently deleted.

4. **To go ahead and delete the sheet (data and all), click Delete.**

   Excel deletes the worksheet.

WARNING

Deleting a sheet is one of those actions that you can't take back with the Undo button on the Quick Access toolbar. This means that after you click the Delete button, you've kissed your worksheet goodbye, so don't do this unless you're *certain* that you aren't dumping needed data. Also, keep in mind that you can't delete a worksheet if that sheet is the only one in the workbook. Excel won't allow a workbook file to be completely sheetless.

## Changing the sheets

Excel enables you to rearrange the order of the sheets in your workbook by moving or copying worksheets, as described in the next two sections.

### Moving a worksheet

To move a sheet, use your mouse to drag the sheet's tab left or right to the new position in the row of tabs. As you drag the tab, the pointer changes shape to an arrowhead on a dog-eared piece of paper, and a black triangle pointing downward appears above the sheet tabs. When this triangle is positioned where you want the sheet moved, release the mouse button.

You can also move a worksheet by following these steps:

1. **Right-click the tab of the sheet you want to move.**
2. **Click Move or Copy in the shortcut menu that appears.**

   The Move or Copy dialog box shows up.

3. **In the Before Sheet list box, click the name of the worksheet before which you want to move the currently active worksheet.**
4. **Click OK to make it so.**

### Copying a worksheet

If you need to copy a worksheet to another position in the workbook, hold down the Ctrl key as you drag the sheet tab. As you drag, the pointer changes shape to an arrowhead on a dog-eared piece of paper that includes a plus sign (+), and a black triangle pointing downward appears above the sheet tabs. When this triangle is positioned where you want the sheet copied, release the mouse button. Excel creates a copy with a new sheet tab name based on the number of the copy and the original sheet name. For example, if you copy Sheet1 to a new place in the workbook, the first copy is renamed Sheet1 (2) [the next copy would be Sheet1 (3), and so on]. You can then rename the worksheet whatever you want.

You can also copy a worksheet by following these steps:

1. **Right-click the tab of the sheet you want to copy.**
2. **Click Move or Copy in the shortcut menu that appears.**

   The Move or Copy dialog box shows up.
3. **In the Before Sheet list box, click the name of the worksheet before which you want to move the currently active worksheet.**
4. **Select the Create a Copy check box.**
5. **Click OK to copy the sheet.**

   Excel creates the copy and gives the sheet the same name as the original, but with a number appended in parentheses, such as "Sheet1 (2)."



## Editing and formatting multiple worksheets as a group

If you're working on a bunch of worksheets that share essentially the same layout and require the same type of formatting, you might not have to edit and format the sheets individually. Excel offers the welcome capability of editing and formatting more than one worksheet at a time. A collection of two or more selected worksheets is called a *group.*

For example, suppose that you have a workbook that contains annual sales worksheets (named Sales_2023, Sales_2024, and Sales_2025) for three consecutive years. The worksheets share the same layout (with months across the columns and quarterly and annual totals, locations, and types of sales down the rows) but lack standard formatting. To format any part of these three worksheets in a single operation, you resort to group editing, which requires selecting the three sales worksheets.

To create a worksheet group, you must select the tab of each worksheet you want to include in the group. There are two techniques you can use:

- **If the worksheet tabs are non-consecutive:** Click the first sheet tab you want to include in the group, hold down Ctrl, and then click each of the other sheet tabs you want to be part of the group.

» **If the worksheet tabs are consecutive:** Click the first sheet tab you want to include in the group, hold down Shift, and then click the last of the sheet tabs you want to be part of the group.

After you select the last sheet, the Group indicator appears in the title bar of the active document window.

The Group indicator lets you know that any editing change you make to the current worksheet will affect all the sheets that are currently selected. For example, if you select a row of column headings and add bold and italics to the headings in the current worksheet, the same formatting is applied to the same cell selection in all the selected sheets. All headings in the same cell range in the other worksheets are now in bold and italics. Keep in mind that you can apply not only formatting changes to a cell range but also editing changes, such as replacing a cell entry, deleting a cell's contents, or moving a cell selection to a new place in the worksheet. These changes affect all the worksheets you have selected as long as they're grouped together.

After you're finished making editing changes that affect all the grouped worksheets, you can break up the group by right-clicking one of the grouped sheet tabs and then clicking Ungroup Sheets at the top of the shortcut menu. As soon as you break up the group, the Group indicator disappears from the title bar. Any editing or formatting changes that you make once again affect only the cells in the active worksheet.

TIP

To select all the worksheets in the workbook for group editing in one operation, right-click the tab of the sheet where you want to make the editing changes that affect all the other sheets, and then choose Select All Sheets from its shortcut menu.

## Hiding worksheets

Another technique that comes in handy when working with multiple worksheets is hiding particular worksheets in the workbook. Just as you can hide particular columns, rows, and cell ranges in a worksheet (refer to Book 3, Chapter 2), you can also hide entire worksheets in the workbook. For example, you may want to hide a worksheet that contains sensitive (for-your-eyes-only) material, such as the one with all the employee salaries in the company.

As with hiding columns and rows, hiding worksheets enables you to share onscreen or print the contents of the workbook without the data in worksheets that you consider either unnecessary or too private for widespread distribution but which, nonetheless, are required in the workbook. (If, instead, you want to prevent folks from making changes to a worksheet, then you need to protect the sheet as I describe in Book 8, Chapter 4.) Then after you've finished sharing the workbook onscreen or after the workbook is printed, you can redisplay the worksheets by unhiding them.

To hide a worksheet, first make it active by selecting its sheet tab. In the Home tab's Cells group, click the Format command, click Hide & Unhide, and then click Hide Sheet. Alternatively, right-click the worksheet tab and then click Hide. Excel temporarily removes this worksheet's tab from the row of sheet tabs.

To redisplay any of the sheets you've hidden, click the Home tab's Format command, click Hide & Unhide, then click Unhide Sheet to display the Unhide dialog box. Alternatively, right-click any worksheet tab and then click Unhide.

In the Unhide Sheet list box, click the name of the sheet that you want to display once again in the workbook. If you want to restore multiple sheets, hold down Ctrl and click each sheet you want to unhide. Click OK and Excel redisplays the hidden worksheet (or worksheets).

IN THIS CHAPTER

» Creating simple formulas with operators and using AutoSum

» Understanding the operators and their priority in the formula

» Copying formulas and changing the type of cell references

» Building array formulas and using names in formulas

# Chapter 5
# Building Basic Formulas

You can, if you want, use Excel only to store data. Using the tables that you find out about in Book 3, Chapter 6, you can turn Excel into a competent database management system. Nothing wrong with that. However, using Excel only to store data is kind of like having a bicycle and only walking with it everywhere you go: You're missing the best part!

What part of Excel are you missing if you only use the program to store data? One word: *formulas.* They are, hands down, Excel's most powerful and most useful feature. Formulas enable you to take the static, lifeless data you've stored in a worksheet and animate that data to return answers and analyses and generate insights and information. Whether you want to add a few cells together, find the average value in a range, or calculate the tax on an invoice, Excel formulas can get the job done.

So, I hear you thinking, if Excel formulas are so powerful, they must be hideously complex, right? Well, I'm not going to lie to you: Advanced Excel formulas make the Dead Sea Scrolls look like a first-grade reader. That's the bad news. The oh-so-good news is that most Excel formulas are much simpler and very straightforward, and learning how to build these basic formulas doesn't require a graduate degree in math or finance. Are you pumped to learn Excel's most exciting feature? I knew it!

# Getting Started with Formulas

A *formula* is a special type of cell entry that performs a calculation. When you complete the cell entry, two things happen, as demonstrated in Figure 5-1:

- The formula result appears in the cell.
- When you select the cell, the formula itself appears in the Formula bar.

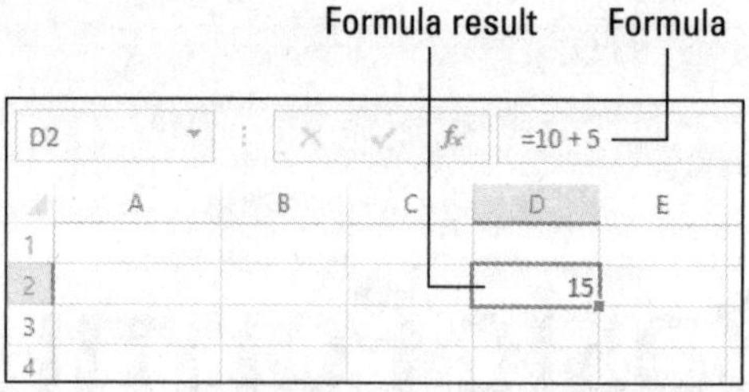


**FIGURE 5-1:** The formula result appears in the cell, while the formula itself appears in the Formula bar.

Here's the formula shown in the Figure 5-1 example:

```
=10 + 5
```

What's going on here? This formula just adds the number 10 and the number 5, resulting in the value 15 that appears in Cell D2 of Figure 5-1. Happily, even this simple formula demonstrates pretty much everything you need to know to get started with Excel formulas. That is, it demonstrates the equal sign (=), operands, and operators:

- **Equal sign (=):** All Excel formulas — from the simple addition formula shown in Figure 5-1 to the most complex statistical calculation — begin with the equal sign (=). This symbol says to Excel, "Hey, everything that follows is a formula, okay?"
- **Operands:** An *operand* provides a bit of data for the formula to work with. In the formula used in Figure 5-1, the operands are the numbers 10 and 5. Operands can be raw data values (which are called *constants*), function results (I talk about functions a bit later; see "Augmenting Formulas with Functions"), or cell or range addresses. If you enter a cell address in a formula, Excel uses the current value of that cell in your formula. For example, Figure 5-2 shows an updated version of the example formula from Figure 5-1. This time, the value 10 is stored in Cell D1, and the value 5 is stored in Cell E1, so here's the updated formula (visible in the Formula bar):

  ```
  =D1 + E1
  ```

**REMEMBER**

The advantage of using cell range addresses instead of constants in formulas is that when you use cell addresses, Excel automatically updates the formula result whenever you change the values in the cells.

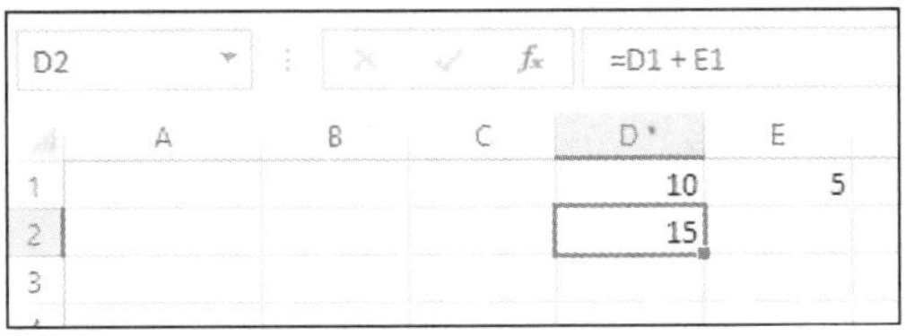


**FIGURE 5-2:** You can use cell addresses as formula operands.

- **Operators:** An *operator* is a special symbol that tells Excel what to do with the operands. As demonstrated in Figure 5-1 and 5-2, the addition (+) operator tells Excel to add the two operands. Other common operands are subtraction (-), multiplication (*), and division (/). (See Table 5-1 later in the chapter for more types of operators.)

So, when you create a formula, you perform these general steps:

1. Select the cell where you want the formula to appear.
2. Type the equal sign (=) to alert Excel that you're building a formula.
3. Type the first operand, such as a constant, function, cell address, or range coordinates.
4. Type an operator.
5. Type the next operand.
6. Repeat Steps 4 and 5 until your formula is done.
7. Complete the cell entry by clicking the Enter button (shown in the margin), pressing Enter, or pressing an arrow key.

# Pointing at formula cells

As you build your formulas you often want to use a cell address as an operand. When you get to that location in the formula, you can either type the cell address or you can click the cell in the worksheet. Clicking the cell is called *pointing* at the cell, and when you point at a cell, Excel inserts the cell address into your formula. (Pointing also works for range operands, where in this case you click and drag over the range you want to use in your formula.)

Using the pointing method to supply a cell address for a formula is often easier and is always a much more foolproof method than entering the cell address by hand. The problem with typing a cell address is that it's all-too easy to type the incorrect row number or column letter (or both), so now your formula is referencing the wrong cell. By contrast, when you click the cell directly, Excel always enters the correct address (assuming you clicked the correct cell!).

Therefore, stick to pointing when building your formulas and restrict typing cell addresses to the odd occasion when you need to enter or edit a cell address and pointing to it is either not practical or just too much trouble.

## Editing formulas

As with numeric and text entries, you can edit the contents of formulas either in their cells or on the Formula bar. To edit a formula in its cell, double-click the cell or press F2 to position the insertion point in that cell. (Double-clicking the cell positions the insertion point in the middle of the formula, whereas pressing F2 positions it at the end of the formula — you can also double-click at the beginning or end of the cell to position the insertion point there.) To edit a formula on the Formula bar, use the I-beam mouse to position the insertion point at the place in the formula that needs editing first.

As soon as you put Excel into Edit mode, Excel displays each of the cell references in the formula within the cell in a different color and uses each color to outline the corresponding cell or cell range in the worksheet. This coloration enables you to quickly identify the cells and their values that are referred to in your formula and, if necessary, modify them as well. You can use any of the four sizing handles that appear around the cell or cell range to modify the cell selection in the worksheet and consequently update the cell references in the formula.

## Using AutoSum to add numbers

Σ

The easiest and often the most used formula that you'll create is one that totals rows or columns of numbers in your worksheet. Usually, to total a row or column of numbers, you can click the Sum command button (shown in the margin) on the Ribbon's Home tab, in the Editing group. When you click Sum, Excel inserts the built-in SUM function into the active cell and simultaneously selects what the program thinks is the most likely range of numbers that you want summed.

TIP

Instead of taking the time to click the Sum button on the Home tab, it's often faster and easier to press Alt+= (equal sign) to insert the SUM function in the current cell and have Excel select the range of cells most likely to be totaled.

Figure 5-3 demonstrates how this works. For this figure, I positioned the cell cursor in Cell B7, which is the first cell where I need to build a formula that totals the various parts produced in April. I then clicked the Sum button (pointed out in Figure 5-3) on the Ribbon's Home tab.

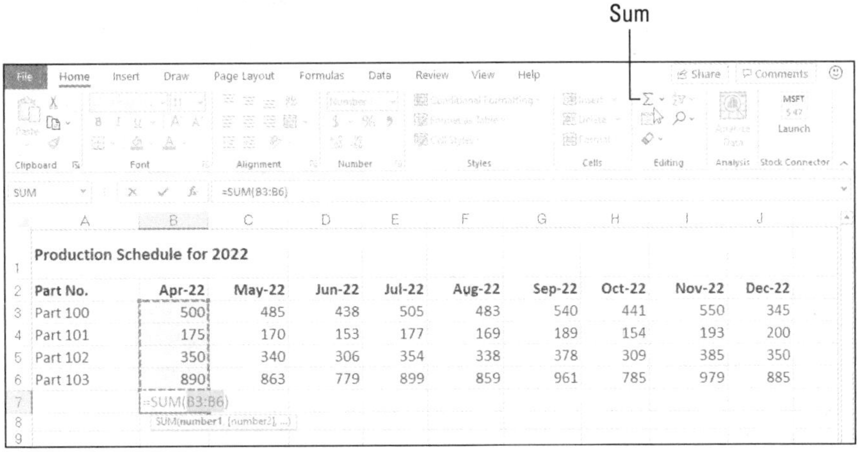


**FIGURE 5-3:** Using AutoSum to create a SUM formula that totals a column of numbers.

As Figure 5-3 shows, Excel inserts an equal sign followed by the SUM function and correctly suggested the cell range B3:B6 as the range to be summed. (Any input you provide for a function, such as a range address, is called a function *argument*. Head over to the "Augmenting Formulas with Functions" section to learn more.) Because Excel correctly selected the range to be summed (leaving out the date value in Cell B2), all I have to do is click the Enter button on the Formula bar to have the April total calculated.

Figure 5-4 shows another example of using AutoSum to instantly build a SUM formula, this time to total the monthly production numbers for Part 100 in Cell K3. Again, all I did to create the formula shown in Figure 5-4 was to select Cell K3 and then click the Sum button. Again, Excel correctly selected B3:J3 as the range to be summed (rightly ignoring Cell A3 with the row title) and input this range as the argument of the SUM function. All that remains to be done is to click the Enter button on the Formula bar to compute the monthly totals for Part 100.

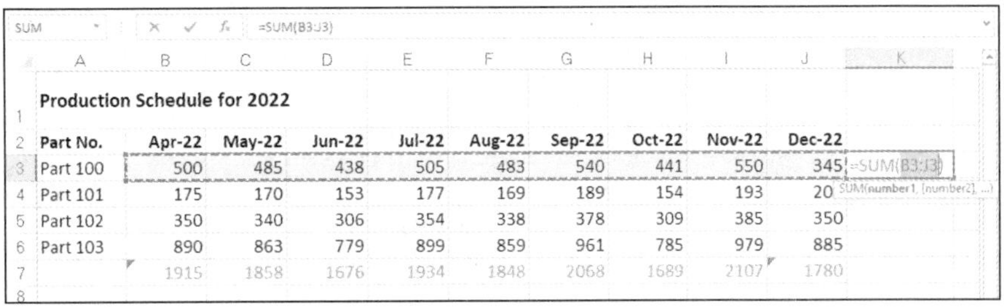


**FIGURE 5-4:** Using the AutoSum feature to create a SUM formula that totals a row of numbers.

If for some reason AutoSum doesn't select the entire or correct range that you want summed, you can adjust the range by dragging the cell cursor through the cell range or by clicking the marquee around the cell range, which turns the marching ants into a solid-colored outline. Then position the mouse pointer on one of the sizing handles at the four corners. When the mouse pointer turns into a thick white arrowhead pointing to the center of a pair of black double-crossed arrows, drag the outline until it includes all the cells you want included in the total.

REMEMBER

All Excel functions enclose their argument(s) in a pair of parentheses, as shown in the examples with the SUM function. Even those rare functions that don't require any arguments at all still require the use of a closed pair of parentheses (even when you don't put anything inside of them).

## Building formulas with computational operators

Many of the simpler formulas that you build require the sole use of Excel's operators, which are the symbols that indicate the type of calculation you want to use. Excel uses four different types of computational operators: arithmetic, comparison, text, and reference. Table 5-1 shows all these operators arranged by type and accompanied by an example.

**TABLE 5-1 The Different Types of Operators in Excel**

| Type | Character | Operation | Example |
|---|---|---|---|
| Arithmetic | + | Addition | =A2 + B3 |
| | – | Subtraction or negation | =A3 – A2 or –C4 |
| | * | Multiplication | =A2 * B3 |
| | / | Division | =B3 / A2 |
| | % | Percent (dividing by 100) | =B3% |
| | ^ | Exponentiation | =A2 ^ 3 |
| Comparison | = | Equal to | =A2 = B3 |
| | > | Greater than | =B3 > A2 |
| | < | Less than | =A2 < B3 |
| | >= | Greater than or equal to | =B3 >= A2 |
| | <= | Less than or equal to | =A2 <= B3 |

| Type | Character | Operation | Example |
|---|---|---|---|
| | <> | Not equal to | =A2 <> B3 |
| Text | & | Concatenates (connects) entries to produce one continuous entry | =A2 & " " & B3 |
| Reference | : | Range operator that includes | =SUM(C4:D17) |
| | , | Union operator that combines multiple references into one reference | =SUM(A2, C4:D17, B3) |
| | (space) | Intersection operator that produces one reference to cells in common with two references | =SUM(C3:C6 C3:E6) |

## More about operators

Most of the time, you'll rely on the arithmetic operators when building formulas in your worksheets that don't require functions because these operators perform computations between the numbers in the various cell references and produce new mathematical results.

The comparison operators, on the other hand, produce only the logical value TRUE or the logical value FALSE, depending on the result of the comparison. For example, say that you enter the following formula in Cell A10:

```
=B10 <> C10
```

If B10 contains the number 15 and C10 contains the number 20, the formula in A10 returns the logical value TRUE. If, however, both Cell B10 and C10 contain the value 12, the formula returns the logical value FALSE.

The single text operator (the so-called ampersand) is used in formulas to join two or more text entries (an operation with the highfalutin' name *concatenation*). For example, suppose that you enter the following formula in Cell C2:

```
=A2 &B2
```

If Cell A2 contains `John` and cell B2 contains `Smith`, the formula returns the new (squashed together) text entry, `JohnSmith`. To have the formula insert a space between the first and last names, include a space as part of the concatenation as follows:

```
=A2 & " " & B2
```

TIP

You most often use the comparison operators with the IF function when building more complex formulas that perform one type of operation when the IF condition is TRUE and another when it is FALSE. You use the concatenating operator (&) when you need to join text entries that come to you entered in separate cells but that need to be entered in single cells (like the first and last names in separate columns).

## Order of operator precedence

When you build a formula that combines different computational operators, Excel follows the set order of operator precedence, as shown in Table 5-2. When you use operators that share the same level of precedence, Excel evaluates each element in the equation by using a strictly left-to-right order.

**TABLE 5-2** Natural Order of Operator Precedence in Formulas

| Precedence | Operator | Type/Function |
|---|---|---|
| 1 | – | Negation |
| 2 | % | Percent |
| 3 | ^ | Exponentiation |
| 4 | * and / | Multiplication and Division |
| 5 | + and – | Addition and Subtraction |
| 6 | & | Concatenation |
| 7 | =, <, >, <=, >=, <> | All Comparison Operators |

Suppose that you enter the following formula in Cell A4:

```
=B4 + C4 / D4
```

Because division (like multiplication) has a higher level of precedence than addition (4 versus 5), Excel evaluates the division between Cells C4 and D4 and then adds that result to the value in Cell B4. If, for example, Cell B4 contains 2, C4 contains 9, and D4 contains 3, Excel would essentially be evaluating this equation in Cell A4:

```
=2 + 9 / 3
```

In this example, the calculated result displayed in Cell A4 is 5 because the program first performs the division (9/3) that returns the result 3 and then adds it to 2 to get the final result of 5.

If you had wanted Excel to evaluate this formula in a strictly left-to-right manner, you could get it to do so by enclosing the leftmost operation (the addition between B4 and C4) in a closed pair of parentheses. Parentheses alter the natural order of precedence so that any operation enclosed within a pair is performed before the other operations in the formula, regardless of level in the order. (After that, the natural order is once again used.)

To have Excel perform the addition between the first two terms (B4 and C4) and then divide the result by the third term (Cell D4), you modify the original formula by enclosing the addition operation in parentheses as follows:

```
=(B4 + C4) / D4
```

Assuming that Cells B4, C4, and D4 still contain the same numbers (2, 9, and 3, respectively), the formula now calculates the result as 3.666667 and returns it to Cell A4 (2+9=11 and 11/3=3.66667).

# Augmenting Formulas with Functions



Excel supports a wide variety of built-in worksheet functions that you can use when building formulas. A *function* is a kind of predefined formula that performs a specific calculation. For example, consider the following formula:

```
=A1 + A2 + A3 + A4 + A5 + A6 + A7 + A8 + A9 + A10
```

You can imagine how tedious that would be to type into a cell. To make your Excel life easier, you can use the SUM function, instead, which sums whatever range address (or addresses) you provide as the function's arguments:

```
=SUM(A1:A10)
```

The most popular built-in function is by far the SUM function, which is automatically inserted when you click the Sum command button on the Ribbon's Home tab. (Keep in mind that you can also use this drop-down button attached to the Sum button to insert the AVERAGE, COUNT, MAX, and MIN functions — see the "Using AutoSum to add numbers" section earlier in this chapter for details.)

## Inserting a function

To use other Excel functions, you can type the function and its arguments, if you happen to know the correct syntax. Otherwise, you can use either the Insert Function button or the Ribbon's Formulas tab.

### Entering a function manually

If you know the name of the function you want to insert and you know its syntax, it's often easier to just type the function manually into your formula. When you begin typing a function name in a formula, Excel's AutoComplete feature kicks in by displaying a drop-down menu with the names of all the functions that begin with the character(s) you've typed. You can then insert the name of the function you want to use by double-clicking its name on this drop-down menu, or highlighting the name and pressing Tab. Excel then inserts the function name along with the open parenthesis as in =DATE. (Now you fill in the rest of the function, add a closing (right) parenthesis, and you're done.

REMEMBER

Excel's function names are all-uppercase affairs, but that doesn't mean you have to type them using only capitals. You can type the function name using lowercase letters and when you complete the formula, Excel will convert the function name to uppercase.

### Using the Insert Function button

*fx*

When you click the Insert Function button on the Formula bar (shown in the margin), Excel displays the Insert Function dialog box, similar to the one shown in Figure 5-5. You can then use its options to find and select the function that you want to use and to define the argument or arguments that the function requires to perform its calculation.

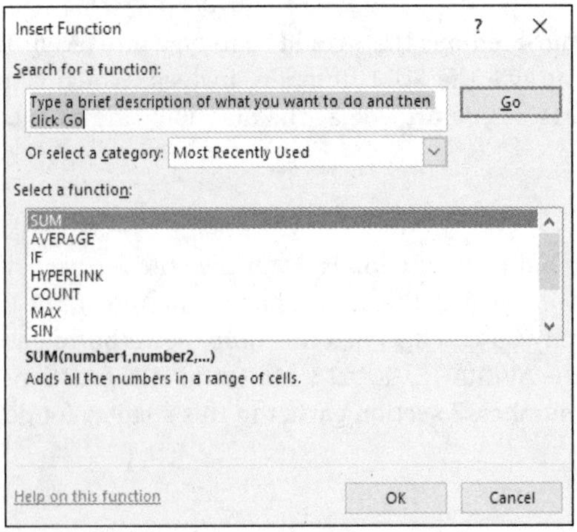


**FIGURE 5-5:** Use the Insert Function dialog box to, you know, insert a function.

To select the function that you want to use, you can use any of the following methods:

- Click the function name if it's one that you've used lately and is therefore already listed in the Select a Function list box.
- Select the name of the category of the function that you want to use from the Or Select a Category drop-down list box (Most Recently Used is the default category) and then select the function that you want to use in that category from the Select a Function list box.
- Replace the text "Type a brief description of what you want to do and then click Go" in the Search for a Function text box with keywords or a phrase about the type of calculation that you want to do (such as "return on investment"). Click the Go button or press Enter and click the function that you want to use in the Recommended category displayed in the Select a Function list box.

When selecting the function to use in the Select a Function list box, click the function name to have Excel give you a short description of what the function does, displayed underneath the name of the function with its argument(s) shown in parentheses (referred to as the function's *syntax*). To get help on using the function, click the Help on This Function link displayed in the lower-left corner of the Insert Function dialog box to open the Help window in its own pane on the right. When you finish reading and/or printing this help topic, click the Close button to close the Help window and return to the Insert Function dialog box.

When you click OK after selecting the function that you want to use in the current formula, Excel inserts the function name followed by a closed set of parentheses on the Formula bar. At the same time, the program closes the Insert Function dialog box and then opens the Function Arguments dialog box, similar to the one shown in Figure 5-6.

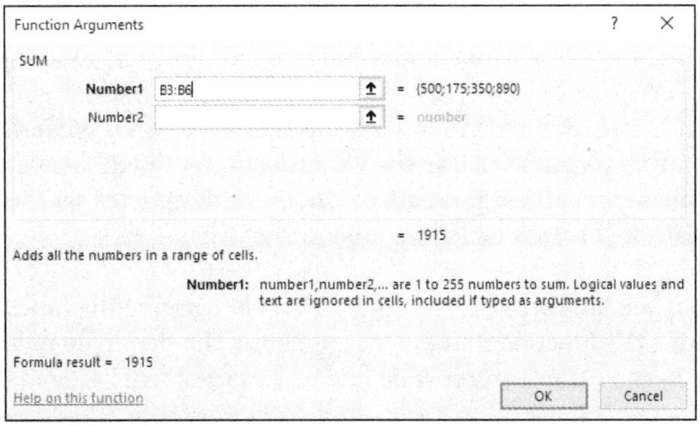


**FIGURE 5-6:** Use the Function Arguments dialog box to specify the arguments for a function.

### Using the Ribbon's Formulas tab

You can also insert a function using the Ribbon's Formulas tab. In the Function Library group, you see drop-down lists for several function categories: Financial, Logical, Text, Date & Time, Lookup & Reference, and Math & Trig. In addition, you can click More Functions to eyeball a few more categories: Statistical, Engineering, Cube, Information, Compatibility, and Web. If the function you want is one you've used lately, it might appear on the handy Recently Used drop-down list. Click the category that contains the function you want and then click the function to insert it into your formula and open the Function Arguments dialog box.

TIP

For your formula-building convenience, note that in the Ribbon's Formulas tab, the Function Library group also includes the same AutoSum button that's available in the Home tab's Editing group.

## Entering function arguments

A function *argument* is an input that gets fed into the function's internal calculations. Almost all functions accept at least one argument, and most functions accept two or more. And, yep, in case you're wondering: Some functions don't require any arguments. For example, the TODAY function returns the current date, with no arguments required.

Function arguments come in two flavors:

- **Required:** Arguments that you must include for the function to return a result.
- **Optional:** Arguments that you can omit and still get a valid result from the function.

All functions — even those that don't take any arguments, such as the TODAY function — follow the function name by a set of left and right parentheses. For example, the TODAY function requires no arguments, so it appears in a formula as TODAY( ). If the function requires arguments, these arguments must appear within the parentheses following the function name. When a function requires multiple arguments, such as the PMT function (used to calculate a loan payment), you must enter the arguments in the order designated by the function's syntax (so that Excel knows which argument is which).

How do you know the proper order? That comes from the function's *syntax*, which specifies the function name, its arguments, the data type of each argument, the order to enter those arguments, and which arguments are required.

The easiest way to see a function's syntax is to type the function's name in a formula followed by the opening (left) parenthesis. Below the cell, Excel displays a ScreenTip that contains the syntax. Figure 5-7 shows the syntax that appears for the PMT function. Look closely and you'll notice three things about this syntax:

- The arguments are displayed in the order you must enter them, separated by commas.
- The current argument (that is, the argument you're about to type or click) is displayed in bold type. When you enter that argument and type a comma, the next argument in the list (if there is one) is displayed in bold.
- Optional arguments are surrounded by square brackets (such as [fv] and [type] for the PMT function).

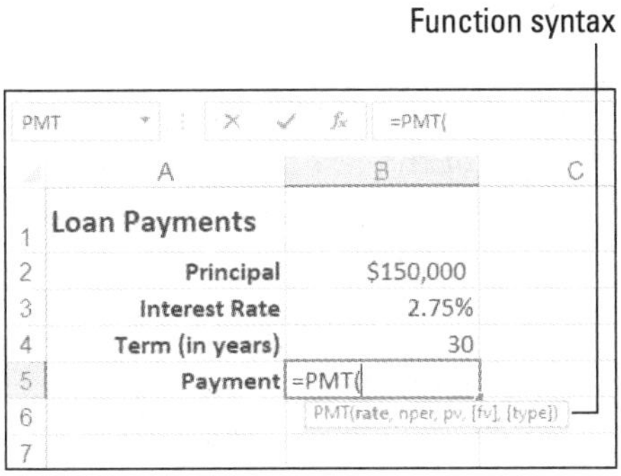


**FIGURE 5-7:** Type the function name followed by the left parenthesis to see a ScreenTip with the function syntax.

If you're not typing the function by hand — that is, you used the Insert Function button or the Formulas tab to get your function off the ground — the function syntax appears in the Function Arguments dialog box. Figure 5-8 shows the Function Arguments dialog box for the PMT function. Again, you can notice three things about the syntax here:

- Although arguments are displayed in the order required by the function (from top to bottom), you can fill in the text boxes in any order you prefer.
- To the right of each argument is a text label that tells you the data type of the argument (such as "number" or "date").
- Required argument names appear in bold type (Rate, Nper, and Pv in Figure 5-8), while optional argument names appear in regular type (Fv and Type in Figure 5-8).

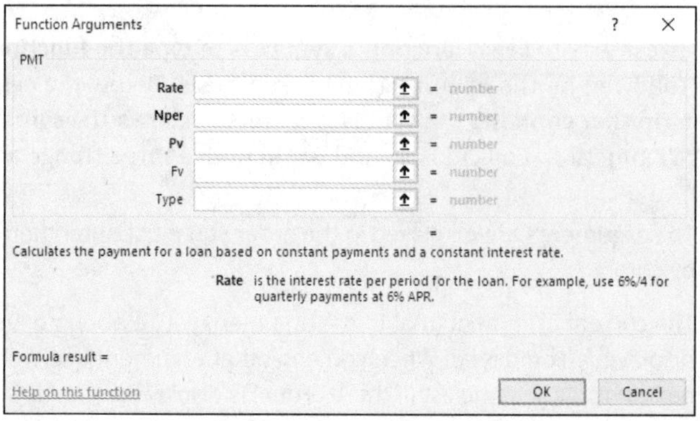


**FIGURE 5-8:** The Function Arguments dialog box shows the function syntax.

When you use the text boxes in the Function Arguments dialog box to input the arguments for a function, you can select the cell or cell range in the worksheet that contains the entries that you want used. Click the text box for the argument that you want to define and then either start dragging the cell cursor through the cells or, if the Function Arguments dialog box is obscuring the first cell in the range that you want to select, click the Collapse Dialog Box button (shown in the margin) located to the immediate right of the text box. Dragging or clicking this button reduces the Function Arguments dialog box to just the currently selected argument text box, thus enabling you to drag through the rest of the cells in the range.

As you define arguments for a function in the Function Arguments dialog box, Excel shows you the calculated result following the heading, "Formula result =" near the bottom of the Function Arguments dialog box. When you finish entering the required argument(s) for your function (and any optional arguments that may pertain to your calculation), click OK to have Excel close the Function Arguments dialog box and insert the function into the formula.

# Copying Formulas

Copying formulas is one of the most common tasks that you do in a typical worksheet that relies primarily on formulas. Although most copy operations for formulas are straightforward, you need to exercise a bit of care to make sure that the copied formula is performing the calculation you want. The next few sections explain what I mean.

## Copying with relative cell references

When a formula uses cell references rather than constant values (as nearly all formulas should), Excel makes the task of copying most formulas straightforward.

(To find out why I added the hedge word "most" in that last sentence, see "Copying with absolute references," next.) The program does this by automatically adjusting the cell references in the original formula to suit the position of the copies that you make. It does this through a system known as *relative cell addresses,* where the column references in the cell address in the formula change to suit their new column position and the row references change to suit their new row position.

Figures 5-9 and 5-10 illustrate how this works. For Figure 5-9, I used the AutoSum button in Cell B7 to build the original formula that uses the SUM function that totals the April sales. The formula in Cell B7 reads

```
=SUM(B3:B6)
```

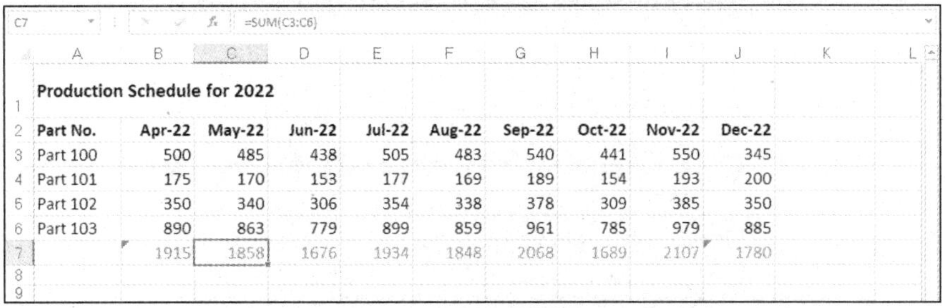

C7 =SUM(C3:C6)

| | A | B | C | D | E | F | G | H | I | J | K | L |
|---|---|---|---|---|---|---|---|---|---|---|---|---|
| 1 | Production Schedule for 2022 | | | | | | | | | | | |
| 2 | Part No. | Apr-22 | May-22 | Jun-22 | Jul-22 | Aug-22 | Sep-22 | Oct-22 | Nov-22 | Dec-22 | | |
| 3 | Part 100 | 500 | 485 | 438 | 505 | 483 | 540 | 441 | 550 | 345 | | |
| 4 | Part 101 | 175 | 170 | 153 | 177 | 169 | 189 | 154 | 193 | 200 | | |
| 5 | Part 102 | 350 | 340 | 306 | 354 | 338 | 378 | 309 | 385 | 350 | | |
| 6 | Part 103 | 890 | 863 | 779 | 899 | 859 | 961 | 785 | 979 | 885 | | |
| 7 | | 1915 | 1858 | 1676 | 1934 | 1848 | 2068 | 1689 | 2107 | 1780 | | |
| 8 | | | | | | | | | | | | |
| 9 | | | | | | | | | | | | |

**FIGURE 5-9:** An original formula copied with the Fill handle across the last row of the data.

I then used the AutoFill feature to copy this formula by dragging the Fill handle to include the cell range B7:J7. (Copying the formula with the cut-and-paste method would work just as well, although it's a little more work.) Note in the cell range C7:J7 that Excel did not copy the original formula to the other cells verbatim. (Otherwise, each of the copied formulas would return the same result, 1915, as the original in cell B7.) If you look at the Formula bar in Figure 5-9, you see that the copy of the original formula in cell C7 reads

```
=SUM(C3:C6)
```

In this copy, Excel adjusted the column reference of the range being summed from B to C to suit the new position of the copy.

Figure 5-10 shows how this works when copying an original formula in the other direction, this time down a column. For this figure, I used the AutoSum button to create a SUM formula that totals all the monthly sales for Part 100 in Row 3. The formula in Cell K3 reads

```
=SUM(B3:J3)
```

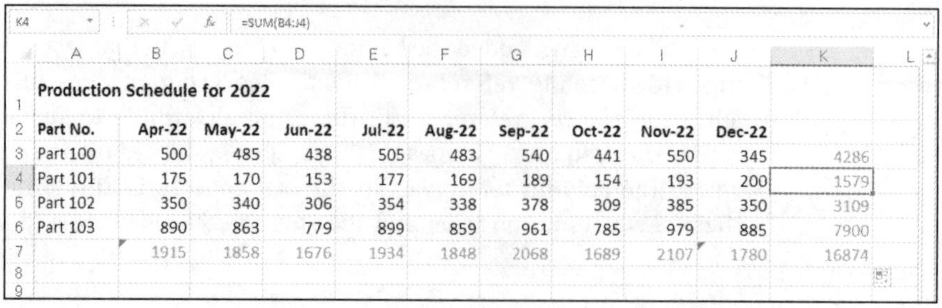

K4 | =SUM(B4:J4)

| | A | B | C | D | E | F | G | H | I | J | K |
|---|---|---|---|---|---|---|---|---|---|---|---|
| 1 | Production Schedule for 2022 | | | | | | | | | | |
| 2 | Part No. | Apr-22 | May-22 | Jun-22 | Jul-22 | Aug-22 | Sep-22 | Oct-22 | Nov-22 | Dec-22 | |
| 3 | Part 100 | 500 | 485 | 438 | 505 | 483 | 540 | 441 | 550 | 345 | 4286 |
| 4 | Part 101 | 175 | 170 | 153 | 177 | 169 | 189 | 154 | 193 | 200 | 1579 |
| 5 | Part 102 | 350 | 340 | 306 | 354 | 338 | 378 | 309 | 385 | 350 | 3109 |
| 6 | Part 103 | 890 | 863 | 779 | 899 | 859 | 961 | 785 | 979 | 885 | 7900 |
| 7 | | 1915 | 1858 | 1676 | 1934 | 1848 | 2068 | 1689 | 2107 | 1780 | 16874 |

**FIGURE 5-10:** An original formula copied with the Fill handle down the last column of the data.

You can then use the Fill handle to copy this formula down the last column of the table to include the cell range by positioning the cell cursor in K3 and then dragging the Fill handle down to select K3:K7. If you were to then position the cell cursor in Cell K4, you would see on the Formula bar that when Excel copied the original formula in Cell K3 down to Cell K4, it automatically adjusted the row reference to suit its new position so that the formula in Cell K4 reads

```
=SUM(B4:J4)
```

## Copying with absolute references

Most of the time, relative cell references are exactly what you need in your formulas to enable Excel to adjust the row and/or column references during copying. However, you'll encounter some situations where Excel should not adjust one or more parts of the cell reference in the copied formula. The most common case is when you want to use a cell value as a constant in all the copies that you make of a formula.

Figure 5-11 illustrates just such a situation. In this situation, you want to build a formula in Cell B9 that calculates what percentage April's part production total (B7) is of the total nine-month production (Cell K7). Normally, you would create the following formula in Cell B9 with all its relative cell references:

```
=B7 / K7
```

However, when you copy this formula across to the range C9:J9 to calculate the percentages for the other eight months (May through December), look what happens: All those cells now show #DIV/0!, an Excel formula error that means division by zero (which is a no-no).

What happened? You can start to understand the problem by thinking about copying the original formula from Cell B9 to C9 to calculate the percentage for May. In this cell, you want the following formula that divides the May production total in Cell C7 by the nine-month total in Cell K7:

```
=C7 / K7
```

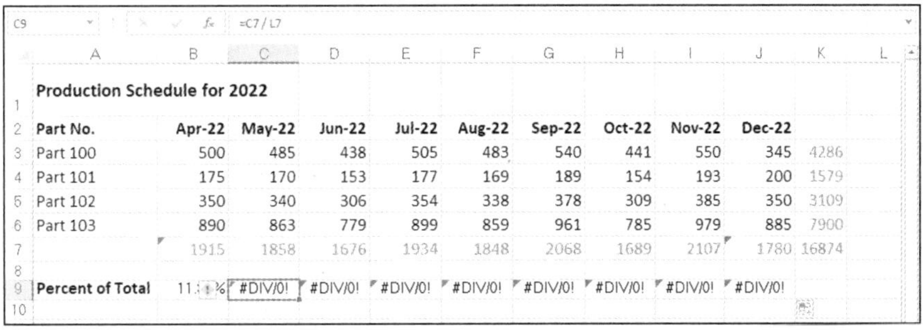

C9 =C7 / L7

| | A | B | C | D | E | F | G | H | I | J | K | L |
|---|---|---|---|---|---|---|---|---|---|---|---|---|
| 1 | Production Schedule for 2022 | | | | | | | | | | | |
| 2 | Part No. | Apr-22 | May-22 | Jun-22 | Jul-22 | Aug-22 | Sep-22 | Oct-22 | Nov-22 | Dec-22 | | |
| 3 | Part 100 | 500 | 485 | 438 | 505 | 483 | 540 | 441 | 550 | 345 | 4286 | |
| 4 | Part 101 | 175 | 170 | 153 | 177 | 169 | 189 | 154 | 193 | 200 | 1579 | |
| 5 | Part 102 | 350 | 340 | 306 | 354 | 338 | 378 | 309 | 385 | 350 | 3109 | |
| 6 | Part 103 | 890 | 863 | 779 | 899 | 859 | 961 | 785 | 979 | 885 | 7900 | |
| 7 | | 1915 | 1858 | 1676 | 1934 | 1848 | 2068 | 1689 | 2107 | 1780 | 16874 | |
| 8 | | | | | | | | | | | | |
| 9 | Percent of Total | 11.[illegible]% | #DIV/0! | #DIV/0! | #DIV/0! | #DIV/0! | #DIV/0! | #DIV/0! | #DIV/0! | #DIV/0! | | |
| 10 | | | | | | | | | | | | |

**FIGURE 5-11:** Copying the formula in cell B9 across produces #DIV/0! errors in the cells C9:J9.

However, if you don't indicate otherwise, Excel adjusts both parts of the formula in the copies, so that C9 incorrectly contains the following formula:

```
=C7 / L7
```

Because Cell L7 is currently blank and blank cells have the equivalent of the value 0, this formula returns the #DIV/0! formula error as the result, thus indicating that Excel can't properly perform this arithmetic operation. (See above section "Copying with absolute references." for details on this error message.)

To indicate that you don't want a particular cell reference (such as Cell K7 in the example) to be adjusted in the copies that you make of a formula, you change the cell reference from a relative cell reference to an *absolute cell reference.* An absolute cell reference contains dollar signs before the column letter and the row number, as in \$K\$7.

If you realize that you need to convert a relative cell reference to an absolute reference as you're building the original formula, you can convert the relative reference to absolute by selecting the cell and then pressing F4. To get an idea of how this works, follow along with these steps for creating the correct formula =B7 / \$K\$7 in Cell B9:

1. **Click Cell B9 to make it active.**
2. **Type = to start the formula; then click Cell B7 and type / (the sign for division).**

   The Formula bar now reads =B7/.
3. **Click K7 to select this cell and add it to the formula.**

   The Formula bar now reads =B7/K7.
4. **Press F4 once to change the cell reference from relative (K7) to absolute (\$K\$7).**

   The Formula bar now reads =B7/\$K\$7. You're now ready to enter the formula and then make the copies.

5. **Click the Enter button (shown in the margin) on the Formula bar and then drag the Fill handle to Cell J9 before you release the mouse button.**

   Figure 5-12 shows the (now correct) results.

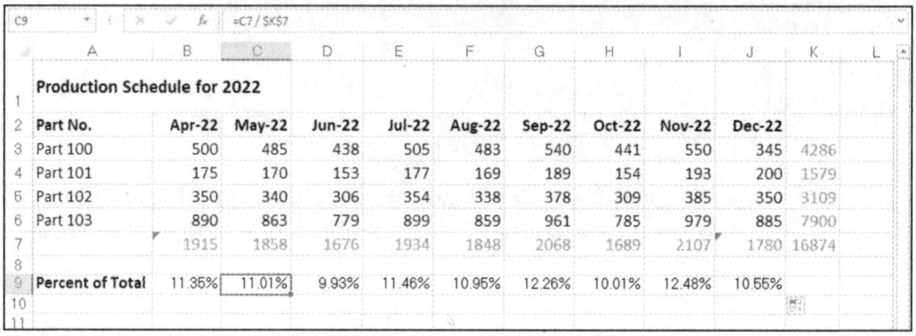

C9
=C7 / $K$7
A B C D E F G H I J K L
Production Schedule for 2022
Part No. Apr-22 May-22 Jun-22 Jul-22 Aug-22 Sep-22 Oct-22 Nov-22 Dec-22
Part 100 500 485 438 505 483 540 441 550 345 4286
Part 101 175 170 153 177 169 189 154 193 200 1579
Part 102 350 340 306 354 338 378 309 385 350 3109
Part 103 890 863 779 899 859 961 785 979 885 7900
1915 1858 1676 1934 1848 2068 1689 2107 1780 16874
Percent of Total 11.35% 11.01% 9.93% 11.46% 10.95% 12.26% 10.01% 12.48% 10.55%


**FIGURE 5-12:** Using an absolute cell reference in the divisor gets rid of the error and produces the correct results.

Like it or not, you won't always anticipate the need for an absolute value until after you've built the formula and copied it to a range. When this happens, you have to edit the original formula, change the relative reference to absolute, and then make the copies again.

When editing the cell reference in the formula, you can change its reference by positioning the insertion point anywhere in its address and then pressing F4. You can also do this by inserting dollar signs in front of the column letter(s) and row number when editing the formula, although doing that isn't nearly as easy as pressing F4.

## Copying with mixed cell references

Some formulas don't require you to change the entire cell reference from relative to absolute to copy them correctly. In some situations, you need to indicate only that the column letter or the row number remains unchanged in all copies of the original formula. A cell reference that is part relative and part absolute is called a *mixed cell reference.*

A mixed cell reference has a dollar sign just in front of the column letter or row number that should not be adjusted in the copies. For example, $C10 adjusts Row 10 in copies down the rows but leaves Column C unchanged in all copies across columns to its right. Another example is C$10, which adjusts Column C in copies to columns to the right but leaves Row 10 unchanged in all copies down the rows. (For an example of using mixed cell references in a master formula, refer to the information on using the PMT Function in the above section "Entering function arguments.")

To change the cell reference that you select in a formula (by clicking the flashing insertion point somewhere in its column letter and row number) from relative to mixed, continue to press F4 until the type of mixed reference appears on the Formula bar. When the Formula bar is active and the insertion point is somewhere in the cell reference (either when building or editing the formula), pressing F4 cycles through each cell-reference possibility in the following order:

- » The first time you press F4, Excel changes the relative cell reference to absolute (C10 to $C$10).
- » The second time you press F4, Excel changes the absolute reference to a mixed reference where the column is relative and the row is absolute ($C$10 to C$10).
- » The third time you select the Reference command, Excel changes the mixed reference where the column is relative and the row is absolute to a mixed reference where the row is relative and the column is absolute (C$10 to $C10).
- » The fourth time you press F4, Excel changes the mixed reference where the row is relative and the column is absolute back to a relative reference ($C10 to C10).

If you bypass the type of cell reference that you want to use, you can return to it by continuing to press F4 until you cycle through the variations again to reach the one that you need.



# Adding Array Formulas

As noted previously in this chapter, many worksheet models use an original formula that you copy to adjacent cells by using relative cell references (sometimes referred to as a *one-to-many copy*). In some cases, you can build the original formula so that Excel performs the desired calculation not only in the active cell, but also in all the other cells to which you would normally copy the formula. You do this by creating an *array formula*. An array formula is a special formula that operates on a collection of values.

Using array formulas can significantly reduce the amount of formula copying that you have to do in a worksheet by producing multiple results throughout the array range in a single operation. Also, array formulas use less computer memory than standard formulas copied in a range. This can be important when creating a large worksheet with many ranges because it may mean the difference between fitting all your calculations on one worksheet and having to split your model into several worksheets.

## Creating an array formula

To get an idea of how you build and use array formulas in a worksheet, consider the sample worksheet shown in Figure 5-13. This worksheet is designed to compute the biweekly wages for each employee. It does this by multiplying each employee's hourly rate by the number of hours worked in each pay period.

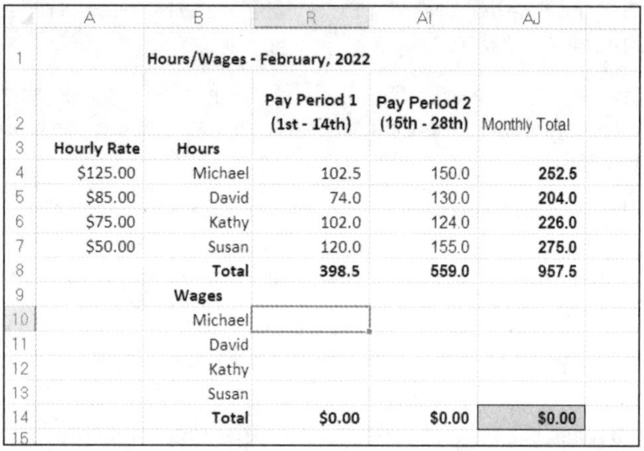

| | A | B | R | AI | AJ |
|---|---|---|---|---|---|
| 1 | | Hours/Wages - February, 2022 | | | |
| 2 | | | Pay Period 1 (1st - 14th) | Pay Period 2 (15th - 28th) | Monthly Total |
| 3 | Hourly Rate | Hours | | | |
| 4 | $125.00 | Michael | 102.5 | 150.0 | 252.5 |
| 5 | $85.00 | David | 74.0 | 130.0 | 204.0 |
| 6 | $75.00 | Kathy | 102.0 | 124.0 | 226.0 |
| 7 | $50.00 | Susan | 120.0 | 155.0 | 275.0 |
| 8 | | Total | 398.5 | 559.0 | 957.5 |
| 9 | | Wages | | | |
| 10 | | Michael | | | |
| 11 | | David | | | |
| 12 | | Kathy | | | |
| 13 | | Susan | | | |
| 14 | | Total | $0.00 | $0.00 | $0.00 |
| 15 | | | | | |

**FIGURE 5-13:** The goal: to calculate each employee's hourly wages for the first pay period.

One way to make these calculations would be to create the following formula in Cell R10 and then copy the formula down to Cells R11 through R13:

```
=A4 * R4
```

That works, but having to copy the formula is an extra step that can be a pain if you have a ton of copies to make. Instead, you can skip the copying step altogether by adding the following array formula in the array range (R10:R13):

```
=A4:A7 * R4:R7
```

This array formula multiplies each of the hourly rates in the 4 x 1 array in the range A4:A7 with the corresponding number of hours worked in the 4 x 1 array in the range R4:R7. This same formula is entered into all cells of the array range (R10:R13) as soon as you complete the formula in the active Cell R10.

**WARNING**

This type of formula is known as a *dynamic array formula,* and it only works in Excel 2019 and later. If you need your array calculation to work in earlier versions of Excel, use the method I describe in the "Building old-fashioned array formulas" section later in this chapter.

Follow along with the steps required to build this array formula:

1. **Ensure that all the cells in the array range are empty.**

   In the example, you'd clear out the range R10:R13, if needed.

2. **Select the first cell in the array range and type an equal sign (=).**

   In the example, you'd make Cell R10 the current cell.

3. **Enter your formula. When you come to an operand that would normally be a cell reference, enter a range reference that contains all the cells in the array.**

   In the example, you'd replace the cell reference A4 with the range reference A4:A7 and you'd replace the cell reference R4 with the range reference R4:R7. Your formula should now look like this:

   ```
   =A4:A7 * R4:R7
   ```

4. **Press Enter or click the Enter button (shown in the margin) in the Formula bar.**

   Presto! Excel adds the array formula not only to the current cell, but to all the cells in the array range, as shown in Figure 5-14. Here, I've selected Cell R11 so you can see that, yep, Excel applies the same array formula to each cell of the array range (R10:R13).

REMEMBER

The process where Excel automatically applies your array formula to the other cells in the range is known in Excel World as *spilling* the data, and the range that gets filled in is called the *spill range.*

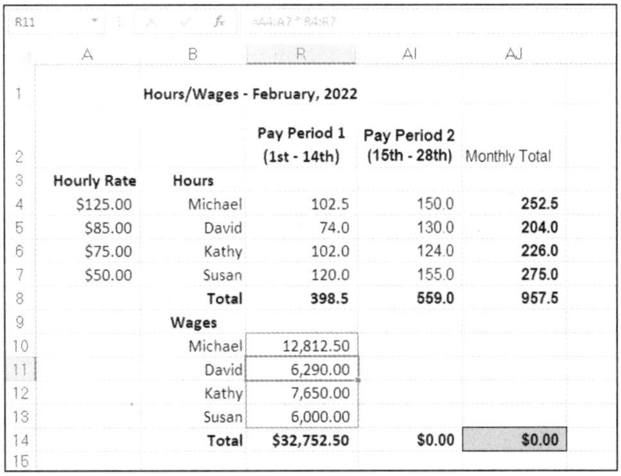

R11 =A4:A7 * R4:R7

| | A | B | R | AI | AJ |
|---|---|---|---|---|---|
| 1 | | Hours/Wages - February, 2022 | | | |
| 2 | | | Pay Period 1 (1st - 14th) | Pay Period 2 (15th - 28th) | Monthly Total |
| 3 | Hourly Rate | Hours | | | |
| 4 | $125.00 | Michael | 102.5 | 150.0 | 252.5 |
| 5 | $85.00 | David | 74.0 | 130.0 | 204.0 |
| 6 | $75.00 | Kathy | 102.0 | 124.0 | 226.0 |
| 7 | $50.00 | Susan | 120.0 | 155.0 | 275.0 |
| 8 | | Total | 398.5 | 559.0 | 957.5 |
| 9 | | Wages | | | |
| 10 | | Michael | 12,812.50 | | |
| 11 | | David | 6,290.00 | | |
| 12 | | Kathy | 7,650.00 | | |
| 13 | | Susan | 6,000.00 | | |
| 14 | | Total | $32,752.50 | $0.00 | $0.00 |
| 15 | | | | | |

**FIGURE 5-14:** An array formula makes short work of hourly wage calculation.

You can use array formulas to complete the rest of the February wage table. In the second cell range, AI10:AI13, you'd enter the following array formula to calculate the hourly wages for the second pay period in February:

```
=A4:A7 * AI4:AI7
```

In the third cell range, AJ10:AJ13, you'd enter the following array formula to calculate the total wages paid to each employee in February 2022:

```
=R10:R13 + AI10:AI13
```

## Editing a dynamic array formula

Although it appears in Figure 5-14 that the dynamic array formula now resides in Cell R11, that's not quite the case. Excel *applies* the formula to that cell (as well as to Cells R12 and R13), but the formula that you see in R11 is only a virtual copy. The actual formula only resides in the cell where you entered the formula (R10, in the example).

Therefore, when you need to edit the array formula, you must first select the same cell that you used to enter the array formula. When you finish your edit and press Enter or click the Enter button, Excel propagates the changes to the rest of the array range.

## Building old-fashioned array formulas

I mentioned earlier that Excel's newfangled dynamic arrays only work with Excel 2019 and later. If you need to keep your worksheets compatible with previous versions of Excel, you can use Excel's old method for building arrays. Going back to the example worksheet shown in Figure 5-13, you can create the following array formula in the array range:

```
={A4:A7 * R4:R7}
```

This array formula looks (and works) just like its dynamic cousin, except that it has those curly brackets — they're called *braces* — surrounding everything that comes after the equal sign (=).

To see how you create this version of the array formula, follow along with these steps:

1. **Make Cell R10 the current cell, and then select the array range R10:R13 and type = (equal sign) to start the array formula.**

   You always start an array formula by selecting the cell or cell range where the results are to appear. Note that array formulas, like standard formulas, begin with the equal sign.

2. **Select the range A4:A7 that contains the hourly rate for each employee as shown, type an * (asterisk for multiplication), and then select the range R4:R7 that contains the total number of hours worked during the first pay period.**

3. **Press Ctrl+Shift+Enter to insert an array formula in the array range.**

   When you press Ctrl+Shift+Enter to complete the formula, Excel inserts braces around the formula and copies the array formula {=A4:A7 * R4:R7} into each of the cells in the array range R10:R13.

WARNING

When entering an old-style array formula, you must press Ctrl+Shift+Enter instead of just the Enter key because this special key combination tells Excel that you're building an older array formula, so that the program encloses the formula in braces and copies it to every cell in the array range. Also, don't try to create this type of array formula by editing it on the Formula bar and then insert curly braces because this doesn't cut it. The only way to create an old-fashioned array formula is by pressing Ctrl+Shift+Enter to complete the formula entry.



## Editing an old-fashioned array formula

Editing old-style array formulas differs somewhat from editing normal formulas. In editing an array range, you must treat the range as a single unit and edit it in one operation (corresponding to the way in which the array formula was entered). This means that you can't edit, clear, move, insert, or delete individual cells in the array range. If you try, Excel displays an Alert dialog box stating "You cannot change part of an array."

To edit the contents of an array formula, select a cell in the array range and then activate Edit mode by clicking inside the Formula bar or by pressing F2. When you do this, Excel displays the contents of the array formula without the customary braces. After you make your changes to the formula contents, you must remember to press Ctrl+Shift+Enter to enter your changes and have Excel enclose the array formula in braces once again.

# Naming Cells and Ranges

Most of your formulas will use a combination of numerical constants, cell references (both relative and absolute), and range references. Although cell and range references provide a convenient method for pointing out the cell location in the worksheet grid, they're not at all descriptive of their content or function when used in formulas. Fortunately, Excel enables you to assign descriptive names to worksheet cells and ranges. Adding such names makes your worksheet formulas immediately more readable by showing the content or function of the cell and range operands.

To get an idea of how names can help to document the purpose of a formula, consider the following formula:

```
=B4 * B2
```

It's a legit formula, but what does it do? It's impossible to say without examining the worksheet in more detail to look for clues.

Now check out the following formula that performs the same calculation but, this time, with the use of names:

```
=Retail_Price * Discount_Rate
```

Ah, that's better: Just by looking at the formula, you can deduce that it's a calculation for determining the sale price of an item. Now the function of the formula is much more comprehensible, not only to you as the creator of the worksheet but also to anyone else who has to use it.

## Defining cell and range names

The most straightforward way to define a name is to follow these steps:

1. **Select the worksheet area you want to name.**

   You can select a cell, a range, or a collection of nonadjacent cells.

2. **Use the Formula bar's Name box to type the name you want to assign to the selection.**

   Figure 5-15 shows an example.

3. **Press Enter.**

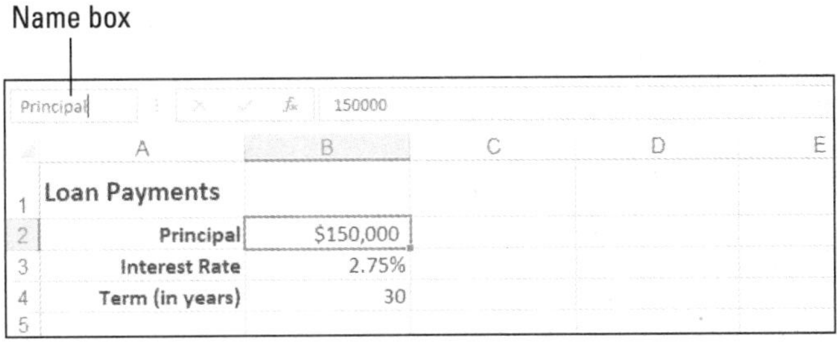


**FIGURE 5-15:** You can define a name using the Formula bar's Name box.

You can also name a selected cell or cell range, or a nonadjacent selection by displaying the Ribbon's Formulas tab then, in the Defined Names group, clicking the Define Name command. Excel opens the New Name dialog box, where you can type the selection's name in the Name text box. If Excel can identify a label in the cell immediately above or to the left of the active one, the program inserts this label as the suggested name in the Name text box.

When you're done, click OK to define the name.

REMEMBER

When naming a range, note that the name must begin with a letter rather than a number, contain no spaces, and not duplicate any other name in the workbook.

## Using names in building formulas

After you assign a name to a cell or range in your worksheet, you can then click the name from the Use in Formula button's drop-down menu on the Ribbon's Formulas tab to paste it into the formulas that you build.

For example, in the sample Autumn 2022 Furniture Sale table shown in Figure 5-16, after assigning the discount rate of 15% to the name, discount_rate, you can create the formulas that calculate the amount of the sale discount.

To do this, you multiply the retail price of each item by the discount_rate constant using the Use in Formula command button by following these steps:

1. **Make Cell D3 active.**
2. **Type = (equal sign) to start the formula.**
3. **Click Cell C3 to select the retail price for the first item and then type * (asterisk).**

   The formula on the Formula bar now reads, =C3*.

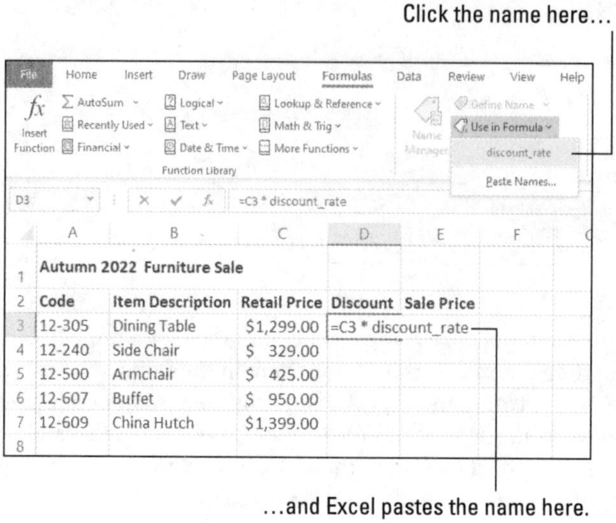


**FIGURE 5-16:** In the Use in Formula list, click the name you want to paste into your formula (such as the name discount_rate).

4. **On the Ribbon's Formulas tab, in the Defined Names group, click the Use in Formula button.**

   Excel opens the Use in Formula drop-down menu, which lists your defined range names.

5. **Click the name discount_rate.**

   The formula now reads =C3*discount_rate.

6. **Click the Enter button on the Formula bar to input the formula in Cell D3.**

   Now, all that remains is to copy the original formula down Column D.

7. **Drag the Fill handle in Cell D3 down to Cell D7 and release the mouse button to copy the formula and calculate the discount for the entire table.**

## Creating names from column and row headings

In the Ribbon's Formulas tab, you can use the Create from Selection command to automatically create column and row names from the existing column and row headings in a table of data. Create from Selection defines column names from the labels used as column headings in the top or bottom row of the table, the row names from the labels used as row headings in the leftmost or rightmost column, or any combination of these headings.

For example, the sample worksheet in Figure 5-17 illustrates a typical data layout that uses column headings in the top row of the data and row headings in the first column of the data.

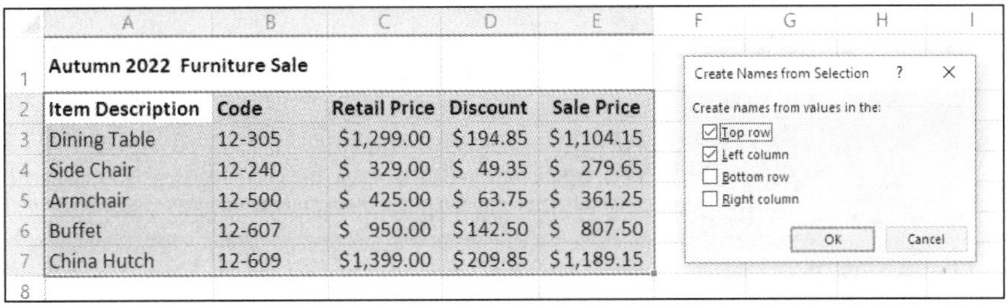


**FIGURE 5-17:** Creating names from the row and column headings in a worksheet data range.

You can assign these labels to the rows and columns in the data by using the Create from Selection command button as follows:

1. **Select the data cells, including those with the column and row labels that you want to use as names.**

   For the example shown in Figure 5-17, you select the range A2:E7.

2. **On the Formulas tab, in the Defined Names group, click the Create from Selection command.**

   Excel opens the Create Names from Selection dialog box that contains four check boxes: Top Row, Left Column, Bottom Row, and Right Column. The program selects the check box or boxes in this dialog box based on the arrangement of the labels in your data. In the example shown in Figure 5-17, Excel selects both the Top Row and Left Column check boxes because the data contains both column headings in the top row and row headings in the left column.

3. **If necessary, select the check boxes that correspond to the layout of your data.**

4. **Click OK to assign the names to your data.**

Note that when you select both the Top Row and Left Column check boxes in the Create Names from Selection dialog box, Excel assigns the label in the cell in the upper-left corner of the range to the data portion of the range you selected (that is, the part of the range that doesn't include the row and column headings). In the example illustrated in Figure 5-17, Excel assigns the name Item_Description (the heading for Column A) to the cell range B3:E7.

Excel also defines each column heading as the name of that column's data. For example, Excel assigns the name Retail_Price to the cell range C3:C7. Similarly, Excel defines each row heading as the name of that row's data. For example, Excel assigns the name China_Hutch to the cell range B7:E7.

## Managing names

As you assign names in your workbook, their names appear in the Name Manager dialog box. You open this dialog box by displaying the Formulas tab and, in the Defined Names group, clicking the Name Manager command.

The Name Manager enables you to do any of the following:

- **Define a new name:** Click New to open the New Name dialog box. (See "Defining cell and range names" earlier in this chapter.)
- **Edit an existing name:** Click the name you want to modify and then click Edit to open the Edit Name dialog box. Change the name, comment, or reference (but not the scope), and then click OK.
- **Delete an existing name:** Click the name and then click Delete. When Excel asks you to confirm the deletion, click OK.
- **Filter the names:** Click the Filter button and then click a filter option (Names Scoped to Worksheet, Names Scoped to Workbook, Names with Errors, Names without Errors, Defined Names, or Table Names) from its drop-down menu.

WARNING

Be careful that you don't delete a name that is already used in formulas in the worksheet. If you do, Excel returns the #NAME? error value to any formula that refers to the name you deleted!

IN THIS CHAPTER

» Analyzing data in a hurry

» Formatting trends and sorting, filtering, and analyzing data

» Using PivotTables to summarize data

# Chapter 6

# Analyzing Data

Sometimes it's not enough to just enter data in a worksheet, cobble together a few formulas, and sprinkle a little formatting to make things presentable. You're often called on to divine some inner meaning from the jumble of numbers and formula results that litter your worksheets. In other words, you need to *analyze* your data to see what nuggets of understanding you can unearth.

This chapter looks at a few basic analytic techniques that you can apply to the data in your worksheets. First you learn various Excel features that offer quick-and-not-all-that-dirty analyses of some data. The chapter then examines conditional formatting, where you use colors, icons, and other cute visual aids to examine data trends and outliers. Next up are tables, which enable you to sort and filter ranges of data, just like the pros. You then dive into some ridiculously useful methods for trying out different scenarios with "what-if" analysis. Finally, the chapter closes with a quick look at Excel's powerful PivotTable feature, which lets you take a massive pile of data and summarize it into a nice, neat tabular format.

## Getting Quick Analyses from Excel

When you're in a hurry to analyze data in a worksheet, take advantage of the Analyze Data command, sparklines, and forecast sheets. These tools can help you examine data closely, recognize trends, and foretell the future. Better keep reading.

# Running a rough-and-ready data analysis

Excel's Analyze Data feature peers into your worksheet and comes up with tables and charts it thinks are insightful. The tables and charts appear in the Analyze Data task pane, as shown in Figure 6-1.

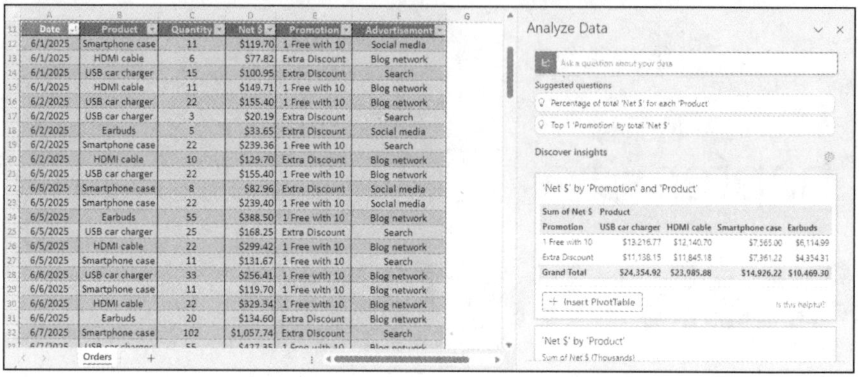


**FIGURE 6-1:** Examining data in the Analyze Data task pane.

To run a data analysis, start by clicking in a worksheet range with data that deserves more attention. Then go to the Home tab and click the Analyze Data button.

You're invited to scroll through items in the Analyze Data task pane to see worksheet data in a new light. While you're at it, you can take advantage of these amenities in the task pane:

- **Pinpoint one area for analysis:** Enter a question in the text box (or click a suggested question) to rerun the analysis and aim it at a narrower subject.
- **Refine the analysis:** Click the Which Fields Interest You the Most? button (shown in the margin). A new window opens in the task pane so that you can choose which columns or rows to analyze and whether you want to total or average data. Click the Update button after you make your choices.

- **Insert a PivotTable or PivotChart in your worksheet:** Click the Insert button below a PivotTable or PivotChart to place the item on a new worksheet in your workbook. Check out "Summarizing Data with PivotTables" to learn all about PivotTables and PivotCharts.

TIP

Scroll to the bottom of the Analyze Data task pane and click the Show All *X* Results link to see the numerous tables and charts Excel is capable of generating (where *X* is the total number of available tables and charts).

## Seeing what the sparklines say

You can place a micro-chart of data in a single cell in your worksheet. Excel refers to these micro-charts as *sparkline* charts. You can create three types of sparkline charts: line, column, or win/loss. All three show you, at a glance, trend information for a range of data you select. Excel places a sparkline chart in the cell immediately to the right of the row of cells you use to create the chart. Figure 6-2 shows some example sparklines. In this case, the cells in Column H use the line type of sparkline to show the trend of the data in Columns B through G.

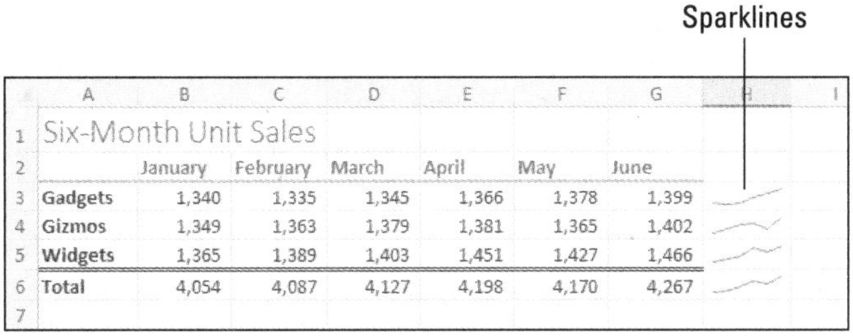


| | A | B | C | D | E | F | G | H | I |
|---|---|---|---|---|---|---|---|---|---|
| 1 | Six-Month Unit Sales | | | | | | | | |
| 2 | | January | February | March | April | May | June | | |
| 3 | Gadgets | 1,340 | 1,335 | 1,345 | 1,366 | 1,378 | 1,399 | | |
| 4 | Gizmos | 1,349 | 1,363 | 1,379 | 1,381 | 1,365 | 1,402 | | |
| 5 | Widgets | 1,365 | 1,389 | 1,403 | 1,451 | 1,427 | 1,466 | | |
| 6 | Total | 4,054 | 4,087 | 4,127 | 4,198 | 4,170 | 4,267 | | |
| 7 | | | | | | | | | |

**FIGURE 6-2:** Sparklines in action.

Follow these steps to create a sparkline chart:

1. **Select the cell where you want the chart to appear.**
2. **On the Insert tab, in the Sparklines group, click the button for the sparkline type you want to insert: Line, Column, or Win/Loss.**

   The Create Sparklines dialog box appears.
3. **Drag in a row or column of your worksheet to select the cells with the data you want to analyze.**
4. **Click OK in the Create Sparklines dialog box.**

To change the look of a sparkline chart, click the sparkline and then click the Sparkline contextual tab. There you will find commands for changing the color of the line or bars, choosing a different sparkline type, and doing one or two other things to pass the time on a rainy day. Click the Clear button to remove a sparkline chart.

TIP

You can also create a sparkline chart with the Quick Analysis button. Drag over the cells with the data you want to analyze. When the Quick Analysis button (shown in the margin) appears, click it, click Sparklines in the pop-up window, and then choose Line, Column, or Win/Loss.

# Generating a forecast sheet

A *forecast sheet* is a worksheet and chart that aim to, if not actually predict the future (wouldn't *that* be handy!), give you a sense of what the future might have in store based on the historical data you have. Figure 6-3 shows an example forecast sheet, which has three main components:

- **Historical data:** The original data you used for the forecast. In Figure 6-3, this is the sales data in the range A1:B22 for the years 2004 through 2024.
- **Forecast data:** The data that Excel projects into the future based on the historical data. This data has three columns, from left to right (Columns C, D, and E in Figure 6-3): Forecast, the predicted values based on your historic data; Lower Confidence Bound, the lowest prediction values for the forecast period; and Upper Confidence Bound, the highest prediction for the forecast period.
- **Forecast chart:** A line chart showing the historical data followed by the data for the three forecast predictions.

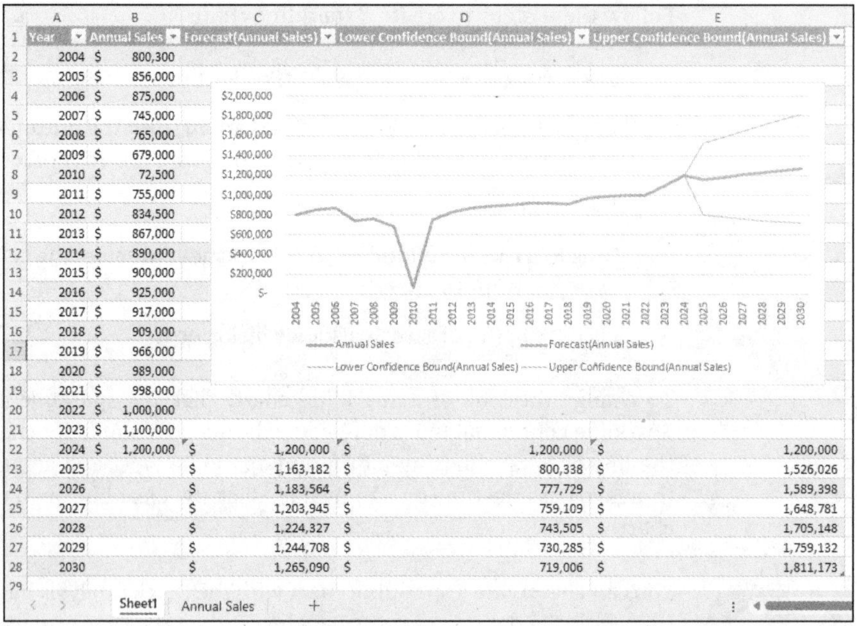

| Year | Annual Sales | Forecast(Annual Sales) | Lower Confidence Bound(Annual Sales) | Upper Confidence Bound(Annual Sales) |
|---|---|---|---|---|
| 2004 | $ 800,300 | | | |
| 2005 | $ 856,000 | | | |
| 2006 | $ 875,000 | | | |
| 2007 | $ 745,000 | | | |
| 2008 | $ 765,000 | | | |
| 2009 | $ 679,000 | | | |
| 2010 | $ 72,500 | | | |
| 2011 | $ 755,000 | | | |
| 2012 | $ 834,500 | | | |
| 2013 | $ 867,000 | | | |
| 2014 | $ 890,000 | | | |
| 2015 | $ 900,000 | | | |
| 2016 | $ 925,000 | | | |
| 2017 | $ 917,000 | | | |
| 2018 | $ 909,000 | | | |
| 2019 | $ 966,000 | | | |
| 2020 | $ 989,000 | | | |
| 2021 | $ 998,000 | | | |
| 2022 | $ 1,000,000 | | | |
| 2023 | $ 1,100,000 | | | |
| 2024 | $ 1,200,000 | $ 1,200,000 | $ 1,200,000 | $ 1,200,000 |
| 2025 | | $ 1,163,182 | $ 800,338 | $ 1,526,026 |
| 2026 | | $ 1,183,564 | $ 777,729 | $ 1,589,398 |
| 2027 | | $ 1,203,945 | $ 759,109 | $ 1,648,781 |
| 2028 | | $ 1,224,327 | $ 743,505 | $ 1,705,148 |
| 2029 | | $ 1,244,708 | $ 730,285 | $ 1,759,132 |
| 2030 | | $ 1,265,090 | $ 719,006 | $ 1,811,173 |



**FIGURE 6-3:** A forecast sheet.

Follow these steps to create a forecast sheet and add it to your workbook:

1. **Select the data Excel needs for forecasting purposes.**

   Select data in two corresponding columns or rows. One column or row must contain date or time values. Moreover, the date or time values must be recorded at regular intervals. For example, date value cells could record dates on the first of each month; time value cells could record times at the top of each hour.

2. **On the Data tab, in the Forecast group, click the Forecast Sheet button.**

   The Create Forecast Worksheet window appears. It shows what the chart portion of the forecast sheet will look like after you create it.

3. **Use the Forecast End spin button to specify how far into the future you want the forecast to extend.**

4. **Click the Create button.**

   Excel adds a worksheet to your workbook. It forecasts future trends in the form of a worksheet and a chart. I hope you like what you see.

# Eyeballing Trends and Outliers with Conditional Formatting

When you have a worksheet full of values, how can you tell when a particular value is exceptional in some way? The unfortunate answer is that, most of the time, it's really hard. All those numbers and dates and whatever just blend together, and making sense of the data seems hopeless.

Ah, but that's where Excel's Conditional Formatting tool comes to the rescue. This tool enables you to apply certain formatting attributes, such as bold text or a fill color, to a cell when the value of that cell meets a required condition. For example, if your worksheet tracks weekly sales, you might set up Excel's Conditional Formatting tool to alert you if a sales figure falls below what is required for you to break even. Now that cell will stick out like the proverbial sore thumb and your data will make a little more sense.



Select the cells that are candidates for conditional formatting and follow these steps to tell Excel when and how to format the cells:

1. **On the Home tab, in the Styles group, click the Conditional Formatting button.**

   Excel drops down a list of conditional formatting types.

2. **Choose Highlight Cells Rules or Top/Bottom Rules on the drop-down list.**

You see a submenu with choices about establishing the rule for whether values in the cells are highlighted or otherwise made more prominent:

- **Highlight Cells Rules** opens a continuation menu with options for defining formatting rules that highlight the cells in the cell selection that contain certain values, text, or dates, or that have values greater or less than a particular value, or that fall within a specified range of values.
- **Top/Bottom Rules** opens a continuation menu with options for defining formatting rules that highlight the top and bottom values, percentages, and above and below average values in the cell selection.
- **Data Bars** opens a palette with different color data bars that you can apply to the cell selection to indicate their values relative to each other using bars that appear within each cell.
- **Color Scales** opens a palette with different three- and two-colored scales that you can apply to the cell selection to indicate their values relative to each other using colors.
- **Icon Sets** opens a palette with different sets of icons that you can apply to the cell selection to indicate their values relative to each other using icons.

3. **Click an option on the submenu.**

If you choose either Highlight Cells Rules or Top/Bottom Rules, you see a dialog box similar to the one in Figure 6-4.

If you choose any other conditional formatting type, Excel applies the formatting and you're done, so you can skip the rest of these steps.

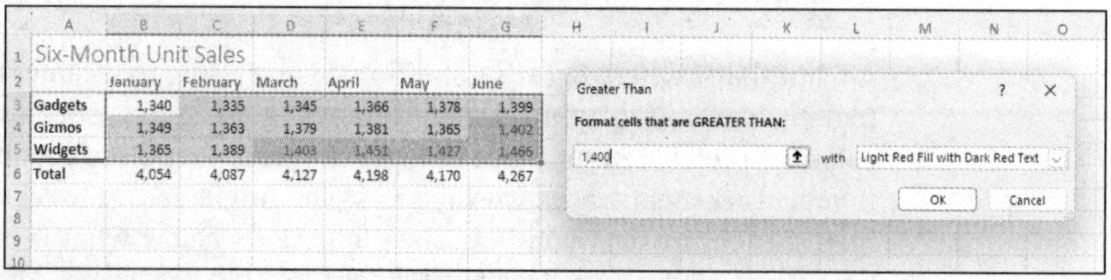


**FIGURE 6-4:** Establishing a conditional format for data.

4. **On the left side of the dialog box, establish the rule for flagging data.**

5. **On the With drop-down list, choose how you want to call attention to the data.**

   For example, you can display the data in red or yellow. You can choose Custom Format on the drop-down list to open the Format Cells dialog box and choose a font style or color for the text.

6. **Click OK.**

To remove conditional formats, select the cells with the formats, go to the Home tab, click the Conditional Formatting button, and choose Clear Rules ⇨ Clear Rules from Selected Cells.

You can also establish conditional formats by selecting cells and pressing Ctrl+Q or clicking the Quick Analysis button (shown in the margin). In the pop-up window, choose the Formatting tab and then click Greater Than or Top 10% to create a highlight-cell or top/bottom rule.

# Managing Information in Tables

Although Excel is a spreadsheet program, many people use it to keep and maintain simple databases called *tables*, such as the one shown in Figure 6-5. Addresses, inventories, and employee data are examples of information that typically is kept in tables. These pages explain how to sort and filter a table to make it yield more information. Sort a table to put it in alphabetical or numeric order; filter a table to isolate the information you need.

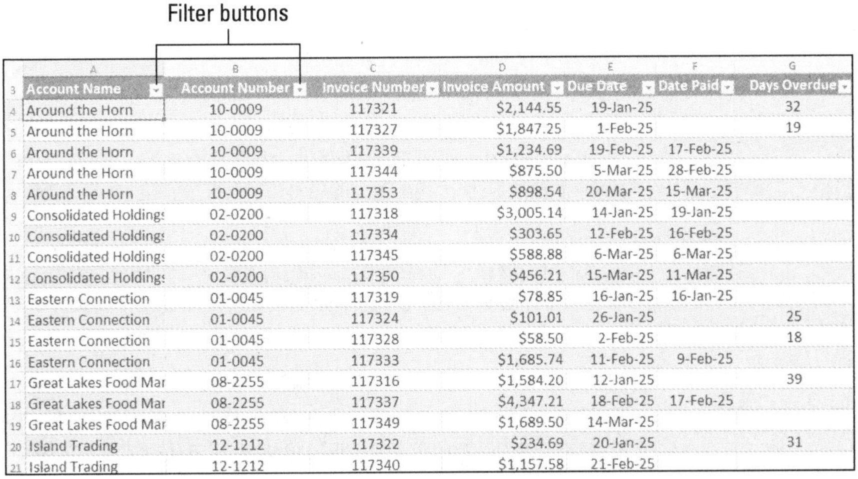


| | A | B | C | D | E | F | G |
|---|---|---|---|---|---|---|---|
| 3 | Account Name | Account Number | Invoice Number | Invoice Amount | Due Date | Date Paid | Days Overdue |
| 4 | Around the Horn | 10-0009 | 117321 | $2,144.55 | 19-Jan-25 | | 32 |
| 5 | Around the Horn | 10-0009 | 117327 | $1,847.25 | 1-Feb-25 | | 19 |
| 6 | Around the Horn | 10-0009 | 117339 | $1,234.69 | 19-Feb-25 | 17-Feb-25 | |
| 7 | Around the Horn | 10-0009 | 117344 | $875.50 | 5-Mar-25 | 28-Feb-25 | |
| 8 | Around the Horn | 10-0009 | 117353 | $898.54 | 20-Mar-25 | 15-Mar-25 | |
| 9 | Consolidated Holdings | 02-0200 | 117318 | $3,005.14 | 14-Jan-25 | 19-Jan-25 | |
| 10 | Consolidated Holdings | 02-0200 | 117334 | $303.65 | 12-Feb-25 | 16-Feb-25 | |
| 11 | Consolidated Holdings | 02-0200 | 117345 | $588.88 | 6-Mar-25 | 6-Mar-25 | |
| 12 | Consolidated Holdings | 02-0200 | 117350 | $456.21 | 15-Mar-25 | 11-Mar-25 | |
| 13 | Eastern Connection | 01-0045 | 117319 | $78.85 | 16-Jan-25 | 16-Jan-25 | |
| 14 | Eastern Connection | 01-0045 | 117324 | $101.01 | 26-Jan-25 | | 25 |
| 15 | Eastern Connection | 01-0045 | 117328 | $58.50 | 2-Feb-25 | | 18 |
| 16 | Eastern Connection | 01-0045 | 117333 | $1,685.74 | 11-Feb-25 | 9-Feb-25 | |
| 17 | Great Lakes Food Mar | 08-2255 | 117316 | $1,584.20 | 12-Jan-25 | | 39 |
| 18 | Great Lakes Food Mar | 08-2255 | 117337 | $4,347.21 | 18-Feb-25 | 17-Feb-25 | |
| 19 | Great Lakes Food Mar | 08-2255 | 117349 | $1,689.50 | 14-Mar-25 | | |
| 20 | Island Trading | 12-1212 | 117322 | $234.69 | 20-Jan-25 | | 31 |
| 21 | Island Trading | 12-1212 | 117340 | $1,157.58 | 21-Feb-25 | | |

**FIGURE 6-5:** A table in a worksheet.

## Converting a range to a table

Before you can use Excel's table tools, you need to convert your standard-issue worksheet range into a table. Follow these steps:

1. **Select the range you want to turn into a table.**

   If the range has column headings, be sure to include those headings in your selection.

2. **On the Home tab, in the Styles group, click the Format As Table button and select a table style in the gallery.**

   The Create Table dialog box appears.

3. **If the cells you want to format include headers, the labels at the top of column rows that describe the data in the columns below, select the My Table Has Headers check box.**

4. **Click OK.**

   Excel converts your range into a full-fledged table and also tacks on the Table Design contextual tab to the Ribbon.

## Sorting a table

*Sorting* means to rearrange the rows in a table based on the data in one or more columns. Sort a table on the Account Name column, for example, to arrange the table in alphabetical order by account name. Sort a table on the Invoice Amount column to arrange the rows in numerical order by invoice amount. Sort a table on the Due Date column to arrange the table's rows chronologically from earliest to latest due date.

Here are all the ways to sort a table:

- **Sorting on a single column:** Click any cell in the column you want to use as the basis for the sort. For example, to sort item numbers from smallest to largest, click in the Item Number column. Then use one of these techniques to conduct the sort operation:

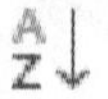

  - *Ascending sort:* On the Data tab, in the Sort & Filter group, click the Sort Lowest to Highest button (shown in the margin) to sort a text field A to Z, a numeric field from lowest to highest, or a date field from earliest to latest.

  - *Descending sort:* On the Data tab, in the Sort & Filter group, click the Sort Highest to Lowest button (shown in the margin) to sort a text field Z to A, a numeric field from highest to lowest, or a date field from latest to earliest.

- *Sorting via the filter button:* Click the column's filter button (shown in the margin) to open the drop-down menu, then click the field's ascending or descending sort command (the name of which depends on the field's data type). If you don't see the filter buttons, then on the Data tab, in the Sort & Filter group, click the Filter button.

» **Sorting on two or more columns:** On the Data tab, in the Sort & Filter group, click the Sort button. You see the Sort dialog box, as shown in Figure 6-6. Use the Sort By list to choose which column you want to sort with and use the Order list to specify the order in which you want to sort. To add another column for sorting, click the Add Level button. When you're ready, click OK to run the sort.

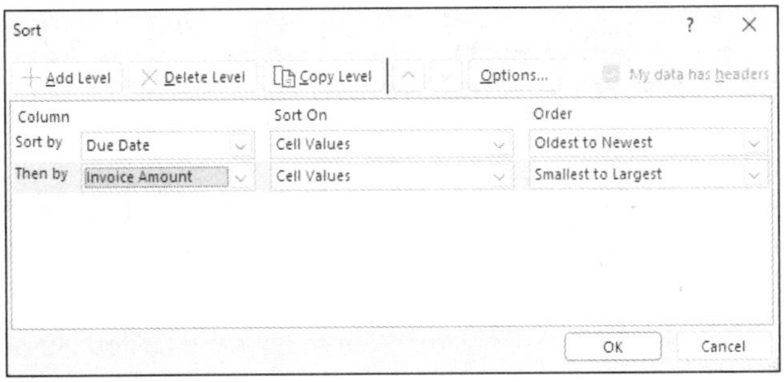


**FIGURE 6-6:** Sort to arrange the table data in different ways.

## Filtering a table

*Filtering* enables you to reduce a large table of data into a subset that meets the criteria you specify. In a table of accounts receivable data, for example, you might want to filter the table to show only those rows where the Date Paid column is blank. Similarly, you might want to filter that table to show only those items for a particular customer or those rows where the invoice amount is greater than $1,000.

Begin by clicking the filter button associated with the column that you want to use as the basis of your filter. (If you don't see the filter buttons in your table, then on the Data tab, in the Sort & Filter group, click the Filter button.)

In the column drop-down list that appears, tell Excel how you want to filter the table:

» **Filter by exclusion:** On the drop-down list, deselect the Select All check box and then select the check box next to each item you *don't* want to filter out, as shown in Figure 6-7. Click OK to put the filter into effect.

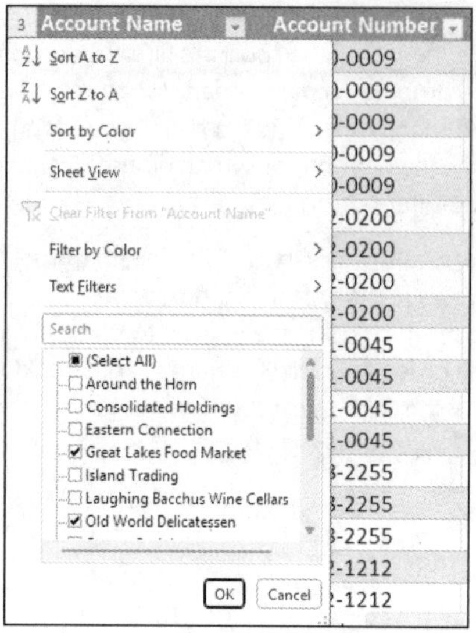


**FIGURE 6-7:** Filtering a worksheet by selecting just the unique columns values you want displayed.

» **Filter with criteria:** On the drop-down list, click *X* Filters, where *X* is Text, Number, or Date, depending on the data type of the column, and then click a filter operation on the submenu.

For more control, click Custom Filter to open the Custom AutoFilter dialog box. Choose an operator (equals, is greater than, or another) from the drop-down list, and either enter or choose a target criterion from the table on the right side of the dialog box. You can search by more than one criterion. Select the And option button if a row must meet both criteria to be selected, or select the Or option button if a row can meet either criterion to be selected. Click OK to apply the filter.

REMEMBER

To see all the data in the table again — that is, to *unfilter* the table — on the Data tab, in the Sort & Filter group, click the Clear button.

# What If You Used What-If Analysis?

One of the most common data-analysis techniques is *what-if analysis*, for which you set up worksheet models to analyze hypothetical situations. The "what-if" part means that these situations usually come in the form of a question: "*What* happens to the monthly payment *if* the interest rate goes up by 2 percent?" "*What* will the sales be *if* you increase the advertising budget by 10 percent?" Excel offers several what-if analysis tools, of which I cover two in the following sections: Goal Seek and data tables.

# Experimenting with Goal Seek

What if you already know the formula result you need and you want to produce that result by tweaking one of the formula's input values? For example, suppose that you know that you need to have $100,000 saved for your children's college education. In other words, you want to start an investment now that will be worth $100,000 at some point in the future.

This is called a *future value* calculation, and it requires three parameters: the term of the investment; the interest rate you earn on the investment; and the amount of money you invest each year. Assume that you need that money 18 years from now and that you can make a 4 percent annual return on your investment. Here's the question that remains: How much should you invest each year to make your goal?

Sure, you could waste large chunks of your life guessing the answer. Fortunately, you don't have to, because you can put Excel's Goal Seek tool to work. Goal Seek works by trying dozens of possibilities — called *iterations* — that enable it to get closer and closer to a solution. When Goal Seek finds a solution (or finds a solution that's as close as it can get), it stops and shows you the result.

You must do three things to set up your worksheet for Goal Seek:

- Set up one cell as the *changing cell,* which is the formula input cell value that Goal Seek will manipulate to reach the goal. In the college fund example, the formula cell that holds the annual deposit is the changing cell.
- Set up the other input values for the formula and give them proper initial values. In the college fund example, you enter 4 percent for the interest rate and 18 years for the term.
- Create a formula for Goal Seek to use to reach the goal. In the college fund example, you use the FV function, which calculates the future value of an investment given an interest rate, term, and regular deposit.

When your worksheet is ready for action, here are the steps to follow to get Goal Seek on the job:

1. **On the Data tab, in the Forecast group, click What-If Analysis and then click Goal Seek.**

   The Goal Seek dialog box appears.

2. **In the Set Cell box, enter the address of the cell that contains the formula you want Goal Seek to work with.**
3. **In the To Value text box, enter the value that you want Goal Seek to find.**

4. **In the By Changing Cell box, enter the address of the cell that you want Goal Seek to modify.**

   Figure 6-8 shows an example model for the college fund calculation as well as the completed Goal Seek dialog box.

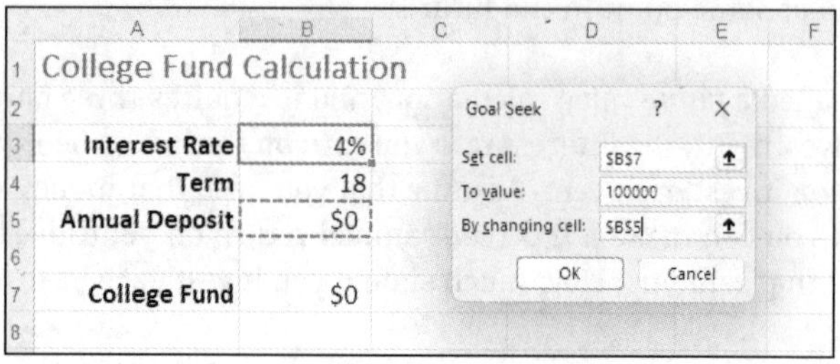


**FIGURE 6-8:** Using Goal Seek to calculate the annual deposit required to end up with $100,000 in a college fund.

5. **Click OK.**

   Goal Seek adjusts the changing cell value until it reaches a solution. When it's done, the formula shows the value you entered in Step 3. Figure 6-9 shows the result of the college fund calculation (Cell B5): you'd have to save $3,899 per year to meet your goal.

6. **Click OK to accept the solution.**

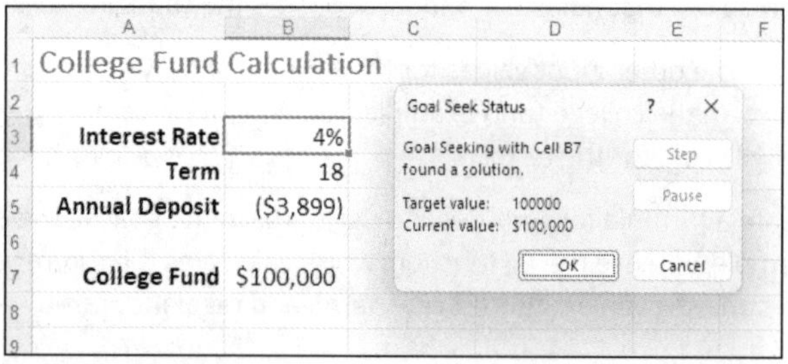


**FIGURE 6-9:** Goal Seek took all of a second or two to find a solution.

## Kicking your analysis up a notch with data tables

If you want to study the effect that different input values have on a formula, one solution is to set up the worksheet model and then manually change the formula's input cells. For example, if you're calculating a loan payment, you can enter different interest rate values to see what effect changing the value has on the payment.

The problem with modifying the values of a formula input is that you see only a single result at one time. A better solution is to set up a *data table*, which is a range that consists of the formula you're using and multiple input values for that formula. Excel automatically creates a solution to the formula for each different input value.

WARNING

Don't confuse data tables with the Excel tables that I talk about earlier in this chapter. Remember that a data table is a special range that Excel uses to calculate multiple solutions to a formula.

## Creating a basic data table

The most basic type of data table is one that varies only one of the formula's input cells. Not even remotely surprisingly, this basic version is known far and wide as a *one-input data table*. Here are the steps to follow to create a one-input data table:

1. **Type the input values.**

   - To enter the values in a column, start the column one cell down and one cell to the left of the cell containing the formula, as shown in Figure 6-10.
   - To enter the values in a row, start the row one cell up and one cell to the right of the cell containing the formula.

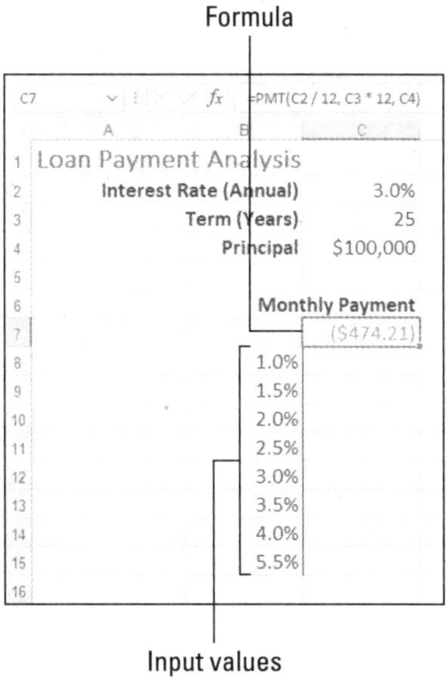


**FIGURE 6-10:** This data table has the input values in a column.

2. **Select the range that includes the input values and the formula.**

   In the example shown in Figure 6-10, you'd select the range B7:C15.

3. **On the Data tab, in the Forecast group, click What-If Analysis and then click Data Table to open the Data Table dialog box.**

4. **Enter the address of the *input cell,* which is the cell referenced by the formula that you want the data table to vary.**

   That is, for whatever cell you specify, the data table will substitute each of its input values into that cell and calculate the formula result. You have two choices:

   - If you entered the input values in a row, enter the input cell's address in the Row Input Cell text box.
   - If the input values are in a column, enter the input cell's address in the Column Input Cell text box. In the example shown in Figure 6-10, the data table's input values are annual interest rates, so the column input cell is C2, as shown in Figure 6-11.

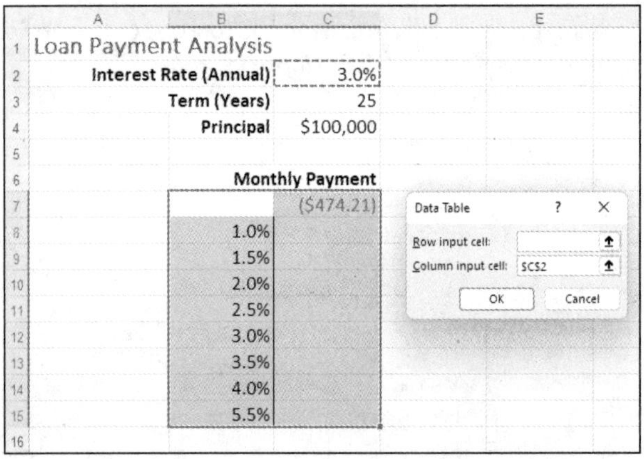


**FIGURE 6-11:** Enter the address of the input cell.

5. **Click OK.**

   Excel fills the input table with the results. Figure 6-12 shows the results of the example data table.

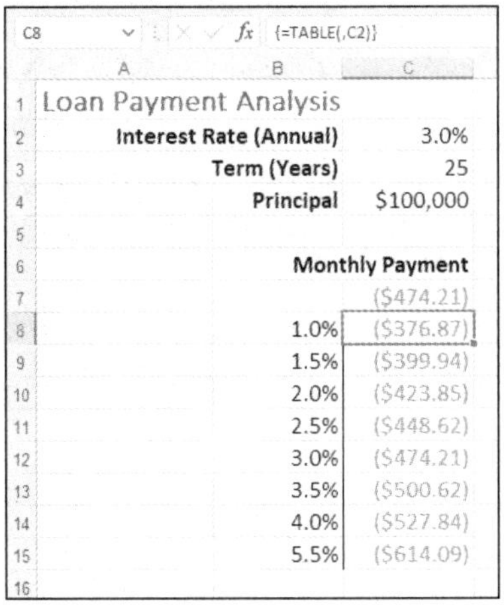


**FIGURE 6-12:** The data table results.

## Creating a two-input data table

Rather than vary a single formula input at a time — as in the one-input data table I discuss in the preceding section — Excel also lets you take things to the next level by enabling you to set up a *two-input* data table. As you might have guessed, a two-input data table is one that varies two formula inputs at the same time. For example, in a loan payment worksheet, you could set up a two-input data table that varies both the interest rate and the term.

To set up a two-input data table, you must set up two ranges of input cells. One range must appear in a column directly below the formula, and the other range must appear in a row directly to the right of the formula. Here are the steps to follow:

1. **Type the input values:**
   - To enter the column values, start the column one cell down and one cell to the left of the cell containing the formula.
   - To enter the row values, start the row one cell up and one cell to the right of the cell containing the formula.

   Figure 6-13 shows an example.

2. **Select the range that includes the input values and the formula.**

   In the example shown in Figure 6-13, you'd select the range B7:F15.

3. **On the Data tab, in the Forecast group, click What-If Analysis and then click Data Table to open the Data Table dialog box.**

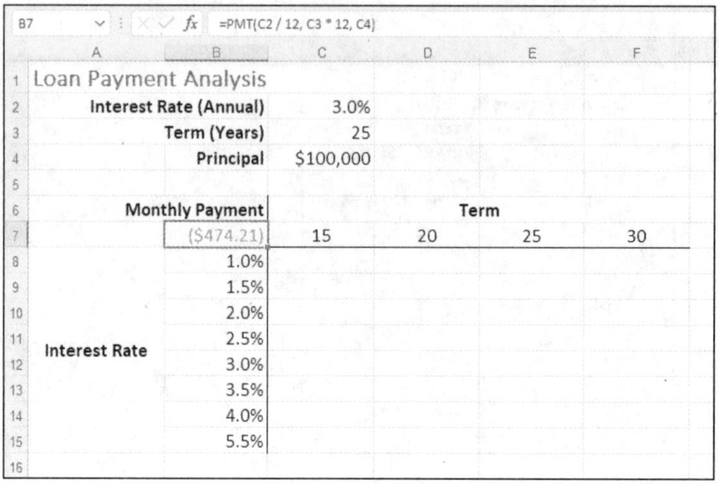


**FIGURE 6-13:** For a two-input data table, enter one set of values in a column and the other in a row.

4. **In the Row Input Cell text box, enter the cell address of the input cell that corresponds to the row values you entered.**

   In the example shown in Figure 6-13, the row values are term inputs, so the input cell is C3 (see Figure 6-14).

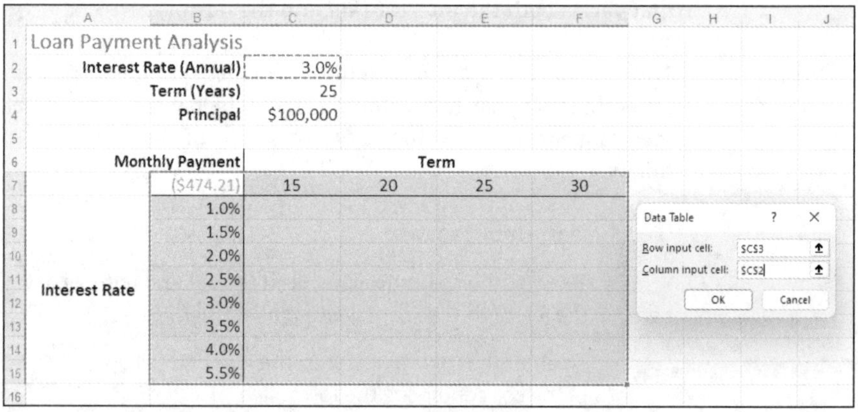


**FIGURE 6-14:** Enter the addresses of the input cells.

5. **In the Column Input Cell text box, enter the cell address of the input cell you want to use for the column values.**

   In the example shown in Figure 6-13, the column values are interest rate inputs, so the input cell is C2 (refer to Figure 6-14).

6. **Click OK.**

   Excel displays the results. Figure 6-15 shows the results of the example two-input data table.

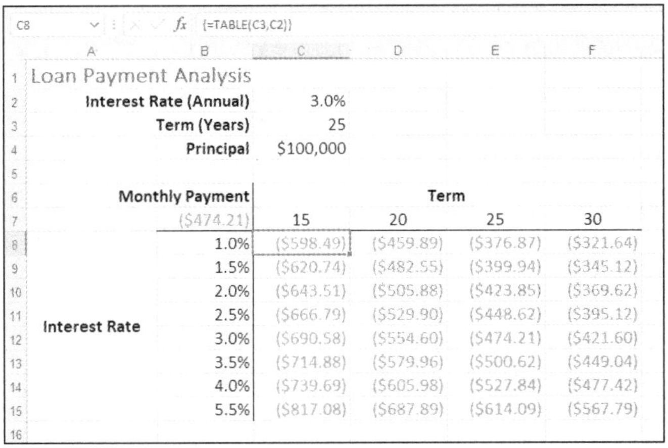

C8 fx {=TABLE(C3,C2)}

| | A | B | C | D | E | F |
|---|---|---|---|---|---|---|
| 1 | Loan Payment Analysis | | | | | |
| 2 | | Interest Rate (Annual) | 3.0% | | | |
| 3 | | Term (Years) | 25 | | | |
| 4 | | Principal | $100,000 | | | |
| 5 | | | | | | |
| 6 | | Monthly Payment | | Term | | |
| 7 | | ($474.21) | 15 | 20 | 25 | 30 |
| 8 | | 1.0% | ($598.49) | ($459.89) | ($376.87) | ($321.64) |
| 9 | | 1.5% | ($620.74) | ($482.55) | ($399.94) | ($345.12) |
| 10 | | 2.0% | ($643.51) | ($505.88) | ($423.85) | ($369.62) |
| 11 | Interest Rate | 2.5% | ($666.79) | ($529.90) | ($448.62) | ($395.12) |
| 12 | | 3.0% | ($690.58) | ($554.60) | ($474.21) | ($421.60) |
| 13 | | 3.5% | ($714.88) | ($579.96) | ($500.62) | ($449.04) |
| 14 | | 4.0% | ($739.69) | ($605.98) | ($527.84) | ($477.42) |
| 15 | | 5.5% | ($817.08) | ($687.89) | ($614.09) | ($567.79) |
| 16 | | | | | | |

**FIGURE 6-15:** The two-input data table results.

# Summarizing Data with PivotTables

*PivotTables* give you the opportunity to summarize data in a long worksheet list and in so doing analyze the data in new ways. You can display data such that you focus on one aspect of the list. You can turn the list inside out and perhaps discover things you didn't know before.

When you create a PivotTable, what you really do is turn a multicolumn table into a table for the purpose of analysis. For example, the four-column list in Figure 6-16 records items purchased in two grocery stores over a four-week period. The four columns are

- **Item:** The items purchased
- **Store:** The grocery store (Safepath or Wholewallet) where the items were purchased
- **Cost:** The cost of the items
- **Week:** When the items were purchased (Week 1, 2, 3, or 4)

This raw list doesn't reveal anything; it's hardly more than a data dump. However, as Figure 6-16 shows, by turning the list into PivotTables, you can tease the list to find out, among other things:

- How much was spent item by item in each grocery store, with the total spent for each item (Sum of Cost by Item and Store)
- How much was spent on each item (Sum of Cost by Item)

» How much was spent at each grocery store (Sum of Cost by Store)

» How much was spent each week (Sum of Cost by Week)

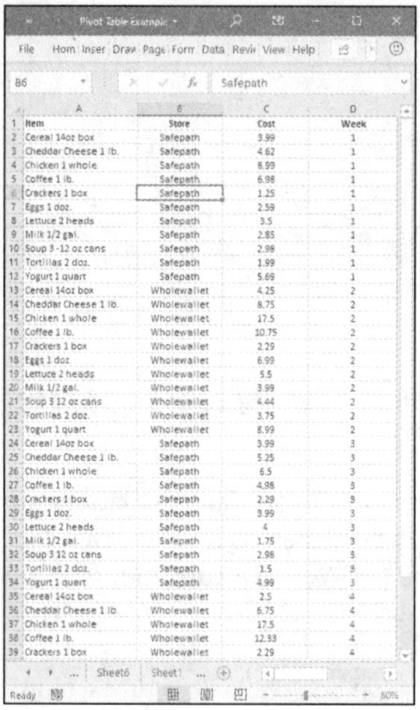

**Sum of Cost by Item and Store**

| Sum of Cost | Column Labels | | |
|---|---|---|---|
| Row Labels | Safepath | Wholewallet | Grand Total |
| Cereal 14oz box | 7.98 | 6.75 | 14.73 |
| Cheddar Cheese 1 lb. | 9.87 | 15.5 | 25.37 |
| Chicken 1 whole | 15.49 | 35 | 50.49 |
| Coffee 1 lb. | 11.96 | 23.08 | 35.04 |
| Crackers 1 box | 3.54 | 4.58 | 8.12 |
| Eggs 1 doz. | 6.58 | 15.49 | 22.07 |
| Lettuce 2 heads | 7.5 | 9 | 16.5 |
| Milk 1/2 gal. | 4.6 | 6.49 | 11.09 |
| Soup 3 12 oz cans | 2.98 | 8.88 | 11.86 |
| Soup 3 -12 oz cans | 2.98 | | 2.98 |
| Tortillas 2 doz. | 3.49 | 8.25 | 11.74 |
| Yogurt 1 quart | 10.68 | 17.98 | 28.66 |
| Grand Total | 87.65 | 151 | 238.65 |

**Sum of Cost by Item**

| Row Labels | Sum of Cost |
|---|---|
| Cereal 14oz box | 14.73 |
| Cheddar Cheese 1 lb. | 25.37 |
| Chicken 1 whole | 50.49 |
| Coffee 1 lb. | 35.04 |
| Crackers 1 box | 8.12 |
| Eggs 1 doz. | 22.07 |
| Lettuce 2 heads | 16.5 |
| Milk 1/2 gal. | 11.09 |
| Soup 3 12 oz cans | 11.86 |
| Soup 3 -12 oz cans | 2.98 |
| Tortillas 2 doz. | 11.74 |
| Yogurt 1 quart | 28.66 |
| Grand Total | 238.65 |

**Sum of Cost by Store**

| Row Labels | Sum of Cost |
|---|---|
| Safepath | 87.65 |
| Wholewallet | 151 |
| Grand Total | 238.65 |

**Sum of Cost by Week**

| Row Labels | Sum of Cost |
|---|---|
| 1 | 45.43 |
| 2 | 77.2 |
| 3 | 42.22 |
| 4 | 73.8 |
| Grand Total | 238.65 |

**FIGURE 6-16:** A raw multicolumn list (left) turned into meaningful PivotTables (right).

REMEMBER

Make sure that the list you want to analyze with a PivotTable has column headers. Column headers are the descriptive labels that appear across the top of columns in a list. Excel needs column headers to construct PivotTables.

## Getting a PivotTable recommendation from Excel

The easiest way to create a PivotTable is to let Excel do the work. Follow these steps:

1. **Select a cell anywhere in your data list.**
2. **On the Insert tab, in the Tables group, click the Recommended PivotTables button.**

   The Recommended PivotTables dialog box appears, as shown in Figure 6-17. This dialog box presents a number of PivotTables.

3. **Scroll the list of PivotTables on the left side of the dialog box, selecting each one and examining it on the right side of the dialog box.**

4. **Select a PivotTable and click OK.**

   The PivotTable appears on a new worksheet.

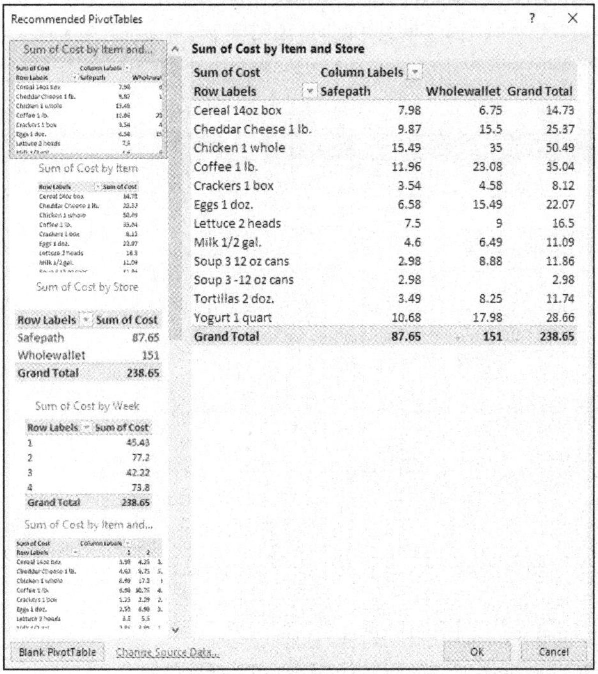


**FIGURE 6-17:** These PivotTables come highly recommended.

## Creating a PivotTable from scratch

Follow these steps to create a PivotTable on your own:

1. **Select a cell anywhere in your data list.**

2. **On the Insert tab, in the Tables group, click the PivotTable button.**

   Excel selects what it believes is your entire list, and you see the PivotTable from Table or Range dialog box. If the list isn't correctly selected, click outside the dialog box and select the data you want to summarize.

3. **Select the New Worksheet option and click OK.**

   You can select the Existing Worksheet option and select cells on your worksheet to show Excel where you want to place the PivotTable, but in my experience, creating it on a new worksheet and moving it later is the easier way to go.

   The PivotTable Analyze tab and PivotTable Fields task pane appear, as shown in Figure 6-18. The task pane lists the names of fields, or column headings, from your table.

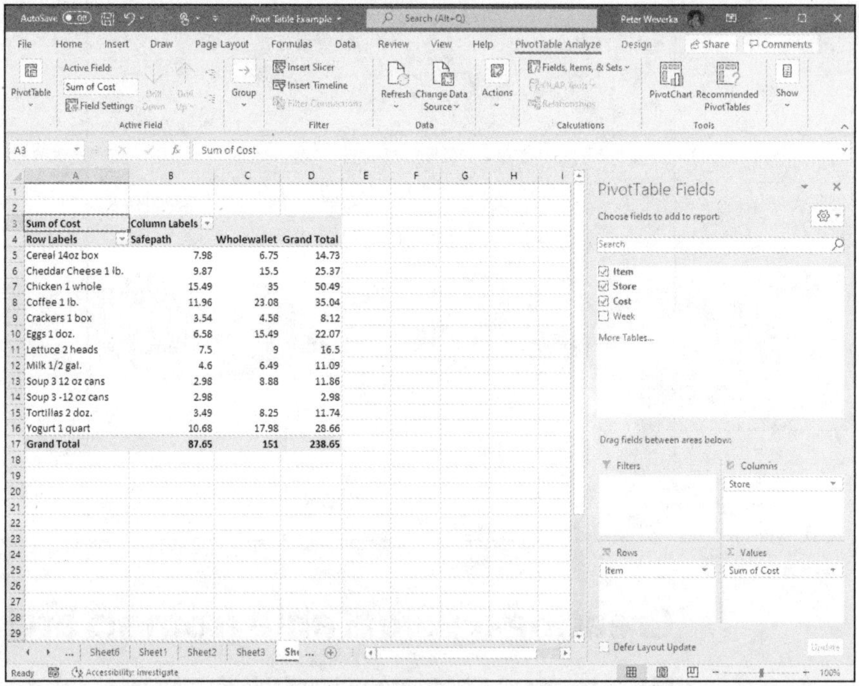


**FIGURE 6-18:** Constructing a PivotTable on the PivotTable Analyze tab.

4. **In the PivotTable Fields task pane, drag field names into the four areas (Filters, Columns, Rows, and Values) to construct your PivotTable.**

   As you construct your table, you see it take shape onscreen. You can drag fields in and out of areas as you please. Drag one field name into each of these areas:

   - **Rows:** The field whose data you want to analyze.
   - **Columns:** The field by which you want to measure and compare data.
   - **Values:** The field with the values used for comparison.

- **Filters (optional):** A field you want to use to sort table data. (This field's name appears in the upper-left corner of the PivotTable. You can open its drop-down list to sort the table; see "Sorting a table," earlier in this chapter.)

## Putting the finishing touches on a PivotTable

Go to the PivotTable Design tab to put the finishing touches on a PivotTable:

- **Grand Totals:** Excel totals columns and rows in PivotTables. If you prefer not to see these "grand totals," click the Grand Totals button and choose an option to remove them from rows, columns, or both.
- **Report Layout:** Click the Report Layout button and choose a PivotTable layout on the drop-down list.
- **PivotTable Styles:** Choose a PivotTable style to breathe a little color into your PivotTable.

TIP

To construct a chart from a PivotTable, go to the PivotTable Analyze tab and click the PivotChart button. The Insert Chart dialog box opens. Book 3, Chapter 7 explains how to navigate this dialog box.

IN THIS CHAPTER

» **Familiarizing yourself with some charting basics**

» **Inserting, activating, and adjusting charts and chart elements**

» **Making your charts look good**

Chapter 7

# Visualizing Data with Charts

One of the best ways to analyze your worksheet data — or get your point across to other people — is to display your data visually in a chart. Excel gives you tremendous flexibility when you're creating charts; it enables you to place charts in separate documents or directly on the worksheet itself. Not only that, but you have dozens of different chart formats to choose from, and if none of Excel's built-in formats is just right, you can further customize these charts to suit your needs.

This chapter takes an in-depth look at Excel's charting feature. You will learn how to create charts, review Excel's different chart types, and format every aspect of your charts.

## Learning Some Crucial Chart Basics

Excel enables you to build impressive and useful charts with just a few mouse clicks, which is awesome. However, to ensure you get the chart that's best suited to your data — and, therefore, to save you further clicks down the road when you realize you need to change the chart in some way — it helps to learn a few charting fundamentals. The next few sections take you through these not-even-close-to-painful preliminaries.

## Reviewing chart parts

Before getting down to the nitty-gritty of creating and working with charts, review some chart terminology that you need to become familiar with. Figure 7-1 points out the various parts of a typical chart. I explain most of these parts in Table 7-1.

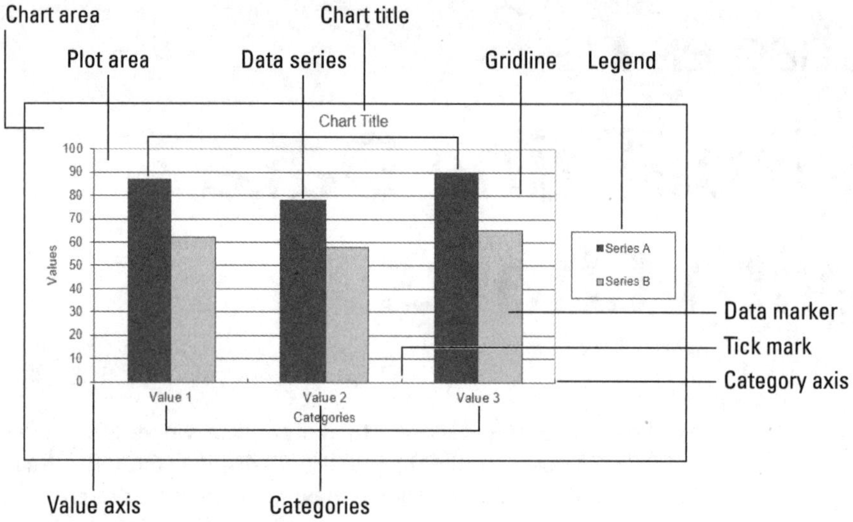


**FIGURE 7-1:** The elements of an Excel chart.

**TABLE 7-1** The Elements of an Excel Chart

| Element | Description |
|---|---|
| Categories | A grouping of data values on the category (horizontal) axis. Figure 7-1 has three categories: Value 1, Value 2, and Value 3. |
| Category axis | The axis (usually the horizontal — or X — axis) that contains the category groupings. |
| Chart area | The area on which the chart is drawn. You can change the color and border of this area. |
| Chart title | A short, descriptive name for the chart. |
| Data marker | A symbol that represents a specific data value. The symbol used depends on the chart type. In a column chart such as the one shown in Figure 7-1, each column is a marker. |

| Element | Description |
|---|---|
| Data series | A collection of related data values. Normally, the marker for each value in a series has the same pattern. Figure 7-1 has two series: Series A and Series B. These are identified in the legend. |
| Data value | A single piece of data. Also called a *data point.* |
| Gridlines | Optional horizontal and vertical extensions of the axis tick marks. These can make data values easier to read. |
| Legend | A guide that shows the colors, patterns, and symbols used by the markers for each data series. |
| Plot area | The area bounded by the category and value axes. It contains the data points and gridlines. |
| Tick mark | A small line that intersects the category axis or the value axis. It marks divisions in the chart's categories or scales. |
| Value axis | The axis (usually the vertical — or Y — axis) that contains the data values. |



## Understanding how Excel converts worksheet data into a chart

Creating an Excel chart usually is straightforward and often you can create one in only a few mouse clicks. However, a bit of background on how Excel converts worksheet data into a chart can help you avoid some charting pitfalls.

When Excel creates a chart, it examines both the shape and the contents of the range you've selected. From this data, the program makes various assumptions to determine what should be on the category axis, what should be on the value axis, how to label the categories, and which labels should show within the legend.

The first assumption Excel makes is that there are more categories than data series. This assumption makes sense, because most graphs plot a small number of series over many different intervals. For example, a chart showing monthly sales and profit over a year has two data series (the sales and profit numbers) but 12 categories (the monthly intervals). Consequently, Excel assumes that the category axis (the X axis) of your chart runs along the longest side of the selected worksheet range.

The chart shown in Figure 7-2 is a plot of the range A1:D3. Because, in this case, the range has more columns than rows, Excel uses each column as a category. Conversely, Figure 7-3 shows the plot of the range A1:C4, which has more rows than columns. In this case, Excel uses each row as a category.

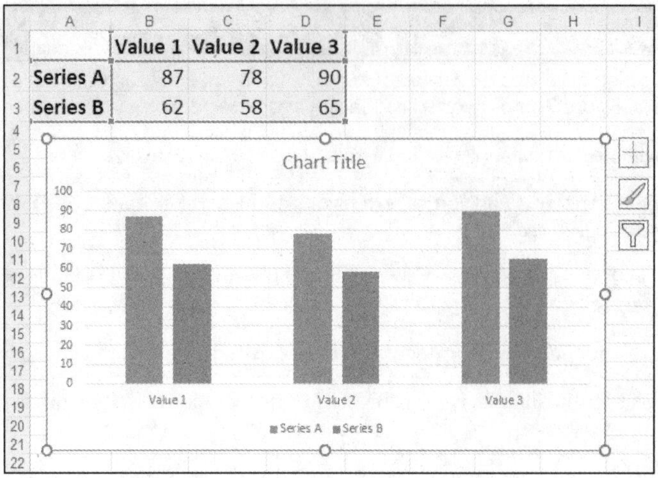


**FIGURE 7-2:** A chart created from a range with more columns than rows.

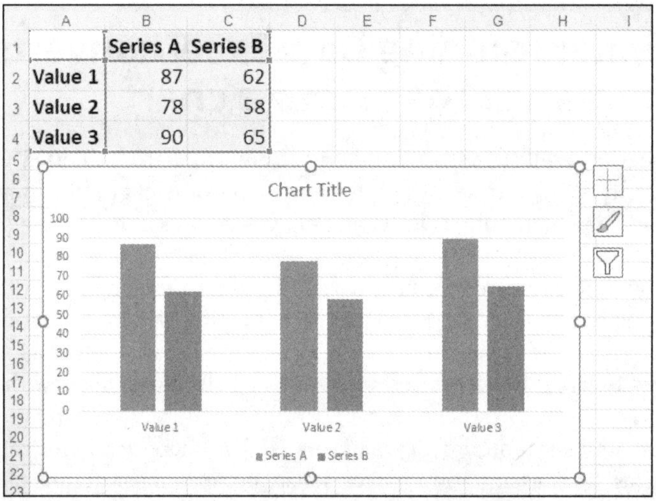


**FIGURE 7-3:** A chart created from a range with more rows than columns.

The second assumption Excel makes involves the location of labels for categories and data series:

- For a range with more columns than rows (such as in Figure 7-2), Excel uses the contents of the top row (Row 1 in Figure 7-2) as the category labels, and the far-left column (Column A in Figure 7-2) as the data series labels.
- For a range with more rows than columns (such as in Figure 7-3), Excel uses the contents of the far-left column (Column A in Figure 7-3) as the category labels, and the top row (Row 1 in Figure 7-3) as the data series labels.

REMEMBER

If a range has the same number of rows and columns, Excel uses the columns as categories. Also, Excel uses the top row for the category labels and the far-left column for the data series labels.

## Getting to know Excel's chart types

To help you create a chart that best presents your data, Excel offers quite a few chart types, each of which is designed to visualize particular types of data. Table 7-2 summarizes the available chart types.

**TABLE 7-2** **Excel's Chart Types**

| Chart Type | Button | Description |
|---|---|---|
| Area |  | Shows the relative contributions over time that each data series makes to the whole picture. |
| Bar chart |  | Compares distinct items or shows single items at distinct intervals. A bar chart is laid out with categories along the vertical axis and values along the horizontal axis. |
| Box & Whisker |  | Visualizes several statistical values for the data in each category, including the average, the range, the minimum, and the maximum. |
| Bubble |  | Similar to an XY chart, except there are three data series. In the third series, the individual plot points are displayed as bubbles. |
| Column |  | Compares distinct items or shows single items at distinct intervals. A column chart is laid out with categories along the horizontal axis and values along the vertical axis. |
| Combo |  | Contrasts two sets of data, with one chart overlying the other to make it easy to compare the two. |
| Doughnut |  | Like a pie chart, shows the proportion of the whole that is contributed by each value in a data series. The advantage of a doughnut chart is that you can plot multiple data series. |
| Funnel |  | Shows how values change across multiple stages of a process. |
| Histogram |  | Groups the category values into ranges — called *bins* — and shows the frequency with which the data values fall within each bin. |
| Line |  | Shows how a data series changes over time. The category (X) axis usually represents a progression of even increments (such as days or months), and the series points are plotted on the value (Y) axis. |
| Map |  | Compares values and categories across geographical regions, such as countries, states, provinces, counties, or postal codes. |

*(continued)*

**TABLE 7-2** *(continued)*

| Chart Type | Button | Description |
|---|---|---|
| Pie | | Shows the proportion of the whole that is contributed by each value in a single data series. The whole is represented as a circle (the "pie"), and each value is displayed as a proportional "slice" of the circle. |
| Radar | | Makes comparisons within a data series and between data series relative to a center point. Each category is shown with a value axis extending from the center point. |
| Stock | | Designed to plot stock-market prices, such as a stock's daily high, low, and closing values. |
| Sunburst | | Displays hierarchical data as a series of concentric circles. The top level is the innermost circle; each circle is divided proportionally according to the values in that level. |
| Surface | | Analyzes two sets of data and determines the optimum combination of the two. |
| Treemap | | For hierarchical data, shows a large rectangle for each item in the top level, then divides each rectangle proportionally based on the value of each item in the next level. |
| Waterfall | | Shows a running total as category values are added (positive values) or subtracted (negative values). |
| XY (or scatter) | | Shows the relationship between numeric values in two different data series. It can also plot a series of data pairs in XY coordinates. |

# Forging a Fresh Chart

When plotting your worksheet data, you have two basic options: You can create an embedded chart that sits on top of your worksheet and can be moved, sized, and formatted; or you can create a separate chart sheet. Whether you choose to embed your charts or store them in separate sheets, the charts are linked with the worksheet data. Any changes you make to the data are automatically updated in the chart. The next few sections discuss each of these techniques and show you a few other ways to mess with your newfangled chart.

## Inserting a recommended chart

With close to 100 possible chart configurations, the Excel chart tools are certainly comprehensive. However, that can be an overwhelming number of choices if you're not sure which type would best visualize your data. Rather than wasting a great deal of time looking at dozens of different chart configurations, the Recommended Charts command examines your data and then narrows down the possible choices to about ten configurations that would work with your data.

Follow these steps to insert a recommended chart:

1. **Select the data that you want to visualize in a chart.**

   If your data includes headings, be sure to include those headings in the selection.

2. **On the Insert tab, in the Charts group, click Recommended Charts.**

   The Insert Chart dialog box appears with the Recommended Charts tab displayed.

3. **Click the chart type you want to use.**
4. **Click OK.**

   Excel inserts the chart.

TIP

A faster way to insert a recommended chart is to select the data that you want to plot (including the headings, if any), then click the Quick Analysis button (shown in the margin). Click Charts to display Excel's recommended chart types for your data, then click the chart type you want to use.

## Creating an embedded chart

If you want full access to all of Excel's chart types, then creating an embedded chart is the easiest way to go because the basic steps require just a few mouse movements, as the following steps show:

1. **Select the range you want to plot, including the row and column labels if there are any.**

   Make sure that no blank rows are between the column labels and the data.

2. **On the Insert tab, in the Charts group, drop down the list for the chart type you want.**

   Refer to Table 7-2 to figure out which Ribbon drop-down list you need to use for the chart type you want.

   Excel displays a gallery of chart types, as shown in Figure 7-4 for the Column type.

3. **Click a chart type.**

   Excel embeds the chart.

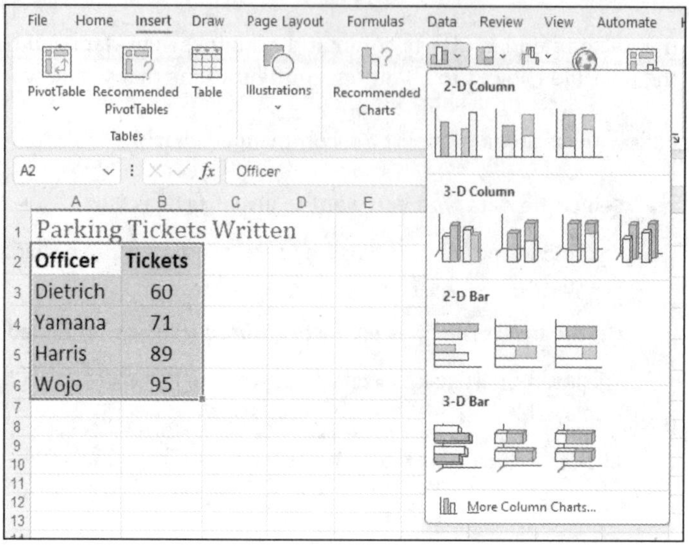


**FIGURE 7-4:** Pull down a list in the Charts group to display a gallery of the selected chart types.

4. **Position the chart on the sheet using the following techniques:**
   - To move the chart, click and drag the chart border.
   - To size the chart, click and drag a chart corner or the middle of any side of the chart border.

TIP

When dragging a chart corner, hold down the Shift key to keep the same relative height and width. Also, hold down Alt to align the chart with the worksheet gridlines.

Figure 7-5 shows an embedded chart. Note, too, that when the chart is activated, Excel also displays two contextual tabs on the Ribbon: Chart Design and Format. You'll learn about many of the controls on these tabs later in this chapter.

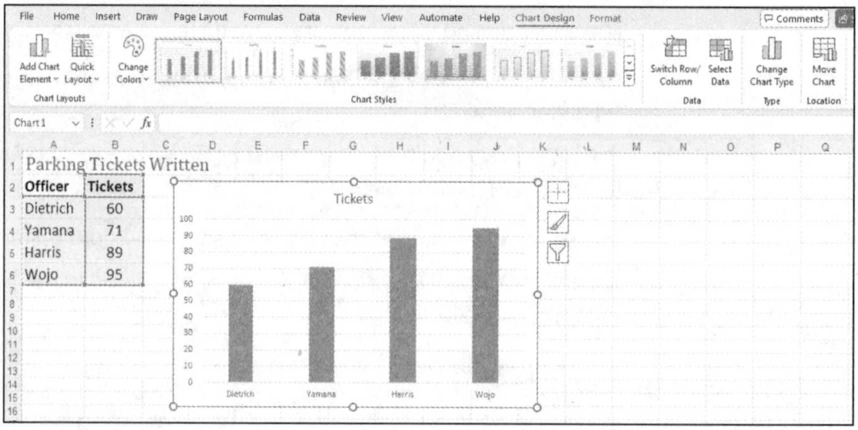


**FIGURE 7-5:** After Excel embeds the chart, it displays the Chart Design and Format contextual tabs.

## Creating a chart in a separate sheet

If you don't want a chart taking up space in a worksheet, or if you want to print a chart on its own, you can create a separate chart sheet. Excel gives you a very easy way to do this, but first here are the official steps:

1. **Select the range you want to plot, including the row and column labels if there are any.**

   Make sure that no blank rows are between the column labels and the data.

2. **Right-click the worksheet tab before which you want the chart sheet to appear, and then click Insert.**

   Excel displays the Insert dialog box.

3. **Click Chart.**
4. **Click OK.**

   Excel creates the chart sheet and adds a default chart.

Now here's the easy method: select the data you want to chart and then press F11.

## Activating a chart

Before you can work with chart types, format a chart, edit the data source, or do any of the work in the rest of this chapter, you need to activate a chart. How you do this depends on the kind of chart you're dealing with:

- For an embedded chart, click inside the chart area.
- For a chart sheet, click the sheet tab.

## Moving a chart between a chart sheet and a worksheet

Whether you create an embedded chart or a chart sheet, you may decide later that you prefer to switch the chart from one position to another. Excel makes this task straightforward:

1. **Activate the chart you want to move (as explained in the previous section).**

2. **On the Chart Design contextual tab, in the Location group, click Move Chart.**

   Excel displays the Move Chart dialog box.

3. **You have two choices:**

   - To move the chart to a separate chart sheet, select New Sheet and then (optionally) type a name for the chart sheet.
   - To embed the chart in a worksheet, select Object In and then use the drop-down list to select the worksheet you want to use.

4. **Click OK.**

   Excel moves the chart.

## Changing the chart type

After you've created a chart, you may decide that the existing chart type doesn't display your data the way you want. Or you may want to experiment with different chart types to find the one that best suits your data. Fortunately, the chart type isn't set in stone; you can change it at any time.

For an embedded chart, here's the easiest way to change the chart type:

1. **Activate the chart you want to change.**
2. **On the Insert tab, in the Charts group, drop down the list for the chart type you want.**

   Refer to Table 7-2 to know which drop-down list you need to use for the chart type you want.

   Excel displays a gallery of chart types.

3. **Click a chart type.**

   Excel changes the chart type.

For both embedded charts and chart sheets, you can use the following method:

1. **Activate the chart you want to change.**
2. **On the Chart Design contextual tab, in the Type group, click Change Chart Type.**

   Excel displays the Change Chart Type dialog box.

3. **Click a chart type category.**

4. **Click the chart type you want.**
5. **Click OK.**

   Excel changes the chart type.

# Selecting Chart Elements

An Excel chart is composed of elements such as axes, data markers, gridlines, and text, each with its own formatting options. Before you can format an element, however, you need to select it. Excel offers two techniques:

- Click the chart and then move the mouse pointer over the chart element you want to select. When the mouse pointer is correctly positioned over the element, Excel displays a banner identifying the element. When the banner appears, click the element to select it.
- Click the chart and then, on the Format contextual tab, in the Current Selection group, drop down the Chart Elements list to display all the elements in the current chart, as shown in Figure 7-6. Click the element you want to select.

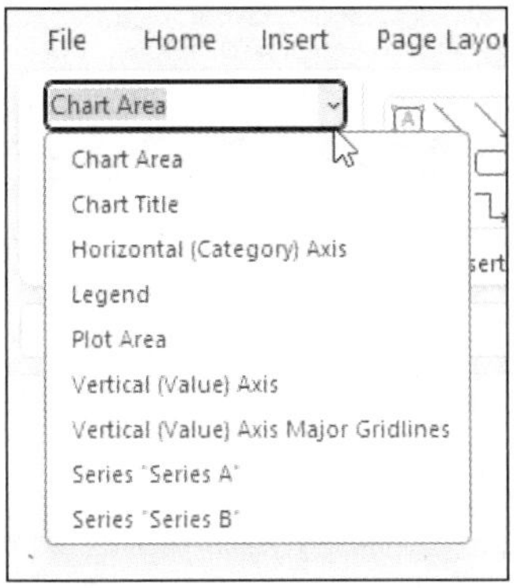


**FIGURE 7-6:** In the Chart Elements list, click the element you want to work with.

# Dressing Up Your Charts

The default charts that Excel produces certainly get the job done, but they lack a certain oomph. Charts are a tool for visualizing your data, so feel free to emphasize the "visual" part of that by formatting your charts to not only make them more attractive, but also to make the information they convey easier to understand.

You'll find all the chart formatting options on the contextual tabs that get tacked on to the Ribbon when you activate a chart. The two tabs to work with are

- **Chart Design:** This tab controls the overall look of the chart. Use the Chart Layouts group to add elements to a chart and to select from a gallery of predefined layouts that control elements such as the chart title, the legend, gridlines, and axes. Use the Chart Styles group to select from a gallery of predefined styles that control formatting such as the data series color, the series markers, the chart area color, and more.
- **Format:** This tab enables you to apply formatting to the selected chart element.

REMEMBER

If you format an element and then decide that you don't like what you've done, you can revert the element to its original style. Click the element and then, on the Format contextual tab, in the Current Selection group, click Reset to Match Style.

## Formatting chart elements

If you want to format a particular chart element, the Format contextual tab offers several options for most chart elements. However, the bulk of your element formatting chores will take place in the Format task pane, the layout of which depends on the element. Excel offers two methods for displaying the Format pane for a particular element:

- Select the element and then, on the Format contextual tab, in the Current Selection group, click Format Selection.
- Right-click the element and then click Format *Element,* where *Element* is the name of the chart item (such as Axis).

Either way, Excel displays the Format *Element* pane, where *Element* is the name of the selected element. For example, Figure 7-7 shows the Format Chart Title pane.

TIP

While the Format pane is displayed, you can switch to the formatting options for another chart element just by clicking that element.

Many versions of the Format pane offer two main tabs that appear just below the pane title. In Figure 7-7, these tabs are named Title Options and Text Options. Here's what they represent:

- ***Element* Options:** Offers formatting options that are specific to the selected element (where *Element* in the tab name is a reference to the selected element). When you select this tab, Excel displays some or all of the following subtabs:

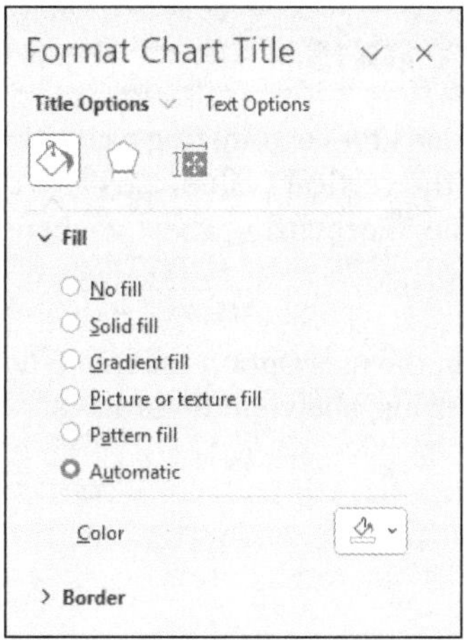


**FIGURE 7-7:** Use the Format Chart Title pane to format the chart title.

| Icon | Name | Formats |
|---|---|---|
|  | Fill & Line | The element's background and it's line or border. |
|  | Effects | The element's shadow, glow, soft edges, and 3D format. |
|  | Size & Properties | The element's height, width, alignment, and properties. |
|  | Options | Options specific to the element, such as the legend position. |

» **Text Options:** Offers formatting options related to the element's text. Note that elements that have no text (such as the plot area) don't offer this tab. When you select this tab, Excel displays the following subtabs:

| Icon | Name | Formats |
|---|---|---|
|  | Text Fill & Outline | The color and outline of the element's text. |
|  | Text Effects | The element's text effects: shadow, reflection, glow, soft edges, 3D format, and 3D rotation. |
|  | Textbox | The alignment, margins, and other options for the box that surrounds the element's text. |

## Formatting a chart axis

Excel offers quite a few useful options for customizing a chart's axes. Select either the horizontal (category) axis or the vertical (value) axis and then open the Format Axis pane, as I describe in the "Formatting chart elements" section, earlier in this chapter.

Click the Axis Options tab and then the Axis Options subtab (shown in the margin) to display the axis formatting controls, shown in Figure 7-8.

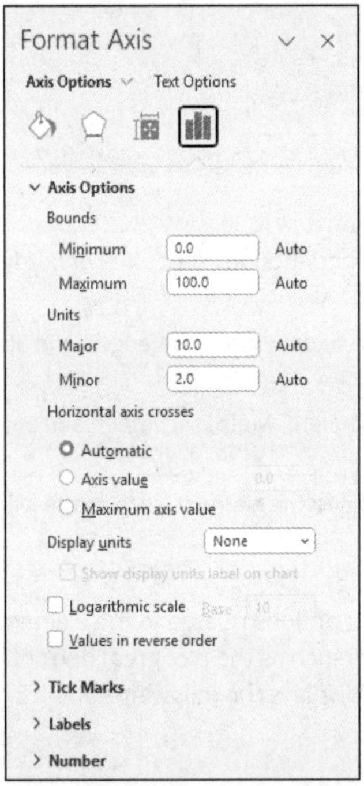


**FIGURE 7-8:** In the Format Axis pane, use the Axis Options subtab to enhance the look of your chart axes.

You can format the scale of your chart axes to set things such as the range of numbers on an axis and where the category and value axes intersect. If you're formatting the vertical (value) axis, the layout shown in Figure 7-8 appears. (The Axis Options tab for the horizontal [category] axis is similar.)

For the axis scale, set the Minimum and Maximum values. For the axis units, set the Major and Minor values.

REMEMBER

The major units are where the axis labels appear. The minor units are those that appear between the labels.

You can also control where the horizontal (category) axis crosses the vertical (value) axis. You have three choices:

- **Automatic:** This places the horizontal axis at the bottom of the chart (that is, at the minimum value on the vertical axis).
- **Axis value:** Click this option and then type your own value for where you want the horizontal axis to cross.
- **Maximum axis value:** Click this option to place the horizontal axis at the top of the chart.

For the axis tick marks, open the Tick Marks category and use the Major Type and Minor Type lists to set where the major and minor tick marks appear.

## Displaying and formatting chart gridlines

Adding horizontal or vertical gridlines can make your charts easier to read. For each axis, you can display a major gridline, a minor gridline, or both. The positioning of these gridlines is determined by the numbers you enter for the axis scales. For a value axis, major gridlines are governed by the Major unit, and minor gridlines are governed by the Minor unit. (The Major and Minor units are properties of the value axis scale. I talk about how to adjust these values earlier in the chapter, in the section "Formatting a chart axis.") For a category axis, major gridlines are governed by the number of categories between tick labels, and minor gridlines are governed by the number of categories between tick marks.

To display gridlines for the active chart, you have two choices:

- **Horizontal gridlines:** On the Chart Design contextual tab, in the Chart Layouts group, click Add Chart Element, click Gridlines, and then click either Primary Major Horizontal or Primary Minor Horizontal.
- **Vertical gridlines:** On the Chart Design contextual tab, in the Chart Layouts group, click Add Chart Element, click Gridlines, and then click either Primary Major Vertical or Primary Minor Vertical.

After you have gridlines displayed, you can display the Format pane to mess around with the width, style, arrows, and line caps of your gridlines.

## Adding chart text

One of the best ways to make your charts more readable is to attach some descriptive text to various chart elements. Excel works with three types of text: titles, legends, and data labels.

### Adding titles

Excel enables you to add four kinds of titles to the chart:

- **Chart title:** This is the overall chart title, and you use it to provide a brief description that puts the chart into context. Activate the chart, choose Chart Design ➪ Add Chart Element ➪ Chart Title, and then click either Centered Overlay Title (the title appears within the plot area) or Above Chart (the title appears above the plot area and Excel reduces the plot area to fit the title). Delete the default title, type your own title, then use Excel's standard font formatting tools to fancy-up the title as needed.
- **Horizontal axis title:** This title appears below the horizontal (category) axis, and you use it to provide a brief description of the category items. Activate the chart and choose Chart Design ➪ Add Chart Element ➪ Axis Titles ➪ Primary Horizontal. Delete the default title and type your own title.
- **Vertical axis title:** This title appears to the left of the vertical (value) axis, and you use it to provide a brief description of the value items. Activate the chart, choose Chart Design ➪ Add Chart Element ➪ Axis Titles ➪ Primary Vertical. Delete the default title and type your own title.
- **Depth axis title:** This title appears beside the depth (z) axis in a 3D chart, and you use it to provide a brief description of the depth items. Activate the chart, choose Chart Design ➪ Add Chart Element ➪ Axis Titles ➪ Depth. Delete the default title and type your own title.

### Adding a chart legend

If your chart includes multiple data series, you should add a legend to explain the series markers. Doing so makes your chart more readable and makes it easier for others to distinguish each series.

To add a legend to the active chart, choose Chart Design ➪ Add Chart Element ➪Legend, and then click one of the legend position options (Right, Top, Left, or Bottom).

## Adding data marker labels

You can add text to individual data markers. By default, these data labels show only the value of the underlying data point, but you can also include the series name and either the category name or the X and Y value (depending on the chart).

To display data labels, first activate the chart and then select the series you want to work with. (If you want to display labels for all the series, don't select any series). Then choose Chart Design ➪ Add Chart Element ➪ Data Labels and click a position (usually Center, Left, Right, Above, or Below). Display the Format Data Labels pane, click the Label Options main tab, click the Label Options subtab (shown in the margin), and then select the check boxes for the items you want to appear in the label (such as Series Name).

IN THIS CHAPTER

» **Maximizing Copilot's usefulness**

» **Using Copilot for analysis, formula building, and conditional formatting**

» **Asking Copilot to sort, filter, and visualize your data**

# Chapter 8
# Automating Excel with Copilot

Google the phrase "Excel is hard" and you'll soon see that a distressing number of people agree with that sentiment. I've written many Excel books over the years, and it has always been my goal to move folks from the "Excel is hard" gulag to the "Excel is amazing!" summer camp. Perhaps you've read some or all of the previous seven chapters here in Book 3 and are feeling a little more positive about your relationship with Excel. If so, great! — my work here is done, at least as far as Excel goes.

But if Excel still presents a challenge to you, then there's one more trick that you can try to get on better terms with all this spreadsheet business. If you're fortunate enough to have a Microsoft Copilot license to go along with your Office 365 subscription, then you've got yourself a powerful AI-fueled partner to help you with a wide variety of Excel tasks. Whether it's creating formulas, extracting text, applying conditional formatting, looking up a value, or spotting a trend, Copilot can do the heavy lifting for you. All you have to do is tell Copilot what you want. (If you're brand new to Copilot, you might want to peruse Book 2, Chapter 9, where I talk more about what Copilot is and how it works.)

In this chapter, you discover how Copilot can help you analyze, manipulate, visualize, manage, and automate Excel data. Yep, Excel can be hard, but Excel plus Copilot is amazing.

# Getting Copilot on the Job

How do you know if you have Copilot access? Display Excel's Home tab and then look way over to the right side of the Ribbon. If you see a Copilot button (shown in the margin), then you have AI ready to roll.

Clicking the Copilot button displays the Copilot pane. As shown in Figure 8-1, the Copilot pane offers a few prompt examples, as well as a text box at the bottom where you enter your prompt. In Figure 8-1, notice that Copilot has already identified the worksheet range that contains data (A11:F132, in this case).

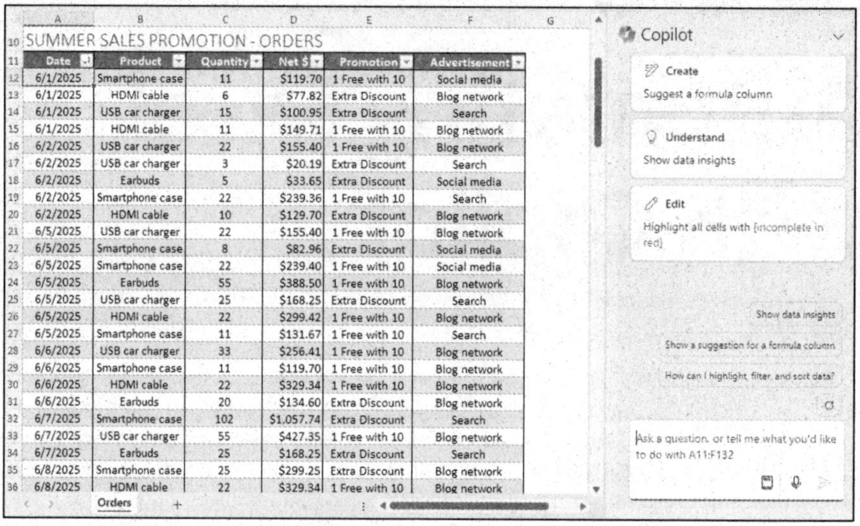


| Date | Product | Quantity | Net $ | Promotion | Advertisement |
|---|---|---|---|---|---|
| 6/1/2025 | Smartphone case | 11 | $119.70 | 1 Free with 10 | Social media |
| 6/1/2025 | HDMI cable | 6 | $77.82 | Extra Discount | Blog network |
| 6/1/2025 | USB car charger | 15 | $100.95 | Extra Discount | Search |
| 6/1/2025 | HDMI cable | 11 | $149.71 | 1 Free with 10 | Blog network |
| 6/2/2025 | USB car charger | 22 | $155.40 | 1 Free with 10 | Blog network |
| 6/2/2025 | USB car charger | 3 | $20.19 | Extra Discount | Search |
| 6/2/2025 | Earbuds | 5 | $33.65 | Extra Discount | Social media |
| 6/2/2025 | Smartphone case | 22 | $239.36 | 1 Free with 10 | Search |
| 6/2/2025 | HDMI cable | 10 | $129.70 | Extra Discount | Blog network |
| 6/5/2025 | USB car charger | 22 | $155.40 | 1 Free with 10 | Blog network |
| 6/5/2025 | Smartphone case | 8 | $82.96 | Extra Discount | Social media |
| 6/5/2025 | Smartphone case | 22 | $239.40 | 1 Free with 10 | Social media |
| 6/5/2025 | Earbuds | 55 | $388.50 | 1 Free with 10 | Blog network |
| 6/5/2025 | USB car charger | 25 | $168.25 | Extra Discount | Search |
| 6/5/2025 | HDMI cable | 22 | $299.42 | 1 Free with 10 | Blog network |
| 6/5/2025 | Smartphone case | 11 | $131.67 | 1 Free with 10 | Search |
| 6/6/2025 | USB car charger | 33 | $256.41 | 1 Free with 10 | Blog network |
| 6/6/2025 | Smartphone case | 11 | $119.70 | 1 Free with 10 | Blog network |
| 6/6/2025 | HDMI cable | 22 | $329.34 | 1 Free with 10 | Blog network |
| 6/6/2025 | Earbuds | 20 | $134.60 | Extra Discount | Blog network |
| 6/7/2025 | Smartphone case | 102 | $1,057.74 | Extra Discount | Search |
| 6/7/2025 | USB car charger | 55 | $427.35 | 1 Free with 10 | Blog network |
| 6/7/2025 | Earbuds | 25 | $168.25 | Extra Discount | Search |
| 6/8/2025 | Smartphone case | 25 | $299.25 | Extra Discount | Blog network |
| 6/8/2025 | HDMI cable | 22 | $329.34 | 1 Free with 10 | Blog network |

**FIGURE 8-1:** Click the Home tab's Copilot button to bring up the Copilot pane.

REMEMBER

Copilot in Excel only works with files that reside on OneDrive or SharePoint, so be sure you've parked your workbook somewhere in either cloud before going any further.

TIP

For the best results with Copilot in Excel, your data should be clean, consistent, and well-formatted. Here's what this means in practice:

- **Use tables.** Copilot performs best when the data it has to analyze is organized into a table.
- **Use clear headers.** Your table should have only a single row of headers and the headers themselves should be clear and descriptive. Avoid using vague or overly complex labels. For example, instead of "Col A," use "Sales Revenue."

Also, avoid using special characters in headers, as these can interfere with formula generation and data interpretation.

- **Use consistent data types.** Ensure that each column contains consistent data types (for example, all dates in one column, all numbers in another). Mixed data types can confuse Copilot and lead to less accurate suggestions or results.
- **Avoid merged cells.** Merged cells can create issues for Copilot when analyzing your data. Keep your cells unmerged to ensure data integrity and proper functioning.
- **Remove empty rows and columns.** Get rid of any empty rows or columns within your data, as these gaps can confuse and mislead Copilot.
- **Normalize data.** Normalize your data where possible, such as converting all date formats to a standard format or ensuring all text entries use consistent capitalization.
- **Keep your data in a single worksheet.** If possible, keep all the data to the same sheet. While Copilot can reference multiple sheets, it's generally more effective when all relevant data is easily accessible on one sheet.
- **Clean your data.** Before using Copilot, clean your data to remove any duplicates, errors, or inconsistencies. Clean data leads to more accurate insights and recommendations.



# Analyzing Data

Excel offers tons of analysis tools, many of which I cover in Book 3, Chapter 6. The biggest problem with these tools is knowing which one to use on your data. ChatGPT helps you solve that problem by automatically choosing the best analysis tool based on your prompt.

For example, using the data shown in Figure 8-1, suppose I simply want to know which product sold the most units. Do I create a formula? Do I filter the data? Do I create a PivotTable? Or do I just prompt Copilot, like so:

*Which product sold the most units?*

Copilot gets right to work analyzing the data, then displays its results, as shown in Figure 8-2. In this case, Copilot analyzed the data by creating a PivotTable. Clicking the Add to a New Sheet button tells Copilot to create a new worksheet that includes the PivotTable.

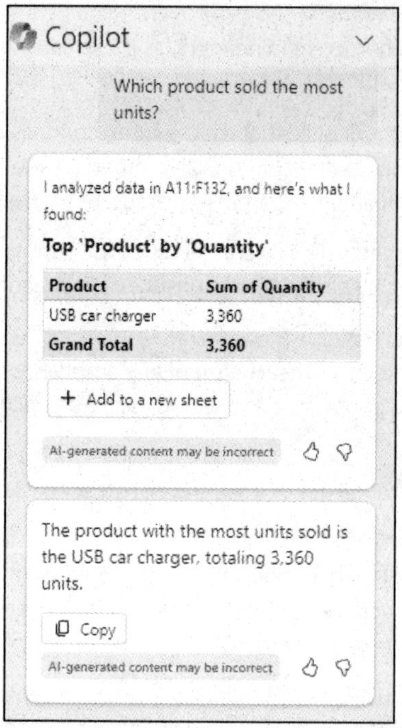


**FIGURE 8-2:** Copilot used a PivotTable to analyze the data according to the prompt.

For the most part, you can prompt Copilot to analyze your data using natural language queries. Here are some examples:

- *How many units did we sell in the West region in June?*
- *What is the year-over-year growth for each product line?*
- *Can you show me the total profit margin for all products in 2024?*

For more specific types of analysis, you can tailor your prompts accordingly, as the following sections demonstrate.

## Data cleaning

Your analysis is only as good as the data you put into it. Fortunately, Copilot can help by cleaning your data for you:

- *Remove duplicate entries from the customer database.*
- *Fix any errors in the dates column where the format is inconsistent.*
- *Identify and fill in the missing values in the sales dataset.*

## Basic data summarization

You can ask Copilot to summarize your data:

- *Summarize the sales data by region for the last quarter.*
- *What are the average sales for each product category?*
- *Find the average sales per customer and create a distribution chart.*
- *Show me the variance and standard deviation for monthly sales figures.*



## Trend analysis

Copilot can spot trends in your data:

- *Identify the sales trend over the past year.*
- *Plot a line graph showing the monthly sales trend for the last two years.*
- *Highlight any noticeable seasonal patterns in the sales data.*

## Forecasts

If you want to know what's ahead based on historical data, you can ask Copilot to generate a forecast from that data:

- *Predict the sales for the next quarter based on the past year's data.*
- *What will be the expected revenue if the current growth trend continues?*
- *Forecast the product demand for the next six months.*

## PivotTables

If you're pretty sure your analysis requires a PivotTable, you can prompt Copilot to generate one:

- *Create a PivotTable to analyze sales by region and product category.*
- *Aggregate the sales data by month and region in a PivotTable.*
- *Show total revenue for each product in the PivotTable format.*

## What-if and sensitivity analysis

Copilot is on friendly terms with what-if analysis and sensitivity analysis:

- *What would happen to our profits if the cost of goods sold increases by 10 percent?*
- *Perform a sensitivity analysis to see how different pricing strategies affect revenue.*
- *Model the impact on total revenue if we increase our marketing spend by 20 percent.*

## Scenario analysis

You can also Copilot to use scenarios to analysis your data:

- *Compare the best-case, worst-case, and most likely revenue scenarios for next year.*
- *Show how different discount rates would impact overall sales volume.*
- *Simulate the financial outcomes if we expand into two new markets next year.*

## Advanced analysis queries

Almost no query is too advanced for Copilot to handle:

- *What percentage of total sales is contributed by the top 20 percent of customers?*
- *How does the sales performance of the new product line compare to the existing ones?*
- *Which regions are underperforming compared to the national average?*

# Creating Formulas

Formulas are one of Excel's most powerful weapons, but they can also be one of the trickiest to learn and one of the hardest to implement without errors. You can ignore the steep formula learning curve (and minimize errors) by getting Copilot to create formulas for you.

Depending on the structure of your data and the specifics of your prompt, Copilot will offer to enter the formula it creates either in a new column of your table (if the formula applies to every row in your table) or in a cell.

Figure 8-3 shows an example of Excel creating a formula and offering to enter it for you in Cell D12, which you can make happen by clicking the Insert Cell button.

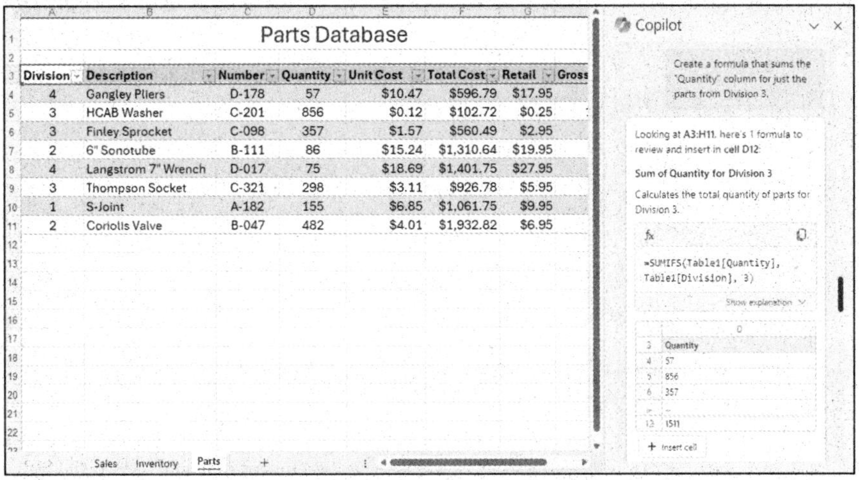


**FIGURE 8-3:** Clicking (in this case) Insert Cell adds Copilot's generated formula to the worksheet.

The next few sections offer various sample prompts you can use with Copilot in Excel to create formulas.

# Basic mathematical formulas

First off, a few basic formulas as a warmup:

- *Create a formula to calculate the total sales by multiplying the quantity by the price per unit.*
- *Add a new column that shows the difference between the target and actual sales.*
- *Create a formula to add up the total expenses in this row.*

## Statistical formulas

Statistics doesn't have to be scary any longer:

- *Calculate the average sales per region in a new column.*
- *Create a formula to find the median sales value in this dataset.*
- *Add a column that calculates the standard deviation of the monthly sales.*

## Text formulas

Get Copilot's help with text-manipulation formulas:

- *Create a formula to combine the first name and last name into a full name column.*
- *Add a column that extracts the first three letters of each product code.*
- *Generate a formula that checks whether the email addresses contain "@" and mark those that don't as invalid.*
- *Create a formula to split the text in the "Full Name" column into separate "First Name" and "Last Name" columns.*
- *Add a column that converts all the text in the "Product Name" column to uppercase.*
- *Generate a formula that removes any extra spaces from the text in the "Address" column.*

## Logical formulas

Logical formulas are among the trickiest in Excel's repertoire, but Copilot eats them for breakfast:

- *Add a new column with a formula that shows "Yes" if the sales exceed $10,000 and "No" otherwise.*
- *Create a formula to check whether the delivery date is within seven days of the order date.*
- *Add a formula to determine whether the quantity ordered is greater than the quantity in stock.*

» *Create a formula that combines IF, AND, and OR to check whether sales are above $10,000 and the product is in stock or on backorder.*

» *Add a column that uses the COUNTIF function to count how many times a specific product was sold.*

» *Generate a formula to highlight rows where the sales are below the average and the profit margin is less than 20 percent.*

## Date and time formulas

Copilot does date and time formulas, no problem:

» *Create a formula to calculate the number of days between the order date and the delivery date.*

» *Add a new column that extracts the month from the order date.*

» *Generate a formula to calculate the year-over-year growth by comparing the current year's sales to the previous year's.*

## Lookup and reference formulas

Lookup formulas can leave even the most advanced Excel formula jockey scratching their head. Why not get Copilot to do them for you:

» *Create a formula that uses VLOOKUP to find the price of a product based on its code.*

» *Add a column that uses INDEX and MATCH to retrieve the region based on the sales rep's name.*

» *Generate a formula using HLOOKUP to find the tax rate based on the state code.*

## Conditional formulas

If Copilot can create conditional formulas, then you should let it:

» *Create a formula using IF to assign a bonus if the sales exceed $15,000.*

» *Add a new column that uses IFERROR to return "N/A" if a division by zero occurs.*

» *Generate a formula using IF to categorize sales as "High," "Medium," or "Low" based on thresholds.*

## Financial formulas

The world of Excel finance is fine with Copilot:

- *Create a formula to calculate the compound interest on an investment.*
- *Add a column that calculates the monthly loan payment.*
- *Generate a formula to calculate the net present value (NPV) of future cash flows.*

## Array formulas

If array formulas scare you, make Copilot do them:

- *Create a formula that multiplies the sales by the corresponding commission rate across all rows.*
- *Add an array formula that sums only the positive numbers in this range.*
- *Generate a formula that returns the largest value in a range that meets multiple criteria.*
- *Create a formula that returns a unique list of product categories.*
- *Add a column that ranks the sales amounts using the RANK.EQ function.*
- *Generate a formula using the FILTER function to display only the sales above $10,000.*

## Nested formulas

Yep, Copilot doesn't get flummoxed when a formula requires nesting one function inside another:

- *Create a nested formula that calculates the bonus based on sales tier: 5% if sales > $10,000, 3% if sales > $5,000, otherwise 0%.*
- *Add a formula that combines INDEX and MATCH to find the corresponding region based on sales rep and product.*
- *Generate a formula that nests IF statements to categorize data into "High," "Medium," or "Low" based on multiple conditions.*

# Highlighting Data

Conditional formatting (refer to Book 3, Chapter 6) is one of the more user-friendly analysis techniques, but that doesn't mean you can't save a bit of time by getting Copilot to do the work for you.

After Copilot has analyzed your request and your data, it tells you what it's going to do, as shown in Figure 8-4. In this case, you need to click Apply to add the conditional formatting to your data.

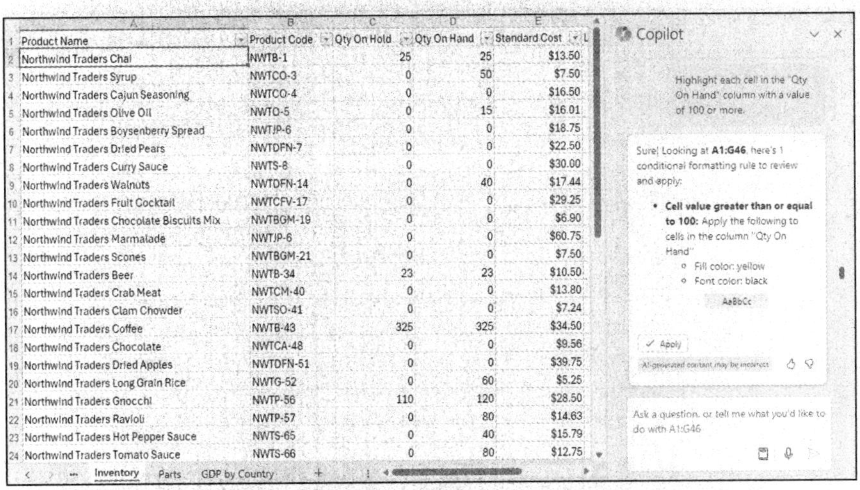


**FIGURE 8-4:** Click Apply to put Copilot's suggested conditional formatting into effect.

The next few sections provide a few examples.

## Basic conditional formatting

Here are a few basic conditional formatting prompts to wet your whistle:

- *Highlight all cells in the "Sales" column that are greater than $10,000.*
- *Apply a green fill to cells in the "Profit Margin" column that are above 20 percent.*
- *Format the cells in the "Due Date" column to turn red if the date is in the past.*

## Top/bottom rules

Copilot is happy to create top/bottom conditional formatting rules:

- *Highlight the top 10 percent of sales values in the "Sales" column.*
- *Apply a format to the bottom five scores in the "Test Results" column.*
- *Use a conditional format to highlight the top three performers based on the "Total Score" column.*

## Data bars, color scales, and icon sets

Copilot knows everything there is to know about data bars, color scales, and icon sets:

- *Add data bars to the "Revenue" column to visualize the sales amounts.*
- *Apply a three-color scale to the "Temperature" column to show low, medium, and high values.*
- *Use icon sets to mark cells in the "Stock Level" column with a green up arrow for high levels, yellow for medium, and red down arrow for low levels.*

## Highlighting duplicates

Looking for duplicates? Copilot can help:

- *Highlight all duplicate values in the "Customer ID" column.*
- *Apply a conditional format to the "Email" column to highlight any duplicates.*
- *Mark any duplicate rows based on the "Order Number" and "Customer Name" columns.*

## Custom formula-based conditional formatting

Formula-based conditional formatting rules can be hard to understand, but they're a snap when Copilot does them for you:

- *Apply a conditional format to highlight cells in the "Delivery Date" column if the delivery is more than seven days from the order date.*
- *Use a formula to highlight rows where the "Sales" column is greater than the "Target Sales" column.*
- *Format cells in the "Discount" column that are greater than the average discount value.*

# Sorting and Filtering Data



Excel's sorting and filtering tools (refer to Book 3, Chapter 6) are relatively straightforward if you stick to the basics, but they can often get a bit hairy in more complex scenarios. Copilot can help you sort and filter your data, no matter how complicated your needs.

With sorting and filtering, what usually happens is that after Copilot examines your data, it will tell you what's required and then display an Apply button, as shown in Figure 8-5. Click Apply to put Copilot's solution into effect.

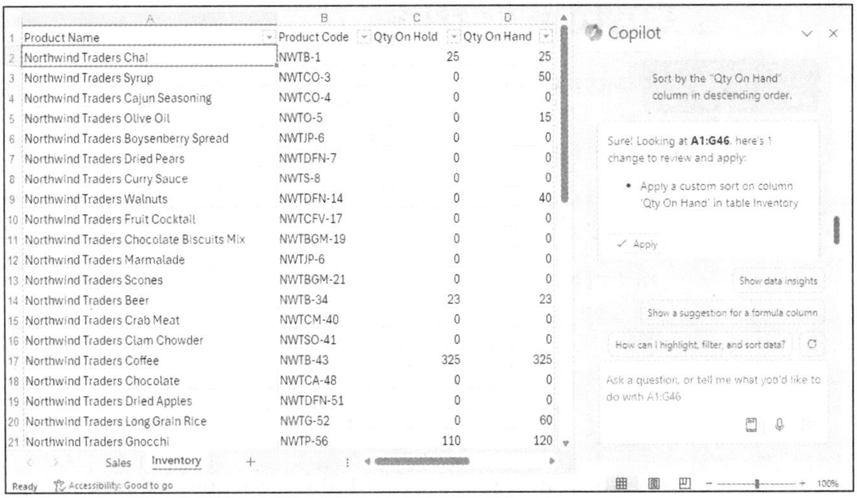


**FIGURE 8-5:** Click Copilot's Apply button to put its sorting or filtering solution into effect.

The next few sections provide you with enough prompt examples to give you a sense of how this part of Copilot for Excel works.

## Basic sorting

Here are the simple sorting prompts to get you started:

- *Sort the "Sales" column in descending order.*
- *Sort the data alphabetically by "Customer Name."*
- *Sort the "Order Date" column from oldest to newest.*

## Sorting by multiple criteria

Need to sort on two or more fields? There's a prompt for that:

- *Sort the data first by "Region" in ascending order, then by "Sales" in descending order.*
- *Sort by "Department" alphabetically and then by "Employee Name" alphabetically.*
- *Sort the table by "Priority" from highest to lowest, then by "Due Date" from oldest to newest.*

## Custom sorting

Sorting on custom field values is tricky, but not for Copilot:

- *Sort the "Status" column using a custom order: "High," "Medium," or "Low."*
- *Sort the "Day of the Week" column using the order: Monday, Tuesday, Wednesday, and so on.*
- *Sort the "Project Phase" column by the sequence: Planning, Execution, Review, Closure.*

## Basic filtering

Here are some straightforward filtering requests that you can send to Copilot:

- *Filter the "Sales" column to show only values greater than $10,000.*
- *Filter the data to show only rows where the "Status" is "Completed."*
- *Filter the "Category" column to display only "Electronics" and "Appliances."*

## Filtering by date

You can ask Copilot to filter your data using date criteria:

- *Filter the "Order Date" column to show only orders placed in the last 30 days.*
- *Show only records where the "Due Date" is next week.*
- *Filter the "Hire Date" column to display only employees hired in 2023.*

## Filtering by text criteria

You can ask Copilot to filter your data using text criteria:

- *Filter the "Product Name" column to show only products that contain the word "Pro".*
- *Display rows where the "Comments" column contains the word "Urgent."*
- *Filter the "City" column to show only entries that start with "New."*



## Filtering by number criteria

You can ask Copilot to filter your data using numeric criteria:

- *Show only rows where the "Quantity" column is greater than 50.*
- *Filter the "Revenue" column to display only values between $5,000 and $20,000.*
- *Display only the top 10 values in the "Sales" column.*

## Advanced filtering

If your filtering needs are a bit more complicated, get Copilot to figure it all out for you:

- *Filter the data to show rows where "Region" is "North" and "Sales" is greater than $5,000.*
- *Display only rows where "Status" is "In Progress" and "Due Date" is in the next 7 days.*
- *Filter the table to show only entries where "Category" is "Electronics" and "Stock Level" is below 100.*

## Sorting and filtering combined

Want to sort *and* filter your data? Ambitious! But Copilot gets the job done without breaking a sweat:

- *Sort the data by "Revenue" in descending order and then filter to show only rows where "Category" is "Books."*
- *First filter the "Department" column to show only "Marketing," then sort the "Employee Name" column alphabetically.*
- *Filter the "Sales" column to show values greater than $1,000 and then sort by "Order Date" from newest to oldest.*

# Visualizing Data

As I showed in Book 3, Chapter 7, Excel offers tons of ways to visualize your data in a chart. If you don't feel like generating a chart by hand, then Copilot is only too happy to step in and get the job done for you.

After Copilot has analyzed your prompt and figured out your data, it displays a thumbnail of the chart, as shown in Figure 8-6. If you like what you see, click Add to a New Sheet to insert the chart into its own sheet.

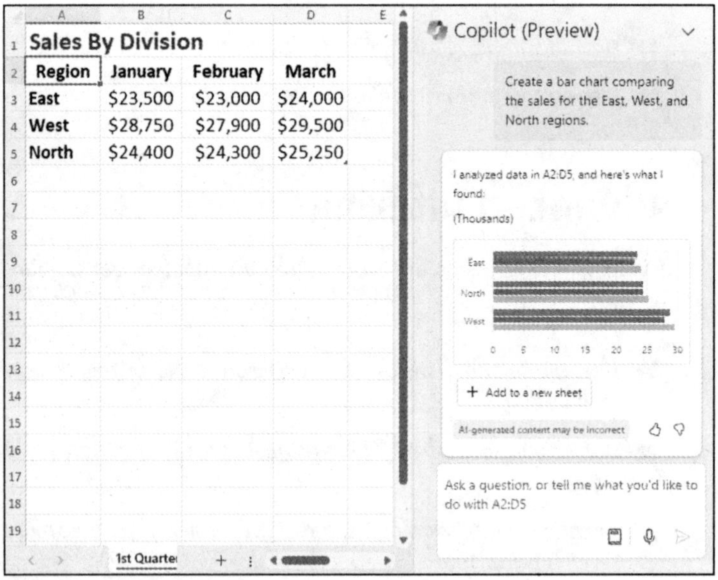


**FIGURE 8-6:** Click Add to a New Sheet to insert Copilot's suggested chart into your workbook.

The next few sections provide you with a few examples of prompts for creating charts with Copilot.

## Basic charts

Here are a few prompts for simple charts to get the ball rolling:

- *Create a bar chart to compare sales across different regions.*
- *Generate a line chart showing the trend of monthly revenue over the past year.*
- *Make a pie chart to display the market share of each product category.*



## Advanced charts

Here are some prompts for more involved charts:

- *Create a stacked bar chart to show the breakdown of sales by product within each region.*
- *Generate a clustered column chart comparing quarterly profits for each year.*
- *Make a waterfall chart to illustrate the contribution of various factors to the overall profit.*

## Combination charts

Need multiple chart types in the same chart? Copilot is on it:

- *Create a combination chart with sales as columns and profit margin as a line.*
- *Generate a chart that combines a bar chart for revenue and a line chart for expenses.*
- *Make a dual-axis chart showing temperature and precipitation data.*

## Highlighting data trends

Trends are almost always easier to work with when they're visualized, and Copilot can help:

- *Create a line chart to highlight the trend in sales over the last five years.*

- *Generate a scatter plot to show the relationship between advertising spend and sales.*
- *Make a chart to display the trend in customer satisfaction scores over time.*

## Comparative analysis

Here are some visualization prompts for comparing stuff:

- *Create a side-by-side bar chart comparing sales and profits for each product category.*
- *Generate a radar chart to compare performance metrics across different departments.*
- *Make a bubble chart to compare market share, sales, and profit margin for various products.*

## Pie and donut charts

Hungry for some pie or donut charts? Copilot can serve those up for you:

- *Create a pie chart showing the percentage of total sales contributed by each region.*
- *Generate a donut chart to illustrate the distribution of expenses across different categories.*
- *Make a pie chart that displays the proportion of customers in each loyalty tier.*

## Histograms and box plots

Histograms and box plots (refer to Book 3, Chapter 7) are no problem for Copilot:

- *Create a histogram to display the distribution of sales figures.*
- *Generate a box plot to show the spread and outliers in employee performance scores.*
- *Make a histogram of the frequency of order quantities.*

## Data distribution and density

Here are some prompts you can modify when you need to visualize data distributions and densities:

- *Create a heat map to visualize the density of sales across different regions.*
- *Generate a histogram to show the distribution of customer ages.*
- *Make a density plot to illustrate the concentration of sales in various price ranges.*



## Geographical data visualization

Copilot is happy to map your data:

- *Create a map chart showing sales by state.*
- *Generate a filled map to illustrate the population density across different regions.*
- *Make a map that visualizes revenue by country.*

## Sparklines and small multiples

If you're a fan of tiny charts (particularly the sparklines that I talk about in Book 3, Chapter 6), Copilot can make some for you:

- *Create sparklines in each row to show the sales trend over time.*
- *Generate a series of small line charts for each product category to display monthly sales trends.*
- *Make a set of sparklines to illustrate the performance of different investment portfolios.*

# 4

# PowerPoint 365

# Contents at a Glance

IN THIS CHAPTER

- » Getting your presentation off to a fine start
- » Populating slides with text and other riffraff
- » Reusing slides from other presentations
- » Taking advantage of presentation masters
- » Organizing your presentation with an outline

Chapter 1

# Putting Together a PowerPoint Presentation

It is probably not a stretch to claim that, in terms of market share, PowerPoint is the most dominant software program in the world. In 2023, Microsoft said that PowerPoint had 95 percent of the presentation graphics market, which is ridiculously high, particularly when strong competitors such as Google Slides and Apple Keynote have been around for a while. And with many of our kids learning and using PowerPoint in school, this dominance is poised to continue into the foreseeable future. In short, we live in a PowerPoint world.

So, learning how to get along in this world is important, and this is what the four chapters here in Book 4 can help you do. The focus is on a PowerPoint "middle way" that avoids the two most common PowerPoint faults: drab, lifeless presentations that are ineffective because they bore the audience to tears, and *PowerPointlessness* — those overly fancy formats, transitions, sounds, and other effects that have no discernible purpose, use, or benefit. With the middle way, you learn how to create attractive presentations that offer visual interest without sacrificing clarity. In this chapter, you start your middle way journey by exploring the basics of cobbling together a presentation.

# Producing a New PowerPoint Presentation

Everything you create in PowerPoint is called a *presentation*. Most people get a new presentation off the ground by using PowerPoint's blank template, but there are quite a few templates available that just might be able to save you some work. (Book 2, Chapter 3 explains templates in detail and how to create your own templates.)

Follow these basic steps to create a presentation:

1. **Choose File ⇨ New.**

   The New window, shown in Figure 1-1, appears.

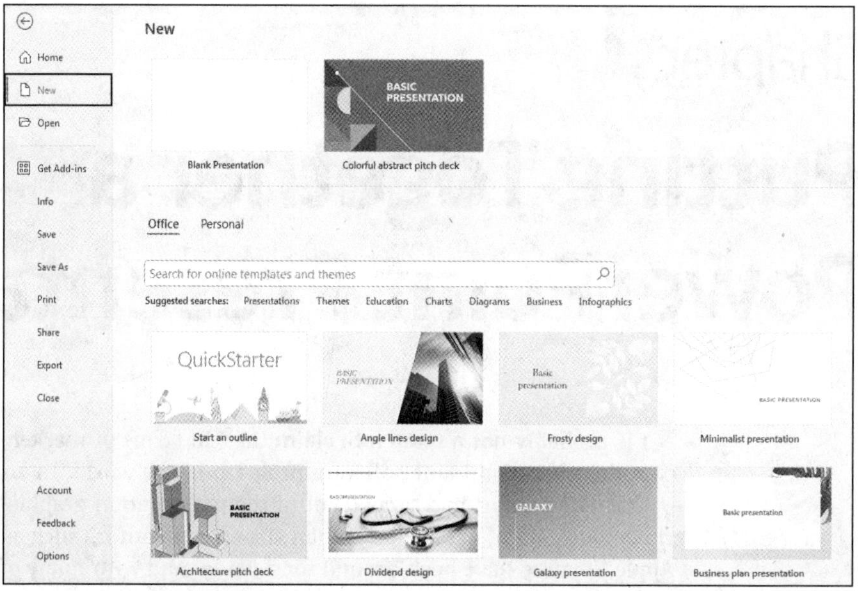


**FIGURE 1-1:** To create a presentation, choose a template in the New window.

2. **Click the template you want to use as the basis for your new document.**

   Use these techniques in the New window to choose a template and create a document:

   - **Create a blank presentation.** Click Blank Presentation to create a bare-bones presentation with few styles. Blank Presentation is the default template for creating documents, which means that's what you get when you press Ctrl+N to create a new presentation without opening the New window. If you go this route, you can skip the rest of this procedure.

- **Create a presentation from a displayed template.** Click a template to examine it in a preview window similar to the one shown in Figure 1-2. Click the Create button in the preview window to create a document from the template.

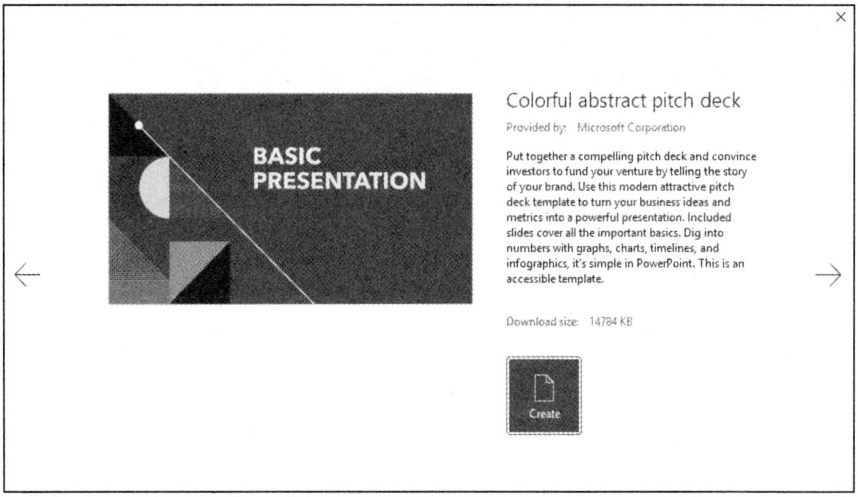


**FIGURE 1-2:** When you click a template in the New window, PowerPoint displays a preview.

- **Create a presentation from an online template.** Type a search term in the Search For Online Templates and Themes text box and then press Enter. (Alternatively, you can click one of the suggested search terms that appear just below the text box). Templates that match your search term appear in the New window. You can click a template to examine it closely in a preview window (refer to Figure 1-2). Click the Create button to create a document from the template.
- **Create a presentation from a personal template.** Click the Personal tab and then click a template to create a presentation from that file. A personal template is one that you created or copied to your computer or network. Book 2, Chapter 3 explains how to create templates. The Personal tab appears in the New window only if you've created templates or copied them to your computer.

3. **Click the Create button in the preview window.**

   Your new PowerPoint presentation opens.

# Perusing the PowerPoint Window

Before getting down to the specifics of putting together a presentation, take a second or three to get to know a few landmarks of the PowerPoint window. For reference, Figure 1-3 shows the PowerPoint window as it appears when a new, blank presentation has just been launched. (I also closed the Designer task pane that PowerPoint usually displays. If you close it, too, you can get it back whenever you feel like it by choosing Home ➪ Designer.)

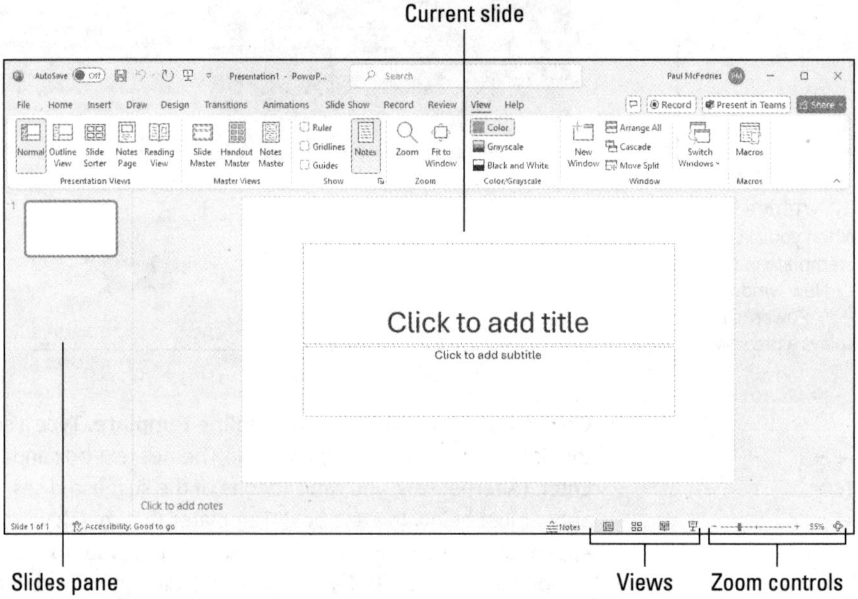


**FIGURE 1-3:** A few PowerPoint features to know.

The PowerPoint window comes with a few standard Office 365 doodads, including the Ribbon, the Quick Access toolbar, and the Search box. Here's a quick rundown of the PowerPoint-specific features that are pointed out in Figure 1-3:

- **Slides pane:** Displays thumbnail versions of all the slides in your presentation.
- **Current slide:** Displays the contents of whatever slide is currently selected in the Slides pane.
- **Views:** Offers different ways of displaying the presentation content. Refer to the "Changing views" section later in this chapter.
- **Zoom controls:** Enable you to increase or decrease the magnification of the current slide.

TIP

One of PowerPoint's most useful features is the Fit Slide to Current Window button (shown in the margin), which hangs out in the lower-right corner of the screen, to the right of the Zoom controls. Click this button to automatically resize the zoom level so that the current slide fills the content area of the PowerPoint window.

## Changing views

PowerPoint offers two methods to switch to a new view:

- **View buttons on the status bar:** Click a View button — Normal, Slide Sorter, Reading View, or Slide Show — on the status bar to change views.
- **View tab:** On the View tab, click a button in the Presentation Views or Master Views group.

## Looking at the different views

Depending on the task at hand, some of PowerPoint's views are better than others. Here's a survey of the different views with suggestions about using each one:

- **Normal view for examining slides:** Switch to Normal view (the status bar button is shown in the margin) and select a slide in the Slides pane when you want to examine a slide. In this view, thumbnail slides appear in the Slides pane, and you can see your slide in all its glory in the rest of the window.
- **Outline view for fiddling with text:** Switch to Outline view when you want to enter or read text. The words appear in outline form on the left side of the screen. Outline view is ideal for editing the text in a presentation and you learn all about it later in this chapter in the "Building a Presentation from an Outline" section.
- **Slide Sorter view for moving and deleting slides:** In Slide Sorter view (shown in the margin), you see thumbnails of all the slides in the presentation (use the Zoom slider to change the size of thumbnails). From here, moving slides around is easy, and seeing many slides simultaneously gives you a sense of whether the different slides are consistent with one another and how the whole presentation is shaping up. The slides are numbered so that you can see where they appear in a presentation.
- **Notes Page view for reading your speaker notes:** In Notes Page view, you see notes you've written to aid you in your presentation, if you've written any.

You can write notes in this view as well as in the Notes pane in Normal view. Check out "Adding notes," later in this chapter.

- **Reading View for focusing on slides' appearance:** In Reading View (shown in the margin), you also see a single slide, but it appears fullscreen with the View buttons and with buttons for moving quickly from slide to slide. Switch to Reading View to proofread slides and put the final touches on a presentation. You can shut down Reading View and return to your previous view by pressing Esc.
- **Slide Show view for running the presentation:** Click Slide Show view (shown in the margin) to run your presentation. For the details on presenting, head over to Book 4, Chapter 4..
- **The Master views for a consistent presentation:** The Master views — Slide Master, Handout Master, and Notes Master — are for handling *master styles,* the formatting commands that pertain to all the slides in a presentation, handouts, and notes. To switch to these views, go to the View tab and click the appropriate button. Head over to the section "Peeking Behind the Curtain: The Slide Master" to learn about master slides and master styles.

# It's All About the Slides

The heart and soul of any presentation is the collection of slides that comprise the bulk of its content and that serve as both the focal point and the organizing structure of your talk. The slides are the bridge between your audience — who, for the most part, have no idea what you're going to talk about — and you, who (at least theoretically!) knows exactly what you want to say. Building an effective presentation consists mostly of creating and organizing slides, which in turn involves four things:

- The content — text and graphics — presented on each slide
- The organization of the content presented on each slide
- The formatting applied to each slide: fonts, colors, background, and so on
- The organization of the slides within the context of the entire presentation

The bulk of this chapter and Book 4, Chapter 2, take you through various PowerPoint techniques and tricks that support these four design ideas.

## Adding a Slide to the Presentation

When you start a new presentation using the Blank Presentation template, the resulting file starts off with a single slide (refer to Figure 1-3) that uses a layout called the Title Slide, because you normally use it to add a title and subtitle for your presentation. After you have done that, you then add more slides to your presentation so that you can add the content. Thumbnails of the slides appear on the left in the Slides pane, and a full-size version of the currently selected size appears on the right.

Before you get to the specifics of adding a slide, you should understand that all slides contain some combination of the following three elements:

- **Title:** This is a text box that you normally use to add a title for the slide.
- **Text:** This is a text box that you normally use to add text to the slide, which is usually a collection of bullets.
- **Content:** This is a container into which you add any type of content, including text, a picture, clip art, a SmartArt graphic, a chart, a table, or a movie. In some cases, PowerPoint displays placeholders for specific types of content. For example, a Picture placeholder can contain only a picture.



In each case, the new slide contains one or more placeholders and your job is to fill in the placeholder with your text or a content object. Each slide uses some combination of title, text, and content placeholders, and the arrangement of these placeholders on a slide is called the *slide layout.*

PowerPoint offers the following nine layouts:

- **Title Slide:** A slide with two text boxes — a larger one for the overall presentation title and a smaller one for the subtitle.
- **Title and Content:** A slide with a title placeholder and a content placeholder.
- **Section Header:** A slide with two text placeholders, one for the description and one for the title of a new presentation section.
- **Two Content:** A slide with a title placeholder and two content placeholders placed side by side.
- **Comparison:** A slide with a title placeholder, two content placeholders placed side by side, and two text placeholders above each content placeholder.
- **Title Only:** A slide with just a title placeholder.
- **Blank:** A slide with no placeholders.

» **Content with Caption:** A content placeholder with two text placeholders to the left of it — one for the content title and another for the content description.

» **Picture with Caption:** A picture placeholder with two text placeholders to the left of it: one for the picture title and another for the picture description.

Besides the predefined layouts, you can also create custom layouts that use any combination of title, text, and content placeholders, organized in any way you want on the slide.

## Inserting a new slide

Here are the steps to follow to add a slide with a predefined layout:

1. **In the Slides pane, click the slide after which you want the new slide to appear.**

2. **On the Home tab, in the Slides group, click New Slide.**

   Alternatively, on the Insert tab, in the Slides group, click New Slide.

   PowerPoint unveils a gallery of slide layouts.

3. **Click the slide layout you want to use.**

   PowerPoint inserts the new slide.

## Duplicating a slide

If you have a slide in the current presentation that has similar content and formatting to what you want for your new slide, you can save yourself a bunch of time by inserting a duplicate of that slide and then adjusting the copy as needed. Here are the steps to follow to duplicate a slide:

1. **In the Slides pane, click the slide you want to duplicate.**

   If you have multiple slides you want to duplicate, you can save time by selecting all the slides at once. You find out how later in this chapter (refer to "Selecting slides").

2. **On the Home tab, in the Slides group, click New Slide (or choose Insert ⇨ New Slide) to display the gallery of slide layouts.**

3. **Click Duplicate Selected Slides.**

   PowerPoint creates a copy of the slide and inserts the copy below the selected slide.

TIP

A quicker way to duplicate a slide is to select it, press Ctrl+C to copy it, and then press Ctrl+V to paste it. If you want the copy to appear in a particular place within the presentation, select the slide after which you want the copy to appear and then press Ctrl+V.

TIP

Yet another way to create a duplicate of a slide is hold down Ctrl as you click and drag it. When you drop the slide, PowerPoint creates a copy of the slide in the new location.

## Reusing a slide from another presentation

One of the secrets of PowerPoint productivity is to avoid redoing work you've performed in the past. If you have a slide with boilerplate legal disclaimer text, why re-create it in each presentation? If you create an organization chart slide and your organization hasn't changed, you don't need to build the chart from scratch every time you want to add it to a presentation.

In the preceding section, I talked about how to duplicate a slide from the current presentation. However, the far more common scenario is that the slide you want to reuse exists in another presentation. Here are the steps to follow to take a slide from an existing presentation and reuse it in the current presentation:



1. **In the Slides list, click the slide after which you want the other slide to appear.**
2. **On the Home tab, in the Slides group, click New Slide (or choose Insert ➪ New Slide) to display the gallery of slide layouts.**
3. **Click Reuse Slides.**

   PowerPoint displays the Reuse Slides task pane.
4. **You now have two ways to proceed:**
   - If you see the file you want in the Recommended PowerPoint Files list, click the file.
   - Otherwise, click Browse to open the Choose Content dialog box, click the presentation you want to use, and then click Open.

   PowerPoint adds the presentation's slides to the Reuse Slides task pane, as shown in Figure 1-4.
5. **If you don't want the formatting of the original slide to appear in the new slide, deselect the Use Source Formatting check box.**
6. **Click the slide you want to reuse.**

   PowerPoint inserts the slide into the presentation.

**FIGURE 1-4:** After you select a presentation, PowerPoint displays its slides in the Reuse Slides task pane.

# Filling Out a Slide with Data

After you've added one or more slides, the next step is to fill in the placeholders. The next few sections take you through some of the details. For now, you should know that the content placeholder contains eight icons grouped together in the middle of the box, as shown in Figure 1-5. These icons represent the eight main types of content you can add to the placeholder, and clicking each icon launches the process of inserting that content type.

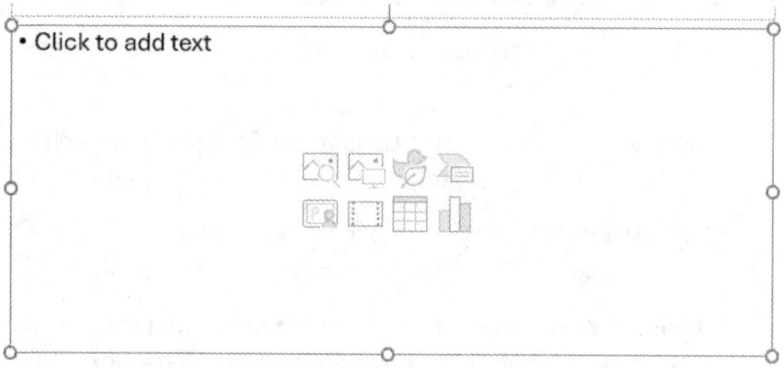


**FIGURE 1-5:** Use the icons inside an empty content placeholder to insert the corresponding content type.

## Adding text

With a title or text placeholder, click inside the placeholder to enable editing and then type your text. In a content placeholder, PowerPoint assumes you'll be adding bullet points, so the bullet format is on by default. Press Enter at the end of each bullet to start a new bullet. You can also use the keyboard shortcuts in Table 1-1 to work with bullet items.

**TABLE 1-1** **Keyboard Shortcuts for Working with Slide Bullets**

| Press | To |
|---|---|
| Alt+Shift+Right arrow | Demote a bullet to a lower level |
| Alt+Shift+Left arrow | Promote a bullet to a higher level |
| Alt+Shift+Down arrow | Move a bullet down |
| Alt+Shift+Up arrow | Move a bullet up |

REMEMBER

Note, too, that after you create a new bullet (but before you add any text to that bullet), you can convert the bullet to regular text by pressing Backspace.

## Adding a graphic or video

Inserting a graphic or a video into a content placeholder is straightforward:

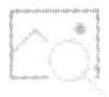

- **Stock Images:** On the Insert tab, in the Images group, click Pictures, then click Stock Images; alternatively, click Stock Images (shown in the margin) in the content placeholder. In the Stock Images dialog box, click the image and then click Insert.

- **Picture:** On the Insert tab, in the Images group, click Pictures, then click This Device; alternatively, click Pictures (shown in the margin) in the content placeholder. In the Insert Picture dialog box, click the picture and then click Insert.

- **Icon:** On the Insert tab, in the Illustrations group, click Icons; alternatively, click Insert an Icon (shown in the margin) in the content placeholder. In the Icons tab of the Stock Images dialog box, click the icon and then click Insert.

- **SmartArt:** On the Insert tab, in the Illustrations group, click SmartArt; alternatively, click Insert a SmartArt Graphic (shown in the margin) in the content placeholder. In the Choose a SmartArt Graphic dialog box, click the layout and then click OK.

- **Camera feed:** On the Insert tab, in the Camera group, click Cameo and then click This Slide; alternatively, click Insert Cameo (shown in the margin) in the content placeholder. Use the Camera Format contextual tab to set up your camera, then click Record. When you're camera-ready, press **R** to start the recording and when you're done, press **S** to stop the recording. Click Close (X) to insert the recording into your slide.

- **Video:** On the Insert tab, in the Media group, click Video and then click This Device; alternatively, click Insert Video (shown in the margin) in the content placeholder. In the Insert Video dialog box, click the video file and then click Insert.

## Creating a photo album presentation

A special kind of graphic presentation is a *photo album* where each slide displays one or more photos. This feature is an easy way to show a series of related images without going to the trouble of creating separate slides for each image. You can load the image from your hard disk or directly from a digital camera. PowerPoint even lets you make photo adjustments such as rotating the images and setting the color contrast and brightness.

Here are the steps to follow to create a photo album presentation:

1. **On the Insert tab, in the Images group, click Photo Album and then click New Photo Album.**

   PowerPoint displays the Photo Album dialog box. (Figure 1-6 shows this dialog box with some photos added.)

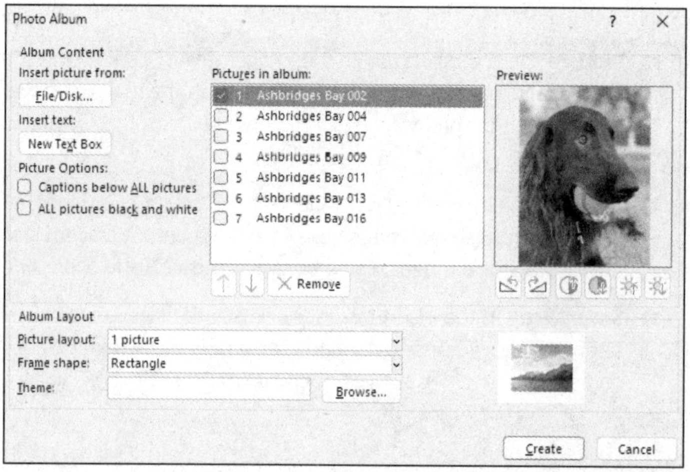


**FIGURE 1-6:** Use the Photo Album dialog box to set up a presentation of photos.

2. **To add pictures to the album, click File/Disk, use the Insert New Pictures dialog box to select the photos you want, and then click Insert.**
3. **In the Picture layout list, click the layout you want to use for each slide (the number of pictures per slide and whether a slide includes a title).**

   WARNING

   If you select a layout with a title, PowerPoint adds a Title placeholder to every slide in the presentation. If you have dozens or hundreds of pictures, you might not want to add that many titles, so consider a non-title layout, instead.
4. **If you clicked a layout other than Fit to Slide in Step 3, use the Frame Shape list to select the type of frame you want to appear around each picture.**
5. **If you clicked a layout other than Fit to Slide in Step 3 and you want the picture filename to appear with each picture, select the Captions Below All Pictures check box.**
6. **To adjust an image, select its check box, then use the buttons below the Preview area to adjust the rotation, contrast, and brightness of the picture.**
7. **Click Create.**

   PowerPoint creates a title slide and the photo album slides.

If you need to make changes to the photo album, choose Insert ⇨ Photo Album ⇨ Edit Photo Album.

## Adding a table

If you want to present data that would look best in a row-and-column format, use a table. PowerPoint gives you four methods, all of which are available by first choosing Insert ⇨ Table. The menu that appears offers the following four options:

- **Grid:** In the grid that appears at the top of the menu, hover the mouse over the square that represents the numbers of columns and rows you want in your table, then click that square to insert the table.
- **Insert Table:** Click this command — or, in the content placeholder, click Insert Table (shown in the margin) — to display the Insert Table dialog box. Type the Number of Columns and the Number of Rows, and then click OK.
- **Draw Table:** Click this command and then click and drag a large rectangle inside the content placeholder to represent the entire table. Click and drag vertical lines to create columns, and horizontal lines to create rows.
- **Excel Spreadsheet:** Click this command to insert an Excel worksheet in the content placeholder.

## Adding a chart

If you have numeric results to present, one surefire way to make your audience's eyes glaze over is show them a slide that is crammed with numbers. Most slides show the "big picture," and nothing translates numeric values into a digestible big-picture format better than a chart. The big news is that PowerPoint uses Excel and its powerful worksheet and charting capabilities. This change means that adding a chart to a PowerPoint slide is not that much different from creating a chart in Excel, which I explain in detail in Book 3, Chapter 7.

Here are the steps to follow:

1. **On the Insert tab, in the Illustrations group, click Chart; alternatively, click Insert Chart (shown in the margin) in the content placeholder.**

   PowerPoint brings the Insert Chart dialog box to the fore.

2. **Click a chart type on the left side of the dialog box, click a chart subtype, then click OK.**

   PowerPoint launches Excel, adds sample data to a worksheet, and inserts a chart based on that sample data into the slide. As shown in Figure 1-7, the worksheet data appears in a separate Excel window and when the chart is selected, you see the Chart Design and Format contextual tabs in the Ribbon.

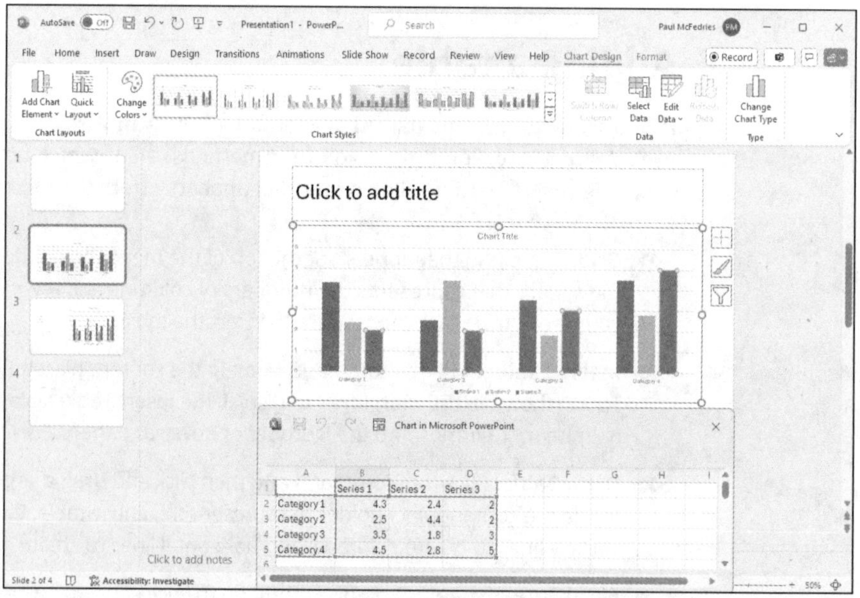


**FIGURE 1-7:** PowerPoint uses Excel to add a chart to a slide.

3. **Adjust the worksheet labels and values as needed.**

   Each time you confirm a change to a cell (for example, by pressing Enter), the change is reflected automatically on the PowerPoint chart.

4. **When you're done, close the Excel window.**

   Note that Excel doesn't allow you to save the workbook as a separate file.

REMEMBER

If you want to make changes to the underlying data, click the chart to select it, then, on the Chart Design contextual tab, in the Data group, click Edit Data.

## Adding notes

When you're trying to figure out the content of your presentation, it's always best to keep the actual amount of information on a slide to a minimum — just the high-level points to provide the framework for the topics you want to present. How, then, do you keep track of the details you want to cover for each slide? What if you want to provide those details to your audience, too? The answer to both questions is to use PowerPoint's notes.

Notes let you have paper printouts that contain both your slides and additional information you enter in notes. Consider the following ways you can use notes:

- As your presentation notes
- As additional detailed handouts for your audience
- As a copy of your presentation with a blank area for your audience to take their own notes: Have you ever been to a conference where they distribute hard copies of the presentations with three-slides-per-page printouts with lines for notes and wanted to do the same thing? Keep reading and find out how.
- As a student guide: If you use a presentation as your primary teaching medium, you can put additional information on notes pages for your learners.
- As an instructor's guide: Again, if you teach from your presentation, you might have points you want to make or other information associated with a particular slide. Add this information as notes, and you have your instructor's guide, perfectly in sync with the information you're giving your learners.

WARNING

Try to avoid the dreaded *triple delivery*, where you have the same text on the slide, on the slide notes you hand out to your audience, and spoken aloud during the presentation.

To create notes, click inside the Click to Add Notes box — this is called the Notes page — that appears below the slide. If you want more room to type, you have two choices:

- » Click and drag the separator bar at the top of the Notes page. Drag the bar up until the Notes page is the size you want, and then release the bar. This gives you less room for the slide, but you can also return the Notes page to its original size after you've added your notes.
- » On the View tab, in the Presentation Views group, click Notes Page to see the full Notes page box.

If you're creating printouts for your audience, you might want to consider using the master formatting tools on the Notes Master. On the View tab, in the Master Views group, click Notes Master to open the Notes Master view. In the Notes Master, you can specify a header and footer and add the date and page numbers. You can also specify how the text within the note body itself will appear by formatting the font. When you're done fooling around with the Notes Master, on the Notes Master tab, click Close Master View.

To print your notes, follow these steps:

1. **Choose File ⇨ Print to display the Print window.**
2. **In the Print Layout list, click Notes Pages.**

   The Print Layout list is the unnamed list box that appears just below the Slides text box.
3. **In the Color/Grayscale list, click Pure Black and White to print the notes in black and white.**

   If you need to print your notes in color, click Color, instead.
4. **Select the other print options you want to use.**
5. **Click Print.**

Notes pages print in portrait layout, with a half-sized representation of your slide on the top portion of the page and your text on the bottom portion.

# Getting Copilot to Help

If your Office 365 account includes a Copilot subscription, then you've got access to a powerful AI assistant that can help you with almost anything related to building a presentation. If you're new to Copilot, you might want to head back to Book 2, Chapter 9 to learn what Copilot is all about.

How do you know whether Copilot is available? Display PowerPoint's Home tab, then scan way over to the right and look for the Copilot button (shown in the margin). If you see that button, click it to fire up the Copilot task pane. You then use the text box to prompt Copilot for what you need.

Not sure what Copilot can do? Here's a few Copilot prompts to help you get started:

- *Create a presentation about* X. Replace *X* with a presentation topic.
- *Create a presentation from* /file. As soon as you type /, Copilot displays a list of recent files. If you don't see what you want, start typing the name of the Word or PDF file, then click the file when it appears in the list.
- *Create a slide about* X. Replace *X* with a slide topic.
- *Add an image/icon of* X. Replace *X* with an image or icon idea.
- *What are some strong titles for this presentation?*
- *What are some ways I can make this presentation read better?*
- *Organize this presentation.*
- *Explain this presentation in X sentences.* (Replace *X* with a number, such as *three* or *five*.)
- *What are the key dates mentioned in this presentation?*
- *Summarize this presentation.*



# Messing Around with Slides

It will be a rare — oh, who am I kidding: it will be a *nonexistent* — person who builds a polished and ready-for-primetime presentation in one shot. And the more slides you have in your presentation, the less polished the product will be and the more you'll need to intervene to get your slide show up to snuff. I'm not talking major renovations, here. Whether it's rearranging the order of some slides or changing a slide's layout, PowerPoint offers straightforward tools and techniques for getting your presentation just right.

## Selecting slides

To do anything with slides, your first task is always to select the slide or slides. Here are the techniques you can use in the Slides pane:

- To select a single slide, click it.
- To select multiple, consecutive slides, click the first slide, hold down Shift, and then click the last slide.
- To select multiple, nonconsecutive slides, click the first slide, hold down Ctrl, and click each of the other slides.
- To select all the slides, click any slide and then press Ctrl+A. If your mouse-clicking finger needs a workout, then, on the Home tab, in the Editing group, click Select and then click Select All.

## Rearranging slides

If you need to change the order that your slides appear in the presentation, PowerPoint gives you two different methods, either of which you can use in the Slides pane or in the Slide Sorter view (choose View ⇨ Slide Sorter or click the status bar's Slide Sorter button, shown in the margin):

- Click the slide you want to move, press Ctrl+X, select the slide after which you want the moved slide to appear, and then press Ctrl+V.
- Click and drag the slide and drop it below the slide after which you want it to appear.

## Changing the layout of a slide

If the original layout you applied to a slide is not what you want, you can change it by following these steps:

1. **Select the slide or slides you want to change.**

2. **On the Home tab, in the Slides group, click Slide Layout (shown in the margin).**

   PowerPoint displays a gallery of slide layouts.

3. **Click the layout you want to use.**

   PowerPoint converts the slide or slides to the new layout.

## Hiding a slide

Not every slide in your presentation is necessarily suitable for every audience. For example, a budget presentation may include sensitive financial data. It's fine to present that data to company executives, but you won't want to show that data to company outsiders such as analysts and investors.

Instead of creating a separate presentation that doesn't include the sensitive slides, you can use your current presentation and temporarily hide those slides that you don't want to present to a particular audience.

Hiding a slide prevents it from displaying during an onscreen slide show. By hiding slides, you can create mini presentations from a master presentation without deleting any slides. You can hide slides, give the presentation, and then unhide them.

1. **Select the slide or slides you want to hide.**
2. **Right-click any selected slide.**
3. **Click Hide Slide.**

   PowerPoint hides the slide or slides.



REMEMBER

PowerPoint marks a slide as hidden by displaying a slash through the slide number in the Slides pane or the Slider Sorter view. To unhide any slide, right-click it and then click Unhide Slide.

## Deleting a slide

As you build your presentation, you might find that a particular slide just doesn't work any longer. The slide might contain information that you no longer need; the slide might be no longer relevant; or the slide might have info that's out of date.

Fortunately, you don't need to burden your presentation with slides that are no longer pulling their weight. Here are the steps to follow to delete one or more slides from your presentation:

1. **Select the slide or slides you want to remove.**
2. **Right-click any selected slide.**

WARNING

PowerPoint doesn't give you a chance to confirm the deletion, so before moving on to Step 3, double-check that you really, really want to delete the selected slide or slides.

3. **Click Delete Slide.**

   PowerPoint removes the slide or slides from your presentation.

## Defining slide footers

In a large presentation, you can easily lose track of what slide number you're working with or viewing. Similarly, if you work with a lot of presentations, you can easily get confused as to which presentation you're currently working on. To help overcome these and other organizational handicaps, take advantage of the footers that PowerPoint enables you to display on a presentation's slides.

By default, PowerPoint does not display the footer in each slide. (Or, more accurately, it displays a blank footer in each slide.) To display the footer, you need to activate the footer content, as follows:

1. **If you only want the footer to appear in certain slides, select those slides.**
2. **On the Insert tab, in the Text group, click Header and Footer.**

   PowerPoint displays the Header and Footer dialog box, as shown in Figure 1-8.

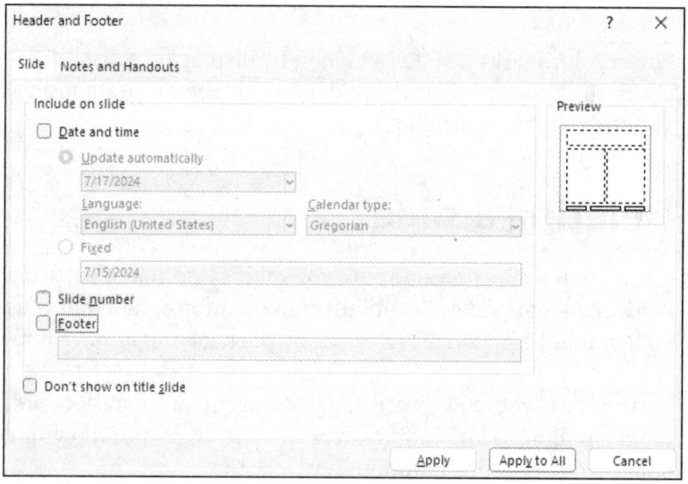


**FIGURE 1-8:** Use the Header and Footer dialog box to specify the data that you want to appear in the slide's footer.

REMEMBER

The "header" part of the Header and Footer dialog box doesn't apply to slides, which can't have headers. Instead, it applies to notes (refer to "Adding notes," earlier in this chapter) and handouts (refer to "Printing slide handouts," later in this chapter). To add a header to your presentation's notes and handouts, use the controls on the Notes and Handouts tab.

3. **To display the date and time in the lower-left corner of the slide, select the Date and Time check box and then click one of the following options:**
   - *Update automatically:* Select this option to always display the current date and time. Use the list provided to select the format of the date and time display.
   - *Fixed:* Select this option to specify a fixed date and time. Note, however, that you can type any text you like into the Fixed text box.
4. **To display the current slide number in the lower-right corner of the slide, select the Slide number check box.**
5. **To display text in the lower middle of the slide, select the Footer check box and then type your text into the box provided.**
6. **If you don't want the footer text to appear on the presentation's title slide, select the Don't Show on Title Slide check box.**
7. **To display the footer, click one of the following buttons:**
   - *Apply to All:* Displays the footer on every slide in the presentation.
   - *Apply:* Displays the footer on just the currently selected slides.

REMEMBER

By default, PowerPoint configures the footer with the date and time placeholder in the lower left of the slide, the slide number in the lower right, and the footer text in the lower middle. You can move these placeholders around and perform other footer customizations by using the Slide Master view. You can find the details on how to do so later in this chapter (check out "Peeking Behind the Curtain: The Slide Master").

## Printing slide handouts

Handouts are printouts of your slides — just the slides, no notes. Audience members often appreciate having copies of your slides. They can concentrate more on your presentation and less on taking detailed notes when you supply the presentation handouts.

To print your handouts, follow these steps:

1. **Choose File ➪ Print to display the Print window.**
2. **In the Print Layout list, click Full Page Slides.**

   The Print Layout list is the unnamed list box that appears just below the Slides text box.
3. **In the Print Layout list's Handouts group, click the layout you want to use for each handout page.**

   These layouts set the number of slides you want to appear on each page (the default is six) and (for layouts that include four or more slides) the slide order on each page: horizontal (that is, left to right across the page) or vertical (top to bottom down the page).
4. **If you want PowerPoint to add a thin border around each slide, click the Frame slides command to activate it.**
5. **In the Color/Grayscale list, click Pure Black and White to print the notes in black and white.**

   If you need to print your handouts in color, click Color, instead.
6. **Select the other print options you want to use.**
7. **Click Print.**

To modify the default handout layout, use the Handout Master by choosing View ➪ Handout Master. Use the following techniques to customize the Handout Master:

- » To change the orientation of the handout pages, click Handout Orientation, and then click either Portrait or Landscape.
- » To change the aspect ratio of the slides that appear on each handout page, click Slide Size, and then click either Standard (4:3) or Widescreen (16:9). If you're feeling ambitious, you can click Custom Slide Size to define your own size.
- » To change the number of slides that appear on each handout page, click Slides Per Page, and then click the number of slides you want: 1, 2, 3, 4, 6, or 9.
- » To remove one or more handout placeholders, in the Handout Master tab's Placeholders group, deselect any of the following check boxes: Header, Footer, Date, or Page Number.

When all is said and done with the Handout Master, click Close Master View to get out of there.

# Building a Presentation from an Outline

You might think outlines are useful only for organizing text in your Word documents, but they can be an essential part of building a presentation, as well. In PowerPoint, outlines offer a convenient way of organizing the content of your presentation hierarchically:

- The top level of the outline hierarchy consists of the slide titles.
- The second level of the outline hierarchy consists of the subtitle in the first slide and the main bullet points in subsequent slides.
- Lower levels of the outline hierarchy consist of the lower levels of bullet points in subsequent slides.

Using PowerPoint's Outline pane, you can build your presentation from scratch by entering outline text as you would in, say, a Word outline. You can promote or demote items to different levels with just a keystroke or mouse click. Best of all, because the Outline pane gives you a big-picture view of your presentation, you can adjust the overall organization by cutting and pasting or clicking and dragging outline text.

Before you get started, display the Outline pane: in the View tab's Presentation Views group, click Outline View.



## Creating the outline by hand

For a new presentation, the Outline pane shows the number 1 and an icon. The number is the slide number and the icon represents a slide; together they're the outline equivalent of the initial (empty) slide added to each new presentation. This is the top level of the outline hierarchy and, as I mention earlier, it consists of the slide titles. Remember that each item in the outline corresponds to a text object on a slide: title, subtitle, bullet point, and so on.

### Creating the top level

The best way to begin the outline is to create and title the slides to complete the top-level hierarchy. Here are the steps to follow:

1. **In the Outline pane, to the right of the slide's icon, type the slide title.**

2. **Press Enter.**

   PowerPoint creates a new slide.

3. **Repeat Steps 1 and 2 until you've created all your slides.**

Figure 1-9 shows a presentation with the slide titles entered into the Outline pane.

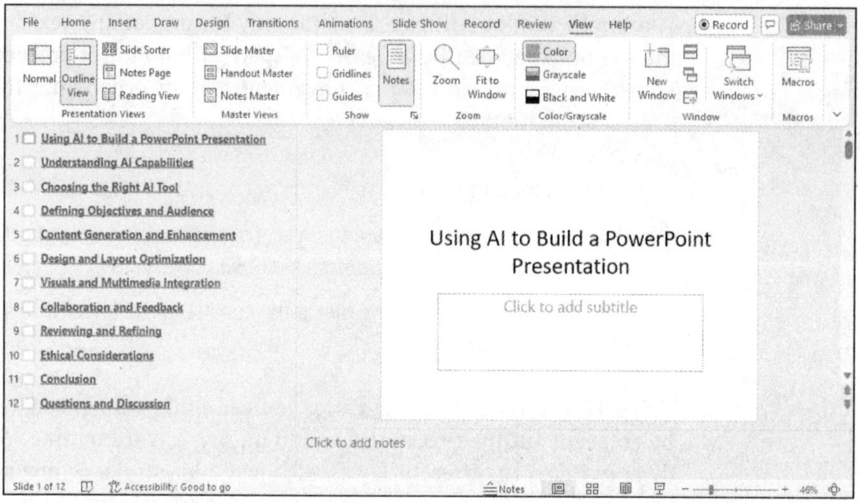


**FIGURE 1-9:** Begin the presentation outline by creating the slides and entering the slide titles in the Outline pane.

## Creating the second level

The second-level outline consists of items such as slide subtitles and the main bullet points that comprise the bulk of your presentation. Follow these steps to create the second level:

1. **In the Outline pane, move the cursor to the end of the title of the slide you want to work with.**

2. **Press Ctrl+Enter.**

   The outline item created by PowerPoint depends on the slide's text layout:

   - For a Title Slide layout, the new outline item corresponds to the subtitle text box placeholder.
   - For any of the text layouts, the new outline item corresponds to a bullet in the text box placeholder.

3. **Type the item text.**

4. **To create another item on the same level, move the cursor to the end of the current item and press Enter.**
5. **Repeat Steps 1 through 4 until you've completed the second level.**

Figure 1-10 shows an outline with some second-level items added.

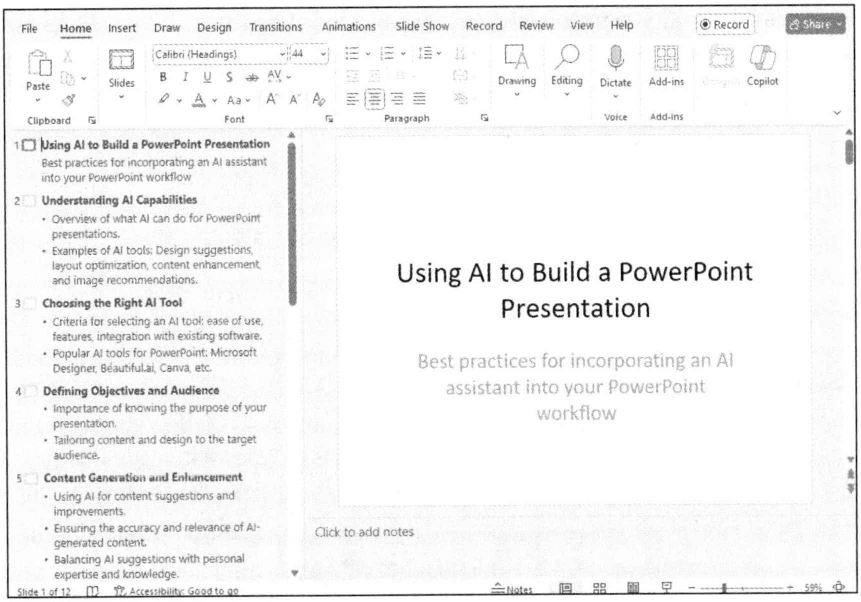


**FIGURE 1-10:** The outline with some second-level outline items.



## Creating lower levels

To create the third and lower levels of the outline, use the following steps:

1. **Follow the steps from the previous section to start a new second-level item.**
2. **Press Tab.**

   PowerPoint demotes the item to the next lower level.

   REMEMBER

   If you accidentally demote an item, you can promote it to a higher level by placing the cursor anywhere inside the item and then pressing Shift+Tab.
3. **Type the item text.**

4. **To create another item on the same level, move the cursor to the end of the current item and press Enter.**
5. **Repeat Steps 1 through 4 until you have completed the outline.**

## Creating an outline from a text file

If you've already sketched out the slide titles and headings for your presentation in a text file, you can import the text file and have PowerPoint convert it automatically to an outline. Before you do that, you may need to modify the text file as follows:

- Each slide title must be flush left in the text file.
- First-level headings must begin with a single tab.
- Second-level headings must begin with two tabs.

To convert the text to a PowerPoint presentation outline, you have two choices:

- Choose File ➪ Open to display the Open window, then click Browse to display the Open dialog box. In the Files of Type list (the unnamed list to the right of the File Name text box), click All Outlines. Click the text file, and then click Open.
- Start a new presentation or open an existing presentation. In the Outline pane, move the cursor to where you want the text file outline to appear. On the Home tab, in the Slides group, click New Slide, click Slides from Outline, click the text file, and then click Insert.

## Creating an outline from a Word file

Given the hierarchical structure of a PowerPoint outline, you won't be in the least bit surprised to hear that you can convert Word's own outline hierarchy — the styles Heading 1, Heading 2, and so on — into a PowerPoint outline. Here are the details:

- PowerPoint interprets a Heading 1 style as a top-level item in a presentation outline. In other words, each time PowerPoint comes across Heading 1 text, it starts a new slide and the text associated with the Heading 1 style becomes the title of the slide.
- PowerPoint interprets a Heading 2 style as a second-level item in a presentation outline. So, each paragraph of Heading 2 text becomes a main bullet (or subtitle) in the presentation.

- PowerPoint interprets the styles Heading 3, Heading 4, and so on as lower-level items in the presentation outline.

To convert a Word outline into a PowerPoint presentation, you have two choices:

- **Choose File ➪ Open to display the Open window, then click Browse to display the Open dialog box.** In the Files of Type list (the unnamed list to the right of the File Name text box), click All Outlines. Click the Word file, and then click Open.
- **Start a new presentation or open an existing presentation.** In the Outline pane, move the cursor to where you want the Word file outline to appear. On the Home tab, in the Slides group, click New Slide, click Slides from Outline, click the Word file, and then click Insert.

WARNING

PowerPoint won't convert the Word document if it's open elsewhere, so be sure to close it before attempting to import the outline.

## Controlling the display of outline levels

If you're working with a long presentation, the Outline pane might show only a small number of the slides. To keep the big picture in view, you can tell PowerPoint to show less outline detail. Here are the techniques to use in the Outline pane to expand and collapse the outline levels:

- To hide the levels for a single slide, double-click the slide icon or right-click inside the slide's outline text and then click Collapse.
- To display the levels for a single slide, double-click the slide icon or right-click the slide's outline title and then click Expand.
- To hide the levels for all the slides, right-click any slide's outline text and then choose Collapse ➪ Collapse All.
- To display the levels for all the slides, right-click any slide's outline text and then choose Expand ➪ Expand All.

## Editing the presentation outline

The Outline pane's big picture view not only lets you easily see the overall organization of your presentation, but it also makes modifying that organization easy. That is, by editing the outline, you also edit the organization. Besides editing the text itself, you can also change the outline levels.

Changing levels means moving items down or up within the outline hierarchy. To demote an item means to move it lower in the hierarchy (for example, from second level to third); to promote an item means to move it higher in the hierarchy (for example, from second level to top level). Here are the techniques to use to change an item's level:

- **To demote an item:** Click anywhere inside the item and press Tab.
- **To promote an item:** Click anywhere inside the item and press Shift+Tab.

# Peeking Behind the Curtain: The Slide Master

One of PowerPoint's templates might be just right for your presentation. If so, great! Your presentation's design will be one less thing to worry about on your way to an effective presentation. Often, however, a template is just right except for the background color, title alignment, or font. Or perhaps you need the company's logo to appear on each slide. Using the template as a starting point, you can make changes to the overall presentation so that it's just right for your needs.

However, what do you do if your presentation already has a number of slides? It'll probably require a great deal of work to change the background, alignment, or font on every slide. Fortunately, PowerPoint offers a much easier way: the Slide Master, which is available for every presentation. The Slide Master acts as a kind of "design center" for your presentation. The Slide Master's typefaces, type sizes, bullet styles, colors, alignment options, line spacing, and more are used on each slide in your presentation. Not only that, but any object you add to the Slide Master — a piece of clip art, a company logo, and so on — also appears in the same position on each slide.

The beauty of the Slide Master is that any change you make to this one slide, PowerPoint propagates to all the slides in your presentation. Need to change the background color? Just change the background color of the Slide Master. Prefer a different type size for top-level items? Change the type size for the top-level item shown on the Slide Master. You can also make separate adjustments to the masters of the nine standard layouts (Title Slide, Title and Content, and so on).

# Viewing the Slide Master

To get the Slide Master onscreen, head over to the View tab then, in the Master Views group, click Slide Master to display the Slide Master view, shown in Figure 1-11.

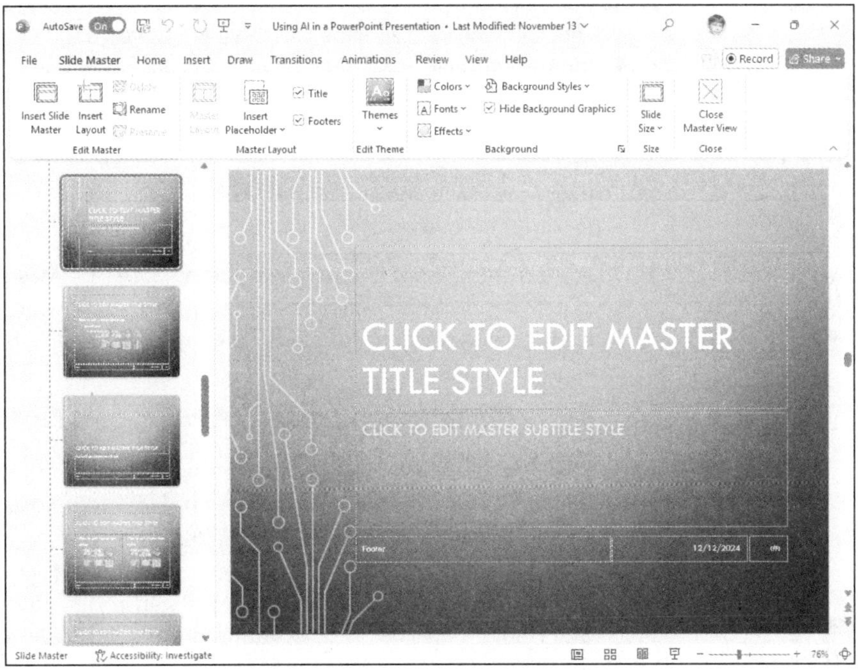


**FIGURE 1-11:** Each presentation comes with its own Slide Master, which acts as a "design center" for the slides.



The Master view shows several master slides on the left, with the Slide Master at the top, the nine standard layouts below it, followed by a couple of extra layouts. Click the master you want to work with and then use the following techniques to customize it:

- To select a placeholder, click it.
- To delete a placeholder, select it and then press Delete.
- To size a placeholder, position the mouse pointer over one of the placeholder's sizing handles (the circles and squares that appear at the corners and border midpoints). The pointer changes to a two-headed arrow. Click and drag the sizing handle to the position you want.

- To move a placeholder, position the mouse pointer over one of the placeholder borders (but not over a sizing handle). The pointer changes to a four-headed arrow. Click and drag the placeholder to the position you want.
- To format a layout's theme, select it and then choose Slide Master ⇨ Themes and use the controls that appear.
- To add a placeholder to one of the layout slides, choose Slide Master ⇨ Insert Placeholder, and then click the placeholder type you want: Content, Text, Picture, Chart, Table, SmartArt, Media, Online Image, or Cameo.
- To toggle the title on and off for a layout, click the layout and then choose Slide Master ⇨ Title.
- To toggle the footers on and off for a layout, click the layout and then choose Slide Master ⇨ Footers.
- To add a custom layout to the Slide Master, choose Slide Master ⇨ Insert Layout. To supply a name to the new custom layout, click it and then choose Slide Master ⇨ Rename. Use the Rename Layout dialog box to type a new name and click Rename.
- To remove a layout from the Slide Master, click the layout and then choose Slide Master ⇨ Delete.
- To display an object — such as clip art or a text box — on every slide, click the Insert tab and then insert the object into the master.

Note, too, that after you select a master, you can format the text, background, bullets, and colors as if you were working in a regular slide. When you're done, choose Slide Master ⇨ Close Master View.

## Using multiple Slide Masters

Although having a consistent look among your slides should be a prime design goal for any good presentation, that doesn't mean you have to use precisely the same formatting and design on every slide. Some of the most effective presentation designs are ones that apply a particular design to groups of related slides. Why would you need to do this? Here are some examples:

- For a budget presentation, you might use a green color scheme on income-related slides and a red color scheme on expense-related slides.
- In a presentation that includes both sensitive and nonsensitive material, you could add a "For Internal Use Only" graphic to the slides with sensitive material.

- If your presentation has multiple authors, you might want to display the author's name, signature, or picture on each of the slides they created.

This would seem to defeat the efficiency of the Slide Master, except that PowerPoint allows you to have more than one Slide Master in a presentation. You can then apply a layout from one of the Slide Masters to the appropriate slides, and any changes you make to that Slide Master will affect only those slides.

To create another Slide Master, you have two choices:

- To create a default Slide Master, choose Slide Master ➪ Insert Slide Master (or press Ctrl+M).
- To create a duplicate of an existing Slide Master, right-click the Slide Master and then click Duplicate Slide Master. This technique is useful if your new Slide Master is similar to an existing Slide Master. By duplicating it and then tweaking the new Slide Master as required, you avoid having to create the new Slide Master from scratch.

After you create another Slide Master, make your adjustments to the layouts, as required. To apply the new Slide Master to a slide, change the slide's layout, as described earlier (refer to "Changing the layout of a slide"). PowerPoint adds a new section to the Layout gallery, and the new Slide Master's layouts are in that section.

IN THIS CHAPTER

» Using themes to apply fonts, colors, and backgrounds with just a few clicks

» Creating and customizing themes to suit your style

» Using easy methods for formatting slide text

» Leveraging powerful and practical formatting tips and techniques

» Perfecting slide formatting with simple guidelines

# Chapter 2

# Formatting Slides

When it comes to presentations, content is all-important. Populating your slides with accurate, up-to-date, and useful information is the royal road to a good presentation that won't waste your audience's time or test its patience. However, good content doesn't represent the entire journey. These days, your presentation must also look every bit as good as the information it contains. It may not be fair, but it's almost always true that if your presentation looks like you spent very little time on the formatting, most people will also assume you spent very little time on the content.

To avoid that fate, you must consider the look of your slides to be at least as important as the text and other content. Fortunately, you rarely have to spend the same amount of time on formatting and design as you do on building content. That's because PowerPoint has some powerful and useful formatting and design tools that make it easier to create eye-catching slides with very little effort. You explore these formatting and design tools in this chapter.

# Applying a Slide Theme

By far the easiest and fastest way to apply high-quality design and formatting to a presentation is to use a theme. For PowerPoint, a *theme* is a predefined collection of formatting options that control the colors, fonts, and background used with each slide in the presentation. PowerPoint built-in themes are nice on their own, but you can also customize any aspect of the theme to tweak the design to what you want.

## Choosing a predefined theme

Applying one of PowerPoint's predefined themes takes just a few mouse clicks, as the following steps show:

1. **If you'll be applying the theme to certain slides only, select the slides.**
2. **Click the Design tab.**
3. **Click the Themes drop-down button (shown in the margin).**

   PowerPoint displays a gallery of themes, as shown in Figure 2-1.

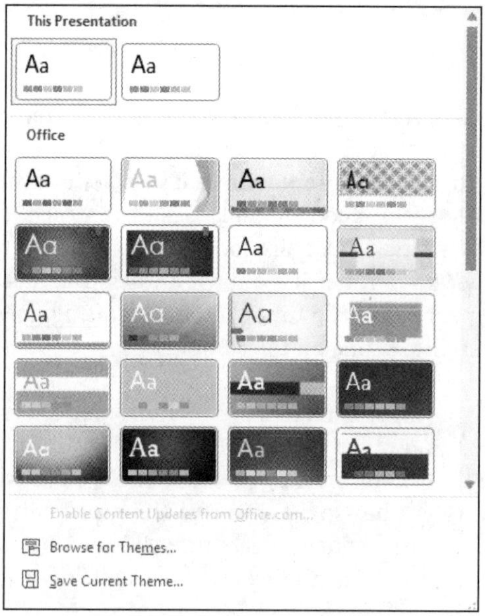


**FIGURE 2-1:** You can apply a theme to one or more slides or to the entire presentation.

4. **You have two choices:**

- If you want to apply the theme to all the slides in the presentation, click the theme.
- If you want to apply the theme to only the selected slides, right-click the theme and then click Apply to Selected Slides.

REMEMBER

Before choosing a theme, remember that if you hover the mouse pointer over a theme, PowerPoint temporarily applies the theme to the displayed slide so you can get a better idea of the theme design.

## Changing the theme colors

If the colors that come with a predefined theme are not quite what you want, you can change them individually. However, if you want to avoid the drudgery of getting your text, line, background, and fill colors to match, PowerPoint comes with more than 20 built-in color schemes that do the hard work for you. Follow these steps to apply a color scheme:

1. **If you want to apply the colors to certain slides only, select the slides.**
2. **Click the Design tab and then click the Variants drop-down button (shown in the margin).**
3. **Click Colors to display a gallery of color schemes, as shown in Figure 2-2.**

   Each color scheme has eight color swatches: The first is the background color, the second is the text color, and the rest are "accent" colors that PowerPoint uses with content such as charts and SmartArt diagrams.
4. **If you only want the color scheme applied to the selected slides, right-click the color scheme you want and then click Apply to Selected Slides. Otherwise, click the color scheme you want to apply to all the slides.**

## Creating custom theme colors

If a particular color scheme isn't quite right for your needs, or if you want to create a color scheme to match your company colors, you need to create a custom scheme. Follow these steps:

1. **If you want to base your custom color scheme on an existing design, follow the steps in the "Changing the theme colors" section to apply the color scheme you want to use.**

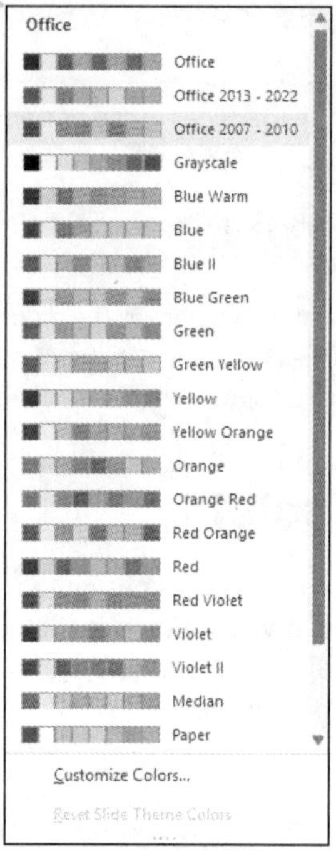


**FIGURE 2-2:** Use the Colors gallery to click the color scheme you want to apply.

2. **Click the Design tab, click the Variants drop-down button (shown in the margin), click Colors to display a gallery of color schemes, and then click Customize Colors.**

   PowerPoint displays the Create New Theme Colors dialog box, shown in Figure 2-3.

3. **Use the following drop-down lists to select the text and background colors:**
   - *Text/Background 1 - Dark:* This is the dark text color that PowerPoint applies when you choose a light background color.
   - *Text/Background 2 - Light:* This is the light text color that PowerPoint applies when you choose a dark background color.
   - *Text/Background 3 - Dark:* This is the dark background color that PowerPoint applies when you choose a light text color.
   - *Text/Background 4 - Light:* This is the light background color that PowerPoint applies when you choose a dark text color.
4. **Use the various Accent drop-down lists to choose the accent colors.**
5. **Use the Hyperlink and Followed Hyperlink drop-down lists to choose link colors.**

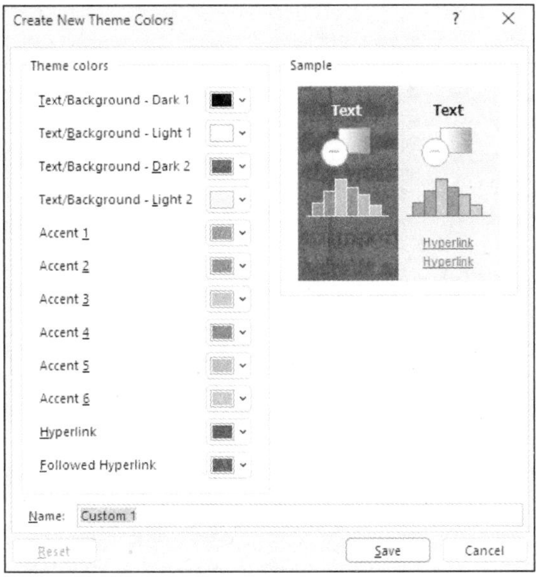


**FIGURE 2-3:** Use the Create New Theme Colors dialog box to create a custom color scheme.

6. **In the Name text box, type a name for the new color scheme.**
7. **Click Save.**

   PowerPoint saves your custom color scheme, which now appears at the top of the Colors gallery in the Custom section.

## Changing the theme fonts

Each theme defines two fonts: a larger font for title text and a smaller font for body text. The typeface is usually the same for both types of text, but some themes use two different typefaces, such as Arial for titles and Times New Roman for body text. You can change the fonts used in the current theme by following these steps:

1. **Click the Design tab and then click the Variants drop-down button (shown in the margin).**
2. **Click Fonts.**

   PowerPoint displays a gallery of font combinations, as shown in Figure 2-4.
3. **Click the fonts you want to use.**

   PowerPoint applies the theme fonts to all the slides in the presentation. Note that there's no way to apply the fonts to only selected slides.

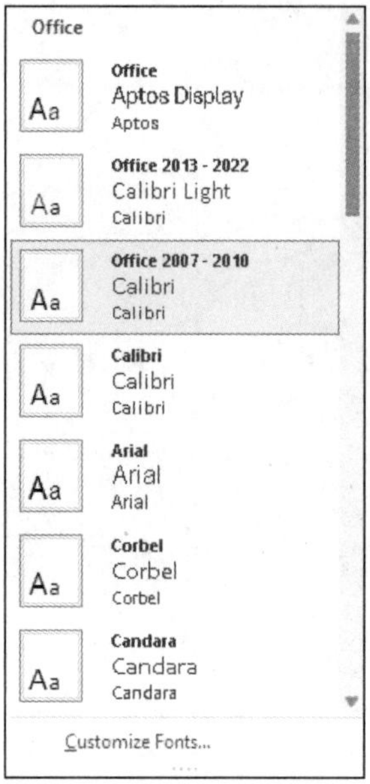


**FIGURE 2-4:** Click Theme Fonts and then click the font combination you want to apply.

## Creating custom theme fonts

If none of PowerPoint's theme fonts are exactly what you want to use in your presentation, you can quickly create your own custom combination. Follow these steps:

1. **If you want to base your custom theme fonts on an existing font combination, follow the steps in the "Changing the theme fonts" section earlier in this chapter to apply the font combination you want to use.**

2. **Click the Design tab, click the Variants drop-down button (shown in the margin), click Font to display a gallery of fonts, and then click Customize Fonts.**

   PowerPoint displays the Create New Theme Fonts dialog box, shown in Figure 2-5.

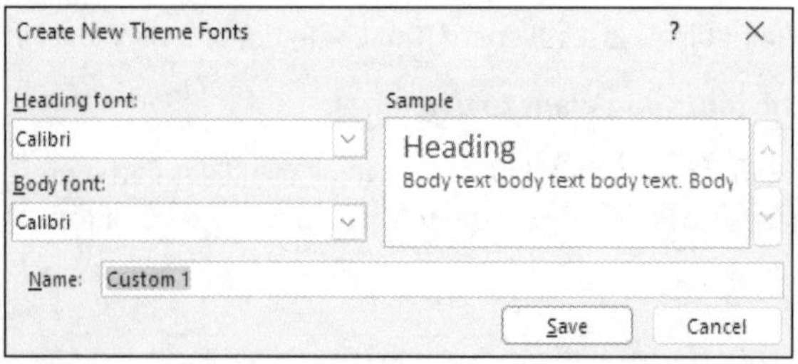


**FIGURE 2-5:** Use the Create New Theme Fonts dialog box to create your custom font combination.

3. **Use the Heading font list to choose the typeface you want to use for titles.**

4. **Use the Body font list to choose the typeface you want to use for the body text.**

5. **In the Name text box, type a name for the new theme fonts.**

6. **Click Save.**

   PowerPoint saves your custom font pairing, which now appears at the top of the Fonts gallery in the Custom section.

## Applying theme effects

PowerPoint defines a number of effects that govern the look of objects such as shapes, SmartArt diagrams, and chart markers. Here are the steps to follow to apply these theme effects:

1. **Click the Design tab and then click the Variants drop-down button (shown in the margin).**

2. **Click Effects.**

   PowerPoint displays a gallery of effects, as shown in Figure 2-6.

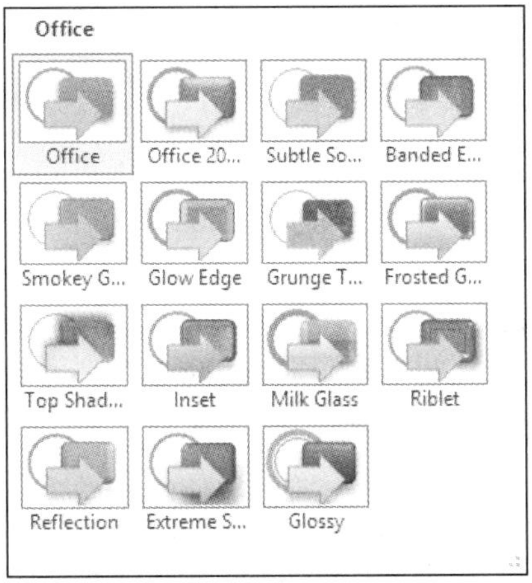


**FIGURE 2-6:** Click Theme Effects and then click the effect you want to apply.

3. **Click the effect you want to use.**

   PowerPoint applies the effect to all the slides.

## Changing the slide background

Most themes offer a solid color background, which is usually a good choice because you don't want your background interfering with the slide content. However, each theme gives you a choice of background colors, as well as your choice of fill effects, such as gradients, pictures, or textures. Note, too, that PowerPoint automatically adjusts the text color if you choose a darker or lighter background color.

Here are the steps to follow to change the slide background style:

1. **If you'll be applying the background to certain slides only, select the slides.**
2. **Click the Design tab and then click the Variants drop-down button (shown in the margin).**
3. **Click Background Styles.**

   PowerPoint offers up a gallery of backgrounds, as shown in Figure 2-7.

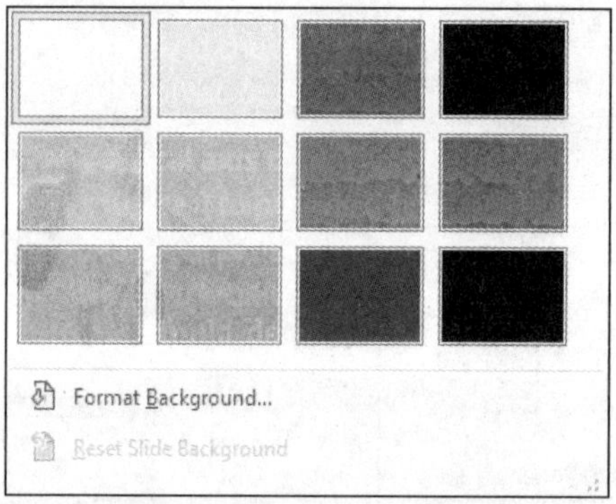


**FIGURE 2-7:** Click Background Styles and then click the background you want to use.

4. **If you only want the background applied to the selected slides, right-click the background you want and then click Apply to Selected Slides. Otherwise, click the background you want to apply to all the slides.**

If you want more control over the design of the background, choose Design ⇨ Format Background ⇨ Background (or right-click the slide background and then click Format Background). The Format Background task pane appears. Use the Fill section to choose the type of fill you want (Solid Fill, Gradient Fill, Picture or Texture Fill, or Pattern Fill) and then use the displayed controls to configure the fill.

TIP

If a background style includes a picture, you can hide the picture by choosing Design ⇨ Format Background to display the Format Background pane, then select Hide Background Graphics.

## Creating a custom theme

If you go to the trouble of choosing a theme and then customizing that scheme with effects and with either predefined or custom colors and fonts, you probably don't want to go through the entire process the next time you want the same theme for a presentation. Fortunately, you don't have to because PowerPoint enables you to save all of your theme details as a custom theme. Nice. Here are the steps to follow:

1. **Use the techniques from the past few sections to customize a theme and its colors, fonts, and effects.**
2. **If you applied the theme only to certain slides, select one of those slides.**
3. **Click the Design tab.**
4. **Click the Themes drop-down button (shown in the margin) and then click Save Current Theme.**

   PowerPoint displays the Save Current Theme dialog box.
5. **Use the File Name text box to type a name for the custom theme.**
6. **Click Save.**

   PowerPoint saves the theme as an Office Theme file.

Your saved theme will now appear in the Themes gallery's Custom section.

TIP

If you want to use your custom theme as the default theme for all new presentations, click the Design tab, display the Themes gallery, right-click your custom theme, and then click Set as Default Theme.

## Reusing a slide theme from another presentation

If you created a custom theme in another presentation, but you didn't save that theme as an Office Theme file, you can still reuse that theme in a different presentation. Here are the steps to follow to take a theme from an existing presentation and reuse it in the current presentation:

1. **Select the slides to which you want the theme applied.**
2. **Choose Home ➪ New Slide (or Insert ➪ New Slide) to display the gallery of slide layouts.**

3. **Click Reuse Slides.**

   PowerPoint displays the Reuse Slides task pane.

4. **Click Browse.**

   PowerPoint brings in the Browse dialog box.

5. **Click the presentation you want to use and then click Open.**

   PowerPoint adds the presentation's slides to the Reuse Slides task pane.

6. **Right-click any slide in the Reuse Slides pane and then click one of the following commands:**

   - *Apply Theme to All Slides:* Applies the theme to every slide in the current presentation.
   - *Apply Theme to Selected Slides:* Applies the theme only to the selected slides in the current presentation.

# Formatting Slide Text

When formatting the slide text, you should strive for an attractive look (by, for example, avoiding too many typefaces in each slide), but your focus must be on maximizing readability, particularly if you'll be presenting to a large audience. Fortunately, PowerPoint offers a wide variety of font formatting options, as the next few sections show.

## PowerPoint's font buttons

When the cursor is active inside a text placeholder, the buttons in the Slides tab's Font and Paragraph groups become available. Table 2-1 summarizes the controls in the Font group.

TIP

If you want to apply any font formatting to a single word, you don't need to select the entire word. Instead, just position the insertion point anywhere within the word, then apply the formatting. If you want to apply font formatting to an entire paragraph, note that triple-clicking anywhere within that paragraph will select the whole thing, just like that.

**TABLE 2-1** **PowerPoint's Font Formatting Buttons**

| Button | Name | Description |
|---|---|---|
| Calibri (Body) | Font | Displays a list of font faces |
| 32 | Size | Displays a list of font sizes |
| B | Bold | Toggles bolding on and off |
| I | Italic | Toggles italics on and off |
| U | Underline | Toggles underlining on and off |
| S | Shadow | Toggles letter shadows on and off |
| ab | Strikethrough | Toggles the strikethrough effect on and off |
| AV | Character Spacing | Sets the amount of space between each character |
| | Text Highlight Color | Applies the displayed color to the text background or displays a palette of text background colors |
| A | Font Color | Applies the displayed color to the text or displays a palette of text colors |
| Aa | Change Case | Displays a list of cases |
| A | Grow Font | Increases the font size |
| A | Shrink Font | Decreases the font size |
| A | Clear Formatting | Removes all font formatting |

Table 2-2 summarizes the controls in the Paragraph group.

TIP

If you want to apply any paragraph formatting to a single paragraph, you don't need to first select the entire paragraph. Instead, just position the insertion point anywhere within the paragraph, then apply the formatting.

## Easier formatting

One of the secrets of PowerPoint productivity is to learn how to apply formatting quickly so you can spend more time getting your content just so. To that end, PowerPoint offers quite a few methods that enable you to apply formats quickly, as the next few sections show.

**TABLE 2-2** **PowerPoint's Paragraph Formatting Buttons**

| Button | Name | Description |
|---|---|---|
| | Bullets | Converts the current paragraph to a bullet or displays a list of bullet styles |
| | Numbering | Converts the current paragraph to a numbered list or displays a list of numbered list styles |
| | Line Spacing | Displays a list of paragraph line spacing values |
| | Text Direction | Displays a list of text orientation options |
| | Decrease Indent | Decreases the paragraph indent |
| | Increase Indent | Increases the paragraph indent |
| | Add or Remove Columns | Specifies the number of columns in which the paragraph is displayed |
| | Align Text | Displays a list of vertical alignment options |
| | Align Left | Aligns each line in the current paragraph with the left margin |
| | Center | Centers each line in the current paragraph between the margins |
| | Align Right | Aligns each line in the current paragraph with the right margin |
| | Justify | Aligns each line in the current paragraph with both margins |
| | Convert to SmartArt | Converts a bulleted list to a SmartArt diagram |

## Formatting from the keyboard

When you're entering content on a slide, knowing some common keyboard shortcuts helps so you do not have to switch over to the mouse to get your formatting chores accomplished. It's not in the same league as Word, but PowerPoint does offer a decent number of formatting shortcuts via the keyboard, as shown in Table 2-3.

## Using the Format Painter

It can take a fair amount of work to get some text or a paragraph formatted just right. That's bad enough, but things get worse if you then have to repeat the entire procedure for another selection. The more times you have to repeat a format, the less likely you are to begin the whole process in the first place.

**TABLE 2-3** **PowerPoint's Formatting Keyboard Shortcuts**

| Press | To apply the following format |
|---|---|
| Ctrl+B | Bold |
| Ctrl+I | Italics |
| Ctrl+U | Underline |
| Shift+F3 | Cycle case |
| Ctrl+= | Subscript |
| Ctrl++ | Superscript |
| Ctrl+> | Grow font |
| Ctrl+] | Grow font size by one point |
| Ctrl+< | Shrink font |
| Ctrl+[ | Shrink font size by one point |
| Ctrl+Shift+F | Display the Font dialog box with font selected |
| Ctrl+L | Align left |
| Ctrl+E | Center |
| Ctrl+R | Align right |
| Ctrl+J | Justify |
| Ctrl+Shift+C | Copy formatting from selection |
| Ctrl+Shift+V | Paste formatting to selection |
| Ctrl+Space or Ctrl+Shift+Z | Clear character formatting |

Fortunately, PowerPoint offers the Format Painter tool that can remove almost all the drudgery from applying the same formatting to multiple selections. Here are the steps to follow to use Format Painter to apply existing formatting to another section:



1. **Position the insertion point within the text or paragraph that has the formatting you want to copy.**

2. **On the Home tab, in the Clipboard group, click Format Painter (shown in the margin).**
3. **Click the text or paragraph that you want to receive the formatting.**

   PowerPoint transfers the formatting from the selected text to the new text.

Where Format Painter really shines is applying formatting to multiple sections of text. Here are the steps:

1. **Position the insertion point within the text or paragraph that has the formatting you want to copy.**

2. **On the Home tab, in the Clipboard group, double-click Format Painter (shown in the margin).**
3. **Click the text or paragraph that you want to receive the formatting.**

   PowerPoint transfers the formatting from the selected text to the new text and leaves the Format Painter button activated.

4. **Repeat Step 3 for each of the other areas that you want to format.**
5. **When you're done, click the Format Painter button to deactivate it.**

## Replacing fonts

An important design guideline is to use typefaces consistently throughout your presentation. Sometimes, however, typefaces can become inconsistent. For example, you might insert some slides from another presentation that use a different font; you might collaborate on a presentation and the other person might use some other typeface; or you might start using Verdana or Helvetica having forgotten that you were previously using Arial.

Whatever the reason, going through the entire presentation and replacing the wrong fonts is a real productivity killer. Fortunately, you can avoid this drudgery by using PowerPoint's Replace Font feature. Here's how it works:

1. **On the Home tab, in the Editing group, drop-down the Replace list and then click Replace Fonts.**

   The Replace Font dialog box appears, as shown in Figure 2-8.

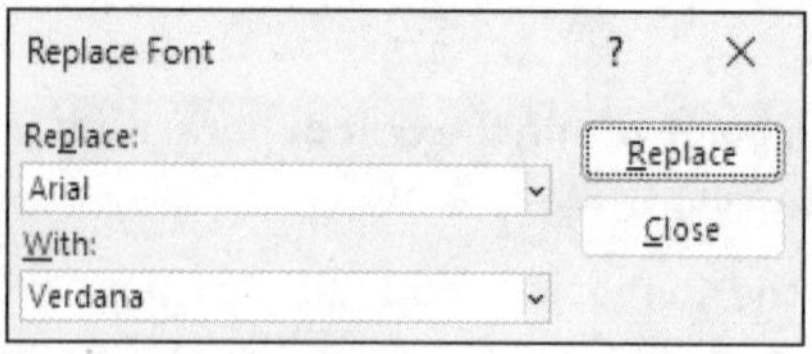


**FIGURE 2-8:** Use the Replace Font dialog box to replace all instances of one typeface with another.

2. **Use the Replace list to click the typeface you want to replace.**
3. **Use the With list to click the typeface to use as the replacement.**

4. **Click Replace.**
5. **If you have other typefaces you want to replace, follow Steps 2 through 4 for each one.**
6. **Click Close.**

## Creating advanced text shadows

The Shadow button (shown in the margin) in the Home tab's Font group creates a basic text shadow, which may be all you need. However, if you want your text to really stand out — which, after all, is the purpose of shadowed text — then you need to use PowerPoint's advanced shadow settings, which are part of its WordArt text effects.

Six effects are available in all — Shadow, Reflection, Glow, Bevel, 3-D Rotation, and Transform — and you access them by selecting text, displaying the Shape Format contextual tab then, in the WordArt Styles group, click Text Effects (shown in the margin).

Here are the steps to follow to create an advanced shadow effect:

1. **Select the text you want to format.**
2. **On the Shape Format contextual tab, in the WordArt Styles group, click Text Effects (shown in the margin) and then click Shadow.**

   PowerPoint displays a gallery of shadow effects.
3. **If the effect you want appears in the gallery, click it and skip the rest of these steps.**

   Otherwise, click Shadow Options to display the Format Shape task pane with the Text Options tab displayed, the Text Effects subtab selected, and the Shadow section opened, as shown in Figure 2-9.
4. **Use the Presets list to select the basic shadow style you want to start with.**
5. **Use the following controls to configure the shadow effect:**
   - *Color:* Sets the color of the shadow. Shades of gray are the best choices for shadows. If you want to use another color, be sure to use one that is lighter than the color of the original text.
   - *Transparency:* Specifies how much of the slide background appears through the shadow (where 0% means no background appears, and 100% means no shadow appears).

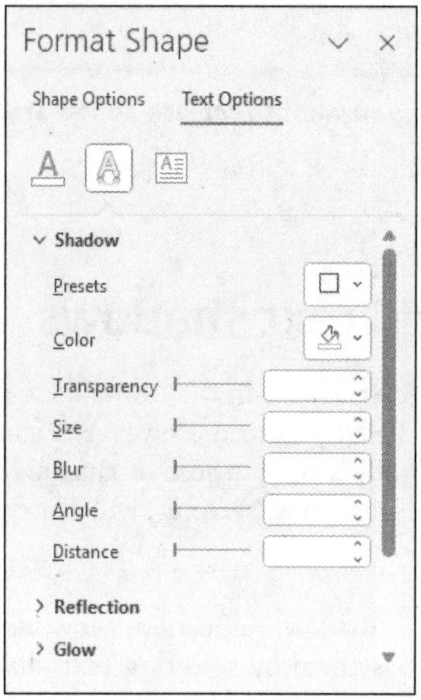


**FIGURE 2-9:** In the Format Shape task pane, use the Shadow section of the Text Effects subtab to create an advanced text shadow.

- *Size:* Sets the size of the shadow relative to the existing text (where 100% means the shadow text is the same size as the original text).
- *Blur:* Specifies the amount of blur applied to the shadow edges.
- *Angle:* Sets the shadow angle, in degrees, relative to the original text. The angle is measured clockwise. For example, a 45-degree angle means the shadow runs down and to the right, a 90-degree angle is straight down, and so on.
- *Distance:* Specifies the distance, in points, that the shadow lies from the original text.

6. **Click Close (X) to close the Format Shape pane.**

# Formatting Tips and Techniques

By its nature, PowerPoint needs to be a cross between a word-processing program and a graphics program. So, although PowerPoint's text features are not as good as Word's and its graphics features don't rival those found in high-end packages such as Photoshop, the sum of its text and graphics features results in a powerful combination. To help you take advantage of that power, the next few sections offer a few useful tips and techniques for creating and formatting text, graphics, and other objects.

## Selecting slide objects

Before you can mess around with one or more objects on a slide, you first need to select them. Here are the basic techniques to use:

- To select a single slide object, click it.
- To select multiple slide objects, click the first one you want in your selection, hold down Shift, and then click each of the other objects you want in the selection. If you select an object accidentally, keep the Shift key pressed and click the object again to deselect it.
- To select multiple slide objects in the same vicinity, use the mouse to drag a rectangular area around each object you want to select.
- To select all the objects on the slide, press Ctrl+A.

REMEMBER

When you select a slide object, PowerPoint displays a contextual tab with formatting commands related to that object. The name of the contextual tab always contains the word Format, but the full name depends on the type of object selected: Shape Format, Picture Format, Graphics Format, and so on.

## Using drawing guides to position objects

One of the little things that differentiates a solid presentation design from an amateur one is the proper alignment of objects on each slide. For example, if you have two or three shapes or icons running along the bottom of a slide, this arrangement looks best when the bottom edges of each image are aligned.

Unfortunately, aligning edges is not always easy, particularly if your mouse skills aren't that great. One way to work around this problem is to take advantage of PowerPoint's Align commands, which you can view by selecting the objects you want to align and then, on the Format contextual tab that appears, click Align (shown in the margin). This displays a list that includes the following commands:

- **Align Left:** Aligns the objects on the left edges of their frames.
- **Align Center:** Aligns the objects on the horizontal center of their frames.
- **Align Right:** Aligns the objects on the right edges of their frames.
- **Align Top:** Aligns the objects on the top edges of their frames.
- **Align Middle:** Aligns the objects on the vertical middle of their frames.
- **Align Bottom:** Aligns the objects on the bottom edges of their frames.

- **Distribute Horizontally:** Aligns the objects so that they're evenly spaced horizontally.
- **Distribute Vertically:** Aligns the objects so that they're evenly spaced vertically.

These commands work well, but PowerPoint offers an alternative method that is often even faster: the drawing guides. These guides are dashed lines — one vertical and one horizontal — that display over the slide area. When you click and drag an object near one of these guidelines, PowerPoint snaps the object to the line. This feature makes quickly aligning a few objects an easy task.

To set up the drawing guides, follow these steps:

1. **Right-click an empty section of a slide and then click Grid and Guides.**

   PowerPoint displays the Grid and Guides dialog box.

2. **Select the Display Drawing Guides on Screen check box.**

   While you're here, make sure the Display Smart Guides When Shapes Are Aligned check box is selected. With this feature enabled, as you drag an object near another, PowerPoint displays two horizontal lines when the two shapes are aligned vertically, or two vertical lines when the two shapes are aligned horizontally.

3. **Click OK.**

   PowerPoint displays the drawing guides.

4. **Click and drag the guides to position them where you want.**
5. **To add another guide, hold down Ctrl and then click and drag an existing guide.**

   To delete one of these extra guides, click and drag it off any edge of the current slide.

TIP

You can also toggle the drawing guides on and off by pressing Alt+F9.

## Nudging an object

The drawing guides and the smart guides are great for aligning objects. However, there are times when you want to arrange objects in some way other than aligning them along their edges. You can do this most quickly by clicking and dragging the objects with your mouse, but that's not the most accurate method. If you need precise positioning of an object, PowerPoint offers two methods:

» Press the left, right, up, or down arrow keys. Each time you press one of these keys, PowerPoint nudges the object in the arrow's direction by 0.083 inches ($\frac{1}{12}$ of an inch).

TIP

The number of inches to which PowerPoint nudges an object when you press an arrow key is called the *grid spacing*. To change it, right-click an empty section of the slide, click Grid and Guides to display the Grid and Guides dialog box, use the Spacing list to type or select the grid spacing you want to use (or use the Spacing spin box to set a custom spacing value), and then click OK.

» Hold down Ctrl and press the left, right, up, or down arrow keys. Each time you do this, PowerPoint nudges the object in the arrow's direction by one pixel.

## Recoloring a picture

One common problem that often comes up when putting together a presentation is that a clip art or other picture has just the right image for your presentation, but the colors clash with the existing colors in your presentation. PowerPoint enables you to work around this kind of problem by changing one or more of the picture's colors to match your presentation. This is called the Recolor feature and you follow these steps to use it:

1. **Click the picture to select it.**
2. **On the Picture Format contextual tab, in the Adjust group, click Color.**

   PowerPoint displays a gallery of color variations.
3. **Click the effect you want to use to recolor the picture.**

   PowerPoint applies the recoloring to the selected picture.

## Compressing pictures to reduce presentation size

If you use lots of graphics in your presentation, you can easily end up with a presentation file that's tens or even hundreds of megabytes in size. That may not matter if you have lots of disk space and won't be sharing your presentation. However, if you plan on putting the presentation on the web, emailing the presentation file, or sharing the presentation over a network, then the smaller the file size the better.

PowerPoint has a Compress Pictures feature that you can use to knock a presentation down to size. The following steps show you how to use this feature:

1. **Click the image you want to compress.**

2. **On the Picture Format contextual tab, in the Adjust group, click Compress Pictures (shown in the margin).**

   PowerPoint displays the Compress Pictures dialog box.

3. **In the Resolution section, select the target output resolution you prefer: HD (330 ppi), Print (220 ppi), Web (150 ppi), or Email (96 ppi).**

   In each case, the resolution is measured in *pixels per inch* (*ppi*), which tells you how dense the pixels are packed together in the image. Higher ppi values produce images of higher quality and greater size; lower ppi values generate images of lower quality and smaller size.

4. **Click OK.**

   PowerPoint compresses the presentation images.

## Repeating a shape at evenly spaced intervals

One easy way to build an interesting image from scratch is to draw a shape and then repeat the shape several times, with each new copy of the shape offset by some amount. For example, instead of using a line to separate one part of a slide from another, you could use a series of small circles or some other shape. Unfortunately, this task is difficult to do by hand because getting the offsets identical for every shape is hard when you are using the mouse to drag the shapes into position.

Fortunately, PowerPoint provides an extremely easy alternative method that always gets the offsets exactly right. Here are the steps to follow:

1. **Create and position the original shape.**

   TIP

   Rather than clicking a shape (on the Insert menu, in the Illustrations group, click Shapes and then click the shape you want) and then drawing the tool on your slide, PowerPoint offers a faster way to get a default shape: Hold down Ctrl as you click the shape. PowerPoint adds a default shape in the center of the slide. You can then move, size, and format the shape as needed.

2. **Click the original shape to select it.**

3. **Press Ctrl+D.**

   PowerPoint creates a copy of the original shape.

4. **Drag and/or nudge the copy until it's offset from the original by the amount you want.**

5. **Press Ctrl+D again.**

   PowerPoint creates another copy of the shape and offsets the copy by the same amount that you specified in step 4.

6. **Repeat Step 5 until you've created all the shapes you need.**

## Forcing shapes and text to get along

If you want to display a shape such as an oval or rectangle with text inside, you don't need a separate text box. Instead, draw your shape and then type the text. PowerPoint automatically centers the text within the shape. If the text you type is wider than the shape, PowerPoint automatically wraps the text onto a new line within the shape.

So far so good, but shapes and text don't always work together so easily. If you continue typing, eventually your text will spill over the borders of the shape, which is not an attractive look. To prevent this situation, PowerPoint gives you two choices:

» **Expand the shape to accommodate the text:** In this case, PowerPoint automatically increases the boundaries of the shape to ensure the text fits completely inside it. Right-click the shape and then click Format Shape to open the Format Shape task pane. Display the Text Options tab, click the Textbox subtab (shown in the margin), and then select the Resize Shape to Fit Text option.

» **Shrink the text to fit inside the existing shape:** In this case, PowerPoint leaves the shape as is and reduces the font size to make the text fit inside the shape. Right-click the shape and then click Format Shape to open the Format Shape task pane. Display the Text Options tab, click the Textbox subtab, and then select the Shrink Text on Overflow option.

TIP

Another way to fit more text inside a shape is by reducing the margins that surround the text. Right-click the shape and then click Format Shape to open the Format Shape task pane. Display the Text Options tab, click the Textbox subtab, and then specify new values in the Left, Right, Top, and Bottom spin boxes.

### Specifying the default formatting for a shape

If you find yourself constantly applying the same fills, line or arrow styles, colors, or effects to a specific shape, you can set that formatting as the default for the shape. Follow these steps:

1. **Add the shape and format it with the options you want to use as the default.**
2. **Right-click the shape.**
3. **Click Set as Default Shape.**

   PowerPoint will now apply the formatting to each new shape.

## Slide Formatting Best Practices

I've shown in this chapter that PowerPoint has a fistful of tools and features for tweaking the formatting of your slides. Like any program with a large number of options, the temptation is to try them all to get a feel for what PowerPoint is capable of. However, *trying* the formatting features is one thing, but actually *using* all of them is quite another. If you lay on the formatting too thick, you run the risk of hiding the slide content under too many layers of fonts, colors, images, and effects.

To help you avoid that all-too-common fate, here are a few formatting considerations to keep in mind when working on your slides:

- **When in doubt, opt for simplicity.** The most effective presentations are almost always the simplest ones. This doesn't mean that your slides must be dull, plain affairs. There's nothing wrong with formatting, and a judicious use of fonts, colors, effects, and particularly images can greatly enhance your message. Simplicity in presentations just means that whatever formatting you add must not interfere with your content and must not overwhelm the senses of your audience.
- **Remember your message.** Before even opening a new PowerPoint file, think about the overall message that you want your presentation to convey. Then, when you format each slide, ask yourself whether each formatting tweak has an enhancing or, at worst, a neutral effect on your message. If the answer is "No," don't add the formatting.

- **Think about your audience.** Some designs suit certain audiences better than others. For example, if you're presenting to children, a bright, happy design with kid-friendly images will work, whereas a plain, text-heavy design will induce naptime. By contrast, if you're presenting to managers or the board of directors, you need a design that gets straight to the point and has little in the way of frills.
- **Think about your company's image.** I mean this in two ways. First and most obviously, if your company has a set color scheme or style, your presentation should reflect that. Second, if your company is known as one that's staid or bold, serious or fun, your presentation shouldn't conflict with that image.
- **Be consistent across all your slides.** This means using the same typeface and type size for all your titles, using consistent bullet styles throughout the presentation, using the same or similar background images on all slides, and having the company logo in the same place on each slide. The more consistent you are, the less work your audience has interpreting the formatting for each slide, so the more they can concentrate on your content.
- **However, don't use the same layout on every slide.** To help keep your audience interested, vary the layout from slide to slide.
- **Choose an easily read typeface.** For the typeface, use sans serif fonts (the ones without the little "feet" at the letter tips), such as Arial, Comic Sans MS, Microsoft Sans Serif, and Verdana. These typefaces are easier to read than serif typefaces (the ones with the little "feet") and are a much better choice than fancy, decorative typefaces, which are very difficult to decipher from a distance.
- **Use an appropriate type size for best readability.** For the type size of your slide content, don't use anything smaller than the default sizes. In particular, never use a type size smaller than 20 points because it will be nearly impossible for your audience to read. If your audience is older, or if you're presenting in a large hall, consider using type sizes even larger than the PowerPoint defaults.

  REMEMBER

  PowerPoint uses a 44-point type for the slide titles, 32-point type for top-level items, 28-point type for second-level items, 24-point type for third-level items, and 20-point type for fourth- and fifth-level items.
- **Make color choices to enhance clarity.** For maximum readability, be sure to have a significant contrast between the text color and the slide's background color. Dark text on a light background is usually best. Also, don't use a background image unless it's relatively faint and the text stands out well against it.

- **Use landscape slide orientation.** Always use the landscape (horizontal) orientation for your slides. The portrait (vertical) orientation reduces the available width, so each bullet point takes up more vertical space, which makes the slides look overcrowded.
- **Edit your slide content.** Finally, and perhaps most importantly, design your slides so that they don't include too much information. Each slide should have at most four or five main points; anything more than that and you're guaranteed to lose your audience by making them work too hard.

IN THIS CHAPTER

» Creating attractive transitions between slides

» Applying animation effects to text, images, bullets, and charts

» The dos and don'ts of effective animations

» Adding interactivity with hyperlinks and action buttons

Chapter 3

# Creating Dynamic Presentations

In Book 4, Chapter 2, I mentioned that your goal when formatting your slides should be to achieve a balance between eye candy and content. That is, although you need to tweak your slide fonts, colors, and effects to a certain extent to add visual interest, you don't want to go so far that your message gets buried under an avalanche of formatting.

The same idea applies to the slide show as a whole, particularly if you want to add some dynamism to the presentation with slide transitions and object animations. These are fine additions to any presentation, but going overboard and therefore overwhelming your content is ridiculously easy to do. This chapter gives you the details and techniques that can help you create the dynamic and interesting slide shows that audiences crave, but always remember that the message is the most important thing in any presentation.

# Animation Guidelines

Before you learn how to apply slide transitions and object animations, it's worth taking a bit of time now to run through a few guidelines for making the best use of slide show animations:

- **Use effects to enhance, not detract from, your content.** The goal of any animation should always be to enhance your presentation, either to emphasize a slide object or to keep up your audience's interest. Resist the temptation to add effects just because you think they're cool or fun because chances are that most of your audience won't see them that way.
- **Remember that transitions can be useful.** Using some sort of effect to transition from one slide to the next is a good idea because it adds visual interest, gives the audience a short breather, and helps you control the pacing of your presentation.
- **Remember that transitions can be distracting.** A slide transition is only as useful as it is unremarkable. If everybody leaves your presentation thinking "Nice transitions!", then you have a problem because they *should* be thinking about your message. Simple transitions such as fades, wipes, and dissolves add interest but don't get in the way. On the other hand, if you have objects flying in from all corners of the screen, your content will seem like a letdown.
- **When it comes to transitions and animations, variety is *not* the spice of life.** Avoid the temptation to use many different transitions and animations in a single presentation. Just as slide text looks awful if you use too many fonts, your presentations will look amateurish if you use too many animated effects.
- **Keep up the pace.** For transitions, use the Fast setting to ensure that the transition from one slide to another never takes more than a few seconds. Also, avoid running multiple object animations at the same time because it can take an awfully long time for the effect to finish, and audiences *never* like having their time wasted on such things.
- **Match your animations to your audience.** If you are presenting to sales and marketing types, your entire presentation will be a bit on the flashy side, so you can probably get away with more elaborate animations; in a no-nonsense presentation to board members, animations and transitions should be as simple as possible.

# Setting Up a Slide Transition

A *slide transition* is a special effect that displays the next slide in the presentation. For example, in a *fade* transition, the next slide gradually materializes, while in a *blinds* transition the next slide appears with an effect similar to opening Venetian blinds. PowerPoint has nearly 50 different slide transitions, and for each one you can control the transition speed, the sound effect that goes along with the transition, and the trigger for the transition (a mouse click or a time interval).

Here are the steps to follow to apply a slide transition to one or more slides:

1. **If you only want to apply the transition to certain slides, select the slides you want to work with.**

2. **On the Transitions tab, in the Transition to this Slide group, click the Transition Effects button (shown in the margin).**

   PowerPoint unfurls the Transition Effects gallery, as shown in Figure 3-1.

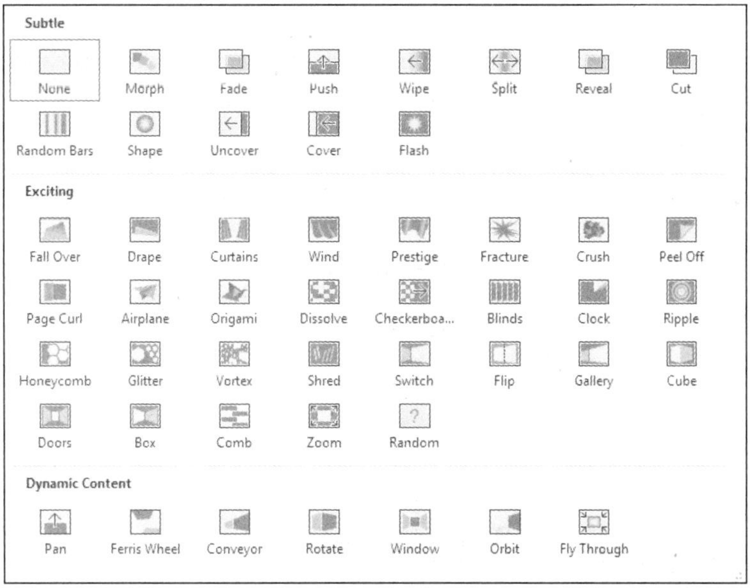


**FIGURE 3-1:** Use the Transition Effects gallery to apply a built-in slide transition to the selected slides.

3. **Click the transition effect you want.**

   PowerPoint previews the transition effect on the current slide.

4. **In the Timing group of the Transitions tab, use the Sound list to click the sound that you want to play during the transition.**

   There are four special cases:

   - *[No Sound]:* Click this item to run the transition without a sound effect.
   - *[Stop Previous Sound]:* If the previous slide transition used a long-running sound effect, click this item to stop that sound.
   - *Other Sound:* Click this item to display the Add Audio dialog box. Click the sound file you want to use and then click OK.
   - *Loop Until Next Sound:* Click this command to repeat the chosen sound effect until the next effect begins.

     WARNING

     There are very few circumstances where the Loop Until Next Sound option is appropriate, so exercise some caution with this command. Unless your looped sound is a pleasant snippet of music (that loops smoothly) or an effect that requires some time — such as a ticking clock — the constant noise will just distract or annoy your audience.

5. **Use the Duration spin box to set the length, in seconds, of the transition.**
6. **Choose the method by which you want to move to the next slide:**
   - *On Mouse Click:* Select this check box to advance the slide when you click the mouse.
   - *Automatically After:* Select this check box to advance the slide after the minutes and/or seconds that you specify in the spin box.
7. **If you want to use the transition for all the slides in the presentation, click Apply to All. (If you don't click this option, the transition applies to only the selected slides.)**

PowerPoint indicates that a slide has an applied transition by adding a star icon with "speed lines" below the slide number in the Slides list.

# Defining Slide Animations

Many years ago, someone defined *fritterware* as any software program that offered so many options and settings that you could fritter away hours at a time tweaking and playing with the program. PowerPoint's animation features certainly put it into the fritterware category because whiling away entire afternoons playing with transitions, entrance effects, motion paths, and other animation features isn't hard. So, consider yourself warned that the information in the next few sections might have adverse effects on your schedule.

While a slide transition is a visual (and sometimes auditory) effect that plays during the switch from one slide to another, an *animation* is a visual effect applied to a specific slide element, such as the slide title, bullet text, or chart data markers.

PowerPoint comes with a number of predefined animations for different types of objects. How you apply these effects depends on the object:

- **Slide title, picture, clip art, or table:** The animation effect applies to the entire object.
- **Bulleted list:** You can apply the animation effect to the entire list or by first-level paragraphs.
- **Chart:** You can apply the animation effect to individual chart elements, such as a series or category.
- **SmartArt:** You can apply the animation effect to individual SmartArt graphic elements, such as a level or a branch.

## Animating a slide title, picture, clip art, or table

Here are the steps to follow to apply an animation effect to a slide title, picture, clip art, or table:

1. **Click the object you want to animate.**

2. **On the Animations tab, in the Animation group, click the Animation Styles button (shown in the margin).**

   PowerPoint drops down the Animation Styles gallery, shown in Figure 3-2.

3. **Click the type of animation you want.**

   PowerPoint applies the animation and runs a preview on the slide object.

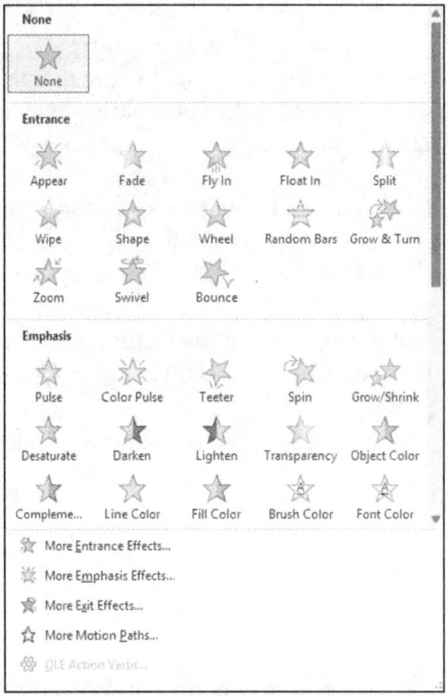


**FIGURE 3-2:** Use the Animation Styles gallery to apply a predefined animation effect to the selected object.

## Animating a bulleted list

Here are the steps to follow to apply an animation effect to a bulleted list:

1. **Click the bulleted list.**

2. **On the Animations tab, in the Animation group, click the Animation Styles button (shown in the margin).**

   PowerPoint unlocks the Animation Styles gallery.

3. **Click the type of animation you want.**

   PowerPoint applies the animation and runs a preview on the bulleted list.

4. **On the Animations tab, in the Animation group, click Effect Options and then click one of the following:**
   - *As One Object:* Applies the animation effect to the entire list
   - *All At Once:* Applies the animation effect separately to each item in the list but runs the effect on the entire list at once.

- *By Paragraph:* Applies the animation effect to the first-level bullets in sequence. For example, suppose your slide has two first-level bullets, each with three second-level bullets. This option begins by displaying the first of the slide's first-level bullets along with its second-level bullets; it then displays the second of the slide's first-level bullets along with its second-level bullets.

## Animating a chart by series or category

If you use charts in your presentations, you can animate the components of the chart, such as the series or the categories. Here are the steps to follow to apply an animation effect to a chart:

1. **Click the chart.**
2. **On the Animations tab, in the Animation group, click the Animation Styles button (shown in the margin).**

   PowerPoint sends in the Animation Styles gallery.

3. **Click the type of animation you want.**

   PowerPoint applies the animation and runs a preview on the chart.

4. **On the Animations tab, in the Animation group, click Effect Options and then click one of the following:**
   - *As one object:* Applies the effect to the entire chart.
   - *By Series:* Applies the effect to each data series, one series at a time. For example, if you have a bar chart that shows quarterly sales figures by region, you could display the bars one quarter at a time.
   - *By Category:* Applies the effect to each data category, one category at a time. For example, if you have a bar chart that shows quarterly sales figures by region, you could display the bars one region at a time.
   - *By Element in Series:* Applies the effect to each data marker in each series, one marker at a time. For example, if you have a bar chart that shows quarterly sales figures by region, you could display the bars for each region one quarter at a time.
   - *By Element in Category:* Applies the effect to each data marker in each category, one marker at a time. For example, if you have a bar chart that shows quarterly sales figures by region, you could display the bars for each quarter one region at a time.

## Animating a SmartArt graphic

If you use a SmartArt diagram to show a process, hierarchy, cycle, or relationship, you can animate the diagram's levels or shapes in various ways. Here are the steps to follow to apply an animation effect to a SmartArt diagram:

1. **Click the Smart Art diagram.**

2. **On the Animations tab, in the Animation group, click the Animation Styles button (shown in the margin).**

   PowerPoint asks the Animation Styles gallery to put in an appearance.

3. **Click the type of animation you want.**

   PowerPoint applies the animation and runs a preview on the SmartArt diagram.

4. **On the Animations tab, in the Animation group, click Effect Options and then click one of the following (note that not all options are available for all types of Smart Art):**

   - *As one object:* Applies the effect to the entire diagram.
   - *All at once:* Applies the effect to all the shapes in the diagram at once, with slightly different timings for each shape.
   - *One by one:* Applies the effect to each shape in the diagram, one shape at a time.
   - *By branch one by one:* Applies the effect to each branch in the hierarchy, one shape at a time.
   - *By level at once:* Applies the effect to each level in the diagram, one level at a time.
   - *By level one by one:* Applies the effect to each level in the diagram, one shape at a time.

## Customizing an animation

Applying a predefined animation might give you exactly the effect you want. If so, great! But once you apply an animation, PowerPoint offers a few options that enable you to customize various aspects of the animation. Click the slide object to which you applied the animation, then consider the following controls on the Animations tab:

- **Effect Options:** Displays a menu that offers several options for modifying the animation effect. The available options depend on the animation and on the slide object you're animating.
- **Add Animation:** Opens a gallery of animations that you can use to apply multiple animations to the selected object.
- **Animation Pane:** Displays the Animation Pane, which you can use to adjust the starting point and duration of an animation, reorder the animations if you're using more than one, and perform other animation-related tasks.
- **Start:** Sets the trigger for the animation:
  - *On Click:* Starts the animation when you click your mouse.
  - *With Previous:* Starts the animation at the same time as the previous animation.
  - *After Previous:* Starts the animation when the previous animation finishes.
- **Duration:** Sets the length of the animation, in seconds.
- **Delay:** Sets the time, in seconds, before the animation begins after it has been triggered.
- **Preview:** Runs the animation.

# Setting Up Hyperlinks and Action Buttons

Most slide shows are linear affairs, meaning that you begin with the first slide and then display the rest of the slides in order until the slide show is complete. As I discuss in Book 4, Chapter 4, PowerPoint makes linear presentations easy to navigate by enabling you to progress to the next slide or animation just by clicking.

However, not all presentations proceed from slide to slide:

- Someone in the audience may ask you to return to the previous slide because they missed something or has a question.
- You may need to return to a previously viewed slide for further discussion or clarification.
- You may need to jump ahead to a slide later in the presentation if you realize that the next few slides are not relevant or useful to your audience.
- You may want to start the presentation over again without leaving the slide show.

- You may want to temporarily exit the presentation by running a program, displaying a web page, or starting another PowerPoint presentation.

Each slide show offers controls that enable you to perform many of these tasks, but they often require navigating shortcut menus, which is not very attractive in the middle of a presentation. An alternative is to set up objects in your presentation that perform specific actions when you click them. PowerPoint offers four types of these navigation objects:

- **Link (also called a hyperlink):** This is a word or phrase in a text box, SmartArt graphic, picture, or image that acts just like a link in a web page or document. That is, when you click the link, the linked web page or document appears.
- **Action object:** This is a picture, shape, image, or other object that performs a specified action when you click it. Actions include navigating to a slide, running a program, running a macro, or linking to a web page or document.
- **Media object:** This is a video file, music file, or sound file that plays when you click it.
- **Action button:** This is a special shape object with an icon that represents its function. For example, there are action buttons for Previous, Next, Beginning, and End. In most cases, PowerPoint defines a default action for the button. For example, the default action for the Previous button is to navigate to the previous slide in the presentation.

The next few sections take you through the methods you use to add these types of objects to your presentation.

REMEMBER

The biggest drawback to links and action buttons is that PowerPoint offers no easy way to insert them into all your slides. You can add a link or other action object to a master slide, but the link or action doesn't work when you run the slide show.

## Adding a text link

PowerPoint gives you two methods for constructing a link:

- Using PowerPoint's AutoCorrect feature to create links automatically
- Specifying the link information by hand

The next two sections discuss each method.

## Creating a link using AutoCorrect

The easiest way to create a link in PowerPoint is to type the address into your document. As long as the address is a network path or a web address, PowerPoint will automatically convert the text into a link.

If this method doesn't work for you, you need to turn on this feature by following these steps:

1. **Choose File ⇨ Options.**

   The PowerPoint Options dialog box shows up.

2. **Click Proofing.**
3. **Click AutoCorrect Options.**

   The AutoCorrect dialog box materializes.

4. **Display the AutoFormat As You Type tab.**
5. **Select the Internet and Network Paths with Hyperlinks check box.**
6. **Click OK to return to the PowerPoint Options dialog box.**
7. **Click OK.**

## Creating a link by hand

For more control over your links, you need to use PowerPoint's Link command, which lets you create links to web pages, documents, slides, and even email addresses. Here are the steps to follow:

1. **Either select the text or image that you want to use for the link or select the position in the document where you want the link to appear.**

   If you don't select anything beforehand, the link text will be the link address.

2. **On the Insert tab, in the Links group, click the Link button (shown in the margin).**

   The Insert Hyperlink dialog box strolls in, as shown in Figure 3-3.

   You can also display the Insert Hyperlink dialog box by pressing Ctrl+K or by right-clicking the selected text and then click Link.

3. **If you didn't select text in advance, use the Text to Display text box to specify the link text.**

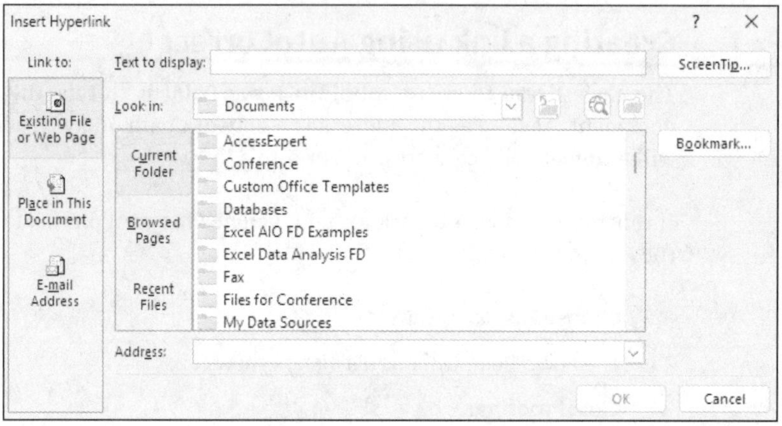


**FIGURE 3-3:** Use the Insert Hyperlink dialog box to create your link by hand.

4. **Click the type of link you want to create:**

   - *Existing File or Web Page:* Use the Address text box to type the location of the file or web page you want to link to. You can enter any of the following: a web address; a path to another PowerPoint document; a path to a document from a different application on your hard drive; or a network path to a document on your company's intranet.
   - *Place in This Document:* Click a relative slide object — such as First Slide or Next Slide — or a specific slide in the current presentation.
   - *Email Address:* Fill in the Email Address (or click an address in the Recently Used EMail Addresses list) and Subject text boxes.

5. **To define a ScreenTip for the link, click ScreenTip, type the tip in the ScreenTip Text box, and click OK.**

   REMEMBER

   The ScreenTip is the pop-up message that PowerPoint displays when you place the mouse pointer over the link. If you don't specify a ScreenTip, PowerPoint uses the link address as the default ScreenTip.

6. **Click OK.**

   PowerPoint inserts the link.

## Working with links

If you right-click a link, the shortcut menu that appears contains the following commands:

- **Edit Link:** Displays the Edit Hyperlink dialog box, which is identical to the Add Hyperlink dialog box.

- **Open Link:** Opens the linked document.
- **Copy Link:** Copies the link to the Clipboard.
- **Remove Link:** Deletes the link.

## Assigning an action to an object

To assign an action to an object such as a picture, icon, or chart, follow these steps:

1. **Click the object you want to work with.**
2. **On the Insert tab, in the Links group, click Action.**

   PowerPoint sends along the Action Settings dialog box.

3. **Select the Hyperlink To option.**

   PowerPoint enables the associated list box, as shown in Figure 3-4.

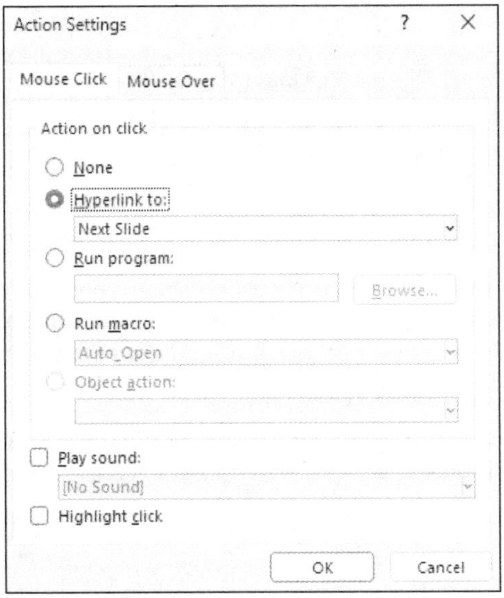


**FIGURE 3-4:** Use the Action Settings dialog box to assign an action to an object.

REMEMBER

If you want to link to another program, instead, select the Run Program option and then click Browse. Use the Select a Program to Run dialog box to click the program's executable file, click OK, and then skip to Step 5.

4. **Use the Hyperlink To list to choose the action you want PowerPoint to perform when you click the object:**
   - *Next Slide:* Navigates to the next slide in the current presentation.
   - *Previous Slide:* Navigates to the previous slide in the current presentation.
   - *First Slide:* Navigates to the first slide in the current presentation.
   - *Last Slide:* Navigates to the last slide in the current presentation.
   - *Last Slide Viewed:* Navigates to the last slide that you viewed in the current presentation.
   - *End Show:* Navigates to the next slide in the current presentation.
   - *Custom Show:* Links to a custom slide show. Use the Link to Custom Show dialog box to click the custom slide show and then click OK. (I talk about custom slide shows in Book 4, Chapter 4.)
   - *Slide:* Navigates to a specific slide in the current presentation. Use the Hyperlink to Slide dialog box to click the slide, and then click OK.
   - *URL:* Links to a web page. Use the Hyperlink to URL dialog box to type the page address, and then click OK. (Note, too, that the URL text box is preloaded with the text `http://`. Change that to `https://`.)
   - *Other PowerPoint presentation:* Links to a slide in a different PowerPoint presentation file. Use the Hyperlink to Other PowerPoint File dialog box to click the file, and then click OK. In the Hyperlink to Slide dialog box, click the slide you want to link to in the other presentation, and then click OK.
   - *Other File:* Links to another file. Use the Hyperlink to Other File dialog box to click the file, and then click OK.
5. **(Optional) If you want PowerPoint to play a sound when you click the object, select the Play Sound check box, and then use the associated list to choose the sound you want to hear.**
6. **(Optional) If you want PowerPoint to display a highlight around the object when you click it, select the Highlight Click check box.**
7. **Click OK.**

## Inserting a media object

If you insert a media file such as a video, music clip, or sound file into a slide, PowerPoint gives you two choices for playing the media:

- **Automatically:** PowerPoint plays the media automatically when you navigate to the slide.
- **When Clicked:** PowerPoint plays the media when you click it.

The latter is an action setting. If you originally set up the media to play automatically, you can change to the action setting by following these steps:

1. **Click the media object you want to work with.**
2. **On the Insert tab, in the Links group, click Action.**

   PowerPoint conjures the Action Settings dialog box.
3. **Select the Object Action option.**
4. **In the Object Action list, click Play.**
5. **Click OK.**

REMEMBER

Another way to set up media to play when clicked is to select the media placeholder and then, on the Playback tab, in the Video Options or Audio Options group, use the Start list to choose When Clicked On item.

## Inserting an action button

PowerPoint's action buttons are shapes with predefined icons. Most of the action buttons also come with default actions, so they're often the easiest way to set up actions in a presentation. Table 3-1 lists the 12 PowerPoint action buttons that you can insert into your slides.

**TABLE 3-1 PowerPoint's Action Buttons**

| Button | Name | Default Action |
|---|---|---|
|  | Previous | Hyperlink To⇨Previous Slide |
|  | Next | Hyperlink To⇨Next Slide |
|  | First | Hyperlink To⇨First Slide |
|  | Last | Hyperlink To⇨Last Slide |
|  | Home | Hyperlink To⇨First Slide |

*(continued)*

**TABLE 4-3** ***(continued)***

| Button | Name | Default Action |
|---|---|---|
|  | Information | None |
|  | Return | Hyperlink To⇨Last Slide Viewed |
|  | Movie | None |
|  | Document | Run program |
|  | Sound | Play Sound⇨Applause |
|  | Help | None |
|  | Blank | None |

To insert an action button, follow these steps:

1. **Select the slide into which you want to insert the action button.**
2. **On the Insert tab, in the Illustrations group, click Shapes.**

   PowerPoint unrolls the Shapes gallery.
3. **Scroll down to the Action Buttons section and then click the action button you want to use.**
4. **Click and drag a rectangle on the slide to draw the shape. When you release the mouse button, PowerPoint displays the Action Settings dialog box.**
5. **Specify the action you want associated with the button.**
6. **Click OK.**

## Using a link to run a macro

Like Word, Excel, Outlook, and Access, PowerPoint supports Visual Basic for Applications (VBA) macros. A *macro* is a script that contains one or more statements that perform some action (such as adding a slide or changing PowerPoint settings). If you want to set up an object to perform a specialized task when clicked, you need to encapsulate that task in a PowerPoint macro and then set up the object to run the macro.

For this to work, you must save your file as a macro-enabled presentation:

1. **Choose File⇨Save As.**

   The Save As window appears.

2. **Click More Options**

   The Save As dialog box thunders in.

3. **In the Save as type list, click PowerPoint Macro-Enabled Presentation.**
4. **Type a filename and select a location for the file.**
5. **Click Save.**

REMEMBER

If PowerPoint displays a Security Alert bar telling you that macros are disabled, click Enable Content, select the Enable this Content option, and then click OK.

Once you've done that and added your macro to the presentation, you can set up the object to run your macro by following these steps:

1. **Click the object you want to work with.**
2. **On the Insert tab, in the Links group, click Action.**

   PowerPoint unveils the Action Settings dialog box.

3. **Select the Run Macro option.**

   If the Run Macro option is disabled, it means you don't have any VBA macros in your presentation, so you'd better get on that.

4. **Use the Run Macro list to choose the name of the macro you want to run.**
5. **If you want PowerPoint to play a sound when you click the object, select the Play Sound check box, and then use the Play Sound list to click the sound you want to hear.**
6. **If you want PowerPoint to display a highlight around the object when you click it, select the Highlight Click check box to activate it.**
7. **Click OK.**

IN THIS CHAPTER

» Rehearsing your slide show

» Recording narration for a single slide or an entire presentation

» Forging a custom slide show

» Starting and navigating a slide show

# Chapter 4
# Delivering a Presentation

Once you have your slides set up with content (refer to Book 4, Chapter 1), formatting (Book 4, Chapter 2), and transitions and animations (Book 4, Chapter 3), you're ready to start thinking about the slide show that you'll be presenting. There isn't a ton that you have to do to prepare for the slide show, but there are a few tasks you should consider. These include rehearsing the timings of each slide, adding narration to individual slides or even the entire presentation, and putting together a custom slide show.

With all that done, you're almost ready to deliver your presentation. I say "almost" because it would be a good idea to take a few minutes now to familiarize yourself with PowerPoint's tools for navigating and annotating a slide show.

You explore all these PowerPoint techniques and more in this chapter. Let the show begin!

# Rehearsing Slide Timings

PowerPoint has a little-used feature that can greatly improve your presentations. The feature is called Rehearse Timings and the idea behind it is simple: You run through ("rehearse") your presentation, and while you do this PowerPoint keeps track of the amount of time you spend on each slide. This is useful for two reasons:

- » If you have only so much time to present the slide show, Rehearse Timings lets you know if your overall presentation runs too long or too short.
- » After the rehearsal, you can examine the time spent on each slide. If you have consecutive slides where you spend a short amount of time on each, consider consolidating two or more of the slides into a single slide. Conversely, if you have some slides where you spend a great deal of time, consider splitting each one into two or more slides to avoid overwhelming your audience.

PowerPoint also gives you a third reason to use Rehearse Timings: You can save the resulting timings and use them to run a slide show automatically. You find out how later in this chapter (check out "Setting up an automatic slide show").

Open the presentation you want to rehearse, collect any notes or props you'll use during the presentation, and then follow these steps to rehearse your slide timings:

1. **On the Slide Show tab, in the Set Up group, click Rehearse Timings.**

   PowerPoint starts the slide show and displays the Recording toolbar, as shown in Figure 4-1.

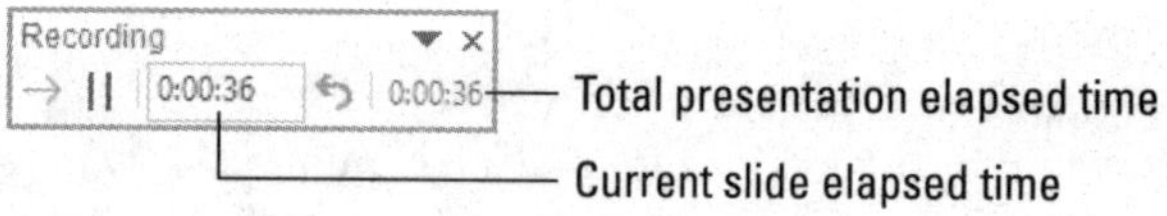


**FIGURE 4-1:** The Recording toolbar appears while you rehearse your slide timings.

2. **Present the slide exactly as you would during the actual presentation.**
3. **When you're ready, click Next (shown in the margin) to move on to the next slide.**

   Note that PowerPoint resets the current slide elapsed time value to 0:00:00.

   REMEMBER

   If you mess up or get stuck on a slide, you have a couple of choices:

   - You can start the timing of that slide over again by clicking the Repeat button (shown in the margin).

- If you just need a second or two to gather your thoughts, click Pause (shown in the margin), instead.

4. **Repeat steps 2 and 3 for the entire presentation.**

   When the presentation is done, PowerPoint displays the total presentation time and asks whether you want to save the slide timings.

5. **To save the timings, click Yes; otherwise, click No.**

If you elected to save the timings, PowerPoint displays your presentation in the Slide Sorter view (on the View tab, in the Presentation Views group, click Slide Sorter), which shows the timing of each slide, as shown in Figure 4-2.



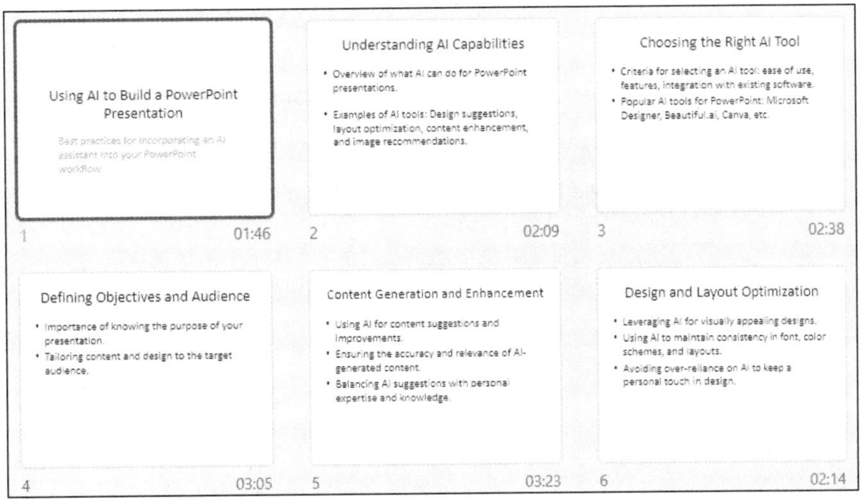


**FIGURE 4-2:** After you rehearse your slide timings, the Slide Sorter view shows the results for each slide.

# Adding Voice and Video

Part of the appeal of a good presentation is that the audience feels like they're being told a story. Some words or images appear on a screen, but a person presents the underlying narrative for those words and images. There's something about a live human voice explicating some idea or process that's appealing on a deep level.

However, there might be times when you require a recorded voice for some or all of a presentation:

» You might have a slide that consists of a recorded greeting from the CEO or someone else at your company.

» You might have several slides where an expert does the presenting. If that person can't be at your presentation, you need to record their material.

» You might be setting up an automatic presentation and so require recorded narration for the entire show.

PowerPoint can handle all these situations by enabling you to record voice and/or video for one or more slides or for the entire presentation.

## Recording narration for a slide

If you just need narration for a single slide, PowerPoint enables you to embed a narration sound object in the slide. With your microphone plugged in and at the ready, here are the steps to follow:

1. **Select the slide in which you want to embed the narration.**
2. **On the Record tab, in the Record group, click Audio.**

   PowerPoint displays the Record Sound dialog box, shown in Figure 4-3.

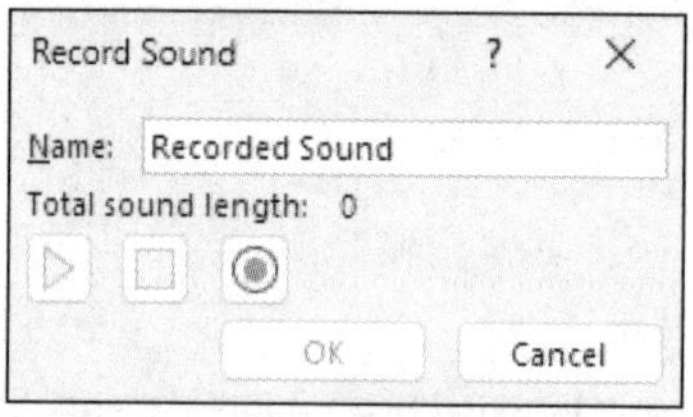


**FIGURE 4-3:** Use the Record Sound dialog box to record narration for a single slide.

3. **Type a Name for the recorded sound.**

4. **Click the Record button (shown in the margin).**
5. **Run through your narration.**

6. **Click the Stop button (shown in the margin).**

7. **If you want to listen to your recording, click Play (shown in the margin).**
8. **Click OK.**

   PowerPoint adds a sound icon to the slide.

To control when the narration sound file plays, click the sound icon and then, on the Playback tab, in the Audio Options group, use the Start list to select one of the following:

- **In Click Sequence:** The narration begins based on the order of clicks defined in the slide, where that order also includes clicks configured to trigger any animations defined on the slide. You can use the Animation Pane (choose Animations ➪ Animation Pane) to mess around with the slide's click sequence (refer to Book 4, Chapter 3).
- **Automatically:** The narration begins as soon as you display the slide.
- **When Clicked On:** The narration begins when you click the sound icon.



## Making a cameo appearance

Depending on the venue and the size of the audience, it can be easy for people to forget about the person presenting the slide show. Sometimes that's exactly what you want because you want folks focusing on your content instead of on you. But if you prefer to keep yourself in the picture, so to speak, you can do that literally by inserting on a slide a *cameo*, which is a live video feed from your device camera. The cameo usually appears as a circle in the lower-right corner of the slide, although you're free to alter the style and position of the cameo.

Follow these steps to insert and customize a cameo:

1. **If you want the cameo to appear on a particular slide, navigate to that slide.**
2. **On the Record tab, in the Camera group, click Cameo and then click one of the following:**
   - *This Slide:* Inserts the cameo on the slide you displayed in Step 1.
   - *All Slides:* Inserts the cameo on every slide in your presentation.

   PowerPoint inserts the cameo on the slide (or slides) and displays the Camera Format contextual tab, as shown in Figure 4-4.
3. **Click and drag the cameo object to the position on the slide that you prefer.**
4. **On the Camera Format tab, in the Camera group, click the Preview button to toggle the video feed.**
5. **On the Camera Format tab, use the tools in the Camera Styles group to customize the cameo object as you see fit.**

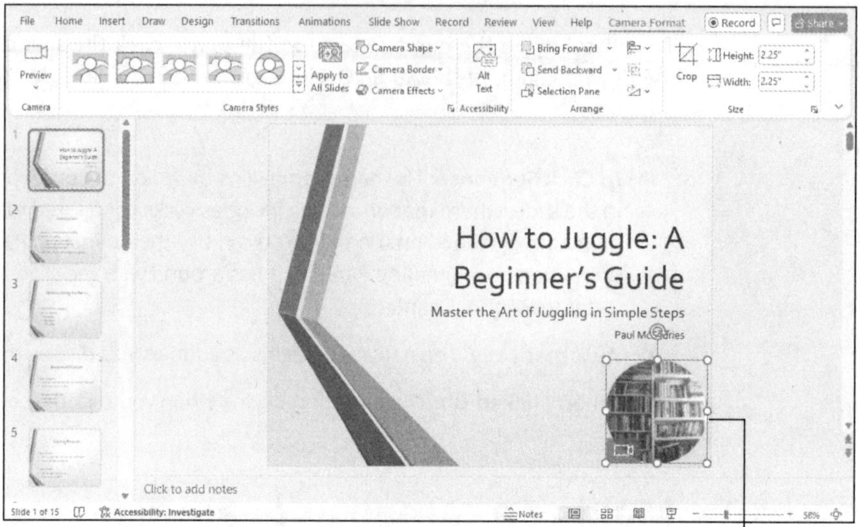
How to Juggle: A Beginner's Guide
Master the Art of Juggling in Simple Steps
Click to add notes
Live video feed

**FIGURE 4-4:** A cameo inserted on a slide.

## Recording a presentation

In some situations, you might want to record your entire presentation and then either play back that recording instead of presenting the slide show live or export the recording to a video file that you can share. Your recording includes the following:

- **Narration:** An audio recording of your voice as you present each slide.
- **Cameo:** A video recording of you as seen through your device camera.
- **Annotations:** Markings you add to each slide using the pen, highlighter, or laser pointer tools.
- **Slide timings:** The duration you spend on each slide.

Collect your notes, comb your hair, pull up your microphone, and then follow these steps to record a presentation:

1. **If you want your recording to begin at a particular slide, navigate to that slide.**
2. **On the Record tab, in the Record group, click one of the following:**
   - *From Current Slide:* Starts the recording from the slide you displayed in Step 1.
   - *From Beginning:* Starts the recording from the first slide.

   PowerPoint displays the recording screen, shown in Figure 4-5.

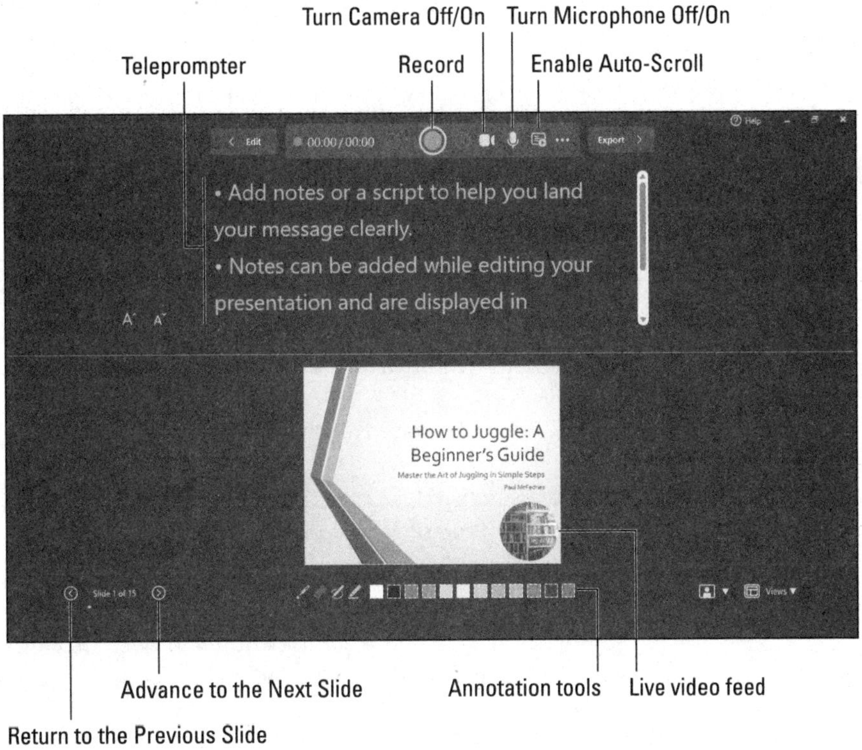


**FIGURE 4-5:** Use the recording screen to record your presentation.

3. **Use the Teleprompter section to write your script or notes for each slide.**

   Use the Advance to Next Slide button to navigate the slides. When you're done, click Return to the Previous Slide until you're back to the slide where you want to start the recording.

   TIP

   During the recording, you can press Ctrl+Down arrow to scroll the Teleprompter text down (or, if need be, press Ctrl+Up arrow to scroll the text up). If you prefer the Teleprompter text to scroll automatically, click the Enable Auto-Scroll button (pointed out in Figure 4-5). In the toolbar that appears, use the Scroll Speed slider to set the speed of the scrolling, then click Play.

   REMEMBER

   If you don't want to use the Teleprompter, you can hide it by clicking Views and then click either Presenter View (which shows the current slide, the next slide, and the current slide's notes) or Slide View (which shows just the current slide).

4. **You can toggle voice and video as follows:**

   - *Voice:* Click Turn Microphone Off/On to toggle the microphone. You can also press Ctrl+M.
   - *Video:* Click Turn Camera Off/On to toggle the camera. You can also press Ctrl+K.

5. **Click Record (or press R).**

   After a brief countdown, PowerPoint starts the recording.

6. **Run through your notes or script for the slide.**
7. **(Optional) Use the annotation tools to mark up the slide.**

   I talk about PowerPoint's slide annotation tools a bit later, in the "Annotating slides" section.

8. **When you're done with the current slide, click Advance to Next Slide.**
9. **Repeat Steps 6 through 8 for each slide in the presentation.**

When you're done, you have two choices:

- Click Edit (and then click Exit when PowerPoint asks you to confirm) to return to the regular PowerPoint window.
- Click Export to export your recording to an MP4 video file. (If you return to PowerPoint and then decide you want to export the recording after all, on the Record tab, in the Export group, click Export to Video.) In the Export to Video screen that appears, type a name and select a location for the file. If you're ambitious, you can click Customize Export to choose the video quality, what you want to include, and whether you want to override the slide timings. Click Create Video to make it so.

REMEMBER

If you make a mess of your recording on a particular slide or on your entire presentation, or just think you'd like to try it once more — this time *with feeling* — then you need to first wipe out the existing recording. On the Record tab, in the Edit group, click Clear Recording and then click either Clear Recording on Current Slide or Clear Recordings on All Slides.

# Creating a Custom Slide Show

Having two or more versions of a presentation is common. Here are some examples:

- You might have a short version and a long version of a presentation.
- You might want to omit certain slides depending on whether you're presenting to managers, salespeople, or engineers.

» You might have "internal" and "external" versions; that is, you might have one version for people who work at your company and a different version for people from outside the company.

You could accommodate these different scenarios by creating copies of the presentation and then removing or reordering the slides as appropriate. However, that sure sounds like a lot of work, it wastes disk space, and it's annoying when one slide changes and you have to make the same change in every version of the presentation that includes the slide.



A much better solution is to define one or more custom slide shows, which is a customized list of slides and the order you want them to appear. Follow these steps to create a custom slide show based on the slides in the current presentation:

1. **On the Slide Show tab, in the Start Slide Show group, click Custom Slide Show, and then click Custom Shows.**

   PowerPoint introduces you to the Custom Shows dialog box.

2. **Click New.**

   PowerPoint offers the Define Custom Show dialog box for your consideration.

3. **In the Slide Show Name text box, type a name for the custom slide show.**
4. **Use the Slides In Presentation list to select the check box beside each slide you want to include in the custom show.**
5. **Click Add.**

   PowerPoint adds the slides to the Slides In Custom Show list, as shown in Figure 4-6.

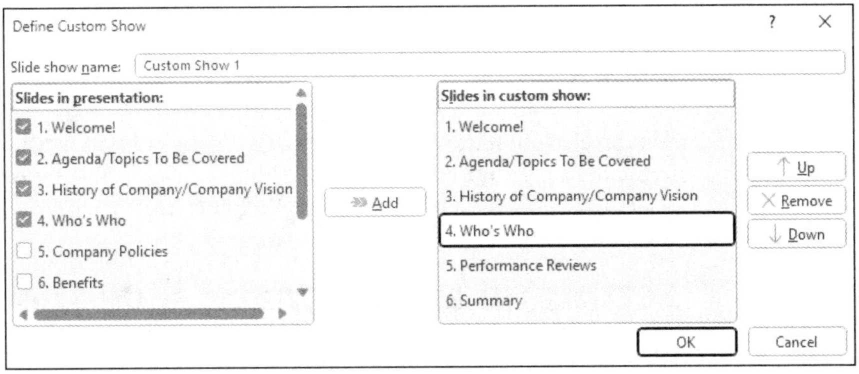


**FIGURE 4-6:** Use the Define Custom Show dialog box to specify which slides you want in the custom show and the order in which those slides appear.

6. **To reorder the slides, click a slide in the Slides In Custom Show list and then click either Up or Down.**
7. **To delete a slide, click the slide in the Slides In Custom Show list and then click Remove.**
8. **Click OK.**

   PowerPoint returns you to the Custom Shows dialog box and displays the name of your custom slide show in the Custom Shows list.
9. **Click Close.**

# Running a Slide Show

With your slides laid out, the text perfected, and the formatting just right, you're now ready to present your slide show. The next few sections show you how to start, navigate, and annotate a slide show.

## Setting some slide show options

If you rehearsed the slide show timings as described earlier in this chapter, before starting the slide show you need to decide whether you want PowerPoint to advance the slides automatically based on those timings. If you do want the slides to advance automatically then, on the Slide Show tab, in the Set Up group, select the Use Timings check box. (Even if you use automatic slide timings, you can still control the slide show manually, as described later in the "Navigating slides" section.)

Similarly, if you've recorded narration and you want to hear that narration during the show then, on the Slide Show tab, in the Set Up group, select the Play Narration check box.

TIP

You can also opt to run your slide show with any animation. On the Slide Show tab, in the Set Up group, click Set Up Slide Show to open the Set Up Show dialog box. Select the Show Without Animation check box, then click OK.

## Setting up an automatic slide show

What do you do if you want to show a presentation at a trade show, fair, or other public event, but you cannot have a person presenting the slide show? Similarly, what do you do if you want to send a presentation to a customer or prospect and you cannot be there to go through the slide show yourself?

In these and similar situations, you can configure the presentation to run automatically. Here are the steps to follow:

1. **Record the presentation.**

   Refer to "Recording a presentation," earlier in this chapter, to learn how this works.

2. **On the Slide Show tab, in the Set Up group, click Set Up Slide Show.**

   PowerPoint displays the Set Up Show dialog box.

3. **Select the Browsed at a Kiosk option.**

   PowerPoint selects (and disables) the Loop Continuously Until 'Esc' check box.

4. **In the Advance Slides section, double-check that the Using Timings, If Present option is selected.**

5. **Click OK.**



## Starting the slide show

PowerPoint gives you several ways to launch a slide show:

- » To start the slide show from the first slide, choose Slide Show ➪ From Beginning (or press F5).

- » To start the slide show from a particular slide, navigate to that slide and then choose Slide Show ➪ From Current Slide, or click the Slide Show icon (shown in the margin) in the PowerPoint status bar (or press Shift+F5).
- » To start a custom slide show, choose Slide Show ➪ Custom Slide Show, and then click the show you want in the list that appears.

## Navigating slides

With your slide show running, you now need to navigate from one slide to the next. By far the easiest way to do so is to use the mouse, and PowerPoint gives you two choices:

- » Click the mouse to advance to the next slide.
- » Turn the mouse wheel toward you to advance to the next slide.

If you have animations defined in a slide, clicking the mouse or turning the wheel toward you also initiates those animations in the order you defined.

For other navigation techniques and slide show controls, right-click the slide show to view a shortcut menu with the following commands:

- **Next:** Moves to the next slide in the presentation.
- **Previous:** Moves to the previous slide in the presentation. (You can also turn the mouse wheel forward.)

  TIP

  To return to the first slide, hold down the left mouse button and press the right mouse button for about two seconds, until you hear a beep.

- **Last Viewed:** Jumps to the last slide displayed in the presentation. (This will be different from the previous slide if you used a hyperlink or action button to jump from a different slide.)
- **See All Slides:** Displays thumbnails of the slides in the presentation. Click the slide you want to present next.
- **Magnify Slide:** Displays a rectangle that indicates the area to be magnified. Position the rectangle over the area you want to expand, then click to magnify it. Press Esc to return to the regular magnification.
- **Custom Show:** Displays a menu of the custom slide shows defined for the current presentation. Click the custom show that you want to view.
- **Show Presenter View:** Switches to Presenter view, which shows the current slide, a thumbnail of the next slide, and the current slide's notes.
- **Screen:** Displays a menu with commands to change the slide show screen. To blank the screen temporarily, click Black Screen or White Screen. (Click the screen again to return to the presentation.) Click Show Taskbar to get access to the Windows taskbar.
- **Pointer Options:** Displays a list of annotation tools. I discuss these tools later in the "Annotating slides" section.
- **Start Subtitles:** Displays subtitles for your slide show narration.
- **Subtitle Settings:** Enables you to configure subtitles.
- **Camera:** Displays a list of cameras connected to your device, which enables you to switch cameras if you're using cameos in your presentation.
- **Keep Slides Updated:** When activated, updates the presentation slides based on changes made to the PowerPoint file, even while you're presenting. This is handy if you have presentation coauthors making changes to the PowerPoint file behind the scenes.
- **Pause:** Temporarily stops the slide show. To restart the presentation, right-click the screen and then click Resume.
- **End Show:** Stops the slide show.

## Navigating the slide show from the keyboard

PowerPoint gives you quite a few keyboard alternatives for navigating and controlling the slide show. These are useful alternatives because displaying the shortcut menu can look unprofessional, and pressing a key or key combination is also usually faster. Table 4-1 lists the available keyboard shortcuts for navigating a slide show.



**TABLE 4-1** Slide Show Keyboard Navigation Techniques

| Press | To |
|---|---|
| N | Advance to the next slide or animation (you can also press the spacebar, Enter, right arrow, down arrow, or Page Down keys) |
| P | Return to the previous slide or animation (you can also press Backspace, left arrow, up arrow, or Page Up keys) |
| *n*, Enter | Navigate to slide number *n* |
| S | Pause/resume an automatic slide show (you can also press plus [+]) |
| B | Toggle black screen on and off (you can also press period [.]) |
| W | Toggle white screen on and off (you can also press comma [,]) |
| Ctrl+A | Change the mouse pointer to an arrow (for example, if the mouse is currently displayed as a pen or eraser) |
| Ctrl+T | Display the Windows taskbar |
| Esc | End the slide show (you can also press hyphen [-] or Ctrl+Break) |

## Annotating slides

While you are running a slide show, you might need to augment a slide by adding comments, markup, diagrams, or other annotations. PowerPoint enables you to do this by changing the regular mouse pointer into a pen. You get a choice of several different pen types (ballpoint, felt tip, and highlighter) and you can choose from a large palette of colors for each pen type.

To switch to and use the pen pointer, follow these steps:

1. **Right-click the slide show, click Pointer Options, and then click a pen type: Pen or Highlighter.**

   If you only want to point things out rather than annotating them, choose the Laser Pointer option rather than a pen.

2. **Right-click the slide show, click Pointer Options, click Ink Color, and then click the color you prefer.**
3. **Click and drag on the slide to make your annotations.**
4. **To erase pen marks, right-click the slide show, click Pointer Options, and then click one of the following:**
   - *Eraser:* Changes the pointer to an eraser. You then click the ink you want to remove.
   - *Erase All Ink on Slide:* Removes all ink annotations from the current slide.
5. **When you're done annotating, right-click the slide show, click Pointer Options, click Arrow Options, then click Automatic.**

You can also use the keyboard techniques in Table 4-2 when annotating a slide.

**TABLE 4-2**

## Annotation Keyboard Techniques

| Press | To |
|---|---|
| E | Erase all annotations in the current slide |
| Ctrl+P | Change the mouse pointer to a pen |
| Ctrl+E | Change the mouse pointer to an eraser |

# 5

# Outlook 365

# Contents at a Glance

IN THIS CHAPTER

- » Setting up and configuring email accounts
- » Using hidden Outlook options and features to send messages
- » Dealing with incoming messages with useful tricks and shortcuts for
- » Organizing your Inbox with powerful rules

Chapter 1

# Sending and Receiving Email

It wasn't all that long ago that people were mourning the demise of letter writing. The evil twin influences of reduced leisure time and overexposure to television were usually cited as the reasons for the passing of a once-popular pastime. Now, however, letter writing is making a big comeback. That's not to say that you'll see mail carriers' mailbags groaning under the weight of epistles, postcards, and *billets-doux* as folks try to catch up on their correspondence. No, the real force behind this resurgence of the written word is email. In corporations and colleges, at home and on the road, people who would never even consider putting pen to paper are exchanging electronic missives and messages in staggering numbers.

Office 365 users can get in on this email frenzy as well using Outlook's email features. This chapter gets you up to speed with Outlook's email capabilities by getting your accounts configured and then showing you around the app. You figure out how to compose messages, check for new mail, read received messages, reply to these messages, and do lots more. Outlook is a powerful program with many useful features and options hidden in obscure corners of the interface. This chapter also shines light on those murky corners to bring out the best in Outlook and help you make your email chores faster and more efficient.

# Setting Up Your Accounts

You can't do anything with Outlook until you've configured the app with one or more accounts. The next couple of sections take you through this vital and necessary task.

## Setting up your initial account

When you launch Outlook 365 for the first time, the program examines your Microsoft account for an email address, which it then displays in a dialog box, as shown in Figure 1-1.

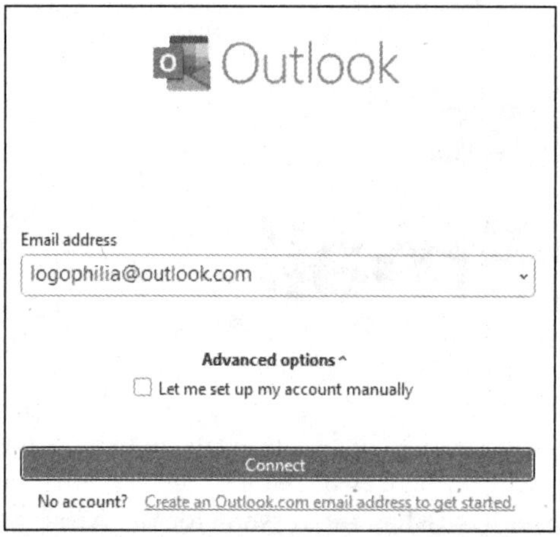


**FIGURE 1-1:** Your first Outlook task is to set up an email account.

At this point, you have three choices:

- If the address displayed in the Email Address list is correct, you don't need to do anything.
- If the address displayed in the Email Address list isn't the one you want to configure, use the list to choose the correct address.
- If the address list doesn't include the address you want to configure, type the correct address in the text box.

Outlook can configure a variety of email accounts automatically, including accounts from Microsoft 365, `Outlook.com`, Hotmail, Gmail, iCloud, and Yahoo.

If you're configuring any of these accounts, click Connect to make it so. To get through these dialog boxes, you need your email address and your email account password.

For other accounts, particularly accounts that use the IMAP (Internet Message Access Protocol) and POP (Post Office Protocol) types, you'll usually need to set up the account by hand, which you can do by clicking Advanced Options, selecting the Let Me Set Up My Account Manually check box, and then clicking Connect. If you elect to input your mail server settings manually, then you also need the following information:

- For an IMAP or POP email account, you need the domain names of the incoming and outgoing mail servers, the ports those servers use, as well as your email account username (this is often your email address). See your email provider's support pages to learn if there is any other info you need.
- For a Microsoft Exchange account, you need the name of the Exchange Server and the name of your Exchange mailbox.

## Adding more accounts

Most people use Outlook with a single account, but if you have multiple accounts you need throughout the day, Outlook is up to the challenge.

To add another account, you have a couple of ways to get started:

- At the bottom of the Navigation pane (refer to the next section and to Figure 1-2, in particular, to learn the Outlook window layout), click Add Account.
- Choose View ⇨ View Settings to open the Settings window, click the Accounts category on the left then, in the Email Accounts subcategory that Outlook displays by default, click Add Account.

Type or select an email address, click Continue, and then follow the screens that appear, which vary depending on the email service and the type of account.

TIP

Once you have multiple accounts configured in Outlook, you need to decide which is the *primary* account, which is the one Outlook automatically uses when you send messages (although you can change to another account before sending a message). Choose View ⇨ View Settings to open the Settings window, click the Accounts category on the left, click Manage next to the account you want to use as the primary, then click Set as Primary Account.

## Removing an account

If you add an account and later decide that you no longer need it in Outlook, follow these steps to remove it with no hard feelings:

1. **Choose View ➪ View Settings.**

   You can also click Settings (shown in the margin) in the toolbar at the top of the Outlook window.

   Outlook coughs up the Settings window.

2. **Click the Accounts category on the left.**

   Outlook displays the Email Accounts subcategory.

3. **Click Manage next to the account you want to remove.**
4. **Click Remove.**
5. **If you see the Remove Account dialog box, select either Remove From This Device or Remove From All Devices, then click OK.**

# Getting Acquainted with Outlook

You're now free to start firing off missives, notes, memos, tirades, harangues, and any other kind of digital correspondence that strikes your fancy. And, of course, you'll also want to read any incoming messages that others have sent your way.

Before you get that far, however, you should take a few moments to acquaint yourself with the Outlook interface as it appears when you're using the Mail app.

## Surveying the Outlook window

You can begin your tour by taking a closer look at the Outlook window so that you can find your way around. Figure 1-2 points out a few of the major landmarks.

Here's a summary of what's pointed out in Figure 1-2:

- **App bar:** Displays icons that represent the apps that are available with Outlook. The icon for the Mail app appears at the top of the app bar and is shown in the margin. To display the names of the apps, choose View ➪ View Settings, click the General category, click the Appearance subcategory, then click the Show App Names switch to On.

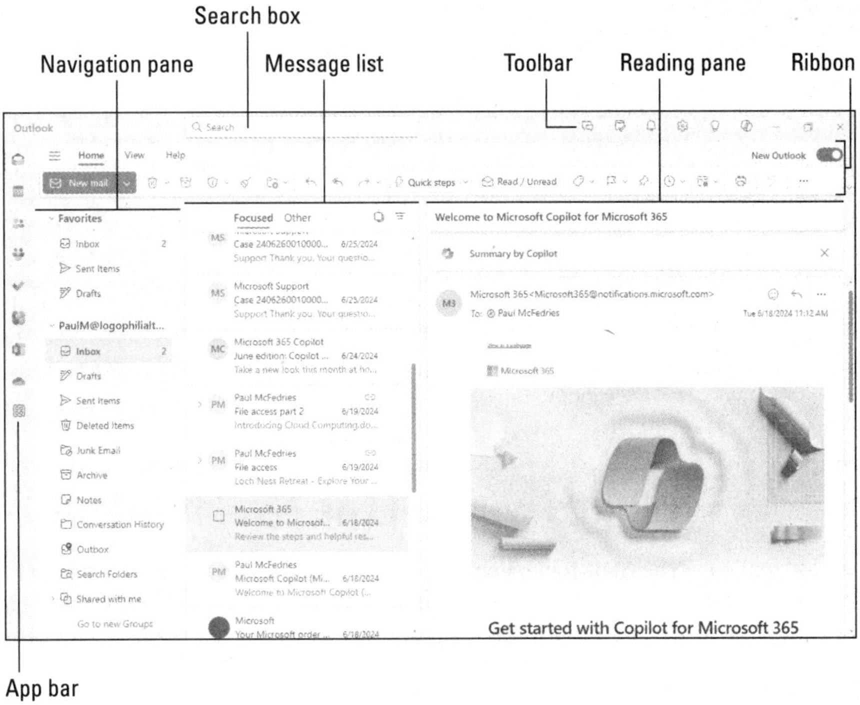


**FIGURE 1-2:** Some of the main sights of the Outlook window.

- **Navigation pane:** In the Mail app, displays the folders associated with your email account (or accounts), which is why this feature is also called the *folder pane*. The Navigation pane is divided into a Favorites section at the top followed by a section for each email account. Click the Show/Hide Navigation Pane icon (shown in the margin) to toggle the Navigation pane.

  If you never use the Favorites section of the Navigation pane, you should hide it to give your other folders more room to breathe. Choose View ➪ Layout ➪ Folder Pane ➪ Hide Favorites, or hover the mouse pointer over the Favorites section heading, click the Favorites icon (shown in the margin) that appears, then click Hide Favorites.

- **Search box:** Enables you to search Outlook for the item you want to read or work with.
- **Toolbar:** Contains icons for several Outlook features, most notably Settings and Copilot. This feature is sometimes called the *command bar.*
- **Ribbon:** Contains buttons for accessing all the Outlook features. The configuration of the Ribbon changes depending on the task you're performing in Outlook.

By default, Outlook displays the simplified Ribbon, which is cleaner than the classic Ribbon, adapts to the task at hand, and is customizable. If you prefer the classic (non-adaptable, non-customizable) Ribbon, either choose View ➪ Layout ➪ Ribbon ➪ Classic Ribbon, or click the Ribbon Display Options button (shown in the margin) that appears to the right of the Ribbon, then click Classic Ribbon.

- **Message list:** Displays the email messages you've received.
- **Reading pane:** Displays the contents of the message that's currently selected in the message list. If you prefer the Reading pane to appear below the message list (which gives more horizontal room to both), choose View ➪ Layout ➪ Reading Pane ➪ Show On the Bottom.

## What's with all the Mail folders?

The Mail folders serve as storage areas for different types of messages. I'll show you how to create folders and move messages between them later in this chapter, but for now, here's a rundown of the main default folders (the names of which will vary slightly depending on the type of email account):

- **Inbox:** Holds all your incoming messages. When you start Outlook, it displays the contents of the Inbox folder by default.
- **Drafts:** Stores outgoing messages that you've saved but not yet sent.
- **Sent Items:** Keeps a copy of each message you send.
- **Deleted Items:** Holds the items (messages and other folders) you delete.
- **Junk Email:** Stores messages that Outlook's Junk Email filter has deemed to be spam.
- **Archive:** Keeps those messages that are important enough to keep, but that don't merit their own folder.
- **Outbox:** Stores messages waiting to be sent the next time you're online.

## Displaying Outlook's settings

Outlook offers quite a few settings that enable you to customize the program to suit your working style. I mention quite a few of these settings throughout this chapter, but for now here are the two methods you can use to access the settings:

- Choose View ➪ View Settings.

- Click the Settings icon (shown in the margin) in the toolbar at the top of the Outlook window.

Either way, Outlook offers up the Settings window, shown in Figure 1-3. You click a category in the left pane, a subcategory in the middle pane, then use the settings that appear in the right pane to perform your customizations. When you make one or more changes, be sure to click Save to put those changes into effect.

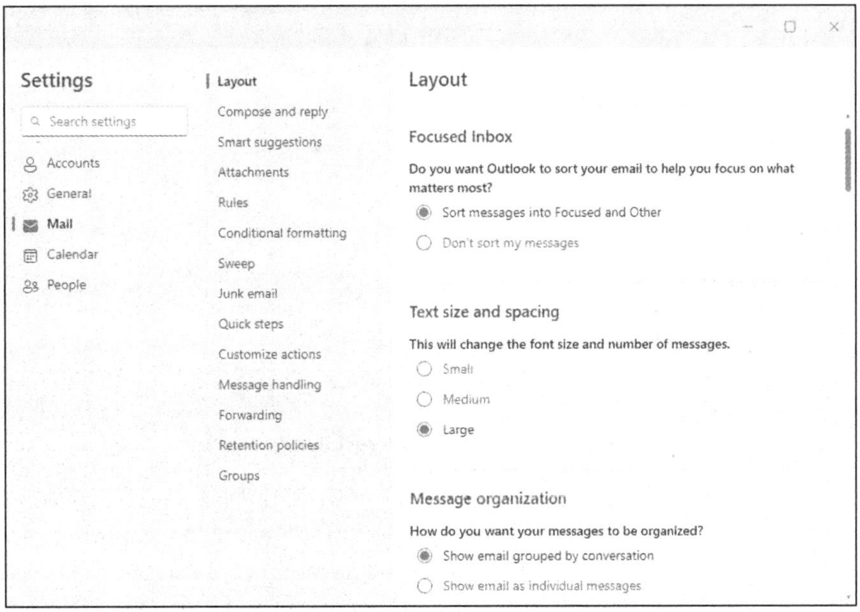


**FIGURE 1-3:** The Settings window is where you customize Outlook to suit your style.



# Shipping Out a New Message

Outlook offers many features and options for sending messages to other people. In this section, you learn the basics of composing and sending a message, and then you learn many other useful techniques that will help you to get your email-sending chores done faster and easier.

## Composing a message

Composing a message in Outlook is not all that different from composing a letter or memo in Word. You just need to add a few extra bits of information, such as your recipient's email address and a description of your message.

Follow these steps to compose and send a basic email message:

1. **Click New Mail.**

   Keyboard fans can alternatively press Ctrl+N or Ctrl+Shift+M.

   Outlook forges a new message in the Reading pane, as shown in Figure 1-4.

   If you'd prefer to open the new message in a separate window, click the Open in New Window button (shown in the margin), which appears in the upper-right corner of the Reading pane.

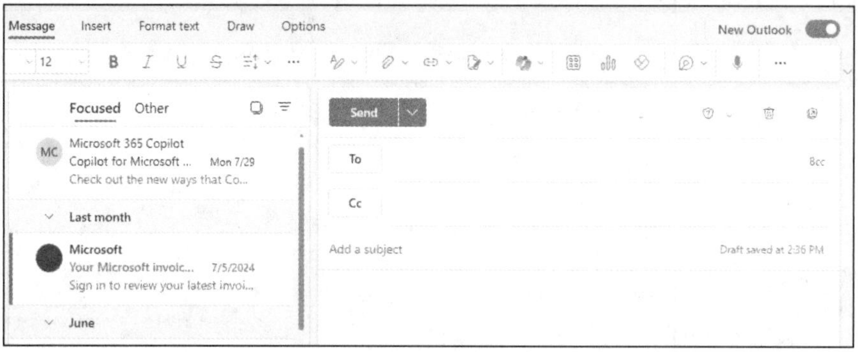


**FIGURE 1-4:** Use the message composition window to enter the email addresses of your recipients, the Subject line, and the body of the message.

2. **In the To field, type the recipient's address.**

   If you want to send the message to multiple recipients, press Enter or type a semicolon (;) or comma (,) after each address.

3. **In the Cc field, type the addresses of any recipients you want to receive copies of the message.**

   Again, separate multiple addresses by pressing Enter or by typing a semicolon or comma after each.

4. **In the Subject field, type a brief description of the message.**

   This description will appear in the Subject column of the recipient's mail client, so make sure that it accurately describes your message.

5. **Use the box below the Subject field to type your message.**

   You can use any of the formatting options found in the Ribbon's Message tab or Format Text tab.

   REMEMBER

   If you want to increase the chances that another person sees your message, you can *mention* that person in the email body by typing @ and then selecting the person's name from the list that appears. Most people have Outlook configured to generate a separate notification when they're mentioned in an email (refer to "Controlling message notifications," later in this chapter).

6. **Click Send (or press Ctrl+Enter).**

   Outlook sends your message.

## Composing a message with Copilot's help

If your Office 365 subscription includes access to the Copilot AI assistant, then Copilot is available in Outlook to help you draft your messages. To get Copilot on the job while you're composing a message, you have a couple of choices:

- When you first launch the new message, click the Draft with Copilot link that appears in the message area. (You can also press slash (/) and then click Draft with Copilot in the menu that appears.)
- Choose Message ➪ Copilot ➪ Draft with Copilot.

Outlook displays the Draft with Copilot box, as shown in Figure 1-5.

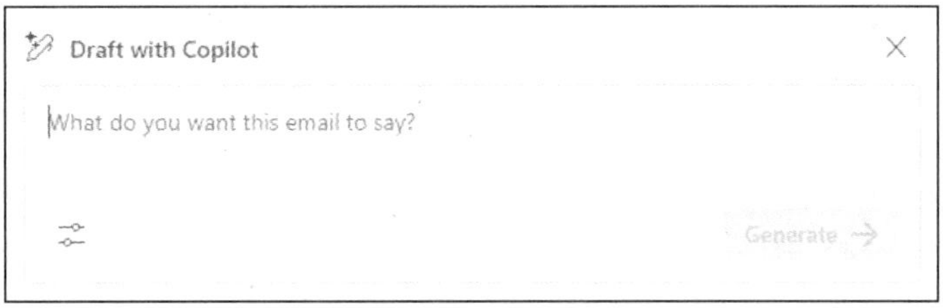


**FIGURE 1-5:** Use the Draft with Copilot box to prompt Copilot to create a draft of your message.

Now describe to Copilot what you want in your email. If you're not sure what to type, here are a few examples you can mine for ideas:

- *Write an email to congratulate the team on a successful product launch.*
- *Compose a fun message inviting people to the annual street party.*
- *Draft a diplomatic email asking our neighbor to stop letting his dog use our yard as a toilet.*
- *Write an apologetic email asking Thomas to extend the writing deadline.*

You can also click the Generation Options icon (shown in the margin) and then click a message Tone (Direct, Neutral, Casual, Formal, or Make It a Poem) as well as the message length (Short, Medium, or Long).

When you're ready, click Generate to make Copilot do its thing.

Once Copilot has written the draft, you have the following choices:

- **Keep It:** Click this button if you're happy with the draft and want to leave the text in your message.
- **Retry:** Click this button if you think Copilot can do better.
- **Anything You'd Like to Change?:** Use this text box to ask Copilot to make a change to the output.

- **Edit Prompt:** Click this icon (shown in the margin) to choose from a list of prefab refinements. Here are some examples:
  - Make it longer
  - Make it sound more formal
  - Make it a poem
- **Discard:** Click this button if the draft is a write-off and you'd prefer to start over.

REMEMBER

This is a draft that Copilot has generated for you, so at this point you should give the generated text the fine-toothed-comb treatment to look for errors and to put the text into your own voice.

## Scheduling a send

When you compose an email and click Send, Outlook dutifully ships out your message right away. However, you might want your email delayed until a certain time or even a certain day. For example, you might want a newsletter email to go out at midnight tonight. Similarly, you might prefer that a message to your team be delivered first thing Monday morning.

Whatever the reason for the delay, you can set up a message to be sent later, by following these steps:

1. **Create, address, and write your email in the usual way.**
2. **Click the arrow to the right of the Send button.**
3. **Click Schedule Send.**

   Outlook sends in the Schedule Send dialog box.

4. **If one of the two offered dates and times works for you, go ahead and click it and then ignore the rest of these steps. Otherwise, click Custom Time.**

   Outlook opens the Set Custom Date and Time dialog box, which offers a calendar and a time list box.

5. **In the calendar, select the date on which you want your message fired off.**
6. **In the list box, select or enter the time you want to send the message.**
7. **Click Send.**

   Outlook makes a note to send your message on the date and time you specified.

## Undoing a send

It's a rare emailer who hasn't experienced "post-Send" regret, which is the sinking feeling in the pit of your stomach that comes when you realize you've just posted a long lament about the sad state of your love life to the entire company.

The Outlook programmers must have experienced that regret a time or two themselves because they did something about it: They created the Undo Send feature. By default, Undo Send isn't activated, so first follow these steps to activate this welcome setting:

1. **Choose View ⇨ View Settings.**

   Outlook opens the Settings window.

2. **Click the Mail category and then click the Compose and Reply subcategory.**
3. **Scroll down to the Undo Send setting, then use the slider to set the number of seconds you want Outlook to wait before sending each message.**

   You can set a delay period of up to ten seconds.

4. **Click Save.**

Now, after you click Send, Outlook displays the Sending pop-up, shown in Figure 1-6, which stays onscreen for the number of seconds you specified in the previous steps. Crucially for those of us with overly sensitive Send trigger fingers, that pop-up includes an Undo button. Click Undo and Outlook plucks your message out of the outbox and opens it again so that you can make whatever changes you need (or toss the message in the trash). Whew!

**FIGURE 1-6:** Right after you send a message, you can change your mind by clicking Undo.

## Using the People app list to specify recipients

When you're composing a message, you can use Outlook's People app (check out Book 5, Chapter 2) to add recipients without having to type their addresses. Here are the steps to follow to use the People app to specify your recipients:

1. **In the message composition window, click the To button.**

   Outlook displays the Add Recipients dialog box.

2. **Locate the contact you want to send the message to.**

3. **Click the contact's Add as a Recipient button (shown in the margin).**
4. **Repeat Steps 2 and 3 for all the recipients you want to include in your message.**
   - *To:* Adds the recipient to the message's To field.
   - *Cc:* Adds the recipient to the Cc field.
   - *Bcc:* Adds the recipient to the Bcc field.
5. **Click Save.**

   Outlook returns you to the message composition window with the recipient(s) added.

6. **To specify the recipients that receive courtesy copies (also called carbon copies) of the message, click the Cc button and then follow Steps 2 through 5.**
7. **To specify the recipients that receive blind courtesy copies (also called blind carbon copies) of the message, click the Bcc icon to the right of the To field, click the Bcc button that now appears, and then follow Steps 2 through 5.**

REMEMBER

Bcc (blind courtesy copy) is similar to Cc, except that addresses in this field aren't displayed to the other recipients.

## Attaching a file to a message

The information you want to send to the recipient might exist in a Word document, Excel spreadsheet, or some other file. In that case, you can attach the file to your message and Outlook sends along a copy of the file when you send the message.

Here are the steps to follow to attach a file to a message:

1. **Start a new message and fill in the addresses, subject, and body.**
2. **Choose Insert ➪ Attach File ➪ Browse This Computer.**

   Outlook displays the Open dialog box.
3. **Click the file you want to attach and then click Open.**

   Outlook attaches the file to the message.

If the file resides on OneDrive, you can share a link to the file instead of attaching it. Choose Insert ➪ Attach File ➪ OneDrive to open the OneDrive file picker, select the file, then click Share Link.

## Setting message options



Before sending your message, you might want to specify a few extra options, such as specifying a different account, asking for a delivery receipt or setting the importance and sensitivity levels. You can find all of these items in the Options tab of the new message. Here is a summary of the most useful of these message options:

- **Show Bcc:** Select this check box to add a Bcc field to the message.
- **Show From:** Select this check box to add a From field to the message. This option is useful if you have Outlook set up with two or more accounts. Outlook normally uses the default account when you send a message, but you can use the From field to click the account you'd prefer to use when sending the message.
- **Set This Item as High Priority:** Sends the message with high priority, which the recipient's email app will mark accordingly (usually with a red exclamation point). Use this option when your message is important.
- **Set This Item as Low Priority:** Sends the message with low priority, which the recipient's email app will mark accordingly (usually with a downward-pointing arrow). Use this option when your message is not even remotely important.

- **Request Delivery Receipt:** Select this check box to set up the message to request an automatic reply that confirms the message was delivered to the recipient.

  WARNING

  Very few mail servers honor requests for delivery receipts.

- **Request Read Receipt:** Select this check box to set up the message to request an automatic reply that confirms the message was read by the recipient.

## Creating and inserting signatures

In email circles, a *signature* is an addendum that appears as the last few lines of a message. Its purpose is to let the people reading your email know a little more about the person who sent it. Although signatures are optional, many people use them because they can add a friendly touch to your correspondence. You can put anything you like in your signature, but most people just put their name, profession and/or title, their company name and address, other contact information (such as a cell number), and maybe a quote or two that fits in with their character.

Fortunately, you don't have to type your signature by hand in each message. Outlook has a Signatures feature that lets you define one or more signatures and then insert a signature into individual messages or into every message you send.

To create a signature, follow these steps:

1. **Choose View ⇨ View Settings.**

   Outlook escorts the Settings window onto the screen.

2. **Click the Accounts category.**
3. **Click the Signatures subcategory.**

   Outlook displays the Signatures pane.

4. **Type a name for your signature.**
5. **Use the large text area to type and format your signature.**
6. **Click Save.**
7. **To add another signature, click New Signature, then follow Steps 4 through 6 to define it.**
8. **To have Outlook add a signature to the end of every new message you compose, use the For New Messages list to click the signature you want to use.**

9. **To have Outlook add a signature to the end of every new reply and forward you compose, use the For Replies/forwards list to click the signature you want to use.**

10. **Repeat Steps 1 to 3 to set up default signatures for your other email accounts.**

11. **When you're done, click Save.**

If you elected not to set up default signatures, you can insert a signature by hand. When you're in the message composition window, choose Insert ⇨ Signature, and then click the signature you want to insert.

# Reading Incoming Mail

Of course, you won't be spending all your time firing off notes and missives to friends and colleagues. Those people will eventually start sending messages back, and you might start getting regular correspondence from mailing lists, administrators, and other members of the email community. This section shows you how to retrieve messages, read them, and use Outlook's many tools for dealing with your messages.



## Retrieving messages

For most account types — including `Outlook.com`, Gmail, iCloud, and Yahoo accounts — message retrieval happens automatically. That is, as soon as the email server receives an incoming message, it notifies Outlook and the message gets delivered to that account's Inbox right away. For other account types, particularly IMAP and POP accounts, Outlook checks periodically for new messages.

Whether your account's messages are delivered automatically or periodically, Outlook does enable you to manually check for new messages, a process that Outlook calls *syncing:*

- » On the View tab, click Sync (shown in the margin).
- » Press F9

Outlook connects to each of your accounts in turn, checks for waiting messages, and retrieves any it finds.

## Controlling message notifications

Outlook makes sure you know a message has arrived by giving you no less than three notifications:

- It plays a brief sound.
- It displays a new item in the Notifications pane.
- It displays a desktop notification in the lower-right corner of the screen that shows you the sender's name, the message subject, and the first two lines of the message. You can also use the desktop notification to run various tasks on the message, as shown in Figure 1-7.

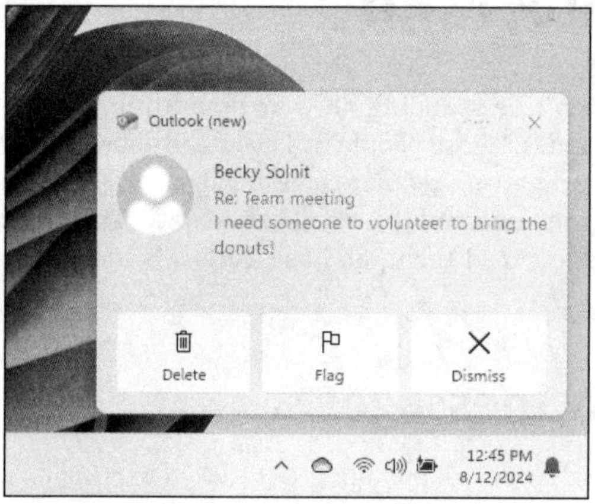


**FIGURE 1-7:** A desktop notification for a new message.

If you think this is overkill, you can turn off one or two of the notifications. Or, if you don't want to be disturbed, you can turn off all of them. Follow these steps:

1. **Choose View ➪ View Settings.**

   The Settings dialog box shows up for work.

2. **Click the General category.**
3. **Click the Notifications subcategory.**
4. **If you don't want to be disturbed by Outlook's email notifications, click the Mail switch to Off. Otherwise, leave the switch On and click Mail to display the notification settings for email.**

The New Email section offers the following settings:

- *Notification Style:* Click Desktop to receive a desktop notification like the one shown in Figure 1-7; click None to skip the desktop notification.
- *Only From Favorite People:* Click this switch On to get an email notification only when the message was sent by someone you've designated as a favorite.
- *Play Sound:* Click this switch Off to bypass the sound effect that plays for each new message.

The Reactions section (refer to "Reacting to a message," later, to learn about reactions) offers the following settings:

- *Notification Style:* Click Alert to receive a reaction notification in the upper-right corner of the screen; click None to skip the desktop notification.
- *Show in Notifications Pane:* Click this switch Off if you don't want to see reaction notifications in the Notifications pane.
- *Play sound:* Click this switch Off to bypass the sound effect that plays for each new message.

Reading pane Mentions section (a mention is when someone precedes your name with the @ symbol in a message; check out "Composing a message," earlier) offers just the following setting:

- *Show in Notifications Pane:* Click this switch Off if you don't want to see mention notifications in the Notifications pane.

5. **Click Save.**

   Outlook puts your notification settings into effect.



## Reading a message

With your messages received, you can now start reading them. The easiest way to do so is to click a message in the Inbox folder and then read the message body using the Reading pane. If you prefer to open the message in a separate window, double-click the message. (If you have notifications turned on, as I describe in the previous section, you can also open an incoming message by clicking either its desktop notification or its item in the Notifications pane.)

Unread messages appear in the message list in boldface type with a solid, blue border to the right of the message. After you've selected a message for at least three seconds and then moved to a different message, Outlook displays the first message in regular type to indicate that you've read it. You can toggle whether a message is read or unread by choosing Home ➪ Read/Unread. You can also mark a message as read by pressing Ctrl+Q and mark a message as unread by pressing Ctrl+U.

By default, Outlook organizes messages by *conversation*, which refers to an original message and all of its replies, replies to replies, and so on. That's a sensible setup because it makes it easy to follow the trend of the conversation and locate a particular reply. Conversations also keep your inbox neat, because the entire conversation resides within a single message in the inbox.

TIP

Still, many people don't like organizing messages by conversations *because* all the messages are hidden within the original message. These people prefer to have all their messages out in the open. If you fall into this camp, you can turn off Outlook's default Conversation view by choosing View ➪ View Settings, click the Mail category, click the Layout subcategory, then, in the Message Organization section, select Show Email as Individual Messages.

## Getting Copilot to summarize a message

If your Office 365 account includes a subscription to Microsoft Copilot, one of the handy perks you get is the generation of email summaries by Copilot. Basically, Copilot examines the message text, then restates the message to give you just the highlights. It's not all that useful for short missives, but for that coworker who writes novel-length dispatches, having these summarized can save you oodles of time.

To press Copilot into service, click the message and then click the Summary by Copilot box that appears near the top of the Reading pane.

## Replying to a message

If you receive a message from someone who needs some information from you, or if you think of a witty retort to a friend's or colleague's message, you'll want to send a reply. Instead of requiring you to create a new message from scratch, Outlook (like all email programs) has a "Reply" feature that saves you the following steps:

- Outlook starts a new message automatically.
- Outlook automatically addresses the reply to the original sender.

» Outlook inserts the original Subject line but adds "Re:" to the beginning of the line to identify this message as a reply.

» Outlook adds the header and the text of the original message to the body of the new message.

Follow these steps to reply to a message:

1. **Click the message to which you want to reply.**
2. **Start the reply by clicking one of the following buttons on the Home tab:**

   - *Reply:* Sends the reply only to the person who sent the original message (any names in the Cc line are ignored). Note that Outlook also provides two Reply buttons in the Reading pane: one at the top and one at the bottom. You can also press Ctrl+R.

   - *Reply All:* Sends the reply not only to the original author, but also to anyone else mentioned in the Cc line. Note that Outlook also provides a Reply All button at the bottom of the Reading pane if the message was addressed to multiple recipients. You can also press Ctrl+Shift+R.
3. **In the message window, type your reply.**
4. **Click Send.**



## Reacting to a message

Some messages require only a minimal response, which could be as little as a word or two. For these kinds of responses, an alternative is to send a *reaction*, which is an icon that summarizes your feelings about the message. Outlook offers a half dozen reaction icons: Like, Heart, Celebrate, Laugh, Surprised, and Sad.

To send a reaction, click the message, click the Reaction icon (shown in the margin) in the Reading pane, then click the reaction type you want to send. Note that if you hover the mouse pointer over the Like reaction, which is a hand doing a thumb's up gesture, Outlook offers you several different skin tones.

## Forwarding a message

Instead of replying or reacting to a message, you might prefer to forward the message to another person. For example, you might receive a message in error, or you might think that a friend or colleague might receive some benefit from reading a message you received.

As with replying, when you forward a message Outlook creates a new message and inserts the original text in the message body. It also adds the original Subject line with Fw: (to identify this as a forwarded message).

Follow these steps to forward a message:

1. **Click the message you want to forward.**
2. **On the Home tab, click Forward (shown in the margin), or press Ctrl+F.**
3. **Use the address boxes to specify one or more recipients.**
4. **In the message body, type a brief note explaining why you're forwarding the message (this is optional but is good email etiquette).**
5. **Click Send.**

## Dealing with attachments

If you receive a message with one or more attachments, Outlook gives you a number of options for dealing with the files. When you select a message with an attachment, the Reading pane shows an icon for the file in the message header. Pull down the attachment menu (or right-click the attachment) and then click one of the following commands:

- **Preview:** Displays the attachment in a separate preview window. Depending on the file type, the preview window will offer other options for dealing with the file, such as saving it to your device or opening it in its associated app.
- **Open:** Launches the associated program and loads the file.

  WARNING

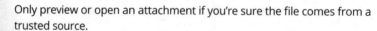

  Only preview or open an attachment if you're sure the file comes from a trusted source.
- **Save to OneDrive:** Saves the file to your OneDrive.
- **Copy:** Places a copy of the file on the Clipboard.
- **Save As:** Opens the Save As dialog box so that you can save the attachment to your device.

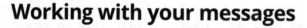

## Working with your messages

When you have a message displayed, you can do plenty of things with it (besides reading it, of course). You can archive it, save it to a file, move it to another folder, delete it, and more. Most of these operations are straightforward, so I'll just summarize the basic techniques here:

- **Pinning a message:** If a message contains important information or is one that you refer to quite often, you can prevent the message from getting lost among your other emails by *pinning* the message, which means the message always appears at the top of the message list. On the Home tab, click Pin This Message (shown in the margin). You can also hover the mouse pointer over the message in the message list and then click the Pin This Message icon that appears.
- **Moving a message to a different folder:** On the Home tab, click Move to a Folder (shown in the margin; you can also press Ctrl+Shift+V) and then use the drop-down list to choose the destination. You can also click and drag the message and drop it on the destination folder.

  REMEMBER

  You should create your own folders in Outlook to store related messages. To create a folder, right-click the account header in the Navigation pane and then click Create New Folder. To create a new subfolder, right-click the folder in which you want to create the new folder, then click Create New Subfolder. Type a name for the folder or subfolder and then click Save.
- **Archiving a message:** On the Home tab, click Move This Message to Your Archive Folder (shown in the margin). You can also press Backspace.
- **Report a phishing message:** On the Home tab, click Report Phishing (shown in the margin). To report junk email, instead, pull down the Report Phishing menu and then click Report Junk.
- **Saving a message:** Instead of storing the message in a folder, you might prefer to save it to a file. To do so, right-click the message and then click Save As. In the Save As dialog box, select a location, type a filename, and then click Save.
- **Deleting a message:** If you want to get rid of a message, click it and then press Delete or click the toolbar's Delete button. (You can also hover the mouse pointer over the message in the message list and then click the Delete icon that appears.) Note that Outlook doesn't really delete the message. Instead, it just moves it to the Deleted Items folder. (So another deletion technique is to click and drag the message and drop it on Deleted Items.) If you change your mind and decide to keep the message, open the Deleted Items folder and move the message back. To permanently remove a message, open the Deleted Items folder and delete the message from there.



## Snoozing a conversation

Sometimes you might want to remove a conversation from your Inbox temporarily. For example, if you're busy, you might not want a conversation's frequent notifications interrupting your train of thought.

You can remove a conversation temporarily from your Inbox by using Outlook's handy snooze feature, which sends the conversation to bed until a date and time you specify. The conversation is still available in the Snoozed folder, should you need to check in.

To snooze a conversation, follow these steps:

1. **Click the conversation in the message list.**
2. **Click Snooze (shown in the margin).**

   Gmail displays a drop-down list with some suggested dates and times. What these items mean is that Outlook will remove the conversation from the Inbox (and store it in the Snoozed folder) until the date and time you specify.
3. **If you see a date and time that works for you, click it and skip the rest of this procedure.**
4. **Click Choose a Date.**

   Outlook opens the Set Custom Date and Time dialog box.
5. **Either click one of the suggested dates and times and then click Save (and skip the rest of these steps) or click Custom Time.**

   Outlook offers another dialog box that offers a calendar and a time list box.
6. **In the calendar, select the date on which you want the snooze period to end.**
7. **In the time list, select the time you want the snooze to end.**
8. **Click Save.**

   Outlook makes a note to restore your conversation on the date and time you specified.

## Setting up a vacation responder

Remember the days when you'd go on vacation for a couple of weeks and leave your work behind? No, I don't either! These days, we live in a cruel world where every person who sends you a message expects an instant reply. And it's a sure sign of pending cultural collapse that you're expected to reply right away even when you're on vacation. Boo!

Okay, fine. Maybe you do have to reply while you're out of the office, but there's no rule (yet) that says you have to reply immediately. Unfortunately, your correspondents might not know you're away, so to forestall an angry "Why didn't you answer my message in less than ten seconds?" follow-up, set up a vacation responder. A *vacation responder* is an automatic reply that gets fired off to everyone who has the temerity to send you a message while you're trying to have a relaxing vacation with your family.

Here are the steps to plow through to create a vacation responder or any type of automatic reply:

1. **Choose View ⇨ View Settings.**

   The Settings page arrives.

2. **Click the Accounts category.**
3. **Click the Automatic Replies subcategory.**
4. **Click the Turn On Automatic Replies switch to On.**
5. **If you only want your automatic replies to go during a specified time, select the Send Replies Only During a Time Period check box, then use the Start Time and End Time controls to specify that time period.**
6. **In the large text box below the Send Automatic Replies Inside Your Organization text, compose the reply that Outlook will send to people in your company.**

   Feel free to spruce up your reply text with any of the formatting options that loom just above the text box.

7. **If you want Outlook to send out automatic replies to folks not in your company, leave the Send Replies Outside Your Organization check box selected.**
8. **If you want Outlook to respond only to messages from people in your contacts list, select the Send Replies Only to Contacts check box.**
9. **In the second large text box (the one below the Send Replies Only to Contacts check box), compose the reply that Outlook will send to people outside of your company.**
10. **Click Save.**

## Categorizing a message

You can improve the organization of your Inbox by applying one or more categories to some or all of your messages. Outlook comes with six categories, which out of the box are named after their associated colors: Blue, Green, Orange, Purple, Red, and Yellow. These are not very meaningful, of course, so Outlook enables you to rename each category to suit your needs.

To apply a category, click the message, click the Home tab's Categorize This Item icon (shown in the margin), and then click the category you want. If you prefer to create your own category, click New Category, instead, type a name, click a color, then click Save.

To manage your categories, choose View ➪ View Settings, click the Accounts category, then click the Categories subcategory. (Alternatively, choose Home ➪ Categorize This Item ➪ Manage Categories.) From here (refer to Figure 1-8), you can create, rename, delete, and favorite categories. (Favoriting a category adds it to the Favorites section of the Navigation pane.)

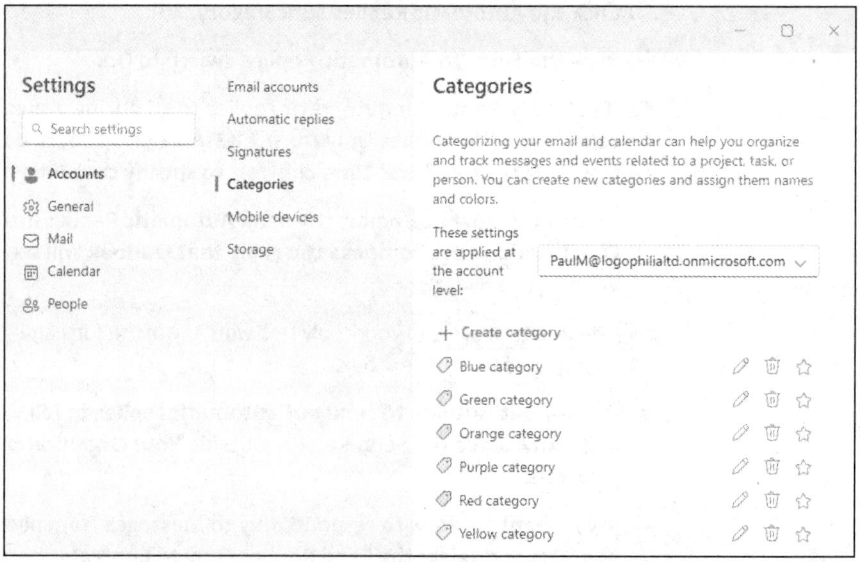


**FIGURE 1-8:** Use the Categories settings to manage your account's categories.

## Setting a message follow-up flag

Outlook enables you to flag a selected message as a reminder to follow up on the message in some way. You have two choices:

- On the Home tab, either click the Flag icon (shown in the margin) to set the default flag. (You can also hover the mouse pointer over the message in the message list and then click the Flag icon.) The default is the Today flag, meaning that you want to perform the follow-up sometime today.
- On the Home tab, pull down the Flag list and then click the flag type you want: Today, Tomorrow, Next Week, and so on. If none of the prefab times works for you, click Custom and then use the Set Flag Date and Time dialog box to set a due date for the flag.

To mark a flagged message as complete, pull down the Home tab's Flag list and then click Mark Complete. You can also hover the mouse pointer over the message in the message list, then click the Flag icon, which turns into a checkmark icon (shown in the margin).

# Using Rules to Process Messages Automatically

With email long entrenched on the business (and home) landscape, email chores probably take up alarming chunks of your time. Besides composing, reading, and responding to email, basic email maintenance — flagging, moving, deleting, and so on — also takes up large swaths of otherwise-productive time.

To help ease the email time crunch, Outlook lets you set up "rules" that perform actions in response to specific events. Here's a list of just a few of the things you can do with rules:

- Move an incoming message to a specific folder if the message contains a particular keyword in the subject or body, or if it's from a particular person.
- Automatically delete messages with a particular subject or from a particular person.
- Flag messages based on specific criteria (such as keywords in the subject line or body).
- Have Outlook notify you with a custom message if an important message arrives.
- Have copies of messages you send stored in a specific folder, depending on the recipient.



## Creating a rule from scratch

Clearly, rules are powerful tools that shouldn't be wielded lightly or without care. Fortunately, Outlook comes with a Rules configuration that makes the process of setting up and defining rules almost foolproof. Here are the steps to follow:

1. **Choose View ⇨ View Settings.**
2. **Click the Mail category, then the Rules subcategory.**

3. **If you have multiple accounts, select the account to which you want your rule to apply.**

4. **Click Add New Rule.**

   Outlook displays the Rules tab, as shown in Figure 1-9.

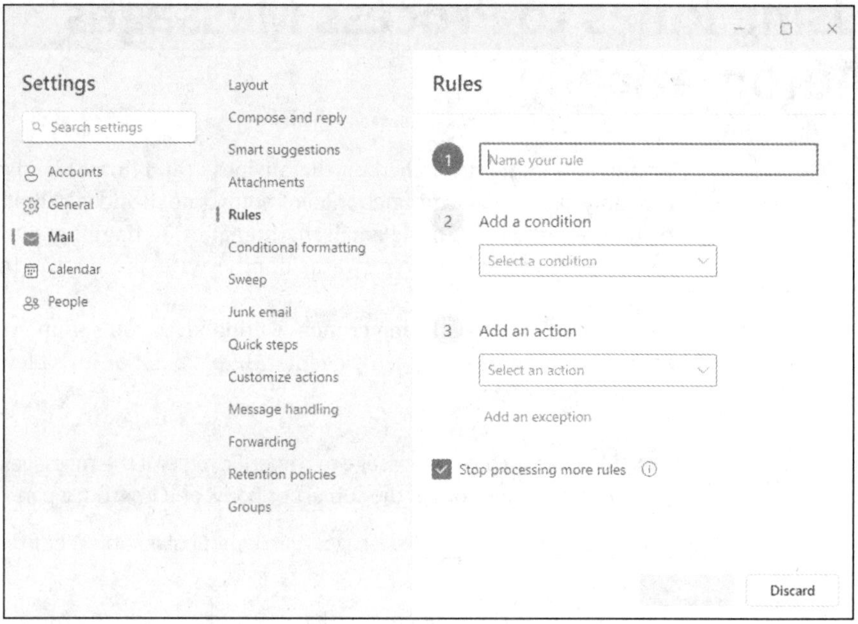


**FIGURE 1-9:** Use the Rules tab to define your new rule.

5. **Type a descriptive name for your rule.**

   The next step is to define the criteria that will cause Outlook to invoke this rule. In other words, what condition or conditions must a message meet to apply the rule to that message?

6. **In the Add a Condition list, select the condition you want to use.**

   Note that some conditions don't require extra info from you. For example, if you choose the condition, I'm On the Cc Line, then Outlook triggers the rule if your email address is included in the Cc field of any incoming message.

   However, many conditions do require extra info. For example, if you select the From condition, then you need to specify the sender email address that you want to trigger the rule. Conditions that require more data will display a control (such as a text box or calendar picker) that you can use to complete the condition.

7. **If the condition requires more information from you, use the displayed control to enter that info.**

8. **(Optional) To create another condition for your rule, click Add Another Condition, then repeat Steps 6 and 7.**

   Now you specify the action or actions that you want Outlook to take for messages that meet the conditions you specified.

9. **In the Add an Action list, select the action you want to apply to the messages.**

10. **If the action requires more information from you, use the control that appears to specify that data.**

11. **(Optional) To specify another action for your rule, click Add Another Action, then repeat Steps 9 and 10.**

12. **(Optional) To specify an exception to the rule, click Add an Exception, use the Add an Exception list to select an exception type, then fill in any extra info that the exception requires.**

13. **Click Save.**

    Outlook adds your new rule to the Rules tab.



You can use the Rules tab to maintain your rules. For example, each rule you've defined has a switch beside it that toggles the rule on and off. You can change a rule by clicking its Edit Rule icon (the pencil). To get rid of a rule, click its Delete icon (the trashcan).

## Creating a rule from a message

It's common to create a rule because of a message you've received. It might be a particular sender whose messages you want moved to a specific folder or a particular subject line that you want to be alerted about. For a limited set of conditions and actions, Outlook enables you to create a new rule based on one or more properties of an existing message.

Right-click the message from which you want to create the rule, click Rules, and then click Create Rule. Outlook displays the Create a Rule dialog box, shown in Figure 1-10.

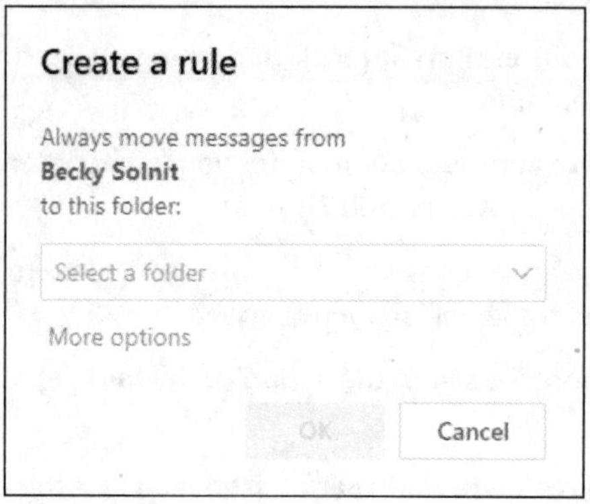


**FIGURE 1-10:** Use the Create a Rule dialog box to create a new rule from the properties of an existing message.

You have two ways to proceed:

- By default, Outlook assumes you want to move all messages from the sender of the message to a particular folder. If that's what you want your rule to do, use the Select a Folder list to specify the folder, then click OK.
- If you want your rule to have a different condition (or multiple conditions) or a different action (or multiple actions), click More Options to open the Rules tab of the Settings dialog box. Now follow the steps I painstakingly outlined in the previous section to set up your rule.

IN THIS CHAPTER

» **Creating contacts from scratch, from email messages, and from data files**

» **Editing contacts**

» **Adding a photo for a contact**

» **Sorting, exporting, and other vital contact tasks**

» **Phoning, emailing, and chatting with contacts**

# Chapter 2
# Managing Your Contacts

Whether it's working with clients, colleagues, or suppliers, contacting people is a big part of most people's working day. It can also be a time-consuming part of your day if you are constantly looking up information about people, whether it is their phone numbers, physical addresses, email addresses, web addresses, and so on. Streamlining these tasks — a process known as *contact management* — can save you lots of time and make your work more efficient.

Outlook's contact management happens in the People app. This app gives you amazing flexibility for dealing with your ever-growing network of coworkers, customers, friends, and family. Yes, you can use People to store mundane information such as phone numbers and email addresses, but you can also preserve the minutiae of each person's life: their birthday, their anniversary, the name of their significant other, and even their web page address. Even better, the People app enables you to reduce the number of steps it takes to perform many tasks. For example, if you want to email someone in your People list, rather than creating the message via the Mail app and addressing it to the contact, you can perform both actions at once by initiating the email request directly from the People app.

This chapter takes you inside the People app and shows you how to add and edit contacts; import contact data from other programs; phone and email contacts; and customize the People view.

# Exploring the People App

When you first display the People app by clicking People (shown in the margin) or by pressing Ctrl+3, you won't see much of anything. I talk about how to populate the People app with new entries in the next few sections. Once you've done that, your People app will look like the one shown in Figure 2-1.

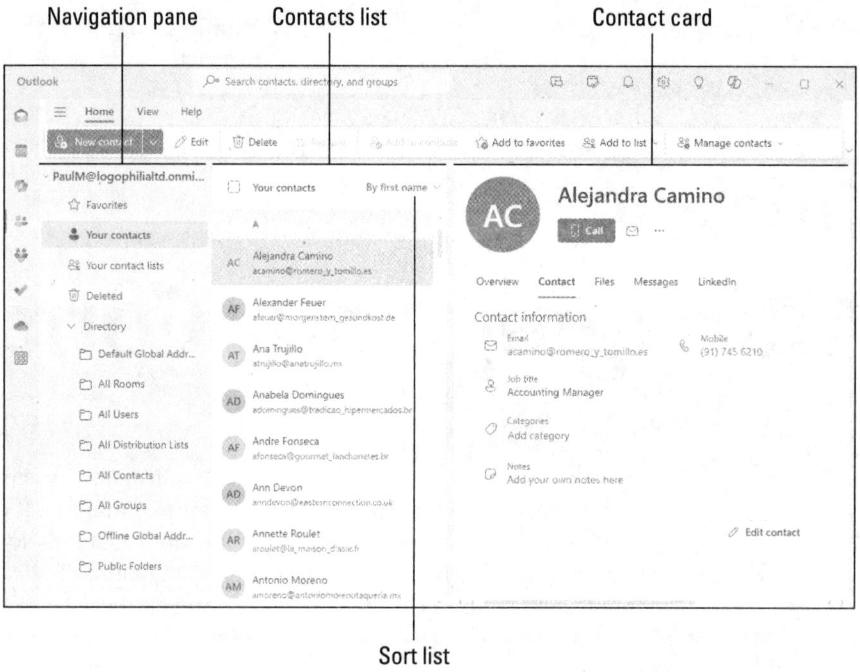


**FIGURE 2-1:** How the People app looks once you have added a few contacts.

As you can see, Outlook presents each contact as a card that shows some of the information you've entered: name, email address, phone number, job title, and notes.

To navigate the contacts, you have a few options:

- Press the Down arrow key to move to the next card.
- Press the Up arrow key to move to the previous card.
- Press Page Down or Page Up to move down or up, respectively, several contacts at a time.
- Use the vertical scroll bar to move up and down through the cards.

- Click inside the Search Contacts, Directory, and Groups box at the top of the People window and then start typing the name of the contact you want to work with. When that person shows up in the search results, click that contact to display their card.
- Click a letter button to display all the letters, then click the letter you want to jump to.

# Adding a New Contact

That next-to-empty People app is not very useful, so you should get right down to adding some new cards. This section shows you various methods of setting up new contacts. You first learn how to add a contact by hand, then I show you several easier methods for adding contacts, including how to import contact data from other programs.

## Creating a new contact from scratch

The basic procedure for creating a new contact by hand is straightforward:

1. **Choose Home ⇨ New Contact or press Ctrl+N.**

   Outlook displays an unnamed window for creating a contact, shown in Figure 2-2.

2. **Fill in as many of the fields as you need.**
3. **Click Save.**

Most of the fields you see are straightforward; you just type in the appropriate data. However, the next few sections give you some details about certain fields in the General form.

### The name fields

Use the First Name and Last Name text boxes to type the name of the contact. To enter more detailed information for the contact, click the Add Name Field button and then click a field from the list that appears: Title (Mr., Ms., and so on) Suffix (Jr., III, Esq., and so on), Middle Name, Nickname, Pronunciation First Name, and Pronunciation Last Name.

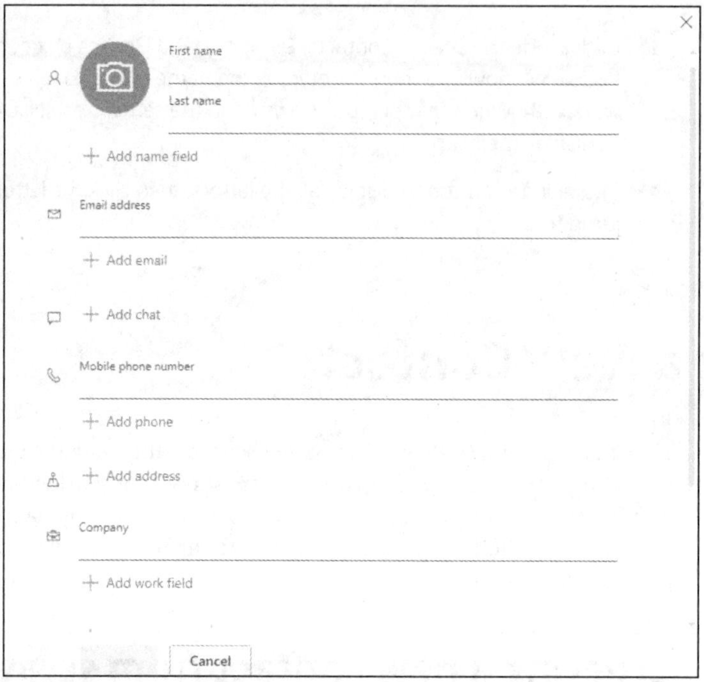


**FIGURE 2-2:** Use this nameless window to enter data for your new contact.

## The Email Address field

Use the Email Address field to — yep — type the contact's email address. If your contact uses multiple email addresses, click the Add Email button to create a new field. Outlook can hold up to three email addresses for each contact.

## The Chat field

Click Add Chat to create a Chat field that you can use to add an instant messaging handle for the contact.

## The Phone Number fields

Use the Mobile Phone Number field to type the contact's mobile number. To store more numbers, click Add Phone, click a type (Mobile, Home, Business, or Other), and then type the number in the new field that appears.

## The Address fields

Click Add Address and then click a type (Home Address, Business Address, or Other Address) to display the fields for entering a physical address: Street, City, State/Province, Zip/Postal Code, and Country/Region. You can click Add Address to specify multiple physical addresses for the contact.

### The Work fields

Use the Company field to type the name of the place where the contact works. To add other work-related fields, click Add Work Field, click a field type (Title, Department, Office Location, or Pronunciation Company Name), and then fill in the data in the field provided.

### The Categories field

Click Categorize and then click the category you want to apply to the contact. If this is the first time you're categorizing a contact, click New Category, type the category name, select a color, then click Save.

REMEMBER

Once you create a category, the People app adds a Categories folder to the Navigation pane and adds your new category as a subfolder. You can click a category subfolder to see all the contacts to which you've assigned that category.

### The other fields

Click Add Others, click a field type (Personal Web Page, Significant Other, Birthday, or Anniversary), then fill in the data in the field that shows up.

## Creating a contact from an email message

Another quick way to add someone to your People list is to create the new contact item from an existing email message. Here are the steps to follow:

1. **In Outlook's Mail app, click a message from the person you want to add to your contacts.**
2. **In the message header, click the sender's name or email address.**

   Outlook displays a contact card for the sender.
3. **Click the Contact tab.**
4. **Click Add to Contacts.**

   Outlook opens a new contact form and fills in the First Name, Last Name, and Email Address fields with the sender's info.
5. **Fill in the rest of the person's contact data.**
6. **Click Save.**

   Outlook adds the sender to your contacts list.

Open the message in its own window, choose Move to Folder ⇨ Other Folder ⇨ People. Outlook displays a new Contact window, fills in the person's Full Name and Email address, and adds the email message body to the Notes field.

## Importing contact data

If you have your contact data in some other application, chances are you will be able to import that data into Outlook and save yourself the hassle of retyping all that information. Outlook comes with an Import Contacts feature that makes the task easy.

Your first task is to use your current contact management app to export the contacts to a comma-separated values (CSV) file. With that done, here are the steps to follow to import those contacts into Outlook's People app:

1. **In the People app, on the Home tab, click Manage Contacts, then click Import Contacts.**

   The Import Contacts dialog box clocks in.

2. **Click Browse.**

   The Open dialog box reports for duty.

3. **Locate and click the CSV file you want to import.**
4. **Click Open.**

   Outlook adds the file to the Import Contacts dialog box.

5. **Click Import.**

   Outlook imports the contacts, just like that.

6. **Click Close.**

## Creating a contact list

If you regularly send email messages or meeting requests to a particular group of people, specifying each person every time you create a new message or meeting gets old in a hurry. And the more people in your group, the more time you waste.

You can eliminate this drudgery entirely by setting up a *contact list*. This is a special People app item that does nothing more than hold the names and email addresses of multiple people. They can either be folks from your contacts list or other people whose names and addresses you enter by hand, and they're called the *members* of the list. After you create the contact list, you can use the list as the recipient of an email message or meeting request, and Outlook sends the item to every person on the list.

Follow these steps to create a contact list:

1. **In the People app, on the Home tab, pull down the New Contact menu and then click New Contact List, or press Ctrl+L.**

   Outlook displays the New Contact List dialog box. Figure 2-3 shows a version of this dialog box with a few members added and an email address about to be added.

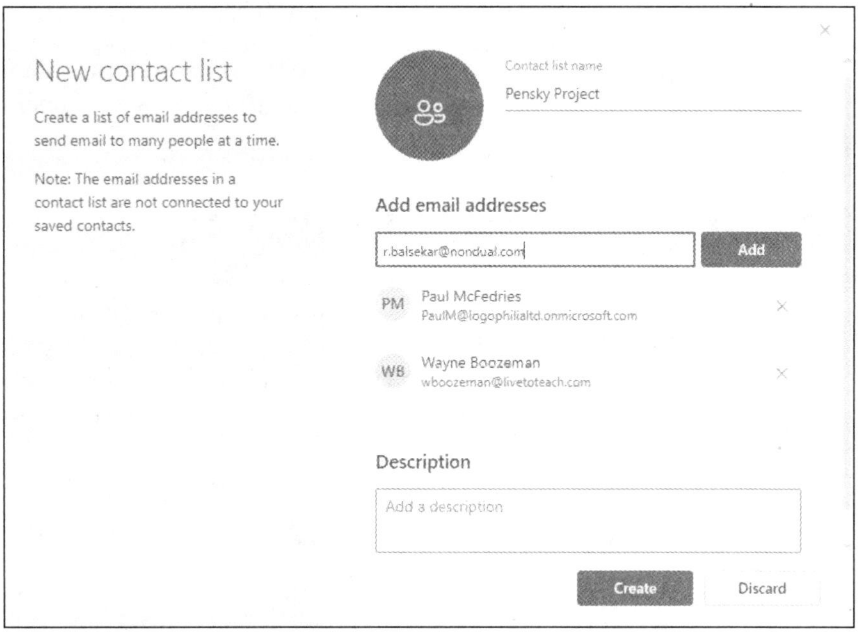


**FIGURE 2-3:** Use the New Contact List dialog box to add members to your contact list.

2. **In the Contact List Name text box, type a name for the list.**
3. **Use the following methods to add members to the list:**
   - *To add someone from your contacts list:* Start typing the name of the person, then click the contact when they appear in the search results.

Managing Your Contacts

- *To add someone from outside your contacts:* In the Add Email Address text box, type the email address of the person you want to include in the list, then click Add.

4. **Repeat Step 3 as needed to add everyone you want in your contact list.**
5. **(Optional) Use the Description text area to describe your contact list.**
6. **Click Create.**

   Outlook creates the list and populates it with the people you specified.

Your freshly created list now appears in the Navigation pane's Your Contact Lists folder. If you need to make changes to your list, click Your Contact Lists, click the list, then click the Home tab's Edit button (or click edit in the contact list's card).

TIP

After you've created a contact list, you can quickly populate the list with people from your contacts. In the People app's list of contacts, select the check box beside each person you want to include in the contact list. Then, on the Home tab, click Add to List, click the name of the contact list, then click Add to This List.

# Working with Your Contacts

Your contacts list is only as useful as it is accurate and up to date. So, it's worthwhile to spend a bit of time maintaining your contacts by correcting erroneous entries, updating changed data, and adding any new information that comes your way. The next few sections show you how to edit contact data and perform a few other maintenance chores.

## Editing contact data

Once you've added some contacts, you'll often have to edit them to either add new information or to change or remove existing information. Outlook gives you two ways to open the currently displayed contact for editing:

- Choose Home ➪ Edit.
- Click the Edit Contact button in the contact card.

Either way, Outlook opens the contact for editing in an unnamed window similar to the one shown earlier in Figure 2-2. Make your edits, then click Save to update the contact.

## Adding a photo for a contact

By default, the "picture" that the People app generates for a new contact just consists of the contact's initials. Boring! If you happen to have a photo of a contact, why not replace those default initials with that photo? Here are the steps required:

1. **Click the person in the contact list.**
2. **Choose Home ➪ Edit or click the Edit Contact button.**

   Outlook opens the contact for editing.
3. **Click the Change Photo button (shown in the margin).**

   The Change Photo dialog box appears, as shown in Figure 2-4.

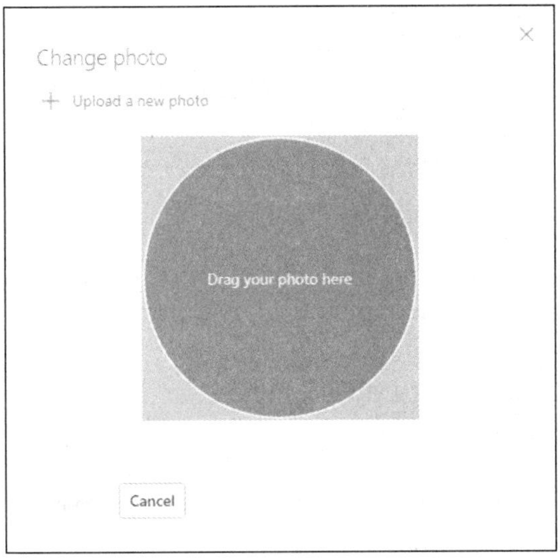


**FIGURE 2-4:** Use the Change Photo dialog box to specify a photo for your contact.

4. **Choose the photo you want to apply using either of the following techniques:**
   - Click Upload a New Photo to get the Open dialog box onscreen, select the photo, then click Open.
   - Use File Explorer to locate the photo, drag the photo file into the Change Photo dialog box, and then drop the photo in the large circle labeled Drag Your Photo Here.
5. **Use the slider below the photo to adjust the magnification.**

6. **Click and drag the photo as needed to get the portion of the image you want to use.**
7. **Click Apply.**

   Outlook replaces the default contact picture with the photo you applied.
8. **Click Save.**

## Designating a contact as a favorite

If there are one or more contacts that you work with frequently, you can save yourself oodles of time by adding those contacts to the People app's Favorites folder, which appears at the top of the Navigation pane. That handy location means you can access your favorite contacts much faster than by constantly having to scroll or search your full contacts list.

Outlook offers a couple of methods for designating a contact as a favorite:

- Click the contact and then choose Home ➪ Add to Favorites.
- Right-click the contact and then click Add to Favorites.

Either way, Outlook plops the contact into the Favorites folder. Click that folder in the Navigation pane to see your faves.

## Deleting contacts

To keep your contacts list neat and relatively tidy, you should delete any entries that you never use. The Contacts app gives you a couple of ways to get rid of unwanted contacts:

- **Delete a single contact:** Either click the contact and then choose Home ➪ Delete, or right-click the contact and then click Delete.
- **Delete two or more contacts:** Select the check box beside each contact you want to remove, then either choose Home ➪ Delete or click the Delete button that appears below the *X* Contacts Selected message (where *X* is the number you've selected). Note that Outlook only supports deleting a maximum of ten contacts at a time.

Either way, Outlook asks if you're sure you want to go through with the deletion. If you're sure you're sure, click Delete to make it happen.

REMEMBER

If you delete a contact accidentally, or if you simply have a change of heart down the road, you'll be happy to hear that you don't need to re-create the contact from scratch. Instead, click the Deleted folder in the People app's Navigation pane. Lo and behold, there are all your deleted contacts! Either click the contact and then choose Home ⇨ Restore, or right-click the contact and then click Restore. Whew!

## Displaying contact activity

The integrated nature of Outlook means that we often deal with a person in a number of ways: read their email; send them email; chat with them; and handle files they've shared. Multiply all this by the dozens of other people you deal with, and finding, for instance, a particular file shared by a particular person can kill a lot of precious time.

If the person you're working with is set up as a contact, however, Outlook offers an often-overlooked method for filtering out other people and items and drilling down to the specific item you're looking for. Open the contact you want to work with and then, in the person's contact card, use the following tabs:

- **Files:** Displays a list of the files the contact has shared with you.
- **Messages:** Displays the chat conversation you've had with the contact. You can use the Type filter to restrict the list to just Teams chats or Outlook chats; and you can use the Date filter to restrict the conversation to within a date range.

## Sorting the contacts

By default, Outlook sorts the contacts in ascending order by the values in the First Name field. If that doesn't work for you, click the Sort list (it should have the value By First Name) that appears above the contacts list (I point out the list location back in Figure 2-1). In the menu that appears, click the sort order you prefer: Last Name, Company, Home City, Work City, or Recently Added.

## Exporting your contacts

If you need a comma-separated values text file for your contacts (say, to import into another app or to use as a backup), follow these steps to export your contacts list to such a file:

1. **Choose Home ⇨ Manage Contacts ⇨ Export Contacts.**

   Outlook deals out the Export Contacts dialog box.

2. **Use the Contacts from This Folder list to choose which folder you want to export.**

   The default is All Contacts.

3. **Click Export.**

   Outlook stuffs your contacts into a file named contacts.csv (for a refresher on comma-separated values [CSV] files, go to the above section "Importing contact data"), which it stores in your device's Downloads folder.

# Performing Contact Tasks

You didn't go to all the trouble of entering or importing contact data just to look up someone's birthday or the name of their significant other. No, with all that information at your fingertips, you'll want to do things that are a bit more substantial. Like what? Well, Outlook gives you lots of choices. For example, you can initiate a phone call to a contact. You can also send an email message to a contact, and you can chat with that person. The following sections give you a quick tour of the methods you use to accomplish these tasks from within the People app.

## Phoning a contact

If your contact's info includes a phone number, you can give that person a ring by displaying their card and then clicking the Call button (or by clicking the phone number that appears in the card). If you see an alert that the Outlook site is trying to open an application, select Always Allow `outlook.office.com` to Open Links of This Type in the Associated App check box, then click Open. Choose the app you prefer to use for calls (such as Skype for Business or Phone Link), click Always, and then follow the instructions.

## Sending an email to one or more contacts

If you have defined at least one email address for one or more contacts, you can send those people a message by following these steps:

1. **Specify the message recipient or recipients:**

   - *Sending a message to one contact:* Click the contact you want to email and then click the email address in that person's contact card.

- *Sending a message to two or more contacts:* In the contacts list, select the check box beside each contact you want to email, then click the Send Email button that appears below the *X* Contacts Selected message (where *X* is the number you've selected).

Outlook creates a new email message with the contact or contacts added to the To field.

2. **Type the Subject line, type the body of the message, and set up any other message options you require.**
3. **Click Send.**

   Outlook ships out the message.

## Starting a chat with a contact

You can initiate a Teams chat from the People app by following these steps:

1. **Click the contact you want to chat with.**

2. **Click the Start a Chat button (shown in the margin) in that person's contact card.**
3. **If you see an alert that the Outlook site is trying to open Microsoft Teams, select Always Allow `outlook.office.com` to Open Links of This Type in the Associated App check box, then click Open.**

   Microsoft Teams opens and launches a new chat. Refer to Book 7, Chapter 3 to learn the ins and outs of chatting in Microsoft Teams.

IN THIS CHAPTER

» Using expert techniques for quickly navigating dates and entering events

» Configuring your Calendar with an extra time zone and custom work weeks

» Creating appointments and events quickly

» Efficiently planning a meeting

# Chapter 3

# Keeping Track of Appointments

In these "whatever-comes-after-busy" days, a common comedic trope is for two people to spend an inordinate amount of time trying to coordinate their schedules to come up with a time for some simple activity, such as having coffee.

> "No, Monday's no good. How about Tuesday morning at 5:30?"
>
> "That doesn't work for me, but I could do Wednesday afternoon at 3:47."

A popular cartoon from *The New Yorker* shows a busy executive on the phone, pointing to his calendar and saying "No, Thursday's out. How about never — is never good for you?"

Never getting together with anyone would certainly simplify everyone's lives, but the extraverts of the world simply won't allow it. So, if we must both meet *and* greet, the least we can do is make the scheduling part faster and more efficient. Fortunately, Outlook's Calendar app is chock-full of collaboration features for helping busy people (that would be all of us) to coordinate their schedules and meet up with a minimum of fuss.

In this chapter, you delve into Calendar's collaboration features for inviting guests to events, sharing your calendar, subscribing to calendars other people have shared, importing and exporting events, and much more.

# Getting Together with the Calendar App

When you display the Calendar app by clicking the Calendar icon (shown in the margin) or by pressing Ctrl+2, Outlook displays a window similar to the one shown in Figure 3-1. As you can see, Calendar is laid out more or less like a day planner or desk calendar. Here are two items to note right up front:

- **Calendar grid:** This takes up the bulk of the Calendar folder and it shows one day at a time, divided into half-hour intervals. The appointments and meetings you schedule appear in this area.
- **Date navigator:** This part of the Navigation pane shows at least six weeks of dates, including the current month, the last few days from the previous month, and the first few days from the next month. As its name suggests, you use the date navigator to change the date shown in the Calendar grid. Dates for which you have already scheduled appointments or meetings are shown in bold type. Note that today's date always has a blue circle around it.

TIP

You don't have to plop all your events into a single calendar. In fact, you really shouldn't since mixing, say, business events with personal events can make your life even more confusing than it already is. Under the date navigator, click Add Calendar, click Create Blank Calendar, then use the Create Blank Calendar dialog box to name your new calendar and choose a color for it.

## Changing the displayed date

Calendar always opens with the current date displayed. However, if you want to work with a different day, the date navigator makes it easy. All you have to do is click a date, and Outlook displays it in the Calendar grid. If the month you need isn't displayed in the date navigator, use either of the following techniques to pick a different month:

- **Move one month:** Click the up-pointing arrow in the month header to move back one month at a time. Similarly, click the down-pointing arrow in the month header to move forward one month at a time. (You can also perform this task in the Calendar grid if you switch to the Month view; see "Changing the number of days displayed," later in this chapter.)

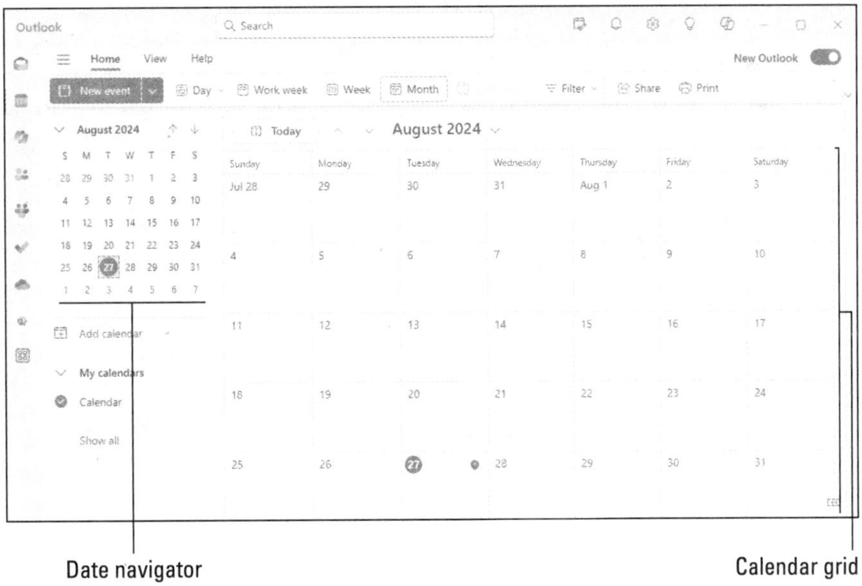


**FIGURE 3-1:** Outlook's Calendar app.

- **Move several months:** Click the month header. A pop-up menu displays all the months of the current year. For a different year, click the up-pointing arrow for an earlier year, or the down-pointing arrow for a later year. Then click the month you want to view.

TIP

To move to today's date, click the Today button that appears in the upper-left corner of the calendar grid.

## Changing the number of days displayed

Calendar's default view is the Month calendar, which shows a month's worth of appointments and meetings (plus usually a few days from the previous month and/or a few days from the next month). However, Calendar is quite flexible, and you can configure it to show two days, three days, a week, or even a month at a time.

The easiest way to change the view is to use Calendar's Day, Work Week, Week, and Month commands to see the following views:

- **Day calendar:** Click Day or press Ctrl+Alt+1.
- **Work week calendar:** Click Work Week or press Ctrl+Alt+2.
- **Week calendar:** Click Week or press either Ctrl+Alt+3 or Alt+- (hyphen).
- **Month calendar:** Click Month or press either Ctrl+Alt+4 or Alt+=.

TIP

If you need to keep track of the week numbers, you can add them to the Month view and the date navigator. Choose View ➪ Calendar Settings to open the Settings dialog box with the Calendar category displayed and the View subcategory displayed. Select the Show Week Numbers check box, then use the list to specify when you want the first week of the year to start. Click Save to make it so.

## Creating a custom view

TIP

You can configure the calendar to display *x* number of days by using either of the following techniques:

- On the Ribbon (either the Home tab or the View tab), pull down the Day list and then select the number of days you want to view at a time in the calendar grid.
- Press Alt+*x*, where *x* is the number of days you want in your custom view. For example, pressing Alt+3 displays the three days beginning with whatever day is currently selected in the date navigator.

You can display up to seven days using these techniques.

If you find you use a particular custom view frequently, follow these steps to save it:

1. **Make sure Calendar is using the custom view you want to save.**
2. **Choose View ➪ Saved Views and then click Save Current View.**

   The Save Current View dialog box materializes.
3. **Type a name for the custom view.**
4. **Click Save.**

   Outlook saves your view.

To apply your saved view, choose View ➪ Saved Views and then click the saved view in the list that drops down. To work with a saved view, choose View ➪ Saved Views, click the right-pointing arrow beside the view you want to mess with, and then click one of the following:

- **Open:** Applies the view.
- **Edit:** Displays the Edit View dialog box where you can change the name of the view.
- **Delete:** Removes the view. When Outlook asks you to confirm, click Delete.

## Changing the time scale

By default, the Calendar grid's Day view displays time in half-hour blocks. If that doesn't work for you, you can change the time scale by following these steps:

1. **In Day view, choose View ⇨ Time Scale.**

   Alternatively, right-click the time display on the left side of the Calendar grid and, in the shortcut menu that appears, click Time Scale.

2. **Click the interval you prefer.**

   Your choices are 60, 30, 15, 10, 6, or 5 minutes.

## Configuring the work week

Outlook assumes the work week consists of five days, from Monday to Friday. If your work week is shorter or uses different days (for example, Tuesday through Saturday, or even any number of nonconsecutive days), you can configure the Work Week view that the Calendar displays. Here are the steps to follow:

1. **Choose View ⇨ Calendar Settings**

   The Settings dialog box shows up with the Calendar category selected.

2. **Click the Work Hours and Location subcategory.**

   Outlook displays the Work Hours and Location settings, shown in the Figure 3-2.

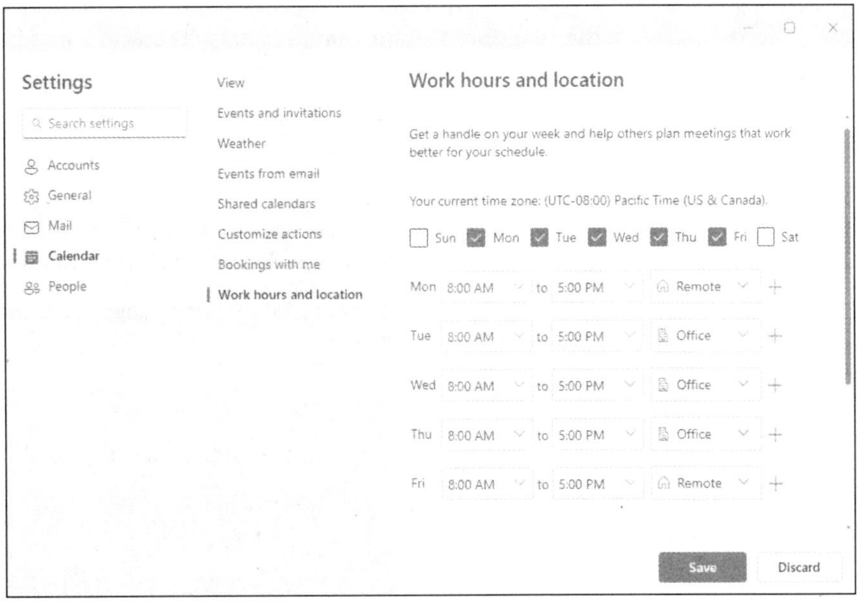


**FIGURE 3-2:** Configuring the work week.

3. **Select the check box for each day you want to include in the Work Week view.**

4. **For each working day, select the time your day starts, the time your day ends, and your location (Office or Remote).**

5. **Click Save.**

TIP

While you're at it, you might want to configure Calendar with the day that you consider to be the start of the week. The default is Sunday, but you can pick any day that makes sense for you. Choose View ⇨ Calendar Settings to open the Settings dialog box with the Calendar category displayed and the View subcategory displayed. Use the Show the First Day of the Week As list to specify which day begins your week, then click Save.

## Displaying a second time zone

If you have colleagues on the opposite coast, clients in Europe, or if you can never figure out what the time is in Indiana, Outlook allows you to display a second time zone in the Day, Work Week, and Week views. Here's how:

1. **In the Day, Work Week, or Week view, right-click the time display, click Time Zones, and then click Edit Time Zones.**

   Alternatively, choose View ⇨ Calendar Settings.

   The Settings dialog box trundles up with the Calendar category and the View subcategory selected.

2. **In the Time Zones group, use the Label text box to type a label that will appear at the top of the current time zone.**

   Labeling the time zones makes it easy to know which one you're working with.

3. **Click the Add Time Zone button.**

   Outlook does just that.

4. **Use the Other Time Zones list to click the time zone you want to add.**

5. **Use the Label text box to type a label that will appear at the top of the second time zone.**

6. **Click Save.**

Figure 3-3 shows the Day view with two time zones displayed.

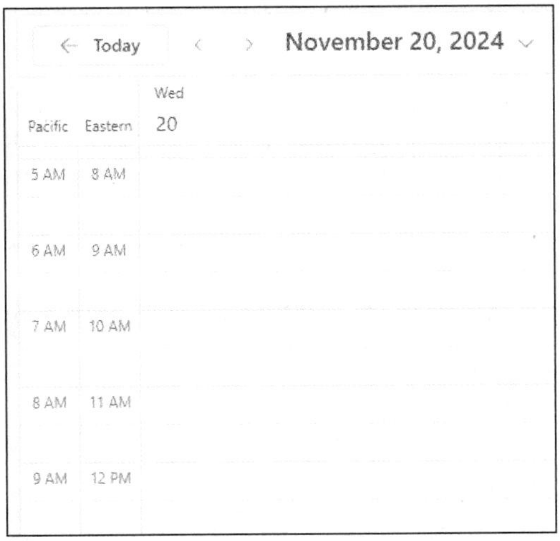


**FIGURE 3-3:** Calendar's Day view with the Eastern and Pacific time zones displayed.

# Items You Can Schedule in Calendar

Calendar differentiates between three kinds of items you can schedule:

- **Event:** An event is the most general Calendar item. It refers to any activity for which you set aside a block of time. Typical events include an appointment, a lunch date, a trip to the dentist or doctor, or a social engagement. You can also create recurring events that are scheduled at regular intervals (such as weekly or monthly).
- **All-day event:** An all-day event is any activity that consumes one or more entire days. Examples include conferences, trade shows, vacations, and birthdays. In Calendar, all-day events don't occupy blocks of time. Instead, they appear as banners above the affected days. You can also schedule recurring all-day events.
- **Meeting:** A meeting is a special kind of event to which two or more people are invited. Outlook has a Scheduling Assistant that lets you set up a meeting and send email messages inviting people to the meeting. Outlook can then track the responses so that you know who is coming to the meeting and who isn't.

The next few sections show you how to create events, all-day events, and meetings.

# Setting Up an Event

Outlook gives you a number of methods for creating events, ranging from simple one-shot appointments to more sophisticated examples that use features such as reminder messages.

## Scheduling a basic event

Here are the steps to wade through to convince Calendar to schedule an event without any bells and whistles:

1. **Decide how much time to block out for the event:**
   - If you need only a half hour, click inside the Day, Work Week, or Week view at the time the event is scheduled to occur.
   - If you need more than a half hour, then in Day, Work Week, or Week view, drag the mouse pointer over the time blocks to select them.
   - If you're working in Month view, click the date of the event to select it, then click the date again.

   Calendar displays the basic version of the form for adding an event, as shown in Figure 3-4.

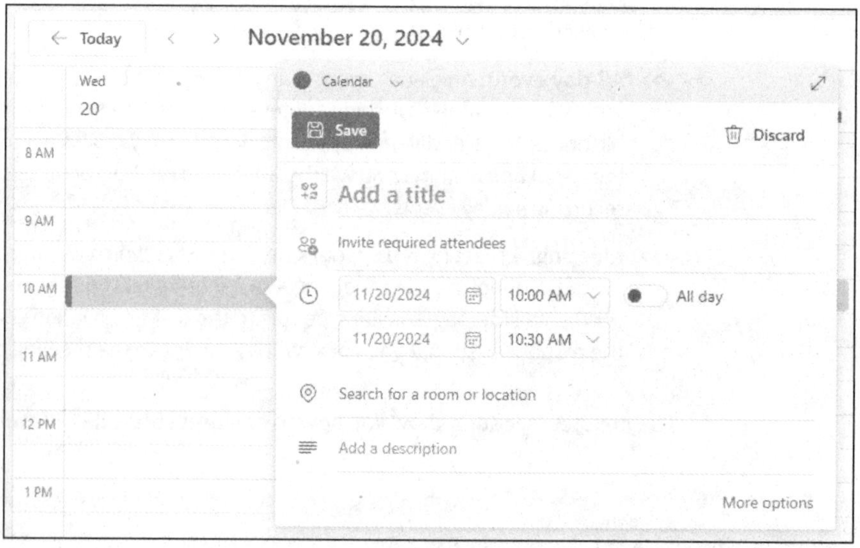


**FIGURE 3-4:** Use this version of the new event form to set up a basic event.

2. **Use the Add a Title text box to type a name for the event.**

   This is the text that will appear in the Calendar grid.

3. **Use the top calendar control and time list to specify the date and time that the event starts.**

4. **Use the bottom calendar controls and time list to specify the date and time the event ends.**

5. **Use the Search for a Room or Location text box to type the location (such as a room number or address) for the event.**

6. **Use Add a Description text box to type notes about the event.**

7. **Click Save.**

   Calendar schedules the event.

## Creating a recurring event

If you have an event that occurs at a regular interval (say, weekly or monthly), Calendar lets you schedule a recurring event. For example, if you create a weekly event, Calendar fills in that event automatically on the same day of the week at the same time for the duration you specify. Here are the steps to follow:

1. **Open the New Event window:**
   - On the Home tab, click New Event.
   - Start a basic event, as I describe in the previous section, then click More Options.

   If you want to add recurrence to an existing event, double-click that event.

2. **Fill in the event particulars, including the title, starting date and time, and ending date and time.**

3. **Click the Recurrence list, which by default shows Don't Repeat.**

   Outlook displays a list of recurrence intervals, shown in Figure 3-5.

4. **Click a recurrence interval.**

   Outlook sends in the Repeat dialog box, which will be filled in with default values based on the recurrence interval you selected. For example, Figure 3-6 shows the version of the Repeat dialog box that shows up when you click the Weekly interval. Steps 5 through 8 that follow are optional. If the default settings in the Repeat dialog box are just what you need, go ahead and skip ahead to Step 9.

5. **Use the Start calendar control to change the date the recurrence begins.**

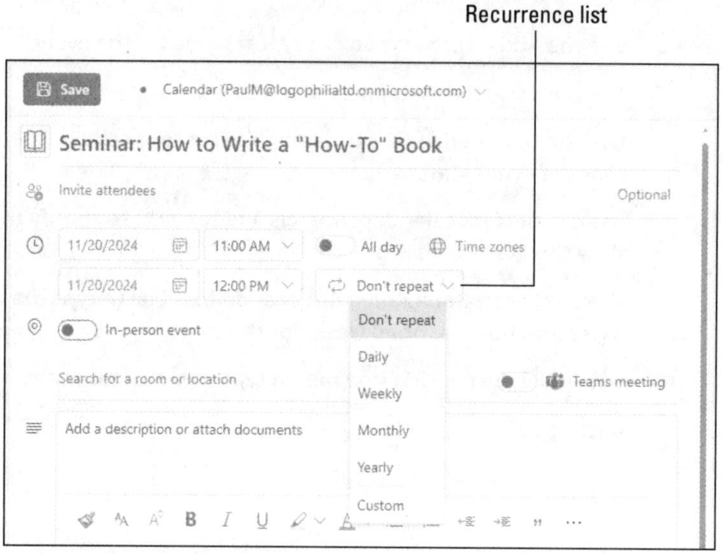


**FIGURE 3-5:** Use the Recurrence list to choose the recurrence interval you want to apply to your event.

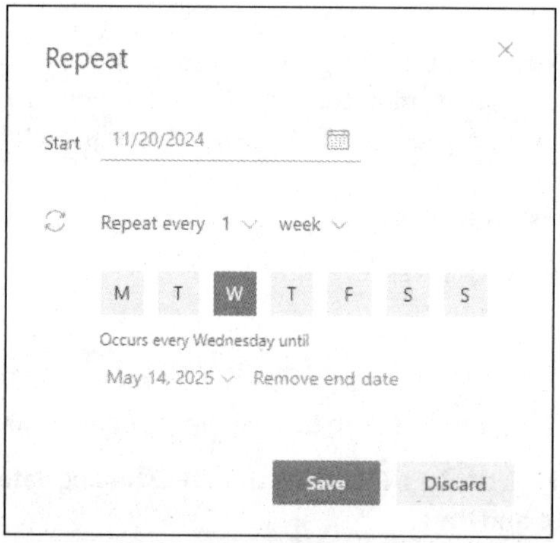


**FIGURE 3-6:** Use the Repeat dialog box to set up a recurring event.

6. **Use the Repeat Every controls to set up the recurrence pattern. Use the right list to click the base interval you want to use: Day, Week, Month, or Year; use the left list to choose a number between 1 and 99.**

7. **Customize the recurrence pattern.**

   How you customize the pattern varies depending on the base interval you selected:

   - *Day:* Use the seven boxes representing the days of the week (M for Monday, the first T for Tuesday, and so on) to toggle the days on which you want the event to repeat. A day is on if its box has a blue background.

- *Week:* Use the seven boxes representing the days of the week to toggle which days you want the event to repeat each week. For example, if you turn on the W and F boxes, then the event will repeat every Wednesday and Friday.
- *Month:* If you select the On Day *N* option, where *N* is the day of the month that appears in the Start date, then Outlook repeats the event each month on the *N*th day of the month. For example, if the Start date is November 20, then the event will recur on the 20th of each month. Alternatively, if you select the On the *M*th *Day* option, where *M* is an ordinal number (such as first, second, or third) and *Day* is the day of the week that corresponds to the Start date, then Outlook repeats the event on the *M*th *Day* of each month. For example, November 20, 2024, is the third Wednesday of that month, so the event would recur on the third Wednesday of each subsequent month.
- *Year:* If you select the On *Month Day* option, where *Month* is the Start date month and *Day* is the Start date day, then Outlook repeats the event each year on the month and day. For example, if the Start date is November 20, 2024, then the event will recur each year on November 20. Alternatively, if you select the On the *M*th *Day* of *Month* option, where *M* is an ordinal number (such as first, second, or third), *Day* is the day of the week that corresponds to the Start date, and *Month* is the month of the Start date, then Outlook repeats the event on the *M*th *Day* of *Month* each year. For example, November 20, 2024, is the third Wednesday of November, so the event would recur on the third Wednesday of each subsequent November.

8. **Specify when you want the recurrence to end.**

   For the Day, Week, and Month recurrence intervals, Outlook supplies a default end date. You can either use the calendar control to choose a different end date, or you can click Remove End Date to let the recurrence go on indefinitely.

   For the Year recurrence interval, Outlook doesn't supply an end date. To add one, click Choose an End Date, then use the calendar that pops up to pick a date.

9. **Click Save.**

   Outlook saves the recurrence and returns you to the event dialog box.

10. **Fill in the rest of the event details, to taste.**
11. **Click Save.**

    Outlook saves your event and adds the event and all of its recurrences to your calendar.

## Getting reminded of an event

When it comes to time management, adding an event to your calendar is really just the first step. What's missing? Right: You have to *remember* the event! That's not a problem if you check out your calendar constantly, but I'm sure you're *way* too busy to do that. A better idea is to get Outlook to check out your calendar constantly and, when it sees that an event is upcoming, to send you a reminder in the form of a notification.

Smartly, Outlook is configured out of the box to automatically remind you of any event 15 minutes before the event starts. If you'd prefer a different reminder time — or no reminder at all — then follow these steps to modify the reminder for a new or existing event:

1. **Open the New Event window:**

   - On the Home tab, click New Event.
   - Start a basic event, as I describe earlier in the "Scheduling a basic event" section, then click More Options.

   If you want to modify the reminder time for an existing event, double-click that event.

2. **Fill in the event particulars, including the title, starting date and time, and ending date and time.**

3. **Click the Reminder list, which by default shows 15 Minutes Before.**

   Outlook displays a list of reminder times, shown in Figure 3-7.

4. **Click a reminder time.**

   If you also want Outlook to send you an email to remind you about the event, follow these steps to make it happen:

   - Click Add Email Reminder.

     The Email Reminder dialog box pops up.

   - Click Add Email Reminder.
   - Select the time interval before the event that you want the email reminder to show up in your Inbox.
   - Type a message to yourself.
   - Click Save.

   If you don't want Outlook to notify you about the event, click Don't Remind Me.

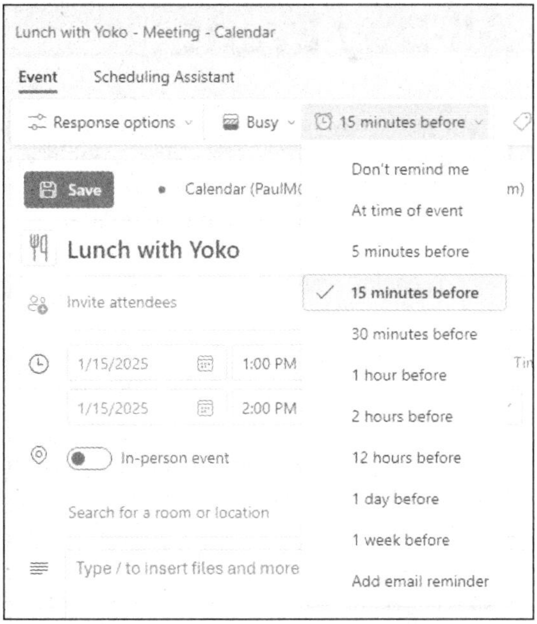


**FIGURE 3-7:** Use the Reminder list to choose the amount of time before the event that you want Outlook to nudge you about it.

5. **Fill in the rest of the event details, as needed.**
6. **Click Save.**

   Outlook saves your event, including your reminder preference.

If you're not happy with Outlook's default reminder time of 15 minutes before each event, follow these steps to customize it:

1. **Choose View ⇨ Calendar Settings**

   The Settings dialog box launches with the Calendar category selected.

2. **Click the Events and Invitations subcategory.**
3. **Use the Default Reminder to select your preferred reminder interval.**

   Or, if you're just not into the reminder thing as a default, choose Don't Remind Me.

4. **Click Save.**

   Outlook saves your setting and will apply it to each new event you create.

# Scheduling an All-Day Event

As I mention earlier, an all-day event is an activity that consumes one or more days (or, at least, the working part of those days). Some activities are obvious events: vacations, trade shows, sales meetings, and so on. But what about, say, a training session that lasts from 9 am to 4 pm? Is that an all-day event or just a long event? From Outlook's point of view, there are two main differences between an all-day event and a regular event:

- » By default, a regular event is marked as "busy" time, so other people know not to schedule events at conflicting times. On the other hand, an all-day event is marked as "free" time.
- » Regular events are entered as time blocks in the Calendar, but all-day events are displayed as a banner at the top of the calendar. This means that you can also schedule regular events on days that you have all-day events.

A good example that illustrates these differences is a trade show. Suppose the show lasts an entire day and you're a sales rep who'll be attending the show. You could schedule the show as a day-long regular event. However, what if you also want to visit with customers who are attending the show? In that case, it would make more sense to schedule the show as an all-day event. This leaves the calendar open for you to schedule regular events with your customers.

Scheduling an all-day event is almost identical to scheduling a regular event, as the following steps show:

1. **Open the New Event window:**
   - On the Home tab, click New Event.
   - Start a basic event, as I describe earlier in the "Scheduling a basic event" section, then click More Options.

   If you want to convert a regular event to an all-day event, double-click that event.
2. **Fill in the event title.**
3. **Click the All Day switch to On.**

   Outlook hides the time controls, shown in Figure 3-8.
4. **Fill in the rest of the event details, to taste.**
5. **Click Save.**

   Outlook saves your all-day event. In the calendar, the all-day event appears above the calendar timeline, as shown in Figure 3-9.

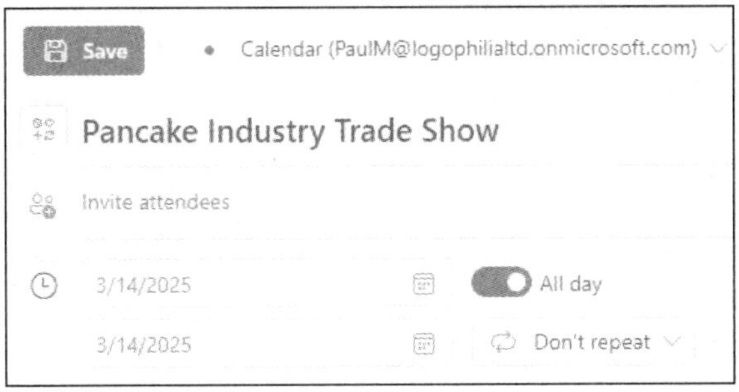


**FIGURE 3-8:** Activate the All Day switch to convert a regular event into an all-day event.

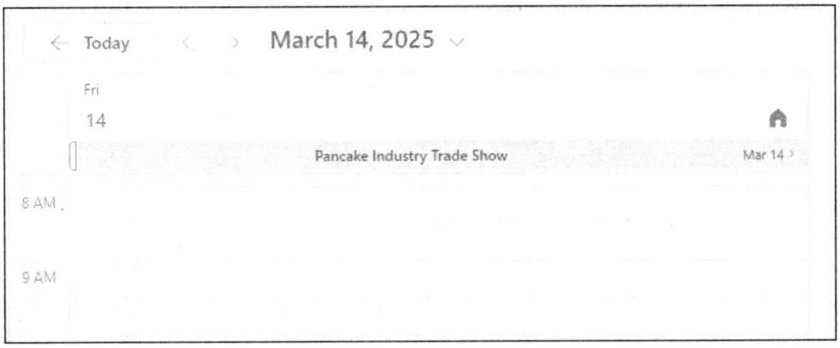


**FIGURE 3-9:** Outlook enters all-day events above the timeline for the scheduled day.

# Requesting a Meeting

Many events are solo affairs (such as dentist appointments or errands) that require no coordination with other people. Other events involve just one or two other people (such as lunches or coffee get-togethers) that can usually be arranged with a couple of instant messages. But then there is the *meeting*, that staple of modern business where a larger number of people gather, either in person or remotely.

Getting folks together for a meeting is never easy, but Outlook solves this dilemma by implementing a couple of time-saving features:

- **Meeting Requests:** These are email messages that you use to set up small meetings. They let the invitees respond to your invitation with a simple click of a button.
- **Scheduling Assistant:** This more sophisticated tool is designed for coordinating larger groups. The Scheduling Assistant feature lets you see in advance the schedule of each invitee, so you can find a suitable time before inviting everyone.

The next two sections show you how to use both features.

## Sending out a new meeting request

If you need to set up a simple meeting that involves just a few people, a basic meeting request is all you need. A meeting request is an email message that asks the recipients to attend a meeting on a particular day at a particular time. The recipients can then check their schedules (although Outlook does this for them automatically) and either accept or reject the request by clicking buttons attached to the message.

To send a meeting request, follow these steps:

1. **Open the New Event window:**
   - On the Home tab, click New Event.
   - Start a basic event, as I describe earlier in the "Scheduling a basic event" section, then click More Options.
2. **Fill in the event title.**
3. **Use the Invite Attendees box to start typing the name or email address of an invitee, then click the invitee when they show up in the search results.**

   If you want to invite everyone in one of your contact lists (refer to Book 5, Chapter 2), start typing the name of the list, then click the name when it appears in the search results.
4. **Repeat Step 3 for each person you want to invite to the meeting.**
5. **If there are people you want to invite whose presence at the meeting is optional, click the Optional link, then use the Invite Optional Attendees box to specify those people.**
6. **Use the Start time controls to specify the date and time that the meeting starts.**

   If you're not sure that your start time will work for everyone, click Find a Time to see each invitee's availability for times close to your proposed start time.
7. **Use the End time controls to specify the date and time the meeting ends.**
8. **If you want each person to attend the meeting in person, click the In-Person Event switch to On.**
9. **Use the Search for Room or Location text box to type the location (such as a room number or address) for the meeting.**
10. **Use the large text box to type notes about the meeting.**

    This message is what will appear in the email invitation that's sent to each person, so be sure to describe your meeting accurately so that people know what the meeting is about. Feel free to format your text to spruce it up a bit.

**11.** **Fill in the rest of the meeting details, as needed.**

**12.** **Click Send.**

Outlook adds the meeting to your schedule and sends out the invitations.

The message the invitee receives will appear similar to the one shown in Figure 3-10. The message includes the meeting times, whether your schedule has a conflict (otherwise you see "No conflicts"), the meeting message, and the list of invitees.

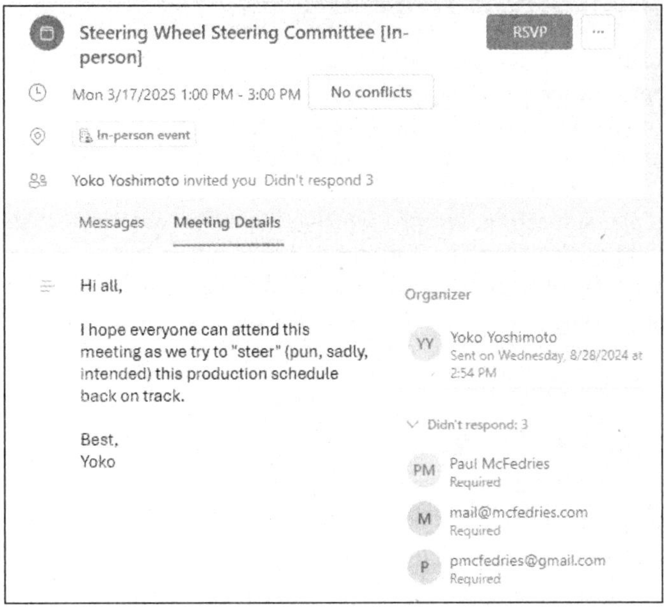


**FIGURE 3-10:** An example of what the meeting request looks like on the recipient's end.

To respond to this request, the recipient clicks the RSVP button, which displays the following buttons:

- **Accept:** Accept the invitation. You can also pull down this list and then click either Yes, In Person (if you'll attend physically) or Yes, Virtually (if you'll attend remotely).
- **Decline:** Decline the invitation.
- **Follow:** Decline the invitation but stipulate to the meeting organizer that you wish to receive information about the meeting.

» **More:** Display a menu with more responses, which includes Maybe (maybe you'll come, maybe you won't); Propose New Time (look for a time that's better for you); Reply to Organizer (send a message just to the meeting organizer); Reply to All Attendees (send a message to everyone invited); and Forward Meeting (pass along the meeting invitation to someone else).

If you Accept the invitation or respond with Maybe, Outlook adds the meeting to your Calendar automatically.

## Planning a meeting

For larger meetings, you can use Outlook's Scheduling Assistant feature to do some advance work. Specifically, you tell Outlook the names of the invitees, and Outlook queries their schedules and shows you when they're free. This lets you choose a convenient time for the meeting before sending out the request.

To plan a meeting, set up a meeting request as described in the previous section, but in particular you need to add all the attendees, including those that are required and those that are optional. When that's done, click the Scheduling Assistant tab. Outlook checks each person's schedule and fills the timeline with blocks that represent each person's existing events and meetings. Figure 3-11 shows an example.

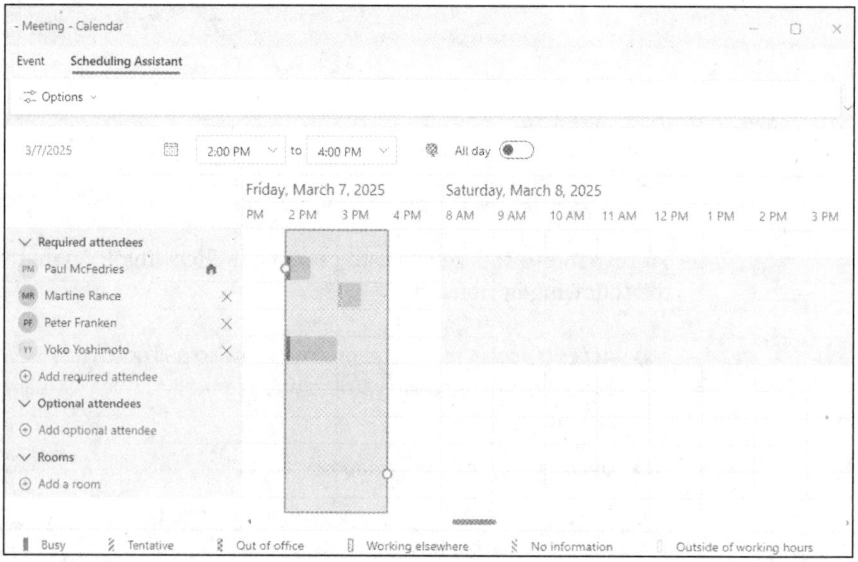


**FIGURE 3-11:** Use the Scheduling Assistant to find a time that works for every attendee.

Now you can adjust your meeting time accordingly. There are three methods you can use:

- Type new values in the meeting's start time and end time controls.
- In the timeline, use the mouse pointer to drag the meeting selection bars left or right. The green bar represents the meeting start time, and the red bar represents the end time.
- In the timeline, move the mouse pointer into the middle of the meeting time (the pointer changes to a grasping hand), then drag the meeting left or right to a new time.

## Tracking a meeting

To monitor the status of the meeting responses, double-click the meeting in your calendar to open the meeting window. The Tracking pane on the right displays a list of the attendees and their current status (Yes, No, Maybe, or Didn't Respond).

## Cancelling a meeting

If you no longer require a meeting, you need to cancel it to alert the attendees. You have two methods to get started:

- In the Calendar grid, double-click the meeting to open it, and then click Cancel.
- In the Calendar grid, right-click the meeting and then click Cancel.

In both cases, Outlook displays a cancellation message addressed to all the meeting participants. Type a message to the attendees and then click Send. Each recipient receives an email message with Canceled in the Subject line and a Remove from Calendar button that they can click to delete the meeting from their calendar.

# 6

# Access 365

# Contents at a Glance

IN THIS CHAPTER

- » Understanding the structure of an Access database
- » Creating your own databases
- » Designing your own tables
- » Building tables with your bare hands

# Chapter 1
# Forging Databases and Tables

Microsoft Access is a *database management system.* This means that Access will not only store your information, but it will also supply you with the means to manage this information — for example, by sorting it, searching it, extracting stuff from it, summarizing it, and so on.

Access is a large, complex, and often intimidating program. However, much of the program's complexity comes from its wealth of features aimed solely at database professionals. If you want just to enter data, access external data, and query and summarize data, then you'll find that a minimum of database theory combined with the right techniques can turn Access into a useable, powerful program. In other words, with the techniques you'll learn in this chapter and the next two, you'll know how to extract meaningful and useful information from whatever jumble of data you now have.

## Understanding Access Databases

In simplest terms, a database is a collection of data with some sort of underlying organization. In most systems, anything related to the data (such as a data entry screen or a query that extracts some of the data) is considered a separate piece of the overall pie. Access, though, is different because its databases consist not only of the basic data, but also of related items you use to work with the data.

If you like, you can think of an Access database as a kind of electronic tool shed. In this tool shed you have not only your raw materials (your data) stored in bins and containers of various shapes and sizes, but you also have a number of tools you can use to manipulate these materials, as well as a work area where all this manipulation happens.

Each Access database consists of a number of different types of objects, but in this mini-book you'll learn about three in particular: tables, forms, and queries. The next three sections introduce you to each type of object.

## Tables: Containers for your data

In Access databases, you store your information in an object called a *table.* Tables are rectangular arrangements of rows and columns, where each column represents a field (a specific category of information) and each row represents a record (a single entry in the table).

Figure 1-1 shows a table of customer data. Notice how the table includes separate fields (columns) for each logical grouping of the data (company name, contact name, and so on).

Customers

| Customer ID | Company Name | Contact Name | Contact Title |
|---|---|---|---|
| ALFKI | Alfreds Futterkiste | Maria Anders | Sales Representative |
| ANATR | Ana Trujillo Emparedados y helados | Ana Trujillo | Owner |
| ANTON | Antonio Moreno Taquería | Antonio Moreno | Owner |
| AROUT | Around the Horn | Thomas Hardy | Sales Representative |
| BERGS | Berglunds snabbköp | Christina Berglund | Order Administrator |
| BLAUS | Blauer See Delikatessen | Hanna Moos | Sales Representative |
| BLONP | Blondel père et fils | Frédérique Citeaux | Marketing Manager |
| BOLID | Bólido Comidas preparadas | Martín Sommer | Owner |
| BONAP | Bon app' | Laurence Lebihan | Owner |
| BOTTM | Bottom-Dollar Markets | Elizabeth Lincoln | Accounting Manager |
| BSBEV | B's Beverages | Victoria Ashworth | Sales Representative |
| CACTU | Cactus Comidas para llevar | Patricio Simpson | Sales Agent |
| CENTC | Centro comercial Moctezuma | Francisco Chang | Marketing Manager |

Record: 1 of 91 No Filter Search

**FIGURE 1-1:** In Access databases, tables store the raw data.

You learn how to work with tables later in this chapter (beginning with the "Designing a Table" section).

## Forms: Making data entry easier

Entering data into a table is unglamorous at best and downright mind-numbing at worst. To make this chore easier, you can create Access database objects called *forms*. Forms provide you with a "template" that you fill in whenever you enter a record. The form displays a blank box or list for each field in the table. Data entry becomes a straightforward matter of filling in the appropriate boxes or selecting data from the lists. As shown in the sample form in Figure 1-2, each box is labeled so that you always know what type of data you're entering. Best of all, each form is easily customizable, so you can move the fields around to make them appear like real-life forms, and you can add fancy effects such as graphics to give your forms visual interest.

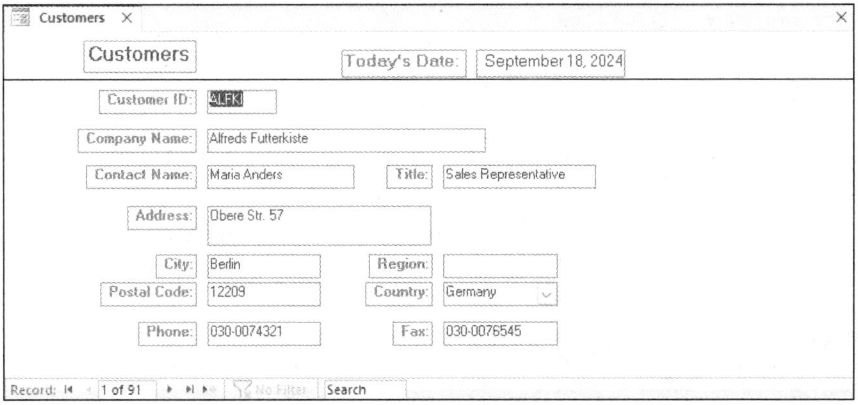


**FIGURE 1-2:** You can use Access forms to make data entry easier.

Refer to the section, "Creating and Using Forms," later in this chapter, to learn more about using Access forms.

## Queries: Asking questions of your data

By far the most common concern expressed by new database users (and many old-timers, as well) is how to extract the information they need from all that data. If you only need to look up a phone number or address, Access has powerful search capabilities (which I cover in Book 6, Chapter 2).

But what if, for example, you have a database of accounts receivable invoices and your boss wants to know right away how many invoices are more than 150 days past due? You could try counting the appropriate records, but if the database is large, you'd probably be out of a job before you finished counting. The better way would be to ask Access to do the counting for you by creating another type of database object: a *query*. Queries are, essentially, questions you ask of your data. In this case, you could ask Access to open the appropriate invoice table, examine the "Past Due" field (or whatever it might be called), and to return a list of all invoices more than 150 days past due.

Queries let you extract from one or more tables a subset of the data. For example, in a table of customer names and addresses, what if you wanted to display a list of firms that are located in France? No problem. You'd just set up a query where you ask Access to extract just those customer records that have "France" in the Country field. The results of such a query are shown in Figure 1-3.

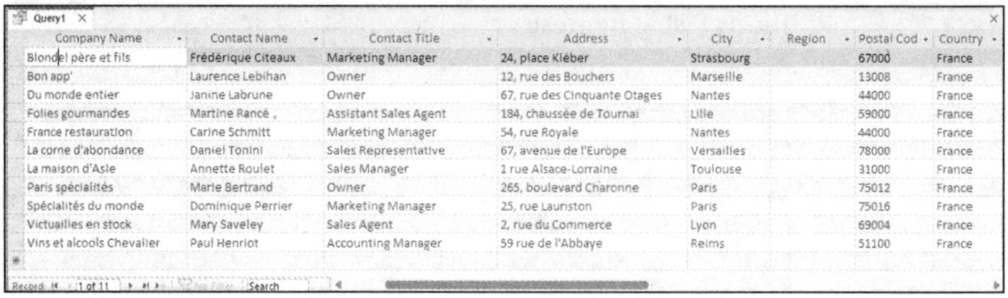


| Company Name | Contact Name | Contact Title | Address | City | Region | Postal Cod | Country |
|---|---|---|---|---|---|---|---|
| Blondel père et fils | Frédérique Citeaux | Marketing Manager | 24, place Kléber | Strasbourg | | 67000 | France |
| Bon app' | Laurence Lebihan | Owner | 12, rue des Bouchers | Marseille | | 13008 | France |
| Du monde entier | Janine Labrune | Owner | 67, rue des Cinquante Otages | Nantes | | 44000 | France |
| Folies gourmandes | Martine Rancé , | Assistant Sales Agent | 184, chaussée de Tournai | Lille | | 59000 | France |
| France restauration | Carine Schmitt | Marketing Manager | 54, rue Royale | Nantes | | 44000 | France |
| La corne d'abondance | Daniel Tonini | Sales Representative | 67, avenue de l'Europe | Versailles | | 78000 | France |
| La maison d'Asie | Annette Roulet | Sales Manager | 1 rue Alsace-Lorraine | Toulouse | | 31000 | France |
| Paris spécialités | Marie Bertrand | Owner | 265, boulevard Charonne | Paris | | 75012 | France |
| Spécialités du monde | Dominique Perrier | Marketing Manager | 25, rue Lauriston | Paris | | 75016 | France |
| Victuailles en stock | Mary Saveley | Sales Agent | 2, rue du Commerce | Lyon | | 69004 | France |
| Vins et alcools Chevalier | Paul Henriot | Accounting Manager | 59 rue de l'Abbaye | Reims | | 51100 | France |

**FIGURE 1-3:** The answer to an Access query that asks, "Which Customer records have 'France' in the Country field?".

You'll learn how to work with queries in Book 6, Chapter 3.

# Creating an Access Database

Although the Northwind Starter Edition sample databases that are available to download (click File, click New, click Northwind Starter Edition, then click Create) are great for experimenting and getting to know the program's features, you'll eventually need to create and work with your own databases. This section shows you a couple of methods for cobbling together a database of your own.

## Creating a blank database

The most direct way to set up a database is to create a blank database container into which you can drop tables, queries, forms, and so on. Here are the steps to follow:

1. **Choose File ⇨ New (or press Ctrl+N).**

   The Backstage view's New screen appears.

2. **Click Blank Database.**

3. **In the File Name text box, type a filename for the new database.**

   By default, Access stores databases in your OneDrive's Documents folder.

   TIP

   To specify a new default database folder, choose File ➪ Options to display the Access Options dialog box with the General tab displayed. To the right of the Default Database Folder option, click Browse, click the folder you want to use, and then click OK. Click OK to close the Access Options dialog box.

4. **To choose a different folder, click the folder icon, use the File New Database dialog box to click a different location, and then click OK.**
5. **Click Create.**

   Access creates the database and displays a new table so you can enter data, as shown in Figure 1-4.



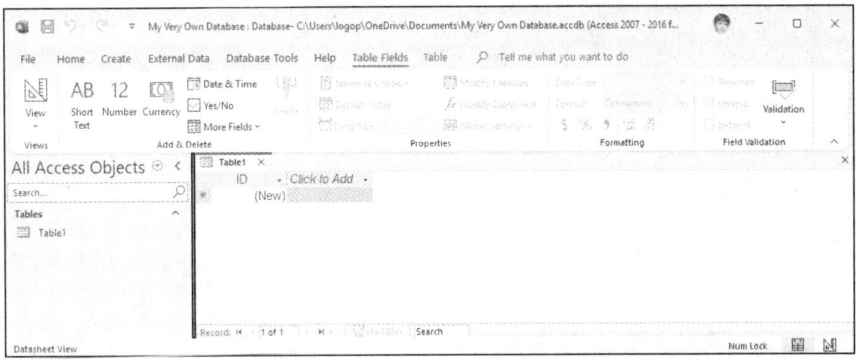


**FIGURE 1-4:** A blank Access database, ready for action.

## Creating a database from a template

Instead of a blank database, you may prefer to use a template to create a database that already has a basic structure in place. Access has more than 20 templates available and you can also find more templates at the Microsoft Office Online site.

Follow these steps to create a new database from a template:

1. **Choose File ➪ New (or press Ctrl+N).**

   The backstage view's New screen appears.

2. **Click the template you want to use.**

   If no template matches what you need, use the Search for Online Templates text box to type a word or two that describes what you want, then press Enter to display the results.

3. **In the File Name text box, type a filename for the new database.**
4. **To choose a different folder, click the folder icon, use the File New Database dialog box to click a different location, and then click OK.**
5. **Click Create.**

   Access creates the database.

Figure 1-5 shows a new database built from a template, in this case the Asset Tracking template.

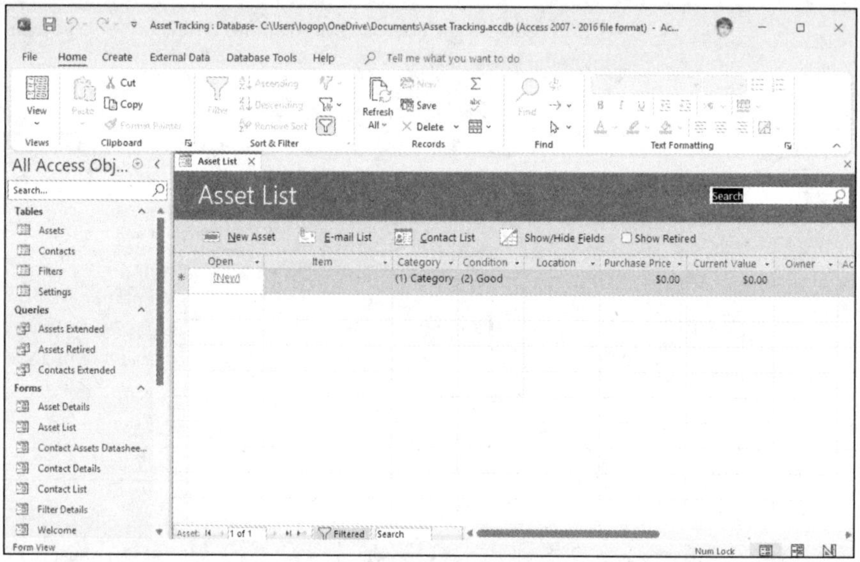


**FIGURE 1-5:** A new Access database based on the Asset Tracking template.

# Working in the Navigation Pane

Below the Ribbon, the Access window is divided into two areas: the Navigation pane on the left and the content area on the right, as shown in Figure 1-6. The Navigation pane lists all the objects that are in the current database, and the content area displays whatever object is currently open.

The Navigation pane is a powerful navigation tool that gives you access (pun semi-intended) to everything that's in your Access database. By default, the Navigation pane is grouped by object: Tables, Queries, Forms, and so on.

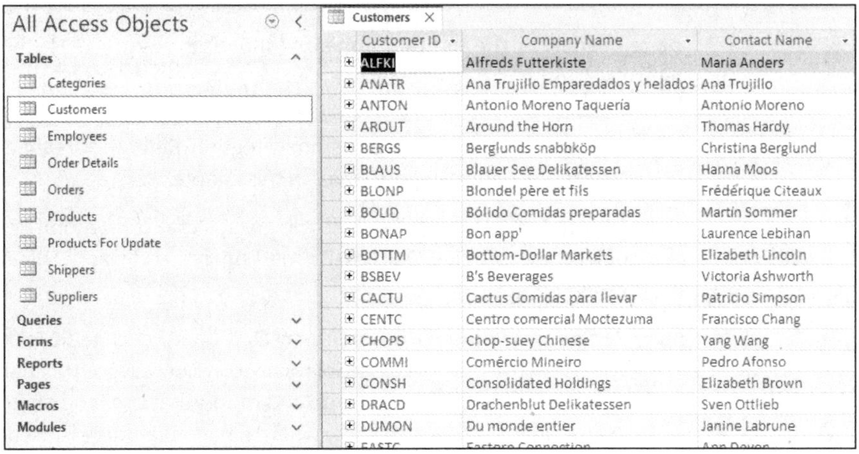


**FIGURE 1-6:** The main Access window offers the Navigation pane on the left and the content window on the right.

Here are a few basic Navigation pane techniques that you need to know:

- To open an object, either double-click the object, or right-click the object and then click Open in the shortcut menu that shows up.

  TIP

  You may find that Access is slightly faster to use if you single-click objects to open them. To set this up, right-click the Navigation pane header, and then click Navigation Options. In the Navigation Options dialog box, under the Open Objects With heading, select the Single-Click option and then click OK.

- To toggle a group between expanded (showing the header and the objects in the group, such as the Tables group in Figure 1-6) and collapsed (showing the header only, such as the Queries and Forms groups in Figure 1-6), click the group header.
- To change the width of the Navigation pane, drag the vertical partition that separates the Navigation pane from the content area.
- To hide the Navigation pane, click the left-pointing arrow (shown in the margin) in the Navigation pane header.
- To display a hidden Navigation pane, click the right-pointing arrow (shown in the margin) in the Navigation pane header.

## Switching the Navigation pane category

The way Access displays the database objects in the Navigation pane depends on the category you choose to display. To display these categories, click the Navigation pane header. In the list that appears (shown in Figure 1-7), the Navigate To Category section has five choices:

- **Custom:** Create your own custom category. (Refer to "Creating a custom Navigation pane category," later in this chapter.)
- **Object Type:** Display the objects in groups that correspond to the Access object types: Tables, Queries, Forms, Reports, and so on. This is the default category.
- **Tables and Related Views:** Display a group for each table in the database. Within each group, Access displays an icon not only for the table itself, but also icons for every query, form, and report that uses the table. This is very useful when you want to know where a particular table is used in the database.
- **Created Date:** Display date-related groups such as Today, Yesterday, Last Week, and Last Month. The objects in each group were created on that date or within that date range.
- **Modified Date:** Display date-related groups where the objects in each group were last modified on that date or within that date range.

## Filtering the Navigation pane by group

When you select a category as described in the previous section, Access populates the Navigation pane with several groups, where the specific groups that appear depend on the category. You can also use these groups to filter the objects that appear in the Navigation pane. Click the Navigation pane header and note that the list that appears (refer to Figure 1-7) includes a Filter By Group section. You have two choices:

- To filter the Navigation pane to show just the objects from a specific group, click that group.
- To remove the filter and show all the objects in the category, click the All *X* item, where *X* depends on the category (for example, All Access Objects or All Dates).

Rather than filtering the Navigation pane to show just the objects from a single group, you can also hide entire groups by following these steps:

1. **Select the category you want to display.**
2. **Right-click the header of the group you want to hide.**

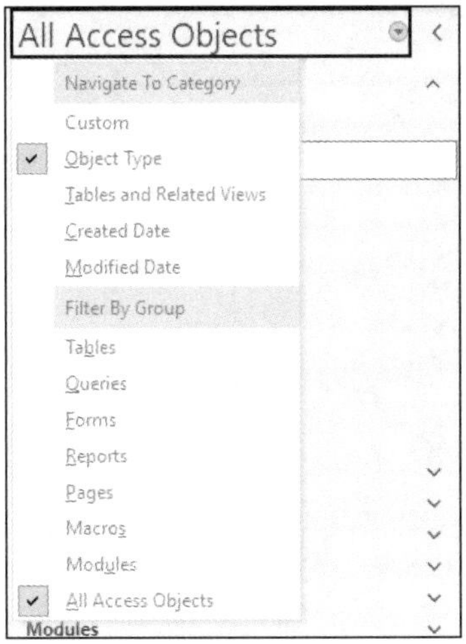


**FIGURE 1-7:** Click the Navigation pane header to choose a different category.

3. **Click Hide.**
4. **Repeat steps 2 and 3 to hide other groups as needed.**

If you have a number of groups you want to hide, here's an easier method (you can also use this method to show groups that you have previously hidden):

1. **Select the category you want to display.**
2. **Right-click the Navigation pane header and then click Navigation Options.**

   Access displays the Navigation Options dialog box, shown in Figure 1-8.
3. **Use the Categories list to click the category you want to work with.**
4. **In the Groups list, deselect the check box for each group you want to hide, and select the check box for each group you want to show.**
5. **Click OK.**

## Creating a custom Navigation pane category

If none of the built-in Navigation pane categories are exactly what you need, you can create a custom category with your own groups. For example, you could create groups for different departments within your company, such as Sales, Marketing, Production, and Personnel. Similarly, you could create different categories for different projects you're working on.

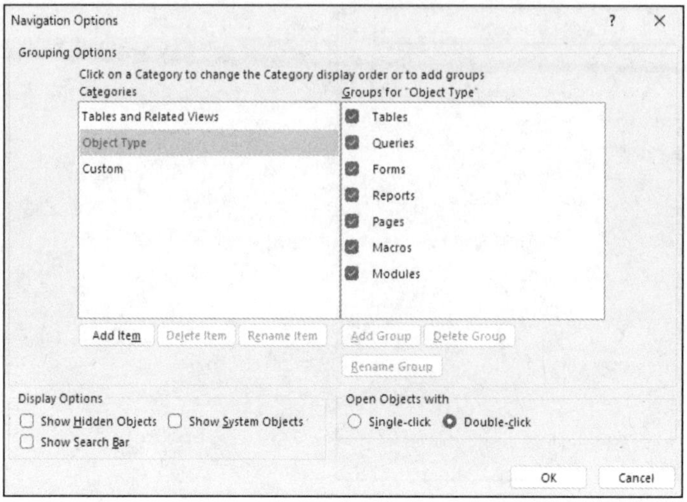


**FIGURE 1-8:** Use the Navigation Options dialog box to hide and show groups within a Navigation pane category.

Here are the steps to follow to create a custom category:

1. **Right-click the Navigation pane header and then click Navigation Options to display the Navigation Options dialog box.**
2. **If you want to use the Custom category, click it. Otherwise, click Add Item, type a name for the new category, and press Enter.**
3. **Click Add Group, type a name for the new group, and press Enter.**
4. **Repeat step 3 to add all the groups you require.**
5. **To change the position of a group, click it and then click the Up and Down arrow buttons.**
6. **Click OK.**
7. **Right-click the Navigation pane header and then click the category you created.**
8. **To assign an object to a group, click and drag it from the Unassigned Objects list and drop it on the group.**
9. **Repeat step 8 to assign all the database objects to a group.**

# Designing a Table

With your database created, you now need to populate it with one or more tables. Before you create a new table, however, you need to plan your table design. By asking yourself a few questions in advance, you can save yourself the trouble of redesigning your table later. For simple tables, you need to ask yourself three basic questions:

- » Does the table belong in the current database?
- » What type of data should I store in each table?
- » What fields should I use to store the data?

The next few sections examine these questions in more detail.



## Does the table belong in the current database?

Each database you create should be set up for a specific purpose. It could be home finances, business transactions, personal assets, or whatever. In any case, once you know the purpose of the database, you can then decide if the table you want to create fits in with the database theme.

For example, if the purpose of the database is to record only information related to your personal finances, it wouldn't make sense to include a table of recipes in the same database. Similarly, it would be inappropriate to include a table of office baseball pool winners in a database of accounts payable invoices.

## What type of data should I store in each table?

The most important step in creating a table is determining the information you want it to contain. In theory, Access tables can be quite large: up to 255 fields and 2 GB in size. In practice, however, you should minimize the size of your tables. This saves memory and makes it easier to manage and search the data easier. Therefore, you should strive to set up all your tables with only essential information.

For example, suppose you want to store your personal assets in a database. You have to decide whether you want all your assets in a single table, or whether it would be better to create separate tables for each type of asset. If you're only going to be entering basic information — such as the date purchased, a description of each item, and its current value — you can probably get away with a single table. More detailed data will almost certainly require individual tables for each asset. For example, a table of books might include information such as the title, the author name, the date purchased, the number of pages, the publisher, and so on. Clearly, such a table wouldn't work for, say, your collection of jewelry.

When you've decided on the tables you want to use, you then need to think about how much data you want to store in each table. In your book collection, for example, would you want to include information on the editor, the publishing date, and the number of people the author thanks in the acknowledgments? This might all be crucial information for you, but you need to remember that the more data you store, the longer it will take you to enter each record.

## What fields should I use to store the data?

Now you're almost ready for action. The last thing you need to figure out is the specific fields to include in the table. For the most part, the fields are determined by the data itself. For example, a table of business contacts would certainly include fields for name, address, and phone number. However, should you split the name into two fields — one for the first name and one for the last name? If you think you'll need to sort the table by last name, then, yes, you probably should use two fields for the name. What about the address? You'll probably need individual fields for the city, state, and postal code.

Here are two general rules to follow when deciding how many fields to include in your tables:

- Ask yourself whether you really need the data for a particular field (or if you might need it in the near future). For example, if you think your table of contact names might someday be used to create form letters, a field to record titles (Ms., Mr., Dr., and so on) would come in handy. When in doubt, err on the side of too many fields rather than too few.
- Always split your data into the smallest fields that make sense. Splitting first and last names is common practice, but creating a separate field for, say, the phone number area code would probably be overkill.

REMEMBER

Don't worry too much about the design process right now. It's straightforward to make changes down the road by, say, adding and deleting fields, so you're never stuck with a bad design.

## Deciding which field to use for a primary key

When you create a table, you'll need to decide which field to use as the primary key. The *primary key* is a field that uses a unique number or character sequence to identify each record in the table. Keys are used constantly in the real world. If you're American, your social security number is a key that identifies you in government records. Most machines and appliances have unique serial numbers. This book (like most books) has a 13-digit ISBN — International Standard Book Number (which appears on the back cover).

Primary keys are useful for a few reasons:

- » Access creates an index for the primary key field. You can perform searches on indexed data much more quickly than on regular data, so many Access operations perform faster if a primary key is present.
- » Keys make it easy to find records in a table because the key entries are unique (things such as last names and addresses can have multiple spellings, which makes them hard to find).
- » A primary key is a handy way to avoid data-entry errors. Since the entries in a primary key field must be unique, there is no chance for someone to, say, enter the same account number for two different customers.



You can set things up so that Access sets and maintains the primary key for you, or you can do it yourself. Which one do you choose? Here are some guidelines:

- » If your data contains a number or character sequence that uniquely defines each record, you can set the key yourself. For example, invoices usually have unique numbers that are perfect for a primary key. Other fields that can serve as primary keys are employee IDs, customer account numbers, and purchase order numbers.
- » If your data has no such unique identifier, let Access create a key for you. This means that Access will set up an AutoNumber field that will assign a unique number to each record (the first record will be 1, the second 2, and so on).

# Creating a Table

Access gives you three main methods to create tables:

- » Using the Datasheet view
- » Using the table Design view
- » Importing data from an external source

The next few sections show you how to wield these tools.

REMEMBER

I might as well mention a fourth method: creating a table from a template. On the Create tab, in the Templates group, click Application Parts and then click the template you want to use (such as Contacts or Tasks). Access adds the new table to the Navigation pane, along with any related database objects that go with the new table.

## Creating a table using the Datasheet view

The most straightforward way to create a table is to use the Datasheet view to build the table on the fly. That is, as you add your fields, you specify the type of data you want in each field: numbers, text, currency values, dates and times, Yes/No fields, and so on. (You can find more detailed information about Access data types later in this chapter in the "Assigning a data type to the field" section.) Since you're in the Datasheet view, you can also populate each field with data as you go.

Here are the steps to follow to create a table using the Datasheet view:

1. **Access gives you two ways to get started:**
   - *Create a new database:* In this case, Access automatically adds a new table to the database.
   - *Create a blank table:* On the Create tab, in the Tables group, click Table.

   Either way, Access displays a new tab for the table and the Add New Field column, which displays Click to Add as the header.
2. **Click the Click to Add header.**

   Access displays a list of the available data types, as shown in Figure 1-9.

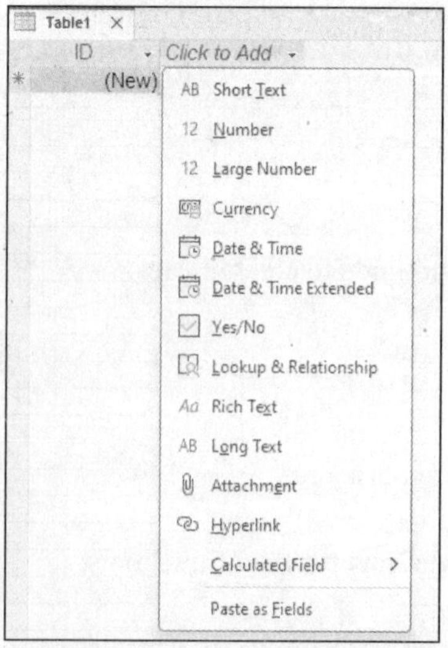


**FIGURE 1-9:** Choose a data type for the field.

3. **Click the data type you want to apply to the field.**

   Access applies the data type, adds a generic name for the field (such as Field1), and opens the field name for editing.

4. **Type the name you prefer to use for the field.**

   Refer to the section "Specifying a name for the field," later in this chapter, to learn the rules you need to follow when assigning a name to a field.

5. **Type a value for the field and press Enter.**
6. **Repeat steps 2 through 5 to define all the fields in your table.**
7. **Choose File ⇨ Save.**

   Access displays the Save As dialog box.

8. **Type a name for the new table and then click OK.**



## Creating a table using the Design view

Working directly in the Datasheet view makes creating tables easy, but there are a few things that you can't do. For example, you can't specify a field description — text that appears in the status bar when you select the field — or a field caption — a text label that appears beside the field when you build a form based on the table. More significantly, the Datasheet view does not enable you to specify a custom data format, an input mask, a validation rule, and a default value.

To get more control over your tables, you need to build them using the Table Design view. To get started, open the Create tab then, in the Tables group, click Table Design. Access creates the new table tab, opens the table in Design view, and displays the Table Design contextual tab, as shown in Figure 1-10.

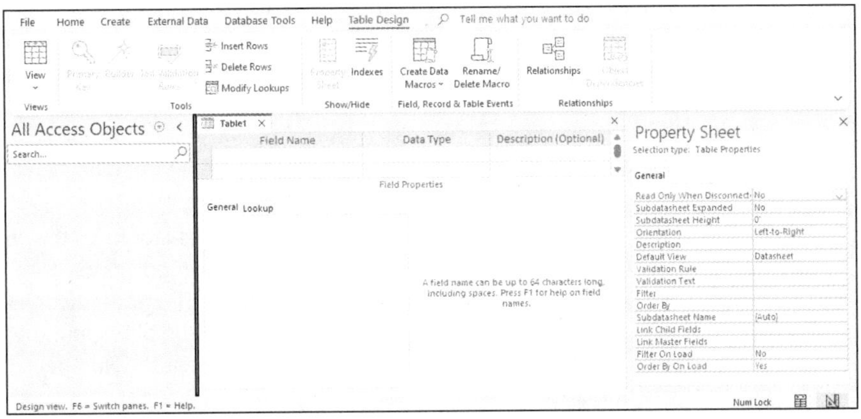


**FIGURE 1-10:** Use the Design view to get maximum control over the construction of your table.

You use the Design view to set up the fields you want to include in your table. For each field, you need to do four things:

1. Type a name for the field.
2. Assign the field's data type.
3. Type a description for the field.
4. Set the field's properties.

The next few sections take you through each of these steps.

## Specifying a name for the field

You use the Field Name column to type a name for the field. This process is generally straightforward, but you need to follow a few rules:

- Names can be up to 64 characters long, so you have lots of room to make them descriptive. One caveat, though: The longer your names, the fewer fields that fit onscreen when it's time to enter data.
- You can use any combination of letters, numbers, spaces, and other characters, but you can't use periods (.), exclamation points (!), backquotes (`), or square brackets ([]).
- Each name must be unique in the table. Access won't let you duplicate field names in the same table.

When you've typed the field name, press Tab to move to the Data Type column.

## Assigning a data type to the field

You use the Data Type column to tell Access what kind of data must appear in the field. This is useful during data entry because if you try to enter the wrong type of data — say, text in a number field — Access displays a pop-up warning and won't let you enter the mismatched data.

Use the drop-down list to click one of the following data types:

- **Short Text:** This is a catch-all type you can use for fields that will contain any combination of letters, numbers, and symbols (such as parentheses and dashes). These fields will usually be short entries (the maximum is 255 characters) such as names, addresses, and phone numbers. For purely numeric fields, however, you should use either the Number or Currency type (discussed in a moment).

- **Long Text:** Use this type for longer alphanumeric entries. Memo field entries are usually several sentences or paragraphs long, but they can contain up to 64,000 characters. These types of fields are useful for long text passages or random notes. In a table of customer names, for example, you could use a memo field to record customers' favorite colors, the names of their spouses and kids, and so on.
- **Number:** Use this type for fields that will contain numbers only. This is particularly true for fields you'll be using for calculations. (Note, though, that fields containing dollar amounts should use the Currency type, described in a moment.)
- **Large Number:** This is also a data type that supports numbers, but in this case the field supports really large (positive or negative) integer values. Specifically, this type (database nerds also call it BigInt) supports integers in the range -9,223,372,036,854,775,808 to 9,223,372,036,854,775,807.
- **Date/Time:** This type is for fields that will use only dates and times. This data type can handle dates from the year 100 right up to the year 9999.
- **Date/Time Extended:** This type is also for fields that will use only dates and times, but it can handle dates from the year 1 up to the year 9999.
- **Currency:** Use this field for dollar values.
- **AutoNumber:** This type creates a numeric entry that Access fills in automatically whenever you add a record. Because this type of field assigns a unique number to each record, it's ideal for setting up your own primary key. (Refer to the section "Deciding which field to use for a primary key," earlier.)
- **Yes/No:** Use this type for fields that will contain only Yes or No values.
- **OLE Object:** This type creates a field that can hold data from other programs (such as a graphic image or even an entire spreadsheet).
- **Hyperlink:** This field type is used for addresses of internet (or intranet) sites or email addresses. When you display the table in Datasheet view, Access configures the addresses as links that you can click.
- **Attachment:** This data type lets you attach documents to a record. Just like an email attachment, a record attachment is a separate file that you can open or save.
- **Calculated:** Sets up the field to be the result of a calculation that you specify using the Expression Builder that appears. Book 6, Chapter 3 offers a detailed description of how the Expression Builder works.
- **Lookup Wizard:** This type displays a combo box from which the user can select from a list of possible values. Selecting this type loads the Lookup Wizard, which takes you through the process of specifying which values to use. You can either designate a field from another database (Access will display the unique values from the field) or enter the values yourself.

When you have selected the data type, press Tab to move to the Description column.

## Typing a description for the field

Use the Description column to enter a description for the field. You can use up to 255 characters, so there's plenty of room. The Description field text appears in the status bar when you're entering data for the field.

## Setting the field properties

Your last task for each field is to set up the field's properties. These properties control various aspects of the field, such as its size and what format the data takes. The properties for each field are displayed in the bottom half of the design window. To change a property, you click the field you want to work with and then click the property.

The properties that appear depend on the data type of the selected field. Space limitations prevent me from covering every possible property, but here's a quick review of the most common ones:

- **Field Size:** In a Text field, this property controls the number of characters you can enter. You can enter a number between 1 and 255, but the size you enter should only be large enough to accommodate the maximum possible entry. In a phone number field, for example, you would set the size to 13 or 14. In a Number field, you select the appropriate numeric type, such as Integer or Single.
- **Format:** This property controls the display of dates and numbers. For example, the Long Date format would display a date as Thursday, August 23, 2025, but the Short Date format would display the date as 8/23/2025. You learn how to build a custom format later in this chapter.
- **Default Value:** This property sets up an initial value that appears in the field automatically whenever you add a new record to the table. For example, suppose you have a table of names and addresses that includes a Country field. If most of the records will be from the same country, you could add it as the default (for example, USA or Canada).

  TIP

  In a Date/Time field, you can make the current date the default value by typing **=Date()** as the Default Value property. For the current time, instead, type **=Time().** To get both the current date and time, type **=Now().**
- **Required:** In most tables, you'll have some fields that are optional and some that are required. For required fields, set their Required property to Yes. Access will then warn you if you accidentally leave the field blank.

» **Indexed:** Tables that are indexed on a certain field make finding values in that field easier. If you think you'll be doing a lot of searching in a field, set its Indexed property to Yes.

## Creating a custom data format

The default formats in the Format drop-down list are fine for many needs, but they may not be exactly what you need. Fortunately, Access has an extensive list of symbols that you can use to build your own custom data formats. Table 1-1 lists these data format symbols.



**TABLE 1-1** Custom Data Format Symbols

| Symbol | Description |
|---|---|
| # | Holds a place for a digit and displays the digit exactly as typed; displays nothing if no number is entered. |
| 0 | Holds a place for a digit and displays the digit exactly as typed; displays 0 if no number is entered. |
| . (period) | Sets the location of the decimal point |
| , (comma) | Sets the location of the thousands separator; marks only the location of the first thousand. |
| % | Multiplies the number by 100 (for display only) and adds the percent (%) character. |
| E+ e+ E– e– | Displays the number in scientific format. E– and e– place a minus sign in the exponent; E+ and e+ place a plus sign in the exponent. |
| / (slash) | Sets the location of the fraction separator |
| $ ( ) – + <space> | Displays the character |
| d | Day number without a leading zero (1 – 31) |
| dd | Day number with a leading zero (01 – 31) |
| ddd | Three-letter day abbreviation (Mon, for example) |
| dddd | Full day name (Monday, for example) |
| m | Month number without a leading zero (1 – 12) |
| mm | Month number with a leading zero (01 – 12) |
| mmm | Three-letter month abbreviation (Aug, for example) |
| mmmm | Full month name (August, for example) |

*(continued)*

**TABLE 1-1** *(continued)*

| Symbol | Description |
|---|---|
| yy | Two-digit year (00 – 99) |
| yyyy | Full year (1900 – 2078) |
| h | Hour without a leading zero (0 – 24) |
| hh | Hour with a leading zero (00 – 24) |
| n | Minute without a leading zero (0 – 59) |
| nn | Minute with a leading zero (00 – 59) |
| s | Second without a leading zero (0 – 59) |
| ss | Second with a leading zero (00 – 59) |
| AM/PM, am/pm, A/P | Displays the time using a 12-hour clock; omit these to use a 24-hour clock |
| / : . – | Symbols used to separate parts of dates or times |
| * | Repeats whatever character immediately follows the asterisk until the field is full; does not replace other symbols or numbers. |
| @ | Holds a place for text |

## Specifying an input mask

One of the major headaches that database administrators have to deal with is data entered in an inconsistent way. For example, consider the following phone numbers:

```
(123)555-6789
(123) 555-6789
(123)5556789
123555-6789
1235556789
```

These kinds of inconsistencies might appear trivial, but they can cause all kinds of problems, ranging from other users misreading the data or improper sorting to difficulties analyzing or querying the data. And it isn't just phone numbers that cause problems. You can also get inconsistencies with social security numbers, ZIP codes, dates, times, account numbers, and more.

One way to avoid such inconsistencies is to add a field description (status bar message) that specifies the correct format to use. Unfortunately, these prompts are not guaranteed to work every time (or even most of the time).

A better solution is to apply an input mask to the field. An input mask is a kind of template that shows users how to enter the data and prevents them from entering incorrect characters (such as a letter where a number is required). For example, here's an input mask for a phone number:

```
(___)___-____
```

Each underscore (_) acts as a placeholder for (in this case) a digit, and the parentheses and dash appear automatically as the user enters the number.

## Using the Input Mask Wizard

The easiest way to create an input mask is to use the Input Mask Wizard. Here are the steps to follow:

1. **Click inside the Input Mask property.**
2. **Click the ellipsis (. . .) button to start the Input Mask Wizard, shown in Figure 1-11.**

   If at this point Access prompts you to save the table, click Yes.

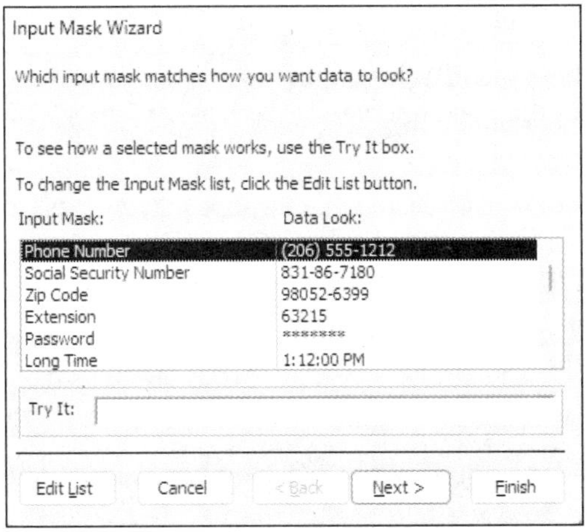


**FIGURE 1-11:** Use the Input Mask Wizard to choose a predefined input mask or to create your own input mask.

3. **In the Input Mask list, click the input mask you want (or one that's close to what you want) and then click Next.**

4. **Use the Input Mask box to make changes to the mask (the next section describes the specifics of which symbols to use), use the Placeholder Character list to choose the character you want to appear in the input mask as a placeholder, and then click Next.**

5. **Click the option that matches how you want the field data stored in the table (click Next after you've made your choice):**

   - *With the symbols in the mask:* Select this option if you want the extra symbols (such as the parentheses and dash in a phone number mask) stored along with the data.
   - *Without the symbols in the mask:* Select this option to store only the data. (The symbols still appear when you view the table, but the symbols aren't stored.)

6. **Click Finish.**

   Access adds the input mask to the Input Mask field.

## Creating a custom input mask expression

If your data doesn't fit any of the predefined input masks, you need to create a custom mask that suits your needs. You do this by creating an expression that consists of three kinds of characters:

- **Data placeholders:** These characters are replaced by the actual data typed by the users. The different placeholders specify the type of character the users must enter (such as a digit or letter) and whether the character is optional or required.
- **Modifiers:** These characters aren't displayed in the mask; instead, they're used to modify the mask in some way (such as converting all the entered characters to lowercase).
- **Literals:** These are extra characters that appear in the mask the same as you enter them in the expression. For example, you might use parentheses as literals to surround the area code portion of a phone number.

Table 1-2 lists the data placeholders you can use to build your input mask expressions.

Table 1-3 lists the modifiers and literals you can use to build your input mask expressions.

You can type your input mask expressions directly into the Input Mask property, or you can modify a predefined input mask using the Input Mask Wizard.

**TABLE 1-2** **Data Placeholders to Use for Custom Input Masks**

| Placeholder | Data Type | Description |
|---|---|---|
| 0 | Digit (0 – 9) | The character is required; the users are not allowed to include a plus sign (+) or a minus sign (-). |
| 9 | Digit or space | The character is optional; the users are not allowed to include a plus sign (+) or a minus sign (-). |
| # | Digit or space | The character is optional; the users are allowed to include a plus sign (+) or minus sign (-). |
| L | Letter (a – z or A – Z) | The character is required. |
| ? | Letter (a – z or A – Z) | The character is optional. |
| a | Letter or digit | The character is required. |
| A | Letter or digit | The character is optional. |
| & | Any character or space | The character is required. |
| C | Any character or space | The character is optional. |

**TABLE 1-3** **Modifiers and Literals to Use for Custom Input Masks**

| Modifier | Description |
|---|---|
| \ | Displays the following character as a literal; for example, \( is displayed as (. |
| "text" | Displays the string text as a literal; for example, "MB" is displayed as MB. |
| . | Decimal separator |
| , | Thousands separator |
| : ; - / | Date and time separators |
| < | Displays all the following letters as lowercase |
| > | Displays all the following letters as uppercase |
| ! | Displays the input mask from right to left when you have optional data placeholders on the left |
| Password | Displays the characters as asterisks so that other people can't read the data |

For example, suppose your company uses account numbers that consist of four uppercase letters and four digits, with a dash (-) in between. Here's an input mask suitable for entering such numbers:

```
>aaaa\-0000
```

Note, too, that input masks can contain up to three sections separated by semicolons (;):

```
First;Second;Third
```

- *First:* This section holds the input mask expression.
- *Second:* This optional section specifies whether Access stores the literals in the table when you enter data. Use 0 to include the literals; use 1 (or nothing) to store only the data.
- *Third:* This optional section specifies the placeholder character. The default is the underscore (_).

For example, following is an input mask for a ZIP code that stores the dash separator and displays dots (.) as placeholders:

```
00000\-9999;0;.
```

## Setting up a validation rule

Another way you can help prevent data-entry errors is to use the Access data validation feature. With data validation, you create rules that specify exactly what kind of data can be entered and in what range that data can fall. You can also specify pop-up input messages that appear when data is entered improperly.

Follow these steps to define the settings for a data validation rule:

1. **Click inside the Validation Rule property.**
2. **Type a formula that specifies the validation criteria.**

   You can either type the formula directly into the property box or you can click the ellipsis (. . .) button and create the formula using the Expression Builder.
3. **If you want a dialog box to appear when the user enters invalid data, click inside the Validation Text property and then specify the message that appears.**

Table 1-4 summarizes the operators you can use when building your validation rule (I discuss these operators in more detail in Book 6, Chapter 3).

For example, suppose you want the users to enter an interest rate. This should be a positive quantity, of course, but it should also be less than 1. (That is, you want users to enter 6% as 0.06 instead of 6.) Here is a Validation Rule property expression that ensures this:

```
>0 And <1
```

**TABLE 1-4** **Data Validation Rule Operators**

| Operator | Description |
|---|---|
| <> *value* | Not equal to — validates the entry only if it's not equal to the specified *value* |
| > *value* | Greater than — validates the entry only if it's greater than the specified *value* |
| >= *value* | Greater than or equal to — validates the entry only if it's greater than or equal to the specified *value* |
| < *value* | Less than — validates the entry only if it's less than the specified *value* |
| <= *value* | Less than or equal to — validates the entry only if it's less than or equal to the specified *value* |
| Like *text* | Validates the entry only if it matches the characters in *text*, including any wildcard characters: ? for single characters and * for any number of characters |
| Between *x* And *y* | Validates the entry only if it's *x* or *y* or anything in between |
| In(*x*,*y*,*z*,. . .) | Validates the entry only if it's the same as one of the items specified in the parentheses |
| Is Null | Validates the entry only if it's blank |
| *exp1* And *exp2* | Validates the entry only if it returns True for both the expressions *exp1* and *exp2* |
| *exp1* Or *exp2* | Validates the entry only if it returns True for at least one of the expressions *exp1* and *exp2* |
| Not *exp* | Validates the entry only if it returns False for the expression *exp* |



## Setting the primary key

Every table should have a primary key so that you have some unique data for each record. To set up a primary key, you need to follow these steps:

1. **Create a field that will contain non-blank entries that uniquely identify each record.**

   If your data doesn't have such a field (such as invoice numbers or customer account codes), all is not lost. Just set up a new field (you could even name it "Primary Key") and assign it the AutoNumber data type.

2. **Place the cursor anywhere in the field row.**
3. **On the Table Design tab, in the Tools group, click Primary Key.**

   Access designates the primary key field by placing a key beside the field name.

## Saving the table

When your table is set up the way you want, you need to save your changes for posterity. (Also, you must save the table before Access allows you to enter data into it.) To do this, follow these steps:

1. **Choose File ⇨ Save (or press Ctrl+S).**

   The first time you do this, Access displays the Save As dialog box.

2. **Use the Table Name text box to type the name you want to use for the table.**

   Table names can be up to 64 characters long, and they can't include exclamation points (!), periods (.), square brackets ([]), or backquotes (`).

3. **Click OK to save the table.**

## Working with fields

Here's a quick summary of a few useful field-related techniques that should come in handy when you're working in the Design view:

- **Selecting a field:** To work with a field, you often need to select it. You do so by clicking the field selection button, which is the column to the left of the field name. To select multiple fields, click and drag the field selection buttons.
- **Moving a field:** The order that you add fields in the Design view grid (top to bottom) is the order that Access displays the fields in the Datasheet view (left to right). If the current field order is not how you want to enter the data, you need to move the fields to get the correct order. To move a field, select it, click and drag the field selection button up or down to the position you want, and then drop the field in the new location.
- **Inserting a new field:** You normally add new fields at the bottom of the Design view grid. However, what if you want to insert the new field somewhere in the middle of the table? You could add the field at the bottom and then move it, but Access gives you a way to save a step. Select the field above which you want the new field to be inserted, then, on the Table Design tab, in the Tools group, click Insert Row. Access creates a blank field above the current field.
- **Deleting a field:** To delete a field you no longer need, select the field, then, on the Table Design tab, in the Tools group, click Delete Rows (or press Delete).

## Switching between the Design and Datasheet views

To add data to your table, you need to switch to Datasheet view, and to make further changes to the table you need to return to Design view. Here are the techniques to use to switch between these two views:

- **Datasheet view:** On the Table Design tab, in the Views group, click View and then click Datasheet View. Alternatively, right-click the table tab and then click Datasheet View.
- **Design view:** On the Table Design tab, in the Views group, click View and then click Design View. Alternatively, right-click the table tab and then click Design View.



# Importing External Data

If the data you want to work with resides in an external data source — usually a local file, a remote file (on a network or on the internet), or data on a server — you need to import it into Access. Depending on the type of data source you're using, Access gives you one or more of the following choices for importing the data:

- Import the source data into a new table in the current database. In this case, Access either creates a new table to hold the data or replaces any data in an existing table. No link is maintained with the original data.
- Append a copy of the records to an existing table. In this case, Access adds the source data to the existing table. If the table does not exist, Access creates it. No link is maintained with the original data.
- Link to the data source by creating a linked table. In this case, Access adds the source data to the new table. A link is maintained with the original data, so if that data changes, the changes are reflected in the Access version of the data.

Access supports a number of data sources, including the following: Access databases, Excel workbooks, text files, XML files, Open Database Connectivity (ODBC) data sources, HTML documents, Outlook folders, SharePoint lists, and dBASE files.

Here are the general steps to follow to import external data in your Access database (the specific steps vary depending on the data source):

1. **Open the External Data tab.**
2. **In the Import & Link group, click New Data Source, then click the data source you want to use.**

   After clicking New Data Source, you click the appropriate From *X* command (where *X* is File, Database, Online Services, or Other Sources), then click the data source. For example, if your data source is a text file, you'd click From File, then click Text File.

   Access displays the Get External Data dialog box. Figure 1-12 shows the version that appears when you're importing data from a text file.

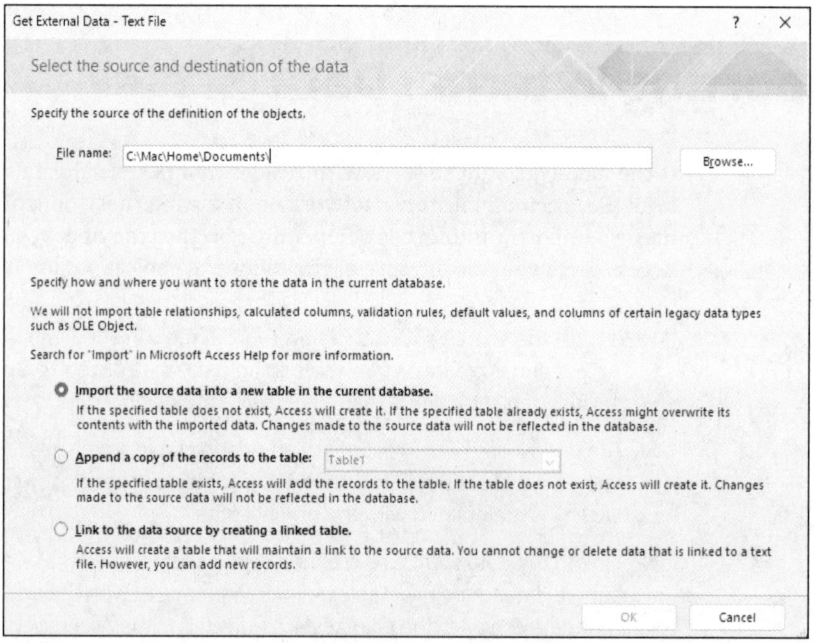


**FIGURE 1-12:** The layout of the Get External Data dialog box varies depending on the data source (such as text, shown here).

3. **Use the File Name text box to type the path and name of the file you want to import.**

   More likely, you'll want to click Browse to select the file using the File Open dialog box.

4. **Select the option that specifies how you want Access to import the data.**
5. **Click OK.**

6. **Follow the dialog boxes that appear (again, these vary according to the data source).**

   When you're done, Access displays the Save Import Steps dialog box.

7. **If you'll be using the same steps to import data later on, select the Save Import Steps check box.**

8. **Click Close.**



# Creating and Using Forms

After you use Access for a while, you quickly come to realize that using a datasheet to enter data into a table is not particularly efficient — you usually have to scroll to the right to get to all the fields, which means you can't display the entire record on the screen — and the no-nonsense row-and-column format of the datasheet is serviceable but not at all attractive.

The datasheet is a reasonable tool if you're only entering one or two records, but if you're entering a dozen records or even a hundred, you need to leave the datasheet behind and use the Access data entry tool of choice: the *form*. A form is a collection of controls — usually labels and text boxes, but also lists, check boxes, and option buttons — each of which represents either a field or the name of a field. Forms not only make data entry easier and more efficient, but thanks to Access's large collection of formatting tools, they can also make data entry more attractive.

## Creating a basic form

By far, the easiest way to create a form is to use one of the predefined form layouts, which let you create a form from an existing table or query with just a couple of mouse clicks. Access has several of these layouts, but you'll use the following three most often:

- **Simple form:** This is a basic form layout that shows the data from one record at a time.
- **Split form:** This layout displays a datasheet on top and a form below. When you click a record in the datasheet, the record data appears in the form.
- **Multiple items form:** This is a tabular layout that shows the field names at the top and the records in rows.

In each case, Access analyzes the table or query and then creates a form using the following guidelines:

- Most text and numeric fields are represented by a simple text box.
- Yes/No fields are represented by a check box.
- In a simple form, if the table has a field that's used as the basis of a one-to-many relationship with another table and the current table is the "one" side of that relationship, the "many" table's related orders are displayed in a subform. For example, the Customers table might have a one-to-many relationship with the Orders table (each customer can place multiple orders), so a simple form built for the Customers data would show a subform that contains each customer's data from the Orders table.

TECHNICAL STUFF

The example of the Customers and Orders tables demonstrates the most common relational model, where a single record in one table — called the *parent table* — relates to multiple records in a second table — called the *child table.* This is called a *one-to-many* relationship. To learn how to create relationships between tables, refer to Book 6, Chapter 2.

- In a simple form, if the table has a field that's used as the basis of a one-to-many relationship with another table and the current table is the "many" side of that relationship, that field is displayed as a drop-down list that contains the values from the related table. For example, in a table of Products, each product comes from one of many suppliers, so in a Products form, the Suppliers field would appear as a drop-down list that contains the names of all the companies in the Suppliers table.

## Creating a simple form

Here are the steps to follow to create a simple form:

1. **In the Navigation pane, click the table or query you want to use as the basis for the form.**
2. **Open the Create tab.**
3. **In the Forms group, click Form.**

   Access creates a form for the table you selected in Step 1.

Figure 1-13 shows a simple form created from the Northwind Customers table. Notice the datasheet on the bottom of the form. This subform shows the current customer's related records from the Order table.

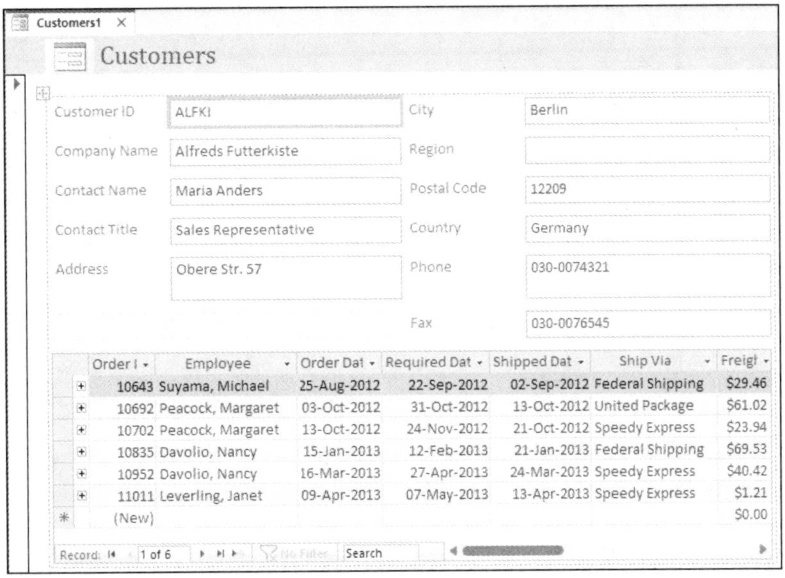


**FIGURE 1-13:** A simple form created from the Customers table.



## Creating a split form

Here are the steps to follow to create a split form:

1. **In the Navigation pane, click the table or query you want to use as the basis for the form.**
2. **Open the Create tab.**
3. **In the Forms group, click More Forms, then click Split Form.**

Figure 1-14 shows a split form created from the Northwind Products table. Notice in the form part that the Supplier field is represented by a drop-down list, which includes the supplier names from the related Suppliers table. The form also includes a Category drop-down list for the items in the related Categories table.

## Creating a multiple items form

Here are the steps to follow to create a form with the multiple items layout:

1. **In the Navigation pane, click the table or query you want to use as the basis for the form.**
2. **Open the Create tab.**
3. **In the Forms group, click More Forms, then click Multiple Items.**

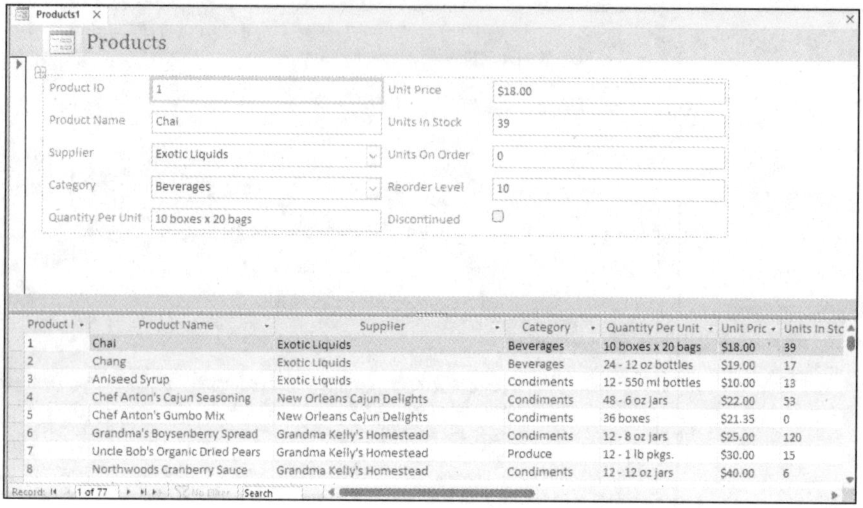


**FIGURE 1-14:** A split form created from the Products table.

Figure 1-15 shows a multiple items layout created from the Northwind Orders table. This form is tabular like a datasheet, but you get easier data entry with controls such as drop-down lists, as shown in Customer and Employee fields in Figure 1-15.

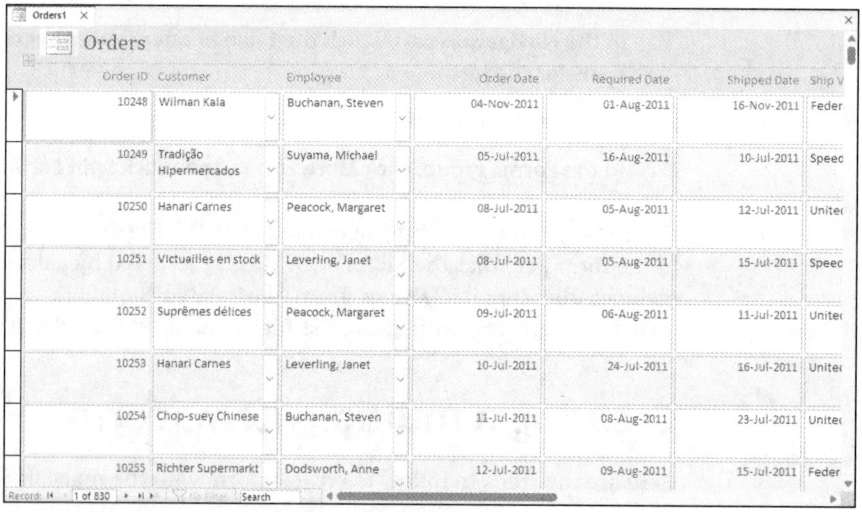


**FIGURE 1-15:** A multiple items layout created from the Orders table.

## Running the Form Wizard

The simple, split, and multiple items forms are all fine for very basic form needs, but it's likely that in most cases the resulting form will not suit your requirements exactly. For a bit more control over your forms, you need to use the Form Wizard which takes you step-by-step through the entire form-creation process. Follow these steps to use the Form Wizard:

1. **In the Navigation pane, click the table or query you want to use as the basis for the form.**
2. **On the Create tab, in the Forms group, click Form Wizard.**

   The first Form Wizard dialog box appears.

3. **The Table/Queries list displays the name of the table or query you clicked in step 1. If this isn't the data you want to work with, use the Table/Queries list to select the data source for the form.**
4. **For each field you want to include in the form, click the field in the Available Fields list and click the > button to add the item to the Selected Fields list. When you're done, click Next.**

   TIP

   If you want to include all the fields in your form, you can do so quickly by clicking the >> button.

   The next Form Wizard dialog box prompts you to choose the layout of the fields.

5. **Select one of the following four options (and then click Next):**
   - *Columnar:* The fields are arranged in columns, and only one record is shown at a time (similar to the Simple Form layout you learned about earlier in this chapter).
   - *Tabular:* The fields are arranged in a table, with the field names at the top and the records in rows (similar to the multiple items layout I mentioned in the previous section).
   - *Datasheet:* The fields are arranged in a Datasheet layout.
   - *Justified:* The fields are arranged across and down the form with the field names above their respective controls.
6. **In the final Form Wizard dialog box, use the What Title Do You Want for Your Form? text box to type a name for your form.**
7. **If you want to use the form right away, leave the Open the Form to View or Enter Information option selected; otherwise, select Modify the Form's Design to open the form in Design view.**
8. **Click Finish to complete the form.**

## Navigating form fields and records

Most forms use a variant of the simple form layout where one record appears at a time and you see all the table's fields appear onscreen. This feature makes navigating the form fields and records using your mouse easy:

- » To navigate to a field, click the field's control (text box, list box, or whatever).
- » To navigate records, use the navigation buttons at the bottom of the form. These are the same navigation buttons that appear at the bottom of a datasheet, so you use the same techniques.

However, when you're entering data in a form, you're most often using the keyboard, so navigating the fields and records using keyboard techniques is usually more efficient. Here are three basic techniques you should know:

- » When you have finished typing data in a field, press Enter. This action causes the field to accept the data you entered into it and then moves the focus to the next field.
- » Press Tab to move from field to field.
- » If shortcut keys are associated with buttons on the form, hold down the Alt key and press the corresponding underlined letter.

Otherwise, to navigate fields and records in a form you can use the keys outlined in Table 1-5.

**TABLE 1-5** **Keyboard Techniques for Navigating Fields and Records in a Form**

| Press | To Move To |
|---|---|
| Tab or right arrow | The next field to the right or, from the last field, the first field in the next record |
| Shift+Tab or left arrow | The previous field to the left or, from the first field, the first field in the previous record |
| Home | The first field |
| End | The last field |
| Page Down | The same field in the next record |
| Page Up | The same field in the previous record |
| Ctrl+Home | The first field of the first record |
| Ctrl+End | The last field of the last record |

IN THIS CHAPTER

- » Getting data into a table
- » Navigating records in a table
- » Taming data by sorting records
- » Working with subsets of data by filtering records
- » Creating powerful relationships between tables

# Chapter 2 Entering, Sorting, and Filtering Data

If data geeks have a motto, it's probably "Garbage in, garbage out" (which the nerdiest of these nerds will shorten to *GIGO*). (British data geeks prefer the motto "Rubbish in, rubbish out" or, yes, *RIRO*.) Lying deep within this simple phrase is a cautionary tale: If the information that goes into a database is inaccurate, incomplete, incompatible, or in some other way invalid, the information that comes out of that database will be outdated, outlandish, outrageous, or just outright wrong.

The moral of the story is that good data hygiene begins with entering the data accurately. I talked a bit about this in Book 6, Chapter 1 when I showed how to set up a table field with an input mask and/or a validation rule. That's an awesome start, but you also need to know how to navigate and work with the data-entry tools that Access offers. That's the task of the first part of this chapter. From there, you also explore the Access features that enable you to sort data, filter data, and relate multiple tables.

# The Population Boom: Entering Data

When it comes to databases, the data is the most important thing. It's right there in the name! So it's crucial to know a few techniques that not only make data entry easier, but also help ensure that data is entered accurately.

## Getting comfy with the Datasheet view

To enter data, you need to open the table's datasheet. You do this by double-clicking the table name in the Navigation pane. Figure 2-1 shows the datasheet window that appears, and it points out the most important features of this screen.

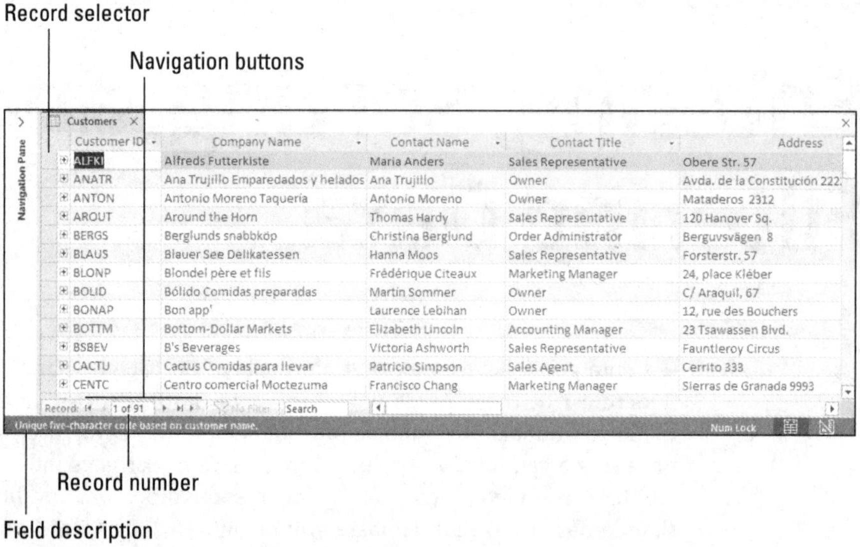


**FIGURE 2-1:** You use the Datasheet view to enter your data into a table.

The datasheet window has the following features:

- **Fields:** Each column in the datasheet corresponds to a field you added to the table (as I describe in Book 6, Chapter 1).
- **Field Names:** These are the buttons at the top of each column. The text is either the name of the field or the field alias, if one exists.
- **Records:** Each row in the datasheet corresponds to a record.
- **Record selectors:** These buttons run down the left side of the window. You use them to select records. They also show icons that give you more information about the record (as I describe later in this chapter).

» **Record number:** This box tells you which record is currently selected and the total number of records in the table. So, if you see the text "1 of 97" in the record number box, it means the cursor is somewhere in the first record and that there are 97 records in the current table.

» **Field description:** If the field has an associated description, it appears in the status bar as you select each field.

» **Navigation buttons:** These buttons enable you to navigate the records. I talk more about table navigation later in this chapter (refer to the section "Navigating records").

## Navigating field-to-field

To make entering your data easier, you need to be familiar with the techniques for navigating the datasheet fields. Using your mouse, you can select a field just by clicking it. If all your fields don't appear onscreen, use the horizontal scroll bar to bring them into view.

Using the keyboard, you can use the keys outlined in Table 2-1.



**TABLE 2-1** Keys for Navigating Fields in the Datasheet

| Key | Description |
|---|---|
| Tab or right arrow | Moves to the next field to the right; if you're in the last field of a record, moves to the first field of the next record |
| Shift+Tab or left arrow | Moves to the previous field to the left; if you're in the first field of a record, moves to the last field of the previous record |
| Home | Moves to the first field of the current record |
| End | Moves to the last field of the current record (Technically, pressing End moves the cursor to the Click to Add "field," which you can use to add a new field to the table on-the-fly) |
| Down arrow | Moves down to the same field in the next record |
| Up arrow | Moves up to the same field in the previous record |
| Ctrl+Home | Moves to the first field of the first record |
| Ctrl+End | Moves to the last field of the last record |

WARNING

When you use the keys in Table 2-1 to move into a field that already contains data, Access selects the data. If you press any key while the data is selected, you'll replace the entire entry with that keystroke! If this isn't what you want, immediately press Esc to restore the text. To prevent this from happening, you can remove the highlight by clicking inside the field or by pressing F2.

## Entering data

Entering data in Access is, for the most part, straightforward. You just select a field and start typing. Here are a few notes to keep in mind when entering table data:

- If you want to replace an entire field value, you can either type in the correct value (Access automatically replaces the selected value with your typing) or press Delete to clear the field.
- If you only want to change one or more characters in a field, press F2 or click inside the field to remove the highlight, and then edit the field accordingly.
- If you're editing a field, you can select the entire contents of the cell by pressing F2.

- When you're editing a record, the record selector sprouts a pencil icon, as shown in the margin. This tells you that the record has unsaved changes.
- If a field contains ##, this means that the field uses the AutoNumber format, so Access will automatically assign numbers to the field.
- When entering dates, use the format mm/dd/yyyy, where mm is the month number (for example, 12 for December), dd is the day, and yyyy is the year. The date format you end up with depends on the Format property assigned to the field.
- When entering times, use the format hh:mm:ss, where hh is the hour, mm is the minutes, and ss is the seconds. You can either use the 24-hour clock (for example, 16:30:05), or you can add am or pm (for example, 4:30:05 pm). Again, the format that's displayed depends on the field's Format property.

  TIP

  You can add today's date to a field by pressing Ctrl+; (semicolon). To add the current time, press Ctrl+: (colon).
- When entering a number in a Currency field, don't bother entering a dollar sign ($); Access will add it for you automatically.

» You save the current record by moving to a different record. If you prefer to save the current record and still remain in edit mode, you have the following methods to choose from:
   - On the Home tab, in the Records group, click Save.
   - Click the record selector.
   - Press Shift+Enter.

## Adding more records

Access always keeps a blank record at the bottom of the table for adding new records (it's the one that has an asterisk in its record selector). The next section tells you how to move around between records, but for now, you can use any of the following methods to select the blank record:

» If you're in the last field of the record directly above the blank record, press Tab.

» On the Home tab, in the Records group, click New.

» Press Ctrl++ (plus sign).

» Click the New Record button on the navigation toolbar (refer to Table 2-2).



## Navigating records

Navigating a table's records is straightforward. You can use the Up and Down arrow keys to move up and down through the records, or you can use Page Up and Page Down for larger jumps. If the record you want appears onscreen, you can click it. (You usually click whatever field you want to edit.) If the record doesn't appear, use the vertical scroll bar on the right side of the datasheet window to bring the record into view.

You can also traverse records using the Datasheet view's navigation buttons, summarized in Table 2-2.

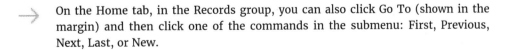

On the Home tab, in the Records group, you can also click Go To (shown in the margin) and then click one of the commands in the submenu: First, Previous, Next, Last, or New.

**TABLE 2-2** Datasheet Navigation Buttons

| Button | Description |
|---|---|
|  | Moves to the first record |
|  | Moves to the previous record |
|  | Moves to the next record |
|  | Moves to the last record |
|  | Moves to the new record |

## Selecting a record

Before you can work with a record, you need to select it:

- To select a single record, click the record selector to the left of the record you want. You can also move to any field in the record and then, on the Home tab, in the Find group, click Select and then click Select in the drop-down menu.
- To select multiple records, click and drag the mouse pointer over the record selector for each record you want to work with.
- To select every record, click the button in the upper-left corner of the datasheet. You can also open the Home tab then, in the Find group, click Select and then click Select All from the drop-down menu. You can also press Ctrl+A.

## Deleting a record

If you need to delete one or more records from the table, follow these steps:

1. **Select the record or records you want to delete.**
2. **Press Delete.**

   Alternatively, on the Home tab, in the Records group, click Delete.

   Access displays a dialog box telling you how many records will be deleted and asking you to confirm the deletion.
3. **Click Yes.**

   Access deletes the record or records.

# Formatting the datasheet

The standard datasheet displayed by Access is serviceable at best. Most people, though, have three major complaints about the default datasheet:

- » Some columns are too small to show all the data in a field.
- » All the fields don't appear in the datasheet window.
- » The characters are a little on the small side, so they're hard to read.

The next few sections show you how to format the datasheet to overcome these problems.

## Changing the datasheet column sizes

The default datasheet assigns the same width to every column. Although this standard width might be fine for some fields, for others it's either too large or too small. Fortunately, Access lets you adjust the width of individual columns to suit each field.

The easiest way to do this is with the mouse. Move the mouse pointer so that it rests on the right edge of the field's column header. The pointer will change to a vertical bar with two arrows protruding from its sides. From here, you have two choices:

- » Drag the mouse to the left to make the column width smaller or drag it to the right to make the width larger.
- » Double-click to size the column width to accommodate the widest field value.

Alternatively, you can follow these steps:

1. **Move the cursor into field you want to adjust.**
2. **On the Home tab, in the Records group, click More and then click Field Width.**

   Access opens the Column Width dialog box, shown in Figure 2-2.

**FIGURE 2-2:** Use the Column Width dialog box to set the width of a field, in characters.

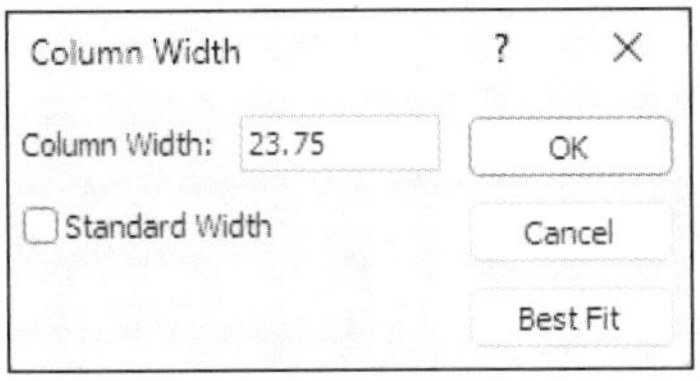

## VIEWING MEMO FIELDS

If you have a field with a large amount of data (a Memo field, for example), expanding the column width to display all the data isn't always practical. Instead, move to the field and press Shift+F2. Access displays the Zoom dialog box to show you more of your data. If you like, you can also use this dialog box to enter more data or edit the existing data. When you're done, click OK to return to the datasheet.

3. **Use the Column Width text box to type the width you want.**

   The width here is measured in characters, where one character is equal to the average width of the default font. The standard column width (which you can enter automatically by selecting the Standard Width check box) is 11.75 characters.

   Alternatively, to get Access to adjust the column width to fit the widest entry in the column, click Best Fit and then skip Step 4.

4. **Click OK.**

   Access adjusts the column width to your specified value.

### Changing the datasheet row heights

Another way to display more data in each field is to increase the height of each datasheet row (you can't do this for individual rows). You have two ways to do this:

- Position the mouse pointer on the bottom edge of any row selector. The pointer will change into a horizontal bar with arrows sticking out of the top and bottom. Drag the mouse up to reduce the row height or click or drag it down to increase the row height.
- On the Home tab, in the Records group, click More and then click Row Height to display the Row Height dialog box (shown in Figure 2-3). Type a new value (in points) in the Row Height text box (or select the Standard Height check box to return the row to the standard height of 14.25 points) and then click OK.

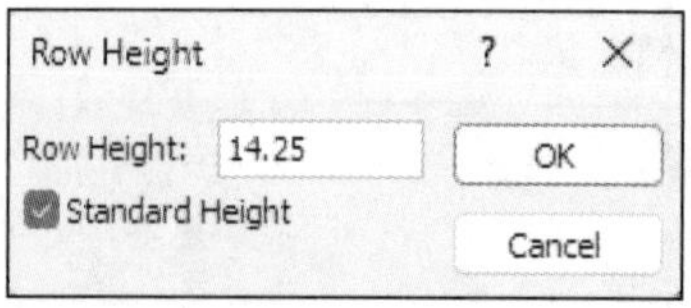


**FIGURE 2-3:** Use the Row Height dialog box to set the height of the datasheet rows, in points.

# Putting Things in Apple-Pie Order: Sorting Records

One way to make sense out of the data in a large table is to *sort* the table. Sorting means that you place the records in alphabetical order based on the data in a field (or numerical order if the field contains numeric or currency data, or temporal order if the field contains dates or times). For example, suppose you have a table of customer names and addresses, and you want to view all the customers who are from Canada. One way to do this is to sort the table by the data in the State field, and all the records with Canada in this field appear together.

## Sorting on a single field

Because sorting is such a common practice, the Access programmers made performing quick sorts on a single field easy. To try this, follow these steps:

1. **Select the field you want to sort on by clicking within that field on any record.**
2. **Click the Home tab.**
3. **In the Sort & Filter group, click one of the following:**
   - *Ascending:* Click this button to sort on the field in ascending order (from A to Z or from 0 to 9).
   - *Descending:* Click this button to sort on the field in descending order (from Z to A or from 9 to 0).

Figure 2-4 shows the Customers table sorted in ascending order on the Country field. Notice that the Country column header now includes an upward-pointing arrow (shown in the margin), which gives you a visual indication that the field is sorted in ascending order. (If the field was sorted in descending order, the arrow would be pointing down, instead.)

REMEMBER

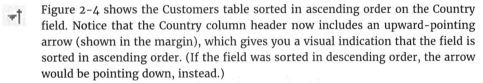

To revert the table to its unsorted state, on the Home tab, in the Sort & Filter group, click Remove Sort.

## Sorting on multiple fields

Although most of your table sorts will probably be on single fields, there will be times when you have to perform a sort on multiple fields. For example, you might want to sort a table by country and then by postal code within each country. For these more advanced sorts, Access provides the Advanced Filter/Sort tool.

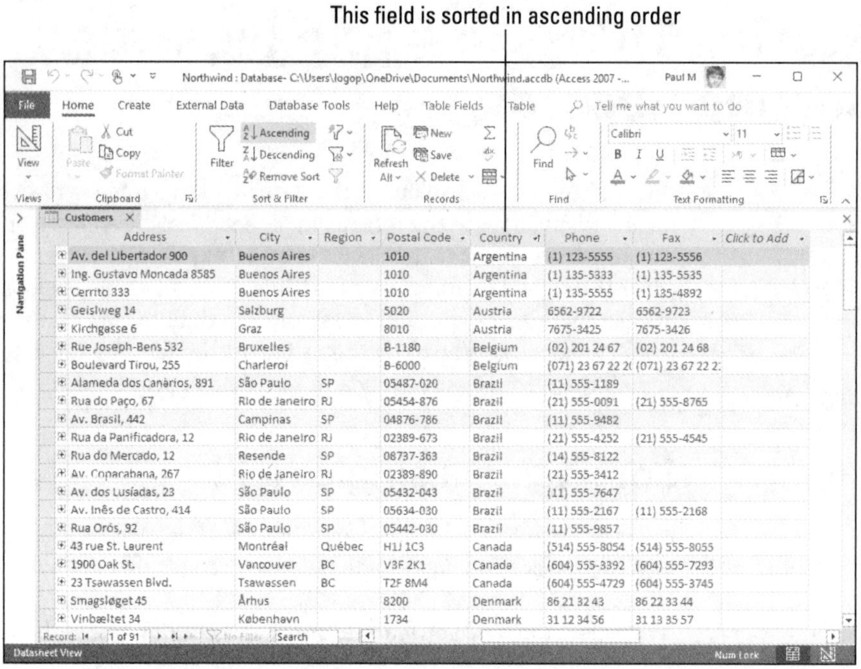


**FIGURE 2-4:** The Customers table sorted on the Country field.

To use this tool, follow these steps:

1. **On the Home tab, in the Sort & Filter group, click Advanced Filter Options (shown in the margin), and then click Advanced Filter/Sort.**

   Access displays a Filter tab.

   You use the columns in the lower pane to select the fields on which you want to sort.

2. **In the first available Field cell, use the drop-down list to click the field you want to use.**
3. **In the Sort cell below the field you just chose, use the drop-down list to click either Ascending or Descending.**
4. **Repeats steps 2 and 3 to choose other fields you want to include in the sort.**

   Figure 2-5 shows a multiple-field sort selection in progress.

REMEMBER

Make sure that the order in which you select the fields reflects the sort priority you want to use. For example, if you want to sort by country and then by postal code within each country, select the Country field in the first column and select then the PostalCode field in the second column.

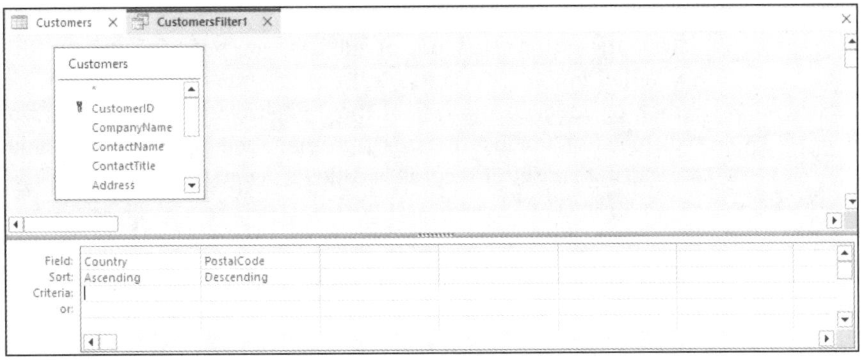


**FIGURE 2-5:** Use the Filter tab to perform sorts on two or more fields.

5. **On the Home tab, in the Sort & Filter group, click Apply Filter (shown in the margin).**

   Access sorts the table.

REMEMBER

To return the table to its unsorted state, on the Home tab, in the Sort & Filter group, click Remove Sort.

# Knocking Things Down to Size: Filtering Data

If you've ever been to a large, noisy gathering, you might have been struck by how easily humans can ignore a cacophony of music and voices around them and concentrate on whatever conversation they're having at the time. Our brains somehow filter out the unimportant noise and let in only what we need to hear.

This idea of screening out the unnecessary is exactly what Access filters do. We often want to work with only some of the records in a large table. The other records are just "noise" that we want to somehow tune out. For example, if you have a table of customer invoices, you might want to work with any of the following subsets of the data:

- Only those invoices from a particular customer
- All the overdue invoices
- Every invoice with an amount greater than $1,000

To work with these kinds of subsets, you need to set up a filter. The idea is that you define the criteria you want to use (such as having the Amount field greater than or equal to 1000), and then, when you apply the filter to the table, Access displays only those records that meet the criteria. When you filter a table, the resulting subset of records is called a *dynaset.*

For example, consider the Order Details table shown in Figure 2-6. This is a table of customer purchases and it has more than 2,000 records, so there's plenty of "noise" to filter out.

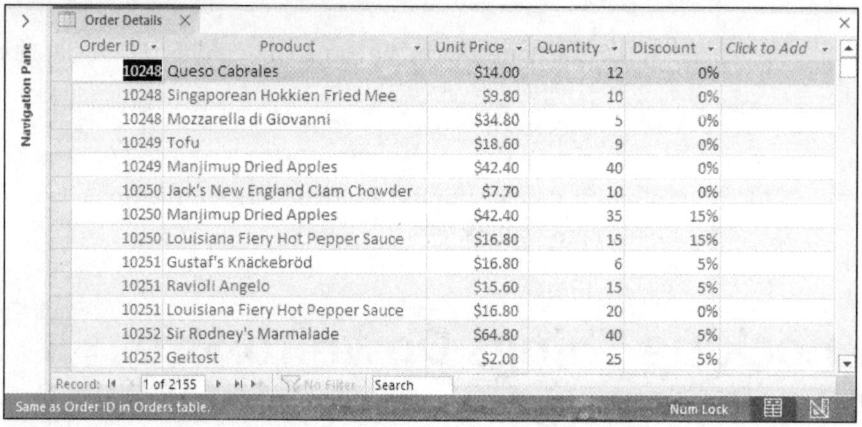

Order Details
Navigation Pane
Order ID
Product
Unit Price
Quantity
Discount
Click to Add
10248 Queso Cabrales $14.00 12 0%
10248 Singaporean Hokkien Fried Mee $9.80 10 0%
10248 Mozzarella di Giovanni $34.80 5 0%
10249 Tofu $18.60 9 0%
10249 Manjimup Dried Apples $42.40 40 0%
10250 Jack's New England Clam Chowder $7.70 10 0%
10250 Manjimup Dried Apples $42.40 35 15%
10250 Louisiana Fiery Hot Pepper Sauce $16.80 15 15%
10251 Gustaf's Knäckebröd $16.80 6 5%
10251 Ravioli Angelo $15.60 15 5%
10251 Louisiana Fiery Hot Pepper Sauce $16.80 20 0%
10252 Sir Rodney's Marmalade $64.80 40 5%
10252 Geitost $2.00 25 5%
Record: 1 of 2155
No Filter
Search
Same as Order ID in Orders table.
Num Lock


**FIGURE 2-6:** The table of customer purchases has more than 2,000 records.

Figure 2-7 shows another view of the same table, in which I've set up a filter to show only a subset of records. In this case, the Product field had to be equal to Queso Cabrales. This shows me all the orders for that particular product. Notice that the dynaset now displays only 38 records, and that the Filtered indicator (pointed out in Figure 2-7) is activated to let you know you're dealing with a subset of the records. (Access also displays Filtered in the status bar.)

In Figure 2-7, notice that the Product column header now includes a filter icon (shown in the margin), which gives you a visual indication that the field is filtered.

The following sections take you through various techniques for filtering records. In each case, when you no longer need to work with the filtered list, you can display all the records once again by opening the Home tab then, in the Sort & Filter group, clicking Remove Filter (shown in the margin).

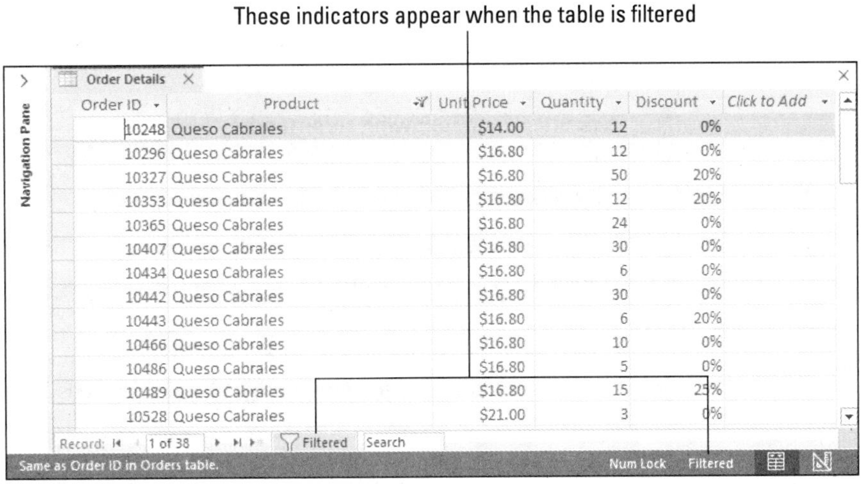
These indicators appear when the table is filtered
Order Details
Order ID
Product
Unit Price
Quantity
Discount
Click to Add
Navigation Pane
10248 Queso Cabrales $14.00 12 0%
10296 Queso Cabrales $16.80 12 0%
10327 Queso Cabrales $16.80 50 20%
10353 Queso Cabrales $16.80 12 20%
10365 Queso Cabrales $16.80 24 0%
10407 Queso Cabrales $16.80 30 0%
10434 Queso Cabrales $16.80 6 0%
10442 Queso Cabrales $16.80 30 0%
10443 Queso Cabrales $16.80 6 20%
10466 Queso Cabrales $16.80 10 0%
10486 Queso Cabrales $16.80 5 0%
10489 Queso Cabrales $16.80 15 25%
10528 Queso Cabrales $21.00 3 0%
Record: 1 of 38
Filtered
Search
Same as Order ID in Orders table.
Num Lock
Filtered

**FIGURE 2-7:** The same table filtered to show only one product's orders.

## Filtering by field value

Access has a feature that enables you to filter a table based on a field value. You select a particular value in a field, and Access then filters the table so that it displays only those records that match the selected value. Follow these steps to use this feature:

1. **In the table, click inside a datasheet cell that contains the value you want to use as the filter basis.**

   In the example I just discussed, I placed the cursor inside a Product field cell that contained the value Queso Cabrales.

2. **On the Home tab, in the Sort & Filter group, click Selection (shown in the margin).**
3. **Click Equals "*value*" (where *value* is the selected field value).**

   Access filters the table to show only those records where the field is equal to the value of the datasheet cell you clicked in Step 1.

## Filtering by partial field value

A similar idea is to filter the table based on part of the text in a given field. For example, you might want to view only those orders where the Product field includes the word "Sauce." In this case, you select the text in the appropriate field, and Access then filters the table so that it displays only those records that include the selected text. Follow these steps to use this feature:

1. **In the table, click inside a datasheet cell that contains the value you want to use, then select the text you want to use as the filter basis.**

2. **On the Home tab, in the Sort & Filter group, click Selection (shown in the margin).**
3. **Click one of the following commands:**
   - *Contains* "value": Displays those records that contain *value* anywhere in the field (where *value* is the text you selected in Step 1).
   - *Begins With* "value": Displays those records where the field begins with *value*. (This command only appears if the text you selected is at the beginning of the current field.)
   - *Ends With* "value": Displays those records where the field ends with *value*. (This command only appears if the text you selected is at the end of the current field.)

   Access filters the table to show only those records where the field matches your criteria.

## Filter excluding field value

Alternatively, you might prefer to display those records that are *not* equal to a specified field value. Again, you select a particular value in a field, but this time Access then filters the table so that it displays only those records that don't match the selected value. Follow these steps to use this feature:

1. **In the table, click inside a datasheet cell that contains the value you want to use as the filter basis.**
2. **On the Home tab, in the Sort & Filter group, click Selection (shown in the margin).**
3. **Click Does Not Equal "*value*" (where *value* is the selected field value).**

   Access filters the table to show only those records where the field is not equal to the value of the datasheet cell you clicked in Step 1.

## Filter excluding partial field value

You may have guessed by now that you can also filter records that don't match part of the text in a given field. For example, you might want to view only those orders where the Product field does not include the word "Tofu." Again, you select the text in the appropriate field, and Access then filters the table so that it displays only those records that don't include the selected text. Follow these steps to use this feature:

1. **In the table, click inside a datasheet cell that contains the value you want to use, then select the text you want to use as the filter basis.**

2. **On the Home tab, in the Sort & Filter group, click Selection (shown in the margin).**
3. **Click one of the following commands:**
   - *Does Not Contain "value"*: Displays those records that don't contain *value* anywhere in the field (where *value* is the text you selected in Step 1).
   - *Does Not Begin With "value"*: Displays those records where the field doesn't begin with *value*. (This command only appears if the text you selected is at the beginning of the current field.)
   - *Does Not End With "value"*: Displays those records where the field doesn't end with *value*. (This command only appears if the text you selected is at the end of the current field.)

   Access filters the table to show only those records where the field matches your criteria.

## Filtering by form

A slightly more sophisticated filter is one that involves multiple values or expressions. These filters come in two styles:

- **"And" filter:** In this type of filter, you specify two or more expressions, and the table is filtered to include only those records that match all the expressions. For example, you might want to display only those orders where the Product field equals Tofu and where the Quantity field is greater than or equal to 25.
- **"Or" filter:** In this type of filter, you specify two or more expressions, and the table is filtered to include only those records that match at least one of the expressions. For example, you might want to display only those orders where the Product field contains Queso Cabrales or Ravioli Angelo.

Note, too, that you can mix and match these filter types.

For these multiple-value filters, Access offers the Filter By Form feature. The next two sections demonstrate how it works.

## Setting up an "and" filter

To set up an advanced filter that shows only those records that meet all the criteria you specify — that is, an "and" filter — follow these steps:

1. **On the Home tab, in the Sort & Filter group, click Advanced Filter Options (shown in the margin), and then click Filter By Form.**

   Access displays the Filter by Form tab.

2. **Specify the criteria you want to use for your filter:**

   - *To use a specific field value as a filter criterion:* Use the field's drop-down list to select the field value.
   - *To use an expression as a filter criterion:* Type the expression into the field. (Refer to Book 6, Chapter 3, to learn more about building criteria expressions.)

   In Figure 2-8, for example, I clicked Tofu in the Product list, and I typed the expression >=25 in the Quantity field.

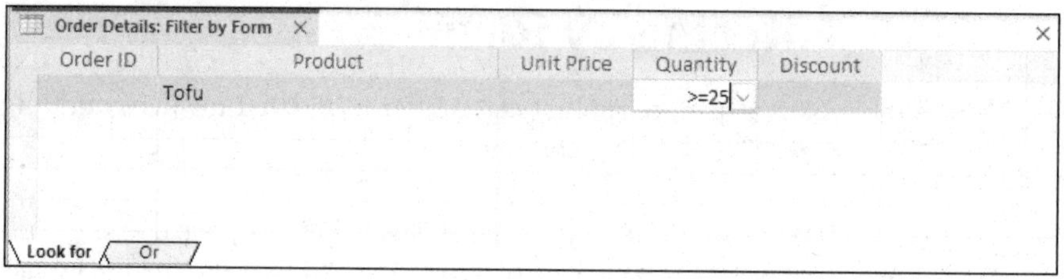


**FIGURE 2-8:** Using the Filter by Form tab to set up an "and" filter on two fields.

3. **On the Home tab, in the Sort & Filter group, click Apply Filter (shown in the margin).**

   Access filters the table to display only those records that match all the criteria you specified in Step 2. Figure 2-9 shows the results of the filter set up in Figure 2-8.

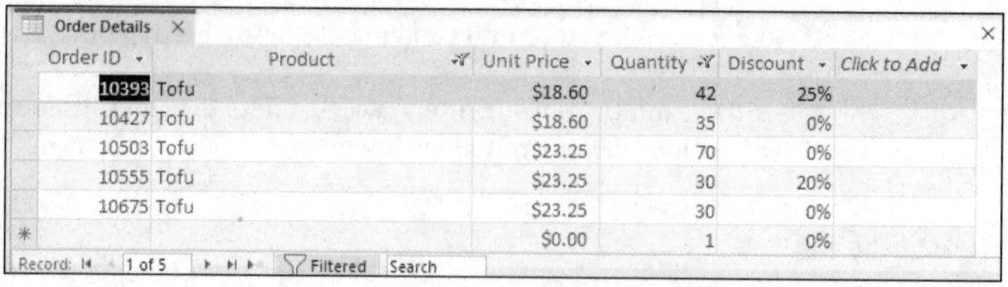

Order Details
Order ID
Product
Unit Price
Quantity
Discount
Click to Add
10393 Tofu $18.60 42 25%
10427 Tofu $18.60 35 0%
10503 Tofu $23.25 70 0%
10555 Tofu $23.25 30 20%
10675 Tofu $23.25 30 0%
$0.00 1 0%
Record: 1 of 5
Filtered
Search


**FIGURE 2-9:** The results of the filter shown in Figure 2-8.

## Setting up an "or" filter

To set up an advanced filter that shows only those records that meet one or more of the criteria you specify — that is, an "or" filter — follow these steps:

1. **On the Home tab, in the Sort & Filter group, click Advanced Filter Options (shown in the margin), and then click Filter By Form.**

   Access displays the Filter by Form tab.

2. **In the Look For sub-tab, specify the first criterion you want to use for your filter:**

   - *To use a specific field value as a filter criterion:* Use the field's drop-down list to select the field value.
   - *To use an expression as a filter criterion:* Type the expression into the field. (Refer to Book 6, Chapter 3, to learn more about building criteria expressions.)

3. **Click the Or sub-tab and then specify another criterion you want to use for your filter.**

   Again, you can either select a field value or type an expression in the second field you want to include in the filter.

   Access adds another Or sub-tab, so you repeat Step 3 to expand your filter as needed.

   For example, in the Look For sub-tab you might click Queso Cabrales in the Product list and in the Or sub-tab you might click Ravioli Angelo in the Product list (as shown in Figure 2-10).

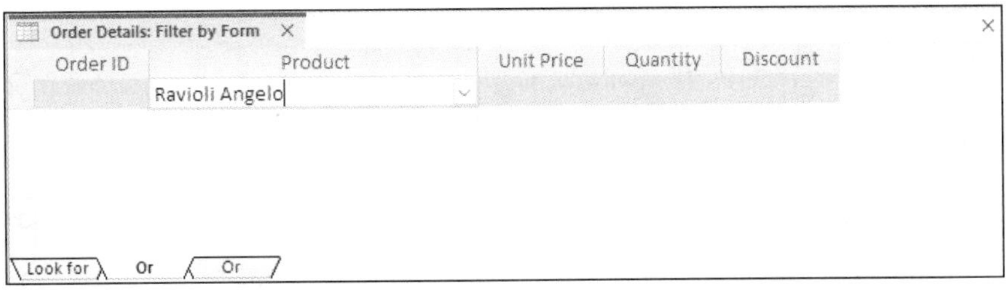


**FIGURE 2-10:** Using the Filter by Form tab to set up an "or" filter on two fields.

4. **On the Home tab, in the Sort & Filter group, click Apply Filter (shown in the margin).**

   Access filters the table to display only those records that match one or more of the criteria you specified in Steps 2 and 3. Figure 2-11 shows the results of the filter set up in Figure 2-10.

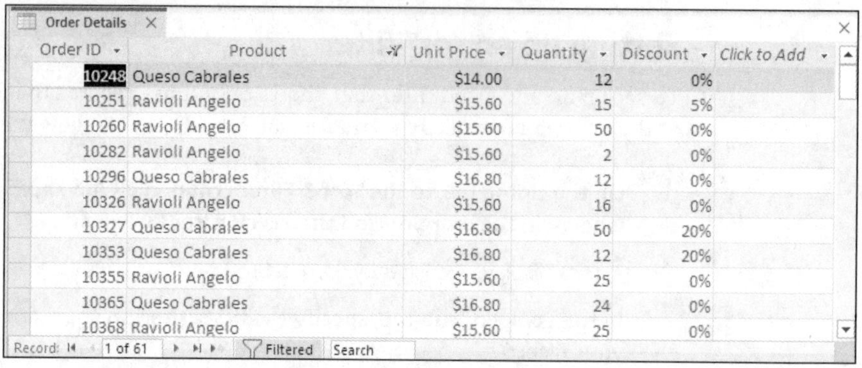

| Order ID | Product | Unit Price | Quantity | Discount | Click to Add |
|---|---|---|---|---|---|
| 10248 | Queso Cabrales | $14.00 | 12 | 0% | |
| 10251 | Ravioli Angelo | $15.60 | 15 | 5% | |
| 10260 | Ravioli Angelo | $15.60 | 50 | 0% | |
| 10282 | Ravioli Angelo | $15.60 | 2 | 0% | |
| 10296 | Queso Cabrales | $16.80 | 12 | 0% | |
| 10326 | Ravioli Angelo | $15.60 | 16 | 0% | |
| 10327 | Queso Cabrales | $16.80 | 50 | 20% | |
| 10353 | Queso Cabrales | $16.80 | 12 | 20% | |
| 10355 | Ravioli Angelo | $15.60 | 25 | 0% | |
| 10365 | Queso Cabrales | $16.80 | 24 | 0% | |
| 10368 | Ravioli Angelo | $15.60 | 25 | 0% | |



**FIGURE 2-11:** The results of the filter shown in Figure 2-10.

## Creating an advanced filter

The most powerful and flexible method for creating a filter is the Advanced Filter/Sort feature. This feature is similar to Filter By Form in that you use criteria to define the filter and you can set up the filter to match some or all of the criteria. The difference is that you create all the criteria in a single window, so it's easier to build advanced filters that use multiple "and" and multiple "or" expressions.

Here are the steps to follow to create an advanced filter:

1. **On the Home tab, in the Sort & Filter group, click Advanced Filter Options (shown in the margin), and then click Advanced Filter/Sort.**

   Access displays a filter tab, which is divided vertically into two sections:

   - The top part of the tab contains a box that includes a list of the table's fields. (If your table is related to one or more other tables — refer to "Relating Multiple Tables," later in this chapter — then you also see a box for each related table.)
   - The bottom part of the tab displays a grid that you use to specify the filter criteria. The grid contains multiple columns and you add a column for each field you want to include in your criteria.

2. **In the grid, use the first available column's Field list to select the field you want to include in your filter.**

   You can also double-click the field name in the top part of the tab, or you can drag the field name from the top part of the tab and drop it in the Field box.

3. **In the Criteria box below your field name, type the criteria.**

   Refer to Book 6, Chapter 3, to learn more about building criteria expressions.

4. **Repeat steps 2 and 3 to filter the table on multiple fields.**

Here's how you create "and" and "or" filters:

- *To create an "and" filter:* Use a different column to select the field you want to work with and then enter the criteria for that field. Make sure all your criteria appear on the same line in the filter grid.
- *To create an "or" filter using the same field:* Enter the second criteria in the or: line that appears below the Criteria: line.
- *To create an "or" filter using another field:* Use a different column to select the field and then enter the second criteria in the or: line below the field.

Figure 2-12 shows an advanced filter that displays those Order Details records where the Product field equals Queso Cabrales and the Quantity field is greater than 25, *or* the Product field equals Ravioli Angelo and the Unit Price field is less than 16.

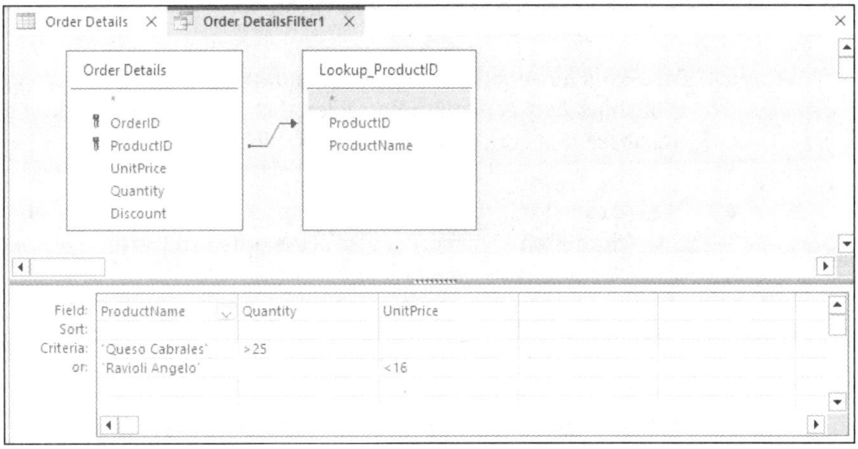


**FIGURE 2-12:** Using the Advanced Filter/Sort tab to set up an advanced filter.

5. **On the Home tab, in the Sort & Filter group, click Apply Filter (shown in the margin).**

Access filters the table to display only those records that match the criteria you specified in Steps 2 through 4. Figure 2-13 shows the results of the filter set up in Figure 2-12.

| Order ID | Product | Unit Price | Quantity | Discount | Click to Add |
|---|---|---|---|---|---|
| 10251 | Ravioli Angelo | $15.60 | 15 | 5% | |
| 10260 | Ravioli Angelo | $15.60 | 50 | 0% | |
| 10282 | Ravioli Angelo | $15.60 | 2 | 0% | |
| 10326 | Ravioli Angelo | $15.60 | 16 | 0% | |
| 10327 | Queso Cabrales | $16.80 | 50 | 20% | |
| 10355 | Ravioli Angelo | $15.60 | 25 | 0% | |
| 10368 | Ravioli Angelo | $15.60 | 25 | 0% | |
| 10407 | Queso Cabrales | $16.80 | 30 | 0% | |
| 10416 | Ravioli Angelo | $15.60 | 20 | 0% | |
| 10438 | Ravioli Angelo | $15.60 | 15 | 20% | |
| 10442 | Queso Cabrales | $16.80 | 30 | 0% | |
| 10535 | Queso Cabrales | $21.00 | 50 | 10% | |
| 10566 | Queso Cabrales | $21.00 | 35 | 15% | |
| 10800 | Queso Cabrales | $21.00 | 50 | 10% | |
| 10889 | Queso Cabrales | $21.00 | 40 | 0% | |
| 10912 | Queso Cabrales | $21.00 | 40 | 25% | |
| 10986 | Queso Cabrales | $21.00 | 30 | 0% | |



**FIGURE 2-13:** The results of the filter shown in Figure 2-12.

# Relating Multiple Tables

Access is a *relational* database system, which means that you can establish relationships between multiple tables. Let's use an example. Suppose you have a database that contains (at least) two tables:

- **Orders:** This table holds data on orders placed by your customers, including the customer name, the date of the order, and so on. It also includes an Order ID field as the primary key.
- **Order Details:** This table holds data on the specific products that comprise each order: the product name, the unit price, and the quantity ordered.

Why not lump both tables into a single table? Well, that would mean that, for each product ordered, you would have to include the name of the customer, the order date, and so on. If the customer purchased 10 different products, this information would be repeated 10 times.

To avoid such data redundancy, the data is kept in separate tables, and the two tables are related on a common field called Order ID. The following two figures show how this works. In Figure 2-14, the first record in the Orders table refers to Order ID 10248. As shown in the Order Details table in Figure 2-15, the first three records also have an Order ID of 10248. Those three records comprise the entire order given by Order ID 10248.

The first Orders record has an Order ID value of 10248

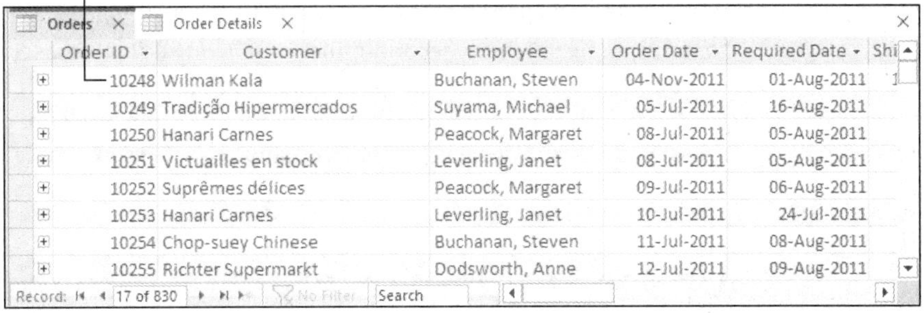

Orders
Order Details
Order ID
Customer
Employee
Order Date
Required Date
Shi
10248 Wilman Kala
Buchanan, Steven
04-Nov-2011
01-Aug-2011
10249 Tradição Hipermercados
Suyama, Michael
05-Jul-2011
16-Aug-2011
10250 Hanari Carnes
Peacock, Margaret
08-Jul-2011
05-Aug-2011
10251 Victuailles en stock
Leverling, Janet
08-Jul-2011
05-Aug-2011
10252 Suprêmes délices
Peacock, Margaret
09-Jul-2011
06-Aug-2011
10253 Hanari Carnes
Leverling, Janet
10-Jul-2011
24-Jul-2011
10254 Chop-suey Chinese
Buchanan, Steven
11-Jul-2011
08-Aug-2011
10255 Richter Supermarkt
Dodsworth, Anne
12-Jul-2011
09-Aug-2011
Record: 17 of 830
No Filter
Search


**FIGURE 2-14:** In the Orders table, the first record has an Order ID value of 10248.

The first three Order Details records use the Order ID value of 10248

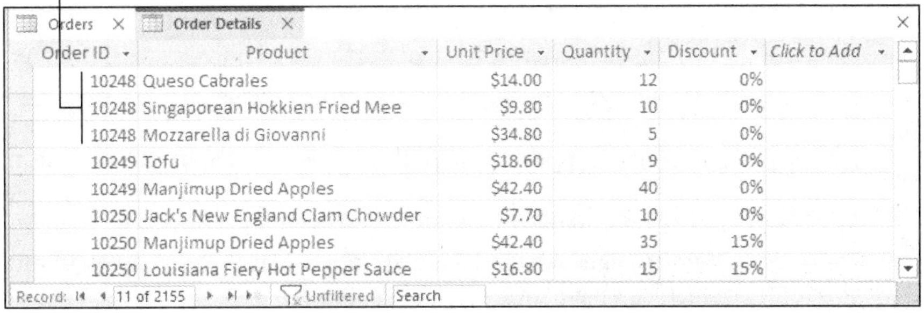

Orders
Order Details
Order ID
Product
Unit Price
Quantity
Discount
Click to Add
10248 Queso Cabrales
$14.00
12
0%
10248 Singaporean Hokkien Fried Mee
$9.80
10
0%
10248 Mozzarella di Giovanni
$34.80
5
0%
10249 Tofu
$18.60
9
0%
10249 Manjimup Dried Apples
$42.40
40
0%
10250 Jack's New England Clam Chowder
$7.70
10
0%
10250 Manjimup Dried Apples
$42.40
35
15%
10250 Louisiana Fiery Hot Pepper Sauce
$16.80
15
15%
Record: 11 of 2155
Unfiltered
Search


**FIGURE 2-15:** The Orders and Order Details tables are related on the common Order ID field, shown here by the first three Order Details records having the Order ID value of 10248.

Note, however, that if two tables are related, you don't need to open the second table to display the related records. In the main table, notice that Access displays plus signs (+) to the left of the first field. These indicate that the table has a related table. Clicking a plus sign displays the related records, as shown in Figure 2-16.

Clicking the plus sign (+)...

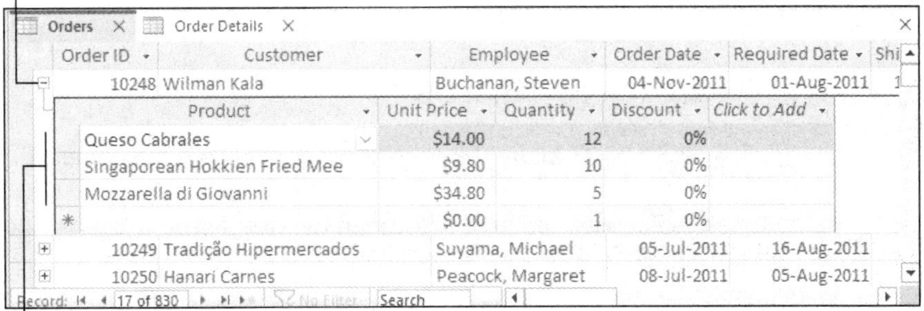

Orders
Order Details
Order ID
Customer
Employee
Order Date
Required Date
Shi
10248 Wilman Kala
Buchanan, Steven
04-Nov-2011
01-Aug-2011
Product
Unit Price
Quantity
Discount
Click to Add
Queso Cabrales
$14.00
12
0%
Singaporean Hokkien Fried Mee
$9.80
10
0%
Mozzarella di Giovanni
$34.80
5
0%
$0.00
1
0%
10249 Tradição Hipermercados
Suyama, Michael
05-Jul-2011
16-Aug-2011
10250 Hanari Carnes
Peacock, Margaret
08-Jul-2011
05-Aug-2011
Record: 17 of 830
No Filter
Search


... to see the related records

**FIGURE 2-16:** Click a plus sign (+) to display the records from the related table.

The Orders and Order Details tables demonstrate the most common relational model, where a single record in the one table — called the *parent table* — relates to multiple records in a second table — called the *child table.* This is called a *one-to-many* relationship. If your data requires that one record in the parent table be related to only one record in the child table, you have a *one-to-one* model. In some cases, you might have data in which many records in one table can relate to many records in another table. This is called a *many-to-many* relationship.

## Understanding referential integrity

Database applications that work with multiple, related tables need to worry about enforcing *referential integrity* rules. These rules ensure that related tables remain in a consistent state relative to each other. For example, suppose your database includes a Customers table for tracking customer data and an Orders table for tracking customer orders. In particular, suppose the Customers table includes an entry for "Seven Seas Imports" and that the Orders table contains nine records for orders placed by Seven Seas Imports. What would happen if you deleted the Seven Seas Imports record from the Customers table? The nine records in the Orders table would no longer be related to any record in the Customers table. Child records without corresponding records in the parent table are called, appropriately enough, *orphans.* This situation leaves your tables in an inconsistent state, which can have unpredictable consequences.

Preventing orphaned records is what is meant by enforcing referential integrity. You need to watch out for two situations:

- » Deleting a parent table record that has related records in a child table.
- » Adding a child table record that is not related to a record in the parent table (either because the common field contains no value or because it contains a value that doesn't correspond to any record in the parent table).

## Relating tables

Now that you know the theory behind the relational model, you can turn your attention to creating and working with related tables in Access. The first step is to establish the relationship between the two tables, which is what this section is all about. Here are the steps to follow:

1. **On the Database Tools tab, in the Relationships group, click Relationships.**

   Access displays the Relationships tab.

2. **On the Relationships Design contextual tab, in the Relationships group, click Add Tables.**

   Access displays the Add Tables task pane.

3. **Double-click each table you want to work with.**

   With each double-click, Access adds a box for the table to the Relationships tab.

   Figure 2-17 shows the Relationships tab with two tables added: Customers and Orders.

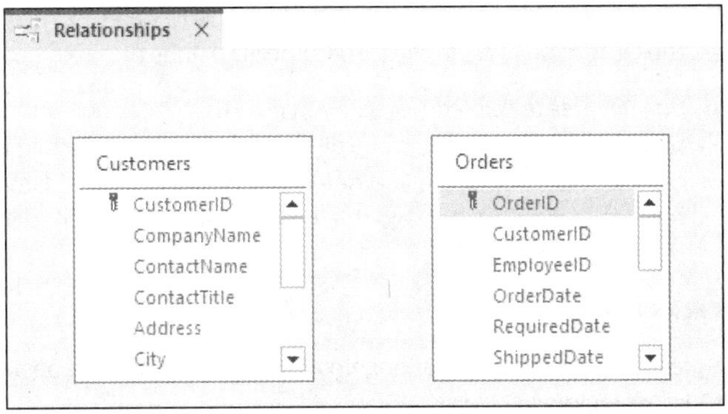


**FIGURE 2-17:** You use the Relationships window to establish relations between tables.

4. **Scroll the table boxes so that in each box the fields you want to use to relate the tables are displayed.**

5. **Drag the related field from one table and drop it on the related field in the other table.**

   In Figure 2-17, for example, I'd drag CustomerID from the Customers table and drop it on CustomerID in the Orders table. Access displays the Edit Relationships dialog box, shown in Figure 2-18.

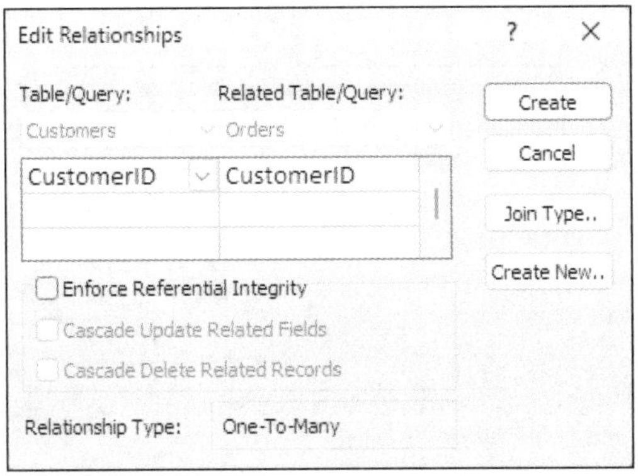


**FIGURE 2-18:** Access displays the Edit Relationships dialog box when you drag a related field from one table and drop it on another.

Entering, Sorting, and Filtering Data

6. **The grid should show the names of the fields in each table that you want to relate. If not, use the drop-down list in one or both cells to click the correct field or fields.**

7. **If you want Access to enforce referential integrity rules on this relation, select the Enforce Referential Integrity check box.**

   If you do this, two other check boxes become enabled:

   - *Cascade Update Related Fields:* If you click this check box and then make changes to a primary key value in the parent table, Access updates the new key value for all related records in all child tables. For example, if you change a CustomerID value in the Customers table, all related records in the Orders table have their CustomerID values updated automatically.
   - *Cascade Delete Related Fields:* If you click this check box and then delete a record from the parent table, all related records in all child tables are also deleted. For example, if you delete a record from the Customers table, all records in the Orders table that have the same CustomerID as the deleted record are also deleted.

8. **Click Create.**

   Access establishes the relationship and displays a join line between the two fields, as shown in Figure 2-19.

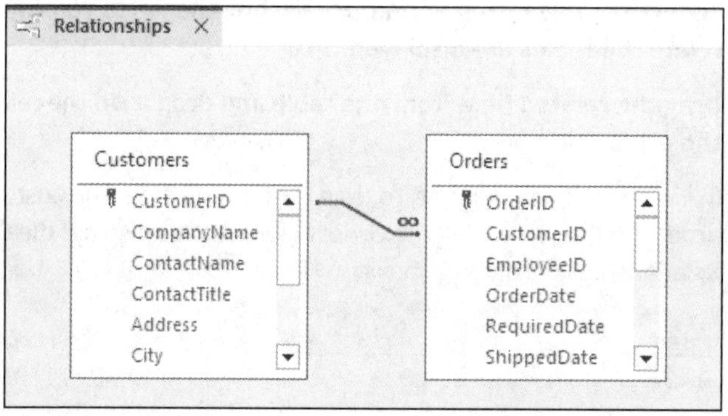


**FIGURE 2-19:** In the Relationships tab, a relationship between two tables is indicated by a join line between the related fields.

IN THIS CHAPTER

» Easily creating simple queries

» Maximizing query power with criteria expressions

» Getting your queries to perform calculations

» Working with multiple tables in a query

» Creating a query to automatically update, append, or delete table records

# Chapter 3

# Querying Data

This chapter gets you up to speed with one of the most powerful concepts in all of Access: queries. Queries are no great mystery, really. Although the name implies that they are a kind of question, thinking of them as requests is more useful. In the simplest case, a query is a request to see a particular subset of your data. For example, showing only those records in a customer table where the country is "Sweden" and the first name is "Sven" would be a fairly simple query to build. (This type of query is known in the trade as a *select query.*)

In this respect, queries are fancier versions of the filters I talk about in Book 6, Chapter 2. As with an advanced filter, you set up a query by selecting field names and specifying criteria that define the records you want to see. However, unlike filters, queries aren't simply a different view of the table data. They're a separate database object that actually extracts records from a table and places them in a dynaset. As you'll see later, a dynaset is much like a datasheet, and many of the operations you can perform on a datasheet can also be performed on a dynaset. (Query results are called dynasets because they're dynamic subsets of a table. Here, "*dynamic*" means that if you make any changes to the original table, Access updates the query automatically, or vice versa.)

The other major difference between a query and a filter is that you can save queries and then rerun them anytime you like. Filters, on the other hand, are ephemeral: When you close the table, any filters you've defined vanish into thin air.

Other types of queries are more sophisticated. For example, you can set up queries to summarize the data in a table, to find duplicate records, to delete records, and to move records from one database into another. You learn about all these query types in this chapter.

# Designing a Simple Query

Although Access has several Query Wizards that you can use to create a query step-by-step, creating a query by hand using the Design view is almost always easier and faster. Follow these steps to get started:

1. **On the Create tab, in the Queries group, click Query Design.**

   Access opens a query design tab and displays the Add Tables task pane.

2. **In the Add Tables pane, double-click the table you want to use as the basis of the query.**

   Access adds a box for the table to the query design tab.

Figure 3-1 shows a query design tab with the Customers table added.

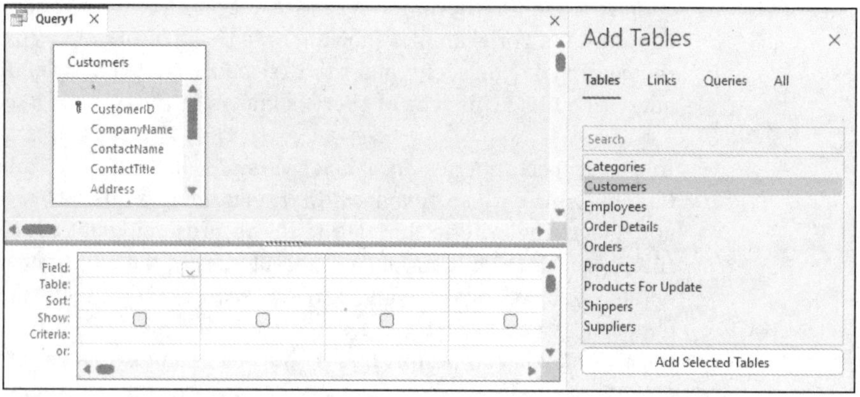


**FIGURE 3-1:** Use the Query Design view to enter fields, sorting options, and criteria for your query.

Similar to the filter window I discuss in Book 6, Chapter 2, the query design tab is divided into two areas:

- **Table pane:** The top part of the tab displays a list box that displays all the fields from your table. Note that this box is resizable, so you can change the height or width as needed.
- **Criteria pane:** The bottom part of the tab is a collection of text boxes (they're called *cells*) where you define the query as I describe in the next few sections.

Note, too, that you can adjust the relative sizes of both panes by vertically dragging the horizontal bar that separates them.

The Criteria pane is also sometimes called the *QBE grid*, where QBE stands for *query by example*, a query design method where you define an example of what you want each dynaset record to look like. As you see in the next few sections, this involves adding the fields you want to a grid and then setting up criteria for one or more of those fields.

## Adding fields to the query

When you've created a new query object, the next step is to build some structure into it by adding one or more fields from the table associated with the query. To add a field, follow these steps:

1. **Click inside the Field cell of the column you want to work with.**

   Access displays a drop-down list in the cell.

   REMEMBER

   Typically, you'd start with the leftmost column and work your way to the right as you add more fields to the query.

2. **Use the drop-down list to click the field you want to work with.**
3. **Repeat steps 1 and 2 to add more fields to the query.**

Note, too, that you can also add fields directly from the Table pane. The two basic techniques are as follows:

- To add a single field, either double-click the field in the field list or drag the name from the field list to the appropriate Field cell in the design grid.

  TIP

  If you want *every* field from the table in your query, the easiest way to do so is to add the special asterisk (*) field that appears at the top of the field list.

- To add multiple fields, hold down Ctrl, click each field you want, and then drag any one of the highlighted fields into a Field cell in the design grid. Access enters each field in its own cell.

Remember that the order in which you add your fields to the Criteria pane is the order in which the fields will appear in the dynaset. If you add fields in the wrong order, you can fix the order using the following techniques:

- **Moving a column:** Select the column by clicking the bar at the top of the column, then drag the column left or right to the new location.
- **Inserting a column:** Drag the field from the field list and drop it on the left edge of an existing column. Alternatively, click the existing column then, on the Query Design tab, in the Query Setup group, click Insert Columns, and then use the new column's Field list to select the field you want to insert.
- **Deleting a column:** Select the column then, on the Query Design tab, in the Query Setup group, click Delete Columns (or just press Delete).

TIP

If you require a field in the Criteria pane but you don't want the field to display in the results — for example, because you want to sort the results on that field or use the field as part of the query criteria — deselect the column's Show check box.

## Specifying the query criteria

The last query design step is to specify the criteria that determine the subset of records you want to work with from the table. For each field that you want to use as part of the criteria, type the criteria expression into the column's Criteria cell in the QBE grid. Your criteria expressions will consist of database field names, literal values, and operators. I go on and on about query criteria later in this chapter (check out the section "Getting Comfy with Query Criteria").

Figure 3-2 shows a QBE grid with several fields from the Customers table and the Country field showing "USA" in its Criteria cell. This tells Access that you only want to see those customers where the Country field equals USA.

## Running the query

With your query design complete, you can now run the query to display the resulting dynaset. You do so by opening the Query Design tab then, in the Results group, click Run. Figure 3-3 displays the results of the query shown in Figure 3-2.

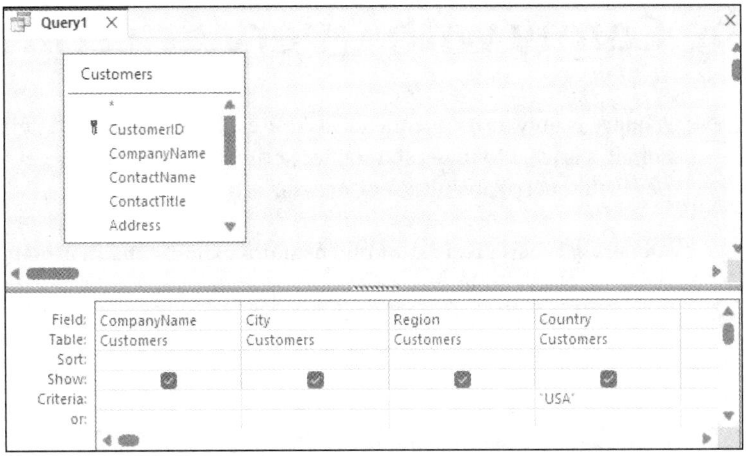


**FIGURE 3-2:** In the QBE grid, type your criteria in the Criteria cells.

| Company Name | City | Region | Country |
|---|---|---|---|
| Great Lakes Food Market | Eugene | OR | USA |
| Hungry Coyote Import Store | Elgin | OR | USA |
| Lazy K Kountry Store | Walla Walla | WA | USA |
| Let's Stop N Shop | San Francisco | CA | USA |
| Lonesome Pine Restaurant | Portland | OR | USA |
| Old World Delicatessen | Anchorage | AK | USA |
| Rattlesnake Canyon Grocery | Albuquerque | NM | USA |
| Save-a-lot Markets | Boise | ID | USA |
| Split Rail Beer & Ale | Lander | WY | USA |
| The Big Cheese | Portland | OR | USA |
| The Cracker Box | Butte | MT | USA |
| Trail's Head Gourmet Provisioners | Kirkland | WA | USA |
| White Clover Markets | Seattle | WA | USA |



**FIGURE 3-3:** The results of the query shown in Figure 3-2.

As you can see, the dynaset is really just a datasheet. You navigate and format it the same way, and you can even edit the records and add new ones. (Any changes you make are automatically applied to the underlying table.), Access gives you two choices for returning to the query design window:

» On the Home tab, in the Views group, click View, and then click Design View.

» In the lower-right corner of the status bar, click the Design View button (shown in the margin).

# Getting Comfy with Query Criteria

A query is only as useful and as accurate as the criteria that define it. For this reason, it's crucial to understand query criteria if you want to get the most out of the powerful query capabilities of Access.

A query's criteria consist of one or more expressions that manipulate the underlying table in some way. The query example shown earlier in Figure 3-2 used a simple literal value — the string "USA" — as its sole expression. When you apply such a logical expression to a field for each record in the table, the dynaset contains only those records for which the expression returned a True result. In the example from Figure 3-2, adding the literal value "USA" to the Country field is equivalent to the following logical formula:

```
Country = "USA"
```

Access builds the dynaset by applying this formula to each record in the table and selecting only those records for which it returns True (that is, those records where the value in the Country field is equal to "USA").

More powerful queries use more complex expressions that combine not only literals, but also operators, table fields, and even built-in functions. Access evaluates the expression on the field in which it was defined and, again, the records where the expression returns a True result are the records that appear in the query dynaset.

The next three sections give you more details about the two main components of a query criteria expression: operands and operators.

## Using operands in criteria expressions

An *operand* is a data value that gets manipulated in some way in an expression. The three operand types that you'll use in your criteria expressions are:

- **Literal:** This is a value that you type directly into the expression. Access recognizes four types of literal: text, numbers, dates and times, and a constant (True, False, or Null).

  REMEMBER

  When you use a date or a time as a literal in a criteria expression, be sure to surround the value with pound signs (#). For example, #8/23/2025# or #3:15 PM#.

» **Field name:** Also called an *identifier*, this is the name of a field from the query's underlying table, surrounded by square brackets; for example, [Country] or [Company Name].

» **Function:** This is a built-in expression that, usually, takes one or more input values — called *arguments* — and processes those values to return a result. For example, the Sum function returns the sum of its arguments. If you apply it to a field, it returns the sum of the field's values, as in this example:

```
Sum([Quantity])
```

## Using operators in criteria expressions

An *operator* is a special symbol that manipulates one or more operands in some way. The most common operators in query expressions are the comparison operators such as less than (<) and greater than or equal to (>=), but Access has many others that enable you to create logical expressions, arithmetic expressions, and more. The next few sections tell you about all the operators defined by Access for use in criteria expressions.

### Comparison operators

You use comparison operators to compare the values in a particular field with a literal value, a function result, the value in another field, or an expression result. Table 3-1 lists the comparison operators used by Access.

**TABLE 3-1 Comparison Operators to Use in Criteria Expressions**

| Operator | Matches records where |
|---|---|
| = (equal to) | The value of the criteria field is equal to a specified value |
| <> (not equal to) | The value of the criteria field isn't equal to a specified value |
| > (greater than) | The value of the criteria field is greater than a specified value |
| >= (greater than or equal to) | The value of the criteria field is greater than or equal to a specified value |
| < (less than) | The value of the criteria field is less than a specified value |
| <= (less than or equal to) | The value of the criteria field is less than or equal to a specified value |

For example, suppose an Order Details table has a Quantity field, and you might want to see just those records where the quantity ordered was greater than 100. To do this, you'd type the following expression in the Criteria cell for the Quantity field (see Figure 3-4; the query results are shown in Figure 3-5):

```
>100
```

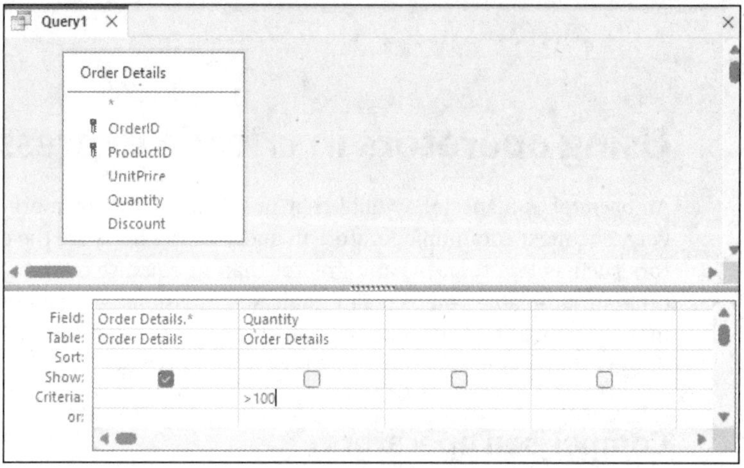


**FIGURE 3-4:** A query designed to show those records in the Order Details table where the Quantity ordered was greater than 100.

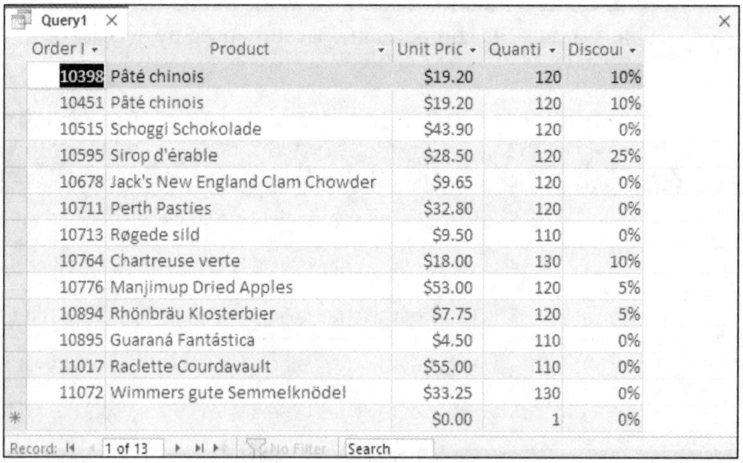

Query1

| Order I | Product | Unit Pric | Quanti | Discou |
|---|---|---|---|---|
| 10398 | Pâté chinois | $19.20 | 120 | 10% |
| 10451 | Pâté chinois | $19.20 | 120 | 10% |
| 10515 | Schoggi Schokolade | $43.90 | 120 | 0% |
| 10595 | Sirop d'érable | $28.50 | 120 | 25% |
| 10678 | Jack's New England Clam Chowder | $9.65 | 120 | 0% |
| 10711 | Perth Pasties | $32.80 | 120 | 0% |
| 10713 | Røgede sild | $9.50 | 110 | 0% |
| 10764 | Chartreuse verte | $18.00 | 130 | 10% |
| 10776 | Manjimup Dried Apples | $53.00 | 120 | 5% |
| 10894 | Rhönbräu Klosterbier | $7.75 | 120 | 5% |
| 10895 | Guaraná Fantástica | $4.50 | 110 | 0% |
| 11017 | Raclette Courdavault | $55.00 | 110 | 0% |
| 11072 | Wimmers gute Semmelknödel | $33.25 | 130 | 0% |
| * | | $0.00 | 1 | 0% |

Record: 1 of 13 No Filter Search

**FIGURE 3-5:** The dynaset produced by the query in Figure 3-4.

REMEMBER

You can tell Access to restrict the dynaset to the first few records or to a percentage of the total. You do this using the Return combo box, which is on the Query Design tab in the Query Setup group. You can either type your own value into the box or select a number or percentage value from the list.

## Arithmetic operators

When you need to build mathematical expressions, use the arithmetic operators shown in Table 3-2.

**TABLE 3-2** Arithmetic Operators for Criteria Expressions

| Operator | Description |
|---|---|
| + (addition) | Adds one value to another |
| - (subtraction) | Subtracts one value from another |
| - (unary) | Changes the sign of a value |
| * (multiplication) | Multiplies one value by another |
| / (division) | Divides one value by another |
| \ (integer division) | Divides one value by another as integers |
| ^ (exponentiation) | Raises one value to the power of a second value |
| Mod (modulus) | Divides one value by another and returns the remainder |

For example, if you want to calculate the *extended total* for an invoice, you first multiply the quantity ordered by the unit price. Assuming you have an Order Details table with Quantity and UnitPrice fields, then your expression would look like this:

```
[Quantity]*[UnitPrice]
```

## The Like operator

If you need to allow for multiple spellings in a text field, or if you aren't sure how to spell a word you want to use, the wildcard characters can help. The two wildcards are the question mark (?), which substitutes for a single character, and the asterisk (*), which substitutes for a group of characters. You use them in combination with the `Like` operator, as shown in Table 3-3.

**TABLE 3-3** The Like Operator for Criteria Expressions

| Example | Description |
|---|---|
| `Like "Re?d"` | Matches records where the field value is Reid, Read, reed, and so on |
| `Like "M?"` | Matches records where the field value is MA, MD, ME, and so on |
| `Like "R*"` | Matches records where the field value begins with R |
| `Like "*office*"` | Matches records where the field value contains the word *office* |
| `Like "12/*/2025"` | Matches records where the field value is any date in December 2025 |

### The Between. . .And operator

If you need to select records where a field value lies between two other values, use the `Between. . .And` operator. For example, suppose you want to see all the invoices where the invoice number is between (and includes) 123000 and 124000. Here's the expression you enter in the invoice number field's Criteria cell:

```
Between 123000 And 124000
```

You can use this operator for numbers, dates, and even text.

### The In operator

You use the `In` operator to match records where the specified field value is one of a set of values. For example, suppose you want to return a dynaset that contains only those records where the Region field equals NY, CA, TX, IN, or ME. Here's the expression to use:

```
In("NY","CA","TX","IN","ME")
```

### The Is Null operator

What do you do if you want to select records where a certain field is empty? For example, an invoice table might have a Date Paid field that, when empty, indicates the invoice hasn't been paid yet. For these challenges, Access provides the `Is Null` operator. Entering this operator by itself in a field's Criteria cell selects only those records whereby the field is empty.

To select records when a particular field isn't empty, use the `Isn't Null` operator.

### Compound criteria and the logical operators

For many criteria, a single expression isn't enough to return the dynaset you want. For example, suppose you're working with a Products table that includes a

UnitsInStock field and you're interested in the products that are currently out of stock. In that case, you'd begin by adding the following expression to the Criteria cell of the UnitsInStock field:

```
=0
```

However, you might be interested in some products that are not only out of stock, but that also have not yet been reordered (where reorders are recorded in the UnitsOnOrder field). For a more complex query like this, you need to set up *compound criteria* where you specify either multiple expressions for the same field or multiple expressions for different fields. The following sections cover the two basic types of multiple criteria: `And` criteria and `Or` criteria.

## Entering And criteria

You use `And` criteria when you want to select records that satisfy each of two or more different expressions. So given *expression1* and *expression2*, a record appears in the dynaset only if it satisfies both *expression1* and *expression2* (which is why they are called `And` criteria).

For example, suppose you want to display all products with no inventory (UnitsInStock=0) and that have not yet been reordered (UnitsOnOrder=0). In this case, you add both the UnitsInStock and UnitsOnOrder fields to the design grid, and use `=0` in the Criteria cells for each field, as shown in Figure 3-6. Figure 3-7 shows the resulting dynaset.

TIP

You can create `And` criteria using a single field by adding the field twice to the design grid and then adding an expression to the Criteria cell for both instances of the field. (To avoid the field appearing twice in the dynaset, deselect one of the Show check boxes.)

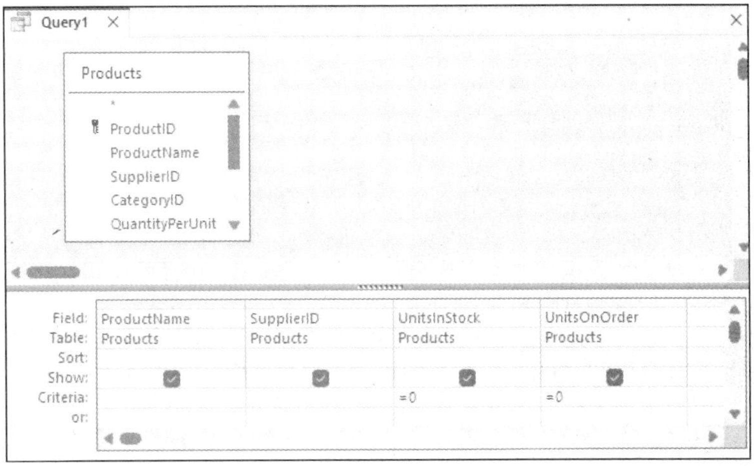


**FIGURE 3-6:** When you enter two expressions in the same row of the design grid, you create an And criterion.

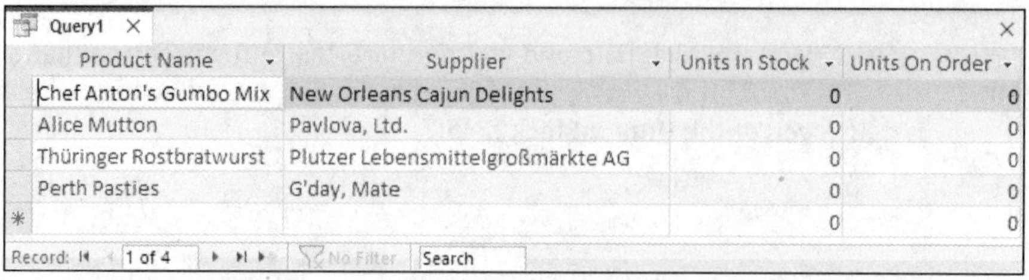


**FIGURE 3-7:** The dynaset produced by the query in Figure 3-6.

## Entering Or criteria

With `Or` criteria, you want to display records that satisfy at least one out of two or more expressions. With two expressions, for example, if the record satisfies either expression (or both), it appears in the query results; if it satisfies neither expression, it's left out of the results. (Again, you're allowed to use more than two expressions if necessary. No matter how many expressions you use, a record appears in the query results only if it satisfies at least one of the expressions.)

For example, suppose you want to select products with an inventory equal to 0 (UnitsInStock=0) or where the reorder quantity is greater than the current inventory (ReorderLevel>UnitsInStock). In this case, you add both the UnitsInStock and ReorderLevel fields to the design grid and enter the criteria expressions on separate lines in the design grid (that's why the Or line appears under Criteria in the grid). Figure 3-8 shows how you set up such a query, and Figure 3-9 shows the results.

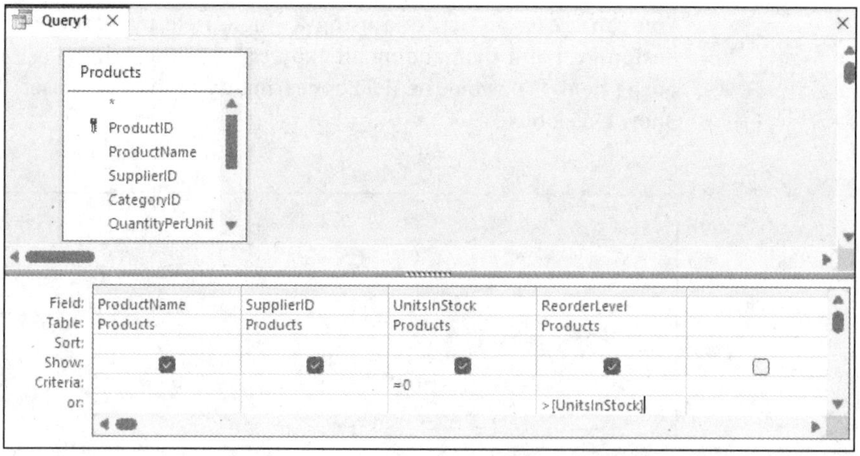


**FIGURE 3-8:** To use `Or` criterion for different fields, enter the expressions on separate lines in the design grid.

TIP

You can create `Or` criteria using a single field by adding the field to the design grid and then typing an expression to the field's Criteria cell and its Or cell.

**FIGURE 3-9:** The dynaset produced by the query in Figure 3-8.

## Combining And and Or criteria

You can construct extremely powerful queries by combining And criteria with Or criteria. For example, in the previous section, you saw a query that returned records where either the inventory was 0 or less than the reorder level. However, both of these conditions are only a concern if no units are on order. In other words, the query should select records where one or both of the following are true:

- The current inventory is 0 *and* there are no units on order (UnitsOnOrder=0)
- The reorder level is greater than the inventory *and* no units are on order.

Figure 3-10 shows this query in the design grid and Figure 3-11 shows the resulting dynaset.

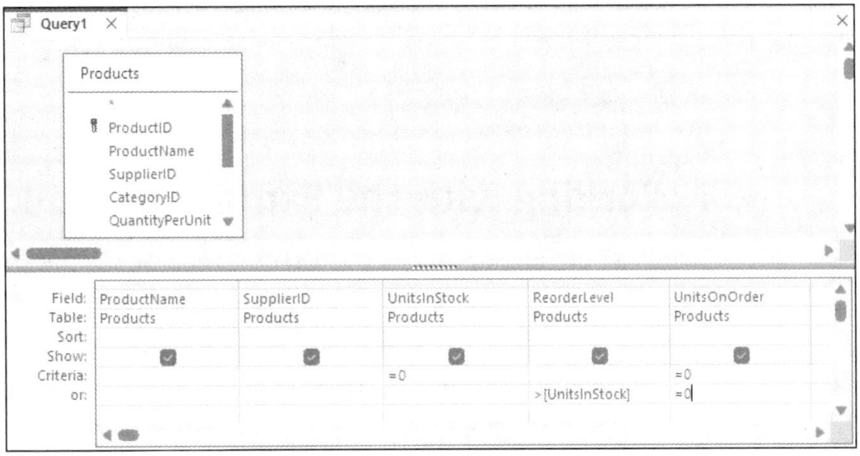


**FIGURE 3-10:** You can combine And criteria and Or criteria in your queries.

| Product Name | Supplier | Units In Stock | Reorder Level | Units On Order |
|---|---|---|---|---|
| Chef Anton's Gumbo Mix | New Orleans Cajun Delights | 0 | 0 | 0 |
| Alice Mutton | Pavlova, Ltd. | 0 | 0 | 0 |
| Thüringer Rostbratwurst | Plutzer Lebensmittelgroßmärkte AG | 0 | 0 | 0 |
| Nord-Ost Matjeshering | Nord-Ost-Fisch Handelsgesellschaft mbH | 10 | 15 | 0 |
| Perth Pasties | G'day, Mate | 0 | 0 | 0 |
| * | | 0 | 0 | 0 |

**FIGURE 3-11:** The dynaset produced by the query in Figure 3-10.

## Logical operators

You use the logical operators to combine or modify True/False expressions. Table 3-4 summarizes Access's six logical operators.

**TABLE 3-4 Logical Operators for Criteria Expressions**

| Operator | General Form | Description |
|---|---|---|
| `And` | *Expr1* `And` *Expr2* | Matches records when both *Expr1* and *Expr2* are True |
| `Or` | *Expr1* `Or` *Expr2* | Matches records when at least one of *Expr1* and *Expr2* are True |
| `Not` | `Not` *Expr* | Matches records when *Expr* isn't True |
| `Xor` | *Expr1* `Xor` *Expr2* | Matches records when only one of *Expr1* and *Expr2* is True |
| `Eqv` | *Expr1* `Eqv` *Expr2* | Matches records when both *Expr1* and *Expr1* are True or both *Expr1* and *Expr2* are False |
| `Imp` | *Expr1* `Imp` *Expr2* | Matches records when *Expr1* is True and *Expr1* is True or when *Expr1* is False and *Expr1* is either True or False |

The `And` and `Or` operators let you create compound criteria using a single expression. For example, suppose you want to match all the records in your Products table where the UnitsInStock field is either 0 or greater than or equal to 100. The following expression does the job:

```
=0 Or >=100
```

# Working with the Expression Builder

Instead of entering complex criteria by hand, Access includes an Expression Builder tool that provides handy buttons for the various operators. The following steps show you how Expression Builder works:

1. **In the QBE grid, click the Field or Criteria cell in which you want to enter the expression.**

2. **On the Query Design tab, in the Query Setup group, click Builder.**

   Access displays the Expression Builder window.

3. **(Optional) If you're creating a calculated column (refer to the section "Setting up a calculated column" to learn more), use the large text box to type the name of the column followed by a colon (:)**
4. **Type some or all of the expression.**
5. **To add an operator to the expression, place the cursor where you want the operator to appear and then either type an operator symbol or click the Operators category and then double-click the operator you want.**
6. **To add a database object to the expression, place the cursor where you want the object to appear, click + to the right of the database filename, use the displayed categories (Tables, Queries, and so on) to find the object, and then double-click the object you want.**

   Figure 3-12 shows the Expression Builder with a couple of fields (Quantity and UnitPrice) added to an expression.

7. **To add a function to the expression, place the cursor where you want the function to appear, click + to the right of Functions, click Built-In Functions, click the function type, and then double-click the function you want.**

   If the function takes arguments (most do), be sure to replace each argument placeholder with an actual operand.

8. **Repeats steps 4 through 7 as necessary to complete the expression.**
9. **Click OK.**

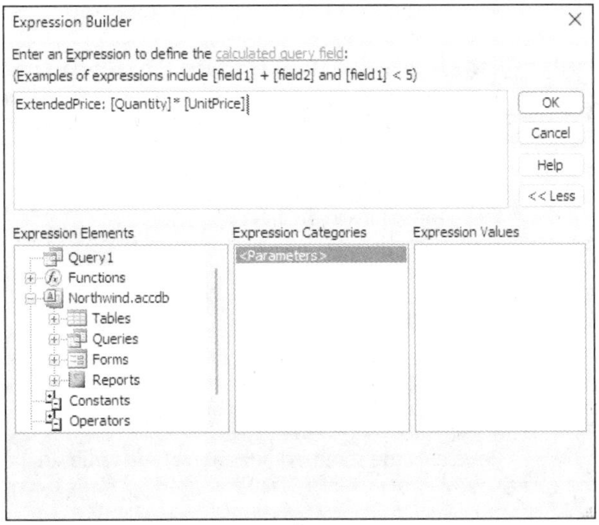


**FIGURE 3-12:** Use the Expression Builder to add text, operators, database objects, and functions to an expression.

Querying Data

# Using Calculations in Queries Like a Pro

The queries you've seen so far have just extracted certain fields and records from the underlying table. This feature is useful, to be sure, because one of the secrets of database productivity is to work only with the data you need, not all the data that exists. However, there's a second database productivity secret: to get the most out of some queries, you have to take the query process a step farther and *analyze* the results in some way. To analyze the dynaset, you need to introduce calculations into your query, and Access lets you set up two kinds of calculations:

- **A totals column:** This is a column in the dynaset that uses one of several predefined aggregate functions for calculating a value (or values) based on the entries in a particular field. A totals column derives either a single value for the entire dynaset or several values for the grouped records in the dynaset.
- **A calculated column:** This is a column in the dynaset where the "field" is an expression. The field values are derived using an expression based on one or more fields in the table.

## Constructing a totals column

The easiest way to analyze the data in a table is to use a totals column and one of the predefined aggregate functions. A number of aggregate operations are available, including functions such as Sum, Avg, Max, Min, and Count, StDev, and Var. The idea is that you add a single field to the QBE grid and then convert that column into a totals column using one of these functions. Table 3-5 outlines the available functions you can use for your totals columns.

**TABLE 3-5** Aggregate Operations for a Totals Column

| Operation | Description |
|---|---|
| Group By | Groups the records according to the unique values in the field |
| Sum | Sums the values in the field |
| Avg | Averages the values in the field |
| Min | Returns the smallest value in the field |
| Max | Returns the largest value in the field |
| Count | Counts the number of values in the field |
| StDev | Calculates the standard deviation of the values in the field |

| Operation | Description |
| --- | --- |
| Var | Calculates the variance of the values in the field |
| First | Returns the first value in the field |
| Last | Returns the last value in the field |
| Expression | Returns a custom total based on an expression in a calculated column |
| Where | Filters the records using the field's criteria before calculating the totals |

## Setting up a totals column

The following steps are required to create a totals column:

1. **Clear all columns from the QBE grid except the field you want to use for the calculation.**
2. **On the Query Design tab, in the Show/Hide group, click Totals.**

   Alternatively, you can right-click the column and then click Totals.

   Access adds a Total row to the QBE grid.
3. **In the field's Total cell, use the drop-down list to select the function you want to use.**

In Figure 3-13, for example, I've selected the Sum function in the Total cell of the UnitsInStock field. Figure 3-14 shows the result of the Sum calculation on the UnitsInStock field. As you can see, the dynaset consists of a single cell that shows the function result.

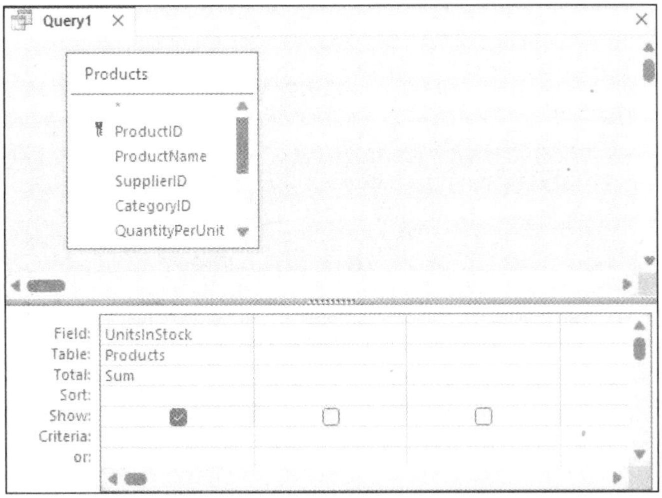


**FIGURE 3-13:** Use the Total cell to choose the aggregate function you want to use for the calculation.

Querying Data

**FIGURE 3-14:** The dynaset shows only the result of the calculation.

## Creating a totals column for groups of records

In its basic guise, a totals column shows a total for all the records in a table. Suppose, however, that you'd prefer to see that total broken out into subtotals. For example, instead of a simple sum on the UnitsInStock field, how about seeing the sum of the inventory grouped by category?

To group your totals, you have to do two things:

- Add the grouping field to the QBE grid to the left of the column you're using for the calculation.
- Make sure the grouping field's Total cell shows Group By.

For example, Figure 3-15 shows the QBE grid with the CategoryID field from the Products table to the left of the UnitsInStock field. Running this query produces the dynaset shown in Figure 3-16. As you can see, Access groups the entries in the Category column and displays a subtotal for each group.

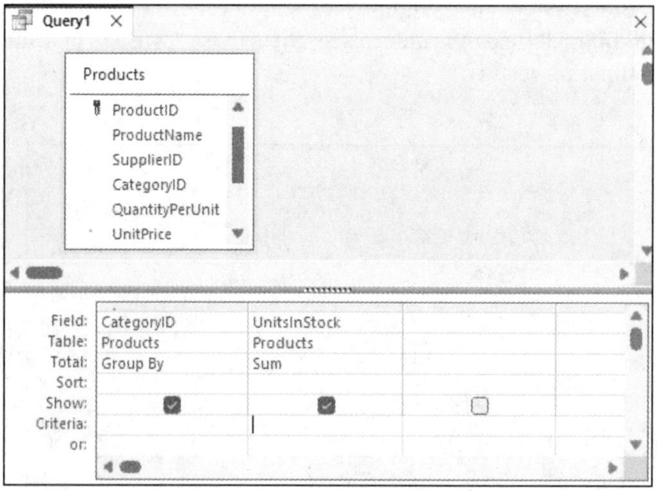


**FIGURE 3-15:** To group your totals, add the field used for the grouping to the left of the field used for the calculation.

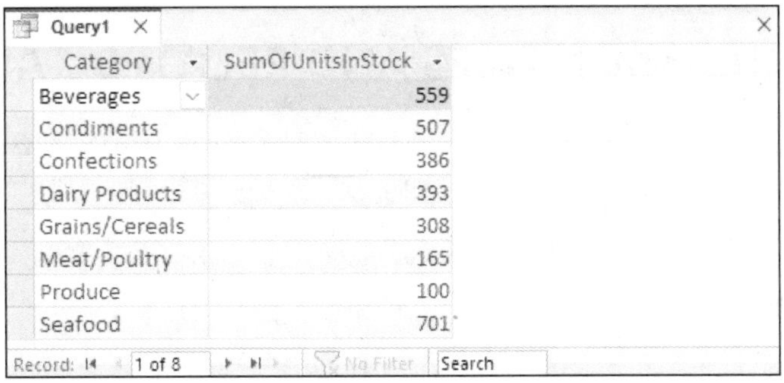


**FIGURE 3-16:** Access uses the columns to the left of the totals column to set up its groupings.

You can extend this technique to derive totals for more specific groups. For example, suppose you want to see subtotals for each supplier within the categories. In this case, you have to add the SupplierID field to the QBE grid to the left of the UnitsInStock column, but to the right of the CategoryID column, as shown in Figure 3-17. Access creates the groups from left to right, so the records are first grouped by Category and then by Supplier. Figure 3-18 shows the dynaset.

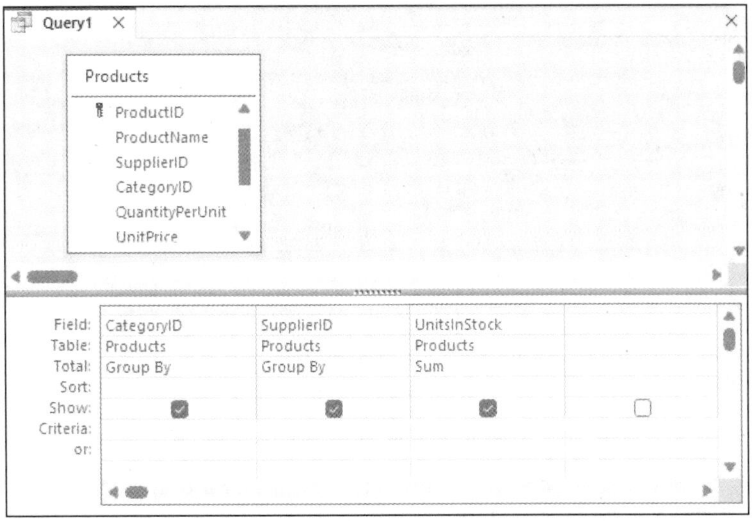


**FIGURE 3-17:** You can refine your groupings by adding more columns to the left of the totals column.

## Setting up a calculated column

The seven aggregate functions available for totals columns are handy, but they may not be what you need. If you'd like to create columns that use more sophisticated expressions, you need to set up a calculated column.

## COLUMN NAMES AND RELATED TABLES

TECHNICAL STUFF

You may be wondering why Access displays the Category and Supplier columns instead of the CategoryID and SupplierID values in the dynaset shown in Figure 3-18. That's because the Products table is related to two tables (among others): Categories and Suppliers. Access uses these relationships to display the category and supplier names instead of only the numbers in the CategoryID and SupplierID fields. Refer to Book 6, Chapter 2 to learn more about table relationships.

Query1

| Category | Supplier | SumOfUnitsInStock |
|---|---|---|
| Beverages | Exotic Liquids | 56 |
| Beverages | Pavlova, Ltd. | 15 |
| Beverages | Refrescos Americanas LTDA | 20 |
| Beverages | Plutzer Lebensmittelgroßmärkte AG | 125 |
| Beverages | Bigfoot Breweries | 183 |
| Beverages | Aux joyeux ecclésiastiques | 86 |
| Beverages | Leka Trading | 17 |
| Beverages | Karkki Oy | 57 |
| Condiments | Exotic Liquids | 13 |
| Condiments | New Orleans Cajun Delights | 133 |
| Condiments | Grandma Kelly's Homestead | 126 |
| Condiments | Mayumi's | 39 |
| Condiments | Pavlova, Ltd. | 24 |
| Condiments | Plutzer Lebensmittelgroßmärkte AG | 32 |
| Condiments | Leka Trading | 27 |

Record: 1 of 49 No Filter Search

**FIGURE 3-18:** The dynaset produced by the query in Figure 3-17.

A *calculated column* is a dynaset column that gets its values from an expression instead of a field. The expression you use can be any combination of operators, field names, and literal values, and there are even a few built-in functions you can use.

Building a calculated column is straightforward: Instead of specifying a field name when adding a column to the dynaset, you type an expression directly in the Field cell using the following general form:

```
ColumnName:expression
```

Here, *`ColumnName`* is the name you want to use for the calculated column and *`expression`* is the calculation.

For example, the Products table contains both a UnitsInStock field and a UnitPrice field. The inventory value is the quantity in stock multiplied by the price of the product. You could set up a calculated column to show the inventory value by entering the following expression as the header of a new column in the QBE grid, as shown in Figure 3-19 (Figure 3-20 shows the resulting dynaset):

```
Inventory Value:[UnitsInStock]*[UnitPrice]
```

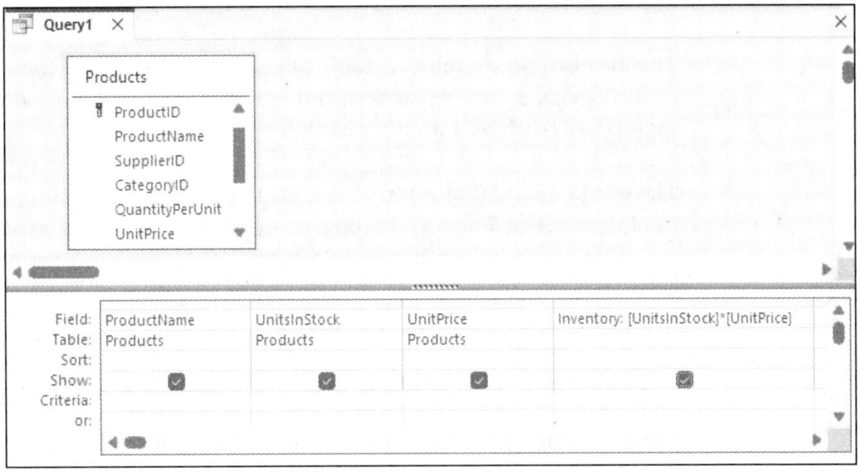


**FIGURE 3-19:** A query set up with a calculated column.

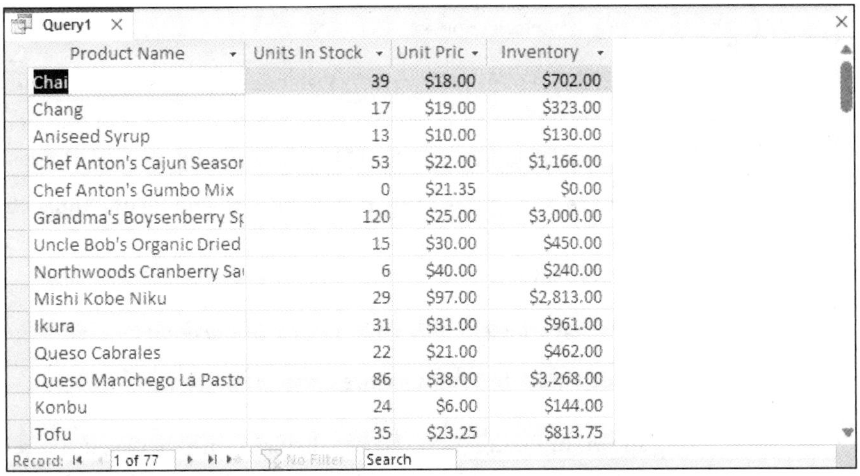


**FIGURE 3-20:** A dynaset with a calculated column.

**TIP**

You can use a calculated column to filter the table by using the calculated column's Criteria cell to enter a criteria expression. For example, if you want to see those products where the inventory value is greater than $3,000, you'd add `>=3000` in the Criteria cell of the calculated column.

# Getting Fancy with a Multiple-Table Query

With a properly constructed relational database model, you'll end up with fields that don't make much sense by themselves. For example, you might have an Order Details table that includes a ProductID field — a foreign key from the Products table. Since this field probably contains only numbers, by itself it would be meaningless to an observer.

The idea behind a multiple-table query is to join related tables and by doing so create a dynaset that replaces meaningless data (such as a product ID) with meaningful data (such as a product name).

The good news is that after you've established a relationship between two tables (as I describe in Book 6, Chapter 2), Access handles everything else behind the scenes, so working with multiple tables isn't much harder than working with single tables.

## Adding multiple tables to a query

To add multiple tables to a query, follow these steps:

1. **Display the Add Tables task pane.**

   You have two choices:

   - Start a new query (Access displays the Add Tables pane automatically).
   - If you're already in the query design window, head over to the Query Design tab then, in the Query Setup group, click Add Tables.

2. **In the Add Tables pane, double-click the name of a table you want to include in the query.**

   Access adds the table to the query's Table pane.

3. **Repeat step 2 to add other tables, as necessary.**
4. **Click the Add Tables pane's Close (X) button.**

As shown in Figure 3-21, Access displays lines between the related tables. These are known in the trade as *join lines* and they run between the fields that define the relation between the two tables. In Figure 3-21, there are two join lines:

» From the Products table's ProductID field (the "one" side of the relation, as marked by the little "1" above the line) to the Order Details table's ProductID field (the "many" side of the relation, as marked by the infinity symbol [∞] above the line).

» From the Order Details table's OrderID field (the "many" side of the relation, as marked by the infinity symbol [∞] above the line) to the Orders table's OrderID field (the "one" side of the relation, as marked by the little "1" above the line).

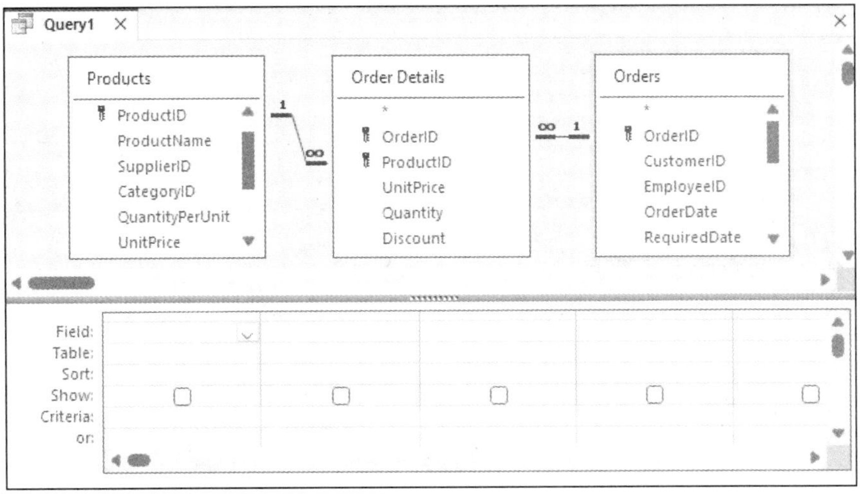


**FIGURE 3-21:** When you add multiple, related tables to the query design window, Access automatically displays the join lines for the related fields.

## Adding fields from multiple tables

With your tables added to the query design window, adding fields to the query is only slightly different than adding them for a single-table query:

» You can still add any field by dragging it from the Table pane to one of the Field cells in the design grid.

» When you choose a field directly from a Field drop-down list, note that the field names are preceded by the table name (for example, Products.SupplierID).

» To lessen the clutter in the Field cells, first use the Table cell to choose the table that contains the field you want. After you do this, the list in the corresponding Field cell will display only the fields from the selected table.

From here, you can set up the query criteria, sorting, top *N* values, totals columns, and calculated columns exactly as you can with a single-table query. Figure 3-22 shows a query based on the Products, Order Details, and Orders tables. The query shows the SupplierID, ProductName, and UnitsInStock (from Products), the Quantity (from Order Details), and OrderDate (from Orders), and a Left In Stock calculated column that subtracts the Quantity from the UnitsInStock. The dynaset will contain just those orders from May 6, 2006 and is sorted on the LeftInStock calculated column. Figure 3-23 shows the resulting dynaset.

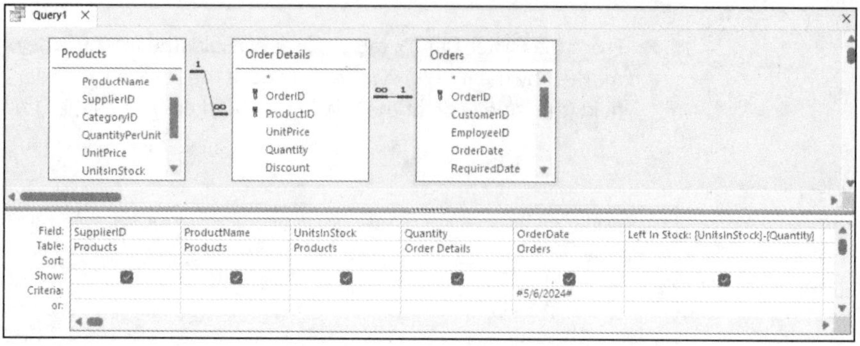


**FIGURE 3-22:** A query with three related tables that includes fields from all the tables.

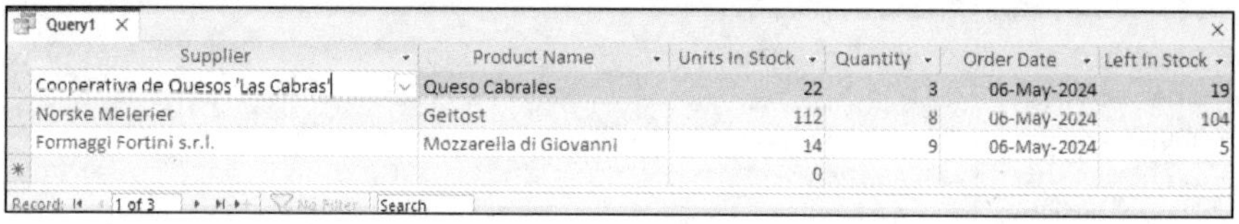


**FIGURE 3-23:** The dynaset returned by the multiple-table query shown in Figure 3-22.

The only thing you have to watch out for is dealing with tables that each have a field with the same name. For example, both the Order Details table and the Products table have a UnitPrice field. To differentiate between them in, say, an expression for a calculated column, you need to preface the field name with the table name, separated either by a dot (.) or an exclamation point (!) like so:

```
[TableName].[FieldName]
[TableName]![FieldName]
```

For example, consider a formula that calculates the extended price for an order, which is the total for a product minus any discount applied. The idea behind this formula is to multiply the unit price times the quantity ordered and subtract the discount. Here's the formula:

```
[Order Details].[UnitPrice]*[Quantity]*(1-[Discount])
```

TIP

When you combine currency values and non-integer values in a calculated column, Access usually displays the results in the General Number format. To apply the Currency format to a calculated column, right-click the column, click Properties, and then click Currency in the Format property list.

# Modifying Table Data with an Update Query

Access, like many programs, has a Replace command that enables you to substitute one piece of text for another either in certain records or throughout a table. Although this command often comes in handy, it simply can't handle some jobs. For example, what if you want to replace the contents of a field with a new value, but only for records that meet certain criteria? Or what if your table includes price data and you want to increase all the prices by five percent?

For these tasks, you need a more sophisticated tool: an *update query*. Unlike a select query, which only displays a subset of the table, an update query makes changes to the table data. The idea is that you select a field to work with, specify the new field value, set up some criteria (this is optional), and then run the query. Access flashes through the table and changes the field entries to the new value. If you enter criteria, only records that match the criteria are updated.

To create and run an update query, follow these steps:

1. **Create a select query that includes the field (or fields) you want to update and the field (or fields) you need for the criteria.**

   Remember, criteria are optional for an update query. If you leave them out, Access updates every record in the table.

2. **When the select query is complete, run it to make sure the criteria are working properly.**

   WARNING

   Update queries can save you a great deal of time, but they must be approached with caution. After you run an update query, Access offers no direct method for undoing the operation. Therefore, always start off with a select query to make sure your criteria are doing what they're supposed to do.

3. **Convert the select query to an update query by displaying the Query Design tab then, in the Query Type group, clicking Update.**

   Access removes the Sort and Show rows from the design grid and replaces them with an Update To row (refer to Figure 3-24).

4. **In the Update To cell for the field you want to change, type the new value or an expression that calculates the new value.**

5. **On the Query Design tab, in the Results group, click Run.**

   Access displays a dialog box to tell you how many rows (records) will be updated.

6. **Click Yes to perform the update.**

After you see what update queries can do, you'll wonder how you ever got along without them. For example, one common table chore is changing prices and, in a large table, it's a drudgery most of us can live without. However, if you're increasing prices by a certain percentage, you can automate the whole process with an update query.

In Northwind's Products table, suppose you want to increase each value in the UnitPrice field by five percent. To handle this task in an update query, you add the UnitPrice field to the design grid and then enter the following expression in the Update To cell:

```
[UnitPrice]*1.05
```

This expression tells Access that you want every UnitPrice field entry increased by five percent. You can also set up criteria to gain even more control over the update. Figure 3-24 shows an update query that raises the UnitPrice field by five percent, but only for those records where the CategoryName field equals "Beverages".

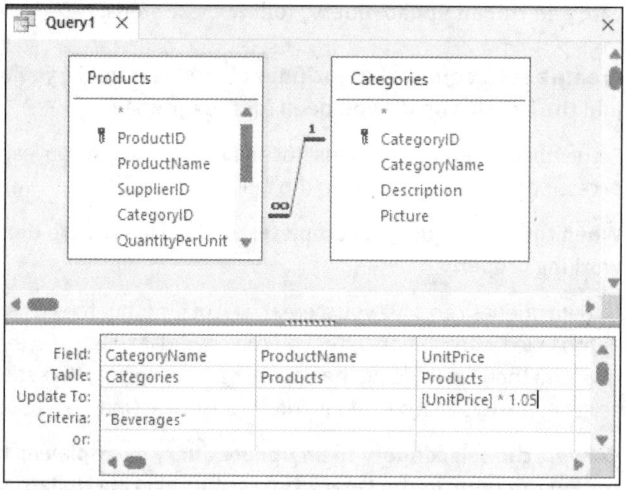


**FIGURE 3-24:** This update query increases the UnitPrice values by five percent for those products where Category Name equals "Beverages".

# Removing Records from a Table with a Delete Query

If you need to delete one or two records from a table, just selecting each record and choosing the Home tab's Delete button (it's in the Records group) is straightforward enough. But what if you have a large number of records to get rid of? For example, you might want to clean out an Orders table by deleting any old orders that were placed before a certain date. Or you might want to delete records for products that have been discontinued. In both examples, you can set up criteria to identify the group of records to delete. You then enter the criteria in a *delete query* and Access deletes all the matching records.

Follow these steps to create and run a delete query:

1. **Create a select query that includes the asterisk "field" (the asterisk represents the entire table), and any field you need for your deletion criteria.**
2. **Enter the criteria and then run the select query to make sure the query is picking out the correct records.**
3. **Convert the select query to a delete query by displaying the Query Design tab then, in the Query Type group, clicking Delete.**

   Access replaces the design grid's Sort and Show lines with a Delete line. The asterisk field will display *From* in the Delete cell, and each criteria field will display *Where* in the Delete cell. Figure 3-25 shows a delete query for the Products table that removes all the records where the Discontinued field is set to True.

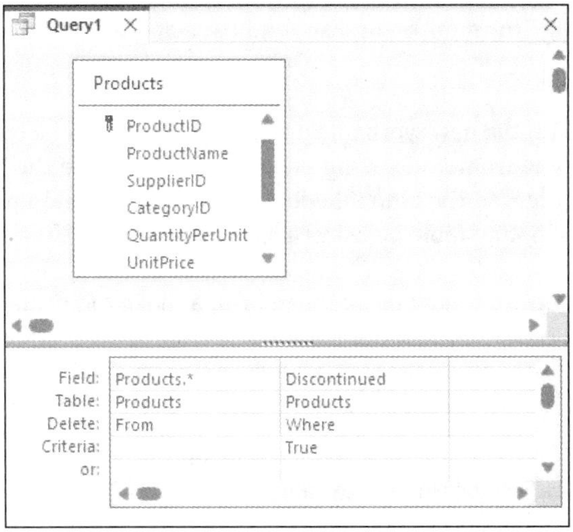


**FIGURE 3-25:** A delete query uses the asterisk field and any fields you need for your criteria.

4. **Run the query.**

   Access analyzes the criteria and then displays a dialog box telling you how many records you'll be deleting.
5. **Click Yes to proceed with the deletion.**

WARNING

The delete query is even more dangerous than the update query because the records you delete are gone for good and nothing can bring them back. Again, setting up and running a select query first is an easy way to avoid wiping out anything important.

# Creating a New Table with a Make Table Query

The results of select queries are called dynasets because they're dynamic subsets of the table data. When I say "dynamic," I mean that if you edit the query records, the corresponding records in the table also change. Similarly, if you edit the table, Access changes the query records automatically. (In either case, you can see the changes by opening the Home tab then, in the Records group, clicking Refresh All.)

This behavior is usually welcome because at least you know you're always working with the most up-to-date information. However, there might be the odd time when this behavior isn't what you want. For example, at the end of the month or the end of the fiscal year, you might want some of your tables to be "frozen" while you tie up things for month- or year-end (this applies particularly to tables that track invoices).

Instead of letting the new work pile up until the table can be released, Access lets you create a table from an existing one. You can then use the new table for your month-end duties, so the old table doesn't need to be held up. You create a new table from an existing table by using a *make table query*.

Here are the steps to follow to create and run a make table query:

1. **Create a select query that includes the fields you want to include in the new table as well as the field (or fields) you need for the criteria.**

   The criteria are optional for a make table query. If you leave them out, Access includes every record in the new table.

2. **When the select query is complete, run it to make sure the criteria are working properly.**

3. **Convert the query to a make table query by displaying the Query Design tab then, in the Query Type group, clicking Make Table.**

   Access displays the Make Table dialog box, shown in Figure 3-26.

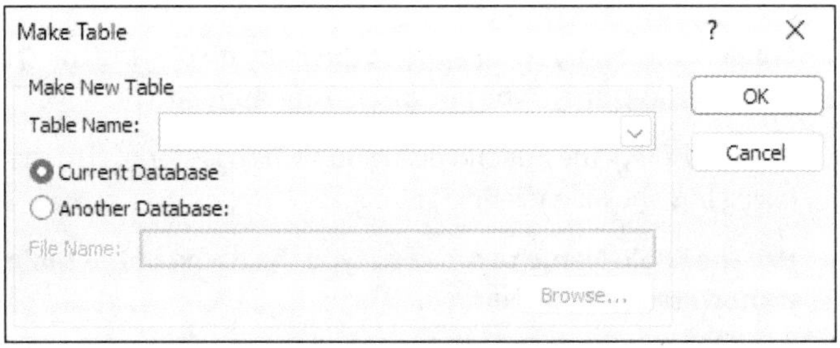


**FIGURE 3-26:** Use the Make Table dialog box to define your new table.

4. **Use the Table Name text box to type the name you want to use for the new table.**
5. **To create the table in the same database, select Current Database.**

   If you prefer to add the table to an external database, select Another Database and type the path and filename of the database in the File Name text box (or click Browse to select the database using a dialog box).
6. **Click OK.**
7. **Run the query.**

   Access displays a dialog box that tells you how many rows (records) will be added to the new table.
8. **Click Yes to create the new table.**

# Adding Records to a Table with an Append Query

Instead of creating an entirely new table, you might prefer to add records from one table to an existing table. You can accomplish this with an *append query.*

Follow these steps to create and run an append query:

1. **Create a select query that includes the fields you want to include in the appended records as well as the field (or fields) you need for the criteria.**

   The criteria are optional for an append query. If you leave them out, Access appends every record to the other table.
2. **When the select query is complete, run it to make sure the criteria are working properly.**

3. **Convert the query to an append query by displaying the Query Design tab then, in the Query Type group, clicking Append.**

   Access displays the Append dialog box, which is identical to the Make Table dialog box shown earlier in Figure 3-26.

4. **Use the Table Name text box to type the name of the table to which you want the records appended.**
5. **If the other table is in the same database, select Current Database.**

   If the other table is in an external database, select Another Database and type the path and filename of the database in the File Name text box (or click Browse to select the database using a dialog box).

6. **Click OK.**

   Access adds an Append To row to the design grid.

7. **For each field in the design grid, use the Append To cell to choose the field in the other table to use for the append operation.**

   WARNING

   If you add the asterisk field to the design grid, its Append To cell will show the name of the other table. In this case, if you add other fields for criteria purposes, make sure these fields have their Append To cells blank.

8. **Run the query.**

   Access displays a dialog box to tell you how many rows (records) will be appended to the table.

9. **Click Yes to append the records.**

# 7

# Microsoft Teams

# Contents at a Glance

IN THIS CHAPTER

» Navigating the Teams app

» Managing your status and profile

» Configuring your settings

» Searching across Teams

» Adding apps, tabs, and other extras

# Chapter 1

# Getting around in Teams

Throughout the first six sections of this book, for the most part I've treated Office 365 as though it was a suite of apps designed for a single person to get their work (or play or creativity or whatever) done. Nowadays, though, around a quarter of the way through the 21st century, getting work (or play or creativity or whatever) done by yourself feels more than a little old-fashioned. In the modern world, especially if you work in an office and/or for some behemoth corporation, you're more likely to be part of a team. And one of the main characteristics of a team is that everyone collaborates with everyone else on the team.

Collaboration is such an important topic now that I devote an entire mini-book to it (that would be Book 8). But the true Office 365 collaboration experience begins right here in Book 7 with an in-depth look at Microsoft Teams. As the name implies, Teams has been designed from the ground up to enable teams of colleagues to work together: keep up with team news, have conversations, chat, share files, meet remotely, and more. The chapters here in Book 7 show you how to use all of these Teams features to make it easier to collaborate with the others on your work team.

In this chapter, you find out how to access all the major features in Teams, update and share your status, use apps and plug-ins, and find people, messages, and files.

## Introducing Teams

Teams brings together communication, collaboration, and online meetings into a single app, complete with strong integration with most of the other Office 365 apps. Teams also has an App store that enables you to connect to additional Microsoft-created features as well as third-party tools like Evernote, Trello, YouTube, and even Zoom. Teams is fully supported on all major operating systems — Windows, macOS, iOS, iPadOS, and Android — through a dedicated app for each. You can also use a browser version of Teams on almost any desktop computer. You can easily hop between a PC at work, a Mac at home, a browser in a hotel, and an iPhone — all from the same account.

Teams provides the following features:

- **Teams and their channels:** In the Teams world, a *team* is a permission-protected online workspace for threaded conversations, file sharing and editing, and channel meetings. A *channel* is a subcategory of a team, used to divide a team into pertinent subtopics. A team and its channels are meant to help move clunky communication and collaboration processes from your email Inbox into a centralized location, with the goal of reducing notifications overall and keeping work better organized. Chapter 2 of this mini-book focuses on teams and channels.
- **Chat:** You use the Chat app to have one-on-one and group private chats with both colleagues and external users of Teams and Skype. Teams chat is similar to other chat apps like WhatsApp, IRC, and Skype, but it has many more features than most of those other tools. Chapter 3 of this mini-book focuses on how to Chat.
- **Calls and meetings:** You can host interactive video conferences within Teams and include anyone inside or outside your organization, or simply start an audio call with a single person. Chat, share your screen, upload files, record meetings, lead webinars, and interact from your desktop or mobile device. This feature is similar to Zoom but provides a lot more capabilities thanks to its deep integration with the rest of Office 365. Chapter 5 of this mini-book tells you much more about meetings.
- **Files:** Access your OneDrive, SharePoint, and Teams files right in the Files app in Teams. You can even bring in files from other services, like Dropbox and Google Drive. Book 7, Chapter 4 covers the Files app.

# Taking a Look Around

This section demystifies the Teams interface. Along the far-left side of the window is the *navigation bar,* which is the vertical pane that holds your basic Teams apps: Activity, Chat, Teams, Calendar, Calls, and so on. You can pin other Teams apps that you install to this bar as well; check out "Enhancing Your Teams Experience with Helpful Extras," later in this chapter, for details.

When you click any of the apps on the navigation bar, Teams opens to a window showing the rail and the main area for that app. The *rail* is the jumping-off point for which app is open and typically lists the most recent or important information in that app. The *main area* contains the actual content for the app you're in. Each app in Teams deals with these areas differently, but the setup stays relatively constant. The Calendar app is the exception; it has no rail but instead takes up the whole space and displays your Office 365 calendar, which is the same calendar you use in Outlook 365. Refer to Figure 1-1 for an overview of the areas in Teams.

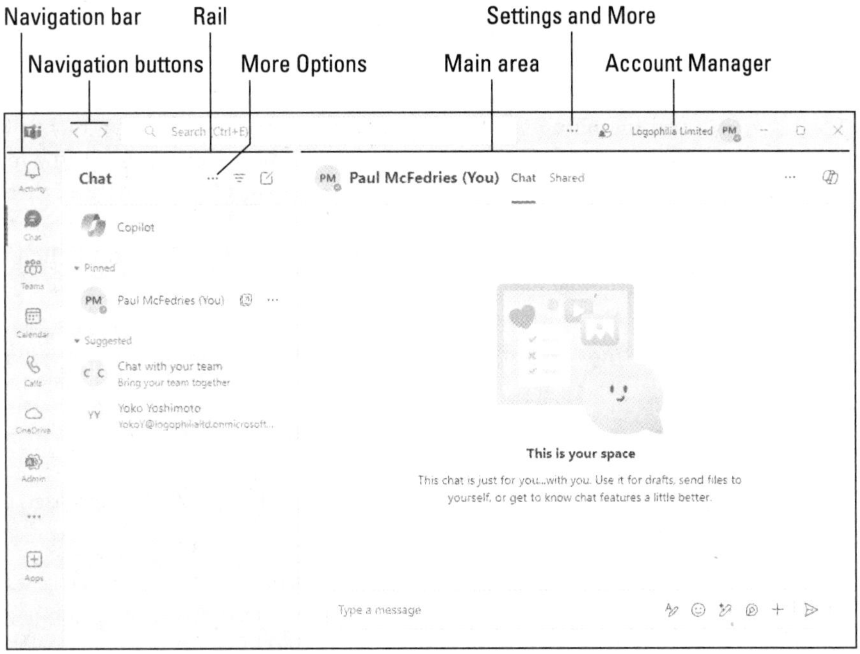


**FIGURE 1-1:** You access the Teams apps via the navigation bar, and most apps have a layout similar to the one shown here for the Chat app.

REMEMBER

As you begin to move around in Teams, keep these navigation tips in mind:

- To switch among Teams apps, click the app name in the navigation bar. The rail may have a title in bold type at the top, such as Teams, Activity, or Chat, depending on the app.

- To the right of the app title, you usually see the More Options button (shown in the margin and pointed out in Figure 1-1). Clicking More Options opens a drop-down menu that offers one or more ways to modify the app view (the commands that appear vary depending on the app).
- Use the Back and Forward navigation buttons (pointed out in Figure 1-1) to navigate previously visited Teams apps.

# Personalizing Teams to Use It Effectively

You can configure Teams to better meet your needs by choosing among the built-in settings and personalization options. The following pages cover how to add or update a profile photo, manage your status and notifications, enable dark mode, and configure your audio and video devices for meetings.

## Adding a profile photo

The first thing any good (or bad, for that matter) Teams user should do is add a profile photo so that your peers and colleagues can attach a face to your name. Adding or updating your photo in Teams updates your profile in all Office 365 apps (though the update can take hours or days to work its way through all the apps).

TIP

Use whatever photo you're comfortable with, but ideally the photo should follow these guidelines:

- The photo should be a straight-on view of your face, with good lighting and a clear contrast between your face and the background.
- It's best if your photo is cropped square or as close to square as possible before you upload. You can't crop or rearrange non-square photos, so do the image work before uploading. A JPEG or PNG image sized to 1024 x 1024 seems to work best.
- Your face should take up as much of the profile photo circle as possible. You don't need to show off your blouse or tie, or anything that might be in the background. Many areas within the Office 365 apps where your photo will show up are small, so the more tightly the image is cropped to your face, the better.

Follow these steps to upload a new or updated profile photo:

1. **Click the Account Manager (pointed out earlier in Figure 1-1).**

   The Account Manager menu opens and displays your photo or initials, status, and other options.

2. **Click the image to the left of your name.**

   If you haven't uploaded a profile photo in the past, the "image" will just be your initials.

   The Change Your Profile Picture window saunters in.

3. **Click Upload.**

   The Open dialog box makes an appearance.

4. **Navigate to the folder that contains the photo, click the file, and then click Open.**

   Teams returns you to the Change Your Profile Picture window and displays the image you selected. If you're not happy with the photo you chose, feel free to repeat Steps 3 and 4 until you find an image that satisfies.

5. **Click Save.**

   Teams updates your profile picture.

## Setting your status

On Teams, your *status* is an indication of your current engagement with the Teams app. The status is useful because it lets others know whether you're available for a meeting, chat, or phone call. For example, if someone wants to invite you to a meeting right now, they'd delay that meeting if your status indicates that you're not currently available.

Your status appears anywhere your profile photo does in Teams, like your Account Manager menu, a chat, or a conversation. If you do nothing with your status, Teams automatically updates the status depending on what you're doing:

- **Available:** You're actively using Teams, and you're not booked in an appointment or sharing a screen in a meeting. The Available status icon is a green circle with a white checkmark.
- **Away:** You haven't interacted with the Teams app for a while (or you've let your computer go into sleep mode). The Away status icon is a yellow circle with clock hands. Figure 1-2 shows the Away status as it appears in the Account Manager menu and also points out several places where the Away icon appears in the Teams interface.

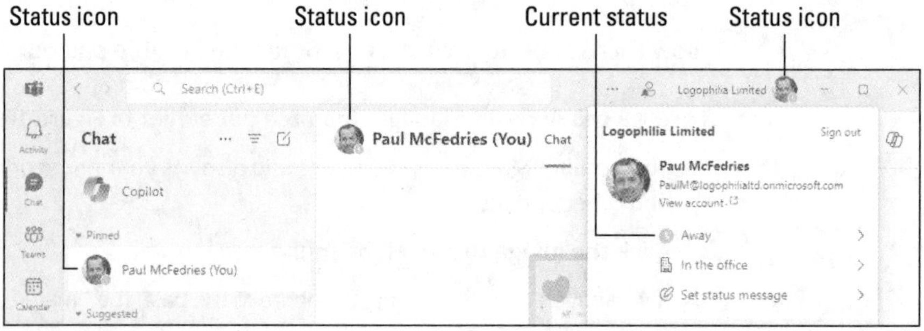


**FIGURE 1-2:** Your current status appears in the Account Manager menu and wherever your profile picture appears.

- **Busy:** You're in an appointment on your calendar (Outlook or Teams) that lists you as busy. The Busy status icon is a solid red circle.
- **Do Not Disturb:** You're in a Teams meeting and you're sharing your screen. The Do Not Disturb status icon is a red circle with a white bar.

However, there might be times when you're technically "available," but you don't want to be contacted because you need to focus on what you're doing. In such cases, you can take control of your status and set it manually to Busy or Away or Do Not Disturb or whatever you think will keep others on your team at bay. You can also set a duration for your manual status and include a status message, which can help direct people who want to reach out to you.

Follow these steps to change your status and status message:

1. **Click Account Manager near the top-right corner of the Teams window.**

   Your Account Manager menu opens.

2. **Click your current status.**

   A drop-down menu with status choices appears, as shown in Figure 1-3.

3. **Click the status you prefer.**

   REMEMBER

   You can't set your status as Available for a duration (probably so that people can't appear to be working when they're not, not that you or I would ever do such a thing).

   TIP

   The Do Not Disturb status blocks most notifications and calls from bothering you, so it's useful when you need some uninterrupted focus time. However, you can provide priority access to certain individuals (maybe your boss?) so that they can circumvent your Do Not Disturb status and get through to you. Refer to the "Setting up priority access" section, later in this chapter, for details.

   Teams changes your status to your chosen option.

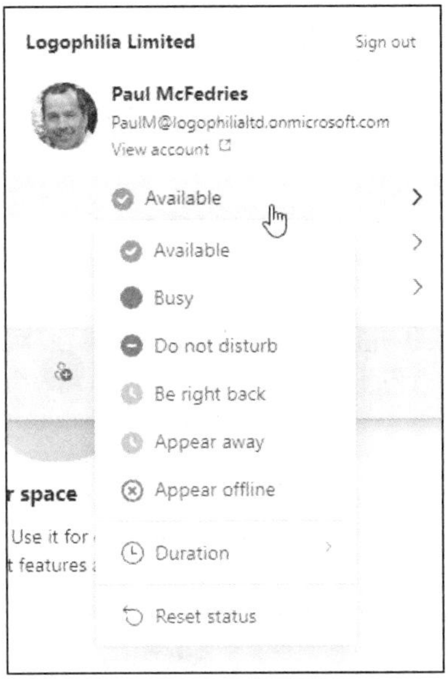


**FIGURE 1-3:** Teams offers a half dozen choices for manually setting your status.

4. **To specify a length of time for your manual status to be in effect, click the new status, click Duration, use the Reset Status After drop-down list to select a time, then click Done.**

   If none of the prefab durations works for you, click Customized, then choose the day and time when you want your status to reset.

5. **To update your status message, click Set Status Message next to your status, then type your message in the large text box that appears.**

   Use the status message to tell people why you're not available or to point them to a resource that might help them when you're not around. The status message automatically displays your out-of-office message (automatic reply) from Outlook when it's set.

   You can also select the Show When People Message Me check box to tell Teams to display your status when someone messages you. Finally, you can also use the Clear Status Message After drop-down list to set the duration of your message.

   REMEMBER

   If you choose to show your status when people message you, your status message displays above any message box a colleague uses to send you a message (for example, in chat or a Team). This feature is incredibly useful for ensuring that people know what to expect when they send you a message.

REMEMBER

You can cancel your manual status at any time by clicking your status and then clicking Reset Status.

TIP

You can quickly set your status using slash commands. In the Teams Search box, type **/available**, **/away**, **/brb**, **/busy**, **/dnd**, or **/offline** (note the forward slash mark before each word) and then press Enter. Refer to the "Saving time with slash commands" section, later in this chapter, for more info on these types of commands.

## Setting up priority access

Priority access enables selected individuals to bypass the Do Not Disturb status if you've set it manually (or you're sharing your screen in a meeting or call). Priority access is useful when you want key people to be able to get hold of you — such as your boss — even when everyone else can't.

Follow these steps to manage your priority access list:

1. **Click Settings and More (shown in the margin) to the left of the Account Manager button.**

   Teams unfurls the Settings and More menu.

2. **Click Settings.**

   Teams introduces you to the Settings pane.

3. **Click Privacy.**

   Just like that, the Privacy settings appear.

4. **Click the Manage Priority Access button.**

   Teams takes you right away to the Manage Priority Access screen.

5. **Use the Search For a Name or Number text box to start typing the name (or phone number) of the person you want to give access to.**
6. **When the person shows up in the search results, click their name.**

   Teams adds the person to your priority access list.

7. **Repeat steps 5 and 6 to add each person you want on your priority access list.**

   You can also remove people from your list by clicking *X* next to their name.

   Your updates are saved automatically. When you're done, just click the Teams app you want to work in next.

## Customizing Teams via settings

Teams comes with a lot of settings, but they're not obvious or easy to find. Still, you might find it worthwhile to take advantage of all the toggles, tick boxes, and features available to configure Teams in a way that works best for you.

To access your settings, click the Settings and More ellipsis (shown in the margin) to the left of the Account Manager button to open the Settings and More drop-down menu, then click Settings.

You should take some time to review the available options. A little time now can save you a lot of time in the future. Options range from choosing how Teams starts up and whether spell-check is enabled to managing notifications in other organizations. You can also manage privacy features, read receipt settings, device settings for video calls, and app permissions, just to mention some.

To navigate Settings, click a category in the Settings pane, then use the controls that appear in the main area of the Teams window.

### Modifying notification settings

Notifications are likely to be the first thing you want to configure. The move to Teams can lead to more total notifications across Outlook and Teams and, well, it doesn't have to be that way. Follow these steps to manage these notification settings:

1. **Click Settings and More (shown in the margin) to the left of the Account Manager button.**

   Teams unpacks the Settings and More menu.

2. **Click Settings.**

   Teams brings in the Settings pane.

3. **Click Notifications and Activity.**

   The Notifications and Activity window appears, as shown in Figure 1-4.

4. **If you prefer not to be bothered at all with notifications, click the Mute All Notifications (Except For Calls and Meetings) switch to On.**

   Note the exceptions here for calls and meetings. Also, by default Teams still allows urgent notifications and priority access notifications. If you'd rather not allow these through, deselect the Always Show Urgent and Priority Contact Notifications check box.

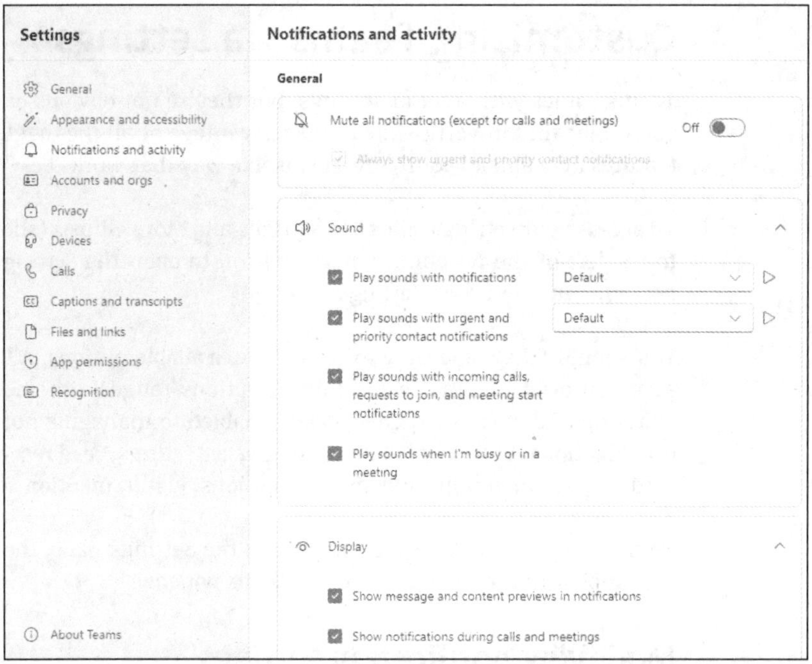


**FIGURE 1-4:** Choose the notification settings that will help you achieve work-life balance.

5. **If you don't mute notifications in step 4, then take your time working through the notification settings in the rest of the window.**

   Teams offers settings for notification sounds and display, chats and channels, meetings, people, and calendar.

TIP

You can manage notifications for specific channels and conversations in each channel. This can help you pare down the notifications that are relevant to you, hopefully reducing your overall notification count in a way that you could never do if you continued working in Outlook exclusively. Head over to Book 7, Chapter 2 for details about channel and conversation options.

## Enabling dark mode or high-contrast mode

Dark mode is one of the most popular features for apps in the modern world, and an app like Teams wouldn't be complete without it. Teams offers both dark mode and high-contrast options in the form of a theme. Follow these steps to manage your theme in Teams:

1. **Click Settings and More (shown in the margin) to the left of the Account Manager button.**

   Teams unloads the Settings and More menu.

2. **Click Settings.**

   Teams asks the Settings pane to step forward.

3. **Click Appearance and Accessibility.**

   The Appearance and Accessibility settings appear.

4. **Use the Theme drop-down list to select Dark or High Contrast.**

   If you've configured Windows to use dark mode, then Teams will follow suit if you select Follow Operating System Theme in the Theme drop-down list.

## Setting up and testing your audio and video devices

Another critical area in your settings is your device listing. Meetings are an essential element of Microsoft Teams, and you want to ensure that your audio and video work correctly before you join a meeting, not *as* you join it. Not only can you use your settings to select your devices, you can also run a test call to ensure that the audio and video are working as expected. Follow these steps to manage your devices:

1. **Click Settings and More (shown in the margin) to the left of the Account Manager button.**

   Teams unveils the Settings and More menu.

2. **Click Settings.**

   Teams requests the presence of the Settings pane.

3. **Click Devices.**

   The Devices window appears.

4. **Under Audio Settings, use the Speaker list to select your speaker and the Microphone list to select your microphone.**
5. **Feel free to adjust the other audio settings, as needed.**
6. **Under Video Settings, use the Camera list to select the camera you want to use.**

7. **Go right ahead and mess around with the other video settings, if you feel like it.**

8. **Scroll back up the screen to find the Make a Test Call button and click it to run your devices through a mock call.**

   This feature starts a call with Teams Echo. You hear a request to record a message. The request shows you how well your speakers sound. Your recording indicates how good your microphone sounds to someone else. Listen for background noises or other distracting sounds, and do your best to minimize them for the best experience in meetings.

TIP

Whenever you need to run a test call again, you can do so quickly by using a slash command. In the Teams Search box, type **/testcall** and then press Enter. (The "Saving time with slash commands" section, later in this chapter, tells you more about slash commands.)

# Noticing Notifications

While you're busy doing your work, Teams is busy monitoring activities such as the following:

- You get mentioned in a conversation.
- You get added to a team.
- Someone replies or reacts to one of your messages.
- You miss a call.
- You get a voice message.

To help keep you in the loop, Teams alerts you when any of the above activities take place. These alerts appear as two types of notifications:

- **Banner:** A pop-up message that shows up temporarily in the Teams app.
- **Activity feed:** These are messages that appear in the Activity app. They also generate indicators in Teams, such as badges and icons that appear in the navigation bar and elsewhere.

Figure 1-5 points out examples of these notifications. (If you're scratching your head over what on Earth an "@mention" might be, stop scratching: You learn all about @mentions in Book 7, Chapter 3.)

**FIGURE 1-5:** Notifications let you know when your team has been active.

# Filtering and Searching

Depending on the size of your team and how many extroverts it contains, Teams can become a very active place. Lots of activity is usually a good thing because it implies interest and engagement, but that doesn't mean that *you* will be interested in or engaged with everything your team generates. Your Teams feeds will consist of both "signal" — content that's relevant to you — and "noise" — content that falls below your threshold of relevance. One of the secrets of Teams success is to reduce the noise so that the signal comes in loud and clear.

One powerful noise reduction method is to *filter* your Activity feed to display only what interests you. You can also drill down directly to the content you need by conducting powerful searches using the Teams Search box.

## Filtering your Activity feed

The Activity app is your one-stop shop for monitoring what's happening within your team — channels, conversations, chats, files, and so on. As shown earlier in

Figure 1-5, a badge on the Activity app icon lets you know when you have unread or missed notifications.

The Activity feed presents actions that you can take in the channels in which you participate. Many people start their workday by checking out what's up on the Activity feed, where you find mentions, replies, and other notifications. Think of it as your Teams Inbox.

However, just as your Outlook Inbox can quickly become overwhelmed with irrelevant messages, your Teams Activity feed can easily become overrun with items that don't interest you or aren't all that important to your work. To make your activity feed more manageable, you can filter it to focus on the information you need. Here are the steps to follow to filter the Activity feed:

1. **Click Activity in the navigation bar.**

   Your Activity feed displays in the rail.

2. Filter the feed by clicking one of the following:

   - **Unread:** Toggles the feed between showing just the items you haven't read yet and showing all the items.
   - **@Mentions:** Toggles the feed between showing just the items that mention you and showing all the items.

   - **Filter:** Click this icon (it's shown in the margin; you can also press Ctrl+Shift+F), then type a word or phrase in the text box that shows up. Teams filters the feed to show just those items that include the word or phrase you typed.

## Searching for a post, message, or other content

How do you find the file your manager mentioned in passing last week? Or recall the name of the movie a colleague suggested during a private chat three months ago? Follow these steps to search Teams for a specific post, message, or file:

1. **Click inside the Search box at the top of the Teams window.**
2. **Start typing a search term.**

   The Search box immediately suggests results, as shown in Figure 1-6. Notice that Teams also displays several filter buttons below the Search text box: Messages, Files, Group Chats, and Teams and Channels.

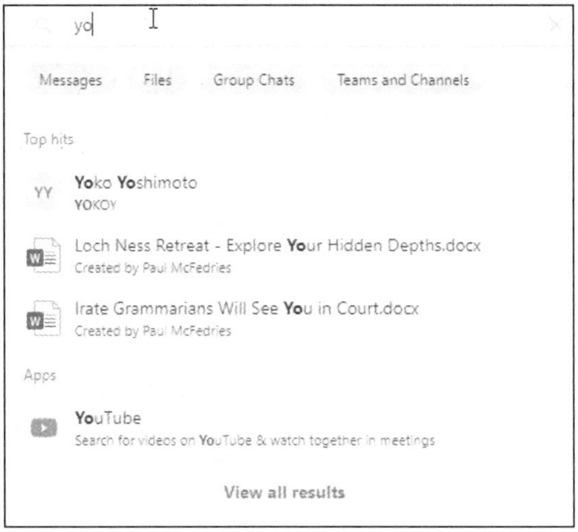


**FIGURE 1-6:** Start typing and Teams immediately displays search results that match what you've typed so far.

3. **(Optional) To filter the search results, click the appropriate filter button.**

   For example, if you know that the item you're looking for is a file, click the Files filter to ask Teams to only display files in the search results.

4. **If you don't see the item you want, click View All Results to display the complete list of matching items.**

5. **Click the item you want.**

   Teams takes you to the item.

## SEARCH TIPS FOR TEAMS AND OFFICE 365

Search is a major topic of discussion, if not a bone of contention, in many organizations. But you can get better results by knowing some key search skills. These tips aren't just for Teams, either — you can use them in the Office 365 home page Search box, any SharePoint Search box, and pretty much anywhere there's a Search box in any app in Office 365. Oh, and they work in Google, too:

- **Filter your results:** Use refiners when available to remove extraneous and irrelevant content. In Teams search, you can filter messages and files using various filters below the Search box, as shown earlier in Figure 1-6.
- **Use quotation marks:** Add quotation marks around a phrase to return results with exactly that phrase. Without quotes, your results will include the terms, but not

*(continued)*

(continued)

necessarily together in the document or message where it was found. For example, *"laptop sales"* will return different results than *laptop sales* with no quotation marks.

- **Use - or NOT:** Filter your results by removing a certain term using a hyphen or the word *NOT* in all caps. If you search *revenue report q1*, you may get results for Q2, Q3, and Q4. Instead, search *revenue report q1 -q2 -q3* or search *revenue report q1 NOT q2 NOT q3*. Hyphens and *NOT* can be used interchangeably, even in the same search query, but you can't use a space after a hyphen whereas you must use a space after *NOT*.
- **Use *:** An asterisk — in this context, called a *wildcard* — at the end of a portion of a word will return results with various forms of the word. The search term *rep** returns *report, repayment, Repo Man*, and other variations on that word. You can use the asterisk only at the end of the word, not the beginning or middle.
- **Put them together:** Go searching for *revenue rep* "laptop sales" q1 -q2 -q3 -q4* and then filter your results using the available refiners. You should notice better or more appropriate results.

## Saving time with slash commands

Everyone loves a shortcut, and Teams provides a list of unique ones called *slash commands*. Enter a slash command into the Teams Search box and you can directly kick off the action for that command. For example, you can set your status by typing **/brb** (for be right back), **/dnd** (for do not disturb), or **/offline** (meaning you can't be reached). Or you can quickly call someone by entering **/call** and providing a name.

Slash commands are especially popular with computer programmers who use Teams, but everyday people can equally benefit.

Follow these steps to use a slash command:

1. **Click inside the Search box at the top of the Teams window.**
2. **Type / (forward slash).**

   A list of available slash commands appears, as shown in Figure 1-7.
3. **Type the command you want to use and press Enter.**

   You can also click the command in the menu.

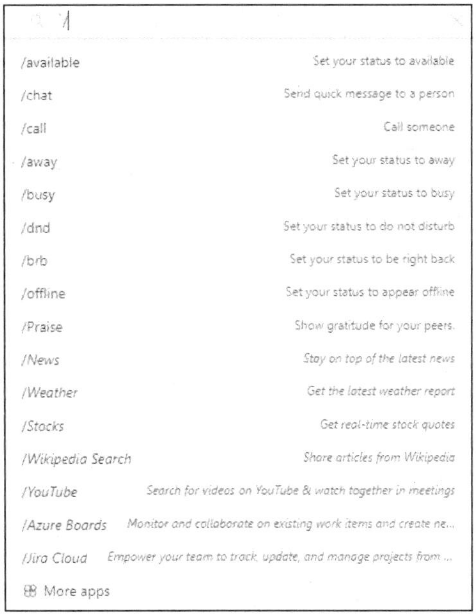


**FIGURE 1-7:** In the Search box, type / to display the slash commands that are at your beck and call.

4. **Enter any additional information needed, depending on the slash** command you use.

   For example, if you want to send a private chat message to someone, after you type **/chat** and press Enter (Steps 2 and 3), a drop-down list of names appears. If the person you want isn't in the list, type the name in the Person Search box above the drop-down list, then click the person when they appear in the search results. Then you can enter the message and press Enter to send it.

# Using Teams to Know Your Colleagues Better

Teams is all about interacting with others, so when you need to know about someone else, the app has your back. The following pages cover how to display a person's profile card and how to find out where they sit in the organization chart (if you have one).

## Viewing a person's profile card

Profile cards abound in Office 365. You can hover over someone's profile photo or initials in almost every app and get more information about them, and Teams is no exception. Teams offers a lot of shortcuts actions through its profile card, too. Figure 1-8 provides a view of the profile card.

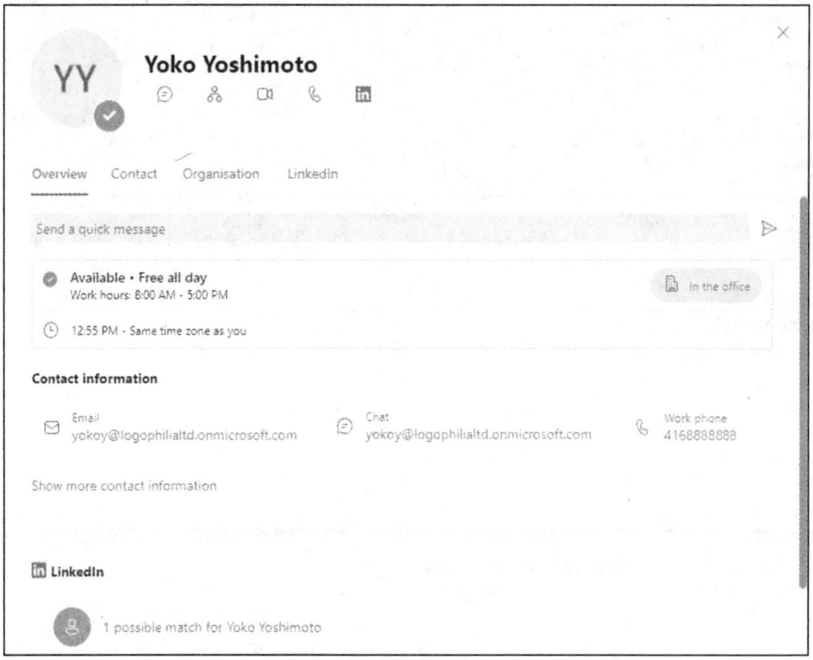


**FIGURE 1-8:** You can garner lots of information about a person from their profile card.

The Teams profile card shows a number of standard facts about the person (as long as the information is provided), including name, job title, organization, phone number, email address, manager, profile photo, and status. Additional information might be included by your organization. But that's not all: Through a profile card, you can also send a private chat message, open an email draft, and start an audio or video call to the person.

Follow these steps to access and use the profile card:

1. **Hover your cursor over another person's photo or initials.**

   When you hover over one of these items, the person's contact information is displayed in the card that pops up.

2. **(Optional) To open the full profile card, click Show More.**
3. **Perform one of the following tasks from the profile card:**

   - *Send a quick message:* Enter your message in the Send a Quick Message box and click Send (shown in the margin).

- *Start (or continue) a chat with that person:* Click the Start a Chat button (shown in the margin).
- *Start an email message addressed to that person:* Click the person's email address.
- *Start a video call with that person:* Click the Start a Video call button (shown in the margin).
- *Start an audio call with that person:* Click the Start an Audio call button (shown in the margin).

Start an Audio and Start a Video both make a Teams call, but the latter starts with your video on. You can disable your video after connecting a video call; likewise, you can enable your video after you start an audio call.

TIP

You can hover over various contact information (such as phone number or email address) and click the Copy icon (shown in the margin) that appears to the right of the info to copy this information and paste it elsewhere. This feature is useful if you're authoring an email in Outlook to a bunch of people and want to quickly grab someone's email address to include.

## Viewing the org chart

One of the most beneficial features of the profile card is the org chart. Click the Org Chart icon (shown in the margin) or click the Organization tab in the full profile card, and a hierarchal tree appears showing where the person sits in the org chart, along with who reports to the same manager.

WARNING

The org chart works only if each employee's manager is identified in the directory. If an org chart doesn't appear or the connections appear incorrect, reach out to your IT team and suggest that they manage who reports to whom, because it's an incredibly useful piece of information to have in one click.

# Enhancing Your Teams Experience with Helpful Extras

A unique feature of Microsoft Teams is the ability to add plug-ins to Teams, chats, meetings, and elsewhere. A *plug-in* is a connection to another app or service, whether it's provided by Microsoft or a third-party tool. An added plug-in in Teams can be a tab in a channel or chat, an app in the Teams navigation bar, and even bots (automated virtual assistants) that interact through natural language chat with you.

A deep dive of Teams apps is beyond the scope of this mini-book, but you should be aware of some of the best apps available out of the box and take some time to investigate whether they'd be useful to you. Available apps include Microsoft-provided ones (to add to the built-in features of Teams) and third-party tools, which bring non-Microsoft tools right into Teams, minimizing the app-jumping fatigue you're likely familiar with.

## Using built-in apps

Teams provides apps out of the box that you can make use of without any installation, as long as your IT team has enabled them for your use. If an app doesn't appear after following the steps below, reach out to your IT team and ask for access. Some of these tools are super handy.

Follow these steps to open and use an existing app:

...

1. **Below your apps in the navigation bar, click View More Apps (the ellipsis shown in the margin).**

   Teams pops up a window of apps.

   The window is organized with already installed apps above and not yet installed apps below.

2. **(Optional) In the Search for Apps text box, type some or all of the name of the app you want to add.**

3. **To add an installed app, click the app.**

   If the app isn't installed, then you need to click the Add button that appears to the right of the app name.

   Teams adds the app to the navigation bar and selects the app so that it appears in the main area.

TIP

The app is added to the navigation bar only temporarily, meaning that when you navigate to another part of the Teams, the app gets removed from the navigation bar. To have the app remain on the navigation bar full-time, right-click the app's navigation bar icon and then click Pin.

Some of the key apps to consider using include:

» **Approvals:** You can send a request or file through an automated approval request right in Teams. Approvals can be sent to an individual or multiple people, and you can manage all sent and received approval requests right in the Approvals app. Templates and built-in connections to Adobe Sign and

DocuSign are available, and you can customize your approval processes using Microsoft Power Automate, which is likely included with your Office 365 subscription.

- **Insights:** The Insights app opens Viva Insights, which provides, well, insight into how you spend your time while working and is intended to promote a healthier mental state through break scheduling, virtual commutes, suggested focus time, and other well-being tools.
- **Shifts:** Manage schedules, reservations, and other aspects of your work with this hourly scheduling feature built into Teams. (Shifts used to be a separate Office 365 app called StaffHub.)
- **Copilot:** Use Microsoft's AI assistant to perform team-related tasks such as generating text and images, summarizing data, and interrogating your Teams activity, as shown in Figure 1-9.

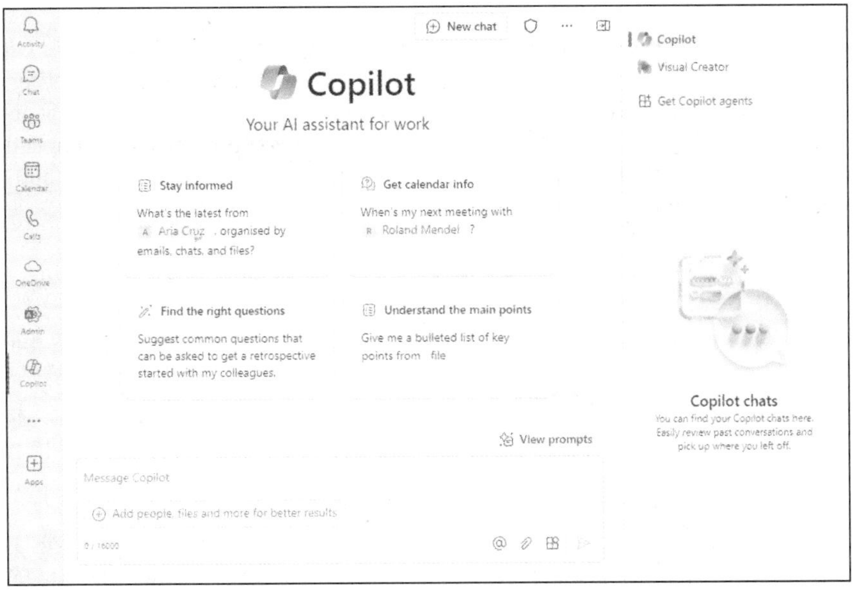


**FIGURE 1-9:** The Copilot app.

**REMEMBER** You can also find built-in apps available in the toolbar under channel and chat message boxes. For example, when you send a message in a channel or private chat, you can click an app icon under the message box to add content from a given app. Click the ellipsis for more app options. From here, you can send an approval request, link directly to a YouTube video, send a praise badge, and create a poll using Microsoft Forms (included with your Office 365 account).

## Using tabs

Apps are useful, but tabs can be even more so because they're so easy to integrate into channels, chats, and meetings. Technically, tabs are also apps, but you typically use the best ones just as tabs, so that's the nomenclature I use here.

Each channel, chat, and calendar appointment includes tabs at the top. There is typically a Posts or Chat tab, a Files tab, a Wiki or Meeting Notes tab, and a big + (plus sign) icon. The + icon is what you want to look for. By clicking this button, you can add an app as a tab so that it's directly accessible in your channel, chat, and meeting with one click.

Teams offers hundreds of tab options for chat and channels. So when would you use a tab? Consider a channel that's being used by a sales team. The team wants to follow their revenue and sales dashboard. They can add a Power BI or Excel tab to display that information from merely one click away (of course, you need to have the dashboard already created).

Or perhaps you have a group chat going with three people with whom you'll be presenting a PowerPoint presentation at a big partner meeting. You can share the PowerPoint file in the chat and then add it as a tab for quick access to edit it right in the chat area. And for your meetings, you can add the agenda as a Word tab so that everyone has quick access; better yet, add the Forms app to create live polls during your meeting.

Follow these steps to add a tab to a channel, chat, or meeting:

1. **In the Channel, Chat, or Meeting Details pane, click the Add a Tab icon (shown in the margin) at the right end of the tab listing at the top of the main area.**

   An unnamed window similar to the one shown in Figure 1-10 appears.

2. **Click the app you want to add as a tab.**

   If you add a Word, Excel, PowerPoint, OneNote, or PDF file as a tab, the file must already exist in the channel or chat's Files tab. (Refer to Book 7, Chapter 4 for more about how to create, organize, and share files in Teams.)

3. **If the app isn't already installed in Teams, follow the prompts to add the app to your Team or chat (depending on where you're adding the tab).**

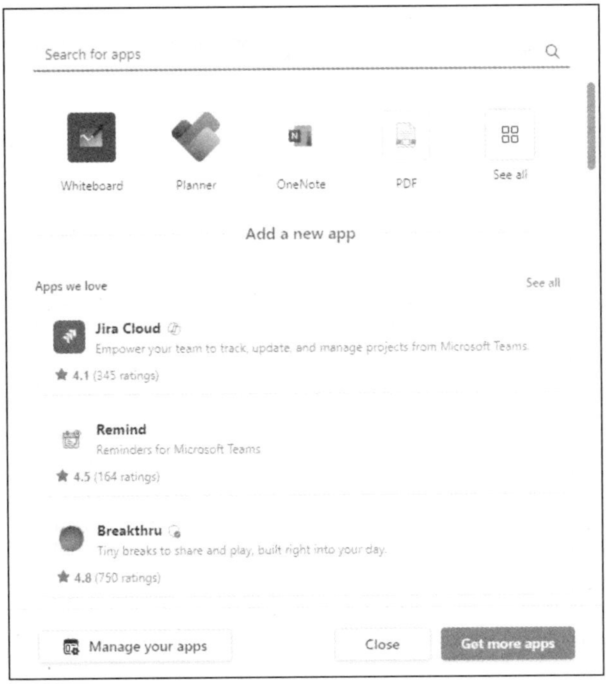


**FIGURE 1-10:** Tab options for a channel (there are more options here than in a chat).

4. **Click Add or Install.**

   Your new tab is now in the tab listing.

   If you're not happy with the name of the tab, click the tab's drop-down arrow (shown in the margin), click Rename, type your preferred name, then click Save.

5. **Click the tab to open it.**

   You can click and drag the tab name left or right to rearrange your tabs.

REMEMBER

To get rid of a tab that's no longer useful, click the tab's drop-down arrow, click Remove, and then click Remove when Teams asks you to confirm.

Your IT team controls whether you have access to and can add tabs. If there aren't many apps available to add as tabs, reach out to IT and ask how the tabs can be made available. Also, if you have guests in your Teams, they can't add tabs to channels.

When it comes to tabs, some key apps are more useful than others. Consider the following list when adding tabs to your channel, chat, or meeting:

- **Office apps:** Word, Excel, PowerPoint, or OneNote files can all be added as tabs. When you open the tab for one of these files, it opens in the web version of the app so that you can edit directly in that tab. Key files can be one click away!
- **PDF:** As with the Office apps, a PDF can be added as a tab as well. Adding a PDF tab is a useful way to have key information at your fingertips. ***Note:*** PDFs with form fields cannot be edited in a tab; the contents of the tab are view only.
- **Website:** Add any website as a tab for quick access to critical information like stock tickers, weather maps, social media feeds, and more. If the website requires you to log in, Teams can't remember that, but in my experience, it asks for your password only about once per day. You can add only websites whose URLs start with https://.
- **Lists:** Microsoft Lists is a list and tracking app included with Office 365. This tab provides direct access to status, tracking, itinerary, and asset management lists right from your channel. (You can't use Lists in chat.)
- **SharePoint:** Add any SharePoint page or document library to a channel (not chat, unfortunately) for quick access to the organization home page, a team home page, or other useful web pages in your network. And if the Files tab isn't enough for you, add another document library to your channel. Refer to Book 7, Chapter 4 for more details on adding a library as a tab, and check out Book 8, Chapter 3 for more on SharePoint.
- **Other Microsoft apps:** If you use other Microsoft apps like Dynamics 365, Power Apps, Power BI, Project, Whiteboard, or Visio, you can have quick access to these through a dedicated tab. Note that some of the apps or features therein come with an additional licensing fee.
- **Third-party apps:** Be on the lookout for any non-Microsoft apps you may already subscribe to. Some of the big ones include ClickUp, Box, Evernote, Intercom, Jira, Trello, YouTube, and Zendesk. Some integrate better than others. Don't buy licenses to one of these apps just because there's a tab; test it by itself first to make sure it gives you what you need.

## Using the Teams App store

The Teams App store is the central place to find all the apps that are available to you. This is helpful because you can experience apps as tabs, connectors, bots, or apps in the navigation bar. But the App store shows you all the apps available in one place.

To access the App store, click the Apps icon in the navigation bar. From here you can view new, featured, and popular apps as well as dozens of app categories and capabilities, as shown in Figure 1-11. If your organization has created custom apps, you find them under a section called Built for Your Org. The Search box is your friend, so make sure to use it! You never know what you might find that could help make you more productive and efficient.

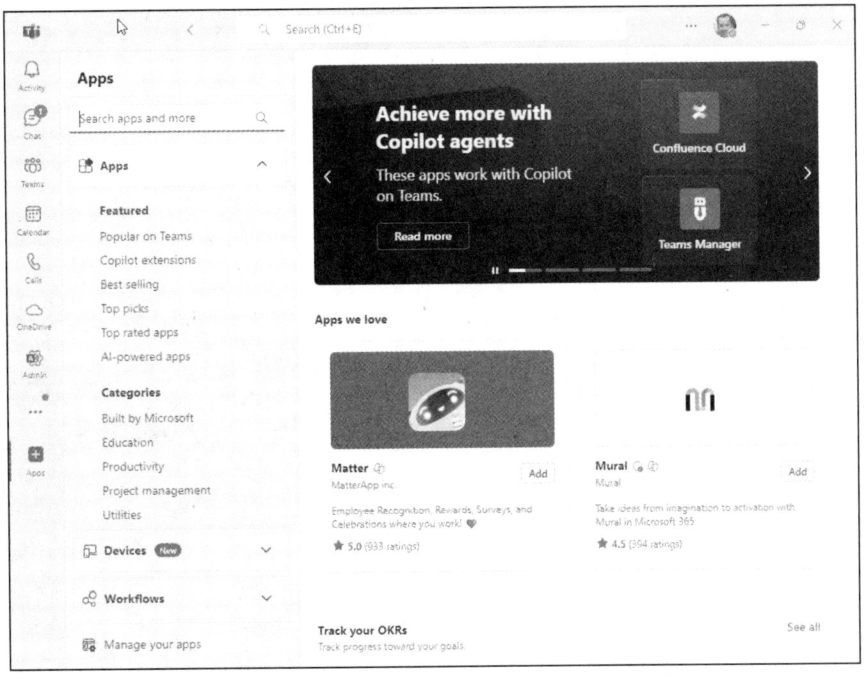


**FIGURE 1-11:** The Teams App store is the central place to find useful apps and install them for your use.

IN THIS CHAPTER

» Understanding the team concept

» Creating and joining teams

» Managing your Teams teams

» Creating channels

» Managing your Teams channels

# Chapter 2

# Getting Up to Speed with Teams and Channels

In the olden days of the 21st century, if several employees were working on the same project, were responsible for the same product, or were part of the same department, those employees had a tough time collaborating with each other. Sure, they had text messaging for short missives, email for longer messages, phone calls for one-on-one conversations, and shared network folders for uploading documents. The problem was that although these technologies are fine on their own, combining them to collaborate on a project or keep members of the same department in the loop got complicated in a hurry. The left hand rarely knew what the right hand was doing.

Teams was created to solve this problem. By organizing related employees as a unit — called a *team* — and bringing technologies such as chat, document sharing, and audio and video calls within the friendly confines of a single app, Teams made collaboration easier and more efficient. Not only did the left hand know what the right hand was doing, but the two could now work together to accomplish a mutual goal.

Although the Teams app comes with lots of moving parts, the two most crucial ones for almost all collaboration tasks are teams and channels. In this chapter, you explore teams by learning what they are, learning how to join them, and even learning how to create your own. You also dive into channels by learning how to add them to a team and how to make the most out of them.

# What's All This About a Team? And a Channel?

As the name implies — or, really, says directly — Microsoft Teams is all about the team, so it's high time to delve into what a team is. There are two senses of the word *team* at work here:

- **Real-world team:** The first sense of the word *team* refers to a collection of work colleagues who are connected to each other in some way. Maybe they all work in the same department or division or office. Perhaps they've all been assigned to the same project. It could be they're working together to bring a new product to market. The key point is that a team is a group of colleagues with something in common.
- **Online team:** The second sense of the word *team* refers to an object within the Microsoft Teams app. In this sense, a team is a secure, online workspace that's designed to enable people to communicate and collaborate with each other.

The connection between these two senses is that a team in Microsoft Teams is composed of several members, each of whom is a member of a real-world team. Whether it's a department, a project, or a product, you create an online team for it and then add each person from the real-world team as a member.

The online team is part of the Teams app and offers a fistful of collaboration and communication tools, including chatting, file sharing and editing, and in-channel team meetings. But the main way that team members share news and keep in touch is through topic-specific portals — called *channels* — that allow for threaded conversations. Every team has at least one channel, and most teams have a bunch of them.

Transparency is the name of the game: Every member of a team has access to pretty much everything in the team, including edit access to all files. For the most part, this access applies to external guests you may invite, too.

# Managing and Working with a Team or Two

Pretty much everything you do in Microsoft Teams is team-related, so getting to know how teams work, how you manage them, and even how to create them, is Teams 101. The next few sections take you through the most important team tasks.

# Joining an existing team

If you click Teams in the navigation bar, there's a good chance there will be an existing team already listed there and this team might have your company name. This is an organization-wide team set up by your Teams administrator, and it includes everyone in your company. In small organizations, this initial team is often the only one that's needed. However, it's far more common for an organization to have lots of teams, with separate teams for each department, division, project, event, group, and so on.

When someone creates a new team, that person — they're known as the team *owner* — usually adds one or more folks to the team, and those people automatically become team members once the team setup is finished. However, adding members is optional, so how do people join a team if they don't get added automatically? There are three possibilities:

- **Join a public team:.** If the team owner made the team public, anybody in the organization can become a member, so joining is just a matter of finding the team and clicking a button.
- **Join a private team with a code.** If the team owner made the team private, the team owner can generate a special code that enables anyone with the code to join the team. The team owner might post the code in a chat, a channel conversation, or an email. If you're not already a team member, you can copy the code and then use it to join the team.
- **Join a private team with a link.** Similarly, the team owner can generate a link to join the team and then share that link via email, text, or social media.

The section "Sharing a team," later in this chapter, goes through the procedures for generating team codes and links, if you're interested.

The next three sections outline the steps involved in each of these possibilities.

## Joining a public team

Follow these steps to join a public team:

1. **Click Teams in the navigation bar.**

   The Teams app appears and displays a list of your teams (that is, the teams of which you're currently a member) in the rail.

2. **At the top of the rail, click Create and Join Teams and Channels (shown in the margin).**

3. **Click Join Team.**

   The main area now lists all the public teams in your organization if there are any. You can scroll through the list or use the Join a Team rail's Type to Search box to find teams by keyword.

4. **When you've found a team to join, move the mouse pointer over the team box and then click the Join Team button that appears (refer to Figure 2-1).**

   Teams adds you as a member of the team, which now appears in the Teams rail.

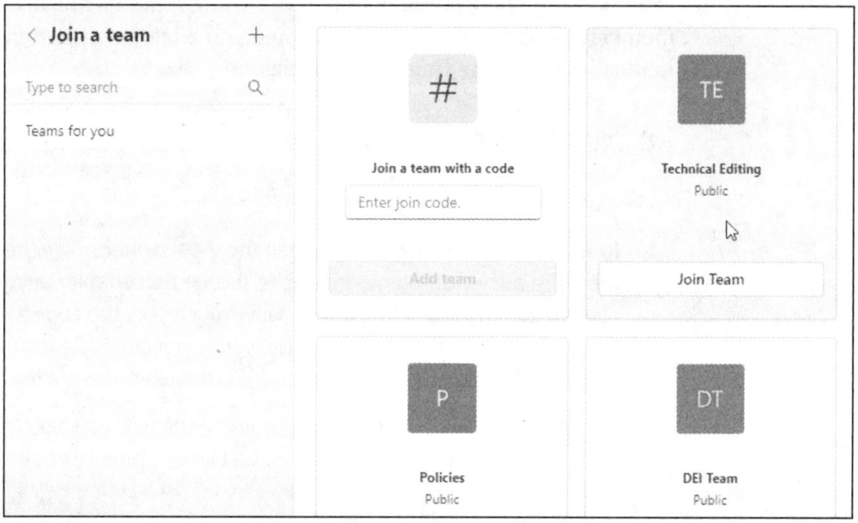


**FIGURE 2-1:** Move the mouse pointer over a public team box to display the Join Team button.

## Joining a private team with a code

Follow these steps to join a private team with a code provided by the team owner:

1. **Copy the team code.**

   Step 1 assumes that the team owner has shared the code somewhere that you have access, such as a channel conversation, a chat, or an email message.

2. **Click Teams in the navigation bar.**

   The Teams rail displays a list of your teams.

3. **At the top of the rail, click Create and Join Teams and Channels (shown in the margin).**

4. **Click Join Team.**

   As shown earlier in Figure 2-1, the main area includes a Join a Team with a Code box.

5. **Paste the copied code inside the Enter Join Code text box.**
6. **Click Add Team.**

   Teams adds you as a member of the team, which now appears in the Teams rail.

## Joining a private team with a link

Follow these steps to join a private team with a link provided by the team owner:

1. **Open the item that contains the link.**

   Step 1 assumes that the team owner has shared the link somewhere that you have access, such as a channel conversation, a chat, or an email message.

2. **Click the link.**

   Teams opens a pop-up that displays info about the team.

3. **Click Join.**

   Teams adds you as a member of the team, which now appears in the Teams rail. For some reason, Teams also opens a new window for the team. That's annoying, so click Close (X) to close the window.



## BEST PRACTICES OF TEAM MEMBERSHIP

For all the advantages offered by being on a team, the Teams app can still have its downsides when people don't use it well. No collaborative app is perfect, after all. Here are some common issues to keep in mind to avoid contributing to the typical pitfalls of collaborative tools:

- Private chat can be distracting from getting work done in a team. Setting your status to Do Not Disturb for blocks of focus time can really help with that.
- Avoid overusing @mentions (refer to Book 7, Chapter 3), especially to channels and Teams.
- Try not to upload files when sending a message. Instead, store and organize the file in an appropriate place ahead of time, and reference that file in the message as a link.

*(continued)*

*(continued)*

- Always use a subject line in a new channel conversation; otherwise, you make it difficult to find when scrolling. Every email needs a subject line; so too should every Teams conversation.
- Avoid posting new conversations to multiple channels very often. Doing so creates internal spam.
- Don't post personal content, such as pictures of your kids or your latest vacation. Keep it professional.

## Opening a team and viewing its channels

Follow these steps to go to a team and visit its channels:

1. **Click Teams in the navigation bar.**

   Your Teams appear in a list in the rail.

2. **Click the name of a team to which you're assigned.**

   Each team consists of one or more channels, whose names appear on the rail under the team name.

3. **Click a channel name and browse its content.**

   Each channel starts off with the following tabs at the top of the main area:

   - **Posts:** This is for announcements and channel conversations. Check out Book 7, Chapter 3 for details.
   - **Files:** Upload and edit files within your team. Refer to Book 7, Chapter 4 for details.
   - **Notes:** Collaborate on channel notes using the OneNote app.

   - **Add a Tab (shown in the margin):** Add new tabs to the channel if you have permission. Refer to the "Using tabs" section in Book 7, Chapter 1 for more about tabs.

4. **When you've finished reviewing your Teams and channels, click Teams in the navigation bar to return to the Teams list.**

## Creating a team

If you have an idea for a collaboration — it might be an upcoming event, an ongoing project, or a bunch of people who have a common interest — and you decide that none of your organization's existing teams are the right fit for this collaboration, you can create a new team. As long as your Teams admin has given you team-creation permission, you can create as many teams as you need. You automatically become the owner of each team you create.

Follow these steps to create a team:

1. **Click Teams in the navigation bar.**

   Your Teams appear in a list in the rail.

2. **At the top of the rail, click Create and Join Teams and Channels (shown in the margin).**

3. **Click Create Team.**

   The Create a Team dialog box pops up in the main area.

   TIP

   These steps take you through the process of creating a new team from scratch. However, you can also create a new team from a template, from an existing team, or from a Microsoft 365 group (not covered in this book, alas). To try out these alternative methods, click the More Create Team Options link, then click the method you want to use in the Create Team rail that appears (From Template, From Another Team, or From Group).

4. **Use the Team Name text box to give your team a name.**

   Make your name brief, but descriptive. If you work for a large company, there's a good chance they have a naming convention you need to follow. Reach out to your IT team for help if you're not sure.

5. **(Optional) Use the Description text box to write a brief description of your group.**

   Although the description is optional, it's a good idea to add one to help people know more about the intended use of the team.

6. **Click Team Type and then click one of the following types:**

   - **Private:** A team that only people who receive an invitation (or a code or a link, as described in the previous section) can join and that only the team members can see in the Teams rail.
   - **Public:** A team that anyone can join and that everyone in the organization can see in the Teams rail.
   - **Org-wide:** A team that automatically includes everyone in your organization. No one is allowed to leave the team, and the team membership is maintained automatically as user accounts are added or deleted. Only a Teams administrator can create an org-wide team.

7. **In the Name the First Channel text box, type a name to use for the team's initial channel.**

   The first channel should be dedicated to a general topic related to the team. Inconveniently, the name "General" isn't allowed because it's a reserved word in Teams. However, a name such as "General Discussion" is perfectly legit. Don't sweat this too much right now because you can always rename the channel down the road (refer to the section "Renaming a channel"," later in this chapter, to learn how).

   Figure 2-2 shows a completed Create a Team dialog box, ready for the next step.

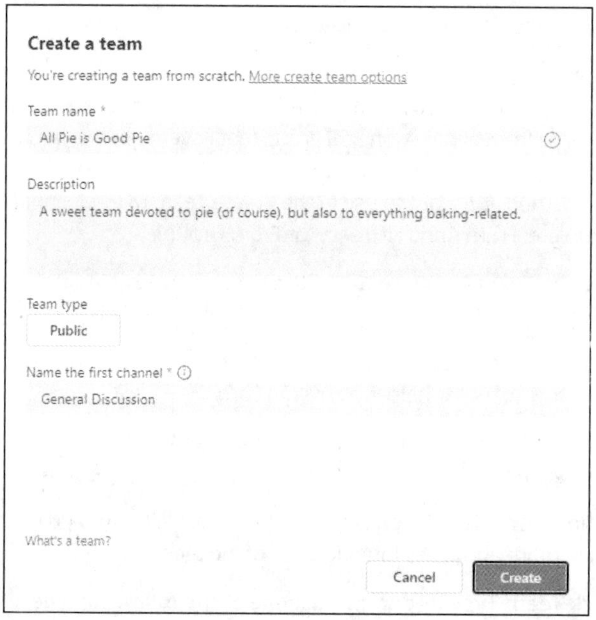


**FIGURE 2-2:** Use the Create a Team dialog box to, you know, create a team.

8. **Click Create.**

   After a second or three, the Add Members dialog box appears.

9. **Use the Type a Name or Email text box to start typing the name of a person you want to add, then click the person when they show up in the results.**

   If your organization allows guests — that is, people from outside your organization — type a guest's email address, then click the Add *Address* as a Guest? item that appears (where *Address* is the email address you typed). Click the guest's Add Name link to include the guest's name. After you finish creating the team, Teams sends an email to the guest to let them know they've been added to the team.

For each person in your organization that you add, Teams offers a drop-down list that enables you to set the person's role with the team. The default role is Member, but you can use a person's drop-down list to make them a team owner, as shown in Figure 2-3.

REMEMBER

When you create a team, you become the owner. You can add more owners and members. Owners can manage the team; members generally take part only in the conversations and content. For large teams, it's a good idea to have two or three owners to help spread out the team management workload.



If you change your mind about adding someone, click the X icon to the right of the person's name or address to remove them from the list.

Note, too, that if you don't want to bother with any of this right now, you can click Skip to bypass adding members. Check out "Adding people to a team," later in the chapter, to learn how to populate a team after you've created it.

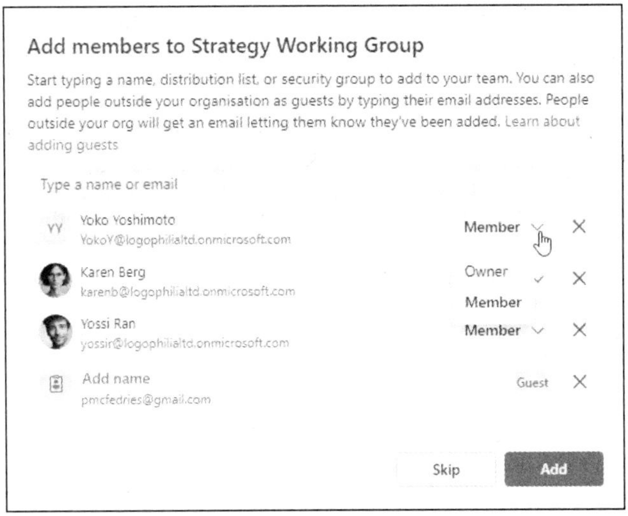


**FIGURE 2-3:** You can make anyone in your organization a team owner.

**10.** **Repeat Step 9 until you've specified everyone you want to add to the team.**

**11.** **Click Add.**

Teams creates the team. Each person in your organization that you added gets a notification in their Activity feed about being added to the team. Emails are sent to any guests you added.

## Adding people to a team

If you're the owner of a team, you can manage the membership of that team, including other owners. Follow these steps to populate a team with new members from both inside your organization and outside it (if guests are allowed):

1. **Click Teams in the navigation bar.**

   Your Teams appear in a list in the rail.

2. **Position the mouse pointer over the team and then click the ellipsis that shows up to open the More Options drop-down menu.**
3. **Click Add Member.**

   The Add Members to *Team* dialog box appears, where *Team* is the name of the team you're working with.

4. **Use the Type a Name or Email text box to start typing the name of a person you want to add, then click the person when they show up in the results.**

   To add a guest from outside your organization (assuming that's allowed in your company), type the person's email address, then click the Add *Address* as a Guest? item that appears (where *Address* is the email address you typed).

   If you change your mind about adding someone, click the X icon to the right of the person's name or address to remove them from the list.

5. **(Optional) For each person in the list who is part of your organization, click the drop-down menu to the right of their name to change their role to Owner if they need added permissions.**

   Owners have full control of a team. Members have fewer rights. Three owners per team is a sweet spot. Fewer, and there aren't enough backups if someone is out; more, and accountability is difficult to rely upon.

6. **Repeat Step 5 until you've specified everyone you want to add to the team.**
7. **Click Add.**

   Teams adds the new members to the team. Each person in your organization that you added gets a notification in their Activity feed about being added to the team. Emails are sent to any guests you added.

## Sharing a team

You can share a team with someone other than by adding a member directly (described in the preceding section, "Adding people to a team"). Sometimes you want to share an open invitation to join a team, or you may want to be able to approve someone's addition.

Teams offers two ways to share an invitation to a team with someone: using a link and using a team code. The next two sections take you through the techniques.

### Sharing a link to a team

Follow these steps to share a link to a team:

1. **Click Teams in the navigation bar.**
2. **Position the mouse pointer over the team and then click the ellipsis next to the team name to open the More Options drop-down menu.**
3. **Click Get Link to Team.**

   The Get a Link to the Team dialog box slides in.
4. **Click Copy.**

   Teams copies the link to your computer's Clipboard. Share the link with an internal person however you prefer (paste it in an email, private chat, or text message).

The invitee should follow the steps in the "Joining a private team with a link" section, earlier in this chapter. This method requires you to approve someone's request to join after the recipient clicks the link. If you prefer to invite someone to the team without the need to approve the request, use the technique in the section that follows.

### Sharing a team code

Follow these steps to share a team code:

1. **Click Teams in the navigation bar.**
2. **Position the mouse pointer over the team and then click the ellipsis next to the team name to open the More Options drop-down menu.**
3. **Click Manage Team.**

   The team opens in the main area.
4. **Click the Settings tab at the top of the main area.**
5. **Click Team Code to expand that section.**

6. **Under the Share This Code. . . heading, click Generate to create the team code.**

   If you don't see the Generate button, it means a code already exists for this team.

7. **Click Copy.**

   Teams copies the team code to the Clipboard. Share the code with an internal person however you prefer (for example, through an email, private chat, or text message).

The invitee should follow the guidance in the "Joining a private team with a code" section, earlier in this chapter. This method does not require approval to join; after the code is entered, the invitee automatically becomes a member.

## Managing team settings

Team ownership is a big responsibility. You hold the keys to the kingdom. You can manage membership, determine whether members can create channels, respond to posts in certain channels, decide which members can use the @mention feature (refer to Book 7, Chapter 3), whether guests are allowed, and a lot more. Although a full overview of ownership best practices is beyond the scope of this mini-book, you should know where to find the various tools.

Follow these steps to manage settings at the team level:

1. **Click Teams in the navigation bar.**
2. **Position the mouse pointer over the team and then click the ellipsis next to the team name to open the More Options drop-down menu.**
3. **Click Manage Team.**

   The team opens in the main area.

4. **Click the Settings tab at the top of the main area.**

   You find many options on this page, as shown in Figure 2-4. Again, the space allotted here does not allow coverage of all these options, but most are self-explanatory.

You can also manage settings at a channel level. To get to those settings, click Teams in the navigation bar, click a team name, and then click the ellipsis next to a channel name. In the More Options drop-down menu that appears, click Manage Channel and then click the Settings tab. As with the team settings, you find some options that you can manage here. The General channel and any private channels have more options than other channels.

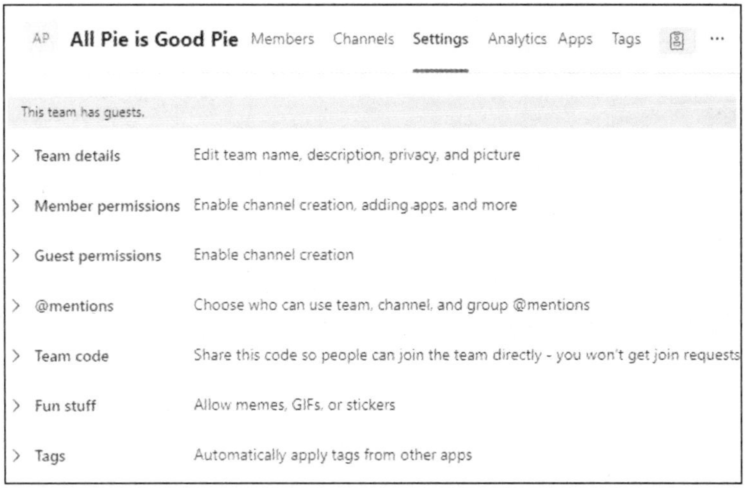


**FIGURE 2-4:** If you're the owner of a team, you should become familiar with these options.



Here's a brief overview of the other tabs with management options on the Manage team page shown in Figure 2-4:

- **Members:** Add and remove members of your team and change the roles of existing members.
- **Pending Requests (not shown in Figure 2-4):** View a list of people to approve or deny who are not members but have received a link to a team and requested access or have been nominated to join a team by an existing member.
- **Channels:** View a list of all channels in a team, with access to various channel-specific management options.
- **Analytics:** View usage metrics of the team, including active participants, meeting information, and inactive channels.
- **Apps:** Manage the apps and tabs that have been added to your team.
- **Tags:** Create and organize subgroups of team members so that it's easier to @mention them without having to @mention a number of individuals or channels.

## Leaving a team

The time may come when you're ready to leave a team — maybe the project has ended, or you're moving on to a new team. To leave a team, you click Teams in the navigation bar, click the ellipsis next to the team name to open the More Options drop-down menu, and then click Leave Team.

REMEMBER

If you're the owner of the team, you can't leave unless there's at least one other owner on the team.

WARNING

You can't automatically re-join a team yourself unless the team is public or you have the Join code. If neither is an option and you want to get back in, ask an owner to add you.

# Getting to Know Channels

Use the channels in your team to separate conversations and files by topic in an organized and efficient manner. Think of channels as next-generation folders in a network shared drive. Don't go haywire with how many channels you create, though. Most people using Teams do best with 10 to 15 active channels at a time. Fewer than that and you may end up overwhelming the few channels you have; more than that and it's hard to keep up with them all. The following sections take you deeper into channels.

## Creating a channel

Both owners and members of a team can create channels as long as the owners haven't disabled the setting for members to create channels. If you're an owner of a large team, you may not want to let members create channels, because it can get out of hand. (In the team's Settings tab, click Member Permissions, then deselect the Allow Members to Create and Update Channels check box. By default, guests aren't allowed to create channels. See "Managing team settings," earlier in this chapter, for more about team settings.)

Follow these steps to create a channel:

1. **Click Teams in the navigation bar.**
2. **Position the mouse pointer over the team and then click the ellipsis next to the team name to open the More Options drop-down menu.**
3. **Click Add Channel.**

   The Create a Channel dialog box barges in.
4. **Use the Channel Name text box to give the channel a moniker.**

   Keep channel names short but descriptive, avoiding acronyms and jargon.

5. **Use the Description box to write a few words about the channel's topic.**

   Don't skimp on the description. The description sets the tone for how members should use the channel.

6. **Use the Choose a Channel Type drop-down list to select one of the following options:**

   - *Standard:* All members of your team have access to the channel.
   - *Private:* Only selected members of your team can access the channel. For more about this type of channel, check out the section "Using private channels" that follows.
   - *Shared:* Only selected people from both inside and outside your organization can access the channel. If you select this option, the Share This Channel with Everyone On the Team check box materializes. Deselect this check box if you prefer to specify which team members have access to the channel.

   WARNING

   You can't switch the type after you create the channel. Therefore, make sure you choose the type that's appropriate for the channel you're creating, because if later you realize that you need to change, say, a standard channel to a private one, you'll need to create an entirely new channel (which is not great because although you can move files to the new channel, you can't move conversations).

7. **Click Create.**

   Teams creates the channel and adds it under the team name in the Teams rail. If you chose Standard in Step 6, your work here is done. If you chose Private or Shared, read on.

8. **Specify who can access your new channel:**

   - *Private channel:* Use the Type a Name or Email text box to start typing the name or email address of a team member you want to add, then click the person when they show up in the results. Repeat for each team member you want to add. You can only add people to a private channel who are already members of the team. When you're ready to move on, click Add.
   - *Shared channel:* Use the Type a Name or Email text box to start typing the name of a team member or the email address of someone outside your organization, then click the person when they show up in the results. Repeat for each person you want to add. When you're done, click Share.

TIP

At the time of publishing, the maximum number of channels per team was 200 (including deleted channels). That said, for the sanity of your team members, you should never come close to approaching this number.

## Using private channels

A private channel offers a protected space inside your team. Although a private channel may seem like a tempting feature to jump into immediately, think through how you want to use any private channel first. It's a complex feature, and creating and owning a private channel is a responsibility that rises almost to the level of owning the team itself. Typical reasons for private channels include:

- » To give managers in the team a place to discuss sensitive topics
- » To give finance and budget professionals a place to discuss financial information

Here are important details to keep in mind about creating a private channel:

- » All members of the private channel must already be members or owners of the parent team.
- » If the team owners are not members of the private channel, they can't access the channel (though the channel name and description do appear to them), which means that you can't rely on them for support or ownership responsibility.
- » Files in the private channel are stored in a SharePoint site separate from the parent team, which can confuse people if they're not used to the concept (refer to Book 8, Chapter 3 to learn more about how SharePoint and Teams interact).
- » Many features of standard channels don't work in private channels, including channel meetings and various apps and tabs.
- » Owning a private channel is a similar responsibility to owning a whole team, and often the people who request or create private channels are not really qualified for the role yet.

REMEMBER

Before you create a private channel, truly convince yourself that you need one. Also, prepare for the eccentricities that come with it, and communicate those issues with members before you create one. A new team is often a better option. You can pin the important channels to the top of the rail so that your list of Teams isn't completely overwhelming. (See the upcoming section for details on pinning a channel.)

TIP

At the time of publishing, the maximum number of private channels per team was 30 and the maximum number of members of a private channel was 250.

## Renaming a channel

If you're not happy with the original name you supplied to a channel, you can follow these steps to change it:

1. **Click Teams in the navigation bar.**
2. **If you don't see the team's channels, click the team to display its channel list.**
3. **Position the mouse pointer over the channel and then click the ellipsis next to the channel name to open the More Options drop-down menu.**
4. **Click Rename Channel.**

   The Edit dialog box shows up.
5. **Edit the channel name and also the description, if that needs to change.**
6. **Click Save.**

   Teams renames the channel.



## Pinning a channel

Your team and channel list can quickly get long and overwhelming. In the meantime, you may be paying attention to only a select few channels at any given time. To deal with that common concern, Teams provides the option to pin your favorite channels at the top of the rail in the Teams app. To pin and organize your favorite channels, follow these steps:

1. **Click Teams in the navigation bar.**
2. **If you don't see the team's channels, click the team to display its channel list.**
3. **Position the mouse pointer over the channel and then click the ellipsis next to the channel name to open the More Options drop-down menu.**
4. **Click Pin.**

   This step places the channel at the top of the rail in a section called Pinned. You can close and expand this section at any time by clicking the caret to the left of the Pinned section. Your pinned channels still display under the team even though they're also displayed in the pinned section.

You can drag pinned channels up or down within the Pinned section to reorder them. To unpin a channel, repeat Steps 1 through 3 but click Unpin.

TIP

For deciphering similarly named channels in your pinned area (especially the General channel from multiple Teams), note that the team icon and name are listed to the left of and below the channel name, respectively.

## Taming channel notifications

Now comes the beauty of Teams. Don't want to hear from a not-so-relevant channel anymore? You can silence some or all of the notifications that would come from that channel except for a personal @mention that specifically references you. (@mentions are explained in Book 7, Chapter 3.) If someone @mentions the channel name, you won't be bothered with a notification that you don't want. To manage notifications on a channel, follow these steps:

1. **Click Teams in the navigation bar.**
2. **If you don't see the team's channels, click the team to display its channel list.**
3. **Position the mouse pointer over the channel and then click the ellipsis next to the channel name to open the More Options drop-down menu.**
4. **Click Channel Notifications.**

   The Channel Notification Settings dialog box hurries in.
5. **Use the All New Posts drop-down menu to select one of the following options:**

   - *Banner and Feed:* You receive two notifications about each new channel post: a banner and an item in your Activity feed.
   - *Only Show in Feed:* You receive one notification about each new channel post: an item in your Activity feed.
   - *Off:* You receive no notifications for new posts.

   If you go with either Banner and Feed or Only Show in Feed, you also have the option of deselecting the Include Replies check box to bypass notifications about each channel post reply that comes in.
6. **Use the Channel Mentions drop-down menu to select a notification setting for @mentions.**

   Your choices here are the same as for posts: Banner and Feed, Only Show in Feed, or Off.
7. **Click Save.**

   Teams applies your new notification settings to the channel.

## Hiding a channel

It can be a challenge to keep your channel list clean without overdoing your pinned channel list. The good news is that you can hide channels that are less relevant to you than others without losing notifications from those hidden channels. Follow these steps to hide a channel:

1. **Click Teams in the navigation bar.**
2. **If you don't see the team's channels, click the team to display its channel list.**
3. **Position the mouse pointer over the channel and then click the ellipsis next to the channel name to open the More Options drop-down menu.**
4. **Click Hide.**

   Teams adds a link named See All Channels to the bottom of the team's channel list. Click See All Channels to open a pane in the main area that displays a complete list of the team's channels, including the ones you've hidden. From here, you can click a hidden channel to access it.



To unhide a channel, click the team's See All Channels link, then click the Show button to the right of the channel you want to restore from purgatory.

IN THIS CHAPTER

» **Understanding the differences between channels and chats**

» **Creating and managing channel conversations**

» **Setting up and participating in private and group chats**

» **Formatting and reacting to messages**

Chapter 3

# Chin-wagging with Channels and Chats

Teams is all about collaborating with colleagues and sometimes that collaboration takes the form of a remote meeting (the subject of Book 7, Chapter 5) or working together on a document (the subject of Book 7, Chapter 4). But much of the time, collaboration just means exchanging messages to brainstorm ideas, spread news, or solve problems. This type of collaboration is so common and so important that Teams gives you not just one, but *two* ways to exchange messages with your Teams-mates: channels and chats.

A channel conversation is a collection of related messages within a channel. A channel (as I describe in Book 7, Chapter 2) is devoted to a topic, so it won't surprise you to hear that a channel conversation is generally centered on some subtopic of the channel. All channel conversations are stored within the channel's Posts tab.

A chat conversation is a collection of messages exchanged between one or more people. That is, a chat in Teams is similar to a chat in whatever text messaging systems you've used in your tech career. All chat conversations are stored in the Teams Chat app.

In this chapter, you explore these two types of Teams communications, get to know the advantages of each, and learn how to use channels and chats to collaborate with your Team.

## Channels versus Chats

Although many people dive right into chat to start conversing with colleagues in Teams, channel conversations have considerably more robust features that might entice you to perform your work-related conversations in a Team rather than in chat. Chat is easy and familiar, but it's often a crutch for people who may not think about organizing information in a way that considers the future.

Chat and channel conversations both provide features like reactions, saving, praise, editing, deleting, memes, GIFs, stickers, approvals, meeting scheduling, formatting, and others. (I discuss these features throughout this chapter.) However, channel conversations come with more features than a chat does. The following features are available in channel conversations but not chat:

- **Channels have more types of posts available.** Conversations in channels can consist of a standard message or an announcement. The latter stands out more and includes a large heading that you can backfill with color or an image.
- **Channel conversations can post in multiple places.** A channel conversation can be posted in multiple channels simultaneously, which creates a separate threaded conversation in each destination, including across different Teams with different audiences. If you want to post a message in multiple chats, you'll be doing a lot of copying and pasting.
- **You can control who can reply.** The author of a new channel conversation can restrict conversation replies to themselves and the Team owners and moderators.
- **You can use subject lines.** Chats seemingly go on forever, offering no context as to what's being discussed unless you read the small text thoroughly each time you stop scrolling. A new channel message can have a subject. In fact, all conversations *should* have a subject; you wouldn't send an email without a subject, right? Same with channel conversations.
- **You receive threaded replies.** Sure, you can reply in a chat, but chat replies are disorganized conversations that could bounce around various topics in a confusing way. A channel conversation can stick to one topic. Need to ask about a semi-related question from that conversation? Start a new conversation to keep all replies on topic.

- **You can copy a link to the message.** Want to point someone directly to a message in a Team? You can copy a link to the message and send the link to the person. Chat doesn't offer a way to link someone directly to a conversation or specific message.
- **Uploaded files get stored in a central spot.** Although uploading a file directly to a message isn't a best practice, if you do it, at least the file will be stored in the Files tab of the channel. Doing the same in chat dumps it in the OneDrive of the sharer, which will last only as long as the person stays in the organization. Files are better stored in a Team for long-term access. Refer to Book 7, Chapter 4 for more information about sharing files in a Team.

Admittedly, one feature of chat that channels don't have is read receipts. If you're a fan of read receipts, only chat supports them. You can manage your read receipts in the Privacy section of your settings. Check out Book 7, Chapter 1 for details on accessing settings.

Chat has its role, but it can also be overused. In most cases, a Team is a better place to send messages or have a conversation because a channel conversation is organized, centralized, and not dependent on any individuals to remain accessible.

Chat is best used for one-off messages that don't have a more strategic Team to take place in. Such messages could include questions, requests, or discussions that aren't closely related to work. Here are a few more aspects to keep in mind about channel conversations and chat:

- Files shared by someone in chat are removed after that person leaves the organization.
- Chats can get overwhelming, with unrelated conversations that happen simultaneously. Channel conversations keep messages better organized.
- Channel conversations have more features than chats.
- In channel conversations, you can @mention specific subsets of the Team membership using a feature called tags. Tags make it possible to, for example, send a notification to all the project managers in a channel message without having to @mention every project manager individually.
- Many organizations don't retain chats nearly as long as they retain conversations in a Team, which means you can't necessarily rely on a history of chats.
- Because chats are private, they don't foster a collaborative environment.
- The cadence of chat implies a quicker turnaround. If you don't need an immediate response, a channel's cadence is closer to email, which can imply you'll respond within a day or two.

» Teams can have more people in them than chats, so you can communicate to a larger audience.

WARNING

True collaboration and work-related conversation and decision-making should be occurring in a Team through channel conversations. Don't let chat be a crutch. It has already become one in many organizations that haven't spent the time and effort training their employees on the best ways to use chats as opposed to channel conversations.

# Conversing in a Channel

A channel conversation is a threaded collection of messages concerned with some subtopic of the channel. Here, *threaded* means that each channel conversation consists of an original message and all the replies that get posted in response to that original message.

For the original message, there are four main types of channel conversations you can initiate:

» **Simple conversation:** A threaded conversation that occurs within a single channel and is posted without a subject line. A simple conversation is useful for brief exchanges with channel members.

» **Conversation with a subject:** A threaded conversation that occurs within a single channel and is posted with a subject line. Except for the simplest exchanges, you should always include a subject when you start a channel conversation. A pithy, well-crafted subject not only identifies the conversation, but it also summarizes the conversation topic and provides welcome context for readers.

» **Announcement:** A threaded conversation with a headline and a subhead, optionally posted to multiple channels. Announcements are useful when you have important news to share.

» **Multichannel conversation:** A threaded conversation that's posted to two or more channels, usually with a subject line. A multichannel conversation is useful when the topic of your conversation is of interest to multiple channels (which could reside in multiple teams).

## Configuring channel moderation

Channel moderation means deciding in advance who's allowed to start a new conversation in the channel. This is an important topic, so it's most unfortunate that

Teams makes what should be a simple process inexplicably complicated. I'll try to untangle the mess in this section.

First, know that Teams does *not* offer moderation settings for private or shared channels. Wait, what?! Yep. Everyone can post to these channel types, which is just bizarre (especially for a shared channel).

Second, Teams *does* offer moderation settings for standard channels, but the settings you see depend on whether the standard channel was the first channel you added when you were creating the team, or a subsequent standard channel. (See? I told you this was annoyingly complicated.) Here are the steps to follow to set up moderation for a team's first standard channel:

1. **Click Teams in the navigation bar.**
2. **If you don't see the team's channels, click the team to display its channel list.**
3. **Position the mouse pointer over the channel and then click the ellipsis next to the channel name to open the More Options drop-down menu.**
4. **Click Manage Channel.**

   The channel's management pane appears in the main area.
5. **Click the Settings tab.**

   Settings should be selected by default, but you never know.
6. **Click Moderation to display its settings, shown in Figure 3-1.**



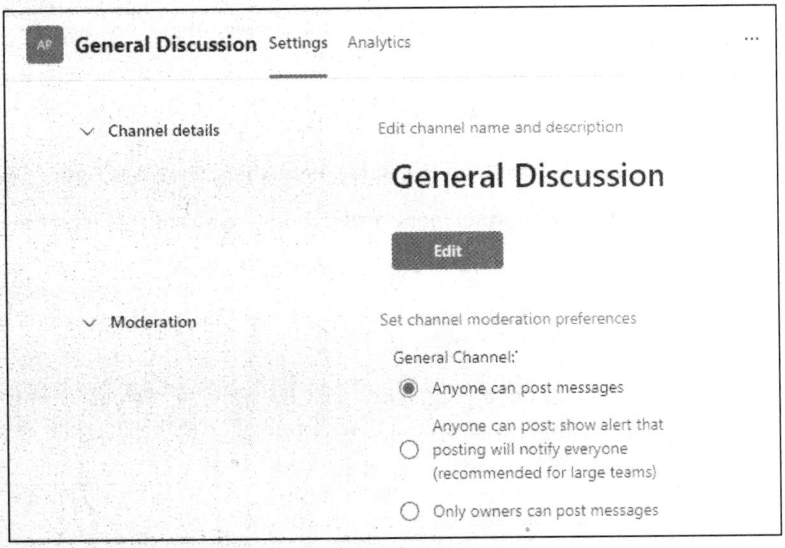


**FIGURE 3-1:** The moderation options for a team's initial standard channel.

7. **Select a moderation option for the channel:**

   - *Anyone can post messages:* Everyone — channel owners, members, and guests — can post messages to the channel. This is the default setting.
   - *Anyone can post; show alert that posting will notify everyone:* Everyone — channel owners, members, and guests — can post messages to the channel. Theoretically, Teams also displays an alert above the posting text box that displays the number of people who'll see the message (the point being that the alert should dissuade people from posting trivial or off-topic messages to a large number of people). I wrote "theoretically" because as I write this the alert box doesn't appear in the current version of Teams.
   - *Only owners can post messages:* Only channel owners can post messages to the channel. Select this option if you prefer to use this channel for one-way communications such as team announcements and updates.

For reasons that my mortal brain can't fathom, Teams offers a completely different set of moderation options for each subsequent standard channel you add to a team. Here are the steps to follow to set up moderation for these standard channels:

1. **Click Teams in the navigation bar.**
2. **If you don't see the team's channels, click the team to display its channel list.**
3. **Position the mouse pointer over the channel and then click the ellipsis next to the channel name to open the More Options drop-down menu.**
4. **Click Manage Channel.**

   The channel's management pane appears in the main area.
5. **Click the Settings tab.**

   Settings should be selected by default, but you never know.
6. **Click Moderation to display its settings, shown in Figure 3-2.**
7. **Use the channel moderation drop-down list to select either On or Off.**
8. **Select a moderation option for the channel.**

   If channel moderation is set to Off, then you have two options, as shown in Figure 3-2:

   - *Everyone can start a new post:* Everyone — channel owners, members, and guests — can start a new conversation in the channel. This is the default setting.

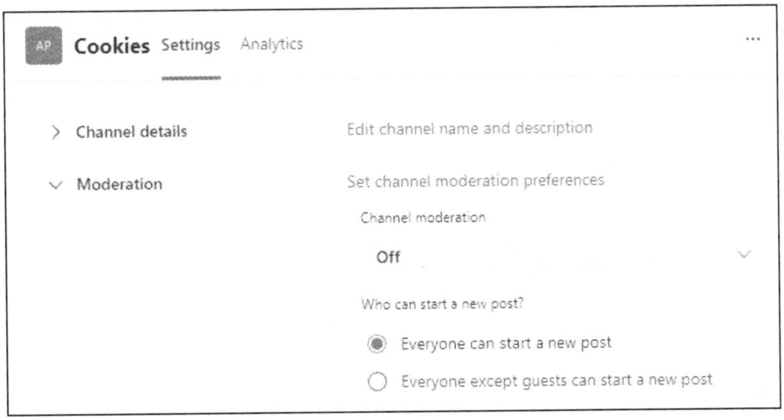


**FIGURE 3-2:** The moderation settings for a team's non-initial standard channels.

- *Everyone except guests can start a new post:* Channel owners and members can start a new conversation in the channel, but channel guests can't.

If channel moderation is set to On, then Teams displays a new collection of moderation settings, as shown in Figure 3-3. With moderation on, only channel moderators can start new conversations in the channel. Who are these moderators? By default, the team owners are the moderators of the channel. However, you can add other moderators by clicking Manage and using the Add or Remove Moderators dialog box to specify the people you want to moderate the channel. You can also use the following settings to control the permissions of the channel's non-moderators:

- *Allow members to reply to channel messages:* Deselect this setting to prevent non-moderators from replying to moderator posts.
- *Allow members to pin channel messages:* Deselect this setting to prevent non-moderators from pinning moderator posts.
- *Allow bots to submit channel messages:* Deselect this setting to prevent chatbots from posting messages to the channel. A *chatbot* (usually shortened to just *bot*) is an app feature that enables channel members to interact with the app by exchanging channel messages.
- *Allow connectors to submit channel messages:* Deselect this setting to prevent connectors (apps) from posting messages to the channel. (Microsoft has announced that connectors will soon be deprecated, so this setting might be gone by the time you read this.)

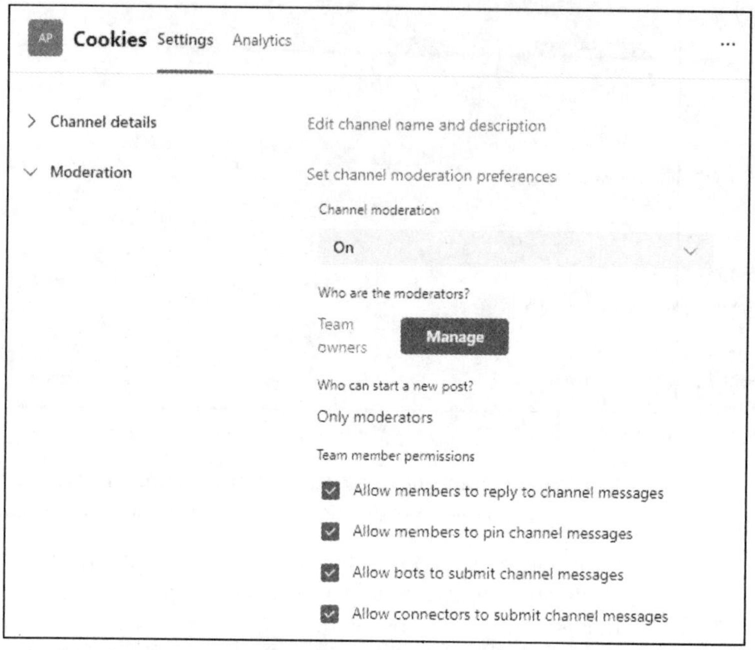


**FIGURE 3-3:** The moderation settings when channel moderation is set to On.

## Getting a conversation off the ground

Assuming you're allowed to launch a new conversation in a particular channel (check out "Configuring channel moderation," earlier in this chapter, to learn why you might not be), here are the steps to plow through to start a conversation in that channel:

1. **Click Teams in the navigation bar and then, in the rail, click the channel you want to post in.**

   You might need to click the team to display its channels. If you still don't see the channel, click the See All Channels link and then click the channel in the list that shows up in the main area.

2. **Click the Start a Post button near the bottom of the main area.**

   A dialog box for composing a post appears, as shown in Figure 3-4.

3. **(Optional) To change your post into an announcement, click Post Type (shown in the margin), and then click Announcement.**

   An announcement stands out much more than a typical post because it adds a banner above the post.

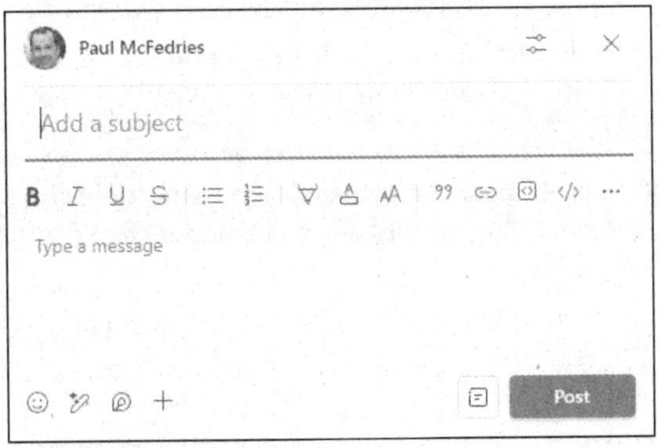


**FIGURE 3-4:** Use this dialog box to compose your channel post.

4. **In the Add a Subject field, type a subject for your conversation.**

   Every conversation should have a subject, just as every email does (or should). A subject keeps the conversation on topic and makes finding it later much easier when you scroll through the posts. A subject like "Quick question" is too vague. A subject line is like a thesis statement: Be specific, detailed, but concise.

   If you turned your post into an announcement in Step 3, then instead of the Add a Subject field you get the Type a Headline banner as well as the Add a Subhead field, as shown in Figure 3-5. Fill in your announcement headline and subhead. Note, too, that you can use the controls in the lower-right corner of the Type a Headline banner to change the background color or add a background image.



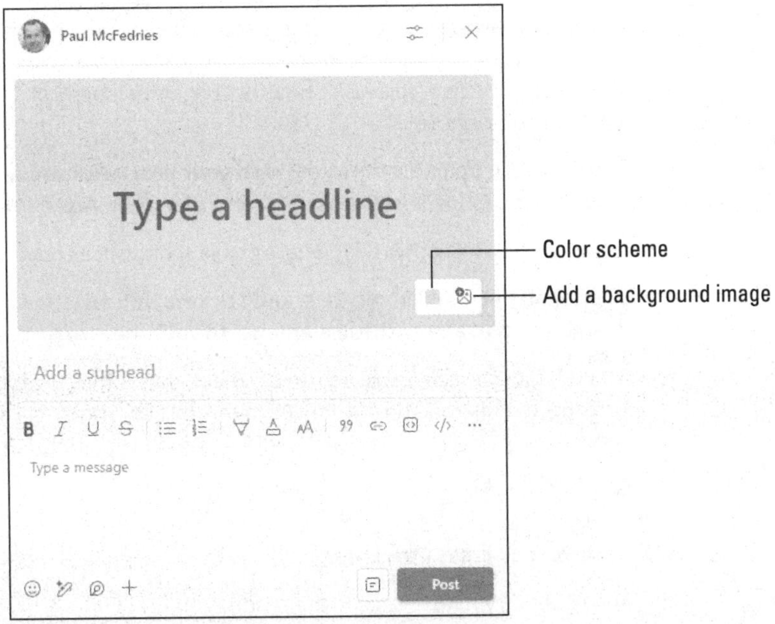


**FIGURE 3-5:** If you turn your post into an announcement, you need to add a headline and a subhead.

5. **(Optional) To restrict who can reply to your message, click Settings (shown in the margin) and then, under the Who Can Reply heading, click You and Moderators.**

6. **(Optional) To cross-post this conversation to multiple channels, click Settings (shown in the margin) and then, under the Post In heading, click Multiple Channels.**

   The Select Cross Post Channels button (shown in the margin) appears above the headline. Click that button to open the Choose Channels dialog box, which offers a list of all the Teams and channels to which you can post. Select the check box to the right of each channel you want to include in your cross-post, then click Update.

7. **Use the Type a Message box to type your message.**

   The toolbar above the Type a Message box offers quite a few options for formatting your text, adding a bulleted or numbered list, and inserting a quotation, link, code block, or code snippet. Click More Options (shown in the margin) to pop up a list with commands for managing indents, adding a horizontal rule, and working with tables.

   You can @mention an individual, a channel, or the team to send notifications if appropriate (I talk more about this useful communications tool a bit later in the "@mentioning in a conversation" section).

   If you'd like to bring Copilot in to help with your message, click the Copilot button (shown in the margin). In the pop-up window that appears, you can either click Rewrite to get Copilot to generate a new (and hopefully improved) version of your message, or you can click Adjust and then click an option from the list that appears (such as Concise or Longer for length, or Casual or Professional for tone).

8. **(Optional) To upload a file along with your post, click the Actions and Apps button (shown in the margin) and then click Attach File.**

   Refer to Book 7, Chapter 4 for details on file sharing in a conversation.

9. **(Optional) Click the Emoji, GIFs, and Stickers button (shown in the margin) to add any of these elements to your message.**

   You can click the applicable item in the menu that comes up; follow any prompts to finish adding the item to your message. Use these sparingly, or avoid them most of the time and dedicate a channel to fun stuff or watercooler discussion. Graphics like these take up a *lot* of space and can drown out important, work-related text amid a GIF or meme war.

10. **Click Post or press Ctrl+Enter.**

    Teams sends your message to the channel.

## Getting in your two cents: replying to a conversation

It's not a conversation if nobody else takes part, so you'll want to reply to a conversation in a channel if you're asked for input or just have something to add.

Follow these steps to reply to a conversation:

1. **Click Teams in the navigation bar and then, in the rail, click the name of the channel where the conversation resides.**

   Alternatively, if you were @mentioned in the message, you receive a notification. Click Activity at the top of the navigation bar to display your notifications in the rail, and then click the notification, which takes you right to the conversation.

2. **At the bottom of the conversation, click Reply.**

   Teams opens a smaller version of the compose box, as shown in Figure 3-6.

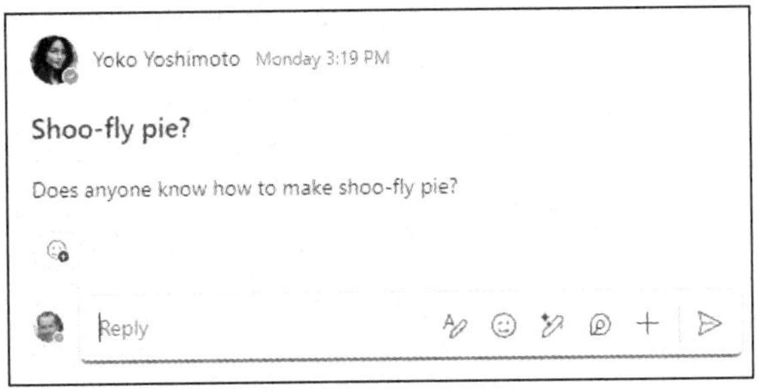


**FIGURE 3-6:** The compose box that appears when you reply to a channel conversation.

3. **(Optional) To display all the formatting options, click the Format icon.**

   You can also press Ctrl+Shift+X.

   Teams display the formatting toolbar above the message box (refer to Figure 3-4, shown earlier).

4. **Type your message, format it as your heart desires, and add anything else you need to fill out your reply.**

   I won't go into all the particulars here. Check out the steps in the earlier section ("Getting a conversation off the ground") for the details.

5. **Click Send (shown in the margin) or press Ctrl+Enter to post your reply.**

   If you didn't open the formatting options in Step 3, you can just press Enter (or click Send) to post a message. When the formatting options are displayed, pressing Enter starts a new line, so that's why you need to press Ctrl+Enter to ship the message.

## @mentioning in a conversation

One of the key features of Teams is the @mention. Taking after Twitter (now, alas, X), Instagram, and Slack, an @ in front of a person, channel, or team name results in a notification to that person, the people who follow the channel, or are members of the Team. The notification appears in their Activity app and indicates to them that they should review the message.

Here are the types of @mention you can use:

- ***@person*:** Notifies the specified *person* about your message. The person must be a member of the team in which the channel conversation is taking place.
- **@channel:** Notifies every member of the current channel about your message.
- ***@channel_name*:** Notifies every member of the channel specified by *channel_name* about your message. The channel must be part of the team in which the conversation is taking place.
- **@team:** Notifies every member of the current team about your message. Alternatively, you can use *@team_name*, where *team_name* is the name of the current team, but why would you?

Follow these steps to @mention in a channel message:

1. **Start or reply to a channel conversation.**

   Check out the sections "Getting a conversation off the ground" and "Getting in your two cents: replying to a conversation," earlier in this chapter, for how to do that.

2. **In the message box, type @.**

   A list of suggested names appears above or below the message box. If the correct suggestion displays, click it and jump to Step 4.

3. **Start typing the person's name, the channel name, or the keyword *team* or *channel* and click it in the suggestions when it appears, or press Enter if it's the first suggestion in the list.**

4. **If @mentioning an individual, change how you want the name to appear in the message, if you want.**

   You can press Backspace to remove portions of the name to address a person more informally or to remove extraneous information, like the recipient's department or location. This is a good idea only if your organization's accounts display names with the first name before the last name, like *John Doe* as opposed to *Doe, John.* The latter does not play well with removing parts of a name when @mentioning.

5. **Enter the rest of your message and press Enter or click Send when you're ready to post it.**

When replying to a conversation, you may not be sure whether you should @mention an individual who's already part of the conversation. If you're in doubt, @mention them to ensure that they get the notification. They can mute the conversation notifications, but an @mention always results in a notification to them.

WARNING

Beware of overusing channel and Team @mentions. Channel @mentions notify all Team members who haven't muted the channel notifications. Team @mentions *always* notify all members of the Team. Especially in large Teams, these actions can essentially become spam. Don't be that person.

TIP

@mentions are no longer unique to Teams. You can also use them in Outlook emails as well as in files and comments in Word, Excel, and PowerPoint. In Outlook, an @mention in the body of the message automatically adds the person to the To field. In the Office apps, the @mentioned person receives an email notification that they've been mentioned with a link to the file. @mentions in these instances are useful for identifying exactly which part of a message, file, or comment is meant for whom.



## Reacting to conversations

Reacting to a conversation means to add an icon as a response, just like on popular social media websites. Teams offers four basic reactions: Like (thumbs-up), Love (heart), Laugh, and Surprised. The most important one is Like. Like lets you acknowledge or agree with a message in an explicit but passive way.

To react to a message, hover your cursor over a message to reveal the row of available reactions, as shown in Figure 3-7, and then click one. If none of the four standard reactions does the job for you, click More Reactions (shown in the margin) to open a pop-up window that offers dozens — nay, *hundreds* — of reaction icons.

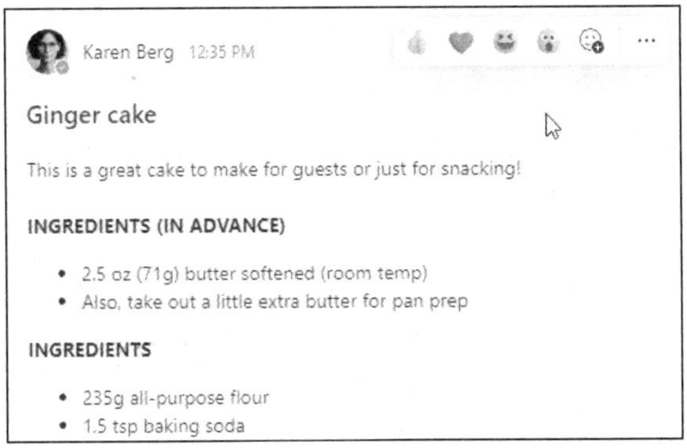


**FIGURE 3-7:** Hover your cursor over a message to display the reaction icons.

## More conversation options to mess with

In Figure 3-7, notice that when you hover your mouse over a channel post, the toolbar of reaction icons also includes the More Options icon (shown in the margin) on the far right. Clicking More Options unfurls a menu that includes the following items:

- **Copy Link:** Copies a link to the post to your computer Clipboard. This is useful when you want to share a message directly with someone else so that they don't have to search for it or you don't need to rewrite it elsewhere. Paste the copied link into a chat, email, or text message. The recipient must be a member of the Team to access the link to the message.
- **Delete:** Deletes the message. Note that you only see this command for messages you've posted.
- **Pin:** Pins a conversation in a channel for easy access and reference. Find the pinned conversation by clicking the information icon (a lowercase *i* in a circle) in the top-right corner of the window. You can pin only one conversation per channel, and you can pin only the first message in a conversation (replies don't have the option).
- **Turn Off Notifications:** Disables notifications on the conversation. This command can be a lifesaver if a conversation goes off the rails and keeps notifying you nonstop. After disabling notifications, the only way you will get a notification from that conversation is if someone @mentions you.
- **Open Conversation in New Window:** Pops out the conversation to a separate window. This is useful if you want to check out something else in the main Teams window while you converse in the popped-out window.
- **Highlights From This Conversation:** Brings in Copilot to summarize the conversation for you. This is useful if the conversation is very long and you're trying to get up to speed with what folks have been saying.
- **Mark as Unread**: Toggles the message status back to unread so that it displays once again in your notifications. This is useful if you want to be able to access the message quickly from your Activity feed rather than scrolling through a long conversation to find it.
- **Share to Outlook:** Sends the conversation in an email to any recipient. Check out the "Sharing a Teams conversation to Outlook" section, later in this chapter, for details.
- **Translate:** Translate the message to your language. This is useful if you work in an organization that uses multiple languages as it enables you to use built-in machine translation to convert the foreign text into your language. Like all automated translation, it's not perfect, but it's typically good enough.

# Bouncing between Teams conversations and Outlook emails

Teams and email will coexist for the foreseeable future, so they should probably work together in some way, right? Well, Teams and Outlook have you covered with a couple of useful tricks up their sleeves. The following section describes how to forward an email to a channel, which helps you avoid having to rewrite or manually copy content into Teams. In the section after that, I talk about how to send a Teams conversation via email to an outside recipient.

## Forwarding an email to a channel

Follow these steps to forward an email to a channel:

1. **Click Teams in the navigation bar.**
2. **If you don't see the team's channels, click the team to display its channel list.**
3. **Position the mouse pointer over the channel and then click the ellipsis next to the channel name to open the More Options drop-down menu.**
4. **Click Get Email Address.**

   The Get Email Address dialog box opens.
5. **(Optional) If you want to control access to the email address, click Advanced Settings, then select the option you want.**

   The default is Only Members of This Team. The alternatives are Anyone Can Send Emails to This Address (risky!) or Only Email Sent from These Domains (you then use the text box to specify one or more domains, separated by commas). Click Save, then go back to Step 3.
6. **Click the Copy button.**

   This copies the email address to your Clipboard.
7. **In Outlook or another email program, open the email you want to forward to Teams and, in the email's To field, paste the email address you copied in the last step.**
8. **Make any edits to the message and remove any attachments you don't want to send with it.**

   Remove any "RE" and "FW" from the subject so that it comes through cleanly. You may even want to update the subject so that the context makes sense to those who will read it in Teams.

9. **Click Send.**

   Teams forwards the email to the channel as the original message for a new conversation.

## Sharing a Teams conversation to Outlook

In the previous sections, I cover how to send an email to Teams, but what about when you want to do the opposite: Send a Teams message or conversation through Outlook? Teams has you covered there as well with the Share to Outlook feature. Follow these steps to share a Teams conversation or message through Outlook:

1. **Click Teams in the navigation bar.**
2. **If you don't see the team's channels, click the team to display its channel list.**
3. **Position the mouse pointer over the channel and then click the ellipsis next to the channel name to open the More Options drop-down menu.**
4. **Click Share to Outlook.**

   This opens a new email with the channel messages included in the body.
5. **In the To, CC, and BCC fields, enter your recipients' email addresses.**

   This feature is called Share to Outlook, but you can send these messages to any email address.
6. **(Optional) Update the subject if necessary.**

   The email will take on the subject of a conversation if there is one, but you don't have to use that.
7. **Select the Include Attachments check box if you want to include attachments.**

   Any files associated with the conversation or message will be attached to the email automatically.
8. **Click Send.**

   Outlook ships out the message.

WARNING

This feature is handy but certainly not perfect. For one thing, you may have to give Teams a moment or two to generate the email, so be patient. Second, if you choose to send any message from a channel conversation, it sends the whole conversation, not just the single message you choose. Last, the resulting email displays some — but not all — formatting that might be applied to a message, and it does not include file links.

# Chatting with Your Team

Although channel conversations are often the best way for teams to communicate, chat is great for keeping connected with close colleagues, checking in with old friends, providing updates to your manager, reminding your student to hand in their work, and submitting your lunch order to the intern. Chat is also where you find the meeting chat for most meetings you attend in Teams.

There are four ways you can chat with people:

- **Quick message:** A brief chat message sent to one person
- **Private chat:** A chat between you and one other person
- **Group chat:** A chat between you and two or more other people
- **Pop-out chat:** A private or group chat that takes place in a separate window

The next few sections take you through these methods and show you a few other chat-related techniques.

## Sending someone a quick message

Probably the fastest way to chat with someone is to send that person a quick message. This method is fast because you don't have to use the Chat app. You can message the person from wherever you happen to be in Teams.

To dash off a quick message, hover your mouse pointer over the person's avatar anywhere in the Teams interface. In the contact card that pops up — Figure 3-8 shows an example — use the Send a Quick Message text box to type your message, then click Send (shown in the margin).

## Starting a private or group chat

You can chat not only with internal people but also anyone outside your organization who is using Teams, Skype for Business, or the consumer version of Skype. These are called *external chats.* As long as you have the email of the recipient, you can send them a message. Similar to guest access in Teams, external chats must be allowed by your IT team. Reach out to them if you can't get it to work.

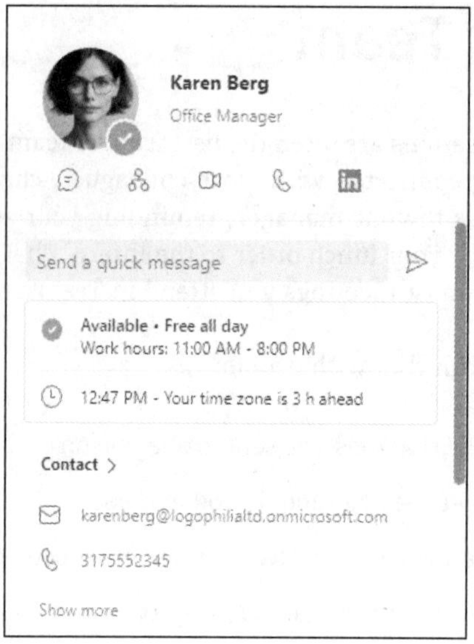


**FIGURE 3-8:** In someone's contact card, use the Send a Quick Message text box to fire off a message to that person.

Whether you want to have a private chat with one other person or a group chat with two or more people, the steps are pretty much the same:

1. **Click Chat in the navigation bar.**

   Any ongoing chats appear in the rail and the last chat you opened appears in the main area.

2. **Click the New Chat icon (shown in the margin) at the top-right of the rail, or press Ctrl+N.**

   The main area changes to a blank window with the To field at the top.

3. **Use the To text box to start typing the name of the person you want to chat with, then click the person when they show up in the results.**

   To chat with someone from outside your organization (assuming that's allowed in your company), type the person's email address, instead.

4. **(Optional) To make this a group chat, repeat Step 3 to add the other recipients to the To field.**

5. **(Optional) To display all the formatting options, click the Format icon.**

   You can also press Ctrl+Shift+X.

   Teams display the formatting toolbar above the message box (refer to Figure 3-4, shown earlier).

6. **Type your message, format it as needed, and add anything else you need to fill out your message.**

   I won't go into all the specifics here. Check out the steps in the earlier section "Getting a conversation off the ground" for the details.

7. **Click Send (shown in the margin) or press Ctrl+Enter to post your message.**

   If you didn't open the formatting options in Step 3, you can just press Enter (or click Send) to post a message. When the formatting options are displayed, pressing Enter starts a new line, so that's why you need to press Ctrl+Enter to ship the message.

## Keeping the chat going: responding to a chat message

Chats are back-and-forth conversations, so once you receive a chat message (you know when a message arrives because a banner appears briefly and you see a badge on the Chat icon in the navigation bar), it's up to you to respond in kind.

To respond to a chat message, first click Chat in the navigation bar, then use the rail to click the chat. From here, Teams gives you four ways to respond to a chat message:



- **Type a response.** Use the Type a Message text box to type your response, format it, if you feel like it, then click Send (shown in the margin).
- **Send a suggested response.** As shown in Figure 3-9, the Chat app displays several boxes above the composing box, where each box is a suggested response. Click one of the suggestions and Chat ships that text back to the sender right away.
- **Reply to an earlier message.** Hover the mouse pointer over the earlier chat message, then click Reply (shown in the margin) in the toolbar that appears. Chat quotes the earlier message. Below that quote, type your reply, then click Send.
- **Send a reaction.** As shown in Figure 3-9, when you hover the mouse pointer over your correspondent's most recent message, a toolbar of reactions appears. Click the reaction you want to send.

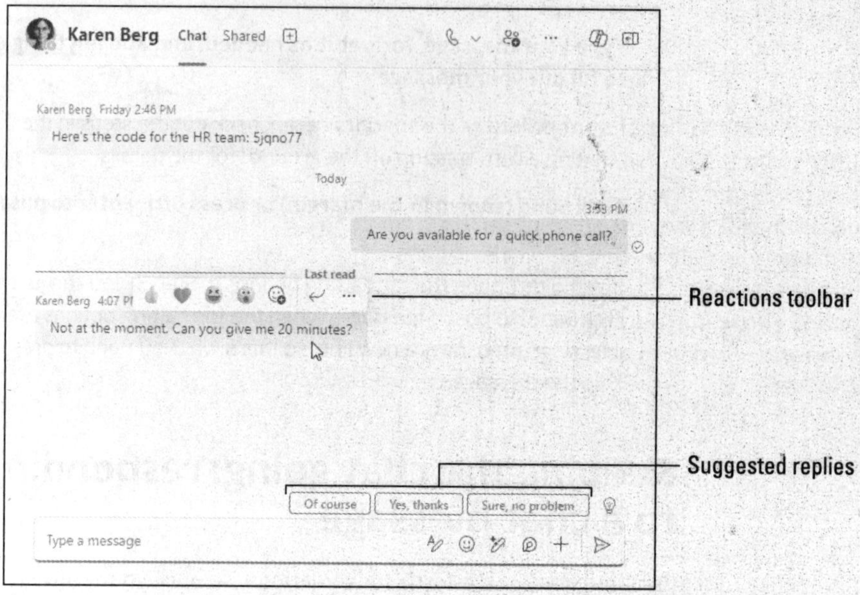


**FIGURE 3-9:** Chat offers several ways to respond to messages you've received.

# Renaming a chat

Group chats appear in the Chat rail named after the chat participants (generally just first names are used). That sounds reasonable, but this system can quickly get overwhelming to manage, especially if you have a lot of group chats whose membership is only slightly different. If you have a chat with a name that's too similar to other chats, consider renaming it. Follow these steps to rename a group chat:

1. **Click Chat in the navigation bar and then, in the rail, click the chat you want to rename.**

   The chat opens in the main area, showing a row of names of any members as well as several tabs along the top (check out Figure 3-10).

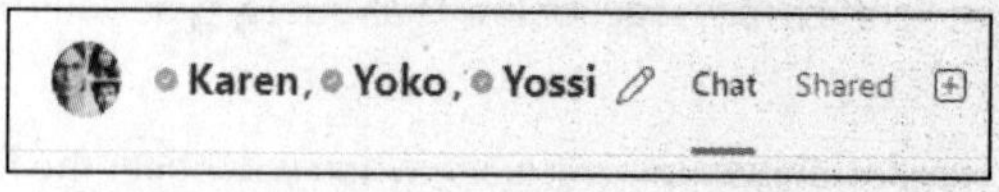


**FIGURE 3-10:** Group chat names consist of the first names of the participants.

2. **To the left of the Chat tab, click the Name Group Chat icon (shown in the margin).**

   The Group Name dialog box sneaks in.

3. **Type the new name in the text box and click Save.**

TIP

Keep the name short; the rail is only so wide.

Teams applies the new name to the group chat.

You can rename a chat as many times as you want. Actually, anyone in the chat can rename the chat, so let others know if you change the name. However, you cannot rename a one-on-one chat (it will always display the one person's name), nor can you change the name of a meeting chat.

## Adding and removing people (including yourself) from a chat

Invariably, you'll need to add people to or remove people from chats you're in. Each chat is equally owned by all the members, so anyone in the chat can perform this action (which could be a bad thing).

### Adding people to a chat

Follow these steps to add someone to a chat:

1. **Click Chat in the navigation bar and, in the rail, click the chat you want to invite someone to.**

   You can add people to a one-on-one chat or a group chat.

REMEMBER

2. **In the top-right corner of the chat's main area, click the View and Add Participants icon (shown in the margin) to reveal a drop-down menu, and then click Add People.**

   The Add dialog box opens.

3. **Enter the name of the person or people you want to add in the Enter Name, Email, or Tag box.**

   Repeat this step as needed to add more folks to the chat.

4. **Click the Add button.**

   If you're adding one or more people to a private chat — that is, you're converting the private chat to a group chat — click Create, instead. Note that in this case Team creates an entirely new chat.

## Removing people from a chat

Follow these steps to remove someone from a chat:

1. **Click Chat in the navigation bar and, in the rail, click the chat you want to remove someone from.**
2. **In the top-right corner of the chat area, click the View and Add Participants icon (shown in th margin).**

   A drop-down menu opens that lists all members of the chat.
3. **Hover your cursor over the name of the individual to be removed and click *X* to the right of their name.**

   Teams asks if you're sure you want to remove the person.
4. **Click Remove.**

   Teams kicks the person out of the chat.

WARNING

The person has been removed and the chat is no longer listed in their chat rail. Anyone in the chat can remove a member of the chat (which can be good or bad). You can remove someone from a meeting chat, but you may run into certain limitations depending on who the participants are, so don't depend on that possibility.

## Leaving a chat

Follow these steps to remove yourself from a chat:

1. **Click Chat in the navigation bar and, in the rail, click the chat you want to leave.**

   You can remove yourself from any chat except a meeting chat for which you are the organizer.
2. **Click the ellipsis next to the chat name to open the More Options drop-down menu; then click Leave.**

   Anyone in the chat can add you back if you need to return.

# Setting chat and message options

When a chat is open in the main area, you see the More Options icon (shown in the margin) near the upper-right corner. Clicking More Options releases a menu that includes the following items:

- **Open Chat in New Window:** Opens the chat in a separate window so that you can keep the chat always available on your computer.
- **Find in Chat:** Displays the Find in Chat pane, which enables you to search for text in the chat.
- **Schedule Meeting:** Opens the New Meeting window so that you can set up a meeting with the members of the chat. (Head over to Book 7, Chapter 5, to learn how to set up meetings in Teams.)
- **Screen Sharing:** Opens the Share Content window, from which you can share your entire screen or a specific window with the chat. (Again, Book 7, Chapter 5 is the place to go for more details.)
- **Mark As Unread:** Toggles the read status of the last message back to unread so that the chat is bolded and any relevant notifications appear.
- **Pin:** Pins the chat to the top of the rail for quick access.
- **Mute:** Disables notifications for this chat. You'll continue to receive notifications if someone @mentions you. A muted chat has a bell with a line through it as its icon.
- **Hide a Chat:** When you want to clean up your chat listing, you can hide a chat. Doing so removes it from your list until someone sends a new message. Note that you can't hide a pinned chat; unpin it first.
- **Delete:** Trashes the chat.



Message options offer their own features. Open the menu by hovering your cursor over a message in a chat, then clicking the More Options ellipsis. The options menu will differ whether you're working with a message someone else sent or one you sent. The options include some of the following key features:

- **Reply:** Sends a reply to the message.
- **Forward:** Sends the message to another private or group chat.
- **Copy Link:** Copies a link to the message to the Clipboard. You can then paste that link in another chat, an email, or a channel post to enable people to go directly to that message.
- **Delete:** Removes the message from the chat (this command is available only to the author of the message).
- **Pin:** Pins the message to the top of the chat.

- **Share to Outlook**: Sends your conversation in an email to any recipient. Head over to the "Sharing a Teams conversation to Outlook" section, earlier in this chapter, for details.
- **Mark as Unread:** Toggles the message status back to unread so the chat is bolded and you'll receive any relevant notifications appear.
- **Translate:** Translates the message to your language.
- **Immersive Reader:** View the message in a larger format or have it read automatically for those with vision impairment

IN THIS CHAPTER

» Taking a tour of Teams' file-related tools

» Creating, sharing, and organizing files

» Understanding how Teams stores and shares files

» Sharing files in channels and chats

# Chapter 4
# Fiddling with Files in Teams

When you start using Teams, you might think that the app is mostly a communications tool. It's not surprising anyone would think that given the seemingly endless ways that Teams enables two or more people to say things to each other: channel conversations, private chats, group chats, meetings, phone calls, and on and on. But Teams is all about collaboration, and in this modern age, collaboration goes far beyond words and includes files. Whether those files are Word documents, Excel spreadsheets, PowerPoint presentations, PDFs, code files, or even simple text documents, collaboration means reading, talking about, and editing files with other members of your team.

The details of file sharing and document collaboration are the subject of Book 8, but before you get that far you should consider how Teams fits into the big file-sharing picture. Teams boasts a large collection of tools and features for working with files. For example, you can create, upload, and edit Office 365 documents without leaving the Teams app. And you can share those documents in a channel or chat for a fully collaborative experience. And after you have files in Teams, you have access to an impressive collection of file management tools. This chapter takes you through the files experience in Teams, including creating, organizing, and sharing them.

# Getting to Know Teams' Files Tools

Teams can accept pretty much any file type, and files can be as large as 250GB. For files on the larger end of the size spectrum, you need to enable OneDrive sync to work on them (as explained in Book 8, Chapter 1).

You can open Word, Excel, PowerPoint, and OneNote files right within Teams. The files open within the browser version of the respective Office app inside Teams; however, if you prefer to work in the desktop version of those apps, you can do that.

In addition to Office files, many other file types either open or show previews in Teams. PDFs, common image file types like PNG and JPG, common video file types like MP4 and WMV, common audio file types like MP3 and WAV, and plenty of other typical file types should open or provide a preview.

Files are such an integral part of the Teams experience that the app gives you multiple ways to upload, create, and manage files:

» **Channels:** Each channel comes with a Files tab. When you upload a file as an attachment to a channel message, Teams stores the file on the Files tab. You can also use a channel's Files tab to upload files, create folders for organizing the files, open a file for editing, and perform various file management tasks.

» **Chat:** Each chat conversation comes with a Sharing tab. When you attach a file to a chat message, Teams stores the file in the Sharing tab (which also includes any web links you've shared during the chat). You can also use a chat's Shared tab to upload files and open a file for editing.

» **OneDrive:** You can access your entire OneDrive right from Teams? Yep, by clicking the OneDrive app in the navigation bar. You don't have to jump to File Explorer (if you're syncing your files) or open OneDrive in the browser to get to it. It's a handy integration to get you to your personal files from your central app for teamwork.

I don't cover OneDrive here (for that you need to check out Book 8, Chapter 2), but the rest of this chapter takes you on a tour of the Files and Sharing tabs.

REMEMBER

Before moving on, you need to get one file-related quirk straight, right off the bat. When you work with a file in Teams, are you working with a copy of that file or with the original? The answer, sort of, is both! Let me explain:

» When you upload to Teams a file from your PC, then you're uploading a copy of that file. Any changes you make to that file in Teams are *not* reflected in the original.

» When you upload to Teams a file from OneDrive, then you're uploading a link to that file. Any changes you make to that file in Teams *are* reflected in the original.

There are scenarios where you'll want to work with a copy of a document (for example, to preserve the original), and scenarios where it's best to work with a link to the original (for example, when you don't want multiple copies of a document floating around).

# Sharing Files in a Team

It's a rare team that doesn't require access to any files. For example, a team working on a business plan will need to work with a Word document. Similarly, another team working on a budget will need to collaborate on one or more Excel workbooks.

In Teams, the most common place to share files is the channel. A channel is a team subset focused on a particular topic, so storing files within the channel makes it easy for channel members to collaborate on files related to that topic.

Teams gives you two ways to add files and folders to a channel:

» **Upload an existing file or folder.** If you already have a file or folder you want to use within Teams, you can upload it to a channel. You can attach a file to a channel post, or you can upload a file or folder via a channel's Files tab. The next two sections explain these techniques.

» **Create a new file or folder.** You can create new folders as well as new, blank Office 365 files without leaving the Teams interface. You can create Word documents, Excel workbooks, and more. Head over to the section "Creating a file or folder in a team," later in this chapter, for the details.



Files and folders you create, upload, or add to Teams are stored in a channel's Files tab. Each Files tab is a front-end for a SharePoint library, and Teams gives you quick access to the channel's underlying SharePoint library in case you want to work with your files directly in SharePoint.

## Attaching a file to a channel post

When it's time to introduce a file to a channel conversation, you can share — or attach, in Teams lingo — the file to a channel post so that the file is easily accessible to the people you're addressing in your message.

Follow these steps to attach a file to a channel message:

1. **Click Teams in the navigation bar and then click the channel where you want to post.**
2. **Click the Start a Post button near the bottom of the main area.**

   A dialog box for composing a post appears.

3. **Click the Actions and Apps button (shown in the margin) and then click Attach File.**

   Teams displays a pop-up menu of file options. Figure 4-1 shows an example. There are four options:

   - **Recent files:** Displays a list of a few files that you've recently opened or edited. These files could be stored in a team, your OneDrive, or elsewhere in Office 365. If the file you want to share appears here, click it.
   - **Attach Cloud Files:** Opens the OneDrive dialog box, which gives you access to all the files in your OneDrive. Click a OneDrive category: My Files, Recent, Shared, or Favorite. Select a file's check box and then click Attach to upload a link to that file to the channel. (Note that you're free to select and upload multiple files at once.)
   - **Browse Teams and Channels:** Opens the OneDrive dialog box and displays the folders in your channel so that you can select files in the channel. But you can also click More Places to access files in other channels and teams if you need to upload a file from elsewhere in Teams.
   - **Upload from This Device:** Launches the Open dialog box, which enables you to upload a file from your hard drive. Select the file, then click Open to upload a copy of the file to the channel.

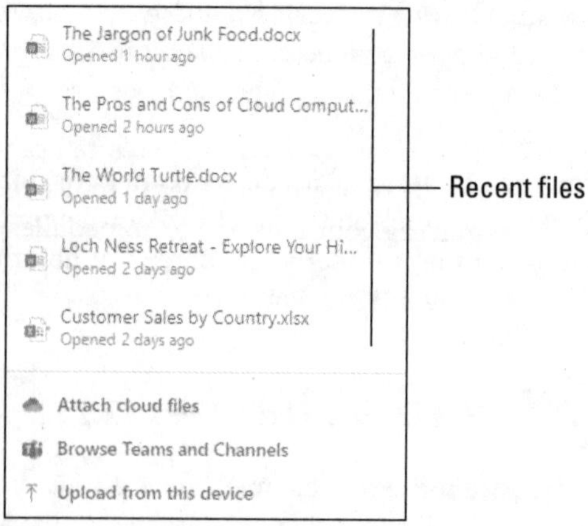


**FIGURE 4-1:** Teams offers several ways to select a file to upload to your channel.

4. **Fill out the rest of your channel message.**

   For all the details about composing a channel post, check out the steps in Book 7, Chapter 3 for creating or replying to a channel conversation.

5. **Click Post or press Ctrl+Enter.**

   Teams sends your message to the channel and adds the file to the channel's Files tab. Figure 4-2 shows a channel message with an attached file (an Excel workbook, in this case).

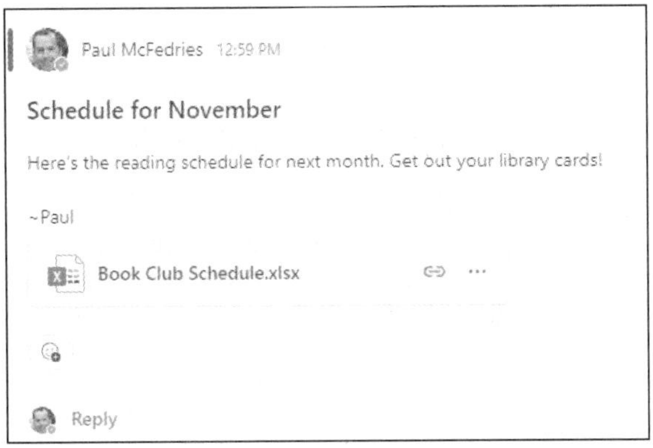

Paul McFedries 12:59 PM
Schedule for November
Here's the reading schedule for next month. Get out your library cards!
~Paul
Book Club Schedule.xlsx
Reply

**FIGURE 4-2** An example of a channel post with an attached file.

## Uploading a file or folder from the Files tab

The Files tab, which is located in the row of tabs in the main window of every channel, is sort of the Windows File Explorer for a channel. On this tab, you can create, upload, and access files for that channel. You can also perform many different file management tasks, such as renaming and moving files.

Uploading a file as an attachment to a channel post (as I describe in the previous section) sends your file straight into the Files tab. That sounds like a good thing, but if the channel ends up with lots of files, the Files tab can quickly become a disorganized mess. A better way to share your files is to use the Files tab directly both to add folders for organizing your files and to upload files into those folders.

Here are the steps to follow to upload a file or folder using a channel's Files tab:

1. **Click Teams in the navigation bar and then click the channel where you want to post.**
2. **Click the Files tab near the top of the main area.**
3. **Click Upload.**

4. **Choose what you want to upload:**
   - *Files:* In the Open dialog box that jogs in, click the file you want to upload and then click Open.
   - *Folder:* In the Select Folder to Upload dialog box that makes an appearance, click the folder you want to upload, then click Upload. When Teams asks you to confirm, click Upload.

   Teams uploads the file or folder and displays it in the Files tab.

TIP

You can upload a file or folder just by locating it using File Explorer, then dragging and dropping it into the Files tab.

## Creating a file or folder in a team

If you require a new file while working in a channel, such as a new Word document or a new Excel workbook, there's no need to switch to Word or Excel, respectively, to create the file, then upload the new file to Teams. Instead, you can stay within Teams and create your new file there. Teams supports creating the following items:

- Folder
- Word document
- Excel workbook
- PowerPoint presentation
- OneNote notebook
- Forms survey
- Visio drawing
- Clipchamp video
- Link

Follow these steps to create a file in a channel:

1. **Click Teams in the navigation bar and then click the channel where you want to create a file.**
2. **At the top of the main area, click the Files tab.**

   A list of the files and folders in this channel appears.

3. **(Optional) If you want to create your file or folder within an existing folder, click the folder to open it.**

4. **Click New.**

   Figure 4-3 shows the list of item types that appears.

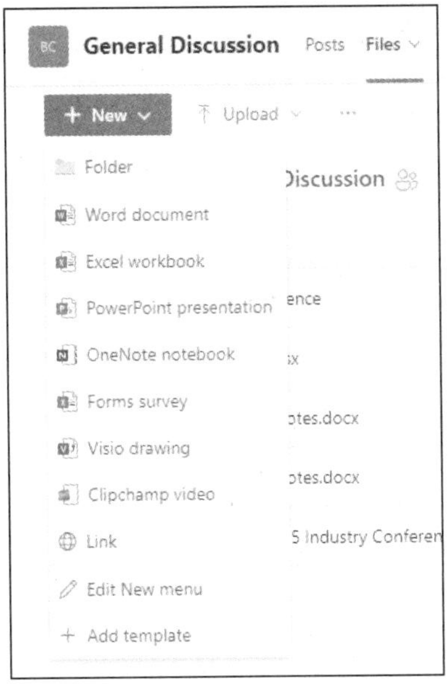


**FIGURE 4-3:** In a channel's Files tab, click New to create a new file or folder.

5. **Click the item type you want to create.**

   Teams prompts you for a name.

6. **Give your file or folder a name and then click Create.**

   If you created a file, the new, blank file opens in the browser version of the respective Office app. You can begin adding content to the file. All your changes are saved automatically.

## Managing files and folders

Once you've got some documents populating a channel's Files tab, the story of those files is only beginning because there's plenty you can do with them. For example, you can click any file to open it. If it's an Office 365 file, it will open in the corresponding online app. Also, hovering the mouse pointer over a file (or selecting the file's check box) displays an ellipsis that, when clicked, displays the file's Actions menu. The items in the Actions menu vary slightly depending on the file type, but they usually include the following commands:

- **Open:** Displays a menu of options for opening the file. For Word, Excel, and PowerPoint documents, your choices are Edit in Teams; Open in Browser (the default); or Open in App. For these file types, you can also click Change Default to select Teams as the default for opening the files.
- **Preview:** Displays a read-only version of the file.
- **Share:** Displays the Share dialog box, which you can use to share a link to the file with one or more recipients.
- **Copy Link:** Copies a link to a file or folder to the Clipboard.
- **Make This a Tab:** Creates a tab in the channel for a Word, PowerPoint, or Excel file. Selecting the tab opens the file for editing in that tab.
- **Delete:** Removes the file or folder from the channel.
- **Download:** Downloads the file or folder to your computer.
- **Rename:** Changes the name of a file or folder.
- **Open in SharePoint:** Displays the SharePoint library that contains the file or folder.
- **Pin to Top:** Displays a file or folder at the top of the Files tab for easy access. For a pinned folder Teams uses a folder icon; for a pinned file, Teams uses a thumbnail image of the file.
- **Move To:** Moves a file (but not a folder) to another folder in the same channel, a different channel in the same team, or a channel in a different team. You can also move the file to a location on OneDrive.
- **Copy To:** Copies a file (but not a folder) to another folder in the same channel, a different channel in the same team, or a channel in a different team. You can also copy the file to a location on OneDrive.

## Understanding where channel files are stored

The files in each channel's Files tab are not stored in Teams. When a team is created, additional workspaces in Office 365 are created alongside it. One of those workspaces is a SharePoint team site. Each team has a SharePoint team site behind it, and all files in a team are stored in the Documents library of that site. I talk more about SharePoint team sites in Book 8, Chapter 3.

REMEMBER

You can access your team's SharePoint site by opening the Files tab of any channel in your team, clicking the ellipsis that appears to the right of the Upload button, and then clicking Open in SharePoint in the menu. This will open your browser and show you the channel's files where they actually live: in the SharePoint site (check out Figure 4-4).

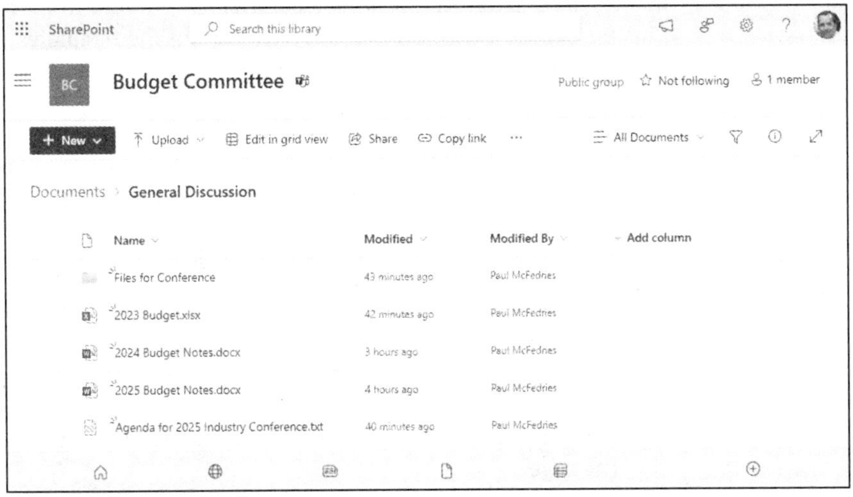


**FIGURE 4-4:** Files in your team actually live in an associated SharePoint site.

The SharePoint site isn't simply another way to look at your team's files. At least at the time of publishing, SharePoint offered more features for dealing with files than the Files tab in Teams does. You may actually need SharePoint to do your work. Some notable examples of options you have in SharePoint and not Teams are to share a file or folder to someone who's not a member of the team; manage access of a file or folder; display a file's version history; restore a file from the Recycle bin; and receive email alerts.

TIP

You can view the rest of the team's files by clicking Documents in the breadcrumb trail, the path of folders above the file and folder listing (refer to Figure 4-4). This will reveal a folder for each channel in your team. You can create additional folders here, but they will not create channels in Teams. To display these extra-channel files in Teams, click the General channel in your team, open the Files tab, and click Documents in the breadcrumb trail under the New button. This is a unique feature available only in a team's General channel.

## Adding a new document library to access in Teams

The Documents library mentioned in the previous section is where all files and folders in a channel's Files tab are stored. But it's not the only library you can have in a SharePoint site, or in your team for that matter. SharePoint is made up of pages, lists, and document libraries, as covered in more detail in Book 8, Chapter 3. Document libraries can have certain file templates, columns, permissions, and other features associated with it that other libraries in the site may not.

Sometimes you might want to have a separate library from the Documents library, and be able to access it in your team. Follow these steps to create a new library and even add it as a tab in your channel if you want:

1. **Click Teams and then click the initial channel of your team.**
2. **Click the Files tab, click the ellipsis next to the Upload button, and then click Open in SharePoint.**

   The SharePoint team site associated with the team opens.
3. **Click the Team icon or initials next to the site name in the top-left of the page.**

   The home page of the site opens.
4. **In the toolbar, click New and then, in the drop-down menu, click Document Library.**

   The Create New Document Library dialog box appears.
5. **Click Blank Library.**

   Alternatively, you can click From Existing Library, click the library you want to use, then click Next.

   SharePoint also offers several templates: Click a template and then click Use Template.
6. **In the dialog box that appears, provide a name and description for your library, and then click Create.**
7. **Add files, folders, columns, and any other content you'd like.**

   Book 8, Chapter 3 offers some guidance.
8. **To add the library to your channel, return to Teams and click the channel in which you want to add the library.**

9. **To the right of the Files tab, click Add a Tab (shown in the margin).**

   The Add a Tab dialog box opens.

10. **Click SharePoint, select the Document Libraries tab, choose your newly created library, and then click Save.**

    Teams adds the document library as a tab in channel.

WARNING

Remember that each team has its own SharePoint site associated with it. A team and its SharePoint site have the same permissions, which can't be uncoupled. You can create a library in a different SharePoint site and add it as a tab in your team, but beware that the permissions could be different. Permissions are important and sometimes difficult to work through, so always think ahead about the implications of the permissions you're working with!

REMEMBER

You can add the new library to as many or as few channels as you want. Be aware, though, that the toolbar and options in this library's new tab don't exactly match those you find in the Files tab. The Files tab is a native experience built into Teams, whereas an added library is built on top of Teams and therefore doesn't have some of the features the Files tab has. As long as you know this going in, you should be fine using your new library resources.

# Sharing Files in a Chat

File sharing in Teams isn't limited to channels. You may want to send a file to one or a few people you've been talking with in a chat. A chat doesn't offer the file management features that a channel does, so you should mostly stick with sharing files via channels. However, if you just want a person or group you're chatting with to have a quick look at a file, then sharing via chat is a reasonable alternative.

## Attaching a file to a chat post



Attaching a file to a chat message is similar to attaching files to a message in a channel, but not quite the same. Follow these steps to add an attachment to a message:

1. **Click Chat in the navigation bar and then begin the private chat or create a new one.**

   Follow the steps outlined in Book 7, Chapter 3, for creating a private chat or group chat.

2. **Click the Actions and Apps button (shown in the margin) and then click Attach File.**

   Teams displays a pop-up menu with the following three options:

   - **Recent files:** A list of a few files that you've recently opened or edited. These files could be stored in a team, your OneDrive, or elsewhere in Office 365. If the file you want to share appears here, click it.
   - **Attach Cloud Files:** Opens the OneDrive dialog box, which gives you access to all the files in your OneDrive. Click a OneDrive category: My Files, Recent, Shared, or Favorite. Select a file's check box and then click Attach to upload a link to that file to the chat. (Note that you're free to select and upload multiple files at once.)
   - **Upload from This Device:** Launches the Open dialog box, which enables you to upload a file from your hard drive. Select the file, then click Open to upload a copy of the file to the chat.

3. **Fill out the rest of your chat message.**

4. **Click Send (shown in the margin) or press Ctrl+Enter to post your message.**

   Teams adds your message to the chat and adds the file to the chat's Shared tab.

## Using the Shared tab in a chat

A chat has a Shared tab at the top of the main area. Shared seems like it would be the chat equivalent of the Files tab in a channel, but it doesn't work the same way as its channel cousin. Instead, the Shared tab in a chat is just a quick way to find files that have already been shared in that chat. As a chat goes on, scrolling up the history of messages seemingly forever to find and access a file would be a real time waster. The Shared tab is the place to go to display all files shared in that chat.

When you click the Shared tab, it shows a central listing of all the files shared in that chat, by whom, and when, as shown in Figure 4-5. Clicking the ellipsis to the right of a file enables you to open the file, download it, copy its link, or make it a tab in the chat. In contrast to a channel's Files tab, the Shared tab doesn't let you upload files, organize them in folders, or perform any file management tasks. The Shared tab in a chat is strictly a way to access files, not manage them.

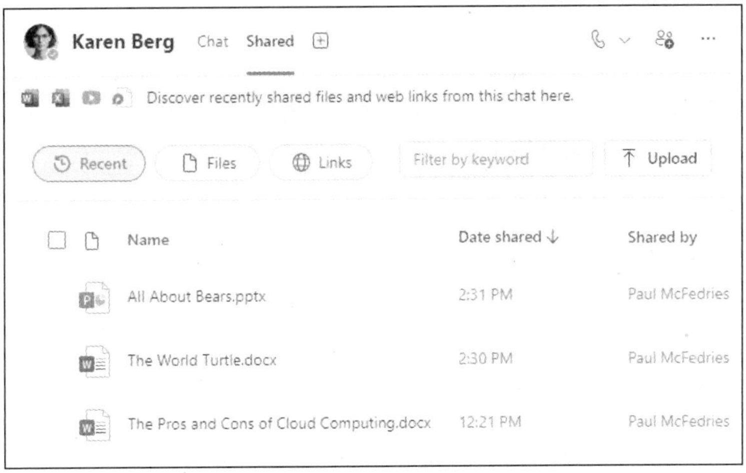


**FIGURE 4-5:** The Shared tab in a chat lists all files that have been shared in that chat.

## Understanding where files shared in a chat are stored

The files shared in a private chat are not stored in Teams. Instead, any file that's shared using the Attach button in a chat is stored in the sender's OneDrive. You can either share an existing OneDrive file — which just changes the permissions of the file and provides a link in the chat — or upload a file.

When you or anyone else in the chat uploads a file, the file gets stored in the sender's OneDrive in a folder called Microsoft Teams Chat Files. This folder is essentially a dumping zone because Teams needs to store the file *somewhere* if the sender didn't store it in a place that makes sense for others to find it when needed.

TIP

After you share a file in a private chat, you *can* move the file from one place in your OneDrive to another (still in your OneDrive) without breaking the link. (Check out Book 8, Chapter 2 for more about what you can do with OneDrive.) That said, rather than dumping files into a catch-all folder, the best experience for you is to upload a file to an appropriate folder in your OneDrive first, and then share the file from OneDrive when you click the Attach icon. You'll likely thank yourself later.

WARNING

Anyone that wants to share a file through chat *must* have a OneDrive account. When you chat with people in a Teams meeting who aren't in the organization, or you chat with Teams or Skype users from other organizations, you often find that they can't share a file. That's most likely because those users don't have the type of Office 365 account that comes with a OneDrive account or they're not allowed to share OneDrive files with people in other organizations. Having no OneDrive account means no file sharing in a chat or meeting chat. To get around this, *you* should share the file with everyone, or the external person can email the file to you and you can upload it in the chat.

IN THIS CHAPTER

» Scheduling a meeting

» Managing meeting options as an organizer

» Making the most of meeting features as a participant

» Accessing recordings of meetings

# Chapter 5
# Getting Together for Online Meetings

A long time ago, most folks worked where they lived. Farmers had their fields and livestock right outside the door, and tradespeople of all descriptions had their tools inside the house. Home was work and work was home, and separating the two would never have occurred to most people. All that changed when the Industrial Revolution came rumbling along. Its muscular machinery mass-produced goods formerly crafted by hand, and the great bulk of its hulking factories and warehouses required huge tracts of land outside cities and towns. The world's butchers, bakers, and candlestick makers had no choice but to leave their homes to ply their trades (or, more likely, some repetitive and soul-destroying subset of a trade) in these faraway enterprises. As a result, for the better part of 200 years, most workers have been leaving their homes and hi-ho, hi-hoing their way to work.

But now a post-industrial (and post-COVID) revolution is taking shape as a steady stream of workers abandon their traditional employment locales. The result is the *remote workforce,* where people toil at home, in a shared office space, hunkered down at the local coffee shop — anywhere but in a standard office.

Nothing wrong with that, but how do these so-called *office-free* workers get some face time? How do they meet? Well, if their organizations use Microsoft Teams, they can gather remotely using video meetings. In this chapter, you get to know the meeting features of Teams, find out what they can do, use them to start or join meetings, and explore their features. An office? Who needs it?

# Getting a Meeting Off the Ground

You can't have a meeting until you or someone else creates it! You can schedule meetings ahead of time or use Teams calling features to kick off ad hoc meetings. Teams lets you create a standard meeting, a webinar (which is basically a standard meeting with a registration page and sign-up process), or a live event, which allows attendees only to watch; live events are best used for town halls, trainings, and large webinars.

## Scheduling a meeting

You can schedule a Teams meeting from both Teams and Outlook. The meeting will display mostly the same information in your Teams and Outlook calendar. The calendar entry is the same in both apps because they both use your one Office 365 calendar. Teams offers more options than Outlook to manage the meeting, though.

### Scheduling a regular Teams meeting

Follow these steps to schedule a regular Teams meeting (as opposed to a channel meeting, discussed next):

1. **In the navigation bar, click Calendar.**
2. **In the top-right corner of the Calendar window click New Meeting.**

   The New Meeting window rises up from the depths.
3. **In the appropriate boxes, enter your meeting name, invitees (required or optional), date and time, description, and other meeting information.**

   Figure 5-1 shows a New Meeting window with the main meeting details filled in.
4. **When you're done setting up your meeting, click the Send button.**

   Teams ships out the meeting invitations.

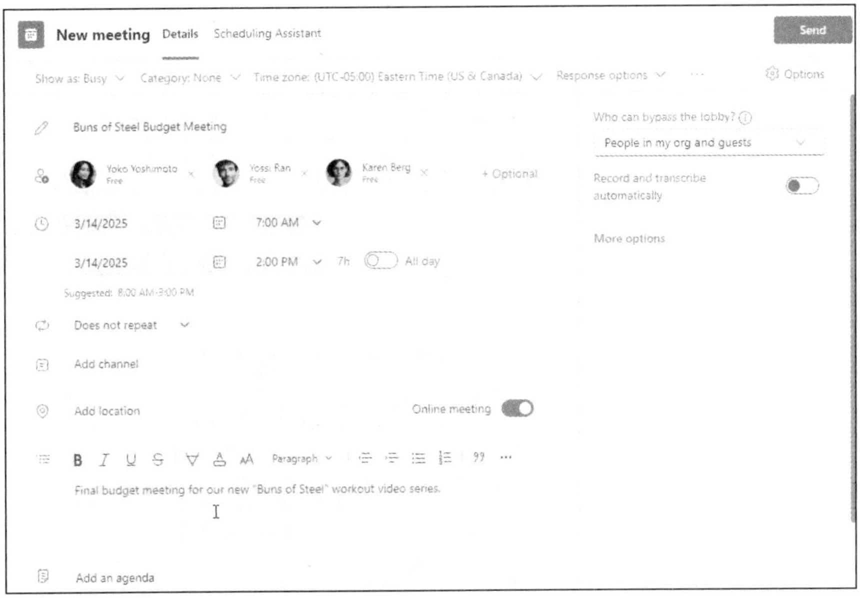


**FIGURE 5-1:** Use the New Meeting window to specify all the particulars of your Teams meeting.

## Scheduling a channel meeting

Channel meetings are a unique meeting feature in Teams. Most people are used to scheduling a meeting with designated invitees — and you can still do that using either Teams or Outlook, as covered earlier in this chapter (refer to the "Scheduling a meeting" section). But a *channel meeting* is a meeting held in a channel and accessible to all members of the channel. Although you can — and should — invite key individuals to a channel meeting, the meeting in the channel is visible and accessible to anyone in the team who has access to the channel.

Once you kick off a channel meeting, Teams adds the meeting as a new conversation in the channel, just as if you had clicked the Start a Post button and posted a message, as covered in Book 7, Chapter 3. This conversation, however, starts with a meeting appointment. The conversation under the initial meeting post comprises the meeting chat. When the meeting is ongoing, visual indicators appear such as a video camera icon next to the channel name in the rail and a purple bar and (partial) list of attendees at the top of the conversation in the main area (check out Figure 5-2).

Channel meetings can be a bit confusing because for most organizations, a channel meeting does *not* automatically invite the whole team to the meeting. Instead, it exists in the channel for anyone to join. So, if you're expecting certain people to join, you need to invite them. Or if you're conducting a class, you should invite all the students in the class.

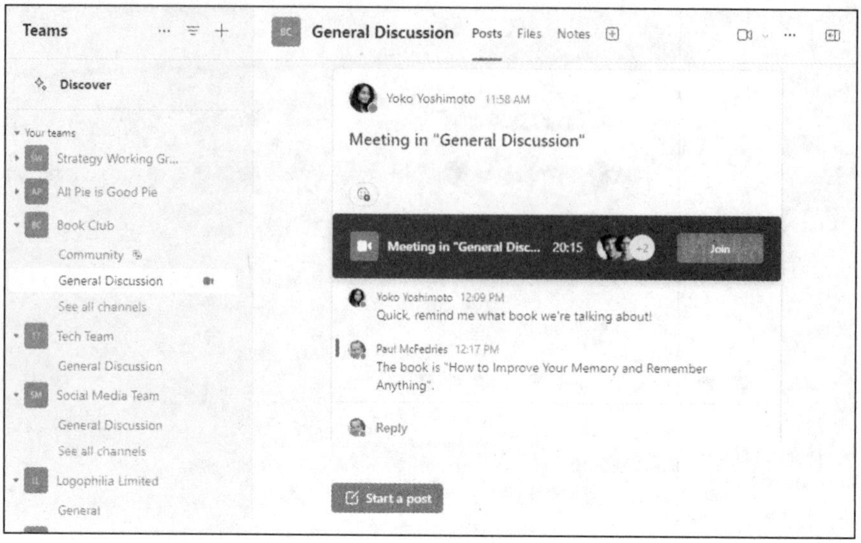


**FIGURE 5-2:** Channel meeting details and chat are listed in a channel, with options to join if the meeting is ongoing.

Follow these steps to schedule a channel meeting:

1. **In the navigation bar, click Teams.**
2. **In the Teams rail, click the channel.**
3. 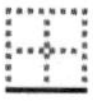 **Click the drop-down arrow next to the Meet Now button (shown in the margin), then click Schedule a Meeting.**

   The New Meeting window (shown earlier in Figure 5-1) comes in from the cold.
4. **Using the appropriate boxes, specify the meeting name, the invitees (required or optional), the starting and ending dates and times, a brief description, and other meeting bric-a-brac.**
5. **When your channel meeting is ready to schedule, click the Send button.**

   Teams hands out the meeting invitations.

## Scheduling a meeting via a chat

If you're in the middle of a private or group chat, you might decide to schedule a meeting with the chat participants. Why not? Here's what you need to do:

1. **In the navigation bar, click Chat.**
2. **In the Chat rail, click the chat.**
3.  **In the chat's message composition box, click Actions and Apps (shown in the margin).**

4. **Click Schedule Meeting.**

   The New Meeting window (shown earlier in Figure 5-1) comes in for a landing. The invitees box comes prefilled with the chat participants.

5. **Fill in the meeting name, the meeting's start and end times, a short description, and any other meeting details that you need.**

6. **Click Send.**

   Teams deals out the meeting invitations to the members of the chat.

## Scheduling a meeting via Outlook

If you happen to be working in Outlook and the inspiration for a meeting comes upon you, you don't need to switch over to Teams because you can get the meeting scheduled right there in Outlook:

1. **In the Outlook navigation bar, click Calendar.**

2. **In the top-left corner of the Calendar window click New Event.**

   TIP

   Another way to schedule a meeting in Outlook is to open an email message from the sender you want to meet with, click the ellipse on the far right of the Home tab, then click Meeting.

   The New Event window rolls in.

3. **Enter the meeting name, the attendees, the meeting's start and end times, a description, and any other meeting specifics you feel are necessary.**

   Note that as soon as you add at least one person to the Invite Attendees box, Outlook automatically sets the Teams Meeting switch to On.

4. **Click Send.**

   Outlook mails the meeting invitations.

## Managing meeting options and participant roles

When scheduling a meeting, you likely shouldn't just click Send and call it a day. Once the meeting is on your calendar, you as the organizer can manage a number of meeting options. The most important task is probably assigning roles to participants, but there are a number of other useful options as well.

To view meeting options, click the Calendar app in the Teams app bar, click the meeting in the calendar, and click the Edit button to expand the meeting from your Teams calendar. Then click Meeting Options in the toolbar at the top of the appointment to open the Meeting Options page. Any changes you make are saved automatically and applied to the meeting immediately.

REMEMBER

If you're scheduling your meeting, you can click the More Options link to display the Meeting Options dialog box, which offers the same settings as the Meeting Options page.

The meeting options are arranged in the following categories:

- **Security:** This section mostly deals with the lobby, which is a holding area for attendees before the organizer admits them into the meeting. You can choose who can bypass the lobby automatically. The Participants pane in the meeting displays the names of anyone waiting in the lobby, and you can let them in during the meeting. Having a lobby helps avoid "Zoom bombing," which is a cheeky term for when outsiders join your meeting without your consent and cause disruption (usually because the meeting link is shared publicly, such as on a website).
- **Audio & Video:** These options let you limit the attendees' ability to enable their microphone or video. These limits prevent or reduce unnecessary interruptions in larger meetings like town halls, webinars, and large training sessions.
- **Engagement:** These options enable you to restrict the engagement of the meeting participants. For example, you can manage whether the meeting chat is always available, available only during the meeting, or not available. You can also toggle Q&A, reactions, and the attendance report.
- **Roles:** Each meeting has three roles: organizer, presenter, and attendee. The organizer is like a super-presenter and is the person who schedules the meeting and can manage the meeting options. Presenters have more options than attendees, but not as many as the organizer. Refer to Table 5-1 for a list of the features available to each role.
- **Recording & Transcript:** In this section you can toggle automatic meeting recording and transcription. You can also specify who can record and transcribe, who has access to the recording or transcript, and whether you want Copilot involved in the transcript.

Roles, in particular, are a critical but underused feature for meetings. Attendees are essentially limited to managing only their own microphone, video, pinning, and traversing shared PowerPoint Live slides. Presenters have more control than attendees, and the organizer holds the keys to the kingdom with control of everything. Table 5-1 covers the features of a meeting and who has access to them.

**TABLE 5-1** **Feature Availability for Each Meeting Role**

| Feature Access | Organizer | Presenter | Attendee |
|---|---|---|---|
| Share video and audio | ✓ | ✓ | ✓ |
| Use meeting chat | ✓ | ✓ | ✓ |
| Request control of a shared screen or app | ✓ | ✓ | ✓ |
| Privately traverse a PowerPoint Live presentation shared by another participant | ✓ | ✓ | ✓ |
| Pin a participant's video | ✓ | ✓ | ✓ |
| Mute other participants | ✓ | ✓ | |
| Share your screen or apps or start PowerPoint Live | ✓ | ✓ | |
| Request control of a presenter's PowerPoint Live presentation | ✓ | ✓ | |
| Remove participants | ✓ | ✓ | |
| Admit participants from the lobby | ✓ | ✓ | |
| Change meeting roles of participants | ✓ | ✓ | |
| Start or stop meeting recording | ✓ | ✓ | |
| Can unmute when hard mute is enabled | ✓ | ✓ | |
| Spotlight a participant's video | ✓ | ✓ | |
| End a meeting | ✓ | | |
| Download meeting participant list | ✓ | | |
| Change meeting options | ✓ | | |
| Start and manage breakout rooms | ✓ | | |

## Launching an immediate meeting

Sometimes you need to have a meeting *right away* and scheduling it from your calendar doesn't make sense. You can call a bunch of people from an ongoing chat, but the Meet Now feature is better.

A Meet Now meeting creates an ad hoc meeting without an associated calendar invitation. From the meeting, you can invite people and use all the typical meeting features outlined in the "Participating in a Meeting" section, later in this chapter. You can start a Meet Now meeting from multiple locations:

- **From a channel:** Open the channel and click the Meet Now button (shown in the margin) in the top-right corner. Doing so starts a channel meeting. When meeting, all other channel members can learn that a meeting is going on, which can be useful when you want people to join if they have the time or the topic is interesting.

- **From your calendar:** Open your Teams calendar and click Meet Now at the top of the window. Doing so starts a private meeting.
- **From a chat:** Open the chat and click the Video Call button (shown in the margin) in the top-right corner of the chat. Or you can use the Video icon that appears under the chat message box.

REMEMBER

When you're in a Meet Now meeting, you can invite specific people to join or share the Join link (check out "Adding people to the meeting," later in this chapter). One of the benefits of a Meet Now meeting over a direct call from a private chat is that you can share the link rather than call people. That way, they can join at their convenience rather than be bothered by a direct call while in the middle of something pressing.

### Using dial-in conference lines

Teams meetings can have conference bridge lines automatically included with a meeting invitation that goes out to recipients. These dial-in lines require an additional license (and cost) for the meeting organizer, but many organizations invest in this feature for two reasons: to provide the most accessibility to join a meeting, and to allow for a more analog backup if Teams happens to be down, which definitely happens sometimes.

You don't have to do anything to include a dial-in line with your meeting. If you have the license, Teams automatically provides a phone number (which, depending on your organization's policies, will either be a toll-free number or a local number) and conference ID in the Join information included at the bottom of every meeting invitation. The conference ID is unique to the meeting, not to a person or organization. Each meeting has its own conference ID, so no one ever has to reserve conference lines.

If you have the license, all your meetings have a dial-in number, and recipients get clear instructions for joining.

## Joining in the Meeting Fun

Meeting invitees can join Teams meetings from the Teams desktop app, the mobile app, or a desktop browser like Microsoft Edge or Google Chrome — no plug-ins or downloads required. This capability is helpful when you're meeting with external invitees who may not use Teams; they don't need the Teams app or a Teams account to attend a meeting. That said, the best experience is always in the Teams desktop app. Keep reading to find out the options and how to use them.

## Joining from a browser

You can use the browser version of Teams to attend a meeting. This is useful for external attendees or those who use a computer that doesn't have Teams installed, or who don't want to log into the desktop app. The browser version is not as feature rich as the desktop app, but it provides all the basic tools needed for leading or attending an online meeting.

TECHNICAL STUFF

Only Microsoft Edge and Google Chrome on both Windows and macOS are fully supported for Teams meetings. Some other browsers will allow you to join, but not all browser features will work. Stick with Edge or Chrome.

REMEMBER

Each Teams meeting invitation includes a Join section at the bottom of the initial email invitation. This section includes a link to join, an associated dial-in number (if you have the feature), a Join code, and other support links. This information is automatically added to every meeting invitation. Figure 5-3 shows an example of Join meeting information in an invitation. The Join information should work for anyone as long as their device doesn't block Teams meeting web addresses.

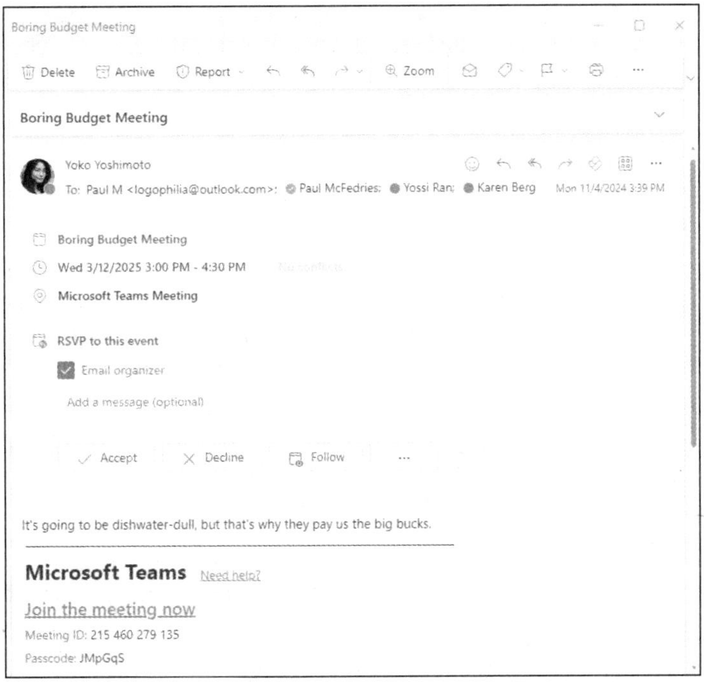


**FIGURE 5-3:** Each meeting invite includes various ways to join the meeting.

Follow these steps to join a meeting from a browser:

1. **In the browser, open the invitation or calendar appointment for the meeting.**

   WARNING

   If you're using Teams, you want to be logged into Teams in your browser via `teams.microsoft.com`. Attendees from outside the organization who don't use Office 365 need to open the meeting appointment in their email or calendar.

2. **Click the Join button (in Teams) or click the Join link at the bottom of the invitation (in any email app).**

   All Teams meeting invitations include a section at the bottom with a link to join the meeting. Anyone using Teams can use this link, but it's especially useful for people who use other email tools like Gmail, Yahoo, AOL, or other email accounts.

3. **Configure your audio, video, and background.**

   Head over to the next section for more information on how to choose your meeting settings.

4. **Click the Join Now button.**

## Joining a channel meeting

How you join a channel meeting depends on how you hear about it:

- **You receive an invitation.** Click the Accept button in the invitation banner that appears.
- **You're a member of the channel.** Open the channel's Posts tab and click the Join button that appears in the meeting post.

Either way, a new window pops up with the meeting settings. I talk about this window in more detail next. For now, you can click Join Now to get inside the meeting.

## Setting your meeting video, audio, and effects options

After you click Join or a link to join a meeting, Teams displays a screen like the one shown in Figure 5-4 to enable you to configure your audio and video equipment as well as any effects you want to use.

**FIGURE 5-4:** Before you join a meeting, you get a chance to set your audio, video, and effects options.

Follow these steps to configure your meeting settings to participate in the meeting:

1. **Click the toggle switch next to the Video icon to enable your video.**

   A preview of your video appears. This preview appears if you have a webcam or a camera attached to your device.

2. **Select your audio device.**

   You can use the computer or an attached audio device, or a Teams-enabled conference room that you connect to. When selecting a room, Teams may automatically detect it. If so, click Join and add this room. If the room was not detected, click Room Audio and enter or select the room name. Not all organizations support rooms.

3. **(Optional) Click the Device Settings icon (shown in the margin) to change your camera, microphone, or speakers.**

   This is necessary only if Teams did not automatically select the right camera, microphone, or speakers.

4. **Click Effects and Avatars and then make your choices:**

   - *Video effects:* Use this tab to set a background image (either a Microsoft-supplied image or your own) or effect or apply a filter to your video feed. You need to have your camera turned on to display these options.

- *Avatar:* If your camera is off, you can use an avatar instead of a live video feed. Click Create Your Avatar to make it so.

5. **Click Join Now to join the meeting.**

   If the meeting has a lobby, you might have to wait a bit until an organizer lets you into the meeting.

# Participating in a Meeting

After you join a meeting, there are a lot of options, best practices, and behavioral considerations to be mindful of. Many of these concepts are important for a meeting facilitator to manage, but plenty of options are available to attendees to maximize their meeting experience, too.

## Adding people to the meeting

If you're in a meeting and realize you forgot to invite someone or want to pull someone in to answer a question or provide either feedback or comic relief (which might be the same thing, depending on the meeting), you can add a person by inviting them or sending them a link to join.

REMEMBER

Anyone in a meeting can invite other people to join the meeting. However, as the meeting organizer you control who gets in as long as you have a lobby where folks must wait before being allowed into the meeting. For more on setting up a lobby, refer to the "Managing meeting options and participant roles" section.

If you're the meeting organizer, when you first join your own meeting Teams displays the Invite People to Join window, shown in Figure 5-5. This window offers three invitation possibilities:

- **Copy Meeting Link:** Places a copy of the meeting link on the Clipboard. You can then paste the link into a channel conversation, chat, email, or text message.
- **Add Participants:** Displays the Participants pane, from which you can invite people as I describe in the steps that follow.
- **Share Via Default Email:** Creates an email message using your default email client. The message includes the necessary info for joining the meeting.

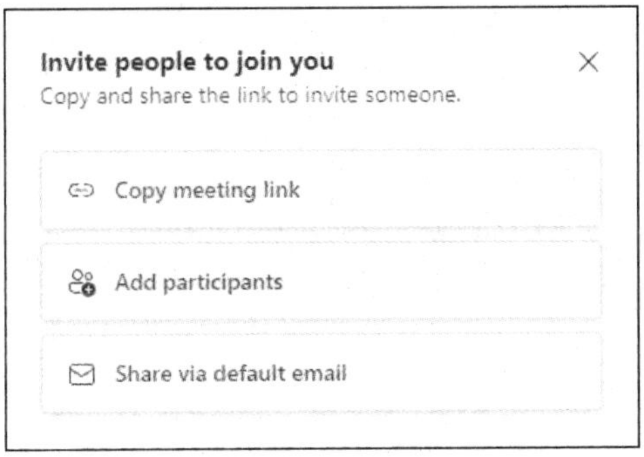


**FIGURE 5-5:** When you first join your own meeting, you can use this window to invite more people.

From within the meeting, you can follow these steps to invite someone to join:

1. **On the meeting toolbar, click People.**

   The Participants task pane slides in.

2. **Use the Type a Name text box to start typing the person's name or email address.**
3. **When the person appears in the list of search results, hover the mouse pointer over the person and then click the Request to Join button that materializes.**

   As an alternative to Steps 2 and 3, Teams provides a few handy participant suggestions below the box. If the person you want to invite appears under the Suggestions heading, hover the mouse pointer over that person and then click the Request to Join button that appears.

   Teams calls (or emails) the person and asks them to join your meeting. If the person clicks Accept, they get to join the meeting.

Alternatively, click the Participants pane's Share Invite button to display a window that offers the Copy Meeting Link and Share Via Default Email sharing options that I discussed earlier in this section.

## Viewing the participants list

To learn who's in a meeting, click the People icon on the meeting toolbar. Teams rolls out the Participants task pane, which offers a list of organizers and attendees in the meeting, as well as invitees who haven't yet joined. Each type of participant is grouped together: organizers first, and then attendees, and then invitees who haven't joined.

The Participants pane is (shown in Figure 5-6) very helpful if you dig into the options. Click the ellipsis to the right of the pane title to open the More Actions drop-down menu to download the current attendance list or lock the meeting (which means that no one else can join the meeting, even people who've been invited). Click the More Options ellipsis to the right of any participant's name to mute, pin, or spotlight them, as well as to change their role, among other options.

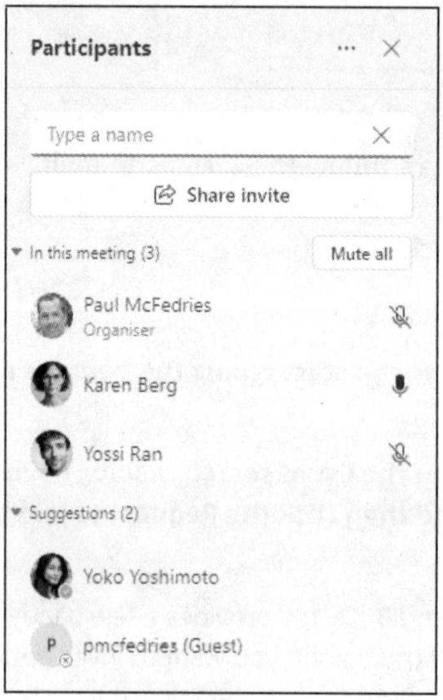


**FIGURE 5-6:** You can quickly learn who is in a meeting by clicking the People icon on the meeting toolbar.

## Changing the view

Once you're in your meeting, you can set view options to control who appears. On the meeting toolbar, click View to display the following view options:

- **Gallery:** Displays up to nine people, typically in a 3x3 format. However, when content is shared, the orientation of the videos can change.
- **Speaker:** Focuses the main display on the active speaker, showing them prominently in a larger section of the screen. Other participants are minimized or arranged in smaller tiles, allowing you to concentrate on the person currently speaking. This view is helpful in meetings with a large number of attendees, where you may want to focus more closely on the speaker without distractions from other video feeds.
- **Large Gallery:** Displays up to 49 people at once, which is useful for large meetings and classes. Click the Select Max Gallery Size option to set the maximum size: 4 people (a 2x2 gallery), 9 people (3x3), 16 people (4x4), or 49

people (7x7). Not that this setting is disabled if your meeting has less than 10 participants showing their video.

- **Together Mode:** Extracts cutouts of participants' video feeds and places them on a virtual background. Use the Select a Scene dialog box to choose the scene you want, then click Apply. Click Change Scene in the bottom-left corner to update the background.
- **Immersive Space (3D):** Transforms your standard meeting into a three-dimensional virtual environment. You and the other meeting participants enter a shared 3D space where avatars represent attendees.
- **Focus on content:** Shifts the spotlight entirely onto the shared screen or document (check out "Sharing your screen and content," a bit later in this chapter), pushing all participant video feeds to the sidelines. Essentially, it's Teams' way of saying, "Look, we know no one actually wants to see Steve's ceiling fan or Janice's cat during this presentation."

## Pinning and spotlighting participants

It can be helpful to highlight key presenters while they're speaking. Doing so not only makes it easier to follow the topic but also helps avoid promoting other participants just because they have their video on and are making noise. Because the screen may change here and there, identifying the individuals who have the floor can keep attention on the key speakers. Teams offers two options for this: pinning and spotlighting.

- **Pin:** All participants can pin individuals they want to keep "pinned" to a visible area on the screen. When you pin someone, you don't affect anyone else's view of the meeting. The person you pin doesn't know you've pinned them. You can pin as many people as the view supports (nine for Gallery view and 49 for Large Gallery view). Together mode doesn't support pinning.
- **Spotlight:** Spotlighting is like a forced pin for everyone and only organizers can spotlight someone. An organizer can spotlight up to seven participants, including that organizer. Spotlighted participants receive a notification that they are spotlighted.

You have two ways to pin or spotlight someone:

- **Right-click the participant's video:** In the shortcut menu that pops up, click either Pin for Me or Spotlight for Everyone. If the person's video isn't currently displayed, click People to open the Participants pane, then follow the techniques described in the next bullet.

- **Participants pane:** On the meeting toolbar, click People to open the Participants pane, hover the mouse pointer over the participant, click the ellipsis that appears to the right of the person's name, and then click either Pin for Me or Spotlight for Everyone.

TIP

A good meeting facilitator makes strong use of spotlighting to ensure that speakers are promoted and always visible to the meeting's participants.

## Muting yourself and others

Silence can be beautiful, especially in an online meeting. Background noises coming through open microphones can create annoying distractions during a meeting. The worst part is that the offender is the only one who doesn't know the impact they're having on the meeting. Teams does its best to try to cancel out background sound, but it's not perfect.

Various mute buttons in Teams are highly useful. If you're not a main participant in a meeting, you should mute yourself. In fact, when you join a large meeting, Teams enables mute automatically. Following are the muting options available to participants in a meeting:

- **Mute:** Click the Mic icon on the meeting toolbar (or press Ctrl+Shift+M) to mute and unmute yourself. This is one of the few icons in the app that indicates its current status rather than the status after you click it. If a line appears through the icon, you're muted.
- **Mute a Participant:** If one participant in particular is making a lot of unproductive noise, an organizer can mute that person in two ways:
  - If the person's video feed is visible, move your mouse pointer over the feed, click the ellipsis to the right of the person's name, and then click Mute Participant.
  - Click People on the meeting toolbar to fire up the Participants pane, move your mouse pointer over the person, click the ellipsis that appears, and then click Mute Participant.

  In case you're wondering, no, you can't unmute someone else; that's a major breach of privacy, which is why it's not available.
- **Mute All:** If your meeting is large, and various unmuted individuals are making noise, muting them one by one is inefficient. Instead, click People in the toolbar to crank up the Participants pane, then click Mute All.

- **Disable attendee microphones:** To not only mute everyone but also prevent everyone from unmuting, turn the Allow Mic for Attendees switch to Off, as I describe earlier in the "Managing meeting options and participant roles" section. You can also turn off this setting during the meeting; check out "Messing with meeting options," later in this chapter.

## Sharing your screen and content

Sharing content is one of the best ways to keep your meeting participants on the same page — sometimes literally! — with regard to the topic at hand. Just don't confuse this concept with sharing a file in a chat (refer to Book 7, Chapter 1) or sending a link via email (that topic is covered in Book 8, Chapter 1). On the meeting toolbar, click the Share icon to display your options. You have a bunch, as shown in Figure 5-7 and explained in the following list:

- **Screen:** Share your entire screen or one of multiple screens if you're lucky enough to use multiple monitors. Choosing this option shares everything on that screen, so if privacy is what you're after, don't use this one.
- **Window:** Share an individual window. This is useful if you want to share one app while using other apps privately, such as to take notes in Word while sharing your browser with the meeting. You can move any other windows around your screen without impacting what appears to the meeting participants on their end; they only get the one window you shared.
- **Microsoft Whiteboard:** Displays a whiteboard in the meeting. You can sketch and draw for brainstorming and notetaking. To display the whiteboard after the meeting, you open the meeting recap in the original appointment in your Teams calendar (check out "Finding Resources after a Meeting," later in this chapter).
- **PowerPoint Live:** You can share PowerPoint presentations using the previous two options, but PowerPoint Live, built right into your meeting, has special features and uses much less bandwidth, meaning crisper video and better sound quality. Refer to the next section, "Using PowerPoint Live," for more details.
- **Excel Live:** Shares an Excel workbook so that everyone in the meeting can not only view the file, but they can also interact with it and even edit it right there in the Teams window. Teams displays a list of some recent Excel workbooks, but you can click either Browse OneDrive or Browse My Computer to open some other Excel workbook.
- **Include Sound:** Click this switch to On to show a video or play music from your device. Make sure to enable this option *before* sharing.

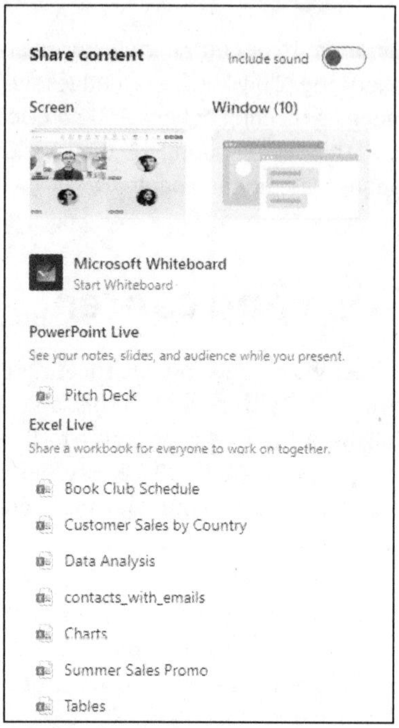


**FIGURE 5-7:** Use the Share Content menu to choose what you want to share.

When you share your screen or window, a toolbar appears in the top-center of the screen. Hover your mouse over the toolbar to expand it. On the toolbar, you can mute your computer audio, give another person control, share your system sounds, and more.

When you're done with your presentation, click Stop Sharing in the sharing toolbar.

# Using PowerPoint Live

PowerPoint slides are probably the most common type of content shared during a Teams meeting, and PowerPoint therefore has a unique relationship with meetings in Teams. The feature is called PowerPoint Live and is available in the Share menu.

The PowerPoint Live section of the Share menu lists your recently opened `.pptx` files from OneDrive, SharePoint, and Teams. If the file you need doesn't appear, you can click Browse to upload it. Or, if you have the file open in the PowerPoint desktop app, you can click Send to Teams in the Home tab to launch your slides right in the meeting.

After you share your slides in the meeting, a "lite" version of PowerPoint's presenter view appears, which shows the current slide, list of slides, slide notes, and other key features. For everyone else in the meeting, the first slide appears, not the details you get. Here are some key features to be familiar with:

- **How to progress through slides:** All participants can move forward and backward through your slides. How anyone views slides is up to them and does not impact what's displayed to others. You can disable this capability by clicking the toolbar's Private View icon to the disabled state. You still control which slide the rest of the meeting attendees are on, even if individuals are progressing through slides on their own.
- **How to take control of slides:** Any presenter in the meeting can click the Take Control button on the meeting toolbar to manage the slides, meaning that nobody should have to say "next slide" ever again. To get control back, you have to click Take Control yourself.
- **Clickable links:** You can include a hyperlink in your slide, which will be live and clickable for everyone while the slides are shared.
- **Access to meeting chat and participant listing**: PowerPoint Live allows access to the meeting chat and the Participants pane, displaying either right next to the shared slides, which are not nearly as easily accessible when you're sharing your screen or window. Learn more about these features in upcoming sections.
- **Pinning and spotlighting**: You can pin and spotlight key people so that they stay front and center while slides are shared. Check out the "Pinning and spotlighting participants" section, earlier in this chapter, for details.

When you've finished your presentation, click Stop Sharing in the toolbar to shut down PowerPoint Live and return to your regular meeting.

## Sharing files in a meeting

Sharing a file for participants to edit during the meeting is identical to uploading a file to a private chat (for private meetings) and to a channel conversation (for channel meetings). Follow these steps to share a file:

1. **On the meeting toolbar, click Chat.**

   The Meeting Chat task pane appears.

2. **In the message composition box, click Actions and Apps (shown in the margin), then click Attach File.**

3. **Click how you want to share the file:**

   - *Attach Cloud Files:* Opens the OneDrive dialog box, which enables you to share a file from your OneDrive. Select the file, then click Attach.
   - *Upload from This Device:* Displays the Open dialog box, which enables you to share a file from your computer. Select the file, then click Open.

4. **Type a message, if you want, then click Send (shown in the margin).**

   Teams shares the file to the meeting chat.

Sharing files as described in the preceding steps is straightforward, but that doesn't mean it's the best option for you. When sharing files for a meeting, you should really share them ahead of the meeting — likely in a designated folder for that meeting — and share the link to the file or folder in the meeting invite. This approach keeps the files organized. When you upload a file in the meeting chat, the file ends up in an unorganized folder. Learn more about sharing files in Teams (in meetings or not) in Book 7, Chapter 4.

## Viewing the meeting chat

Chat is an important aspect of your meeting. It's a place for participants to interact without interrupting ongoing discussion or presentations. Depending on your meeting type, the chat lives in different places. If you're in a private meeting, the chat is listed in the Chat app in Teams, and you can find it there after the meeting. If you're in a channel meeting, chat is part of a conversation in the host channel.

Regardless of meeting type, you access the chat the same way *during* the meeting. On the meeting toolbar, click the Chat icon to open the Meeting Chat task pane. This pane offers all the features that appear in a channel conversation or regular chat. Additionally, messages actively pop up above the meeting at the top-center of the meeting window, so you can follow them as they come in without needing to open the chat.

TIP

Using the meeting options, the meeting organizer can disable the chat entirely or allow its use only during the meeting (refer to the "Messing with meeting options" section, later in this chapter).

## Recording the meeting

Meeting recordings can be useful later for invitees who missed the meeting, for training purposes, or even as an easy way to record yourself presenting slides without needing expensive video editing software.

To record a meeting, on the meeting toolbar, click More, click Record and Transcribe, then click Start Recording.

REMEMBER

For privacy reasons, all participants are informed that they're being recorded. You should also verbally mention that you're going to start recording so that participants can mute themselves and disable their video if they don't want to be included in the recording.

To stop the recording, on the meeting toolbar, click More, click Record and Transcribe, then click Stop Recording.

REMEMBER

If you don't click Stop Recording, the recording stops when the last person leaves the meeting or the organizer ends the meeting.

TECHNICAL STUFF

For a standard private meeting (the meetings most people schedule through Teams or Outlook), the meeting recording is saved in the OneDrive of the person who clicks Start Recording. For a channel meeting, the meeting recording is saved in the Files tab of the host channel. In both cases, the file (it uses the MP4 video file type) is stored in a folder called *Recordings*. Anyone who has access to the channel can open, preview, or download the recording file.

## Using live captions and transcription

Live captions and transcription are of course useful for people with hearing impairment, but they're also handy for anyone surrounded by loud noise. Captions show what is stated. Transcription does the same but also identifies the speaker and can be downloaded after the meeting.

To enable live captions, on the meeting toolbar, click More, click Language and Speech, then click Show Live Captions.

To enable transcription, on the meeting toolbar, click More, click Record and Transcribe, then click Start Transcription.

REMEMBER

After the meeting, the transcript is available to the meeting organizer in the Meeting Recap (check out the "Finding Resources after a Meeting" section, later in this chapter). If you don't need a transcript after, live captions is likely sufficient.

## Reacting and raising your hand

You can make your meeting more inclusive by encouraging people to react to presentations and speakers during the meeting by using meeting reactions. On the meeting toolbar, click React and then click one of the five available reactions: Like (thumbs-up), Love (heart), Applause (clapping hands), Laugh (laughing face), or Surprise (surprised face). Although no record is kept of who reacted how or when, it's a live gauge of participants' views of the content.

TIP

Reactions (especially the thumbs-up) are also useful to get quick answers from participants, such as whether they can hear you and view your shared content without having to come off mute or muddy up the chat.

Also available on the meeting toolbar is the Raise icon (or press Ctrl+Shift+K). Participants can raise their hand to indicate that they have a question or to answer an informal yes/no poll. When a participant raises their hand, an icon of an open palm appears on the video feed. You can view everyone whose hands are raised by clicking People on the meeting toolbar to open the Participants task pane, where the list of raised hands appears in the order in which people clicked the button. (The person at the top of the list has waited the longest.)

To lower a raised hand, the person who raised their hand can click the Raise button again (or press Ctrl+Shift+K). A meeting organizer can forcibly lower someone's raised hand via the Participants pane by hovering the mouse over that person, clicking the ellipsis to the right of their name, and then clicking Lower Hand.

WARNING

Beware of hand raising, however: This is a social contract that everyone in the meeting must be aware of and agree to use completely or not at all. Provide a quick briefing on hand-raising expectations by presenting a "Please raise your hand" slide at the beginning of presentations, or mention that you're not using it (whichever is applicable).

If you don't check in on raised hands every so often, people will get frustrated. Also, if participants don't use the hand but instead jump in verbally with an ad hoc question that you answer, others won't be motivated to raise their hand because anyone can skip the line. Last, if participants don't know to raise their hand, they won't. You can avoid all these issues by using the tips in the previous paragraph.

## Messing with meeting options

Meeting options are available both before the meeting (as I described earlier in the "Managing meeting options and participant roles" section) and during the meeting, when you can change them on the fly. A good meeting facilitator will toggle settings as necessary during the meeting to make it the best experience it can be. Meeting options can be managed only by the meeting organizer.

Follow these steps to manage meeting options during the meeting:

1. **On the meeting toolbar, click More.**
2. **Click Settings.**
3. **Click Meeting Options.**

   The Meeting Options dialog box shuffles in.
4. **Change your meeting options as necessary.**

   I talked about these options earlier in the "Managing meeting options and participant roles" section.
5. **Click Save.**

   Teams puts the new options into effect.

## Using breakout rooms

*Breakout rooms* are separated but connected mini meetings that you can split participants into during a Teams meeting. Breakout rooms are useful for dividing your meeting into smaller groups for easier discussion or brainstorming sessions, and they're popular among teachers and people leading team-building events.

Breakout rooms can be complex, and covering them in detail is beyond the scope of this book. So you may want to learn more about them before using them live in a large event. Testing is always your friend. The meeting organizer has the most control over breakout rooms in a meeting, so make sure that whoever schedules the meeting is knowledgeable enough to use them if they are needed. Here are the general steps for using breakout rooms in a meeting:

1. **On the meeting toolbar, click Rooms.**

   The Create Breakout Rooms task pane bullies its way onto the screen.
2. **Choose how many rooms you need.**

   The maximum is 50.
3. **Choose whether participants will be split into rooms automatically or manually.**

   If you choose the automatic option, you can't assign people manually at the start, though you can move people between rooms after the rooms are opened.

4. **Click Create Rooms.**

   Teams creates the breakout rooms and displays the Breakout Rooms task pane. In this pane, you can create more rooms, delete rooms, rename rooms, manage rooms settings, send an announcement to all rooms, assign participants to rooms, and move participants to different rooms.

5. **When you're ready to start your breakout sessions, click Open to open all rooms.**

   Alternatively, you can open a single room by hovering the mouse pointer over the room, clicking the ellipsis to the right of the room name, then clicking Open.

   When you open one or all rooms, anyone assigned to an open room will leave the meeting and join the room.

When you're ready to close your rooms, on the Breakout Rooms task pane (click Rooms in the meeting toolbar if that pane isn't open), click Close Rooms to close all rooms. To close a single room, hover the mouse pointer over the room, click the ellipsis to the right of the room name, then click Close. When you close one or all rooms, the assignees of the closed rooms will leave the room and rejoin the meeting.

## Leaving and ending the meeting

Anyone in a meeting can leave whenever they want by clicking the Leave button on the meeting toolbar. The meeting automatically ends when everyone leaves. The meeting organizer can also end the meeting, forcing everyone out when the organizer decides it's time. The organizer has a drop-down menu on the Leave button that provides the End Meeting option. If you're the organizer, you should generally end the meeting rather than wait for everyone to leave. The meeting recording, transcript, and other artifacts won't be available until everyone leaves, and sometimes people simply forget to leave.

# Finding Resources after a Meeting

After your scheduled meeting is done, you gain access to the meeting recap, which is a window that provides information about and artifacts from a meeting. To get to this window, you have two choices:

- Click Chat in the navigation bar, click the meeting chat in the Chat rail, then click View Recap.
- Click Calendar in the navigation bar, right-click the meeting, and then click Edit.

The various tabs in the meeting recap window quickly get you to the meeting chat (the Chat tab), files shared in the chat and the meeting recording (the Shared tab), the details of the meeting (the Details tab), the meeting attendance list (the Attendance tab), the whiteboard (the Meeting Whiteboard tab), the breakout rooms (the Breakout Rooms tab), and any questions that were asked and answered (the Q&A tab).

The Recap tab (check out Figure 5-8) offers a general overview of what happened, including direct access to the recording, meeting notes, @mentions, and the meeting transcript (if any).

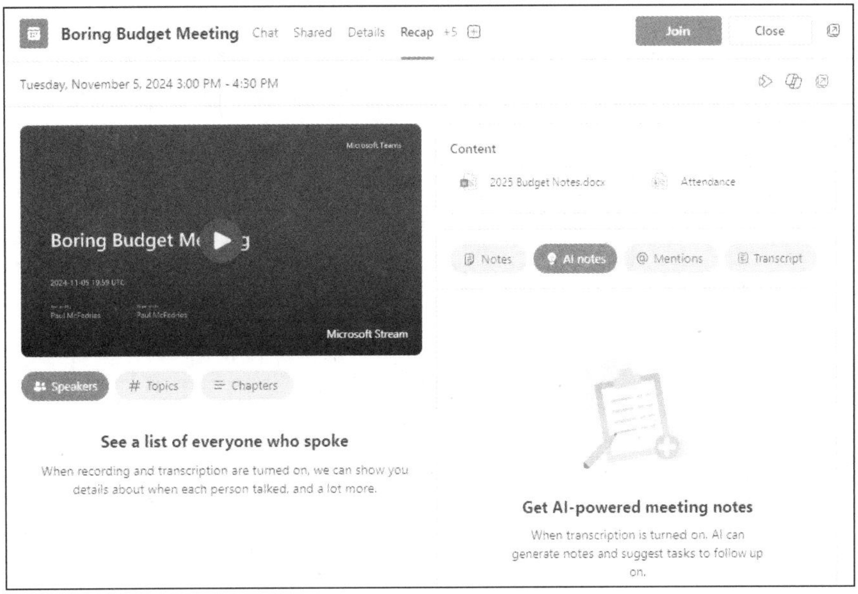


**FIGURE 5-8:** The meeting recap offers a wealth of information about a completed meeting.

For a channel meeting, open the channel, find the meeting conversation in the Posts tab, then click the Open link to open the meeting recap. This recap includes the meeting chat, the attendance list, and the meeting recording.

# 8

# File Sharing and Collaborating

# Contents at a Glance

IN THIS CHAPTER

» Understanding the differences between OneDrive and SharePoint

» Syncing your files for offline access

» Editing files in the browser versus desktop Office apps

» Keeping track of a file's version history

» Restoring accidentally deleted cloud files

» Sharing files with people outside your organization

# Chapter 1 Sharing Files

Long gone are the days when business types worked on memos, budgets, and presentations in splendid isolation. Sure, even today one person might work up a first draft of a file, but for all but the most trivial documents, the next stage is to get a bunch of different fingers in that pie. The chapters here in Book 8 are all about collaborating on files, but modern-day collaboration begins with sharing those files with your team, your department, or with anyone who needs to view or edit the files.

In Office 365, file sharing is a cloud-based affair, with tools like OneDrive and SharePoint enabling you to share files — and even set those all-important permissions — with just a few clicks. This setup is particularly useful for team projects and organizational workflows, ensuring everyone has access to the latest version of each file. It's teamwork at its finest, without the mystery of wondering who spilled coffee on the final draft.

This chapter launches your Office 365 collaboration course by focusing on using OneDrive and SharePoint to share documents, workbooks, presentations, and more. You explore crucial sharing features such as syncing files to your devices, working with file versions, copying and moving files within the cloud, and even how to share files outside your organization. In this chapter and the rest of Book 8, you see that Office 365's file-sharing capabilities streamline the process of working together, making it easy to manage permissions, collaborate in real time, and keep files secure. Call it *splendid collaboration.*

# Knowing when to Use OneDrive or SharePoint

Files in Office 365 get stored in one of Microsoft's cloud storage tools: OneDrive or SharePoint. You can still save files to C drives, flash drives, shared drives, and other local options, but most organizations that use Office 365 are moving to or already store their files in OneDrive for Business, SharePoint Online, and Microsoft Teams. If you have a personal Office 365 account, you get a consumer OneDrive account. Whether you have a business or personal account, you get 1TB of OneDrive storage to mess around with.

The most common source of confusion for new and veteran Office 365 users alike is when to use OneDrive, SharePoint, or Teams for storing and sharing files. As Book 7, Chapter 4, notes, all files shared in Teams chats and channels are actually stored in OneDrive and SharePoint, respectively, behind the scenes. You may think you've never used OneDrive or SharePoint, but if you're creating files in or uploading files to Microsoft Teams — surprise! — you most certainly have used them. Besides being able to access files within Teams through the Files tab in a channel or the Shared tab in a chat, you can also share and retrieve your files from either OneDrive or SharePoint. For these last two options, the following sections clarify when it's best to use them for retrieving, sharing, and storing files.

## When to use OneDrive

OneDrive is perfect for two types of files: personal files that shouldn't be shared and drafts of files you're not yet ready for others to work with. When you're ready to share, that's when you move them to a SharePoint site or Teams channel for collaborative input or reviews.

Although you *can* share files from and collaborate on them without leaving OneDrive, it's usually not your best option. Sharing at the file or folder level, as opposed to storing all working files in one bucket with consistent access, like a Team or SharePoint site, quickly becomes a permissions nightmare. It's especially confusing when each person in a working group shares individual files from their own OneDrive account with the other members of that group as they work on them. You make things much easier for everyone if you upload and collaborate on files that are located in a central SharePoint site or in a Team in Microsoft Teams.

WARNING

Another reason to minimize sharing from your OneDrive is that when someone leaves an organization, their OneDrive is typically retired within 30 days. If your working group depends on critical files that have been shared from someone's OneDrive and that person leaves the organization, you won't be happy to find out one morning that those files are gone for good without warning.



## When to use SharePoint

SharePoint consists of websites. Each site has one or a few owners and its own permissions for the whole site, which owners can change as necessary. In these sites, you can build pages, store and organize files, and do a lot more. SharePoint is best used in two ways:

- **Team sites are best for collaborating.** Team sites have members and most — if not all — of those members have edit access to everything in the site. Team sites are for getting work done. They're also the file storage location behind Microsoft 365 Groups, including Outlook Groups, Viva Engage (an enterprise-level social network platform), and Teams in Microsoft Teams. (Microsoft Teams is covered in Book 7.) Each member of these group types automatically has edit access to the associated team site. But you can create a SharePoint team site by itself; you don't need to use Outlook, Viva, or Teams.
- **Communication sites are perfect for publishing.** These sites are usually accessible to almost everyone in the organization, but most people have only view access. A few people have access to upload, edit, and delete published files. Communication sites generally make up your organization's intranet. A good example of an item published on a SharePoint communication site is a corporate policies listing. The people who write and maintain those files can update the policies when necessary, but most visitors to the site just read the policies; they shouldn't be able to edit them. Communication sites are for everyone's stuff.

If your organization doesn't already have a different process in place, consider drafting your file in OneDrive. When you're ready, move your file to your SharePoint team site where colleagues can provide input and review. You could also draft the file in the team site and leave it there for greatest visibility to your peers (if you were using OneDrive, the file would be private to start whereas in the team site, others can stumble across it and provide useful input along the way), and then call on them later to review the file.

When the file is completed and ready to be widely shared, publish the file to a communication site (if it's meant for wide distribution) or to the team site (if it's something like a template or team-specific documentation for your team to use later). Keep a working copy in your team site so that updates are easy to make and kept private from the rest of the organization while you work on any revisions.

SharePoint, OneDrive, and their integrations with Teams might seem complex. But to put it most simply, you may find yourself moving between OneDrive, SharePoint team sites, and SharePoint communication sites: me, we, us, as illustrated in Figure 1-1.

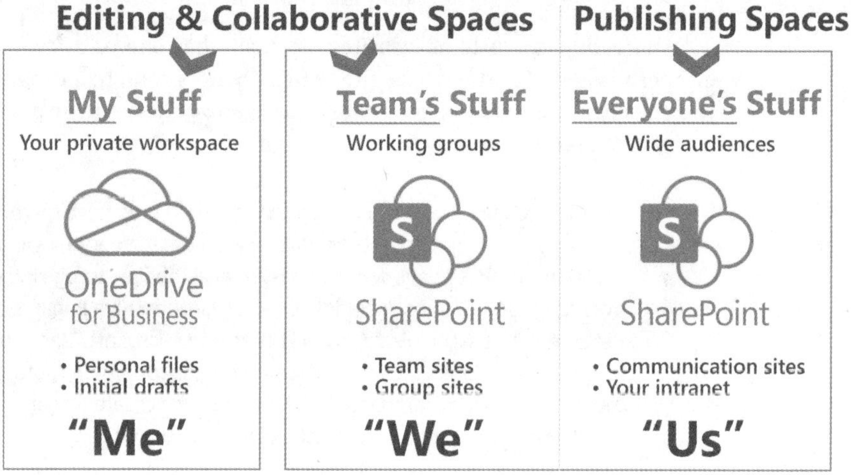


**FIGURE 1-1:** OneDrive for personal drafts (me); SharePoint team sites for collaboration (we); and SharePoint communication sites for publishing (us).

# Syncing Office 365 Files to Your Devices

You're probably familiar with — and likely prefer — accessing files from a shared drive, local hard drive, or other location listed in the left side of Windows File Explorer. You might also need to be able to work on your files even when you don't have an available internet connection. Using OneDrive, you can sync any of your files from Office 365 to any device — computer, tablet, smartphone — and locate them the same way you always have.

But isn't OneDrive just a personal storage space? No, not *just*. In an example of poor marketing that has confused millions worldwide, the name "OneDrive" is used for two distinct functions: the storage space described earlier in the chapter, and a separate tool from Microsoft that you use to sync files from *the other* OneDrive, as well as from your SharePoint sites. This other OneDrive is an app that you install on your devices, and it's a feature that you can't live without.

## Linking OneDrive to your Office 365 business account

To sync files from Office 365, you need to have the OneDrive app installed on your device. If you're running Windows 11, OneDrive is already installed. For earlier versions of Windows and for your other devices, you can get OneDrive for Windows, macOS, iOS, and Android from `https://www.microsoft.com/en-us/microsoft-365/onedrive/download`.

Once OneDrive is installed, you need to link your Office 365 account to the app. Open File Explorer and in the navigation pane on the left, you see an item with a cloud icon (refer to Figure 1-2). If the name of that item is your first name followed by your company name, then you're all set. If the name of the item is your first name followed by Personal, then it means OneDrive is linked only to your personal account. Here are the steps to follow to link OneDrive to your Office 365 account:

1. **Right-click the OneDrive item in File Explorer's navigation pane, click OneDrive in the shortcut menu that appears, then click Settings.**

   The OneDrive Settings window descends from the cloud.

2. **In the navigation pane on the left, click Account.**

   If the account shows your Office 365 account, there's no need to proceed, so feel free to skip lightly but resolutely over the rest of these steps.

3. **Click Add an Account.**

   The Set Up OneDrive dialog box storms in.

4. **Type your email address, then click Sign In, and then specify your password, if prompted.**

   OneDrive shows you the location of your OneDrive folder. If you want, you can click Change Location to choose some other folder, but the default location should be fine.

5. **Click Next.**

   OneDrive links to your Office 365 account and adds your OneDrive to File Explorer's navigation pane. Figure 1-2 shows File Explorer linked to both a personal OneDrive (Paul – Personal) and a business OneDrive (Paul – Logophilia Limited).

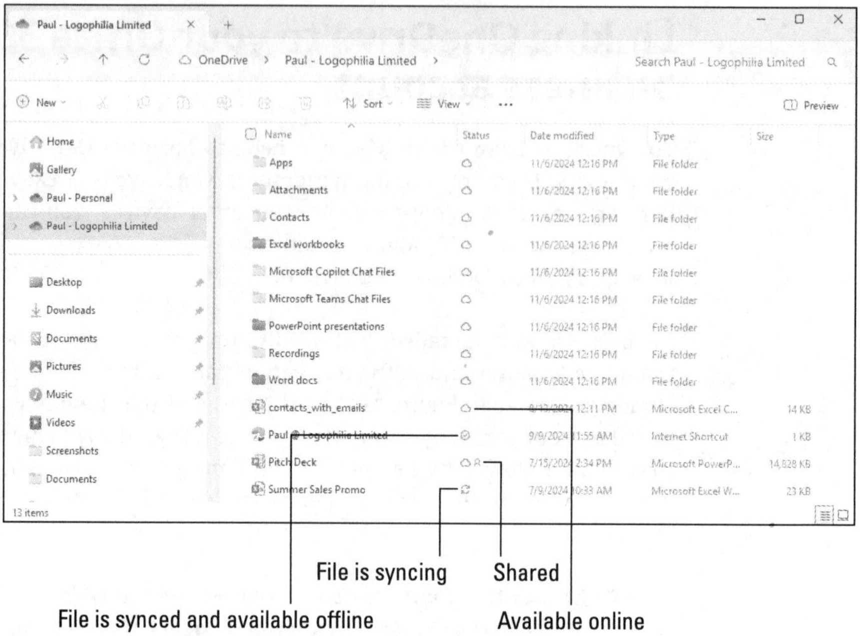


**FIGURE 1-2:** You can link to both a personal OneDrive and a business OneDrive for your Office 365 account.

## Keeping files always available on your device

When you open your OneDrive folders in File Explorer, a little icon appears next to the name of each file and folder. (If you have File Explorer in Details view — pull down the View menu and click Details to get there — the icons appear in the Status column.) There are four main icons to watch for:

- » The blue cloud outline indicates that the file is available only when you have an internet connection; to open one of these files, you have to download it first.

- » The two circular arrows tell you that an offline file has changed so it's being synced to your device.

- » The green check mark inside a circle indicates that you can access the file when you're offline.

- » The generic head and upper body tells you the file or folder has been shared with one or more people or groups.

You probably want files that you use regularly to be accessible offline for times when you're disconnected from the internet. Follow these steps to always keep a file or folder on your device:

1. **Open File Explorer.**
2. **In the left-side navigation, click your OneDrive.**

   Your OneDrive folders and files appear in the main area.
3. **Right-click any file or folder and click Always Keep on This Device.**

   The file or folder downloads to your device and displays a circular blue arrow icon until it's completed downloading. Depending on how much information you're downloading, it may take a while. You can view the status of your sync by clicking the OneDrive icon in the system tray.



TECHNICAL STUFF

Your OneDrive has a lot of space — 1TB for most people — but plenty of computers still don't offer that much space. So, what happens if your synced files start taking up too much space on your device? Follow the preceding steps, but in Step 3, click Free Up Space for the files and folders that take up more than their fair share of your computer.

You can sync and unsync files as you need them. If you intend to be offline for a while, you can save the files you expect to need while you're still at a location with dependable Wi-Fi. If you make edits to files while you're offline, they will sync with the source file in the cloud the next time you're on Wi-Fi.

## Syncing Teams and SharePoint files to your device

You can also use the OneDrive app to sync Teams and SharePoint content to your computer or mobile devices. Teams and SharePoint files don't automatically sync to your device — that could be an insane amount of files — but you can sync the files and folders that are important to you in those Teams or sites. If you don't already have a team or site, refer to Book 7, Chapter 2, or Book 8, Chapter 3, for instructions on creating a team or SharePoint site, respectively. Follow these steps to sync files from Microsoft Teams or a SharePoint team or communication site to your device:

1. **Open the Team or SharePoint site where the files are stored.**
   - *Team site:* Click the channel where the files are stored and then click the Files tab at the top of the main area.
   - *SharePoint site:* Open the site in a browser. If you need access or a link, ask the site owner.
2. **Open the folder you want to sync, or follow the breadcrumb trail all the way to the top level to sync all files.**

3. **In the toolbar above the files, click Sync.**

   This opens a notification from OneDrive that the sync has started. You can click Close to get rid of it. If you're syncing a SharePoint site and you see a notification that the site wants to open OneDrive, be sure to click Open.

4. **Launch File Explorer.**

5. **In the left-side navigation, under your organization name, click the channel or SharePoint site name.**

   The folders and files appear in the main area (refer to Figure 1-3). If needed, follow the steps in the preceding section, "Keeping files always available on your device," to choose files to always have available locally on your device, even if you're not online.

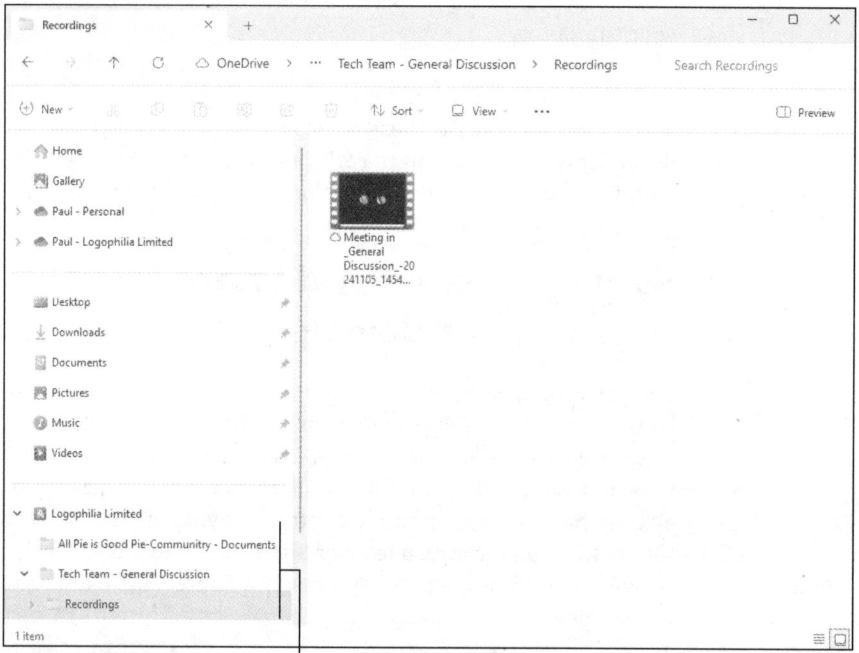


**FIGURE 1-3:** You can sync Teams and SharePoint folders to your device.

WARNING

One of the biggest risks with this feature is that you may forget that other people depend on these files. If you no longer want the files on your device, *don't* delete them! Doing so deletes the files for everyone else as well. Instead, right-click the file or folder in File Explorer and click Free Up Space in the menu that appears.

Alternatively, if you no longer want to sync a particular channel or site, you can tell OneDrive to stop the sync:

1. **Click the OneDrive icon in the system tray.**
2. **Click Help & Settings (shown in the margin) and then click Settings.**

   The OneDrive Settings window appears.
3. **Click the Account category.**
4. **Click the Stop Sync button to the right of the channel or site you no longer want to sync.**

   OneDrive shuts down the sync for the channel or site.



# Staying Sane When Editing Files

In this section, you delve into some details on editing Office files as well as some of the implications that come from making changes to your files.

## Editing Office files in their desktop versus web versions

If you've been using Office 365 for a while, you've probably noticed that Office files — particularly those associated with Word, Excel, PowerPoint, and OneNote — don't always open in the desktop app that you're probably used to.

Instead, these files may open in a browser version of the app. These browser versions are part of Office 365 for the Web, with each app having a similar name: Word for the Web, Excel for the Web, and so on. While these web versions don't have all the same features as their desktop counterparts, the web apps can be pretty good for light tasks, such as reviewing a letter in Word or updating some data in Excel. They're faster to load than the desktop apps, they update quickly when you're editing files with someone else, and they're simpler to navigate and use.

Although the Office 365 for the Web versions continue to progress and add features, they can be limited in what they can do, especially if you have complex needs. The takeaway here is that these apps are entirely worth using, but in the right circumstances. Just be aware of what you need to be able to do.

## Editing Office files with colleagues

One of the benefits of the cloud is the ability for Office files to be opened and edited by multiple people at the same time, which Microsoft calls *coauthoring.* This capability is a major shift from the days of shared drives, when it was not uncommon for a file to be "locked for editing" by someone, seemingly right when you most needed that file.

REMEMBER

You can coauthor in Word, Excel, PowerPoint, and OneNote in the desktop app, web app, or directly in Teams. When someone else is currently working in a file you're editing, their photo or initials pop up in the Ribbon to let you know they're there. As they traverse the file, a cursor or box may appear around the content they're working on. Changes also occur live, right on your screen. For the details on Office coauthoring, head over to Book 8, Chapter 3.

## Keeping track of a file's version history

All OneDrive and SharePoint files provide a version history, which lets you go back in time to view or restore a previous version of your file. Version history is a great way to get a file back without needing IT intervention.

REMEMBER

To use version history, you must access OneDrive or SharePoint in the browser, so begin by opening the OneDrive folder or SharePoint site in your nearest web browser.

If you want to access the version history of a file in a team, switch to Microsoft Teams, click the channel where the file is stored, click the Files tab above the main area, and then click Open in SharePoint in the toolbar below the Files tab; this brings you to the Team's files in the SharePoint team site.

Once the file appears in SharePoint or OneDrive, hover the mouse pointer over the file, click the ellipsis that materializes, then click Version History.

The Version History window that bubbles up shows all the versions for that file and their version numbers. Hover the mouse pointer over a version to expose an ellipsis for the version. Click the ellipsis to unfurl a drop-down menu, from which you can click Open File (to open that version), Restore (to restore that version), or Delete Version (to remove the version if it has information you don't want saved).

TIP

Each version will also list a date and time and who edited the file, creating that version. It's a great way to recover from a corrupted file or to go back to a clean version when someone added too many comments.

# Using the Recycle Bin to Restore Deleted Files

The Recycle Bin in OneDrive and SharePoint can be your saving grace when someone mistakenly deletes a file. It's especially nice because it usually doesn't require IT intervention to help. OneDrive has a Recycle Bin, and each SharePoint site has its own Recycle Bin.



You can delete a file or folder in OneDrive or SharePoint by hovering your mouse pointer over the file or folder, clicking the ellipsis that shows up, then clicking Delete. To delete multiple items, select the check box to the left of each item (you have to hover the mouse pointer over an item to see its check box), then click Delete in the toolbar at the top.

As I'm sure you know from bitter experience, sometimes clicking Delete is a mistake. To access the Recycle Bin and recover a mistakenly deleted file or folder for your OneDrive or for your SharePoint site, follow these steps:

1. **Locate the Recycle Bin in your browser:**

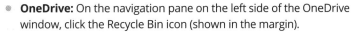

   - **OneDrive:** On the navigation pane on the left side of the OneDrive window, click the Recycle Bin icon (shown in the margin).

   - **SharePoint:** Click Toggle Navigation Pane (shown in the margin) and then click Recycle Bin.
   - **Teams:** There's no direct link to the Recycle Bin in Teams, so you need to open the SharePoint team site from Teams first. In Teams, click the channel where the deleted content used to be stored, click the Files tab above the main area, and then click Open in SharePoint in the toolbar below the Files tab; this brings you to the Team's files in the SharePoint team site. You can then access the Recycle Bin in SharePoint as described in the previous bullet.

2. **Click the file or folder you want to restore.**

   If you're looking to restore multiple files or folders, then for each item hover your mouse pointer over the item and click the check box that appears to the left of the file or folder.

3. **Click Restore in the toolbar above the contents of the Recycle Bin.**

   Your file or folder is returned to its original location, safe and sound.

REMEMBER

You should have up to 93 days to restore a file before it's permanently deleted. If a file you were hoping to restore doesn't appear in the Recycle Bin and you know it was deleted less than 93 days ago, reach out to your IT team. They may have some further options.

# Copying and Moving Files between OneDrive and Teams

You often need to copy or move files between various locations. These actions have different outcomes, so it's important to know how and when to use each.

- **Copy:** This feature creates an exact copy of a file in the location you select. The original version retains its version history and any unique permissions. The copy has no version history and will inherit the permissions of its new home. When you make a copy, two versions of the same file exist. That might be perfectly fine for your situation — just make sure you don't confuse people about which version they should be viewing or editing.
- **Move:** This feature removes a file from one place and drops it in another. The file retains its version history wherever you move it, and it *may* retain its earlier permissions while also inheriting the permissions of its new home. It all depends on where you're moving it from and to; typically, OneDrive will ask you about the permissions before moving.

WARNING

If the file you're copying or moving is used by a number of people, always make sure to communicate the change if it could affect their ability to use that file. Communication is key!

To copy or move a file or folder, follow these steps:

1. **Find the file or folder in OneDrive or Teams.**
2. **Move the mouse pointer over the file, then click the ellipsis to open the Show actions drop-down menu.**

   If you don't see the ellipsis, right-click the file, instead.

   The menu includes the commands Move To and Copy To.
3. **Click the command you prefer, and the Move or Copy dialog box opens.**

4. **Choose your destination.**

   You can choose either your OneDrive or a SharePoint site you have access to. After you select OneDrive or a site, select the document library or folder to place the content in.

5. **Click the Move Here or Copy Here button.**

   OneDrive or Teams moves or copies the file.

# Sharing Files Outside Your Organization



For those times when you need to get a file to someone outside your organization, you have an alternative to attaching a file to an email. In many ways, sharing a file with an external person is preferred: the process is more secure, the sender has more control over the content, the information stays centralized, and you can benefit from the full features for files like coauthoring, version history, and permissions.

You still send an email, but instead of sending a copy of a file to the recipient, include a link to the file's location. You can also share a link to any file or folder and send it in another message type, such as a private chat or even a text message.

## Sharing a file

Sharing a file link has several benefits for both the sender and recipient. All edits are made to a central copy of the file, so you don't have to merge various return copies; you can revoke permissions to the file at will; you can view and manipulate version history; you can take advantage of coauthoring; and you have access to many of the other features referenced in this chapter. An email attachment can do none of those things.

The basic share experience is available in Teams, OneDrive, and SharePoint:

1. **Select what you want to share.**

   - **To share a single file:** Hover the mouse pointer over the file, then click the Share icon (shown in the margin) that appears.
   - **To share multiple files:** For each file you want to share, hover the mouse pointer over the file and select the check box that appears. When you're ready to move on, click the Share icon in the toolbar.

   The Share dialog box shoulders its way onto the screen.

2. **Use the Add a Name, Group, or Email text box to type the address of your external recipient (or recipients).**

3. **Click the Can Edit icon (shown in the margin) and then click the permission you want to give the recipients.**

   Your choices are Can Edit, Can View, or Can't Download.

4. **Type a message to the recipient.**
5. **Click Send to complete the share.**

## Sharing a link

Sharing a link to a file gives you more choices about how you send the link. Here are the steps to follow:

1. **Hover the mouse pointer over the file you want to share, then click the Share icon (shown in the margin) that appears.**

   The Share dialog box walks on.

2. **Use the Add a Name, Group, or Email text box to type the address of your external recipient.**

3. **Click the Link Settings icon (shown in the margin) to the right of the Copy Link button.**

   The Link Settings dialog box appears.

4. **Select the People You Choose option.**

   By selecting this option, you're saying that the recipient you specified in Step 2 can use the link to access the file you specified in Step 1 with the permission you're about the specify in Step 5.

5. **Use the More Settings drop-down list to click the permission you want to give the link recipient.**

   Your choices are Can Edit, Can View, or Can't Download.

6. **Click Apply.**
7. **Click Copy Link.**

   The link to the file is saved to your computer's Clipboard.

8. **Paste the copied link into whatever medium you want to use to share it — email, chat, text message, channel post, or whatever — then send or post the message.**

When recipients click the link you've sent, they may need to log in or provide a passcode to access the file. From there, they have the access you provided (edit or view) and should be able to download the file, unless you disabled that capability in Step 5. Talk to your IT team about the organization's rules for external sharing.

REMEMBER

External sharing can scare a lot of IT people, especially those in the cybersecurity realm. Although sharing files with external people might seem like a security risk, an email with an attachment amounts to the same thing, but with less control. So, if external sharing is not available to you, it's likely because of an IT decision. Reach out to your IT team if necessary.

IN THIS CHAPTER

» Exploring the OneDrive window

» Accessing files shared with you

» Connecting to Teams and SharePoint sites

» Managing permissions

# Chapter 2

# Making the Most of OneDrive

You're onsite with a client or at a coffee shop getting some work done, taking your trusty laptop along for the trip. You go to open a crucial document and — No! — you realize that the file is sitting uselessly on your desktop PC's hard drive at work. That scenario happens often and it can be extremely frustrating. But it can become a scenario of the past thanks to the miracle of cloud computing.

Your Office 365 account includes a bit of personal online real estate in the form of OneDrive, a cloud-based storage service. Documents stored in OneDrive are available from any device and any location that's connected to the internet. Whether you're with a client or at the coffee shop, if you've got Wi-Fi, your files are always just a few clicks away.

However, as I discussed in Book 8, Chapter 1, you can also use OneDrive to share files with people both within and without your organization. OneDrive also makes it easy to access files other folks have shared with you and you can even use OneDrive to access SharePoint and Teams files.

These and other OneDrive features mean that you'll likely be spending quite a bit of time working with OneDrive and its files and folders. That time will be better spent if you're familiar with OneDrive and know how to perform basic tasks such as viewing, selecting, creating, and uploading files and folders. These and other OneDrive techniques are the subject of this chapter. As noted in Book 8, Chapter 1, OneDrive files are accessible from a browser, from Teams (via the OneDrive app), and from File Explorer in Windows. This chapter covers the browser experience because it has more features than what you find in Teams and File Explorer.

# Getting Started in OneDrive

OneDrive can store up to 1TB (that's 1,000GB) of files, which is the standard amount that comes with both personal accounts and work or school accounts.

To get into a personal OneDrive account or a work or school account, you first need to log in. If you're using a personal account (typical logins end in @live.com, @outlook.com, @hotmail.com, or even @xbox.com), go to `https://onedrive.live.com`. To log into a work or school account, go to `https://office.com`.

In either instance, log in, click the App Launcher icon (shown in the margin) and then click OneDrive. If you're using an account through the U.S. government, Germany, or China, you need to talk to your IT team for the specific link.

WARNING

If the browser asks to remember your password, feel free to let it as long as you're not using a public device (like a hotel computer). You don't want someone else to be able to log into your account and wreak havoc in the new playground they found.

TIP

When you're ready to sign out of Office 365 in a web browser, click your profile photo, name, or initials in the top-right corner of the screen and click Sign Out.

When you first log into your OneDrive account, there will likely be few or no folders. Your workplace or school may create some for you, but that depends on the organization. A personal account includes Documents and Pictures folders as well as a personal vault, which is a secure storage location in a personal OneDrive account. Figure 2-1 shows the OneDrive window with numerous folders.

## Navigating the navigation pane

The OneDrive page includes a navigation pane on the left. Rather than trying to decipher what each icon represents, click the Navigation Pane icon (shown in the margin) to open the pane and reveal the name of each icon, as shown in Figure 2-2.

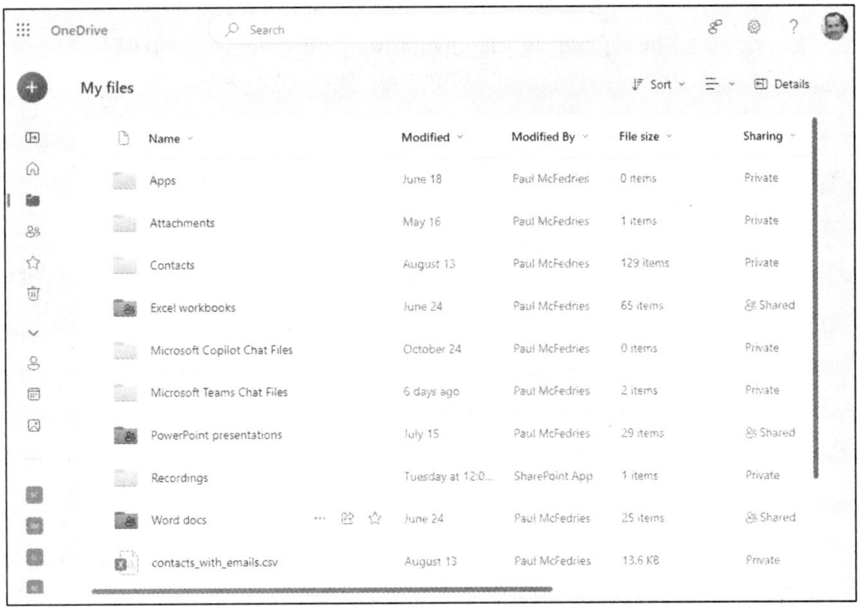


**FIGURE 2-1:** The OneDrive page in List view.

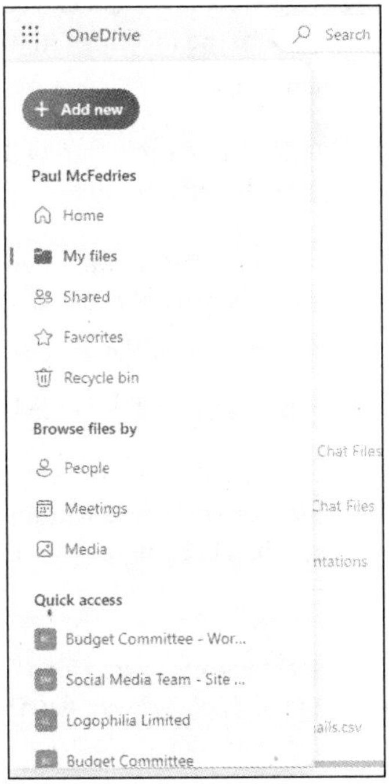


**FIGURE 2-2:** The OneDrive navigation pane.

The top part of the navigation pane (that is, the part just under your name) contains links to some important OneDrive folders:

- **Home:** Displays a few recommended files as well as a list of documents you've worked on recently, which you can filter by file type, name, or person.
- **My Files:** Displays all your OneDrive folders and files.
- **Shared:** Displays all your shared files. Click the With You tab to display the files other folks have shared with you; click the By You tab to display the files you've shared with others. For both types of shares, you can filter the files by type, name, or person.

- **Favorites:** Displays the files and folders you've designated as your favorites. To mark an item as a favorite, display the item, hover the mouse pointer over the item, then click the Favorite icon (shown in the margin).
- **Recycle Bin:** Displays the files and folders you've deleted. Head back to Book 8, Chapter 1, to learn how to work with the Recycle Bin to restore accidentally deleted files and folders.

The Browse Files By section of the navigation pane enables you to view your files according to the people who've shared them, the meetings in which the files were shared, and by media type.

The Quick Access section of the navigation pane offers a few links to display the files associated with some team sites and SharePoint sites.

Finally, the Storage section at the bottom of the navigation pane shows your current OneDrive storage space and how much of it you've used.

## Viewing and locating stuff in OneDrive

There might not be a ton of content in your OneDrive now, but one day you'll have more files and folders than you can shake a stick at (assuming stick-shaking is your thing). When that day comes, you'll be glad you learned the following techniques for locating OneDrive content:

- **Search:** Enter a search term in the Search box to search for a folder or file. The Search box is in the top-center of the OneDrive window. The search engine will look through the contents of files, not just look for names of files.
- **Sort:** Click the Sort button and choose an option (such as Type, Name, or Modified By) and a sort order (Ascending or Descending) to rearrange folders and files in the OneDrive window. Sorting is helpful for finding a folder or file in a long list.

- **View:** Click the Switch View Options button (shown in the margin) to switch views and then click a view:
  - *List:* Displays (refer to Figure 2-1) the folder or filename, the date it was last modified, who modified it, the size (for a file) or the number of items (for a folder), whether the item has been shared, and any recent activity for the item (the Activity column doesn't appear in Figure 2-1, in case you're wondering).
  - *Compact:* Displays the same info as List view, but with less vertical space between each line of folders and files.
  - *Tiles:* Displays the folders and files in thumbnail form (shown in Figure 2-3). Each folder displays a number representing how many files and folders it contains, and each file displays a preview of the document content. Both folders and files show the date when the item was last modified.
- **Details pane:** Select a folder or file (you might want to check out the "Selecting files and folders" section at this point) and Details to open the Details pane (shown in Figure 2-3). You can also display the Details pane by right-clicking a folder or file and choosing Details.

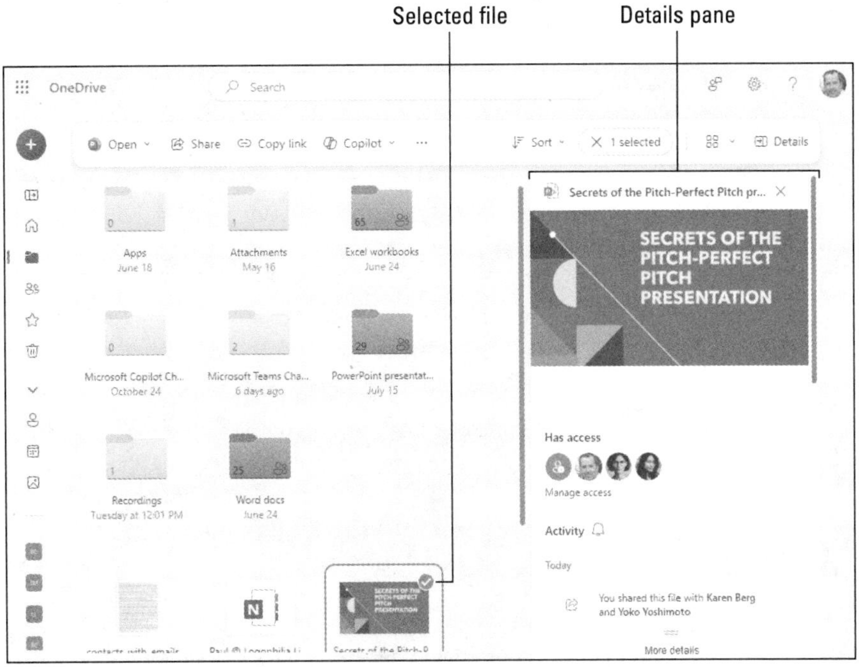


**FIGURE 2-3:** The OneDrive My Files page in Tiles view with the Details pane showing.

# Managing Your OneDrive Content

Think of OneDrive as a cloud version of your My Documents folder. OneDrive likely gives you more space, however, and you can access your files from multiple devices, even one that's not yours, such as a computer in a hotel business center or a public library.

After you accumulate a few folders in OneDrive, getting to the folder you want to open can be an arduous, interminable journey. To help you on your way, OneDrive offers several techniques for going to a folder:

- **The drill-down method:** Starting in the My Files view, click a top-level folder to display its subfolders. If necessary, keep drilling down this way until you reach the file you want to open.
- **The breadcrumb trail method:** Most file storage pages in Office 365, including SharePoint and Microsoft Teams, have a breadcrumb trail, and OneDrive is no exception. This trail lists the path to the folder that is currently open. To backtrack, click the name of a folder on the path, as shown in Figure 2-4.
- **The browser button method:** Click the Back and Forward buttons in your browser to open a folder you previously opened.

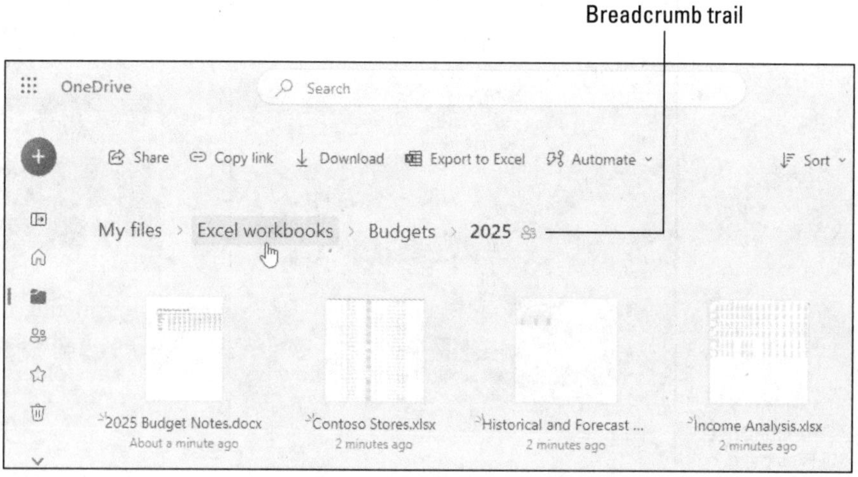


**FIGURE 2-4:** Click a folder name in the breadcrumb trail to open that folder directly.

To return to the top-level OneDrive folder, click My Files either in the breadcrumb trail or in the navigation pane.

TIP

By bookmarking a folder in your browser, you can go straight to a folder without having to navigate to it in OneDrive. After you choose the bookmark (and enter your username and password if you haven't yet signed in), the folder opens.

## Selecting files and folders

Before you can rename, delete, move, copy, or pretty much do anything with a folder or file, you first have to select it. Use these techniques to select a file or folder in OneDrive:

- **In any view:** Click the check box (it's a check circle, actually) that appears when you hover your mouse pointer over a file or folder.
- **In List view or Compact List view:** Click anywhere on the file or folder except for the name. If you click the name, OneDrive opens the file or folder instead of selecting it.

If you want to select multiple files and/or folders, use the check box method to select each item.

## Performing actions on files and folders

Each folder and file stored in OneDrive offers a very list long of actions you can perform on the item. I mean, it's a *long* list. To access the list, hover your mouse pointer over the file or folder, then click the More Actions ellipsis to display a menu like the one shown in Figure 2-5. Some of the key actions you can take from this menu are to open a file, share it, get the link to it, manage permissions, download, delete, move, copy, rename, and view the version history. Most of these features are covered in various sections in Book 8, Chapter 1.

## Creating a folder

Organizing files in OneDrive is no different than organizing them on your local hard drive. In particular, it's best to store related files in the same folder for each access. That means you need to know how to create new folders in OneDrive. Here are the steps to follow:

1. **Open your OneDrive and open the folder in which you want to create the new folder.**
2. **Click the Add New button in the navigation pane.**

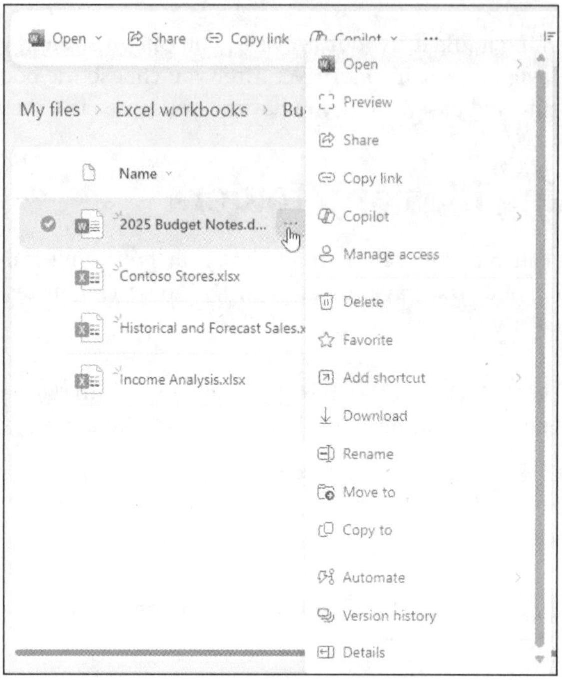


**FIGURE 2-5:** Each file and folder has a big list of actions you can perform om the item.

3. **Click Folder.**

   The Create a Folder dialog box leaps into the fray.

4. **Use the Name text box to type a moniker for your new folder.**
5. **(Optional) Click a folder color.**

   The color determines the background color of the folder's icon in OneDrive.

6. **Click Create.**

   OneDrive adds the new subfolder to the folder you opened in Step 1.

## Creating a file

You're likely used to running the New command in an Office 365 desktop app to create new files. Interestingly, you can also create fresh files from within One-Drive, which can be handy if you're already doing some file-related stuff in One-Drive. When it comes to forging new files, there are minor differences between a personal OneDrive account and a work or school OneDrive account, but they all let you create at least a Word document, Excel workbook, PowerPoint slide show, and OneNote notebook. Follow these steps to create a file in OneDrive:

1. **Open your OneDrive and open the folder in which you want to create the file.**
2. **Click the Add New button in the navigation pane.**

   OneDrive displays a menu of the file types you can create, which includes multiple Office document types.
3. **Click the type of file you want to create.**

   OneDrive opens a new tab and loads the new file into the associated web app. OneDrive provides a generic default name for the file, such as Document for a Word document, Book for an Excel workbook, and Presentation for a PowerPoint presentation.
4. **Click the generic filename to open it for editing, type a proper name for the file, and then press Enter.**

   The web app saves your file under the new name.

TIP

You can continue working with the new file in the web app. To open the file in the desktop app, click the Mode Menu button — it's right next to the Share button, as shown in Figure 2-6 — then click Open in Desktop.

**FIGURE 2-6:** To switch your new file to its desktop app, click Open in Desktop on the Mode Menu.

After a file opens in the desktop app, the AutoSave switch in the top-left of the Office app should be set to On. AutoSave indicates that all changes are automatically saved to OneDrive. So, you don't have to remember to press Save ever again if you're working on Office files from OneDrive. Bliss!

## Uploading files and folders

Creating a file or folder within OneDrive automatically stores that item in the cloud. If you want the convenience of cloud access for some of the files and folders that currently reside on your PC's hard drive, then you need to upload those items to OneDrive.

The easiest way to upload stuff to OneDrive is to first open the OneDrive folder you want to use as the destination. In File Explorer, select your files and folders (multiple folders, if you want!) and then drag and drop them into the OneDrive browser window.

After you drop your files and folders, they immediately begin uploading. Keep an eye on the progress (refer to Figure 2-7 for an example) and don't log off your computer until the upload completes. If there's already a file with the same name as one you're uploading, the progress boxwill ask what you want to do: Replace — that is, overwrite the existing OneDrive file — or Keep Both — that is, upload the file but tack "(1)" onto the name of the uploaded file. This one is important because the warning is easy to miss.

**FIGURE 2-7:** Follow the progress of your upload.

**WARNING**

If you need to upload very large files (gigabytes in size), dozens or hundreds of files simultaneously, or many very large files, don't upload this way. Instead, drag and drop the files into OneDrive in File Explorer and let the OneDrive sync tool do the work as covered in Book 8, Chapter 1; it will pause and resume syncing automatically if your computer is off or your internet connection is disrupted.

# Managing File and Folder Permissions

When you share a file or folder (as explained in Book 8, Chapter 1), you may need to adjust or revoke the sharing permissions at some point. Follow these steps to change the permissions on a file or folder:

1. **Open the OneDrive folder that contains the file or folder you want to mess around with.**
2. **Hover your mouse pointer over the file or folder and then click the More Options ellipsis that materializes.**

   OneDrive displays the More Options menu.

3. **Click Manage Access.**

   Teams dusts off and displays the Manage Access window.

4. **Adjust the permissions using one of the following techniques:**

   - To revoke access to the file for everybody, click Stop Sharing, then click Stop Sharing again when OneDrive asks if you're sure you want to do this. Note that this option is available only for files, not folders.
   - To grant access to someone, click Share to open the Share dialog box. Add the person, choose a permission level (Can Edit, Can View, or Can't Download), and then click Send.
   - To change someone's existing access, click the person in the list of people who have access. OneDrive opens a new dialog box that shows the person's current level of access. Click the current level, then either click the new permission level (Can Edit, Can View, or Can't Download), or click Remove Direct Access to revoke that person's permissions. Click Apply to make it so.

# Adding SharePoint and Teams Files to OneDrive



A high-value trick to collect your files from SharePoint and Teams in OneDrive is the Add Shortcut to OneDrive button. In a SharePoint library or folder, or the Files tab in a Teams channel, the toolbar always includes this option, and clicking the button makes the library or folder display in line with your top-level OneDrive folders. Follow these steps to add a SharePoint library or folder to your OneDrive:

1. **In SharePoint or Teams, open the library or Files tab you want to add as a shortcut.**
2. **Drill down to the folder you want to add as a shortcut (if applicable).**

   TIP

   You're more than welcome to connect the entire library (a whole Team's worth of files!), but you can also add shortcuts for individual subfolders if you don't want all the folders and files above your folder of choice mucking up your OneDrive.

3. **Click the Add Shortcut to OneDrive button in the toolbar.**

   TIP

   Alternatively, in SharePoint or Teams, hover your mouse pointer over a folder name to reveal the Add Shortcut to OneDrive icon (shown in the margin), then click that icon to add a shortcut to the folder.

You receive a notification when the shortcut is added to your OneDrive. Go back to OneDrive, and the folder or library should appear in your My Files folder, as shown in Figure 2-8. You can tell it's a shortcut because it has the arrow icon in the lower-right corner of the folder icon.

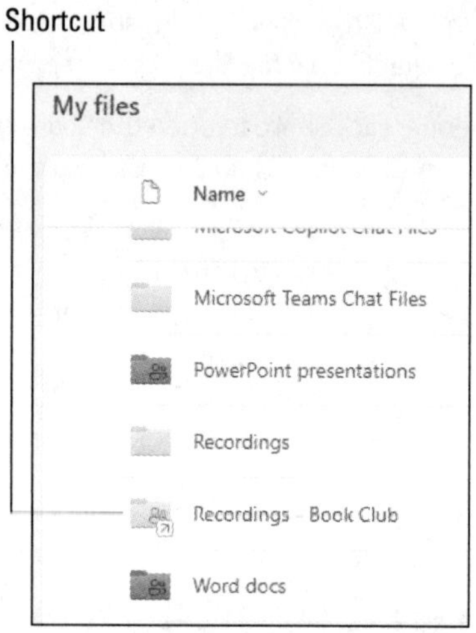


**FIGURE 2-8:** You can add SharePoint content as shortcuts to your OneDrive for easy access in the browser.

If you sync your OneDrive to your computer so that you can access your files via File Explorer, as described in Book 8, Chapter 1, the shortcut folder appears there, too, and you can save those files for offline access. This is a great option for one-off folders or libraries to which you want quick access via your OneDrive without having to sync the SharePoint files separately.

IN THIS CHAPTER

» Getting around SharePoint Online

» Making the most of a SharePoint team site

» Building pages and libraries

» Organizing libraries by metadata and views

# Chapter 3 Collaborating in SharePoint

SharePoint can be a scary term for a lot of people. It may conjure bad memories of ugly web pages, messy folder structures, and bad search results. Those memories arise from the older versions of SharePoint that were installed on local servers. SharePoint Online, however, is modern, mobile friendly, and easy to use, especially compared to its predecessor versions.

SharePoint is an advanced collaboration and publishing system that stores much of the information you might work on when using Office 365. You may not directly encounter SharePoint all that often, but it does a lot of heavy lifting in the background for many Office 365 apps, especially for work and school accounts. This chapter shows you how to create a site and pages within the site. It also covers storing and collaborating on files, managing lists of information, and taking control of who can access the files and folders stored in a SharePoint site.

## Getting Oriented with SharePoint

SharePoint Online is the Office 365 version of SharePoint; it's not a version locally installed on servers. SharePoint Online consists of *sites,* which are similar to public websites that you may use regularly, except that SharePoint in your organization is accessible only by you and your peers. Like the normal websites you're familiar with, a SharePoint site has pages and other areas to store content within the site. Organizations might create *communication sites*, which are used to publish information that needs to be widely available — like corporate policies, document templates, news, events, and resource content. An organization might also build *team sites*, which, in contrast to public websites you're familiar with, allow members to collaborate on and organize ongoing work with a project team, class, or other group. The focus of this chapter is the team site. Most of the features I discuss apply to communication sites as well, but those are likely to be in the hands of your IT or communications teams (though not always!) and are usually used for publishing finalized content to a large audience.

To get started in SharePoint, you open the SharePoint start page, which is also where you find any sites you've recently accessed or updated content in. Follow these steps to access your SharePoint start page:

1. **In your browser, type** `www.office.com` **to open the Office 365 home page.**
2. **Click the Sign In button to enter your work or school account and password to log in.**

3. **Click the app launcher (shown in the margin) and then click SharePoint.**

   The SharePoint home page appears, which lists the sites that you frequently visit, as shown in Figure 3-1.

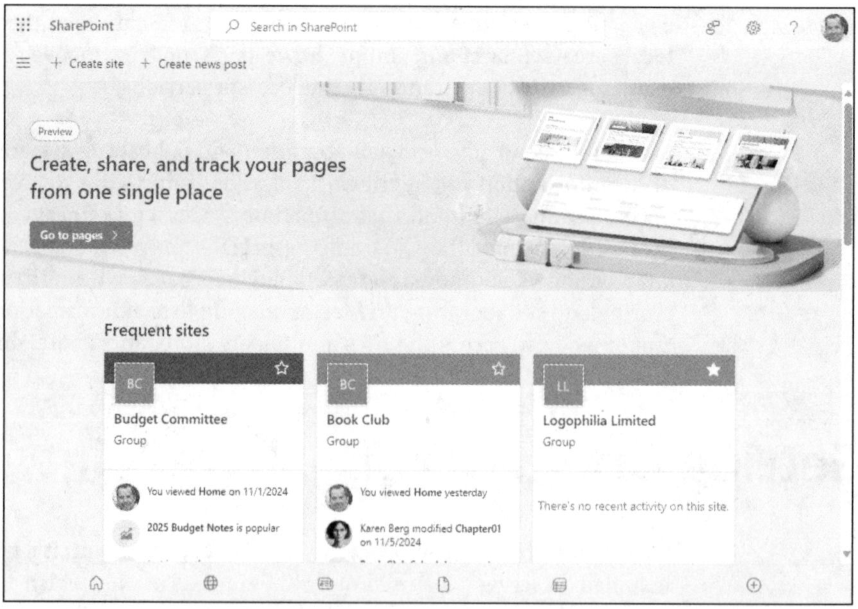


**FIGURE 3-1:** The SharePoint home page.

The SharePoint home page includes the Toggle Left Panel icon (shown in the margin) near the top-left corner. Clicking that icon displays a panel like the one shown in Figure 3-2, which gives you quick access to the following:

- **Following:** A list of the sites you follow (SharePoint's version of bookmarking). Click the See All link to view the complete list of sites you follow. To follow a site, navigate to the site and then click the Follow icon (shown in the margin) near the top-right corner of the page (the icon label changes from Not Following to Following).
- **Recent:** A list of sites you've visited recently. Click See All to display the complete list.
- **Featured Links:** A curated list of links provided by your organization that give you quick access to all the biggest and most important sites in SharePoint. If you happen to be a SharePoint admin, click the Edit link and then click Add to place a SharePoint site in this area.

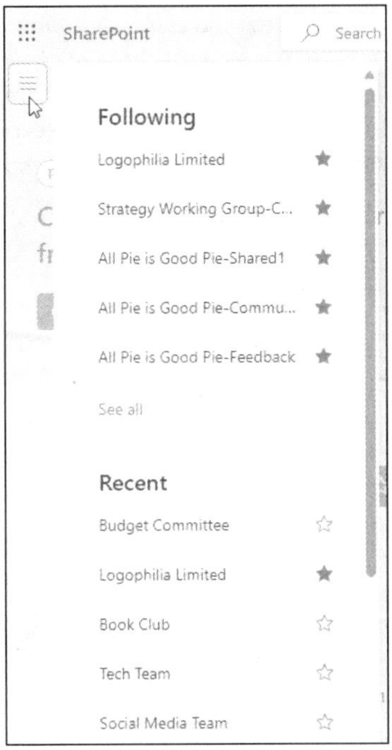


**FIGURE 3-2:** The SharePoint home page's left panel.

Each SharePoint page also features a bunch of icons along the bottom of the page. Here's what they represent:

- **Home:** Returns you to the SharePoint home page.
- **My Sites:** Opens a page with two lists: one for your frequently visited sites and one for the sites you follow.
- **My News:** Displays a list of news posts recommended to you based on sites you interact with the most. News posts are published by members of various sites and centralized on this page.
- **My Files:** Offers a list of recent files you've opened in OneDrive, SharePoint, or Teams.
- **My Lists:** Opens a page with two sections: one for the lists you've visited recently and one for the lists you've marked as favorites. Okay, so what the heck is a "list"? It's something you or another member of your organization created using the Microsoft Lists app. I discuss this app later in the "Taking a Brief Look at Microsoft Lists" section.
- **Create:** Opens a page with a list of items you can create within SharePoint. Later in this chapter you learn how to create the three main types of SharePoint items: a news post, a page, and a site. Within SharePoint you can also create five Office 365 file types: a Word document, an Excel workbook, a PowerPoint presentation, a OneNote notebook, and a Microsoft Lists list.

# Managing SharePoint Team Sites

In SharePoint, a team site plays a number of roles, including organizing files, hosting pages that provide site news and links, and building lists to track things. You may and in fact probably will be included in multiple team sites. And, as the need arises, you can create more team sites.

Team sites are great for projects, business units, classes, affinity groups, user groups, and communities of practice (for example, project managers or customer service representatives across your organization, regardless of which departments they work in).

Safely store information relevant to who has permissions in this one central spot; add and remove people as necessary; share files with outsiders if you need to; and retain a dependable, dedicated spot for all the work that's essentially "owned" by anyone who has permission to access it at any time.

## TEAM SITES VERSUS TEAMS

REMEMBER

Okay, you have team sites in SharePoint and teams in Microsoft Teams. They're the same thing, right? Nope! There's some overlap, but really you're dealing with two different concepts here. The overlapping part comes from the fact that every team in Microsoft Teams has its own SharePoint team site lurking in the background. However, the term *team site* in SharePoint doesn't derive from the word *team* as it's used in Microsoft Teams. Indeed, as you learn in this chapter, you can create a SharePoint team site by itself; a Microsoft team isn't required for a SharePoint team site to exist. In fact, the term *team site* predates Microsoft Teams; SharePoint did it first, and Teams hitched a ride. It's most unfortunate (and most confusing) that Microsoft uses *team* in these two very different contexts, but for the purposes of this chapter, unless specified otherwise, the term *team* refers a team site in SharePoint.

Many organizations remove the capability to create SharePoint sites, so you have to request a site rather than create one yourself. If that's the case, follow your IT team's guidance. But if your SharePoint home page includes the Create Site button near the top-left corner, you can follow these steps to forge a new team site:

1. **From the SharePoint home page, click Create Site in the toolbar near the top-left of the page.**

   SharePoint offers up the Create a Site: Select the Siter Type window.

2. **Click Team Site.**

   SharePoint unveils the Select a Template window.

3. **Click a template that works for your new site.**

   If your organization has created their own templates, you'll find them in the From Your Organization tab.

   SharePoint presents you with a preview of the template you chose.

4. **Click Use Template.**

   If, for some reason, the template doesn't do it for you, click Back and repeat Steps 3 and 4.

   SharePoint prompts you for a name for your new site.

5. **Type the site name.**

   Site names can be up to 256 characters long and can't include any of the following characters:

   ~ " # % & * : < > ? / \ { | } .

As you enter the site name, fields named Site Description, Group Email Address and Site Address suddenly materialize out of thin air. You need to type the site description yourself (this is optional, but I highly recommend it because it helps people understand what the site is for), but SharePoint fills in the group email address and the site address automatically (although you're free to edit these default values, if you'd like).

REMEMBER

The default group email address is your site name, with spaces and any other illegal-for-email characters removed. Of course, that's not a full email address. The actual address uses the following generic format:

```
SiteName@YourOrganizationDomain.com
```

When you add site members and owners (refer to Steps 9 and 10, below), the notifications are sent from the group email address. Emails sent to this address are automatically delivered to all the site owners and members.

If you're wondering what the term *group* means in this context, check out the section "Understanding the connection between SharePoint team sites and Microsoft 365 groups," later in this chapter, to enlighten yourself.

6. **Click Next.**

   SharePoint now asks you to specify your site's privacy settings and language.

7. **In the Privacy Settings drop-down menu, choose Private or Public, and in the Select a Language drop-down menu, choose the language of the site.**

   When selecting your privacy settings, be aware that all SharePoint users in your organizations can find public sites (for example, through the SharePoint search box); private sites can be accessed only by people who are members of the site.

8. **Click Create Site.**

   SharePoint asks you to add members to the site.

9. **(Optional) In the Add Members box, start typing a person's name, then click the person when they appear in the search results.**

   SharePoint adds the person to the list with Member permission. Members have edit access to all content in the site. You can always add members later if you want.

10. **(Optional) To change the person to an owner, click the person's permission list and then click Owner.**

    Owners have full control of a site. A good practice is to have a total of three owners: a primary, a backup, and a secondary backup. Site ownership is a real responsibility, so choose wisely. The site creator is also an owner. You can always add owners later if you want.

11. **Click Finish.**

You're now the proud owner of a new team site, which SharePoint displays for you so that you can add content, members, or whatever you feel like. Hey, it's your team site!

TIP

If your organization allows people from the outside to access your SharePoint sites, you can also add email addresses in the preceding Steps 9 and 10, making them owners or members of your team sites. You should check with your IT team to review any rules that might be in place for these situations.

## Understanding the connection between SharePoint team sites and Microsoft 365 groups

To add some complexity to an already bordering-on-complex topic, creating a team site doesn't just create a site. It creates a permission-protected collection of online workspaces called a Microsoft 365 group. The team site and group are forever linked, have the same name, and retain certain aspects that apply to both entities.

TECHNICAL STUFF

Groups have owner (full control) and member (edit) permissions across all the workspaces in various Office 365 apps that are connected to the group. The SharePoint team site just happens to be one app connected to the group, and if you create a site from SharePoint, that site was the entry point to create the group. When you create a Microsoft Team, that, too, creates a group and a site, though the group works a bit differently than when you create a team site directly. But still, the underlying concept of the group is the same.

When you create a team site in SharePoint, you get a workspace in several Office 365 apps, including the following:

- **Outlook:** Use the group email address to send emails to the group as an entity (the inbox itself) and everyone in the group. Owners can toggle settings to push emails to all members or just to the group as an entity. People external to the organization can email this address, too. Access the group inbox by clicking the team site's Toggle Navigation Pane icon (shown in the margin) and then clicking Conversations.
- **OneNote:** Each team site gets a OneNote notebook for members to use. You can create more OneNote notebooks in any of your document libraries (explained in "Creating a new document library," later in this chapter). This OneNote notebook is meant to be a quick and easy one for anyone in the site to use from the start. Access the notebook by clicking the team site's Toggle Navigation Pane icon and then clicking Notebook.

- **Planner:** Microsoft Planner is a simple but useful project-management tool that lets you assign tasks to people in a collaborative way (similarly to Trello). Each group gets a blank plan. Planner uses the Kanban project management methodology and is free. You can get to the Planner home page for your team site plan by opening the team site, clicking the team site name, clicking Apps, and then clicking Planner.

REMEMBER

You may find the Microsoft 365 group helpful as you're working in your SharePoint team site, changing permissions, or looking for other tools that might help you get work done in the team site. You get these workspaces whether you plan to use them or not, and not using them is a perfectly legitimate choice if it makes sense for you.

REMEMBER

A Microsoft 365 group is not the same thing as a shared mailbox, a security group, or a distribution group. Microsoft 365 groups are in some ways built on the shoulders of those earlier features, but they don't work the same way.

## Finding your way around a team site

When you're in a team site, the site name displays prominently on the top of every page (check out Figure 3-3). Click the Toggle Navigation Pane icon (shown in the margin) to display the navigation pane, which has the following elements:

- **Home:** Takes you back to the site's home page. (Clicking the site icon next to the site name also takes you to the home page.)
- **Conversations:** Opens the site's Outlook app, from which you can manage the site's group email.
- **Documents:** Displays the team site's document library where you can store files. It's the one document library that comes with your site, but you can add more. A document library is like a super folder and is unique to SharePoint. You can find more details about document libraries in the "Working with Document Libraries" section, later in this chapter.
- **Shared With Us:** Opens the Shared With Us page, which lists all the files that others have shared with the team site.
- **Notebook:** Opens the OneNote notebook that comes automatically with a site. You can create more notebooks.
- **Pages:** Displays the Site Pages window, which provides a list of all the pages in your site. Find more about pages in the "Working with SharePoint Pages" section, later in this chapter.

- **Site Contents:** Displays a list of all the team site's document libraries, including Site Pages and Documents. Site Contents displays everything in your site. An alternative way to display your site's contents is to click the Settings icon (shown in the margin) near the top-right corner of the page, then click Site Contents.
- **Recycle Bin**: Open the team site's Recycle Bin folder. When anything is deleted from your site, it goes to the Recycle Bin before being deleted forever. You have up to 93 days to restore a deleted file, page, or other object from the Recycle Bin. Book 8, Chapter 1, has more information on using the Recycle Bin in SharePoint.
- **Edit:** Opens the navigation pane for editing. For each item, click its ellipsis and then click a command: Edit (change the item type, address, and display name), Move Up/Move Down (move the item in the navigation pane), Make Sub Link (makes the item a second-level item of the one above it), or Remove (deletes the item). Click Save to preserve your changes. If the Edit command doesn't show up, it means you don't have the permissions to make changes.

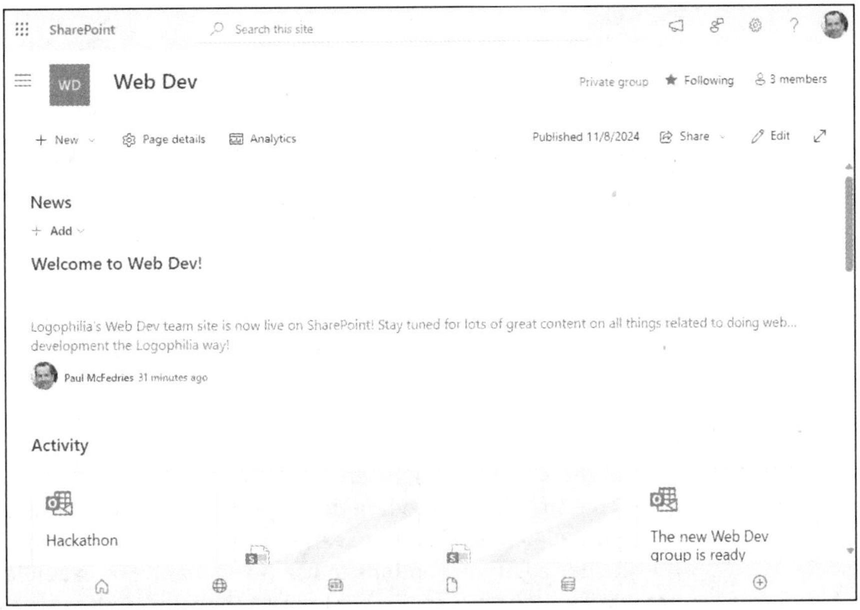


**FIGURE 3-3:** A SharePoint team site.

TIP

If you're ever looking for content in a site and you see no link for it in the navigation pane, you can always hop over to Site Contents. Unless someone removes Site Contents from the navigation pane, the link should be there. If it's not, click the Settings icon (shown in the margin) near the top-right corner of the SharePoint page and then click Site Contents.

## Adding members

If you didn't add members to your team site during setup or you want to add other people, follow these steps to make it happen:

1. **From the home page of your site, click the *X* Members link (where X is the current number of team site members) near the top-right corner of the SharePoint page.**

   SharePoint rolls down the Group Membership pane.

2. **Click Add Members.**

   The Add Members pane slides in.

3. **Use the Add Members text box to start typing a name, the click the person when their name pops up.**
4. **Click the new member's permission list and then choose a permission level: Member or Owner.**
5. **Repeat Steps 3 and 4 to add anyone else you want in the team site.**
6. **Click Save.**

   SharePoint adds the new members.

## Getting familiar with site permissions

You can't talk about SharePoint without talking about permissions. Permissions represent one of the most important, although sometimes most confusing, aspects of a SharePoint site. The biggest takeaway from this section is this: Permissions can be hard to manage, and they always require thought and planning. It takes effort to keep your permissions organized and manageable. If you don't do it, you may regret it later on — in fact, you probably will.

REMEMBER

Each SharePoint site comes with a permissions setup that owners can manage. In fact, the site permissions are built atop the Microsoft 365 group permissions (check out the "Understanding the connection between SharePoint team sites and Microsoft 365 groups" section, earlier in this chapter, for more information), but the site has additional options to use if you want. For example, the site provides permissions that are applicable only to the site; it also provides the ability for anyone in the site to share the whole site or something in the site. An owner can disable that feature, though.

Think of the basic permissions levels as buckets. The group (and therefore the site) has two buckets: one for owners, one for members. The site offers an additional bucket for visitors. If you're in the owner's bucket, you have full control of everything in the whole site (and the group); members have edit access to everything in the whole site (and the group); and visitors can read, open, and download anything in the site, but they can't make changes. If you have a Microsoft team connected to your site, the owners and members groups are the same across the team and the site.

## Adding a site visitor

When you add people to the team site during setup or after the team site is up and running, you can set each person's permission level to member or owner. What about site visitors? For them, you need to follow the steps below:

1. **From the home page of your site, click the Settings icon (shown in the margin) near the top-right corner of the SharePoint page.**

   The Settings pane appears.

2. **Click Site Permissions.**

   The Permissions pane makes an appearance. This pane offers three lists: Site Owners, Site Members, and Site Visitors. Click any list to see who has that permission level.

3. **Click Add Members and then click Share Site Only.**

   The Share Site pane enters laughing.

4. **Start typing the name of the person you want to add as a visitor, then click the person when they appear in the results.**

   SharePoint adds the person to the list of people to add.

5. **Click the Person's permission list and then click Read.**

   Technically, you can choose either Edit or Full Control. What that would mean was that the person would have either editing permission or full control of just the team site, not the rest of the associated group.

6. **(Optional) To send the person an email letting them know about their access to the team, leave the Send Email check box selected and then type a message to include in the email.**

   If an email isn't called for, deselect the Send Email check box.

7. **Click Add.**

   SharePoint adds the visitor and returns you to the Permissions pane, where you now see the person in the Site Visitors list.

## Setting permissions

There are two ways to view and manage your group and site permissions.

- To display the group owners and members, on the top-right of the site's home page, click the *X* Members link (where *X* is the total number of owners and members) to bring the Group Membership pane onto the stage. Under each person's name you see their current role: Owner or Member. You can click the role to open a drop-down menu (refer to Figure 3-4), then click a different role; click Remove from Group to remove them from the Group.

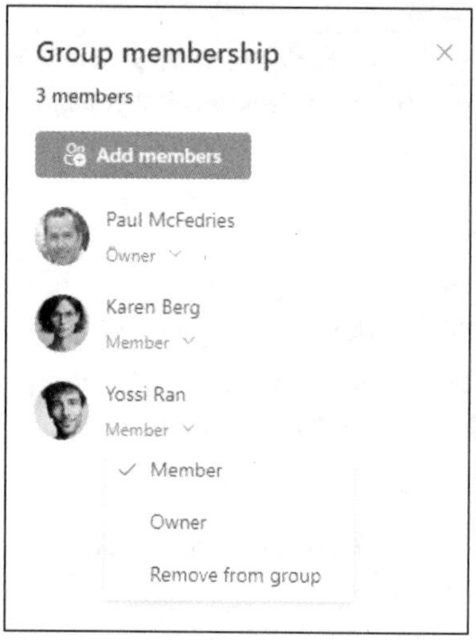


**FIGURE 3-4:** You can view (and change) each person's group permission using the Group Membership pane.

- To learn who has full control, edit access, or read access to *just* the site, click the Settings icon (shown in the margin), click Site Permissions, and in the Permissions pane, click each group name (site owners, site members, site visitors) to expand the list of people or groups in them (refer to Figure 3-5). Names and groups listed here have access to the site only, not the Group (and therefore not any of the other workspaces listed in the "Understanding the connection between SharePoint team sites and Microsoft 365 groups" section, earlier in this chapter). Click the role under a name — full control, edit, read — to open a drop-down menu to change their role if you need to; click Remove to remove them from the site.

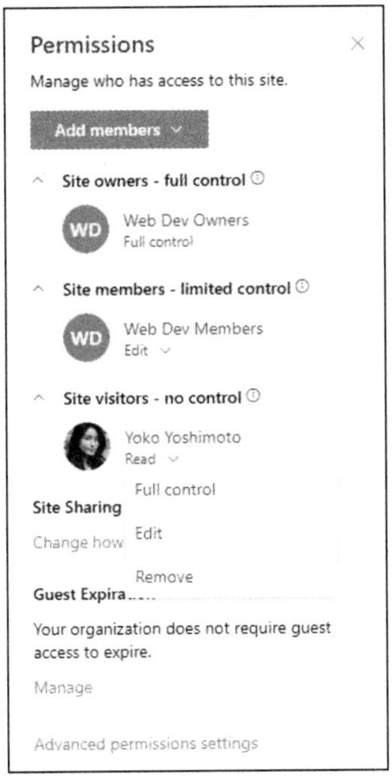


**FIGURE 3-5:** You can view (and change) each person's site permission using the Permissions pane.

## Setting content-sharing permissions

SharePoint offers even further flexibility — or complexity, depending on how you want to look at it — with member-sharing rights. Out of the gate, a team site lets members share parts of the site content as necessary — a file here, a folder there — for input or review from someone who isn't already a member of the group or site. Site owners can manage this feature by clicking the Settings icon, and then Site Permissions, and then, in the Permissions pane that appears, clicking Change How Members Can Share. When the Site Sharing Settings pane opens, you can manage these settings to meet your needs. If nothing in the site is meant to be shared, select the Only Site Owners Can Share Files, Folders, and The Site option and click Save. In that case, anyone who needs to provide input or review of any content in the site needs to be a group or site member. More on sharing files and folders later in this chapter.

## Providing permissions to people outside your organization

You can also add external people to a Microsoft 365 group or a SharePoint team site. There are two ways to do so: grant external access or guest access. Sharing a file or folder with an external person — called *external access* — is done the same way as you share with an internal person, except you use their email address in the sharing options instead of searching for a name (refer to Book 8, Chapter 1).

Granting *guest access*, on the other hand, gives an external person full access to the whole site. You add them to the group or site using the guidance in the "Adding a site visitor" section, earlier in this chapter, but use their email address when selecting the person. When someone has been given guest access, you can send them messages in Teams (if they use Teams) and add them to other sites.

TIP

Think of external access as a push: You're sending someone the file or folder. Guest access is a pull: You're bringing someone into your site to take part as any internal person can. Both your IT team and a Group owner can disable external and guest access, so don't be surprised if it doesn't appear as an option.

# Working with SharePoint Pages

Most people think of a team site as a place to store files, but it's also a great spot to post information to keep people updated and provide easy access to important resources. Pages in SharePoint fit that bill.

Creating a page doesn't require any knowledge of web development, coding, or HTML (though if you do have these skills, you can take SharePoint pages to the next level using the SharePoint Framework, which isn't covered in this book).

A good team site page can be a central point for members to access the files and links they need, or to stay up to date with news and team status. Pages can even list popular, trending, and recent files and pages so that members can know what's going on both in your team site and in other sites in SharePoint.

## Creating a page

This section presents the basic steps involved in creating a page, but subsequent sections explain more about templates as well as the various parts of a page, so you might want to continue reading before you start building pages.

Follow these steps to create a page in a SharePoint team site:

1. **From the team site's home page, click New in the page toolbar that appears under the site name.**

   If the page toolbar doesn't appear, you don't have sufficient access to create a page and need to talk to the site owner.

2. **In the drop-down menu that appears, click Page or News Post.**

   You probably want Page, unless you're posting original news articles on your site. This opens the Page Templates dialog box.

3. **Choose from the available templates.**

   TIP

   There are a few provided templates, but your organization may provide templates for you. Click a template to display a preview. You can also create a template from any page for use later in your site.

4. **Click Create Page.**

   The new page opens in Edit mode.

5. **Make your edits, add sections and web parts, and organize your information so that it's helpful to your audience.**

   Check out the rest of this section for guidance on editing the page.

6. **Click Save as Draft or Publish.**

   WARNING

   If you're not ready to share a new page or update an existing page with everyone in your site, click Save as Draft instead of Publish. Don't click Publish until everything on the page is ready to be seen by everyone in the site.

To return to editing your draft page or published page, click Edit in the page toolbar.

## Enhancing a page with web parts

Pages are composed of sections, and each section contains *web parts,* which are building blocks that you can add to a section that display the content you want to show off. When you're in edit mode on your page, you add sections to the page, then modify the section properties and content. Here's the basic procedure to follow:

1. **To add a new section to your page, click the Add Section button that appears on the bottom edge of the existing section after which you want your new section to appear.**

   SharePoint displays a list of section types.

2. **Click the type of section you want to add.**

   SharePoint inserts the section.

3. **Add a web part to the new section:**

- For most sections, click the Toolbox icon (shown in the margin) on the far-right side of the page, then click an object in the Web Parts section of the Toolbox pane that appears (refer to Figure 3-6). Notice that a toolbar appears above the web part with options for moving the web part, editing its properties, copying it, deleting it, or changing its layout.
- If your new section is multi-column, hover the mouse pointer over the first column, click the + icon that appears, then click a web part in the menu that shows up. Repeat for each of your other section columns.

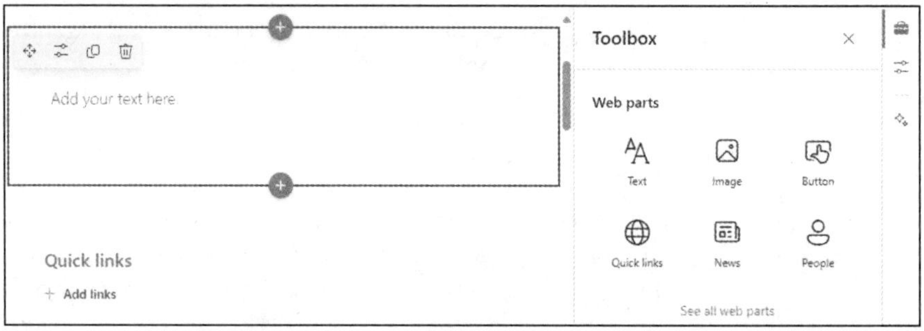


**FIGURE 3-6:** You can use the Toolbox pane to add a web part — such as Text, shown here — to a page section.

4. **Fill in the web part with text, links, or images, depending on the part type.**
5. **Click a section you want to enhance.**

6. **Click the Properties icon (shown in the margin) on the far-right side of the page.**

   SharePoint displays the Section pane (refer to Figure 3-7), which offers a few properties you can adjust for the section you selected in Step 5.

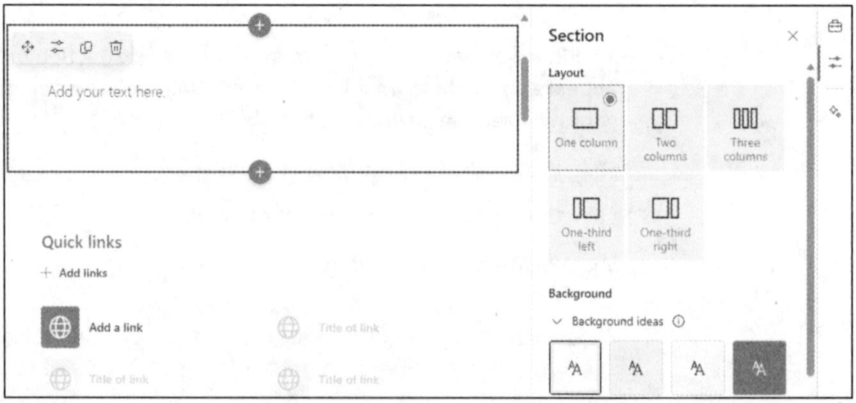


**FIGURE 3-7:** You can use the Section pane to adjust the properties of the selected page section.

7. **Modify the section properties, as you see fit.**
8. **Click the Design Ideas icon (shown in the margin) on the far-right side of the page.**

   SharePoint displays the Design Ideas pane (refer to Figure 3-8), which offers a few design suggestions for the section you selected in Step 5.

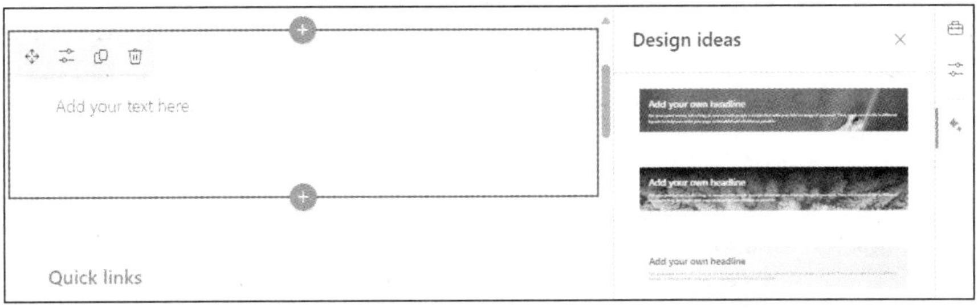


**FIGURE 3-8:** You can use the Design Ideas pane to apply a pre-fab design to the selected page section.

9. **Click the design you want to pally to the page section.**
10. **Click a web part you want to mess with.**
11. **Click the Properties icon (shown in the margin) and then use the pane that shows up (it will have the name of the selected web part) to modify the properties of the web part.**

    Not every type of web part offers properties you can play around with.
12. **Repeat Steps 1 through 11 as needed to populate your page.**

When you're ready to make your page visible to everyone in the site, click Publish. If you're working on a page that was already published, click Republish. If you're not ready to publish the page or updates, click Save as Draft instead; you can come back to it later and publish when you're ready.



# Working with Document Libraries

SharePoint is great for storing and sharing files in multiple ways. You can use folders and metadata tags for sorting and filtering, all within document libraries. In fact, document libraries are the lifeblood of a team site. A document library is like a super folder: it's the first level available to separate files from each other in any SharePoint site. Libraries can have their own permissions, columns for tagging files, and even template files called content types. Libraries also offer advanced settings that let you configure whether folders are allowed (you may want to use only metadata tags to organize your files), whether content will appear in search results, and whether Office files open in the browser app or desktop app when clicked.

Each team site comes with a default document library called Documents. To access this library, click the site's Toggle Navigation Pane icon (shown in the margin) and then click Documents. This default Documents library is where you can start storing your files from the moment your site is created. If your SharePoint team site is connected to a Microsoft team, this library is where all your channel files are stored. Each channel has an associated folder in the Documents library, but owners and members can add other folders as necessary.

You can create more libraries as needed, too. In those libraries, you can create, upload, edit, and share files and folders as well as sort, filter, and group content based on its columns. The following sections explain how to make the most of your libraries.

## Creating a new document library

It makes sense to create a new document library when you need to keep certain files and folders in a separate location, but still within your team site. Maybe you want different permissions on this library because you're sharing it with external collaborators who shouldn't have access to other libraries. Or maybe you want to add specific columns to the files in this library so that you can sort and filter your files by that unique information. Follow these steps to create a new document library:

1. **From the team site's home page, click New in the page toolbar that appears under the site name.**

   If the page toolbar is nowhere to be found, you don't have sufficient access to create a library and need to talk to the site owner.

2. **In the drop-down menu that appears, click Document Library.**

   The Create New Document Library window opens.

3. **Click how you want SharePoint to create the library:**

   - *Blank Library:* Creates a basic library.
   - *From Existing Library:* Displays the Select an Existing Document Library dialog box, from which you select the library you want to use as a starting point. Click and then click Next.
   - *Template:* Click a template to open a preview then, if you like what you see, click Use Template.

   SharePoint prompts you to name your new library.

4. **Type a name and description for your library in the appropriate boxes.**

   Keep the name short and descriptive. Don't skimp on the description; it sets the tone for what the library is intended for.

5. **Leave the Show in Site Navigation check box selected if you want the library to be displayed in the site's navigation pane.**

6. **Click the Create button.**

   SharePoint builds and then opens your new document library, just like that.

REMEMBER

As site members and owners create libraries, the libraries may or may not be added to the navigation pane, depending on the preference of the person creating the library. You can find all the document libraries created by you or anyone else in a site by clicking the Toggle Navigation Pane icon (shown in the margin) and then clicking Site Contents. Everything stored in your site is located here, including any document libraries that don't show up on the navigation pane.

## Uploading files to a document library

After you create a library, you can fill it up with good stuff. Creating and uploading files in a SharePoint library works the same as doing these things in OneDrive, which is covered in detail in Book 8, Chapter 2.

You have various options for adding things to your library:

- **To create folders and Office files:** From the library toolbar, click New and then click Folder or the file type you want to create.
- **To upload multiple files or a single folder from your computer:** From the library toolbar, click Upload and then click either Files or Folder.
- **To upload multiple files and multiple folders from File Explorer:** Select the files or folders in File Explorer and drag them into the library to upload them. You can upload multiple folders this way, which you can't do using the Upload button. Check out Book 8, Chapter 2, for more details.
- **To sync the contents of a library to a device:** You can access your SharePoint files right in File Explorer if you've installed and configured the OneDrive app. Once set up, you can open and edit SharePoint files even if you're offline. Book 8, Chapter 1 is the place to go for more on setting up syncing, and Book 8 Chapter 2 is where I talk about adding SharePoint and Teams files to your OneDrive.

## Opening and editing a file in a document library

You can open Word, Excel, PowerPoint, and OneNote files from within your document library. Click a file's name to open it for viewing or editing in the web version of the app. If you want to open an Office 365 file in the desktop app, select the file by clicking it anywhere except the name, click Open in the toolbar, then click Open in App. (Alternatively, hover your mouse pointer over the file, click the ellipsis that shows up to open the More Actions menu, click Open, and then click Open in App.) Doing so launches the desktop app and opens the file for you. All changes you make to an Office file opened from a SharePoint library are saved automatically.

You can also open other popular file types — such as PDFs, images, videos, and Photoshop files — from within the document library. They open in the browser for you to view, but not edit. Sync the library to your device to be able to open a file from File Explorer in its respective app, especially if you need to edit it. For example, you can open synced images in the Windows Photos app, Photoshop files in Photoshop, and PDFs in Adobe Acrobat to make changes and save them. Updates to files will automatically sync back to SharePoint so that the next person to open them will get the updated version.

## Sharing files from a document library

Just as you can with OneDrive, you can share files and folders from a document library. Additionally, you can share the entire library itself if you want. Keep in mind, though, that a SharePoint team site is meant for collaborative work; ad hoc sharing of individual files and folders isn't really recommended. Instead, consider making a person a member of the site so that they can access the content they need.

Still, some situations require one-off sharing. Breaking permissions can quickly become a nightmare for the site owner, though, so it's best to discuss sharing before your group starts doing it.

Sharing is generally done internally, to people inside your organization who have accounts. However, if your site is set up to allow external sharing, you can also share the content to anyone with an email address. The next section covers how to change the permissions of your document library.

### Managing permissions of a document library

In this section, I take you through the procedures for providing access to an entire document library to people who can't already access the SharePoint team site (you likely have to be a site owner to perform these tasks).

First, follow these steps to stop the document library from inheriting its permissions:

1. **From the document library, click the Settings icon (shown in the margin) near the top-right corner of the page.**

   The Settings pane rumbles in.

2. **Click Library Settings.**

   SharePoint coughs up the Library Settings pane.

3. **Click More Library Settings.**

   SharePoint reveals the full complement of library settings.

4. **Under the Permissions and Management column in the center of the page, click Permissions for this Document Library.**

   The Library Permissions page opens, where you can change a person's or group's existing permissions or add new people individually.

5. **Click the Stop Inheriting Permissions button in the Ribbon and click OK when SharePoint asks if you're sure about this.**

REMEMBER

The permissions of this library are now disconnected from the SharePoint team site, so if you make changes to the site permissions, they will not apply to this library. The library is now an island when it comes to access.

To change existing permissions, follow these steps:

1. **Select the check box next to a person's or group's name.**
2. **Click Edit User Permissions in the Ribbon.**

   The Edit Permissions page appears.

3. **Select the check box for each permission level you want to apply.**

   Stick to the Full Control, Contribute, or Read options unless you're familiar with what the other options do.

4. **Click OK.**

   SharePoint applies the new permissions.

If you want to revoke the permissions of a person or group, select their check box and then click Remove User Permissions in the Ribbon.

Finally, you can create new permissions for the document library by following these steps:

1. **Click Grant Permissions in the Ribbon.**

   The Share dialog box opens, where you can invite people or groups.

2. **In the Enter Names or Email Addresses box, type names of individuals or groups and then click their name when they pop up in the suggestions.**

   If you're inviting people from outside your organization (called "guests" in this context), enter their email addresses individually. Depending on your IT policy, you may or may not have the ability to invite guests. Head back to Book 8, Chapter 1, for more information.

3. **(Optional) Use the large text box to type a message that will be sent with the invitation.**

4. **(Optional) Deselect the Share Everything in This Folder, Even Items with Unique Permissions check box if you don't want the new people to access files or folders that don't inherit permissions from the library.**

   Because anyone in a site can share a file with people outside of the site or library, some content in the library may not have the same permissions as the library itself. If this box is selected, the people you're giving permissions to will be able to access those things anyway. If you deselect this box, the content with unique permissions will not show up for the people you're adding here.

5. **Click Show Options.**

   SharePoint expands the dialog box to display a few more options.

6. **(Optional) Deselect the Send an Email Invitation check box if you don't want to send an automated email to everyone you're giving permissions to.**

   If you're giving permissions to a large group of people, you may not want to send an email out to all those people automatically. Be sure that sending the email makes sense.

7. **In the Select a Permission Level drop-down menu, select which level of access these people will be given.**

   The full control, edit, and read options are the most common selections. The other options are outside the scope of this book.

8. **Click the Share button.**

   The permissions are changed and an email notification goes out to everyone if you left the Send an Email Invitation check box selected in Step 6. If you decided not to send an automated email and the people you added need to know about the library, you should send them a message with a link to the library.

## Sharing a file or folder

In many cases, you just want to share a folder or file in a library. That's a lot easier than dealing with site or library permissions and access issues, and it's something all site owners and members can do.

To share a file or folder in a library, hover your mouse pointer over the file or folder and then click the Share icon (shown in the margin) that fades in. In the Share dialog box that appears, you can choose who needs access and what level of permission they get. The Share dialog box is exactly the same as the one used in OneDrive, so refer back to Book 8, Chapter 2 to learn about the various sharing possibilities.

# Viewing file and folder options

Just as with OneDrive, you have a number of options you can manage for your files and folders. Click the vertical ellipsis to the right of a folder or filename to open the Show Actions menu and display all the options. This menu gives you the ability to download, delete, move, copy, rename, view the version history of a file, and more. Chapter 2 of this mini-book provides more detail into what options are available and what they do.

You can also use Pin to Top to pin up to three files or folders at the top of the page for each folder level in your library. Click Alert Me to get an email when new files are created or existing ones are edited or deleted. Click Check Out to reserve a file for editing just by you (though this concept doesn't allow coauthoring, so it might not suit the practices of your organization).

# Working with columns and views

One big advantage of document libraries in SharePoint is the ability to tag files with *metadata*, which is information *about* a file, like filename, file size, date it was created, who created it, date it was edited last, who edited it last, and so on. Metadata shows up in a library as columns. And you can add custom metadata, too, like document type, customer, or project name to tag files with appropriate categories.



With this information, you can sort, filter, and group your files into views so that you can display the correct files when you need to. For example, maybe you want to categorize all files based on which office branch manages the file so that you can group the files by office branch, then sort them by file type, and filter out files that weren't edited in a given quarter. You have a lot of power to find your files quickly and display them smartly if you put a little time into designing a robust metadata setup.

## Creating or showing a column in a library

When you create or open a library, three columns automatically display under the library toolbar: Name (filename); Modified (when the file was last edited); and Modified By (who edited the file last). You can add more columns to serve your needs. You can reorder columns by clicking and dragging the column title left or right.

To create or show a column in your library, click +Add Column, which is on the right end of the column headers in your library. The Create a Column pop-up that appears (refer to Figure 3-9) provides options that let you either create a new column or show existing columns that SharePoint provides automatically, but are hidden by default.

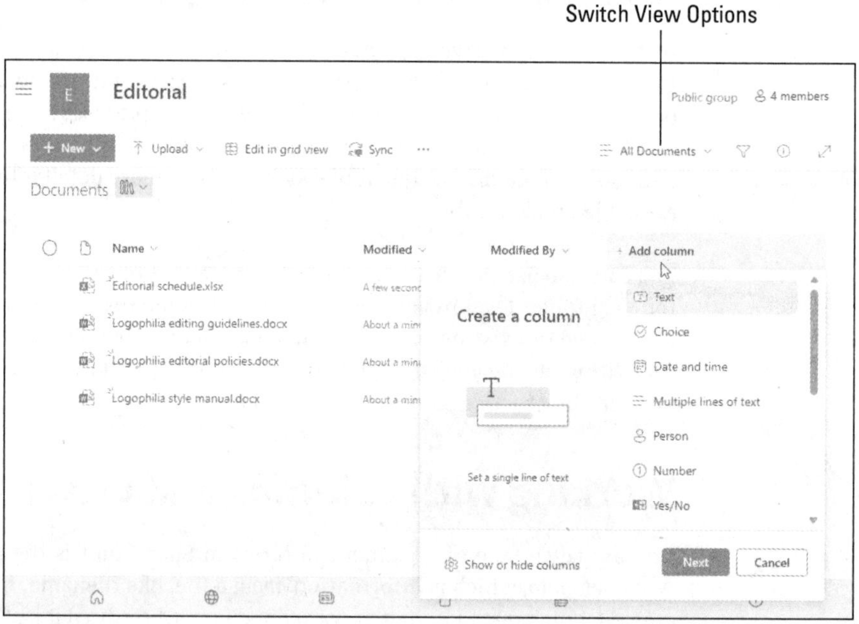


**FIGURE 3-9:** Click Add Column to add custom columns to a document library.

Use the following techniques to modify your library columns:

» **To show an existing column:** Click Show/Hide Columns to open the Edit View Columns pane. In the pane that appears, select the check box next to each column that you want to display. When you're done, click the Apply button at the top of the pane to display your new columns in the library.

» **To create a new column:** Click one of the column types in the menu, click Next, use the Create a Column pane that shows up to provide the required information for your column type, then click Save. I can't cover all the options in this chapter, but Choice columns are great for identifying the status of a file and dividing content by organizational or regional hierarchy. People columns are useful for identifying owners of files, or who is expected to perform the next action in a task. Date columns are great for delivery dates. You can explore a number of other column types.

Metadata can't be applied to folders, so if you're going to make strong use of metadata columns in a library, you may want to avoid using folders because they can muck up the experience. Plus, you don't *need* folders if you're using metadata. A folder is basically just another type of metadata tag, but unlike metadata, you can put a file in only one folder; you can tag a file with as much metadata as you want, meaning you can sort, filter, and group your files into whatever collection makes sense for *right now.* When someone sets up a folder structure, everyone using it is kind of stuck with a structure that made sense back when it was created, but it may not make as much sense now. Metadata is more flexible.

## Creating saved views of your organized information

When you have columns set up in your library, click any of the column names to open a menu that lets you sort, filter, and possibly group by the content in those columns. You can organize the information the way you want and then save that layout as a view. You can create multiple views that display different combinations of sorts, filters, or groupings as well.

A saved view is useful to get quick access to a selection of files that's been sliced and diced to show only the ones that are relevant to that view, like having a folder for all contracts signed in a given year. With metadata, you can create a view that automatically filters a custom column called Document Type to display only contracts, and another custom column called Agreement Year to display only files for that year. Together, these two filters display only contracts from that year.

With metadata, you can tag your files by project, customer, document type, year, and any other tags that make sense. Then sort and filter any appropriate columns to show you all the files that have the tags, and save this information as a view.

SharePoint opens a document library in a default view called the All Documents view, which appears in the Switch View Options list, pointed out earlier in Figure 3-9. To save the current view as a new view, click Switch View Options and then click Save View As. In the Save As dialog box, give your view a name. If you deselect the Make This a Public View check box, it means your saved view is visible only to you. Click Save.

You can continue to modify the layout with different sorting, filtering, and grouping preferences, and create more views based on them as the need arises. All the views for the library are listed in the View menu.

# Taking a Brief Look at Microsoft Lists

I don't have the space in this chapter to cover the Microsoft Lists app in detail, but it's a useful feature to know about. Microsoft Lists is an Office 365 app that builds on a SharePoint feature (also called Lists) with new branding and prettier features. A list is like a document library, but without the files. A list consists of columns and rows containing information organized in a web-friendly way. You can keep these lists in your SharePoint sites.

Lists are useful for tracking, planning, and organizing projects, events, and items. You can sort, filter, and group information into views just as you can in a document library. You can find all Microsoft Lists that were created in a SharePoint team site by going to Site Contents, which you can access either from the navigation bar or by clicking the Settings gear icon.

TIP

The Microsoft Lists app centralizes all your lists from across Office 365. You may use different lists in various SharePoint sites, and you might have some that you've created in your OneDrive for your own use. Easily accessing them all from one place was impossible until Microsoft Lists was introduced; now you don't have to hop from SharePoint site to SharePoint site to display the various lists you might be working on.

You find the Lists app by clicking the Office 365 app launcher in the top-left corner of the suite bar. If Lists doesn't display in the app launcher, click More Apps to find and open the app. The Microsoft Lists home page shows all your recent lists. Click the star on a list to make it a favorite and save it at the top of the page for easy access. You can create lists from here as well.

To create a list, you have two choices:

- On the Microsoft Lists home page, click the New List button.
- In SharePoint, click Create (shown in the margin) in the lower-right corner of the page and then click List.

Either way, the Create a List window joins the fray, as shown in Figure 3-10.

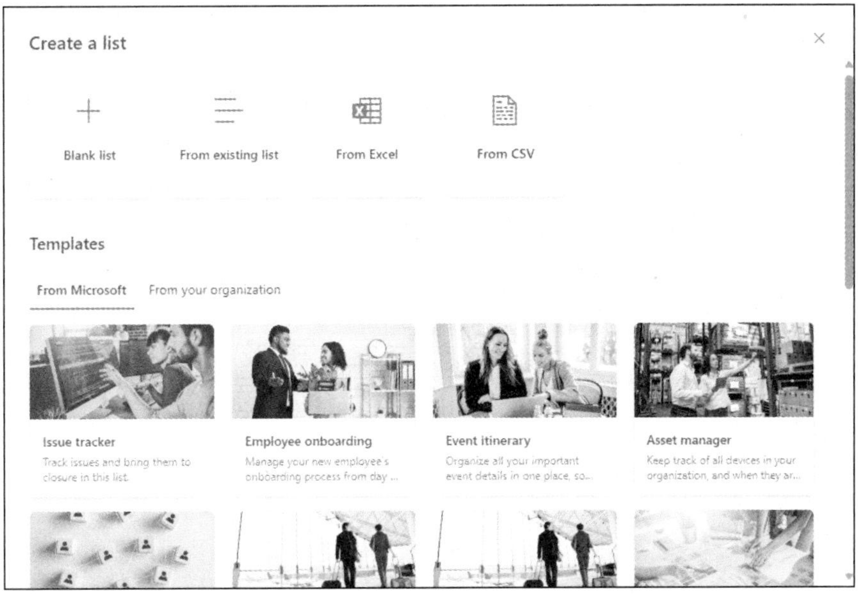


**FIGURE 3-10:** Create a list using existing lists or files (top) or a template (bottom).

Microsoft provides a number of templates for specific uses that already include useful columns. Select one to display a preview of the list template, as shown in Figure 3-11. If you like what you see, click Use Template to create your list from that template. Otherwise, you can create the list from scratch, from an existing list, or you can import either an existing Excel workbook or a comma-separated values (CSV) file. These options are shown at the top of Figure 3-10.

WARNING

When you create a list from the Lists home, make sure you always choose the correct place for it to be created. Many people mistakenly create a list in their OneDrive when they intended to create it in a SharePoint site. If the list is not created in a site, the list isn't accessible to the people who have permissions to that site. You can avoid this problem altogether by creating a list directly in the SharePoint site where it belongs. When you create a list in a site, everyone who has access to the site also has access to the list. After the list is created, it shows up in your Lists app.

TIP

You can find many resources online for guiding you on creating your list, including a number of formatting templates for showing completion status, displaying items in a bulletin board, or creating a custom profile card.

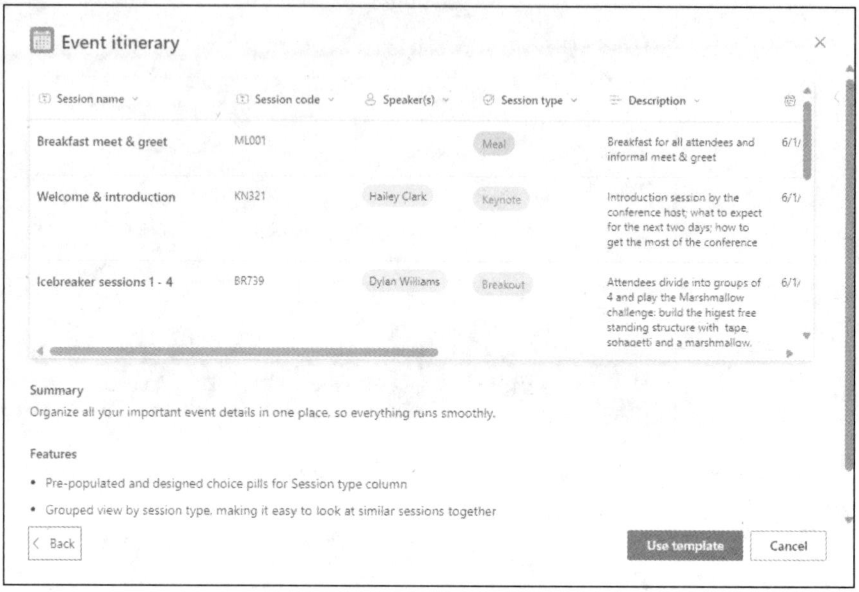


**FIGURE 3-11:** If you select a template to start from, Lists shows the included columns and dummy information as inspiration.

IN THIS CHAPTER

» Controlling file access

» Editing and commenting on other people's files

» Accepting or rejecting suggested edits

» Dealing with comments

# Chapter 4
# Collaborating on Documents

Whether you're a company employee, a consultant, or a freelancer, you almost certainly work with other people in one capacity or another. Most of the time, your work with others is likely pretty informal and consists of ideas exchanged during video meetings, chats, or email messages. However, the modern business world often calls upon people to work with others more closely by collaborating with them on a file, such as a document, a spreadsheet, or a presentation. This work can involve commenting on another person's spreadsheet, editing someone else's document, or dividing a presentation among multiple authors. For all these situations, Office 365 offers a number of powerful collaborative tools. In this chapter, you explore how to use, and get the most out of, these tools.

## Protecting a Document from Mischief

Perhaps you want to submit your file to others for critical review but don't want just any Tom, Dick, or Harriet to look at your file. In that case, Office 365 offers several methods for preventing unauthorized changes to a file.

# Opening a document as read-only

If your goal is to prevent accidental changes to a document, perhaps the easiest way to go about it is to open the document as read-only. You can still make changes to the document, but the only way to save those changes is to use the Save As command to save as a different file.

If you're opening the file yourself, you can open it as read-only by following these steps:

1. **Choose File ➪ Open (or press Ctrl+O).**

   The Open window of the Backstage view appears.

2. **Click Browse.**

   The Open dialog box clocks in.

3. **Open the folder containing the document and then click the document.**

4. **Click the Open button's drop-down list and then click Open Read-Only, as shown in Figure 4-1.**

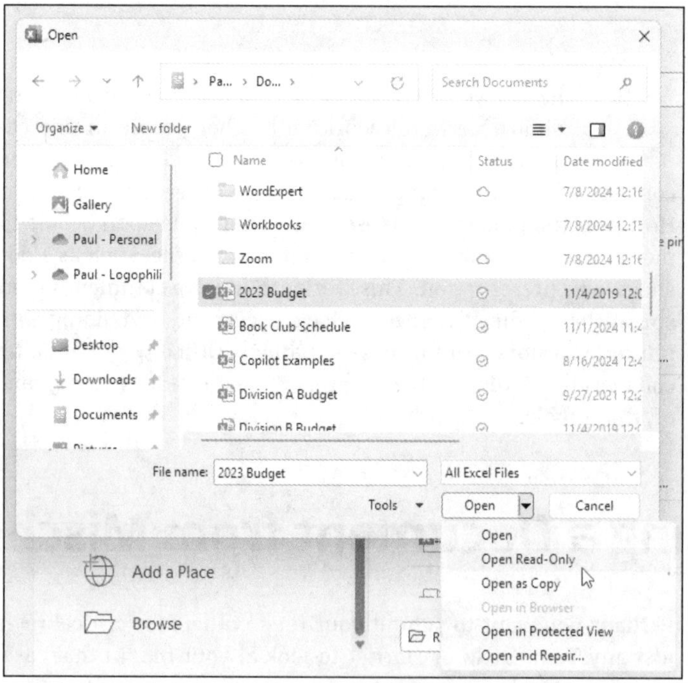


**FIGURE 4-1:** In the Open list, click Open Read-Only to open a document as read-only.

When the application opens the document, it displays "Read Only" beside the document name in the title bar.

If other people will be opening the document, you can add an extra level of safety by telling Word and Excel to recommend that the document be opened as read-only. Follow these steps:

1. **Choose File ➪ Save As.**

   If you're working with a OneDrive file, choose File ➪ Save a Copy, instead.

   The Backstage view's Save As (or Save a Copy) window shows up.

2. **Click Browse.**

   The app fires up the Save As dialog box.

3. **Click Tools and then click General Options.**

   The General Options dialog box appears.

4. **Select the Read-Only Recommended check box.**
5. **Click OK.**
6. **Click Save.**

   The app asks you to confirm you want to replace the file.

7. **Say, "But of course!" and click Yes to finish saving the document.**

When you attempt to open the document now, Word or Excel displays the READ-ONLY information bar under the Ribbon, as shown in Figure 4-2. Close this bar to continue working with the document as read-only. If you want to make changes to the document, you can click Edit Anyway, instead.

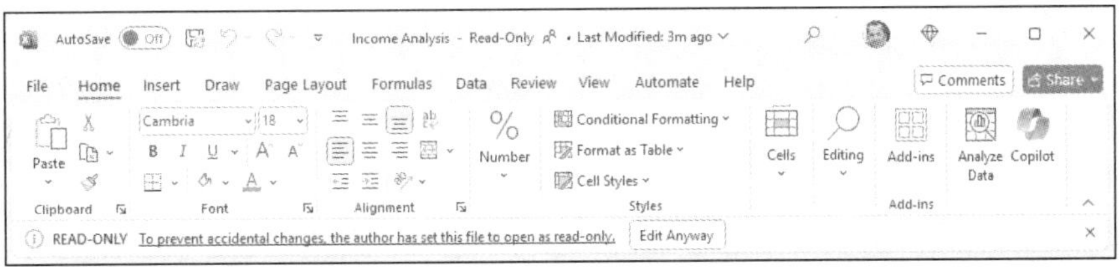


**FIGURE 4-2:** Word or Excel displays this information bar when opening a document that has the Read-only Recommended option activated.

## Marking a document as final

Marking a document as read-only, as I discuss in the previous section, is easily bypassed, but at least the read-only state sends a message that you don't want the file messed with. A slightly stronger message to send is to mark the document as final, which tells everyone that this is the final version of the file. Marking a document as final also prevents typing in the document and disables editing commands.

Is your document truly protected when it's marked as final? Alas, no, anyone who opens the file can easily click a button to edit the document anyway. But by telling users the document is the final version, you at least discourage editing.

Here are the steps to follow to save a document as final:

1. **Open the document you want to work with and make any final edits or format changes.**
2. **Choose File ⇨ Info.**

   The backstage view's Info window appears.
3. **Click the Protect Document (in Word), Protect Workbook (in Excel), or Protect Presentation (in PowerPoint) button, and then click Mark As Final.**

   The app informs you that the file will now be saved and then marked as final.
4. **Say, "Good to know!" and then click OK.**

   The app informs you that the file has been marked as final.
5. **Say, "Okay, okay, I get it!" and then click OK.**

As shown in Figure 4-3, marking a document as final displays the MARKED AS FINAL information bar, disables every option in the Ribbon that would change the document in any way, and prevents editing the document text. Ah, but notice the Edit Anyway button in the information bar. Clicking that button enables all the Ribbon controls as well as document editing.

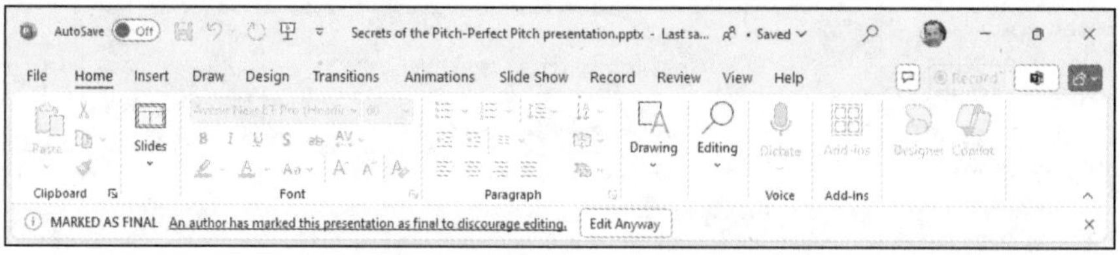


**FIGURE 4-3:** When you mark a document as final, you can't edit the document text and most of the app's Ribbon controls are disabled.

# Protecting a document with a password

In the previous couple of sections, I talked about saving a document as read-only and marking a document as final. Both techniques prevent casual editing of a document, which might be all the protection you need. However, both protections are easily bypassed. What do you do if you *really* don't want unauthorized folks to make any changes to a document?

For that scenario, you need to slap a password on the document. That way, you prevent unauthorized changes by other users, but you (or anyone else to whom you provide the password) can still make changes.

You can assign passwords to Word documents, Excel workbooks, and PowerPoint presentations. In each case, you have two choices:

- **Password to open:** This password is required to view the document. If the user doesn't have this password, they can't even open the document.
- **Password to modify:** This password is required to edit the document's contents. If the user doesn't have this password, they can open the document, but they can't change it in any way.

REMEMBER

The password you use should be a minimum of eight characters (longer is better) and should be a mix of letters and numbers. Note, too, that the Office applications differentiate between uppercase and lowercase letters, so remember the capitalization you use.

## Assigning a password to open a document

If you assign a password to open a document, the program uses the password as a key to encrypt the document contents. The only way to view the document is to supply the password. Here are the steps to follow to assign a password to encrypt a Word document, an Excel workbook, or a PowerPoint presentation:

1. **Choose File ➪ Save As.**

   If you're working with a OneDrive file, choose File ➪ Save a Copy, instead.

   The backstage view's Save As (or Save a Copy) window appears.

2. **Click Browse.**

   The app fires up the Save As dialog box.

3. **Click Tools and then click General Options.**

   The General Options dialog box appears.

4. **In the Password to Open text box, type the password.**

   WARNING

   If you forget your password, there's no way to recover it, so you'll never be able to access your document. Therefore, make sure the password you use is memorable.

5. **Click OK.**

   The Confirm Password dialog box pops up to prompt you to reenter the password for opening the document.

6. **Retype the password.**
7. **Click OK.**

   The app returns you to the Save As dialog box.

8. **Click Save.**

   The app asks you to confirm you want to replace the file.

9. **Say, "Duh!" and click Yes to finish saving the document.**

## Assigning a password to modify a document

If you assign a password to modify a document, the only way to make changes to the document is to supply the password. Here are the steps to follow to assign a password to control the modification of a Word document, an Excel workbook, or a PowerPoint presentation:

1. **Choose File ⇨ Save As.**

   If you're working with a OneDrive file, choose File ⇨ Save a Copy, instead.

   The backstage view's Save As (or Save a Copy) window appears.

2. **Click Browse.**

   The app fires up the Save As dialog box.

3. **Click Tools and then click General Options.**

   The General Options dialog box appears.

4. **In the Password to Modify text box, type the password.**
5. **Click OK.**

   The Confirm Password dialog box pops up to prompt you to reenter the password for modifying the document.

6. **Retype the password.**
7. **Click OK.**

   The app returns you to the Save As dialog box.

8. **Click Save.**

   The app asks you to confirm you want to replace the file.

9. **Say, "Here goes nothing!" and click Yes to finish saving the document.**

In this case, when someone opens the file, Excel prompts them for the password to modify the file. If the user doesn't know the password, they can still view the file by clicking the Read Only button, shown in Figure 4-4.

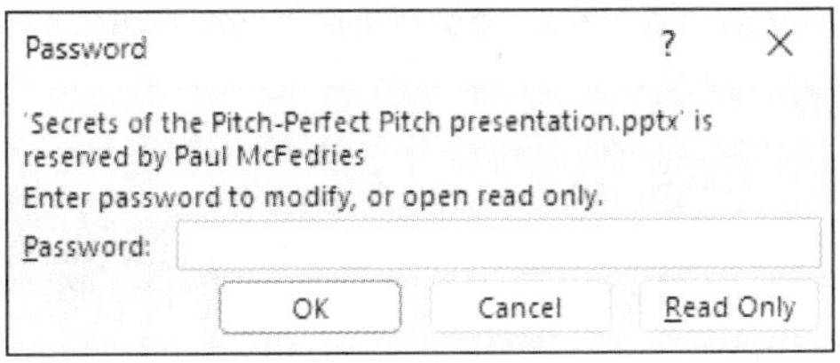


**FIGURE 4-4:** When you open a document with a modification password, either type the password or click Read Only to view the document.

## Encrypting a document

If you have a file that's particularly sensitive, you can add an extra layer of protection by encrypting the file's contents with a password. Here's how:

1. **Open the document you want to protect.**
2. **Choose File ⇨ Info.**

   The backstage view's Info window appears.

3. **Click the Protect Document (in Word), Protect Workbook (in Excel), or Protect Presentation (in PowerPoint) button, and then click Encrypt with Password.**

   The Encrypt Document dialog box makes an appearance.

4. **Type a password and then click OK.**

   WARNING: If you forget your password, you'll never be able to access your document. Therefore, make sure the password you use is memorable.

   The app asks you to enter your password again.

5. **Retype the password and then click OK.**

   The app encrypts the document.

To remove the password (and the encryption) from a document, open the document, choose File ➪ Info, click the Protect Document (or Workbook or Presentation) button, click Encrypt with Password, delete the password, and then click OK.

# Commenting on a Word Document

If someone asks for your feedback on a Word document, you could write that feedback in a separate document or in an email message. However, feedback is most useful when it appears in the proper context. That is, if you have a suggestion or critique of a particular word, sentence, or paragraph, the reader will understand that feedback more readily if it appears near the text in question. To do that in Word, you insert a *comment*, a separate section of text that's associated with some part of the original document.

Comments appear in the Comments pane on the right side of the screen or in balloons as well, if you so choose (check out "Viewing and displaying comments," later in this chapter). Figure 4-5 shows a Word document with a few comments displayed in the Comments pane.

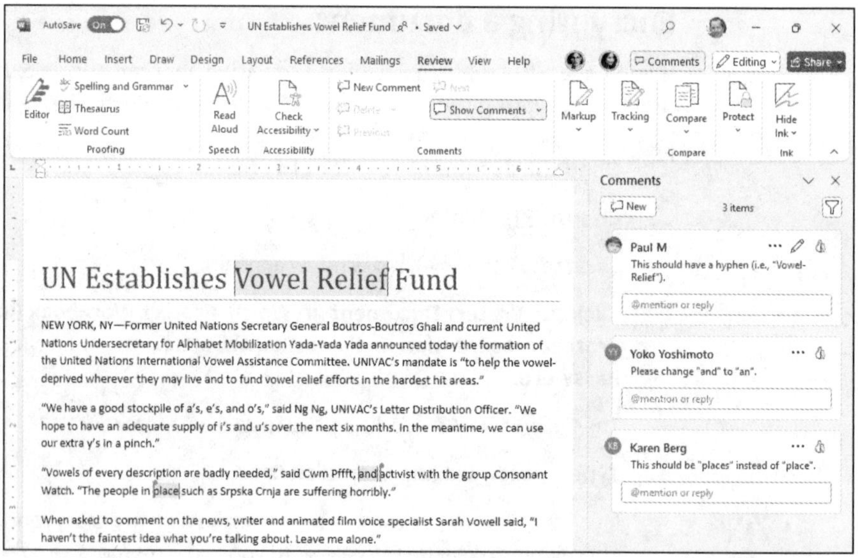


**FIGURE 4-5:** Comments in the Comments pane.

## Entering comments

In my experience, Print Layout view is the best view for entering and reading comments. Comments are marked with the writer's name, the writer's initials, and the date on which the comment was made. Follow these steps to write comments in Print Layout view:

1. **Select the text you want to comment on.**

   If you want to comment on a particular word, you can position the cursor within or immediately to the left or right of the word.

2. **Use one of the following techniques to tell Word you want to enter a comment.**

   - Click the Comments button in the upper-right corner of the screen to display the Comments task pane; then click the New button. The Comments task pane appears, and Word adds a new comment to the pane.
   - On the Review tab, in the Comments group, click the New Comment button. A balloon for entering a comment appears on the right side of the Word window.

3. **Type your comment.**

4. **Click the Post Comment button (shown in the margin; or press Ctrl+Enter).**

   Word adds your comment to the Comments pane and adds a highlight to the text you selected in Step 1.

TIP

Each comment lists the name of the person who wrote it. If a comment you wrote doesn't list your name, go to the File tab, click Options, and enter your username in the General tab of the Word Options dialog box. Select the Always Use These Values Regardless of Sign In to Office check box if you are enrolled in Office 365 and you sign in to `Office.com` under a different name than the one you entered.

## Viewing and displaying comments

The makers of Word want you to be able to view comments when necessary but shunt them aside when comments get in the way. To tell Word how to display comments, go to the Review tab and then, in the Comments group, use the following techniques:

- **Toggle comments on and off:** Click the Show Comments button.
- **Control where comments appear:** Click the drop-down area next to the Show Comments button, then click either Contextual (to display comments as balloons to the right of the associated document text) or List (to display comments as a list in the Comments pane).

## Replying to and resolving comments

To reply to and resolve comments, first display comments in balloons on the right side of the screen or as a list in the Comments task pane (refer to the previous section). Then do the following:

- **Replying to a comment:** Type your reply in the comment's @mention or Reply text box and then click the Post Reply button (shown in the margin; or press Ctrl+Enter). If you want someone in your organization to be notified about the reply, you can @mention that person as part of your response.
- **Resolving a comment:** In the comment, click the More Thread Actions button (the ellipsis) and then click Resolve Thread. Resolving the thread means that the comment is closed to further replies.

## Caring for and feeding comments

Here are a few useful comment-related tasks to help manage your comments:

- **Editing a comment:** In one of your comments (you can't edit other people's comments, however much you might like to), click the Edit Comment icon (shown in the margin). Edit the text, then click Post Comment (the checkmark; or press Ctrl+Enter).

- **Liking a comment:** Click the comment's Like icon (shown in the margin).
- **Going from comment to comment:** On the Review tab, in the Comments section, use the Previous and Next buttons to leap backwards and forwards through the comments.
- **Displaying comments by a specific reviewer:** On the Review tab, in the Markup group, click the Show Markup button, click Specific People, and deselect All Reviewers on the submenu. Choose Show Markup ⇨ Specific People, and then click the name of the reviewer you want to show. To display all comments again, choose Show Markup ⇨ Specific People ⇨ All Reviewers.
- **Deleting comments:** Delete one, all, or some comments:
  - **Deleting a comment:** Click the comment then, on the Review tab, in the Comments group, click the Delete button. You can also click the comment's More Thread Actions button (the ellipsis) and then click Delete Thread.
  - **Deleting all the comments in the document:** On the Review tab, in the Comments group, open the drop-down list on the Delete button and then click Delete All Comments in Document.

- **Deleting all the resolved comments in the document:** On the Review tab, in the Comments group, open the drop-down list on the Delete button and then click Delete All Resolved Comments.
- **Deleting comments made by specific reviewers:** First, isolate comments made by people whose comments you want to delete (refer back to "Displaying comments by a specific reviewer," earlier in this list). Then, on the Review tab, in the Comments group, open the drop-down list on the Delete button and click Delete All Comments Shown.

# Tracking Changes to Documents

A higher level of collaboration occurs when you ask another person to make changes to a document. That is, rather than suggesting changes by using comments, as I talk about in the previous section, the other person makes the changes directly in the document. This method can save you a ton of time and effort, but it can also lead to problems if you don't know what parts of the document the user edited. For example, without knowing what the user changed, you have no way of checking the changes for style or for factual errors.

To avoid such problems, you can have Word track all the changes made to a document. This means that any time you or another person makes changes to the original text — including adding, editing, deleting, and formatting the text — Word keeps track of the changes and shows not only what changes were made, but who made them and when.

When Word's Track Changes feature is activated:

- Changes to a document are recorded in a different color, with one color for each reviewer.
- New text is underlined; deleted text is crossed out. (If deleted text isn't crossed out in your documents, on the Review tab in the Markup group, click the Show Markup button, click Balloons on the drop-down menu, and click Show All Revisions Inline on the submenu.)
- Formatting changes appear to the right of the document in the markup area, pointed out in Figure 4-6.

When you move the mouse pointer over a change, Word displays a pop-up message that tells you the name of the person who made the change, when they made it, and what the change was (check out Figure 4-6 for an example).

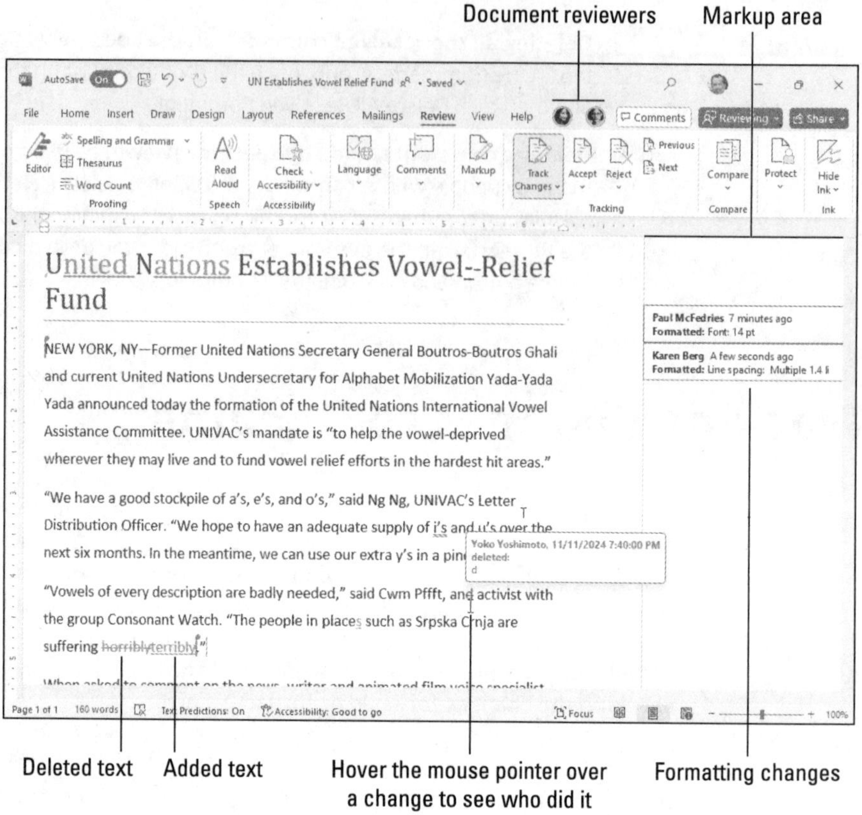


**FIGURE 4-6:** A document with Track Changes turned on.

## Telling Word to start marking changes

To start tracking where editorial changes are made to a document, turn Track Changes on. You can do that with one of these techniques:

- On the Review tab, in the Tracking group, click the top part of the Track Changes button.
- Press Ctrl+Shift+E.
- On the status bar, click the words *Track Changes* so that the status bar reads "Track Changes: On." If the words *Track Changes* don't appear on the status bar and you want to display them there, right-click the status bar and select Track Changes on the pop-up menu.

To stop tracking changes to a document, click the Track Changes button again, press Ctrl+Shift+E again, or click the words *Track Changes* on the status bar so that the words read "Track Changes: Off."

## Reading and reviewing a document with revision marks

Reading and reviewing a document with revision marks isn't easy. The marks can get in the way. Fortunately, on the Review tab, in the Markup group, Word offers the Display for Review menu for dealing with documents that have been scarred by revision marks. Choose options on the Display for Review drop-down list to get a better idea of how your changes are taking shape:

- **Get an idea where changes were made.** Choose Simple Markup. A vertical line appears on the left side of the page to show where changes were made. (This line doesn't appear in Draft and Outline view.)
- **Display where additions and deletions were made.** Choose All Markup. Additions are underlined and deleted text is crossed through.
- **Display what the document would look like if you accepted all changes.** Choose No Markup. All revision marks are stripped away and your document appears as it would if you accepted all changes made to it.
- **Display what the document would look like if you rejected all changes.** Choose Original. You get the original, pristine document back.

### REQUIRING YOUR COLLABORATORS TO TRACK CHANGES

As well as insist that your collaborators track the changes they make to a document, you can compel them to do so. You can lock your document so that all editorial changes made to it are tracked with revision marks.

To lock a document against anyone's making changes without the changes being tracked, go to the Review tab then, in the Tracking group, open the Track Changes drop-down list and choose Lock Tracking. In the Lock Tracking dialog box that shows up, enter and reenter a password, then click OK.

All changes are tracked automatically in a document that has been locked against anyone's turning off the track changes mechanism.

To unlock a document so that you and your collaborators can once again turn the Track Changes feature on or off, open the drop-down list on the Track Changes button and deselect Lock Tracking. Then enter the password in the Unlock Tracking dialog box.

## Accepting and rejecting changes to a document

The point of marking up a document is to later on review the changes and then either incorporate some or all of them into the final version or remove those that aren't useful or suitable. Word offers you several tools to either accept or reject changes.

Note, first, that you can navigate changes in a document from the Review tab. In the Tracking group, click Next to move to the next change in the document; click Previous to go back to the previous change in the document.

### Accepting document changes

For accepting document changes, you've got six methods at your disposal:

- To accept a change, navigate to it and then, on the Review tab in the Tracking group, click the top part of the Accept button.
- To accept a change and automatically move to the next change, navigate to the first change and then, on the Review tab in the Tracking group, drop down the Accept menu and click Accept and Move to Next.
- To accept all the changes in the current document, on the Review tab in the Tracking group, drop down the Accept menu and then click Accept All Changes in Document.
- To accept all the changes in the current document and shut off Track Changes, on the Review tab in the Tracking group, drop down the Accept menu and then click Accept All Changes and Stop Tracking.
- To accept only certain types of changes (such as formatting or insertions and deletions), on the Review tab in the Markup group, use the Show Markup list to turn off the markup for all the changes except the ones you want to accept. Then, on the Review tab in the Markup group, drop down the Accept menu and then click Accept All Changes Shown.
- To accept only the changes made by a particular reviewer, on the Review tab in the Markup group, click Show Markup and then use the Specific People list to turn off the markup for all reviewers except the one you want to accept. Then, on the Review tab in the Markup group, drop down the Accept menu and then click Accept All Changes Shown.

## Rejecting document changes

For rejecting document changes, you've got six methods to work with:

- To reject a change, navigate to it and then, on the Review tab in the Tracking group, click the top part of the Reject button.
- To reject a change and automatically move to the next change, navigate to the first change and then, on the Review tab in the Tracking group, drop down the Reject menu and click Reject and Move to Next.
- To reject all the changes in the current document, on the Review tab in the Tracking group, drop down the Reject menu and then click Reject All Changes in Document.
- To reject all the changes in the current document and shut off Track Changes, on the Review tab in the Tracking group, drop down the Reject menu and then click Reject All Changes and Stop Tracking.
- To reject only certain types of changes (such as formatting or insertions and deletions), on the Review tab in the Markup group, use the Show Markup list to turn off the markup for all the changes except the ones you want to accept. Then, on the Review tab in the Markup group, drop down the Reject menu and then click Reject All Changes Shown.
- To reject only the changes made by a particular reviewer, on the Review tab in the Markup group, click Show Markup and then use the Specific People list to turn off the markup for all reviewers except the one you want to accept. Then, on the Review tab in the Markup group, drop down the Reject menu and then click Reject All Changes Shown.

# Marking changes when you forgot to turn on revision marks

Suppose that you write the first draft of a document and someone revises it, but that someone doesn't track changes. How can you tell where changes were made? For that matter, suppose that you get hold of a document, you change it around without tracking changes, and now you want to display what your editorial changes did to the original copy. I have good news: You can compare documents to display the editorial changes that were made to them. Word offers a command for comparing the original document to a revised edition and another for comparing two different revised editions of the same document.

Follow these steps to compare an original document to its revised copy or two revised copies:

1. **On the Review tab, in the Compare group, click the Compare button.**

   A drop-down list appears (depending on the size of your screen, you may have to choose Compare more than once to get to the drop-down list).

2. **On the drop-down list, choose Compare to compare the original document to its revised edition; choose Combine to compare two editions of the same document that were revised separately.**

   The Compare Documents dialog box or the Combine Documents dialog box appears. These dialog boxes work the same way.

3. **On the Original Document drop-down list, choose the original or a revised edition of the document; if its name isn't there, click the Browse button and select it in the Open dialog box.**

4. **On the Revised Document drop-down list, choose a revised copy, or else click the Browse button and select it in the Open dialog box.**

5. **Click the More button.**

   Word displays more options for comparing or combining documents.

6. **If you so desire, deselect Comparison Settings check boxes to tell Word what you want to compare.**

7. **Click OK.**

   As shown in Figure 4-7, Word splits the screen into three panes. On the right, the top pane shows the original document, and the bottom pane shows the revised document. In the larger left pane, Word displays a new document that displays the changes that were made between the original and the revision. You can save this document if you want to.

TIP

To help with document comparisons, you can tell Word what to display in the Source Documents pane on the right side of the screen. On the Review tab in the Compare group, click the Compare button, click Show Source Documents, and click an option on the submenu. You can hide the source documents, show the original document, show the revised edition, or show both editions (the default).

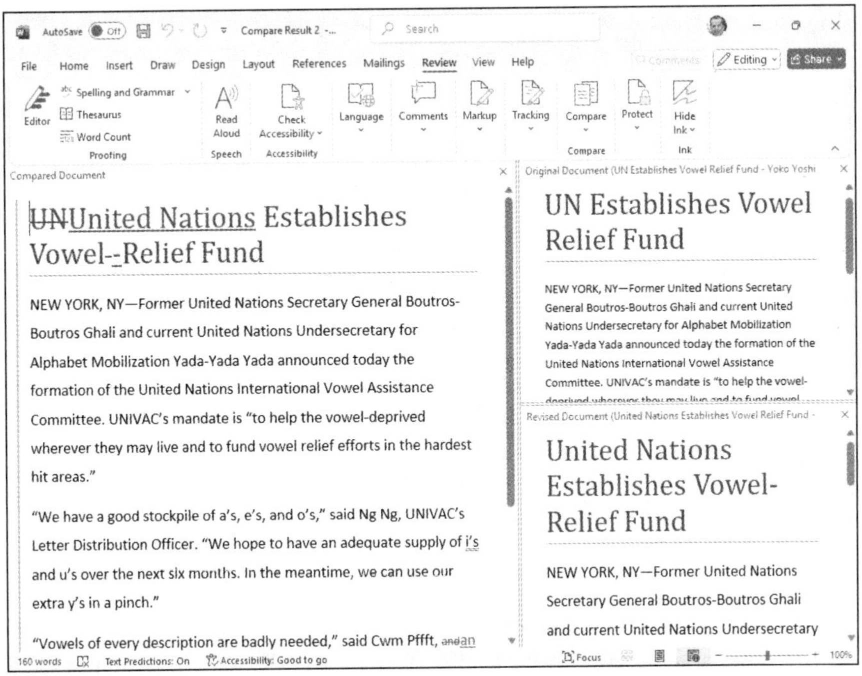


**FIGURE 4-7:** Comparing the changes made between an original document and its revised version.

# Documenting a Worksheet with Notes

If someone else will be viewing or editing a worksheet, they might be confused or mystified by a certain value or formula. To avoid having the person write you a comment (that's the subject of the next section) or, even worse, change the value or formula, you can explain the value or formula by adding a note to the cell.

A *note* is a little explanation that describes part of a worksheet. Each note is connected to a cell. You can tell where a note is because a small red triangle appears in the upper-right corner of the cell to which the note is attached. Move the pointer over one of these triangles and a pop-up box appears containing a note and the name of the person who entered the note, as shown in Figure 4-8.

Starting on the Review tab, in the Notes group, follow these instructions to handle notes:

- **Entering a note:** Click the cell that deserves a note, click the Notes button, and click the New Note on the drop-down list (or right-click the cell and then click New Note). Enter your note in the pop-up box. When you're done, click outside the note box.

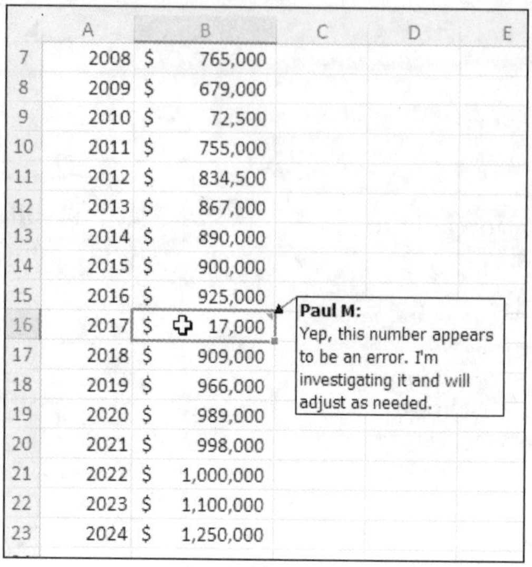
A
B
C
D
E
7 2008 $ 765,000
8 2009 $ 679,000
9 2010 $ 72,500
10 2011 $ 755,000
11 2012 $ 834,500
12 2013 $ 867,000
13 2014 $ 890,000
14 2015 $ 900,000
15 2016 $ 925,000
16 2017 $ 17,000
17 2018 $ 909,000
18 2019 $ 966,000
19 2020 $ 989,000
20 2021 $ 998,000
21 2022 $ 1,000,000
22 2023 $ 1,100,000
23 2024 $ 1,250,000
Paul M:
Yep, this number appears to be an error. I'm investigating it and will adjust as needed.

**FIGURE 4-8:** Notes explain what's what in a worksheet.

- **Reading a note:** Move the pointer over a cell with a small red triangle and read the note in the pop-up box (refer to Figure 4-8). You can also click the cell, click the Notes button, and then click Show/Hide Note (or right-click the cell and then click Show/Hide Note).
- **Showing and hiding all the notes:** Click the Notes button and click Show All Notes on the drop-down list to display or hide all the notes in a worksheet.
- **Navigating notes:** Click the Notes button and then click the Previous Note or Next Note commands on the drop-down list to go from note to note.
- **Editing a note:** Select the cell with the comment, click the Notes button, and then click Edit Note. You can also right-click the cell and then click Edit Note.
- **Deleting notes:** Right-click the cell with the note and then click Delete Note. To delete several notes, select them by Ctrl+clicking and then right-click and choose Delete Note.
- **Deleting all notes (and comments):** Press Ctrl+A to select all cells in the worksheet. On the Home tab, in the Editing group, click the Clear button, and then click Clear Comments and Notes on the drop-down menu. Beware: This command deletes all comments as well as all notes. Don't select it if you want to keep the comments in your worksheet.

TIP

If your name doesn't appear in the pop-up box after you enter a note and you want it to appear there, go to the File tab, choose Options, select the General category in the Excel Options dialog box, and enter your name in the User Name text box.

# Collaborating on a Workbook with Comments

When constructing a workbook is a team affair, consider writing comments to discuss with team members how to make the workbook better. Comments are meant for workbooks being shared. Each comment is attached to a cell. You can tell where a comment is because a purple comment icon appears in the upper-right corner of cells that have been commented on. Write comments to suggest ways to make a workbook better and to reply to others' suggestions.

Starting on the Review tab, in the Comments group, follow these instructions to comment on a workbook you share with others:

- **Entering a comment:** Click the cell that needs a comment and then click the New Comment button. A pop-up box appears for entering a comment. Enter your comment and click the Post Comment button (shown in the margin; or press Ctrl+Enter).
- **Displaying a single comment:** Move the pointer over the cell with the purple icon. The comment appears in a pop-up box.
- **Displaying all comments**: Click the Show Comments button on the Review tab or the Comments button in the upper-right corner of the screen. The Comments pane opens. From there you can read, reply to, and enter comments.

- **Editing a comment you made:** Hover the mouse pointer over the cell that contains the comment. In the pop-up box that appears with the comment text, click the Edit Comment icon (shown in the margin), make your edits, and then click Post Comment (or press Ctrl+Enter).
- **Replying to a comment:** Display the comment and enter your reply in the @mention or Reply text box. Click the Post Comment button (or press Ctrl+Enter) when you finish replying.
- **Going from comment to comment:** Click the Previous Comment or Next Comment button. You can also scroll through comments in the Comments pane.
- **Deleting comments:** Select the cell with the comment and click the Delete button on the Review tab. To delete a comment and all its replies, display it in the Comments pane, click the More Thread Actions button (the ellipsis), and then click Delete Thread.
- **Resolving a thread:** Display the comment in the Comments pane, click the More Thread Actions button (the ellipsis), and then click Resolve Thread. A thread is a collection of comments all aimed at the same cell in a worksheet. Resolve a thread to signal that the discussion about the thread is closed.

# Keeping Others from Tampering with Worksheets

People with savvy and foresight sometimes set up workbooks so that one worksheet holds raw data and the other worksheets hold formulas that calculate the raw data. This technique prevents others from tampering with the raw data. Furthermore, if the worksheet with raw data is hidden, the chance that it will be tampered with is lower; and if the worksheet is protected, people can't tamper with it unless they have a password. These pages explain how to hide a worksheet so that others are less likely to find it. I also tell you how to protect a worksheet from being edited.

## Hiding a worksheet

Follow these instructions to hide and unhide worksheets:

- **Hiding a worksheet:** Right-click the worksheet's tab and choose Hide on the shortcut menu. You can also go to the Home tab, in the Cells group click the Format button, and choose Hide &Unhide ⇨ Hide Sheet.
- **Unhiding a worksheet:** Right-click any worksheet tab and choose Unhide; or go to the Home tab, in the Cells group click the Format button, and choose Hide & Unhide ⇨ Unhide Sheet. Then, in the Unhide dialog box, select the sheet you want to unhide and click OK.

## Protecting a worksheet

*Protecting* a worksheet means to restrict others from changing it — from formatting it, inserting new rows and columns, or deleting rows and columns, among other tasks. You can also prevent any editorial changes whatsoever from being made to a worksheet. Follow these steps to protect a worksheet from tampering by others:

1. **Select the worksheet that needs protection.**
2. **On the Review tab, in the Protect group, click the Protect Sheet button.**

   The Protect Sheet dialog box appears, shown in Figure 4-9. You can also open this dialog box by going to the Home tab, in the Cells group clicking the Format button, and then clicking Protect Sheet.

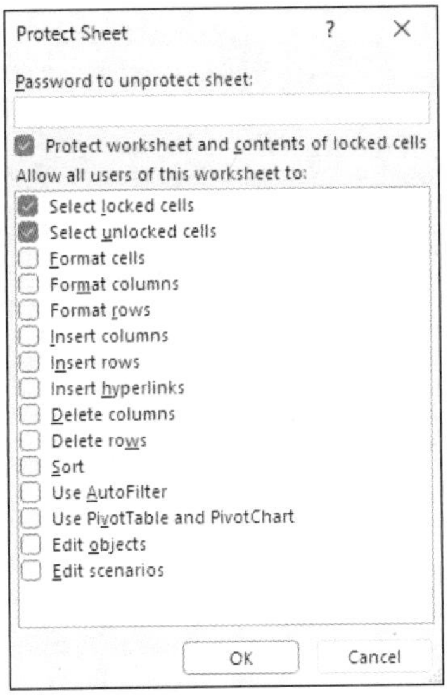


**FIGURE 4-9:** Select what you want to leave unprotected on the worksheet.

3. **(Optional) Type a password in the Password to Unprotect Sheet text box.**

   Specify a password if you want only people with the password to be able to unprotect the worksheet after you protect it.

4. **On the Allow All Users of This Worksheet To list, select the check box next to the name of each task that you want to permit others to do.**

   For example, select the Format Cells check box if you want others to be able to format cells.

   TIP: Deselect the Select Locked Cells check box to prevent any changes from being made to the worksheet. By default, all worksheet cells are locked, and by preventing others from selecting locked cells, you effectively prevent them from editing any cells.

5. **Click OK.**

   If you entered a password in Step 3, you must enter it again in the Confirm Password dialog box and click OK.

To unprotect a worksheet that you protected, go to the Review tab, then in the Protect group, click the Unprotect Sheet button. You must enter a password if you elected to require others to have a password before they can unprotect a worksheet.

# Index

## A



## B

# D

# E

# F

# G



# H



# I

## J



## K



## L



## M

# N



# O

# P

# Q



# R

# S

# T

# U



# V



# W

# Z

## About the Author

**Paul McFedries** has been a technical writer for 30 years (no, that is not a typo). He has been messing around with productivity software since installing WordPerfect and Lotus 1-2-3 on an IBM PC clone in 1986. He has written more than 100 books (nope, not a typo) that have sold more than four million copies worldwide (again, not a typo). Paul's books include the Wiley titles *Excel All-in-One For Dummies*, *Excel Data Analysis For Dummies*, *Teach Yourself VISUALLY Excel*, and *Teach Yourself VISUALLY Windows 11*. Paul invites everyone to drop by his personal website (`https://paulmcfedries.com`) and to follow him on Twitter (`@paulmcf`) and Facebook (`https://www.facebook.com/PaulMcFedries/`).

## Dedication

To Karen and Chase, the best beings in the world.

## Author's Acknowledgments

If we're ever at the same cocktail party and you overhear me saying something like "I wrote a book," I hereby give you permission to wag your finger at me and say "Tsk, tsk." Why the scolding? Because although I did write this book's text and take its screenshots, that represents only a part of what constitutes a "book." The rest of it is brought to you by the dedication and professionalism of Wiley's editorial and production teams, who toiled long and hard to turn my text and images into an actual book.

I offer my sincere gratitude to everyone at Wiley who made this book possible, but I'd like to extend a special "Thanks a bunch!" to the folks I worked with directly: Executive Editor Steve Hayes, Project Editor Thomas Hill, Copy Editor Jennifer Connolly, and Technical Editor Doug Sahlin.

**Publisher's Acknowledgments**

**Associate Acquisitions Editor:** Steve Hayes
**Editor:** Thomas Hill
**Copyeditor:** Jennifer Connolly
**Technical Editor:** Doug Sahlin
**Production Editor:** Tamilmani Varadharaj
**Cover Image:** © OsakaWayne Studios/ Getty Images